THE PADRES ENCYCLOPEDIA

David Porter
Joe Naiman

SPORTS PUBLISHING L.L.C.
sportspublishingllc.com

ISBN: 1-58261-058-4

All photos courtesy of the San Diego Hall of Champions with the exceptions of pages 44, 48, 96, 145, 147, 155, 158, 159, 160, 161, 162, 259, 293, 296, courtesy of AP/Wide World Photos.

Director of Production: Susan M. Moyer
Senior Project Manager: Jennifer L. Polson
Project Manager: Jim Henehan
Cover designer: Kenneth J. O'Brien
Developmental Editor: Erin Linden-Levy
Copy Editor: Cynthia L. McNew

SPORTS PUBLISHING L.L.C.
www.SportsPublishingLLC.com

Acknowledgments

The authors deeply appreciate the invaluable assistance of numerous people and organizations during the preparation of the book. The San Diego Padres Media Guides provided information for the player biographies and the individual and team game, season, and career batting and pitching records. The *San Diego Union Tribune* furnished daily accounts of Padre games and transactions from inception to the present. *Total Baseball VI, The Baseball Encyclopedia, The Sporting News Official Baseball Guide, The Sporting News Official Baseball Register,* and *USA Today* contained data on Padre history, players, and transactions. The National Baseball Library at Cooperstown, New York, also supplied information on Padre players.

Sparky Anderson, Steve Arlin, Dave Campbell, Jerry Coleman, Rollie Fingers, Tim Flannery, Dick Freeman, Steve Garvey, Tony Gwynn, Jay Johnstone, Randy Jones, Fred Kern, Gary Lucas, Jack McKeon, Luis Salazar, Elten Schiller, the late Eric Show, Garry Templeton, Ed Whitson, and Whitey Wietelmann graciously shared their Padre reminiscences. Buzzie Bavasi, Dave Dravecky, Steve Garvey, Tony Gwynn, Ray Kroc, Jack McKeon, Ozzie Smith, Dave Winfield, and Dick Williams told rich Padre anecdotes in their autobiographies.

Bill Swank's recent book, *Echoes from Lane Field,* afforded perspective on Padre minor league history. Russell William Barman's Masters thesis, "From Smith and Bavasi to Kroc," Andy Strasberg and Mark Gugliemo's VHS, *Nineteen Summers,* and Frank Norris' *Journal of San Diego History* article "San Diego Baseball: The Early Years," illuminated our understanding of early Padre history.

We especially wish to thank Mike Pearson and the staff at Sports Publishing L.L.C. for their adept guidance and valuable suggestions, facilitating the planning and writing of this volume. My wife, Marilyn, again demonstrated considerable patience understanding, and support throughout the project.

David Porter

Although only two author names appear in *The Padres Encyclopedia,* the assistance of numerous other people made the book possible.

We wish to express our appreciation to the late Dr. Al Anderson and Phil Collier, Sparky Anderson, Be Barnes, Buzzie Bavasi, Ray Brandes, Greg Eichelberger, Theo Epstein, Glenn Geffner, Brigg Hewitt, Don King, Tom Larwin, Corinne Naiman, Ken Nigro, Frank Pelkey, Julie Reeder, Roger Riley, Karen Slaton, Andy Strasberg, Bill Swank, Glenn Turgeon, and Bill Zavestoski.

We also appreciate the quotes about events at the time or historical eras which were provided by Michael Monk, Galen Cisco, Bruce Bochy, and Rickey Henderson. Other current and past Padres players and coaches were also helpful in giving us the information we needed.

Assistance was also provided by the El Cajon branch of the San Diego County Library System, the City of San Diego main library, the Chula Vista library, the San Diego State University library, and the University of San Diego library, since microfilm research was performed at those various locations at one time or another.

San Diego Hall of Champions was extremely generous in allowing us to use its photographs, and Hall of Champions staff members Don King and Glenn Turgeon were very helpful in the process of identifying the photographs.

The Padres' media relations office not only provided essential information during the research period, but much of the material was possible because of Padres press credentials issued by the media relations office and other efforts of the Padres' media relations staff.

Some of the material had previously been researched for other articles, so acknowledgements are also due for the meteorology department of San Diego State University, the operations department at Montgomery Field, editor Diane Caudle and publisher Kurt Bevacqua of *Baseball Gold,* and former *Online Drive* editors Adam Gordon and Rich Donnelly.

Thanks are also appropriate for Mike Pearson, Erin Linden-Levy, Jennifer Polson, and Kenny O'Brien, and the rest of the Sports Publishing staff who converted this book from a concept to a reality.

Joe Naiman

Contents

Part I

The Formative Years

[1968-1977]

1

The Birth of a Major League Franchise [1968]

San Diego, the bustling metropolis on the southern border of sunny California, has a long baseball heritage. Professional baseball moved to San Diego during the Great Depression. The San Diego Padres played in the Class AAA Pacific Coast League from 1936 through 1968. In 1936, owner Bill Lane, a onetime miner, shifted the Hollywood Stars franchise to San Diego because he did not want to pay an annual $25,000 rental fee to use Wrigley Field. Lane sponsored a local newspaper contest to adopt a new club name. Area resident Don Blackwell won two season tickets after suggesting the club be named the Padres after the brave Franciscan Father Junipero Serra, who had founded the first mission in California over 400 years ago. Works Progress Administration funds financed the construction of Lane Field, a 9,100-seat baseball stadium on tidelands property at the foot of Broadway along the Pacific Coast Highway.

Baseball in San Diego debuted at Lane Field on March 31, 1936. Herman Pillette pitched the Padres to a 6-2 triumph over the Seattle Rainiers before 8,178 spectators. In 1936, San Diego finished second in the Pacific Coast League with 91 victories. The Padres featured several future major-leaguers, including outfielders Ted Williams and Vince DiMaggio, second baseman Bobby Doerr, and shortstop George Myatt. Williams, a gangling youngster who had starred at Herbert Hoover High School in San Diego, batted .271 with eight doubles, two triples, and 11 RBIs in 42 games, while Doerr collected six hits in one game. In 1937, Williams hit .293 with 23 home runs and 98 RBIs, helping the Padres capture the Shaughnessy playoffs for the Pacific Coast League championship. San Diego did not win another league title until 1954.

During the late 1930s, Padre hurlers pitched several masterpieces at Lane Field. In the seven-inning second game of a 1938 doubleheader, Padre manager Frank Shellenback outdueled 18-year-old Seattle right-hander Fred Hutchinson, 2-1. On August 30, 1938, Dick Ward pitched 12.2 hitless innings against Los

Angeles, outdueling Ray Prim, 1-0, on a two-hitter. On May 20, 1939, Dick Stegman hurled 10.2 hitless frames against Salt Lake City. San Diego won that contest in the 12th inning after Stegman had departed.

Left-handed batters found the 325-foot right field fence at Lane Field a favorite batting range. First baseman Jack Graham clouted 48 home runs in 1948 and appeared destined to break Tony Lazzeri's Pacific Coast League record of 60 until pitcher Red Adams of Los Angeles beaned him at mid season. In 1949, outfielder Max West belted 48 homers and first baseman Luke Easter added 25. Easter, who possessed power in all fields, slugged the longest home run ever hit at Lane Field—a 500-foot drive against the center-field scoreboard. On April 3, 1953, outfielder Ted Beard of the Hollywood Stars displayed enormous power at Lane Field. He set a Pacific Coast League record by clouting four home runs in five plate appearances to lift the Stars to a 6-5 victory over the Padres. Each home run traveled about 475 feet to right center field. Third baseman Bob Elliott clouted the two most dramatic home runs in Lane Field history in a playoff game to decide the 1954 Pacific Coast League championship. The onetime National League MVP belted two home runs with five RBIs as the Padres defeated the Hollywood Stars, 7-2.

Owner Bill Lane suffered a heart attack in August 1938 and died later that year. His estate operated the San Diego franchise until 1945 when Bill Starr and his associates acquired it. Starr had caught for the Padres from 1937 to 1939 and was the only Padre to pinch hit for Ted Williams. The Starr group sold the Padres in 1956 for $350,000 to C. Arnholdt Smith, head of the U.S. National Bank and owner of a business conglomerate. Two years later, Smith moved the Padres from termite-ridden Lane Field to beautiful Westgate Park. Westgate Park, which seated around 8,200 people, was built on Smith's property with his money and was named for Smith's Westgate-California Tuna Packing Company. The foul lines measured 320 feet, while center field was 410 feet away. The Padres dedicated Westgate Park against Phoenix on April 29, 1958, attracting crowds of 4,619 and 7,129 for a day-night doubleheader. San Diego captured Pacific Coast League pennants in 1962, 1964, and 1967, the last year Westgate Park was used.

The San Diego city fathers hoped to attract a major-league baseball franchise. In May 1965, the city council approved plans for a 50,000-seat, $27.5 million San Diego Stadium a couple of miles from Westgate Park and directed the city manager to acquire the necessary acreage in Mission Valley for a four-tier structure. Voters passed a city bond to finance stadium construction by an overwhelming 72 percent majority. Construction crews diverted the San Diego River, which flowed through the proposed stadium site, and removed 2.5 million cubic yards of dirt and built the stadium on a dirt mound 40 feet above the playing surface. Stadium construction was completed in 1967. Westgate Park was demolished to make way for Fashion Valley, a shopping center.

San Diego Stadium housed the 1967 San Diego Chargers professional football team and was dedicated on August 26 with an exhibition game between the Chargers and the Detroit Lions. In a two-day open house on February 17-18, 1968, around 15,000 people toured the stadium. The stadium baseball dimensions included the 330-foot foul lines, the 370-foot power alleys, a center-field fence 420 feet away, and a 17-foot high fence surrounding the outfield. On April 5, 1968, the San Francisco Giants played the Cleveland Indians in the first major-league exhibition game at San Diego Stadium. The Padres played their final Pacific Coast League campaign in the new park in 1968, finishing in second place and attracting a season total of 203,000 fans.

C. Arnholdt Smith and Emil J. "Buzzie" Bavasi played crucial roles in securing a major-league baseball franchise for San Diego. Smith consented to pay a then record $10.2 million franchise fee, borrowing over 90 percent of the money. Bavasi initially objected to the price, but Smith moved ahead anyway. Bavasi recollected, "I called Mr. Smith and told him as far as I was concerned, he ought to forget about it. He said no, we committed ourselves to the city to get a baseball club, and he decided to pay the $10 million." Smith, who owned two-thirds of the prospective club, persuaded the City of San Diego to establish the Greater San Diego Sports Association. The Association formulated a strategy to sell the people of San Diego on securing a major league franchise.

C. Arnholdt Smith became principal owner of the Padres. Smith, who was born in Walla Walla, Washington in 1899, moved to San Diego with his parents in 1906. He worked as a grocery store clerk after leaving San Diego High School at age 15 and joined the Bank of Italy (later Bank of America) at age 17. After rising to division vice president by 1932,

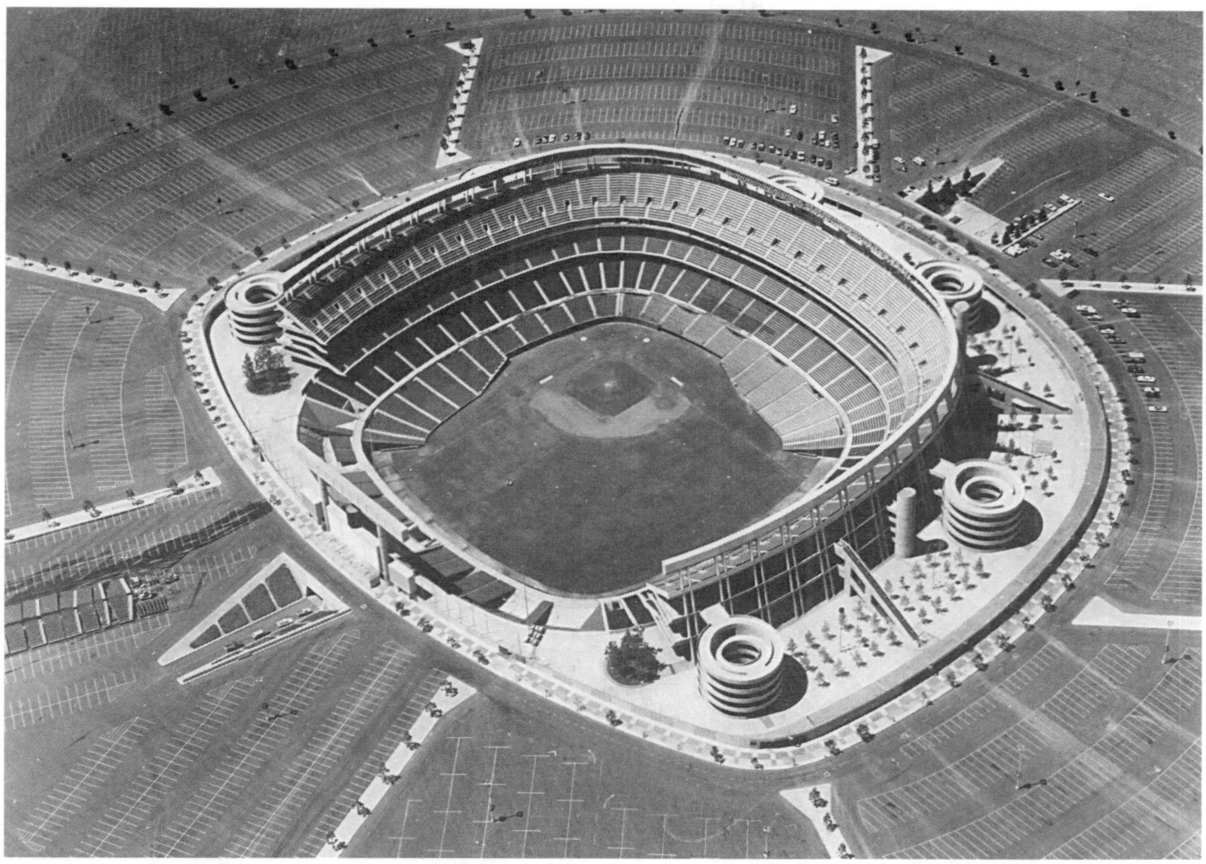

The Padres have played at San Diego Stadium, later named Jack Murphy Stadium and Qualcomm Stadium, since their inception as a major league franchise in 1969.

Smith left Bank of America the next year to join his brother in purchasing the U.S. National Bank of San Diego. He built a financial empire worth an estimated $1 billion by 1973. The Westgate-California Tuna Packing Corporation, created in 1960, formed the nucleus of the enterprise. The $200 million conglomerate encompassed seafood, ground transportation (Yellow Cab), aviation (Air California), insurance, and hotel (Westgate Plaza Hotel) businesses.

Buzzie Bavasi, an expert in internal baseball operations, led the campaign for San Diego to acquire a major-league baseball team. He consented to become club president and own one-third of the team. Bavasi was born in New York City in 1915 and joined the Brooklyn Dodgers organization following graduation from DePauw University in 1938. In 1951, he became vice president and general manager of the Brooklyn Dodgers. He moved with the Dodgers to Los Angeles in 1958 and remained with the club until 1968. During Bavasi's tenure, the Dodgers won six National League pennants and four World Series championships.

National League owners met in Chicago on May 27, 1968 and awarded franchises to the Montreal Expos and San Diego Padres, extending the senior circuit to 12 teams. Montreal won unanimous league approval, but Buffalo, New York, Milwaukee, Wisconsin, and Dallas, Texas, vied with San Diego for the other franchise. The owners nearly awarded the second franchise to Buffalo. Eight owners supported Buffalo, but Horace Stoneham of the San Francisco Giants and Walter O'Malley of the Los Angeles Dodgers held out for awarding the franchise to San Diego. San Diego did not receive the necessary 10 votes for league acceptance until the remaining eight owners joined Stoneham and O'Malley on the 18th ballot.

Bavasi's connections with O'Malley helped San Diego secure the franchise. Bavasi convinced National League owners that San Diego deserved a major-league franchise. According to him, San Diego could support a major-league baseball team with its growing population exceeding one million people. He stressed that the new San Diego Stadium could seat 50,000 people and perhaps could draw one million fans for major-league baseball games in 1969. Bavasi predicted: "If everybody in the city of San Diego attends one game, we'll do all right. That would mean about 675,000 in attendance, and we'll draw the balance from the metropolitan area." San Diego fans had supported the minor-league Padres very well from 1936 through 1967. C. Arnholdt Smith concurred, "Our city now has a major league franchise which it has shown it so richly deserves by the construction of the new stadium and the support it has given our Padres for 33 years." San Diego offered ideal weather conditions for baseball games and the best climate among the five competitors. The sports-minded city possessed a rich minor league baseball heritage and had produced over 100 major-league baseball players. Smith seemingly provided the club solid financial ownership, while Bavasi lent vast experience in baseball operations.

At the October 14 expansion draft, Bavasi favored selecting around 10 veterans and completing the roster with promising minor-league players. He told sportswriter Jack Murphy, "The people of San Diego are too sophisticated to believe that old-timers can help young ball clubs. Our job is to give fans a good show, and I don't think you can do it with veterans." Expansion rules allowed San Diego to select 30 players from other National League clubs.

Preston Gomez managed the Padres from 1969 to April 1972.

The Padres made outfielder "Downtown" Ollie Brown, who had spent parts of four seasons with the San Francisco Giants, their first selection. Brown batted .267 with 13 home runs in 1967 but was suspended for refusal to report to the minor leagues in 1968. Scout Tom Mulcahy considered Brown a fine prospect with good power and a great throwing arm. Pitchers Dave Giusti of the St. Louis Cardinals, Al Santorini of the Atlanta Braves, and Dick Selma of the New York Mets, along with second baseman José Arcia of the Chicago Cubs, were the next four Padre choices. Santorini and Arcia had played under one year in the major leagues.

The next five Padre selections were pitcher Clay Kirby of the St. Louis Cardinals, catcher Fred Kendall of the Cincinnati Reds, outfielder Jerry Morales of the New York Mets, first baseman Nate Colbert of the Houston Astros, and shortstop Zoilo Versalles of the Los Angeles Dodgers. Only Versalles boasted considerable major-league experience. Kirby, Kendall, and Morales spent 1968 in the minor leagues, while Colbert played just 20 games with the Houston Astros. Bavasi recalled, "We got just what we wanted—good young pitchers, speed, and defense."

The Padres filled the remainder of their roster with the following picks:

11. Frank Reberger, pitcher, Chicago Cubs
12. Jerry DeVanon, infielder, St. Louis Cardinals
13. Larry Stahl, outfielder, New York Mets
14. Dick Kelley, pitcher, Atlanta Braves
15. Al Ferrara, outfielder, Los Angeles Dodgers
16. Mike Corkins, pitcher, San Francisco Giants
17. Tom Dukes, pitcher, Houston Astros
18. Rich James, pitcher, Chicago Cubs
19. Tony Gonzalez, outfielder, Philadelphia Phillies
20. David Roberts, pitcher, Pittsburgh Pirates
21. Ivan Murrell, outfielder, Houston Astros
22. Jim Williams, outfielder, Los Angeles Dodgers
23. Bill McCool, pitcher, Cincinnati Reds
24. Bobby Peña, infielder, Philadelphia Phillies
25. Al McBean, pitcher, Pittsburgh Pirates
26. Steve Arlin, pitcher, Philadelphia Phillies
27. Rafael Robles, infielder, San Francisco Giants

28. Fred Katawcik, pitcher, Cincinnati Reds
29. Ron Slocum, catcher, Pittsburgh Pirates
30. Clarence Gaston, outfielder, Atlanta Braves

Of the 30 players drafted, Versalles, Giusti, James, and Katawcik never played for the Padres. James and Katawcik played in the Padre minor-league organization. Bavasi gambled that the younger talent would make the Padres a contender within four years. "If we have to finish last," he philosophized, "we'd rather do it with youngsters who are learning and improving." Coach Whitey Wietelmann admitted the Padres "got players the other teams did not want."

San Diego also completed its minor-league organization. The Padres named Peter Bavasi, son of Buzzie Bavasi, the director of minor league operations.

The Padres shared a Class AA team with the Kansas City Royals at Elmira, New York, under pilot Harry Bright in the Eastern League, sponsored a Class A club at Key West, Florida, under skipper Don Zimmer, and fielded a rookie classification team at Salt Lake City, Utah, under manager Dave Garcia in the Pioneer League.

San Diego did not have lofty expectations for the inaugural 1969 season, which coincided with the City of San Diego's 200th anniversary. Manager Preston Gomez predicted that the Padres would win about 60 games in 1969 and that it would take from five to 10 years to make the Padres a formidable winning team. He realized "we drafted a lot of babies and it will take time for them to develop." Buzzie Bavasi likewise expected the Padres to win only 60 to 65 games their inaugural campaign.

San Diego needed to rely primarily on hitting and defense its initial major-league season. Preston Gomez claimed that outfielders Ollie Brown, Cito Gaston, and Tony Gonzalez matched well offensively with other National League outfields and believed that first baseman Bill Davis, second baseman Roberto Peña, third baseman Ed Spiezio, and shortstop Tommy Dean could provide good defense and furnish limited offensive production. San Diego, however, boasted a pitching staff that had won only 25 National League contests in 1968. Preston Gomez realized that Padre success would depend largely on the pitching quality. Veterans Johnny Podres, Dick Kelley, Dick Selma, and Al McBean formed the nucleus of the Padre staff, but Gomez did not know how the quartet would perform.

2

The Inaugural Season

[1969]

From the outset, owners C. Arnholdt Smith and Buzzie Bavasi struggled to keep the San Diego Padres afloat financially and to gain public recognition for the team as a major-league club. San Diego needed to make payments each year to meet the franchise fee obligations and initially lacked the cash flow to build a successful team. According to Bavasi, "There was never a lot of money from the start."

An enormous geographical disadvantage hindered the Padres in marketing operations. The city is bordered by the Pacific Ocean on the west, Mexico on the south, the desert on the east, and sprawling Los Angeles to the north, limiting the likely Padre fan support to six miles to the west, 30 miles to the south, 20 miles to the east, and 30 miles to the north. The Los Angeles Dodgers had commanded enormous popularity in the San Diego area since 1958, compounding marketing problems. "San Diego," former Padre executive Elten Schiller remarked, "was Dodger territory. San Diegans listened to Dodger games, as announcer Vin Scully enthralled audiences. People did not switch allegiances until a new generation of dads came along."

San Diego faced additional problems. The expansion agreement prevented the Padres from sharing in television revenues until 1972. "Now that's a major source of income to a club," former club publicist Irv Grossman remarked, "and it wasn't there." Padre radio announcers could not entice a large audience from Los Angeles Dodgers games until the public identified with the new franchise. The Padres also needed to lure San Diegans from other recreational activities, including golf, tennis, fishing, surfing, Sunday racing at Caliente, Sunday bullfights in Tijuana, backyard grilling, and beach-going. "How," inquired Bavasi, "can you compete against the good life?"

Before the 1969 season, San Diego made several trades blending younger players with three veterans. On October 21, the Padres purchased first baseman Bill Davis from the Cleveland Indians.

The deal was completed on December 2 when the Indians acquired veteran shortstop Zoilo Versalles. The Padres the next day traded reliever Dave Giusti to the St. Louis Cardinals for third baseman Ed Spiezio, catcher Danny Breeden, outfielder Ron Davis, and pitcher Phil Knuckles. On March 28, San Diego acquired pitcher Tommie Sisk and experienced catcher Chris Cannizzaro from the Pittsburgh Pirates for outfielder Ron Davis and infielder Bobby Klaus. Sisk had compiled a 37-35 mark with a 3.69 ERA in seven major-league seasons, while Cannizzaro had batted .237 in seven years of major-league catching experience. Veteran pitcher Johnny Podres, who had logged a 141-110 record in 14 major-league seasons, came out of retirement on March 21 at age 36 to join the Padres.

A strike threat, meanwhile, delayed spring training. The Major League Players Association was deadlocked in a fierce pension dispute with the owners and had agreed to boycott spring training until the pension dispute was resolved. Over 400 players supported the Major League Players Association's position. New Commissioner Bowie Kuhn persuaded the owners to take a softer line, while the Major League Players Association reduced some of its demands. The strike was resolved in late February, when the owners agreed to increase their contributions to the players' pension funds and increased player benefits.

The Padres spent their first spring training in late February and March at a 25-acre complex developed by the Yuma, Arizona, Recreation and Parks Department. The facility consisted of Keegan Field and three practice playing fields in a cloverleaf shape with a huge ultramodern 12,000 square-foot clubhouse in the center. The exhibition field had a concrete grandstand with 700 box seats, 1,500 reserved seats, and 2,000 bleacher seats. The Keegan Field dimensions were 350 feet down the foul lines, 385 feet in the power alleys, and 410 feet to straightaway center field.

San Diego made an auspicious regular season major-league debut under manager Preston Gomez on April 8, 1969, defeating the Houston Astros, 2-1, before 23,370 fans at San Diego Stadium. The box score for the initial game was:

Houston	AB	R	H	RBI	PO	A	E
Jesus Alou, rf	4	1	3	0	1	0	0
Joe Morgan, 2b	3	0	0	0	3	0	1
Norm Miller, cf	4	0	0	0	1	0	0
Doug Rader, 3b	4	0	1	1	3	2	0
Curt Blefary, 1b	4	0	1	0	8	0	0
Bob Watson, lf	4	0	0	0	0	0	0
Denis Menke, ss	3	0	0	0	1	3	0
John Edwards, c	3	0	0	0	7	0	0
Don Wilson, p	2	0	0	0	0	0	0
Gary Geiger, ph	1	0	0	0	0	0	0
Jack Billingham, p	0	0	0	0	0	1	0
Totals	32	1	5	1	24	6	1

San Diego	AB	R	H	RBI	PO	A	E
Rafael Robles, ss	4	0	0	0	0	0	0
Roberto Peña, 2b	3	1	0	0	1	3	0
Tony Gonzalez, cf	4	0	0	0	3	0	0
Ollie Brown, rf	4	0	1	1	4	0	0
Bill Davis, 1b	3	0	0	0	3	1	0
Nate Colbert, 1b	0	0	0	0	3	0	0
Larry Stahl, lf	3	0	0	0	0	0	0
Ed Spiezio, 3b	3	1	1	1	0	0	0
Chris Cannizzaro, c	2	0	0	0	12	0	0
Dick Selma, p	2	0	2	0	1	0	0
Totals	28	2	4	2	27	4	0

Houston	1 0 0	0 0 0	0 0 0	- 1
San Diego	0 0 0	0 1 1	0 0 x	- 2

2B—Brown. 3B—Alou. HR—Spiezio. SB—Alou, Robles. S—Selma. LOB—Houston 6, San Diego, 5.

Pitchers	IP	H	R	ER	BB	SO
Don Wilson (L)	6	3	2	2	1	4
Jack Billingham	2	1	0	0	0	3
Dick Selma (W)	9	5	1	1	2	12

HBP—By Wilson (Peña). PB—Cannizzaro. BK—Wilson. U—Shag Crawford, Chris Pelekoudas, Doug Harvey, and Frank Dezelan. T—2:14. A—23,370.

San Diego starter Dick Selma hurled a five-hitter, striking out 12 Houston Astros and not allowing a run after the first inning. Rafael Robles, the first Padre batter, reached base safely when Houston second baseman Joe Morgan bobbled his grounder. San Diego third baseman Ed Spiezio homered in the fifth inning off Houston starter Don Wilson, clouting the first round-tripper in Padre annals. An inning later, San Diego right fielder Ollie Brown doubled to score Bobby Peña with the winning run. Selma finished the contest by fanning Denis Menke. Padre pitcher Johnny Podres observed, "We didn't look like any expansion team tonight."

Gene Gregston, unidentified, Carol Smith Shannon, C. Arnholdt Smith, Earl Keller, John McDonald, and Mrs. Gregston. Gregston, Keller, and McDonald were San Diego sports writers. Shannon, Smith's daughter, was chairman of the Padres Board of Directors. Smith served as co-owner of the Padres.

San Diego players and fans jubilantly celebrated the first major-league victory in franchise history. Catcher Chris Cannizzaro raced to the mound and jumped on Selma "like a lion pouncing on its prey." The attendance, however, disappointed San Diego president Buzzie Bavasi, who had hoped that the Padres would draw at least 30,000 people for San Diego's first major-league game. Two days later San Diego blanked Houston, 2-0, sweeping its first three games in franchise history. The Padres exhibited their youth the next day at home, making a club-record five errors against the San Francisco Giants. The Padres drew 123,275 spectators for their first 11 home games, averaging 11,000 people per contest.

San Diego triumphed in nine of 23 games in April and recorded several franchise firsts. On April 12, the Padres turned their first double play in the sixth inning against the San Francisco Giants at San Diego Stadium. San Diego went six consecutive games from April 21 through April 26 without making an error. Third baseman Ed Spiezio made four consecutive hits at home against the Cincinnati Reds on April 26 and April 27. San Diego won its first doubleheader on April 27 over the Cincinnati Reds at home. The Padres edged the Reds, 10-9, in the 13-inning second game, the first extra-inning contest for the franchise.

San Diego continued to establish franchise records in May. On May 2, Al Ferrara clouted the first Padre pinch-hit and grand slam in the fourth inning off George Culver in an 8-5 triumph over the Cincinnati Reds at Crosley Field. The following day, outfielder Ollie Brown belted the first San Diego grand slam on consecutive days in the first inning off Tony Cloninger in a team-best 13-5 triumph over the Cincinnati Reds. The Padres tallied nine runs on seven hits in the first inning of that contest.

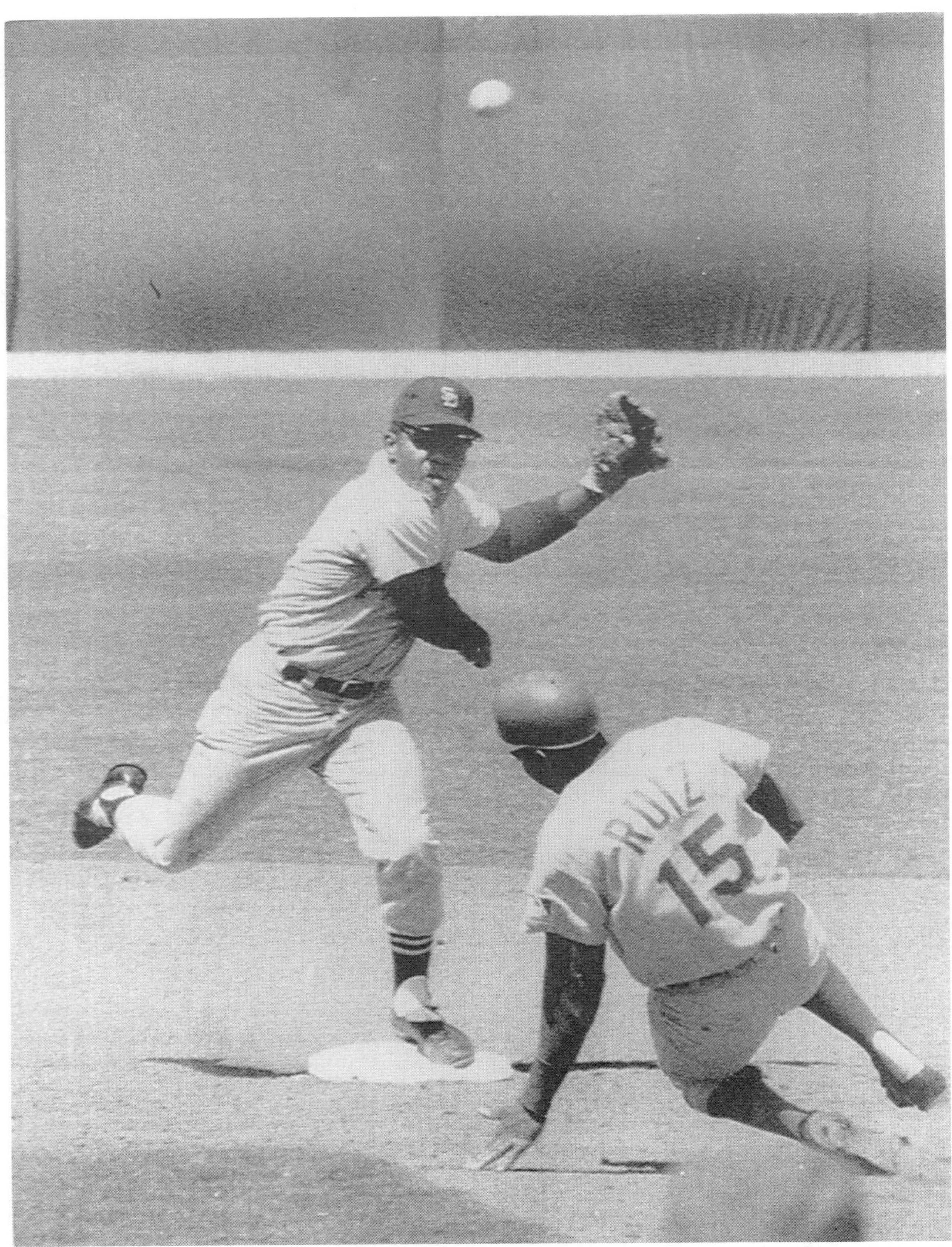

Padres second baseman Roberto Peña forces out Chico Ruiz of the Cincinnati Reds in the first game, won by the Padres, 5-2, on April 17, 1969.

San Diego won two out of three games from the defending champion St. Louis Cardinals in their first meeting from May 9 through May 11 at Busch Stadium. In the May 10 contest, shortstop Bobby Peña reached base safely four times and belted a grand slam in the fourth inning off Steve Carlton in a 5-3 Padre victory. Padre infielders completed a franchise-record five double plays in a 2-1 triumph over the St. Louis Cardinals at San Diego Stadium. First baseman Nate Colbert on May 25 belted the fourth Padre grand slam of the month and the first at home by a Padre in the third inning off Don Nottebart in a 10-2 victory over the Chicago Cubs. San Diego pitchers set a dubious franchise record on May 13 by allowing the Chicago Cubs 19 runs in a 19-0 rout at Wrigley Field.

President Buzzie Bavasi, meanwhile, accelerated the youth movement by trading veteran starting pitchers Al McBean and Dick Selma. On April 17, San Diego sent McBean to the Los Angeles Dodgers for pitcher Leon Everitt and shortstop Tommy Dean. Eight days later, the Padres acquired pitchers Joe Niekro and Gary Ross and shortstop Francisco Libran from the Chicago Cubs for Selma. Niekro had compiled a 24-17 record and 3.84 ERA in two major-league seasons with the Cubs, while Ross had split two decisions in 1968. Manager Preston Gomez inserted Ross and Niekro into the starting rotation with Clay Kirby and Al Santorini. The Padres released catcher Jesse Gonder on April 23 and traded shortstop Jerry DaVanon and first baseman Bill Davis to the St. Louis Cardinals for shortstop John Sipin and catcher John Ruberto, paving the way for Nate Colbert to become the regular first baseman.

San Diego won 24 of its first 54 games and appeared on track to record 72 victories, the most by a first-year expansion team. The Padres won six straight road contests from May 30 through June 4, recording three consecutive wins over the Montreal Expos from May 30 through June 1 and over the Philadelphia Phillies from June 2 through June 4. San Diego homered three times in three separate games between May 25 and June 6. Ollie Brown, Al Ferrara, and Nate Colbert homered in a 10-2 home victory over the Chicago Cubs on May 25, while Ferrara connected once and Brown twice in a 6-2 road win over the Montreal Expos on May 31. Ed Spiezio clouted two homers and Colbert one at home against the Montreal Expos on June 6. Colbert also homered twice in a 5-2 road triumph over the Montreal Expos on June 1 and

"Downtown" Ollie Brown played outfield for the Padres from 1969 through 1972.

Ed Spiezio duplicated the feat on June 10 against the Montreal Expos. Colbert clouted 11 home runs during the club's first 54 games, while catcher Chris Cannizzaro batted over .280 and provided good defense. During the first third of the season, Padres pitchers performed above expectations.

The San Diego honeymoon ended abruptly, however, with a 7-22 June swoon. The Padres lost 11 consecutive games from June 17 through June 25 and 11 of 13 June home contests at San Diego Stadium. The Padres went scoreless for 30 consecutive innings from June 20 through June 24. During that span, the Houston Astros blanked the Padres, 4-0 and 2-0, and the Cincinnati Reds shut out the Padres, 5-0, in consecutive games from June 21 through June 23. Don Wilson of the Astros retired 20 consecutive Padres on June 22. The 19-0 thrashing by the Los Angeles Dodgers on June 28 also symbolized San Diego's plight. The Dodgers tallied 10 runs in the third inning. Padres starter Steve Arlin uncorked three wild pitches in just 2.2 innings.

In an attempt to change club fortunes, San Diego made several roster moves. On June 12, the Padres traded veteran outfielder Tony Gonzalez to the Atlanta

Ed Spiezio played third base for the Padres from 1969 through July 1972.

Braves for catcher Walt Hriniak, infielder Van Kelly, and outfielder Andy Finlay. Kelly homered five days later against Bill Singer of the Los Angeles Dodgers at Dodger Stadium, becoming the Padres' first left-handed batter to clout a round-tripper. On June 27, the Padres placed veteran pitcher Johnny Podres on the voluntary retired list and made him a minor-league pitching instructor. Three days later, the Padres sold minor-league catcher Danny Breeden to the Cincinnati Reds.

The Padres still experienced peaks and valleys. On July 5, San Diego had 21 hits in a 9-8, 12-inning home victory over the Houston Astros, setting franchise records for most safeties and consecutive hits (7). The following day, Dick Kelley hurled a one-hit, 1-0 victory in the second game against the Astros. Outfielder Ivan Murrell set a club record by hitting safely in 15 consecutive games from July 7 through July 25. Catcher Chris Cannizzaro became the first Padre ever selected to the National League All-Star team, but did not appear in the 9-3 All-Star Game victory on July 23 at Washington, D.C. On July 15, Clay Kirby, on the other end of the spectrum, walked 10 San Francisco Giants batters in just 7.2 innings at Candlestick Park. Meanwhile, by the middle of July, the San Diego home attendance average dropped to 9,094 per game in a stadium with a 50,000-seating capacity. Fans seemed disinterested in watching younger, lesser-known players. The player morale sagged as few fans attended games to cheer for the home team. President Buzzie Bavasi still vowed, "Both the team and the crowds could be better and they will get better."

By July 13, San Diego had plunged to a 31-61 record and trailed the Western Division-leading San Francisco Giants by 32 games. Buzzie Bavasi patiently played younger players and built for the future. Buffalo and New Orleans officials asked Bavasi whether the Padres might be willing to relocate for the 1970 season, but Bavasi preferred to keep the club in San Diego. *The San Diego Union* wrote, "Bavasi is captivated by San Diego, and he resists the idea of failure." C. Arnholdt Smith, who left daily club operations to Bavasi, still held no regrets over purchasing the Padres and maintained that the expanding west needed major-league baseball.

During the first week of August, San Diego fell 40 games under a .500 winning percentage. Manager Preston Gomez still claimed that the Padres fielded "the nucleus of a good baseball team" and stressed "it's a lot closer to being a good team than some people think." According to Gomez, Clay Kirby, Al Santorini, Joe Niekro, and other young pitchers were learning to master their craft in the major leagues and consequently would reach their potential sooner. Gomez still expected the Padres to become contenders within five seasons.

By the end of August, San Diego had amassed 54 more losses than victories. Team frustration peaked in a 4-2 loss to the Chicago Cubs at San Diego Stadium on August 13, when second baseman Roberto Peña became the first Padre ejected from a game by an umpire. Peña argued with umpire Chris Pelekoudas after being called out while attempting to steal second base. San Diego nevertheless continued to establish club milestones. In the same game, the Padres converted the first triple play in franchise history in the first inning against the Chicago Cubs. On August 19, Al Santorini became the first San Diego pitcher to clout a home run, connecting against the Montreal Expos at Jarry Park. In the same game, Van Kelly reached base safely four times.

The Padres did not even reach a season home attendance of 500,000 fans until August 26, but they hoped that more people would attend the September games against the other Western Division teams. San Diego swept a four-game series at home against the Los Angeles Dodgers from September 4 through September 7, helping knock them out of contention for the Western Division title. Los Angeles never quite recovered, finishing fourth in the division. In the 3-1 triumph on September 6, Clay Kirby and Tommie Sisk combined to retire 17 consecutive Dodgers batters. Under 35,000 fans attended the four-game series, deeply disappointing San Diego officials. The Padres had attracted over 59,000 fans for their first five home games against the Los Angeles Dodgers.

The franchise appeared in trouble as the 1969 season entered the final three weeks. *The San Diego Union* sportswriter Jack Murphy observed: "It wouldn't be quite accurate to say that major-league baseball in San Diego is a failure. Not yet at least. But most of the evidence suggests that the sport is in a sickly condition." Buzzie Bavasi even acknowledged, "I don't think we made a mistake coming to San Diego, but for the first time, I'm wondering." Nevertheless, Smith and Bavasi still pledged to keep the club there.

San Diego, however, encouraged manager Preston Gomez by winning 12 of its final 21 games. Gomez remarked, "The last month—the way we bounced back—made our 1969 season. A good many of our players were kids when the season started. When it ended, they were men." The Padres spoiled the chances of the Houston Astros and San Francisco Giants to take the Western Division title. The Padres split their remaining four games with the Cincinnati Reds and Houston Astros, losses which neither could afford. On September 17, Padres pitchers surrendered a franchise record 20 hits in a 10-5 setback to Cincinnati at home, but infielder José Arcia belted three doubles the following day in a 7-1 triumph over the Reds. Nate Colbert homered twice in a 9-2 loss to the Houston Astros at the Astrodome.

The San Francisco Giants came into San Diego Stadium September 22 in first place by 1.5 games. The Padres defeated San Francisco in two of three games, dropping the latter 1.5 games behind the Atlanta Braves. San Diego ended the season with two consecutive victories over the Giants at Candlestick Park. On October 1, Nate Colbert knocked in a season-high five runs in a 9-4 win over Giants. The Atlanta Braves were the only contender that the Padres could not match down the stretch. The Braves swept two three-games series from the Padres at San Diego Stadium and Atlanta-Fulton County Stadium to take the Western Division title.

San Francisco slugger Willie Mays became just the second major-leaguer to clout 600 career home runs when he hit a pinch hit home run on September 22 to give the Giants a 4-2 victory over the Padres. The score was tied, 2-2, in the seventh inning when San Francisco manager Clyde King asked Mays to pinch hit with Ron Hunt on second base. Padre rookie pitcher Mike Corkins threw Mays a fastball about belt high. Mays pulled the pitch into the seats near the left-field line for his historic 390-foot home run, joining Babe Ruth as the only sluggers to reach the six-century mark.

The 1969 Padres wallowed around in last place for almost the entire season and finished last in the Western Division with a 52-110 record, 41 games behind the Atlanta Braves. Buzzie Bavasi admitted his club was "terrible" and added, "When we looked down on the field and saw the caliber of players we had, we knew we were in trouble." Seven opposing pitchers hurled two-hitters against the Padres. The youth-oriented club, however, won one more game than the world champion New York Mets did in their sophomore season. The 613,327 home attendance and 512,970 paid attendance for 75 home dates fell far short of the one million envisioned by Smith and Bavasi. Manager Preston Gomez did not reach his preseason goal of 60 victories, but found the Padres' September performance encouraging. Gomez predicted that his team could notch 70 victories in 1970, an 18-game improvement over 1969.

Several young Padres had shown some potential. Nate Colbert, who began the season splitting first base duties with Bill Davis, batted .255 and surprised the San Diego franchise with 24 home runs and 66 RBIs. Ollie Brown paced San Diego starters with a .264 batting average, 20 home runs, and 61 RBIs for a club ranking last in most offensive categories. He also performed well defensively and possessed an excellent throwing arm. Veteran Al Ferrara contributed 14 home runs and 56 RBIs in only 366 plate appearances.

The young pitching staff, meanwhile, gained valuable major-league experience. Twenty-one-year-old starter Clay Kirby performed much better than his 7-20 record indicated and compiled a 3.79 ERA. Al Santorini, another 21-year-old starter, and Joe Niekro led the club in victories with eight each. Santorini yielded only 3.94 runs per nine innings. Niekro led the club in shutouts with three and finished 8-18 with a 3.71 ERA. The Padres' bullpen, however, provided little relief. Reliever Jack Baldschun enjoyed the longest winning streak with five victories between April 24 and May 30, but hard-luck starter-reliever Gary Ross lost

11 consecutive decisions from May 4 through August 31. Veteran catcher Chris Cannizzaro provided a steadying influence on the young Padre pitchers.

President Buzzie Bavasi engineered two winter trades that added two superior infielders, a fine catcher, and two veteran pitchers. The first trade, consummated on the evening of December 4, dispatched pitcher Pat Dobson and second baseman Dave Campbell from the Detroit Tigers for pitcher Joe Niekro. Dobson had blanked opponents in 26 of 40 relief appearances and had compiled a 5-10 record with a 3.60 ERA in 1969, while Campbell had performed well defensively. The next morning, the Padres acquired third baseman Bobby Etheridge, catcher Bob Barton, and pitcher Ron Herbel from the San Francisco Giants for pitcher Frank Reberger. Herbel had compiled a 29-28 record with a 3.53 ERA in six major-league seasons mainly as a middle-inning reliever. Bavasi remarked, "There are eight daily regular positions in baseball, and we've definitely improved ourselves at three of them." Before the 1970 campaign, Gomez boasted, "We're definitely going to be better this year. Just the experience of 1969 for our young players—especially our pitchers—would indicate improvement. But Bavasi's trades have guaranteed it."

3

The Cellar-Dwelling Early Years [1970-73]

The 1970-1973 seasons brought further frustration to San Diego Padres fans. San Diego continued to struggle in last place, averaging just over 60 victories and 99 losses per season. Annual home attendance ranged between 550,000 and 645,000, well short of the 800,000 needed to make the franchise profitable.

In 1970, the Padres made several roster moves during spring training. On March 24, San Diego traded infielder Roberto Peña to the Oakland Athletics for first baseman Ramon Webster. Six days later, the Padres acquired pitcher Gerry Nyman from the Chicago White Sox for pitcher Tommie Sisk. On April 2, the Padres traded pitcher Billy McCool to the St. Louis Cardinals for shortstop Steve Huntz.

First baseman Nate Colbert's three-run homer off Phil Niekro helped San Diego defeat the Atlanta Braves, 8-3, in the April 7 home opener before a season-high 25,215 fans. *The San Diego Union* reported, "It was David slaying Goliath." Starting pitcher Pat Dobson, acquired from the Detroit Tigers, struck out six Atlanta batters in eight innings. The Padres won five of their first 11 road games, but saw fortunes reversed on April 22 at Shea Stadium. Tom Seaver of the New York Mets fanned the last 10 San Diego batters and 19 altogether, tying the major league record at that time for most strikeouts in a single game. He hurled a two-hit, 2-1 masterpiece, allowing just a second-inning home run by outfielder Al Ferrara and a fourth-inning single by second baseman Dave Campbell. The Padres lost five consecutive home games from April 24 through April 28 and ended the month in last place.

San Diego pitchers did not hurl a complete game until their 21st start on April 29, when Pat Dobson fanned 11 batters in a three-hit, 10-0, victory over the Montreal Expos. Only 1,753 fans saw Dobson's masterpiece at San Diego Stadium. Owner Buzzie Bavasi attributed the declining attendance to poor team performance and the lack of divisional rivalries. The sparse attendance at nine home games against the Los Angeles

Dodgers particularly disappointed Bavasi. He stated, "We had figured we'd draw 250,000–300,000 people, but we . . . didn't come close to that."

Although playing well in May, San Diego still drew under 10,000 fans a game. In their first 42 contests through May 21, the Padres outhit, outscored, and outhomered their opponents. Mike Corkins won three consecutive starts in May, while on May 9, Danny Coombs blanked the Montreal Expos, 6-0, on a two-hitter at Jarry Park. On May 23, San Diego set club records with 17 runs, 21 hits, and eight extra-base hits and tied a franchise record with five home runs in a wild five-hour, 29-minute, 15-inning, marathon 17-16 victory over the San Francisco Giants at Candlestick Park. Nate Colbert clouted a home run and hit four singles, while Chris Cannizzaro, Cito Gaston, Ron Slocum, and Steve Huntz also homered. The Giants battered Padres pitching for 23 hits and left 17 runners on base. Cannizzaro enjoyed a season-best 13-game hitting streak from May 8 through May 30.

Cito Gaston played outfield for the Padres from 1969 through 1974.

By the first week of June, San Diego almost ascended from the cellar. The Padres averaged nearly five runs per game and belted 65 home runs through 55 games. On June 2, San Diego exploded for 19 hits and connected for four triples against the Pittsburgh Pirates at Three Rivers Stadium. Chris Cannizzaro, Tommy Dean, and José Arcia each tripled in the seventh inning. The Padres' fortunes began to change 10 days later. In the first game of a June 12 doubleheader, 25-year-old Doc Ellis of the Pittsburgh Pirates blanked San Diego, 2-0, for the first no-hitter in San Diego Stadium history. He faced the Padres for the second time in two weeks, having defeated them, 5-1, 11 days earlier. Ellis did not have good control, walking eight batters and hitting one. The only threat to the no-hitter came in the seventh inning, when second baseman Bill Mazeroski grabbed pinch hitter Ramon Webster's line drive. The catch helped Ellis retire the side in order for just the third time in the game. Padres batters connected solidly only two other times, hitting line drives directly at center fielder Matty Alou. Ellis struck out six Padres, while Pittsburgh first baseman Willie Stargell clouted solo home runs in both the second and seventh innings. In the nightcap, Nate Colbert tripled twice to lift the Padres to a 5-2 victory.

The Padres slumped during the latter part of June, batting just .201 and hitting only 10 home runs. San Diego lost eight consecutive games from June 20 through June 28. On June 22, Don Wilson of the Houston Astros retired 20 consecutive Padres in a 4-1 hurling masterpiece at the Astrodome. Outfielder Ollie Brown did not knock in a run for half a month. Starters Pat Dobson, Al Santorini, and Mike Corkins, along with reliever Tom Dukes, missed significant playing time due to injuries. Starter Clay Kirby went six weeks without a victory, while Dave Roberts lost 10 consecutive decisions from June 12 through September 5.

Buzzie Bavasi and Preston Gomez both patiently waited for the younger, inexperienced players to succeed. San Diego still performed inconsistently during the second half of the 1970 season. Starting pitchers Gary Ross and Al Santorini combined for only three victories before the All-Star break and were optioned to Salt Lake City. On July 15, the Padres purchased veteran starting pitcher Earl Wilson from the Detroit Tigers, but he won only one of seven decisions. The relievers were overworked and became fatigued. Padres defensive errors led to 63 unearned runs in a 103 game span.

The San Diego offense occasionally came alive. On July 1, outfielder Ollie Brown knocked in a then club-record six runs in a 12-7 loss to the San Francisco Giants at Candlestick Park. On July 4, second baseman Dave Campbell stole two bases against the Atlanta

Braves at Atlanta-Fulton County Stadium. In a 9-7 home loss to the Los Angeles Dodgers on July 10, Ivan Murrell, Ed Spiezio, Campbell, and Cito Gaston hit ninth-inning home runs. Four days later, Gaston became the first Padre to appear in an All-Star Game. He went hitless in two plate appearances in a 5-4, 12-inning National League victory at Riverfront Stadium in Cincinnati. On July 26, the Padres overwhelmed the Philadelphia Phillies, 16-2, at Veterans Stadium in their highest scoring production and largest margin of victory of the decade. Al Ferrara homered twice, while Nate Colbert and Steve Huntz added round-trippers.

On July 21, right-hander Clay Kirby hurled one of the best games in franchise history. His masterpiece came against the New York Mets at San Diego Stadium, where he came within three outs of a no-hitter. The Padres fell behind, 1-0, on a first-inning walk, two stolen bases, and a groundout. Kirby started up to the plate with two men out and no runners on base in the bottom of the eighth inning when Gomez removed him. The sparse hometown crowd of 10,373 booed lustily when Cito Gaston struck out as a pinch hitter for Kirby. Irate fans jumped down from the seats and searched for Gomez in the dugout. When police hustled the intruders away, spectators booed the security. The Mets won 3-0, tagging reliever Jack Baldschun for two runs and three hits in the top of the ninth inning. Gomez deprived Kirby of a golden opportunity to lift the last place Padres psychologically and spark local interest in the team. No Padre has yet hurled a no-hitter. "Gomez," Steve Arlin recalled, "felt that's what he needed to do to win the game. He often pinch hit for pitchers in trying to generate runs." Kirby's performance did not improve San Diego's fortunes.

The Padres suffered their earliest elimination from the National League pennant race in franchise history, falling 32.5 games behind the Cincinnati Reds on August 13. The following day, Padres pitchers surrendered eight runs in the fifth inning in a 10-1 loss to the Pittsburgh Pirates at Three Rivers Stadium. On September 1, the Padres sold workhorse reliever Ron Herbel, who was pacing the National League with 64 appearances, to the New York Mets.

The Padres won 13 games in September. On September 4, pitcher Mike Corkins clouted a grand slam off of Jim Merritt of the Cincinnati Reds in the fourth inning of a 15-2 victory at Riverfront Stadium. Two days later, Pat Dobson allowed the Reds only two hits in a 3-2 triumph. The Padres won five consecutive games from September 9 through September 13. On September 13, Clay Kirby fanned 11 Cincinnati Reds in a 5-4 home win. Left-hander Dave Roberts became the first Padre pitcher to hurl two consecutive shutouts, blanking the Los Angeles Dodgers, 4-0, on September 16 at Dodger Stadium and the Atlanta Braves, 5-0, on September 24 at Atlanta-Fulton County Stadium. Besides completing 23 consecutive scoreless innings, he surrendered only 12 earned runs in his final seven starts. On September 26, Nate Colbert homered twice, doubled, and singled in a 7-6 loss to the San Francisco Giants at Candlestick Park. In the season finale at home on October 1, Cito Gaston hit three singles and a double against the Los Angeles Dodgers.

San Diego finished 63-99 in 1970, 39 games behind the first-place Cincinnati Reds and 13 games behind the fifth-place Atlanta Braves. Although falling seven victories short of Manager Preston Gomez's goal, San Diego recorded 11 more victories than in their inaugural season. Gomez stressed, "The players improved themselves and their team even more than they did their record." The Padres defeated the Cincinnati Reds in 10 out of 18 games. Only one other National League team held a season advantage over the Reds. Cincinnati manager Sparky Anderson commented, "I'm glad we don't have to face the Padres in a playoff for the pennant. They have one of the best offenses in baseball." San Diego split season series of 12 games each with the Eastern Division champion Pittsburgh Pirates and the dethroned world champion New York Mets.

The Padres vastly improved their offensive production in 1970, raising their team batting average 21 points to .246. The team clouted a still club record 172 home runs, ranking third in the National League behind the powerful Cincinnati Reds and Chicago Cubs. First baseman Nate Colbert, center fielder Cito Gaston, and right fielder Ollie Brown sparked the Padres' offense. Colbert shattered the San Diego record for most home runs in a season with 38, and he knocked in 86 runs. Gaston batted .318, an astounding 88-point improvement over 1969, to become the first San Diego regular to reach the .300 plateau. Gaston, the lone Padre All-Star selection, also clouted a career-high 29 home runs and led the Padres in hits (186) and RBIs (93). He only had two home runs with 29 RBIs in 1969. Brown enjoyed his best major-league season, hitting .292 with 23 homers and 89 RBIs. Catcher Chris Cannizzaro batted .279, while Al Ferrara, Dave

Campbell, Ivan Murrell, Ed Spiezio, and Steve Huntz all contributed between 11 and 13 home runs.

Pat Dobson anchored the Padres' pitching staff with a 14-15 record, a 3.76 ERA, eight complete games, and 251 innings pitched. The remaining starting pitchers, however, did not fulfill team expectations. Clay Kirby only contributed 10 victories in 26 decisions, while Al Santorini and Gary Ross combined for only three victories. San Diego hurlers allowed too many unearned runs, losing 37 one-run games. Reliever Ron Herbel became the club's first league leader when he paced the National League with 76 appearances, including 12 after being traded to the New York Mets.

The Padres made several off-season trades to strengthen their defense. On October 19, San Diego sold first baseman Ramon Webster to the Oakland Athletics and the next day acquired outfielder Rod Gaspar from the New York Mets to complete the Herbel transaction. On December 1, the Padres obtained shortstop Enzo Hernandez and pitchers Tom Phoebus, Al Severinsen, and Fred Beene from the Baltimore Orioles for pitchers Pat Dobson and Tom Dukes. Three days later, they acquired second baseman Don Mason from the San Francisco Giants for shortstop Steve Huntz. The Padres expected major offensive production in 1971 from Nate Colbert, Cito Gaston, and Ollie Brown and more consistent performances from starting pitchers Clay Kirby, Dave Roberts, Danny Coombs, Al Santorini, and Steve Arlin.

The Padres drew 633,439 fans for 73 home games in 1970, an increase of 20,000 from 1969. The attendance figures, however, were nearly 170,000 short of the amount needed to make a profit and the lowest in the National League. Gomez urged the fans to remain patient as the young players matured. Rumors spread that the Padres would move to Washington, D.C., Toronto, or New Orleans, but determined co-owners C. Arnholdt Smith and Buzzie Bavasi had enough money and patience to keep the Padres in San Diego.

Bavasi predicted that San Diego would win at least 15 more games in 1971, but the Padres failed to live up to his expectations. The San Francisco Giants blanked San Diego, 4-0, on a five-hitter by Juan Marichal in the April 6 home opener before a record crowd of over 34,000 fans. The Padres lost 11 of their first 14 games, including eight consecutive, and struggled in last place. During the losing streak, opponents shut out San Diego twice and never allowed them more than two runs in a game. In the final loss, Padres pitchers surrendered 18 hits in a 10-2 loss to the Los Angeles Dodgers. Crowd attendance dropped below 4,000 at two games.

A ray of hope came on April 11 when first baseman Nate Colbert homered in his first two plate appearances against the Los Angeles Dodgers at Dodger Stadium, giving him three consecutive round-trippers. He tied the club record with six RBIs, while Larry Stahl and Cito Gaston also homered in the 9-7 victory. The Padres batted under .200 in their initial 14 contests and went one four-game stretch with just one extra-base hit. *The San Diego Union* reported that the Padres were "having such a power failure that you'd think they were doing business with Con Edison in New York." No Padre starting pitcher completed a game during the first 14 contests. The team ERA hovered around 6.00, as the staff allowed more than one hit per inning.

The Padres won only five of 21 games in April, falling 11 games behind first place. Fan interest declined because the Padres lost so many games, while the players performed poorly before sparse home crowds. Nate Colbert complained that the small crowds adversely affected team performance. "It [took] away from the game to go out to that big, beautiful stadium in San Diego and see all those empty seats," Colbert said. "If we're losing by a couple of runs in the fifth inning," he added, "they'll leave early."

By mid-May, San Diego was mired in last place with only 10 victories and the worst major-league record. On May 16, the Padres blew a 7-1 lead over the Chicago Cubs, losing 9-8 in 10 innings. Bavasi kept Preston Gomez as manager and blamed the players for the poor team performance. He needed to acquire quality veterans but lacked the money to buy them. Bavasi, therefore, sold or traded his young players for other young players. On May 11, the Padres signed relief pitcher Robert L. Miller, who had been released by the Chicago Cubs, and two days later traded outfielder Al Ferrara to the Cincinnati Reds for outfielder Angel Bravo. On May 19, Bavasi traded catcher Chris Cannizzaro to the Chicago Cubs for infielder Garry Jestadt and cash. On June 11, the Padres acquired outfielder Leron Lee and pitcher Fred Norman from the St. Louis Cardinals for pitcher Al Santorini. San Diego liked Norman's minor-league performance and hoped that Lee would give them a powerful, speedy, left-handed batter. Bavasi resisted offers to give up potential franchise stars Nate Colbert and Clay Kirby.

Despite these transactions, the Padres continued to struggle both offensively and defensively. San Diego suffered a seven-game losing streak from June 16 through June 22, victimized by poor infield defense. Miscues by third baseman Dave Campbell and second baseman Garry Jestadt led to all four of the Houston Astros' runs in a 4-2 setback at home on June 22. In their first 70 games, the Padres made 17 more errors (78), scored 80 fewer runs, and clouted 25 fewer home runs than in 1970.

By midseason, the Padres' front office complained that Gomez was too patient with younger players and too often sought the big inning rather than trying to score one run at a time. The front office also lamented that Padres runners were picked off base too often and that some batters did not try to run out ground balls. They also criticized the lack of public support for the team. General Manager Eddie Leishman expressed concerns about the low attendance. He admitted that the front office couldn't ignore the situation anymore.

San Diego languished with a 33-57 record at the All-Star break. Opponents held the Padres scoreless for 37.2 consecutive innings from July 21 through July 24, blanking the Padres in three consecutive games in late July. The Atlanta Braves shut out San Diego by identical 1-0 scores on July 21 and July 22 at Atlanta-Fulton County Stadium, while the Pittsburgh Pirates triumphed over the Padres, 4-0, on July 23 at San Diego Stadium. The Padres briefly broke out of the slump on July 29, doubling five times in a 5-1 home victory over the Cincinnati Reds. In an attempt to bolster the offense, the Padres on August 10 traded pitcher Robert L. Miller to the Pittsburgh Pirates for outfielder John Jeter and pitcher Eduardo Acosta. On September 7 outfielder Leron Lee generated some of that much-needed offense. He became the first Padre to make five hits in a game, doubling twice and scoring four runs, in an 8-7 win over the Cincinnati Reds.

Clay Kirby, anchor of the Padre starters, pitched several memorable games. On May 9, he threw a franchise-record 161 pitches in a 7-2 home triumph over the Cincinnati Reds. Then on June 10, he struck out 13 New York Mets in a 4-2 victory at Shea Stadium. On August 30, he tied the club record for most season strikeouts with 185 in a 4-3 win over the Cincinnati Reds at Riverfront Stadium. The triumph marked his third consecutive victory. During September, Kirby nearly pitched two consecutive no-hitters. A no-hitter was authored at home by Kirby for 7.1 innings against the Houston Astros on September 13 before John Edwards doubled. Kirby eventually lost the game on an unearned run in the ninth inning.

Clay Kirby pitched for the Padres from 1969 through 1973.

Five days later, Kirby retired the first 21 San Francisco Giants batters at Candlestick Park. Willie McCovey led off the eighth inning with a home run for the Giants' only hit in the 2-1 Padre triumph. In the first game of a September 24 doubleheader, Kirby set a franchise mark by fanning 15 Houston Astros in 15 innings. The Padres played their longest game in franchise history, losing 2-1 in a 21-inning contest. Five days later, Kirby extended his club season record for most strikeouts with 231 in a 4-1, seven-hit, 10-inning home triumph over the Giants. He also set a club mark for Padre pitchers with his 15th victory, retiring the last 10 batters consecutively. Besides ranking fourth in the National League in strikeouts, he boasted an impressive 2.83 ERA.

Other Padre pitchers performed well, too. Reliever Bob Miller won both games of a June 23 home doubleheader against the Houston Astros. Dick Kelley, on July 6, blanked the Houston Astros, 1-0, at home on a one-hitter. On August 11, Dave Roberts outdueled Tom Seaver of the New York Mets, 1-0, in 12 innings before nearly 10,000 fans. Only 4,600 fans saw Steve Arlin best Nolan Ryan of the New York Mets, 3-0, the following night. Arlin ranked second to Milt Pappas in National League shutouts with four through September 3.

The Padres emphasized youth in September. Pitcher Jay Franklin on September 4 became the youngest Padre player to appear in a major-league game at 18 years, 6 months, and 19 days. He pitched in an 11-7 home loss to the Atlanta Braves, with 19-year-old Mike Ivie as catcher. Franklin compiled an 0-1 record with a 6.00 ERA in three games that season and never appeared in another major league game. The much-maligned San Diego defense even turned a triple play in the seventh inning on August 1 at home against the Atlanta Braves.

The Padres hosted the first-place San Francisco Giants in the final three games of the season. The Giants retained the one-game lead over the Dodgers to win the Western Division title, defeating the Padres, 5-1, in the September 30 season finale before 35,000 people. The final home stand drew 65,000 fans. *The San Diego Union* remarked, "At least, baseball in San Diego, circa 1971, ended with a bang, not a whimper."

San Diego again finished last in the Western Division with a 61-100 record and attracted a dismal 549,085 attendance for 69 home dates. The Padres' offensive production fell far short of expectations. San Diego shared last place with the Philadelphia Phillies with a .233 team batting average, scoring only 486 runs and clouting just 96 home runs. The Padres averaged slightly over three runs per game, nearly one less than in 1970. Nate Colbert's home run production fell from 38 to 27, but he led the Padres with 149 hits and 84 RBIs. Cito Gaston batted only .228 with 17 home runs and 61 RBIs, far below his 1970 production. Ollie Brown hit .273 with 55 RBIs and just nine home runs, 16 fewer than in 1970.

In 1971, San Diego hurlers could have sued the Padres for lack of offensive support. They compiled a 3.22 ERA, third best in the National League behind the New York Mets and the Houston Astros. Dave Roberts set a San Diego record and finished second to Tom Seaver in the National League with a 2.10 ERA, but won only 14 of 31 decisions. In his 17 losses, the Padres scored only 22 runs, were blanked five times, and tallied only one run seven times. San Diego scored just 86 runs in the 37 games Roberts pitched. Clay Kirby compiled a 15-13 record with a 2.83 ERA and ranked fourth in the National League in strikeouts with 231. Although recording only nine wins in 28 decisions, rookie Steve Arlin hurled four shutouts, toiled 228 innings, and authored a 3.47 ERA. Fred Norman pitched far better than his 3-12 record indicated, while rookie Ed Acosta split decisions in his six starts. Bob Miller strengthened the Padres' bullpen during his three-month stint. Rookie shortstop Enzo Hernandez provided good defense, but the Padres needed better-fielding second and third basemen.

The abysmal team performance sparked one major off-season transaction. On December 3, 1971, the Padres sent premier starting pitcher Dave Roberts to the Houston Astros for second baseman Derrel Thomas and pitchers Bill Greif and Mark Schaeffer. In 1971, Thomas batted .286 and Greif fanned 152 batters for Oklahoma City of the American Association. President Buzzie Bavasi hoped that Thomas would give the Padres more speed in the infield, at the plate, and on the base paths and that Greif would replace Roberts in the starting rotation.

San Diego, meanwhile, enlisted area businessmen to increase season ticket sales. Bavasi, on January 4, formed the Padres Action Team, a 90-member volunteer group, to sell partial-season tickets. The team offered two partial-season ticket plans of 24 home games for $84. One plan covered home games on Fridays and Sundays, while the other covered home games on Wednesdays and Fridays. The San Diego Chamber of Commerce also pledged to help boost season ticket sales. The Padres hoped that the two plans would help increase season attendance to at least 800,000. Within five weeks, the Padres sold 609 partial-season tickets.

Manager Preston Gomez planned for the Padres to feature team speed and pitching depth in 1972. The Padres fielded the youngest major-league team, averaging around 24 years old. Gomez expected outfielder Leron Lee and infielders John Jeter and Dave Campbell to provide additional team speed and planned to rely on Clay Kirby, Steve Arlin, Fred Norman, Bill Greif, and rookie Mike Caldwell for the starting rotation. Gomez, however, ended up altering his plans. John Jeter broke his arm in spring training and struggled at the plate in 1972, while Derrel Thomas had difficulty reaching base. Ollie Brown struggled at spring training and was put on the trading block. Reliever Al Sevirensen, a New York resident who had recorded eight saves and a 3.47 ERA in 59 appearances in 1971, left spring training camp at Yuma, Arizona and threatened to retire unless traded to an East Coast club. Mike Ivie, a 19-year-old catcher from Georgia and the nation's top draft pick in 1970, walked out of spring training camp the first weekend after having a poor exhibition game. He did not report to the Alexandria, Louisiana farm club until late April and wanted to become a first baseman. Utility infielder Tommy Dean retired at age 26.

San Diego missed the first nine games of the 1972 season because of a players' strike. The players wanted to extend the arbitration principle to salary disputes. Padre players voted unanimously in favor of striking. The strike officially began on April 1, the last Saturday of spring training and five days before the season opener. Marvin Miller, executive director of the Major League Players Association, led the players in a 13-day strike yielding a new contract. The agreement extended the arbitration principle to salary disputes, a concession sending salary levels sharply upward. During the strike, General Manager Eddie Leishman underwent gall bladder surgery. He was later hospitalized with pneumonia and underwent lung surgery.

San Diego defeated the Atlanta Braves, 6-5, in the season opener before 15,000 home fans on April 15, as Kirby bested Phil Niekro. The next day, nearly 10,000 fans saw the Padres split a doubleheader with the Atlanta Braves. Local sportswriter Jack Murphy labeled San Diego "fiercely competitive" and "entertaining." The Padres, however, lost six of their next eight games and were soon mired in last place. San Diego, on April 20, traded pitcher Tom Phoebus to the Chicago Cubs and signed pitcher Ron Taylor, formerly with the Montreal Expos.

San Diego needed a strong leader to improve team fortunes. On April 27, Bavasi fired Gomez, who had compiled a 4-7 record in 1972 and a 180-316 overall record as manager. Bavasi had never removed a manager in his long career as a baseball executive. Gomez knew baseball fundamentals well and had patiently tried to turn a young team into a contender, but he had lacked communication skills with the press. The Cuban native often conversed in Spanish and therefore needed everything translated. Bavasi regarded the managerial change as a public relations move and not a reflection on Gomez's managing ability. Upon being fired, Gomez remarked, "It's a shock to me. But in baseball, it comes with the job. The team was not hitting . . . the situation is very bad. Anyway, I came with a suitcase and I'm leaving with one."

Third base coach Don Zimmer replaced Gomez as manager. Zimmer, a stocky, fiery competitor stressing

Don Zimmer managed the Padres in 1972 and 1973.

pitching and defense, had played infield for 11 seasons with the Brooklyn Dodgers, Los Angeles Dodgers, New York Mets, Chicago Cubs, Cincinnati Reds, and Washington Senators and had piloted from 1969 through 1972 in the Padre farm system. Zimmer had developed a reputation as a determined leader who would not quit. Under Zimmer, the Padres won eight of their first 14 games and nearly reached the .500 winning percentage mark. Sportswriter Jack Murphy observed, "It seems that Zimmer and the San Diego Padres are just right for each other. The players respond to his easy ways, and the job is a piece of cake to Zimmer." On May 5, Bill Greif struck out five consecutive New York Mets at Shea Stadium. Nate Colbert was leading the National League with nine home runs by early May. The leaky Padre defense, however, made six errors on May 7 against the New York Mets at Shea Stadium.

San Diego players and fans began to believe that the Padres could contend for the Western Division title. Over 104,000 fans came to San Diego Stadium for a seven-game home stand from May 15 through May 21 against the Los Angeles Dodgers and Cincinnati Reds. The Padres won three of those contests, including two shutouts by Fred Norman. Norman, who had already blanked the Montreal Expos, 5-0, at Jarry Park on May 13, shut out the Dodgers, 2-0, on May 17 and the Cincinnati Reds, 7-0, on May 21. San Diego drew over 42,000 fans for a three-game series with the Dodgers and over 61,000 for the four-game series, including a doubleheader, with the Reds. Over 196,000 fans attended the first 19 Padre home games. "If we continue to play the way we have lately," Bavasi boasted, "we could draw a million here this season." The attendance figures and improved team performance reassured Bavasi that the Padres could survive in San Diego. The Padres doubled seven times on May 27 against the Reds at Riverfront Stadium. Nate Colbert, Ed Spiezio, and Jerry Morales each doubled twice.

San Diego lost 10 consecutive games from May 29 through June 10. The Padres on May 17 traded struggling outfielder Ollie Brown to the Oakland Athletics for catcher-outfielder Curt Blefary and pitcher Mike Kilkenny, leaving Nate Colbert and Cito Gaston as the only regular position players over age 25. Bavasi claimed that Brown "wasted a lot of talent" and "did not have the competitive desire to do well." During the losing streak, a few developments encouraged San Diego fans. On June 4, the Padres turned a triple play in the ninth inning at home against the Chicago Cubs.

Nate Colbert played first base for the Padres from 1969 through 1974.

Three days later, Clay Kirby hurled 13 consecutive scoreless innings in a 1-0 home loss to the Pittsburgh Pirates. Bill Greif on June 9 picked off Bob Gibson and Lou Brock in the third inning of a 3-2 victory over the St. Louis Cardinals at home.

Rookie infielder Dave Roberts jumped directly to the Padres from the University of Oregon after being selected in the first round of the June free agent draft. He signed on June 7 and played his first professional game that evening, entering in the twelfth inning against the Pittsburgh Pirates. He started his first major-league game on June 10 against the St. Louis Cardinals at third base and remained in the lineup thereafter. Roberts had four hits, including his first major-league home run, on June 29 in an 8-6 win over the Atlanta Braves at San Diego Stadium. He was thrown out three times at the plate the next night in a 4-3 victory over the Cincinnati Reds, but doubled home two runs to tie the game and doubled to start the winning rally in the 13th inning. San Diego also made several other roster changes. On June 11, the Padres traded pitcher Mike Kilkenny to the Cleveland Indians for infielder Fred Stanley and traded catcher Bob Barton to the Cincinnati Reds for catcher Pat Corrales. Nine days later, San Diego sent infielder Rafael Robles to the St. Louis Cardinals for first baseman Mike Fiore and a minor league pitcher.

San Diego returned to last place in the Western Division with a 21-41 record on June 25. The Padres had never avoided the cellar for such a length of time before. Weak hitting, ineffective pitching, and relative youth caused the Padres' woes. Nate Colbert had reached double figures in home runs and knocked in 44 runs by the end of June, but no teammates recorded more than 22 RBIs. Tom Seaver of the New York Mets nearly hurled a no-hitter against the Padres in the first game of a doubleheader on July 4 at Shea Stadium, yielding just a ninth-inning single by Leron Lee in the 2-0 victory.

Steve Arlin, who had triumphed in seven games by June 23 and picked off nine runners at second base in 1972, paced National League pitchers from June 18 through July 18, hurling two one-hitters and three two-hitters and allowing only 40 hits in 79 innings. His masterpieces began on June 18, when he blanked the Pittsburgh Pirates 1-0 on a two-hitter at Three Rivers Stadium. Five days later, he hurled a less dramatic one-hit, 4-1, victory at home against the Giants. Garry Maddox tripled in the second inning for the Giants' lone safety. On July 6, Arlin authored a one-hitter for the first 10 innings in a 1-0, 14-inning win over the New York Mets at Shea Stadium. He gave up two hits in a 3-2 loss to the Mets on July 14 at San Diego Stadium.

Four days later against the Philadelphia Phillies, Arlin hurled the best pitched and longest hitless game in team history. He still had a no-hitter with two men out in the ninth inning and two strikes on Denny Doyle. After Padre manager Don Zimmer moved third baseman Dave Roberts in by 10 feet, Doyle bounced a single over Roberts's head. Doyle's grounder could have been fielded if Roberts had remained in his normal fielding position. Zimmer later apologized to Arlin, who ironically led the major leagues with 21 losses that season. Before Doyle singled, Arlin had pitched 12 consecutive hitless innings over two successive games. He then lost 10 consecutive games before defeating the Los Angeles Dodgers on September 18.

First baseman Nate Colbert enjoyed an outstanding second half of the season. He scored the winning run in the tenth inning to give the National League All-Stars a 4-3 victory on July 25 at Atlanta-Fulton County Stadium. After walking as a pinch-hitter for Met reliever Tug McGraw, he moved to second base on a sacrifice and scored on second baseman Joe Morgan's single to right field. Keyed by Colbert, the rejuvenated Padres won eight of 12 games on their first road trip after the All-Star break.

At Atlanta-Fulton County Stadium on August 1, Colbert emerged as one of the true major-league sluggers while enjoying the one of the best hitting performances in baseball history. He attracted national attention by clouting five home runs, driving in 13 runs, and recording 22 total bases in a doubleheader against the Atlanta Braves. His 13 RBIs for the doubleheader broke the major-league record of 11 held jointly by Earl Averill, Jim Tabor, and Boog Powell, and remains a major-league record for a twinbill. In the first game, Colbert homered off of Ron Schueler in the first inning with two runners aboard and off of Mike McQueen in the seventh inning with the bases empty. In the second inning of the nightcap, he belted a grand slam off of Pat Jarvis. Later the same game, Colbert homered with one aboard off of Jim Hardin in the seventh inning and off of Cecil Upshaw in the ninth inning.

His five home runs in the doubleheader equaled St. Louis Cardinal Stan Musial's major-league standard. Colbert saw Musial set the record in his hometown of St. Louis on May 2, 1954, when he was just eight years old. "When I hit the fourth homer," Colbert recalled, "I was in Busch Stadium that afternoon. I never thought anyone would ever equal that record, certainly not me." His 13 RBIs cracked Jim Bottomley's National League record of 12 for two consecutive games set in 1924 and his 22 total bases for a doubleheader eclipsed Musial's major-league mark of 21 in 1954. His three home runs and eight RBIs in the second game established Padre records.

Colbert and outfielder Rick Monday of the Chicago Cubs were the only major-league players to have three-homer games in 1972. Colbert reached the second deck in left field at San Diego Stadium in a 3-2 triumph over the St. Louis Cardinals. He surpassed the 100 RBI mark with another grand slam in the sixth inning of the second game of a September 7 home doubleheader off of pitcher Jack Billingham in a 5-1 triumph over the Cincinnati Reds.

Injuries, meanwhile, devastated San Diego the second half of the 1972 season. Steve Arlin developed a sore shoulder, Clay Kirby missed 23 days because of elbow problems, and Bill Greif suffered a sore elbow, as well. The decimated pitching staff surrendered 104 runs in a two week span in August. In just five games between August 22 and August 26, Padre starters gave up 22 earned runs and 29 hits in nine innings. Injuries likewise sidelined regular position players. Leron Lee missed six weeks because of a broken finger, while Cito Gaston was sidelined for 42 games because of ankle and shoulder injuries. Dave Campbell appeared in only 33 games because of a torn Achilles tendon in his left ankle. He suffered the severe injury while running to first base in a 2-1 loss to the Chicago Cubs on June 2 and spent the rest of the season recuperating from surgery.

The injury-riddled Padres made several player transactions, most notably on July 9 when they traded third baseman Ed Spiezio to the Chicago White Sox for a minor league pitcher.

San Diego's fortunes bottomed on September 2, when Milt Pappas of the Chicago Cubs hurled an 8-0 no-hitter against the Padres at Wrigley Field. Pappas needed only 98 pitches to dispose of San Diego, striking out six in a game that lasted only two hours and three minutes. He nearly lost his no-hitter twice. In the fifth inning, shortstop Don Kessinger handled Nate Colbert's one-hop smash and nipped Colbert by half a step at first base. In the ninth inning, hard-running Billy Williams rescued Pappas when rookie center fielder Bill North slipped while chasing a routine fly ball by center fielder John Jeter. Pappas still enjoyed a perfect game with two outs in the ninth inning when pinch hitter Larry Stahl stepped to the plate. Stahl, however, walked on a three-two count. The no-hitter remained intact when pinch hitter Garry Jestadt popped out to second baseman Carmen Fanzone.

The Pappas masterpiece may have inspired Padre pitchers. Mike Corkins hurled consecutive 1-0 shutouts against the Giants on September 4 at Candlestick Park and the Braves six days later at home. He and Clay Kirby on September 24 combined on a two-hitter in a 2-1 home victory over the Atlanta Braves. Fred Norman on September 15 set club records for shutouts in a season with six and strikeouts in a nine-inning game with 15 in a 1-0 victory over Don Gullett of the Cincinnati Reds at Riverfront Stadium. The 28 strikeouts by both clubs set a new National League record. The Los Angeles Dodgers, however, rocked him for 14 hits in seven innings in his next home start on September 20. Norman, who owned a wicked screwball, pitched shutouts in all but three of his nine victories and defeated Cincinnati's pennant winners four times. During the second half of the season, he also blanked the Braves, 5-0, at Atlanta-Fulton County Stadium on August 2 and the Cubs, 3-0, at Wrigley Field on September 3.

San Diego again finished last in the Western Division with a 58-95 mark and a corresponding .379 winning percentage. The 13-day strike in early April helped the Padres avoid a 100-loss season. The Padres' starting rotation of Steve Arlin (10-21), Clay Kirby (12-14), Fred Norman (9-11), and rookie Mike Caldwell (7-11) were all saddled with losing records. The team ERA slipped from third in the league in 1971 to 11th in 1972. Johnny Podres replaced Roger Craig as pitching coach following the 1972 season. Aside from Nate Colbert, the Padres supplied little offensive firepower. Colbert tied his club record for most season home runs with 38 and incredibly drove in 111 runs for a team that scored only 488 times and tallied just three runs a game. "It is amazing," infielder Dave Campbell recalled, "how far Colbert could hit the ball on a consistent basis." Left fielder Leron Lee was the only Padre position starter to bat .300.

Manager Don Zimmer remarked, "I know this is the best team we've ever had, but you would not believe it by looking at the standings." He had made bold moves, including demoting infielder Derrel Thomas to Hawaii of the Pacific Coast League for 10 days for disciplinary reasons. "Before he left, he was nothing but trouble," Zimmer claimed. "When he returned, he was never a problem." Zimmer also convinced the front office to keep University of Oregon star infielder Dave Roberts on the roster. The Padres had planned to let their top draft selection take one road trip and then option him to the minor leagues. Zimmer instead inserted the big right-handed hitter as regular third baseman after Dave Campbell underwent an Achilles tendon operation. Roberts batted .244 and switched to second base in September when rookie Dave Hilton joined the club. Zimmer liked Roberts's "fine ability" and "outstanding attitude." Despite these moves, San Diego performed woefully at the plate, on the mound, and in the field. The Padres remained what executive Elten Schiller termed "a ragtag outfit."

Nevertheless, Bavasi liked the young players promoted from the minor leagues in September and was especially impressed with Mike Ivie, converted from catcher to first baseman. The other promising prospects included third baseman Dave Hilton, outfielders John Grubb and Randy Elliott, and pitchers Steve Simpson and Ralph Garcia. "All of those kids were impressive," Buzzie Bavasi observed, "and our accent on youth is starting to pay off." The increased attendance also encouraged Bavasi. The Padres set a then club record by drawing 644,272 fans in 1972, an increase of 86,760 over 1971. Bavasi acknowledged, "How can I be disappointed in the attendance when the club is in last place?" The fine Padre May performance sparked much of the increase. San Diego's first annual Old-timer's Game also drew over 30,000 people on August 18 in a 4-2 loss to the Pittsburgh Pirates. The Padres, however, still needed to draw more than 150,000 additional fans to break even financially. San Diego fared only 26-54 at home as compared to 32-41 on the road. Team promotions, including Diamond Night, failed to attract large crowds. Bavasi conceded, "What we need is to become competitive and win more games."

The Padres made several off-season transactions. Bavasi sought a left-handed power hitter to bat fifth behind Leron Lee and Nate Colbert, but could not make such a deal. San Diego sent center fielder John Jeter to the Chicago White Sox for pitcher Vicente Romo on October 28, traded pitcher Al Severinsen to the New York Mets for left-handed pinch hitter Dave

Marshall on November 30, sold utility outfielder Larry Stahl to the Cincinnati Reds on November 30, and released outfielder-catcher Curt Blefary on December 27. General Manager Eddie Leishman, meanwhile, was seriously ill and unable to travel to Hawaii for the winter meetings. He died December 28.

Rumors abounded that the team might move to Washington, D.C., but on December 22 the Padres announced their intention to remain in San Diego for 1973. The city agreed to help increase ticket sales and promote greater attendance at the Padres' games. Mayor Pete Wilson promised to assist the Padre Action Team in its "mini-season" ticket drive and believed that 10,000 tickets could be sold before the 1973 season. Wilson affirmed, "This is a good young club—better than people realize—and it deserves public support. Up to now, the support hasn't been good enough."

The Padres rested their hopes for the 1973 campaign on their developing pitching staff. Manager Don Zimmer believed that his starters Fred Norman, Steve Arlin, and Clay Kirby, along with reliever Mike Caldwell, comprised the best pitching staff in the National League. He predicted that his club would escape last place and perhaps attain a .500 winning percentage. The 6-16 preseason exhibition record, however, indicated that the Padres would need to rely primarily on pitching and speed. Three rookies, —third baseman Dave Hilton, center fielder Johnny Grubb, and catcher Bob Davis—made the starting lineup. The Padres on April 2 strengthened their bullpen by reacquiring reliever Robert L. Miller, who had been released by the Pittsburgh Pirates. The bench possessed greater depth with Dave Campbell, Jerry Morales, and Derrel Thomas.

For the fourth time in five seasons, San Diego won its opening game, 4-2, on April 6 over the Los Angeles Dodgers before 32,019 San Diego Stadium fans. The Padres scored all their runs off Dodgers ace Don Sutton. Clay Kirby pitched eight innings for the victory, witnessed by the then-fifth-largest crowd to attend a major league game in San Diego. Leron Lee keyed the offense with three hits and two RBIs. The Padres then suffered five consecutive defeats, including a three-game sweep by Western Division rival Atlanta. Only 3,200 fans attended the final contest with the Atlanta Braves. Bill Greif provided a ray of hope on April 15, blanking the Houston Astros, 4-0, on two hits.

San Diego fortunes sagged further on the first extended 1973 road trip. The Padres managed only one victory in eight games against the Houston Astros, Pittsburgh Pirates, and Chicago Cubs. The April 25 game with the Pirates was postponed by rain. San Diego finished April in last place with a 7-15 record, 10 games out of first place. Zimmer's injury-plagued 1973 squad fielded seven rookies and four second-year players, often falling below the 25-player limit. Nate Colbert, who had just become the highest paid player in San Diego history at $70,000 a year, homered only once in his first 22 games. Second baseman Dave Roberts struggled at the plate and was optioned to the minor leagues, while pitcher Steve Arlin was reassigned to the bullpen.

San Diego won only 20 of its first 58 games through June 9, falling 17 games behind first place. The Padres drew 142,000 fans for their first 15 home games, an increase of 19,000 fans, but still ranked second worst in National League attendance. Cito Gaston sparked the offense, hitting safely in 13 consecutive games from May 5 through May 19. The struggling Nate Colbert clouted only four home runs and knocked in 23 runs in the first 58 games. Padre pitchers turned in some notable performances. Mike Caldwell on May 6 blanked the Pittsburgh Pirates 8-0 on two hits at home, but six days later was shelled for eight runs in just three innings against the Atlanta Braves. Bill Greif hurled a two-hit, 4-1 victory over the Cubs on May 7 and blanked the New York Mets, 4-0, on June 1. Steve Arlin returned to the starting rotation and edged the Dodgers, 4-3, on May 23. Dave Roberts, who was batting .375 for Hawaii, was recalled on May 23 and bolstered the Padre offense. He tripled twice on June 12 against the Montreal Expos at Jarry Park.

On June 5 the Padres chose Dave Winfield in the first round of the free agent draft as the fourth overall selection. Winfield, who had starred as a pitcher and outfielder at the University of Minnesota and had won Most Valuable Player honors at the 1973 College World Series, gave San Diego a powerful hitter around which to build the franchise. General Manager Peter Bavasi boasted that Winfield had more physical tools than any free agent the Padres had ever signed. Winfield debuted on June 19 against the Astros, making his first major-league hit and throwing out a runner at second base. The Padres hoped that tall, strong, speedy Winfield would ignite the anemic offense, which ranked last in runs scored. Winfield hit safely in his first six major-league games from June 19 to June 28 and made three hits, including his first home run, in his third major-league contest which was a 7-3 loss to the Astros at San Diego Stadium.

Despite the acquisition of Winfield, San Diego continued struggling off the field. The Padres' financial problems grew so acute that the front office made two cash transactions. On May 26, San Diego purchased infielder Rich Morales from the Chicago White Sox. The infield declined defensively after June 7 when veteran second baseman Dave Campbell was sent to the St. Louis Cardinals for error-prone infielder Dwain Anderson and cash. Five days later, San Diego traded pitcher Fred Norman, who had won only one of his first eight decisions, to the Cincinnati Reds for outfielder Gene Locklear, pitcher Mike Johnson, and cash. Norman helped the Cincinnati Reds win the Western Division title. The Padres promoted promising rookie left-hander Randy Jones to replace Norman. San Diego on June 22 sold pitcher Robert L. Miller to the Detroit Tigers.

The club performance continued to worsen. In the seventh inning on June 13, Jerry Morales hit into the first triple play in franchise history against the Montreal Expos at Jarry Park. The Padres tied a club record June 19 by losing their tenth consecutive home game, 7-3, to the Houston Astros. Pitcher Clay Kirby won only two games and allowed over six earned runs per game through early June but provided a glimmer of hope on June 23 by fanning 13 Cincinnati Reds at San Diego Stadium.

San Diego ranked last in the Western Division with a 33-65 mark at the All-Star break, 29 games behind the first-place Los Angeles Dodgers. Injuries and off seasons by veterans gave the Padres an excellent opportunity to give major-league experience to younger players. San Diego rookies salvaged an otherwise disappointing season. Center fielder John Grubb and right fielder Dave Winfield led the Padres in hitting through July. Second baseman Dave Roberts contributed nine home runs. Padre pitchers also boasted some impressive performances. Steve Arlin on July 5 hurled a 4-0, two hitter over the Los Angeles Dodgers at Dodger Stadium. Bill Greif boasted an impressive 3.34 ERA, outdueling Steve Carlton of the Philadelphia Phillies 3-0 with a two-hitter on August 8. The shutout took only one hour, 30 minutes in the fastest night game in major-league history. Randy Jones, who had posted an 8-1 record and 2.01 ERA at Alexandria of the Texas League, won two of his first five decisions with a 3.00 ERA after joining the Padres on June 12.

John Grubb played outfield for the Padres from 1972 through 1976.

Knuckleballer Phil Niekro of the Atlanta Braves no-hit the Padres, 9-0, on August 5 at Atlanta-Fulton County Stadium. The 34-year-old struck out four and walked three in the first no-hitter of his career and the first ever at the Atlanta park. In the eighth inning, pinch hitter Dave Winfield hit the only solid ball off the workmanlike veteran. The no-hitter was the first by a Brave since 1961 and the third in four years against the Padres. The previous night, pitcher Mike Corkins clouted the last of his three 1973 home runs against the Braves.

September brought more peaks and valleys. Home attendance plummeted to just 1,413 fans, a record low, on September 11 against the Houston Astros. Two days later, Mike Corkins tied a franchise record by hitting three San Francisco Giants batters. Nate Colbert, Dave Roberts, Cito Gaston, and Dave Hilton, on September 26, homered in a 5-1 victory over the Cincinnati Reds at Three Rivers Stadium. On September 29, the Los Angeles Dodgers defeated the Padres, 3-2, before 15,000 fans in seemingly the last major-league game in San Diego. In the fourth inning of that contest, infielder Dave Roberts became the first Padre to clout an inside-the-park home run. President Buzzie Bavasi wept following the game while fans walked sadly around the stadium. Bavasi blamed the limited market for preventing the team from drawing the 800,000 fans needed yearly to make operations profitable. He stated, "We did the best we knew how." The Padres hoped to avoid making up an April rainout game against the Pittsburgh Pirates at Three Rivers Stadium. The National League, however, required San Diego to replay the game on October 1 because the Pirates were battling the New York Mets and St. Louis Cardinals for the Eastern Division crown. Randy Jones defeated Pittsburgh, 4-3, on five hits in that contest, dropping the Pirates out of second place.

San Diego finished last in the National League Western Division for the fifth consecutive season with a 60-102 record, second-worst record in franchise history. Manager Don Zimmer philosophized, "It had to be about as tough a season as any team ever had to go through."

The Padres ranked last in team batting average (.244), RBIs (516), and runs scored (548). First baseman Nate Colbert led San Diego with a disappointing 22 home runs and only 79 RBIs. Third baseman Dave Roberts batted .286 with 21 home runs and 64 RBIs. All but three of his home runs came in the second half of the season. Outfielder John Grubb paced the Padres with a .311 batting average and fielded adeptly. He enjoyed a 10-game hitting streak from May 22 through June 1 and a nine-game hitting streak from June 21 through July 6. He made four hits against the St. Louis Cardinals on May 2 and batted a sizzling .571 with five RBIs in 12 pinch-hit appearances. Catcher Fred Kendall raised his batting average 66 points to .282 and thwarted rivals from stealing bases, while outfielder Jerry Morales increased his batting average 42 points to .281. Outfielder Dave Winfield batted .277 in 56 games, including .471 in 17 pinch-hit appearances, and reached base in five consecutive pinch-hit appearances. He homered as a pinch-hitter against the Braves on August 3 at Atlanta-Fulton County Stadium and knocked in four runs in a 9-0 victory over the New York Mets on August 14.

The starting pitchers fell far short of Zimmer's expectations, ranking next to last in National League ERA. Clay Kirby finished with an 8-18 record and a 4.79 ERA, while Mike Caldwell won only five of 19 times. Although struggling with a 10-17 mark, Bill Greif boasted a splendid 3.21 ERA, blanked three opponents, and hurled three two-hitters. Randy Jones encouraged the Padres with a 7-6 record and led the team with a 3.16 ERA, setting a club season record for the highest winning percentage (.538) by a left-hander. On July 3, he threw just 80 pitches in a 4-1 triumph over Los Angeles at Dodger Stadium. He blanked the New York Mets, 9-0, on August 14, and defeated the Dodgers twice, 4-1 and 3-2. Rich Troedsen won seven of 16 decisions as a combined starter and reliever. The Padres drew 611,826 fans, again missing the 800,000 mark. Bavasi said: "We can't condemn the fans here. If we were winning and didn't draw, it would be a different matter."

The San Diego front office quickly sought to improve the team. First, they planned to give the team financial relief by obtaining a more favorable stadium lease with the City of San Diego. Second, the Padres hoped to secure established major-league players. On October 24, San Diego acquired $70,000-a-year veteran outfielder Matty Alou. In 13 major-league seasons, Alou had a .309 career batting average with 1,761 hits. The following day, the Padres traded pitcher Mike Caldwell to the San Francisco Giants for powerful first baseman Willie McCovey and outfielder Bernie Williams. McCovey, who earned $100,000 a year, gave San Diego its first six-figure player. Upon joining the Padres, McCovey had clouted 413 career home runs, made the All-Star team six times, and earned Most Valuable Player honors in 1969.

On November 7, the Padres acquired second basemen Glenn Beckert and Bob Fenwick from the Chicago Cubs for outfielder Jerry Morales. On November 9, they traded pitcher Clay Kirby to the Cincinnati Reds for outfielder Bobby Tolan and pitcher Dave Tomlin. Although losing a pitching workhorse, the Padres secured a player capable of batting .300 and stealing 30 bases a season. Tolan had batted over .300 in 1969 and 1970 and had led the National League with 57 stolen bases in 1970. San Diego on December 20 traded pitcher Steve Simpson to the New York Mets for pitcher Jim McAndrew.

Lastly, the Padres planned to replace manager Don Zimmer and hire a new coaching staff. "I think that we have a very good chance," Bavasi remarked, "of surprising a lot of people in 1974." The Padres, however, appeared headed to Washington, D.C., for the 1974 season. Topps Chewing Gum even produced 1974 cards of 13 Padre players with the Washington inscription.

4

The Padres Nearly Leave San Diego

[1973-74]

Sparse attendance nearly caused the Padres to leave San Diego for Washington, D.C. The Padres consistently drew under 650,000 fans, ranking last in the National League. During San Diego's third major-league season, owner C. Arnholdt Smith began receiving offers to buy the Padres. Smith initially rejected the various bids because he believed that his club could still flourish in San Diego.

In 1971, the American League Washington Senators moved to Texas and became the Rangers. Republican Representative Joel Broyhill of Virginia on September 22 telegrammed Padre shareholder Carol Shannon Smith, C. Arnholdt Smith's daughter, about moving the Padres to Washington, D.C. "I will insure my personal efforts," Broyhill wired Smith, "to create the proper climate and support for your club here." Owners C. Arnholdt Smith and Buzzie Bavasi announced publicly that they intended to keep the Padres in San Diego. Bavasi, however, met secretly on September 27 with attorney Thomas Kuchel, representing an investor desiring to transfer the Padres to Washington, D.C. He reported that "no offers were made or given."

A conflict over San Diego Stadium advertising rights had prompted Bavasi's meeting with Kuchel. The City of San Diego had allowed companies in direct competition with the Padres' radio and television sponsors and Smith's U.S. National Bank to advertise on panels on each side of the San Diego Stadium scoreboard. A local firm sold advertising panels to Union Oil, Pacific Southwest Airlines, and the Bank of America, which competed directly with the Padres' radio sponsors of Standard Oil, Air California, and the U.S. National Bank. The conflict caused local radio revenue to decline by $400,000, the amount that each major-league club received from national television coverage.

On October 1, Bavasi met with Washington trial lawyer Edward Bennett Williams and Joseph Danzansky, head of the Giant Food Corporation, in the nation's capital. Williams and Danzansky tried to convince Bavasi to move the Padres to Washington, D.C., but the latter still preferred to keep the Padres in San Diego and settle the advertising rights issue with the city. At a sportswriters' meeting in August 1972, Bavasi reiterated his plans to keep the Padres in San Diego. Home attendance increased by nearly 100,000 to 644,000 in 1972.

On November 17, 1972, Danzansky met with Bavasi and Smith in San Diego to discuss buying the Padres. He offered to purchase the Padres for $11,750,000 and move them to Washington, D.C. Smith wondered if he could continue to absorb an annual loss of around $700,000. He had borrowed $10 million to acquire the Padres and was paying $700,000 annual interest, money he had hoped home attendance would cover. Smith's interest payments remained a huge financial drain because the Padres had earned only around $50,000 per year since 1969. Bavasi on December 13 told Mayor Pete Wilson that the Padres were considering leaving San Diego because of the lack of community support.

Buzzie Bavasi served as president of the Padres from 1968 through September 1977.

The next day, Bavasi met with a New York City law firm, headed by former Attorney General John Mitchell, to discuss any legal problems the Padres might have with the City of San Diego if they broke the stadium lease. If economic problems could not be settled with the city, he warned that the team probably would have to move and would strongly consider the invitation to move to Washington. The Washington Armory Board had already offered the Padres more favorable terms to play in Robert F. Kennedy Stadium. San Diego City Attorney John Witt, however, reminded the Padres on December 18 that they had a 20-year binding lease with the city and threatened legal action if they broke the contract by moving to Washington. The Padres decided to remain in San Diego after the city consented to help build ticket sales and promote better attendance at Padre home games.

Owner C. Arnholdt Smith's major financial problems, meanwhile, surfaced in May. *The San Diego Union* sports editor Jack Murphy disclosed that Smith was struggling financially and wanted to sell the Padres. Smith lacked the money to pay the annual $700,000 interest on the $10 million he had borrowed to buy the Padres. Unbeknownst even to co-owner Buzzie Bavasi, he had secretly juggled millions of dollars to keep his massive financial empire afloat. The Securities and Exchange Commission suspended trading in the stock of Westgate-California, the parent company of Smith's empire, and Air California, the airline controlled by Westgate-California. Smith resigned as president, board chairman, and chief executive officer of the U.S. National Bank. The Padres consequently did not have the financial resources to purchase players on waivers, build an effective farm system, or employ sufficient scouts to make the team competitive. "Nobody knew Smith's financial empire was tumbling," Elten Schiller recalled. "Smith was taking from Peter to pay Paul."

Smith on May 5 sold the Padres to Joseph Danzansky's Washington, D. C., group for $12 million. Dentist Robert Schattner and attorney Marvin Willig agreed to help finance the Danzansky purchase. Danzansky, who would become principal owner, handed Smith a $100,000 check as a down payment and was given 45 days to finish financial arrangements, obtain a lease from Robert F. Kennedy Stadium, and secure approval from National League owners. All major Padre player transactions needed the approval of the Danzansky group. Smith did not even tell co-owner Bavasi, who opposed the sale, about the transaction. Bavasi remarked, "I don't see how they can move the franchise in the middle of the season."

The sale, however, faced many obstacles. The Padres needed the unanimous approval of the other National League owners and permission from the city to break the remaining 15 years on their stadium lease. Once these terms were met, Danzansky's group would pay Smith $9 million in cash and sign a note owing $3 million. The Padres would move to Washington, D.C. following the 1973 campaign. Smith probably announced the deal in May, presumably so that he could receive his $9 million right away. The Padre players did not appear surprised by the sale but wondered when the club planned to move. Washington, D.C. citizens looked forward to having a National League club for the first time since 1899.

The Padres on June 8 officially informed the city that they planned to move the franchise to Washington, D.C. for the 1974 season. In a letter to Mayor Wilson, Smith explained that his continuous financial losses forced him to sell the Padres. "It is not and will not, in our opinion, be economically feasible to continue to operate the Padres franchise in San Diego," he stressed. He hoped to arrange a lease termination agreement with the city. In *The San Diego Union* article, Smith contended that San Diego Stadium had originally been constructed for the San Diego Chargers football team. He had wanted the Padres to play their home games in smaller Westgate Park, but the city had insisted that they use the larger San Diego Stadium instead. The $10 million entry fee, the geographical location, and the declining media revenue prevented the Padres from making any money. Smith denounced the $10 million entry fee as a "brutal and completely unwarranted price tag for an expansion franchise." Padre attendance suffered due to the Pacific Ocean on the west, Mexico on the south, the mountains to the east, and the Los Angeles Dodgers loyalties to the north. The team revenue from radio and television broadcasts had plummeted from $600,000 in 1969 to only $185,000 in 1972.

City officials would not allow the Padres to sever their 20-year lease agreement and threatened legal action. City attorney John Witt told National League president Chub Feeney and all National League owners about the lease arrangement. "We intend," he warned "to take whatever legal steps are necessary and appropriate to enforce our contractual rights." Witt added that the city relied on the Padres to help pay the $2.2 million due annually on the $27 million San Diego Stadium and gave notice that the city would file a $12 million breach of contract suit against the National League if the Padres left San Diego. The San Diego City Council concurred that the Padres could not withdraw unilaterally from the 20-year San Diego Stadium lease after just five years. If Smith wanted to end the lease, he needed to make a mutually satisfactory cash settlement with the city. The city originally consented to subsidize the Padres $300,000 annually for the first seven years of the franchise, while the team would give the city eight percent of the gross gate in rent. The subsidy was to be returned to the city over the final 13 years of the lease from yearly revenues based on attendance over 800,000.

San Diego Hall of Champions founder Bob Breithard with Ray Kroc and Ballard Smith.

On June 15, the city obtained a temporary restraining order prohibiting Smith from finalizing the sale before a financial settlement was reached. Witt filed the suit against the Padres, the National League, Smith, Bavasi, and Danzansky. A hearing was scheduled for June 29 on the city's request for a permanent injunction blocking the Padres from ending the San Diego Stadium lease before the 1988 expiration date. The city threatened to file a companion suit for $24 million and triple damages, raising the potential amount against the National League to $84 million. Little Leaguers and other San Diegans wrote protest letters and signed petitions urging the Padres to stay in San Diego.

San Diego Superior Court judge Eli Levenson on July 10 denied the city's request for a preliminary injunction, but ruled that the city could initiate a class action suit for monetary damages against the Padres. Witt obtained an extension of the temporary restraining order to appeal Judge Levenson's decision. On July 19, an appellate court rejected Witt's request to block the Padres' move. The California Supreme Court on August 16 denied the city's petition for a hearing to present its case. The city did not appeal to the U. S. Supreme Court because the latter still considered baseball exempt from antitrust legislation.

The city on August 31 demanded $12 million from the Padres for terminating the San Diego Stadium lease agreement. Witt based the amount on projected income from the Padres over the next 15 years and the revenue the city expected to lose if the team relocated. He asked the San Diego Superior Court to take over the Padres' assets until the team paid the $12 million. He hoped that the $12 million damages would force the Padres to find another buyer who would keep the team in San Diego.

The 12 National League owners met in Chicago on September 19 to discuss the fate of the Padres. Nine of the 12 owners were needed to approve the sale for the Padres to move to Washington, D.C. The National League owners, however, delayed their vote for 30 days because of the city's $12 million demand. On September 21, Judge Levenson of the San Diego Superior Court denied the city's request to seize all the team's assets because no actual breach of contract had occurred. National League owners on October 5 again tabled a vote on the proposed sale to Danzansky after learning that Smith had found a buyer who would keep the Padres in San Diego. They gave Smith 30 days to complete financial arrangements with the prospective buyer.

Marjorie Lindheimer Everett, the largest stockholder in the Hollywood Park race track, wanted to purchase the Padres. Everett, the wife of a retired racing executive, owned nearly 125,000 shares of stock in Hollywood Park worth an estimated $2.6 million. She had sold her shares in her father's race tracks to Gulf & Western for $32 million in cash and stock. Although having sports experience and the cash to bring financial stability to the floundering San Diego franchise, Everett confronted some thorny obstacles. She needed to arrange a more favorable lease with the San Diego City Council so that the Padres could spend more money on acquiring quality players. Everett also had been involved in a bribery, perjury, conspiracy, and mail fraud case resulting in the conviction of former Illinois Governor Otto Kerner. She had sold Kerner race track stock at bargain prices to secure special treatment from him.

Smith's financial and legal problems, meanwhile, worsened in October. The United States controller of the currency on October 18 declared his U.S. National Bank of San Diego insolvent because it had made numerous unwise loans. The Internal Revenue Service claimed that Smith owed $22.8 million in back taxes and interest for 1969 and placed temporary liens on his properties in nine California counties. The Securities and Exchange Commission sued Smith and other Westgate Corporation executives for trying to defraud stockholders of Westgate and the U. S. National Bank.

Negotiations between the Everett group and the city over a new lease stalled in late October. Neil Papiano, Everett's attorney, sought too many financial concessions from the city. He wanted a new lease permitting the Padres to exit San Diego if home attendance did not reach a certain amount and and giving the owners a higher percentage of money from the San Diego Stadium's parking and gate revenue if attendance increased. The city, however, still vowed to pursue the $12 million lawsuit against the Padres should the team leave San Diego. According to Mayor Wilson, the city intended "to prosecute as vigorously as it can and use its resources, legal and political, to keep the franchise here." The impasse continued for nearly a month over the lease. Bavasi acknowledged, "Both sides are being stubborn and I'm very much afraid it will cost [San Diego] a major league team."

In late November, the Everett group agreed to buy the Padres and accepted a new lease arrangement. Smith sold the Padres on November 23 to Marjorie Everett and several other investors for around $10 million. The other investors included Hollywood Park race track board chairman Vern Underwood, composer Burt Bacharach, movie producer Steven Brodie, soft drink executive Mrs. Gene Washburn, Dr. Robert Kerlan, and attorney Papiano. The owners could buy out the new lease if they desired to sell the Padres or move the team from San Diego. The Everett group agreed to pay the city $5 million if they ended the lease before 1975. The penalty for terminating the lease steadily decreased each year thereafter. The new lease let the Padres make more money through concessions, receive one-third of the city's share of stadium parking revenue, and have veto power over the potential advertisers on stadium panels. The city consented to defray the costs of field maintenance and cleanup for four years.

The sale, however, still needed the approval of the other 11 National League owners. Some owners still considered binding the Danzansky group's original $12 million offer to move the Padres to Washington, D.C. Other owners did not want the Padres to move to Washington, D.C.—because major-league baseball had already failed twice there—and favored shifting the Padres to Seattle, New Orleans, or another city committed to building an indoor stadium. Some owners opposed the sale to Everett because she had been involved in the Kerner bribery case. Mayor Wilson, therefore, had the city proceed with its $12 million lawsuit against the National League and authorized Witt to file an antitrust lawsuit against the National League if the owners rejected Everett's bid to buy the Padres.

Two attorneys addressed the National League owners on December 5 in Houston, Texas. Smith's attorney, John Holt, stressed that the owners had three options: (1) approve the sale of the Padres to the Danzansky group for $12 million; (2) endorse the sale of the club to the Marjorie Everett group; or (3) let Smith operate the Padres in San Diego through financial assistance arranged by Holt. Under the third option, Smith had made financial arrangements through Holt to keep the Padres in San Diego without selling the team to the Everett group. Holt's banking friends would make loans to finance the Padres. Smith changed his mind after the meeting, however, and wanted to sell the team. The change disappointed Bavasi, who thought that Smith wanted to keep the Padres. *The San Diego Union* reported, "Bavasi, tears in his eyes and his face ashen, was bitter over the action resulting from an overnight switch in the thinking of Padres' owner C. Arnholdt Smith." Bavasi believed that Smith had made financial arrangements through Holt to keep the Padres in San Diego without selling them to the Everett group. Attorney Neil Papiano, meanwhile, asked the National League owners to approve the sale to the Everett group.

On December 6, the National League owners rejected Everett's bid by an 8-3 margin and conditionally approved the sale of the Padres to Danzansky's Washington, D.C. group. They gave the Danzansky group until December 21 to protect the National League against legal action by the city. The Danzansky group needed to pay the city $5 million in damages for severing the 20-year San Diego Stadium lease. The National League based the $5 million fee on the liquidation clause in the lease with the Everett group. Mayor Wilson, the same day, warned that "the city will wage war against the league on both the legal and political fronts to keep our baseball team in San Diego." The city renewed its application to take over Padre assets and sought a temporary restraining order preventing the team from moving to Washington, D.C.

Six days later, Witt filed an antitrust civil suit in federal court requesting $72 million damages from the National League and other defendants. The other defendants included Smith, the other National League owners, California Congressman Bernie Sisk, baseball commissioner Bowie Kuhn, and Danzansky. Witt accused the defendants of conspiring to prevent the city from taking part in the operation of San Diego Stadium. According to the suit, the defendants had created a monopoly and had conspired to use this monopoly to drive out competitors. Witt argued that the departure of the Padres would cost the city $24 million in revenue and asked that the projected $24 million loss in revenue be tripled for a damage award of $72 million.

A federal judge on December 18 refused to hand down a preliminary restraining order to block the Padres from moving to Washington, D.C. and scheduled a January 30 hearing to consider the city's request for a permanent injunction to stop the Padres from leaving San Diego. The following day, Superior Court judge Levenson again rejected Witt's demand to take over the Padres' assets because it would be difficult to assess the monetary value of the damages. The Padres front office, meanwhile, boxed all their possessions and hired vans to move the team to Washington, D.C., while Topps Chewing Gum produced 1974 baseball cards of 13 Padres players and the team with the Washington inscription.

The National League owners, however, on December 21 rescinded their approval of the Padre sale to Danzansky's Washington, D.C. group. The Danzansky group failed to raise the $5 million to protect the National League from damage suits by the city or to meet the December 21 deadline to acquire the Padres. Danzansky sought to renegotiate his original proposal to Smith, offering the latter a $7 million down payment instead of the $9 million and $3 million in installment payments agreed upon the previous May. Smith, though, did not want to renegotiate Danzansky's original offer and returned the $100,000 deposit check to the Danzansky group.

Smith on December 28 sold the Padres to the Everett group for around $10 million. He wrote the

National League owners that Danzansky had not acquired the Padres in time and stressed that the Everett group could afford to buy the team. The National League owners, on January 9, 1974, again rejected the sale to the Everett group by a 9-3 margin. The Chicago Cubs and the San Francisco Giants were the only National League teams supporting the Padres. Everett's involvement in the race track scandal probably influenced the outcome. The National League owners hoped to find a buyer who would keep the Padres in San Diego for two seasons and then move them to Seattle, New Orleans, or another city building a domed stadium.

The city, meanwhile, protested the National League vote. Mayor Wilson vowed to proceed with the $12 million lawsuit against the Padres and the $72 million antitrust lawsuit against the National League. Four separate groups had approached Wilson about acquiring the Padres and keeping them in San Diego. Wilson indicated that the city could arrange a new stadium lease agreement granting the same concessions offered to the Everett group. The purchaser, of course, would have to pay a penalty if the Padres left San Diego.

Smith, meanwhile, agreed to sell the Padres to Chicagoan Ray Kroc, the 72-year-old chairman and largest stockholder of the McDonald's restaurant chain. Kroc had read in a newspaper article that the National League owners had rejected the Everett group and that the Padres were for sale. He had already built the McDonald's hamburger operation into the nation's largest fast-food chain and had amassed a personal fortune estimated at $500 million. Kroc, who had always wanted to own the Chicago Cubs baseball club, paid Smith $12 million in cash for the Padres on January 25 and vowed to keep the team in San Diego. In his autobiography *Grinding It Out*, he wrote, "I wasn't even considering going into baseball when I was flying out to Los Angeles to meet [my wife] Joan early in 1974 and read the sports stories about the impending sale of the San Diego Padres. I thought to myself, 'My God, San Diego is a gorgeous town. Why don't I go over there and look at the ball park? I've always admired Buzzie Bavasi' . . . and the whole thing sounded very appealing." San Diego players, management, and fans alike welcomed Kroc's move. "Kroc's buying of the club," pitcher Steve Arlin observed, "was a great relief to the players."

Kroc, a Chicago native, had followed baseball since he was seven years old, when his father took him to a Chicago Cubs game. During World War I, he dropped out of high school to join the Red Cross Ambulance Corps. After the war, Kroc played the piano in Chicago bars and restaurants and sold paper cups. He eventually became Midwest sales manager for Lily-Tulip Cup Company. Kroc, in 1937, paid $10,000 for the exclusive sales rights to Prince Castle Multimixer, a machine able to mix six milkshakes simultaneously. In 1954, the McDonald brothers bought eight of Kroc's Multimixers for their San Bernardino, California hamburger restaurant. Kroc was so astonished with volume of business that the McDonald brothers handled that he persuaded them to permit him to market their outlets nationwide. By 1960, the McDonald's restaurants had grown to 228 franchises across the United States and grossed $56 million a year. The next year, Kroc paid $2.7 million to purchase the brothers' outlets and became the owner of McDonald's. By 1970, over 2,500 McDonald's restaurants handled nearly a billion dollars worth of business. When Kroc purchased the Padres, his stock in the McDonald's franchise exceeded $500 million.

Kroc still needed to arrange a lease agreement with the city and secure the approval of the National League owners. After conferring with Smith and Witt, Kroc told reporters, "I'm hopeful [the sale] will work out, it looks very good. Baseball is my sport. I want to have fun with an expensive hobby." Kroc on January 25 accepted a new San Diego Stadium lease with the city, committing the Padres to stay in San Diego through 1980. The new lease contained the same concessions given to the Everett group. The city would operate San Diego Stadium daily during the baseball season and allot the Padres one-third of the parking revenues over a four-year span. The Padres would give the city 50 cents for every gate admission beyond 800,000 in a single season.

On January 31, the National League owners unanimously approved Kroc's acquisition of the Padres. After several agonizing months, they had found a wealthy businessman to own the Padres and keep them in San Diego. Although 72 years old, Kroc still possessed the stamina and energy to stabilize the franchise. Sportswriter Red Smith wrote that Kroc "has plenty of mustard, means to keep the Padres in San Diego, and has done no harm to anybody that bicarbonate soda cannot remedy."

5

The Adolescent Years [1974-77]

For the first time since joining the National League in 1968, the Padres had changed ownership. Ray Kroc's acquisition ended speculation that the team would move to Washington, D.C. His personal involvement soon began to turn the franchise around. Kroc vowed to build a contender gradually and let baseball authorities handle the front office and field manager operations. The new owner took a much keener interest than C. Arnholdt Smith in the Padres. "Smith," pitcher Steve Arlin recalled, "did not care about the team. The players never saw him. Kroc, by contrast, was a great baseball fan."

Kroc also brought more financial stability, possessing monetary resources to make the Padres more competitive and marketable. "His financial support," Los Angeles Dodgers first baseman Steve Garvey observed, "gave the team money to change things." Kroc even bought the Padres an airplane to facilitate travel and installed a lounge for the players and their families. He instituted several other changes, including having McDonald's replace Jack-in-the-Box as sponsor for Bat Night, moving up night games 30 minutes to 7:00 p.m., and placing a home run stripe on the center field fence.

Kroc retained Buzzie Bavasi as president and Peter Bavasi as general manager. The Padres abandoned the old yellow uniforms and adopted a snappier white at home and gray on the road. On February 2, John McNamara, a quiet, evenly dispositioned sound, baseball strategist, replaced Don Zimmer as manager. Zimmer had produced a 114-190 record in his two-year managerial stint. McNamara had spent 24 seasons in the minor leagues, 15 as a catcher and nine as a manager. He had joined the Oakland Athletics as a coach in 1968 and piloted them to an 89-73 record in 1970. Since 1971, he had served as third base coach for the San Francisco Giants. McNamara hired Bill Posedel as pitching coach and Jim Davenport and Jack Bloomfield as other coaches. Whitey Wietelmann was retained as bullpen coach. San Diego anticipated considerable

Willie McCovey played first base for the Padres from 1974 to 1976.

improvement in 1974. The Padres on April 2 sold outfielder Ivan Murrell to the Atlanta Braves and the next day purchased veteran second baseman Horace Clarke from the New York Yankees. First baseman Willie McCovey, outfielders Matty Alou and Bobby Tolan, and second baseman Glenn Beckert were expected to join Dave Winfield and Nate Colbert in giving McNamara considerable offensive production, while Jim McAndrew gave the Padres another starting pitcher.

Over 39,000 fans watched the Padres open their home season on April 9 against the Houston Astros. The crowd cheered wildly when new owner Ray Kroc was introduced before the game, warmly welcoming the instant folk hero who had saved major league baseball in San Diego. By the eighth inning, however, the Padres trailed, 9-2. San Diego committed three errors and made a base-running mistake to end a bases-loaded rally. Ray Kroc grew increasingly frustrated in the press box. When the Padres came to bat in the bottom of the eighth inning, he grabbed the public address microphone and apologized to the startled, cheering crowd, "Ladies and gentlemen, I suffer with you." After Kroc told the crowd that the loyal San Diego fans had "outstripped" the Los Angeles Dodgers by 8,000 fans in opening game attendance, a male streaker darted across the field. As the ballpark turned into bedlam, Kroc confessed, "I've never seen such stupid ball playing in my life."

Kroc's remarks infuriated the Padre players, who contemplated boycotting the next game. Veteran Willie McCovey asserted, "This is a shocking thing. We may have played sloppy. But we're professionals and we know when the hell we play that way. We don't need to be reminded." Houston Astros infielder Doug Rader asked, "What does he think we are, short-order cooks or something?" The following day, baseball commissioner Bowie Kuhn and National League president Charles Feeney demanded that Kroc apologize to his players for publicly reprimanding them. Kroc quickly realized that he would need considerable patience. When the Astros returned to San Diego on June 28, he good-naturedly staged a chef's night and admitted free anyone wearing a chef's hat. Before that game, Rader approached the home plate umpire wearing a chef's hat and an apron and carrying a frying pan. He flipped the starting lineup card with a spatula and asked the umpire, "What's your pleasure—rare, medium, or well-done?"

Financial stability gradually came to the struggling San Diego franchise. San Diego drew 1,075,399 spectators in 1974, smashing the record by 431,127 people and giving the Padres a profit for the first time in franchise history. The Padres attracted 44,504 fans for a May 25 night game against the Cincinnati Reds. Bavasi acknowledged, "The city proved it will support major-league baseball—now it's up to us to do our part." Sportswriter Don Freeman observed, "The town has simply gone bananas over the Padres from blue-collar Chula Vista to blue-chip La Jolla." The listening audience of San Diego Padres broadcasts by Jerry Coleman and Bob Chandler doubled. Kroc's promise to establish a contending club, the excitement among Padre fans that the team did not move, and special club promotions boosted both home attendance and radio ratings.

The acquisitions of veterans Matty Alou, Willie McCovey, and Glenn Beckert gave San Diego fans recognizable players. Players promoted the Padres at McDonald's restaurants and started endorsing commercial products. Kroc initiated special promotions to draw San Diegans to home games. Elten Schiller enlisted San Diego businesses to give away commercial products to fans on special promotion nights. "Kroc," according to eventual club president Dick Freeman, "loved anything new and unique." McNamara's Band, a small but noisy musical group led by Marine Lieutenant Jim Eakle, stirred up fan enthusiasm.

San Diego steadily improved under manager John McNamara. The Padres won a fair percentage of their home games, including a season-best five consecutive victories over Philadelphia and Montreal between April 26 and May 1. Besides triumphing in a majority of their one-run games, San Diego occasionally came from behind in the late innings. The Padres compiled a respectable 42-55 record through July 17 and trailed the fifth-place San Francisco Giants by only 1.5 games.

The Padre offense blossomed in April and May. Derrel Thomas on April 17 had four hits in a 6-1 road victory over the Atlanta Braves. Six days later, Enzo Hernandez tied his club record by stealing three bases in a 10-2 home triumph over the New York Mets. On May 7, Fred Kendall, Thomas, and Dave Winfield homered to lift the Padres to a 5-3, 13-inning victory over the Philadelphia Phillies at Veterans Stadium. Ten days later, Nate Colbert clouted his fifth grand slam as a Padre in the first inning off of Ron Bryant to defeat the Giants 7-3 at Candlestick Park. Willie McCovey on May 19 belted his second grand slam as a Padre to give San Diego a 10-7 win over the Giants in the second game of a doubleheader and the following night knocked in four runs in an 8-6 triumph over Houston at the Astrodome. Bobby Tolan on May 23 had four hits in a 5-4, 13-inning home victory over the Cincinnati Reds.

Similar momentum carried into June. On June 2, San Diego recorded a season-high 17 hits in a 9-6 loss to the St. Louis Cardinals at Busch Stadium. The Padres, on June 9, walked to a 6-5 home triumph over the Cardinals with a record 10 free passes. San Diego, the next day, rallied at home from an 8-0 deficit with nine runs in the last two innings to defeat the Pittsburgh Pirates, 9-8. Derrel Thomas, on June 14, belted an inside-the-park home run in the third inning off of Ernie McNally, as the Padres defeated Montreal, 5-4, at Jarry Park. Two days later, homers by Dave Winfield, Fred Kendall, and Cito Gaston still left San Diego one run short in a 9-8 loss to the Montreal Expos at Jarry Park. On June 18, infielder Rich Morales became the first Padre to steal home in a 9-4 win over the Chicago Cubs at Wrigley Field. The following day, Dan Spillner authored a one-hit, 1-0 shutout against Chicago.

Padre bats remained alive through mid-July. Colbert, McCovey, and Winfield, on July 16, homered in a 5-4 home triumph over the Philadelphia Phillies. The next day, outfielder Bobby Tolan knocked in six runs in a 15-1 rout of the Phillies, tying the franchise record for largest margin of victory.

During the first half of the season, pitching coach Bill Posedel rebuilt the struggling staff. On May 12, Padres pitchers gave up 23 hits in a 15-9, 13-inning home loss to the Dodgers. Gary Ross, Mike Corkins, Rich Troedsen, and Ralph Garcia were demoted to the Hawaii farm club because of high ERA or injuries. Ross and Garcia recorded no decisions with 4.50 and 6.30 ERAs, respectively. Corkins split four decisions with a 4.82 ERA, while Troedsen fared 1-1 with a 8.53 ERA. On May 31 the Padres purchased pitcher Lowell Palmer from the Yankees and the next day released Jim McAndrew, who won only one of five decisions with a 5.57 ERA. After triumphing only once in eight decisions during the first two months of 1974, Steve Arlin was traded on June 15 to the Cleveland Indians. Six days later, the Padres acquired pitchers Brent Strom and Terry Ley from the Indians.

The club momentum changed dramatically in mid-July. Right fielder Bobby Tolan tore ligaments in his right knee against the Phillies on July 18 at San Diego Stadium. Tolan had batted .266 with 40 RBIs in 95 games, enjoying 15-, 12-, and eight-game hitting streaks and hitting safely in 38 of 41 games from May 11 to July 2. His 15-game hitting streak from June 1 to June 17 tied the club record. The Padres collapsed without Tolan, losing 57 of 75 games after July 16 and dropping 10 straight games from August 28 through September 6. San Diego used seven pitchers in a 15-4 loss to the Los Angeles Dodgers on July 31 and in a 9-7 setback to the Atlanta Braves on August 5. Pinch-hitter Enzo Hernandez, providing one of the few bright spots, singled twice in the same inning on September 7 in an 8-4 victory over Houston at the Astrodome.

During the season, the Padres used 15 rookies. Dave Freisleben, Dan Spillner, and Joe McIntosh gained valuable experience in the starting rotation, while reliever Larry Hardy compiled a 9-4 record with two saves and won four consecutive decisions from June 4 through August 17. Freisleben on August 4 pitched 13 consecutive scoreless innings against the Cincinnati Reds. San Diego won that home game the next inning, 1-0. Spillner, on September 11, blanked the Houston Astros, 2-0, at home, striking out 10 batters.

San Diego stumbled to a 60-102 last place finish. The Padres ranked worst in the major leagues in batting percentage (.229), runs scored (541), and pitching (4.58 ERA) and set club pitching records with 124 home runs, 715 walks, and 830 runs allowed. "We didn't win as many games as I thought we would," McNamara conceded, "but I could see progress, especially among the younger players." The injury-plagued Padres used a then-record 43 different players during the season and a record 22 players on May 23 in a 5-4, 13 inning victory over the Cincinnati Reds. The Padres fared only 1-17 against the Atlanta Braves, 2-16 against the Western Division titlist Los Angeles Dodgers, and 3-9 against the Eastern Division winning Pittsburgh Pirates. San Diego split 60 games with the other Eastern Division clubs. Two other calamities befell the Padres in 1974. A fan fell 17 feet onto the field during one game, while bees invaded the stadium at another game. On the positive side, the Padres set club season records for most sacrifice flies (35), walks (562), pinch hits (69), and pinch hitting average (.242)

Dave Winfield batted .265 with 20 home runs and led the Padres with 75 RBIs in his first full major-league season, while the injury-prone Willie McCovey paced San Diego with 22 home runs, placed second with 63 RBIs, and drew 96 walks. John Grubb batted .286, a decline of 25 points. Enzo Hernandez improved his batting average to .232 with 37 stolen bases, while Derrel Thomas raised his batting average to .247 and played better afield. Nate Colbert hit only .207 and clouted just 14 home runs. Dave Roberts and Fred Kendall also struggled at the plate, while injuries limited Glenn Beckert to only 64 games. Randy Jones finished 8-22 with a 4.46 ERA and lost eight consecutive decisions from July 30 through September 13, while Bill Greif fared 9-19 with a 4.70 ERA and set club season records by allowing 127 runs, 118 earned runs, and 224 hits and hitting 14 batters. Mike Corkins established a club season mark with three balks, including two on April 30 against the Montreal Expos.

Major transactions marked the off season. San Diego traded veteran outfielder Cito Gaston to the Atlanta Braves for pitcher Danny Frisella on November 8 and Nate Colbert to the Detroit Tigers for shortstop Eddie Brinkman, pitcher Bob Strampe, and outfielder Dick Sharon in a three-way deal also involving the St. Louis Cardinals on November 18. The Padres sent Brinkman and a player to be named later to the Cardinals for pitchers Alan Foster, Rich Folkers, Sonny Siebert, and Frank Linzy. The deal was completed December 12 when San Diego traded catcher Danny Breeden to St. Louis. On December 6, San Diego sent Derrel Thomas to the San Francisco Giants for second baseman Tito Fuentes and pitcher Butch Metzger.

The Padres also bid for free agent pitcher Catfish Hunter of the Oakland A's. San Diego held the early lead in the bidding, offering him an estimated $3.5 to $4 million on December 20. McNamara had managed Hunter, and Posedel had served as his pitching coach, at Oakland. General manager Peter Bavasi stated, "I don't think we'll lose the services of Jim Hunter due to a deficiency in our offer." The New York Yankees, however, signed him on New Year's Eve to an estimated $3.75 million contract.

Owner Ray Kroc instilled more enthusiasm and confidence in his squad. Before the 1975 season, he hung an inspirational sign in the clubhouse: "Press on—nothing in the world can take the place of persistence. Persistence and determination alone are omnipotent." San Diego released pitcher Vicente Romo on March 28 and veteran second baseman Glenn Beckert on April 28. The Padres sent pitcher Sonny Siebert to the Athletics on May 16 for infielder Ted Kubiak and, on June 24, purchased outfielder Don Hahn from the St. Louis Cardinals.

San Diego led the Western Division for 13 of 15 days from April 12 through April 27. Padre pitchers, paced by Randy Jones, led the major leagues in ERA into late June. Jones blanked Houston 4-0 at the Astrodome on April 21 and the Cincinnati Reds 3-0 on May 8 at Riverfront Stadium. Jones won five straight decisions from May 4 through May 30 and on May 19 hurled the longest one-hitter in franchise history, a 1-0, 10-inning home victory over the St. Louis Cardinals. Five days later, Jones shut out the Pittsburgh Pirates 5-0 at San Diego Stadium on just 68 pitches. On July 3, he pitched a one-hitter in a 2-1 home triumph over the Cincinnati Reds. The game took only two hours, the shortest extra-inning game in franchise history. In the All-Star Game on July 15, Jones also recorded a save for the National League in its 6-3 victory at County Stadium in Milwaukee.

The San Diego offense also came alive. Dave Winfield had four hits and knocked in five runs at home on April 24, but the Los Angeles Dodgers won, 11-6. Other four-hit games were made by John Grubb on

April 27 against the Atlanta Braves and on May 19 against the Chicago Cubs, by Tito Fuentes on June 14 against the New York Mets, and on July 2 and September 23 against the Los Angeles Dodgers, and on June 9 by Enzo Hernandez against the Philadelphia Phillies. Mike Ivie on July 1 belted a grand slam and knocked in five runs in a 10-1 rout of Los Angeles at Dodger Stadium. The following day, the Padres had eight consecutive hits in the fifth inning against the Dodgers.

Manager John McNamara acknowledged: "Last year we didn't have the talent to stop a losing streak. This year we do." Infielder Mike Ivie added, "It feels good to come into a locker room knowing everybody is in a winning frame of mind." Not all Padres fared well. After playing just four games, infielder Dave Hilton missed most of the season battling infectious hepatitis. San Diego optioned outfielder John Scott to Alexandria of the Texas League in late June after he had only one hit in 24 plate appearances over two seasons. As a pinch runner, he scored the winning run five times and stole two bases.

San Diego shared third place as late as July 9, but injuries slowed the Padres after the All-Star break. Dave Winfield was tied for the National League lead in home runs and ranked near the top in RBIs before suffering wrist injuries at midseason. He missed 19 games and ended the season batting .267 with just 15 homers and 76 RBIs. Other players needed to pick up the slack. The Padres won five consecutive games from July 25 through July 28 and recorded season highs with 11 runs on September 9 against the Cincinnati Reds and 18 hits on August 28 against the Montreal Expos. Willie McCovey tied a club record with three doubles on August 24 to help defeat the Phillies at home, while Dave Roberts hit safely in 14 consecutive games from August 23 through September 4. Randy Jones pitched exceptionally well at home, blanking the Pittsburgh Pirates, 1-0, on July 22 and the Atlanta Braves, 4-0, on August 1. On September 23, he became the first 20-game winner in Padres history, defeating the Los Angeles Dodgers, 6-4, at home. Nevertheless, San Diego struggled much of the second half of the season and lost eight straight contests from September 14 through September 21. Reliever Joe McIntosh lost his last seven decisions starting with July 30. On September 24, Padre pitchers surrendered a season-high 14 runs and 18 hits to the Dodgers. San Diego occasionally enjoyed luck even when not hitting well. Although they got only one hit on July 19 against the Chicago Cubs at San Diego Stadium, the Padres won, 2-1. John Grubb singled off Steve Stone in the seventh inning for the lone Padre hit.

Native Americans, meanwhile, protested that outfielder Gene Locklear, a full-blooded Lumbee Indian and accomplished artist, should see more playing time. Locklear batted .321 in 100 games, but did not have enough plate appearances to qualify for the National League batting title. He had four hits in a 3-0 victory over the Cincinnati Reds on May 8 at Riverfront Stadium and two hits with three walks in a 5-4 loss to the Pittsburgh Pirates on May 14. He enjoyed a 12-game hitting streak from June 22 through July 2 and knocked in four runs in an 8-6 triumph over the Montreal Expos on August 20 at Jarry Park. Despite Native American protests, manager John McNamara preferred to use him as a pinch hitter off the bench. Locklear batted .292 with 14 hits as the club's top pinch-hitter.

San Diego escaped the cellar for the first time, placing fourth in the National League Western Division with a 71-91 record. The Atlanta Braves and the Houston Astros finished below the Padres. San Diego set a franchise record for victories and boosted club attendance by 206,000 people to 1,281,747. Manager McNamara confided, "Our goal was to get out of last place, which we did, but our objective was to play .500 ball, and we might have made it if it hadn't been for injuries." He added, "We improved and proved to ourselves and to the rest of the league that we are competitive."

During 1975, pitcher Randy Jones became the first San Diego-developed superstar. Jones, who lost 22 games in 1974, almost single-handedly gave respectability to the beleaguered Padres and hurled 18 complete games. Under rookie pitching coach Tom Morgan, he compiled a 20-12 mark, led National League pitchers with a 2.24 ERA, tied Fred Norman's club shutout record (6), and finished second to Tom Seaver in the National League Cy Young Award balloting. Jones exhibited great control with his sinkerball, inducing many ground balls and hurling very short games. His masterpieces included two one-hitters, two two-hitters, one three-hitter, and three four-hitters. On July 15, he threw a scoreless ninth inning in relief to record a save for the National League in the 1975 All-Star Game.

Padre pitchers, led by Jones, finished sixth in the National League and eighth in the major leagues with a 3.48 ERA. Brent Strom worked behind Jones in the starting rotation, compiling an 8-8 record with a 2.55 ERA. Dave Freisleben struggled with a 5-14 mark and 4.28 ERA, while Dan Spillner logged a 5-13 record with a 4.26 ERA. Dave Tomlin performed well in 67 games out of the bullpen, while Danny Frisella, Bill Greif, and Rich Folkers gave the Padres bullpen depth.

For the second consecutive year, San Diego finished last in the major leagues in runs scored (552). They batted only .244 and clouted just 78 home runs. The Padres set club records for doubles (215), sacrifice hits (133), and sacrifice flies (46). Dave Winfield again led the Padres with 76 RBIs, while Willie McCovey paced San Diego with 23 home runs and contributed 68 RBIs. His home runs and RBIs set club marks for left-handed batters. Tito Fuentes led the club with a .280 batting average and helped the Padres convert a record 163 double plays. He set a club record with 130 singles. Mike Ivie played his first full major-league season, splitting duties between third base and first base. He did not begin playing third base until the end of spring training, and he batted .249, set a club rookie record with 46 RBIs, and tied another with eight home runs. Ivie made the Topps and *Baseball Digest* All-Rookie teams and connected with a grand slam in a 10-1 victory over Los Angeles at Dodger Stadium on July 1. The leaky Padre defense, however, paced the National League with 188 errors. John Grubb set club records for a left-handed batter with 36 doubles and 149 hits.

During the off season, San Diego made several transactions. On October 20, the Padres acquired veteran outfielder Willie Davis from the St. Louis Cardinals for outfielder Dick Sharon. San Diego acquired infielder Rudy Meoli on November 4 from the California Angels to complete a September 17 deal in which the Padres had traded pitcher Gary Ross for infielder Bobby Valentine. San Diego on December 11 solidified its infield defense by obtaining veteran third baseman Doug Rader from the Houston Astros for pitchers Joe McIntosh and Larry Hardy. On April 5, the Padres acquired outfielder-pinch hitter Merv Rettenmund from the Cincinnati Reds for infielder Rudi Meoli and cash. San Diego also traded pitcher Danny Frisella to the St. Louis Cardinals for pitcher Ken Reynolds on April 8 and sold catcher Randy Hundley to the Chicago Cubs five days later. The Padres also sought free agent pitcher Andy Messersmith of the Los Angeles Dodgers, but the latter signed a three-year $1 million package with the Atlanta Braves on April 10, 1976.

San Diego, sparked by pitcher Randy Jones, again performed well the first half of 1976. Jones captured an incredible 16 of 19 decisions before the All-Star break and garnered National League Pitcher of the Month honors in April and May. He recorded a season-high seven strikeouts against the Los Angeles Dodgers on April 14 and St. Louis Cardinals on April 23. Between May 17 and June 22, he tied Christy Mathewson's long-standing mark of 68 consecutive innings without surrendering a walk. The streak ended when Jones walked catcher Marc Hill of the San Francisco Giants on a full count to lead off the eighth inning at San Diego Stadium. His sixteenth victory came on July 8 against the Chicago Cubs at Wrigley Field. He started for the National League in the 1976 All-Star Game at Veterans Stadium in Philadelphia and was the winning pitcher in a 7-1 triumph. Manager John McNamara was the first Padre to serve as a coach in an All-Star Game.

Dave Winfield ignited the Padre offense during the first half of the season. On April 13, he clouted the first grand slam of the 1976 major-league season in the seventh inning against Los Angeles at Dodger Stadium. Winfield enjoyed another four-RBI game on April 23 against the St. Louis Cardinals and belted a second grand slam on May 21, connecting at home off of Gary Nolan of the Cincinnati Reds in the first inning. Four Padres enjoyed four-hit games, including John Grubb against the Atlanta Braves on April 9, Tito Fuentes against the St. Louis Cardinals on April 24, and Willie Davis and Mike Ivie against the San Francisco Giants on June 23. Doug Rader tripled twice against the Giants on May 17 and knocked in four runs on May 25 against the Los Angeles Dodgers, while Jerry Turner did the latter against the Atlanta Braves on June 26.

The Padres enjoyed success against the Giants at Candlestick Park, scoring a season-high 12 runs there on May 17 and a season-best 16 hits there on May 17 and June 23. The Padres set a club home attendance record for a doubleheader on June 13 with 43,473 fans against the Philadelphia Phillies. San Diego swept the doubleheader, 5-0, and 4-3. The Padres defeated the San Francisco Giants eight days later to move into second place, only five games behind the Cincinnati Reds.

A disastrous second-half slump, however, began after a 5-2 triumph over the Los Angeles Dodgers on July 4. The Padres stood in third place in the Western Division, only 6.5 games behind the Cincinnati Reds. The Chicago Cubs blanked San Diego three straight contests from July 5 through July 7 at Wrigley Field. After salvaging the series finale against the Cubs, the Padres lost four consecutive games to the Philadelphia Phillies from July 9 through July 11 at Veterans Stadium. Philadelphia pitchers shut out San Diego twice and limited the Padres to only five runs in the series. San Diego relinquished third place to the Houston Astros on August 27, fourth place to the San Francisco Giants on September 15, and ended the season just three games ahead of the last-place Atlanta Braves. On September 29, infielder Doug Rader belted the last grand slam of the 1976 National League season in the first inning at home against the Cincinnati Reds.

The Padre offensive production sputtered during the second half of the season. Clean-up hitter Dave Winfield missed the last month of the season with a leg injury. He batted .291 with 53 RBIs before the All-Star break, but hit just .267 with only 16 RBIs thereafter. Eleven of his 13 home runs came before June 18. Winfield clouted over 20 percent of all Padre home runs and tied the club mark with three stolen bases in the second game of a doubleheader against the San Francisco Giants on September 5. After batting .283 the first half of the season, center fielder Willie Davis hit just .246 following the All-Star break. Disenchanted second baseman Tito Fuentes batted .276 the first half and only .248 the second half. Third baseman Doug Rader slumped badly in July and August, while shortstop Enzo Hernandez finished the season with a .256 batting average after hitting .300 through mid-June. Willie McCovey split first base duties with Mike Ivie, batting only .203 with seven home runs until being sold to the Oakland Athletics on August 30. Ivie, meanwhile, enjoyed a 10-game hitting streak from August 16 to August 29 and hit in 35 of his final 44 games from August 10 through October 3. He played only two games at third base in 1976, being used almost exclusively at first base.

The lack of run production likewise hurt the Padre pitching staff. Ace Randy Jones struggled during the second half with just a 6-11 mark, but seven of his losses were by one run and three of his setbacks came when San Diego was blanked. The Padres batted only .232 behind him during the first half and .211 throughout the second half. His production also declined for the second half because of injuries suffered in an automobile accident and nerve damage in his left arm. He underwent arm surgery shortly after the end of the season to help repair the nerve damage. Brent Strom won eight of 17 decisions before the All-Star break but ended the season 12-16. After winning six of his first seven decisions, Dave Freisleben lost eight consecutive decisions and ended the campaign 10-13. San Diego labored with just eight or nine pitchers much of the season because of injuries to Dan Spillner and Alan Foster. The acquisitions of Rick Sawyer from the New York Yankees and Tom Griffin from Houston bailed out the Padres. Collectively, Sawyer and Griffin won nine of 15 decisions.

Nevertheless, the second half produced a few highlights. San Diego had 16 hits in a 9-3 home victory over the Houston Astros on August 6, when both Fred Kendall and Jerry Turner had four hits. The Padres stole four bases against the San Francisco Giants on September 5 and Los Angeles Dodgers on October 3. Padres with four-RBI games included John Grubb against the Atlanta Braves on August 2, Fred Kendall against the Houston Astros on August 6, Enzo Hernandez against the St. Louis Cardinals on August 16, Mike Ivie against the Pittsburgh Pirates on August 24, and Doug Rader against the Cincinnati Reds on September 29.

San Diego finished in fifth place in the National League Western Division with a 73-89 record, one notch below 1975. In a statistical oddity, the Padres played 82 road games and just 80 home contests. Weak hitting again stymied the Padres, who ended next to last in runs scored (570) and home runs (64). Opposition pitchers shut out San Diego a league-leading 23 times. The Padres, however, set season marks with 216 doubles and 92 stolen bases. Although establishing a club record with 42 home victories, San Diego finished only 19-29 in one-run games and just 17-32 against left-handed pitchers. Manager John McNamara explained, "Some of the older players ran out of gas, there were injuries and we just stopped hitting." The Padres established club marks for most victories (73) and attendance (1,458,478), the latter for the third consecutive season. Padre pitchers set team records for most games completed (47), fewest strikeouts (652), and fewest home runs allowed (87).

Randy Jones, who anchored the Padre pitching staff, set season club records for wins (22), complete

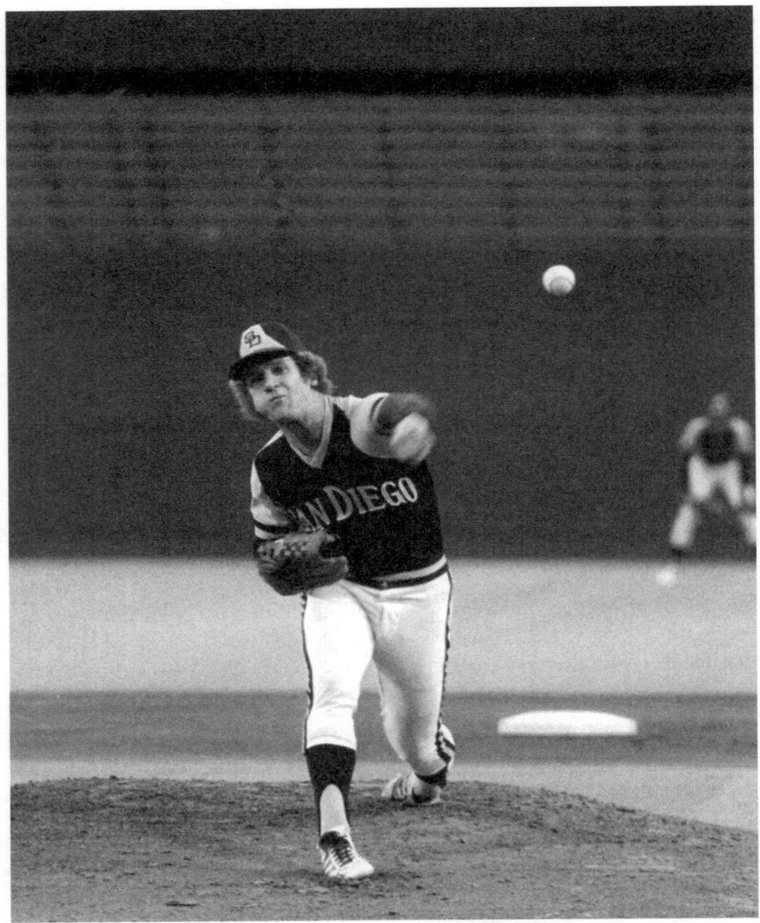

Randy Jones pitched for the Padres from 1973 through 1980.

games (25), and innings pitched (315), leading the National League in all three categories. He also established team season records for starts (40) and consecutive complete games (5). His 22-14 overall mark and 2.74 ERA helped him earn AP, UPI, and *The Sporting News* All-League team honors and *TSN* National League Pitcher of the Year accolades. Jones finished 12-5 at home and 12-9 on the road and fanned 93 batters to become the first National League pitcher since World War II to win 20 games without striking out 100 hitters.

Jones triumphed over every National League team at least once and finished 13-6 against Western Division clubs, defeating the Houston Astros, Los Angeles Dodgers, and San Francisco Giants three times each. He won all three decisions against the Philadelphia Phillies, hurling shutouts each time. Jones pitched 11 games under two hours, including just one hour and 31 minutes against Philadelphia on July 20 for the fastest National League contest that year and one hour and 38 minutes against the Montreal Expos to notch his 20th win of the year. He twice went 10 innings to notch a victory, besting the San Francisco Giants, 4-3, on May 30 and the Houston Astros, 2-1, on July 28. Although making only six hits in 103 plate appearances, he set a major-league fielding record for most chances without an error (112).

Jones became the first Padre National League Cy Young Award winner, beating out Jerry Koosman of the New York Mets. Only Bob Gibson of the 1970 St. Louis Cardinals and Steve Carlton of the 1972 Philadelphia Phillies had previously won the Cy Young Award for second division clubs. Jones, who joined Mike Marshall as the only pitchers to win the award after finishing second the season before, beamed, "It's a boyhood dream." Padres coach Bob Skinner observed, "Randy's pitches are too good to take—and not good enough to hit," while Steve Arlin recalled, "Jones always kept his infielders in the game." Announcer Dave Campbell added, "People reveled in his success. He drew 10,000 to 15,000 additional people to games and received standing ovations even when warming up."

Reliever Bruce Metzger was switched to the bullpen at spring training and responded brilliantly, winning his first 10 decisions with a 1.78 ERA and recording 13 saves through August 25. He ran out of stamina down the home stretch, ending 11-4 with a 2.93 ERA and 16 saves. Metzger became the first Padre to earn *The Sporting News'* National League Rookie Pitcher of the Year Award and tied Pat Zachry of the Cincinnati Reds for BBWAA National League Rookie of the Year honors. He established a major-league record with 77 appearances by a rookie, breaking Larry Hardy's 1974 mark. Metzger also set several club records, including most appearances (77), saves (16), and consecutive games won (10), and defeated every Western Division club, finishing 8-3 with a 2.93 ERA and nine saves against those opponents. He won three of four decisions with two saves against the Atlanta Braves and fared 2-0 with three saves against the Los Angeles Dodgers. Metzger went 3-1 with a 2.92 ERA and seven saves against the Eastern Division and was not scored on in 50 of his 77 appearances. He hurled 19 innings over 12 games before yielding his first earned run against the Chicago Cubs on May 14.

Dave Winfield again sparked the offense, leading San Diego with 13 home runs and plating 69 runs. His batting average rose 16 points to .283. "Winfield," coach Whitey Wietelmann claimed, "could do everything. He could run, field, throw, hit, hit with power." Mike Ivie paced the Padres with a .291 batting average and 70 RBIs, knocking in three runs in the season finale against the Los Angeles Dodgers to edge Winfield. He enjoyed 29 games with at least two hits, but contributed only seven home runs. Jerry Turner hit .366 in September to finish with a .267 batting average, while Willie Davis set a club record with 10 triples.

For the first time, all four Padre farm clubs captured league titles in 1976. Honolulu-based Hawaii won the Western Division of the Pacific Coast League with a 77-68 record after defeating Tacoma in a one-game playoff. Manager Roy Hartsfield guided Hawaii over Salt Lake City in three of five games to take the Pacific Coast League crown. Amarillo, Texas stood atop the Western Division of the Texas League with an 81-54 mark, finishing three games ahead of El Paso. Under manager Bob Miller, Amarillo defeated Shreveport in three of five games to earn the Texas League crown. Reno, Nevada placed third in the regular California League standings with a 75-62 mark, but triumphed over Salinas in three out of four games under manager John Goryl to take the California League title. Under manager Cliff Ditto, Walla Walla, Washington compiled a 46-26 record to finish eight and one-half games ahead of Eugene, Oregon for the Southern Division crown in the Northwest League and prevailed over Portland in two of three games to win the Northwest League playoffs.

Following the 1976 season, San Diego made numerous transactions. On October 22, the Padres sold infielder Dave Hilton, outfielder John Scott, and infielder-catcher Dave Roberts to the Toronto Blue Jays. On November 5, San Diego sold pitcher Chuck Hartenstein to the Toronto Blue Jays. On December 8, the club acquired center fielder George Hendrick from the Cleveland Indians for outfielder John Grubb, catcher Fred Kendall, and shortstop Hector Torres. San Diego also entered the free agent market for the first time. On December 14, the Padres dramatically

Butch Metzger relieved for the Padres from 1975 through May 1977.

strengthened their bullpen by signing Rollie Fingers of the Oakland Athletics to a six-year $1.6 million contract and raised their power potential by signing catcher Gene Tenace to a five-year $1.8 million contract. Fingers and Tenace had both starred on several championship Oakland Athletics clubs.

In early 1977, San Diego made several more roster moves. On January 20, the Padres released outfielder Willie Davis, who departed for the Japanese Baseball League. San Diego reacquired catcher-third baseman Dave Roberts on February 16 from the Blue Jays for pitcher Jerry Johnson. Padre second baseman Tito Fuentes on February 23 joined the Detroit Tigers as a free agent. San Diego sold pitcher Ken Reynolds to the Blue Jays on March 21 and Rich Folkers to the Milwaukee Brewers on March 23. After releasing pitcher Alan Foster on March 29, the Padres signed second baseman Gary Sutherland on April 6.

The new year brought sadness off the field, as two ex-Padres died. Dan Frisella, who pitched for the

New York Mets from 1967 through 1972, the Atlanta Braves in 1973 and 1974, San Diego in 1975, and the St. Louis Cardinals and Milwaukee Brewers in 1976, died in a dune buggy accident at age 30 near Phoenix, Arizona on January 1, 1977. He compiled a 1-6 record with nine saves and a 3.12 ERA in 1975 for the Padres and a 34-40 record with 57 saves and a 3.32 ERA in 10 major league seasons. Ron Willis, who hurled for the St. Louis Cardinals from 1966 through 1969 and the Houston Astros in 1969 and ended his major league career with San Diego in 1970, died at age 34 in Memphis, Tennessee on November 21, 1977. Willis split four decisions with four saves and a 4.02 ERA in 1970 for the Padres and posted an 11-12 record with 19 saves and a 4.02 ERA during five major-league seasons.

Despite the new acquisitions, San Diego endured another disappointing season in 1977, resembling Dr. Jekyll and Mr. Hyde. The Padres mustered three five-game winning streaks from May 28 through May 31, August 9 through August 12, and August 29 through September 3. Dave Freisleben and Dan Spillner both enjoyed five-game winning streaks. On the other hand, San Diego endured two eight-game losing streaks from April 24 through May 1 and June 20 through June 28.

Rollie Fingers relieved for the Padres from 1977 through 1980.

At one stretch, Bob Shirley lost nine consecutive decisions. The Padres scored 12 runs four times between April 10 and May 30 and made 16 hits three times, twice in consecutive games against the New York Mets on July 30 and July 31.

San Diego split a four-game series with the Cincinnati Reds at Riverfront Stadium to open the season. In the series finale on April 10, Bob Shirley struck out 11 Cincinnati Reds in a 12-4 romp. Eight days later, Gene Tenace homered twice and knocked in five runs in a 12-6 rout of the Braves at Atlanta-Fulton County Stadium. Bob Shirley on April 22 established a club record by retiring 25 consecutive Astros in a 4-2 victory at the Astrodome. The injury bug struck the Padres a few days later. Shortstop Enzo Hernandez, who had enjoyed his best major-league season in 1976, suffered a back injury in late April and spent nearly all of the 1977 campaign on the disabled list. He appeared in just seven games, mostly as a late-inning defensive replacement.

May started well but tested the club will. Dave Winfield enjoyed a season-high 16-game hitting streak from May 3 through May 21. Randy Jones on May 4 hurled the shortest nine-inning home game in franchise history. It took only one hour, 29 minutes for Jones to defeat the Philadelphia Phillies, 4-1. On May 17, the Chicago Cubs pounded Tom Griffin and several other San Diego pitchers for 24 hits in a 23-6 rout at Wrigley Field. Padres hurlers had never surrendered that many runs in a major-league game. Four days later, San Diego defeated the Montreal Expos, 11-8, in a wild 21-inning marathon at Olympic Stadium. The five-hour, 33-minute contest marked the longest road game in club history. On May 24, the Padres set a dubious club mark by stranding 17 runners but still defeated the Braves, 4-3, at Atlanta-Fulton County Stadium.

On May 17, San Diego traded struggling reliever Butch Metzger to the St. Louis Cardinals for pitchers John D'Acquisto and Pat Scanlon. After winning 11 decisions in 1976, Metzger had recorded no victories or saves in 17 games and saw his ERA balloon to 5.48 in 1977. The Padres in mid-May optioned Brent Strom, who had lost both decisions in 1977 after winning 12 games in 1976. Strom later underwent surgery for the removal of bone chips in his left elbow. In his first start as a Padre on May 22, John D'Acquisto set a club mark with four wild pitches against the Montreal Expos at Olympic Stadium.

On May 29, owner Ray Kroc fired manager John McNamara. The personable McNamara had compiled a 21-28 record in 1977 and a 224-310 ledger for the Padres since 1974 with sixth-, fourth-, and fifth-place finishes. Coach Bob Skinner served as interim manager for one game, guiding the Padres to a 3-2 triumph over the Houston Astros. Chicago Cubs first base coach Alvin Dark, who had managed four major-league clubs and produced three first-place finishers, took over the reins on May 30 and guided San Diego to a 48-65 mark thereafter.

The Padres initially responded well to the managerial change. Mike Ivie set a franchise record with five doubles in a double-header on May 30 against the San Francisco Giants at Candlestick Park. Three of Ivie's doubles came in the second game of the doubleheader. San Diego doubled four times, including Ivie twice and Doug Rader and Jerry Turner once each, in the seventh inning of the first game. Dave Winfield clouted a solo home run in a 1-0 victory over Los Angeles on June 3 at Dodger Stadium. The only other National League 1-0 game decided by a home run came on August 22, when Padre Gene Tenace connected against the Pittsburgh Pirates at Three Rivers Stadium.

Alvin Dark managed the Padres from May 1977 to March 1978.

Published reports soon indicated that at least 10 Padres disliked Dark as manager and wanted to be traded. On June 8, San Diego sold veteran Doug Rader, who complained about Dark's ban of beer on team flights, to the Toronto Blue Jays.

To bolster their offensive power, San Diego acquired outfielder Dave Kingman on June 15 from the New York Mets for infielder Bobby Valentine and pitcher Paul Siebert. Kingman batted .238 with 11 home runs and 39 RBIs in just 56 games, belting several memorable round-trippers. On June 21, he became only the third Padre to drive a home run into the second deck in left field in the second inning off of John Candelaria of the Pittsburgh Pirates. Kingman clouted two grand slams in August, his first coming in the sixth inning on August 5 off of Paul Reuschel of the Chicago Cubs at Wrigley Field and his second coming in the first inning on August 21 off of Tom Underwood of the St. Louis Cardinals at Busch Stadium. The Padres, however, sold Kingman on September 5 to the California Angels and on September 29 sold pitcher Rick Sawyer to the Montreal Expos.

Other Padres displayed hitting prowess during the second half of the season. In the second game of a July 26 doubleheader, Gene Richards established a franchise record and tied a National League extra-inning record by making six hits, including five singles and a double, in seven official plate appearances against the Montreal Expos in a 16-inning, 4-3 victory. George Hendrick knocked in five runs with two doubles and a home run on July 30 in an 8-6 triumph over the New York Mets at Shea Stadium. Bill Almon plated five runs with a home run and a double on August 17 to help defeat the Cincinnati Reds, 7-4, at Riverfront Stadium.

San Diego Stadium witnessed a major milestone in late August. Speedster Lou Brock of the St. Louis Cardinals swept past Ty Cobb's career stolen base mark of 892, making his record-breaking steal in a 4-3 loss to the Padres on August 29 before 19,656 fans at San Diego Stadium. He established the baseball milestone on his second steal of the night, pilfering second base in the seventh inning. Shortstop Bill Almon missed the ball and tag on a wild throw from the catcher. Brock, who later remarked, "I thought Ty Cobb's record was unattainable," achieved the feat in his 16th full major league season at age 38. The six-time All-Star selection, who helped the Cardinals to three National League pennants and two World Series titles in the 1960s, later became the 14th major-leaguer to reach 3,000 hits.

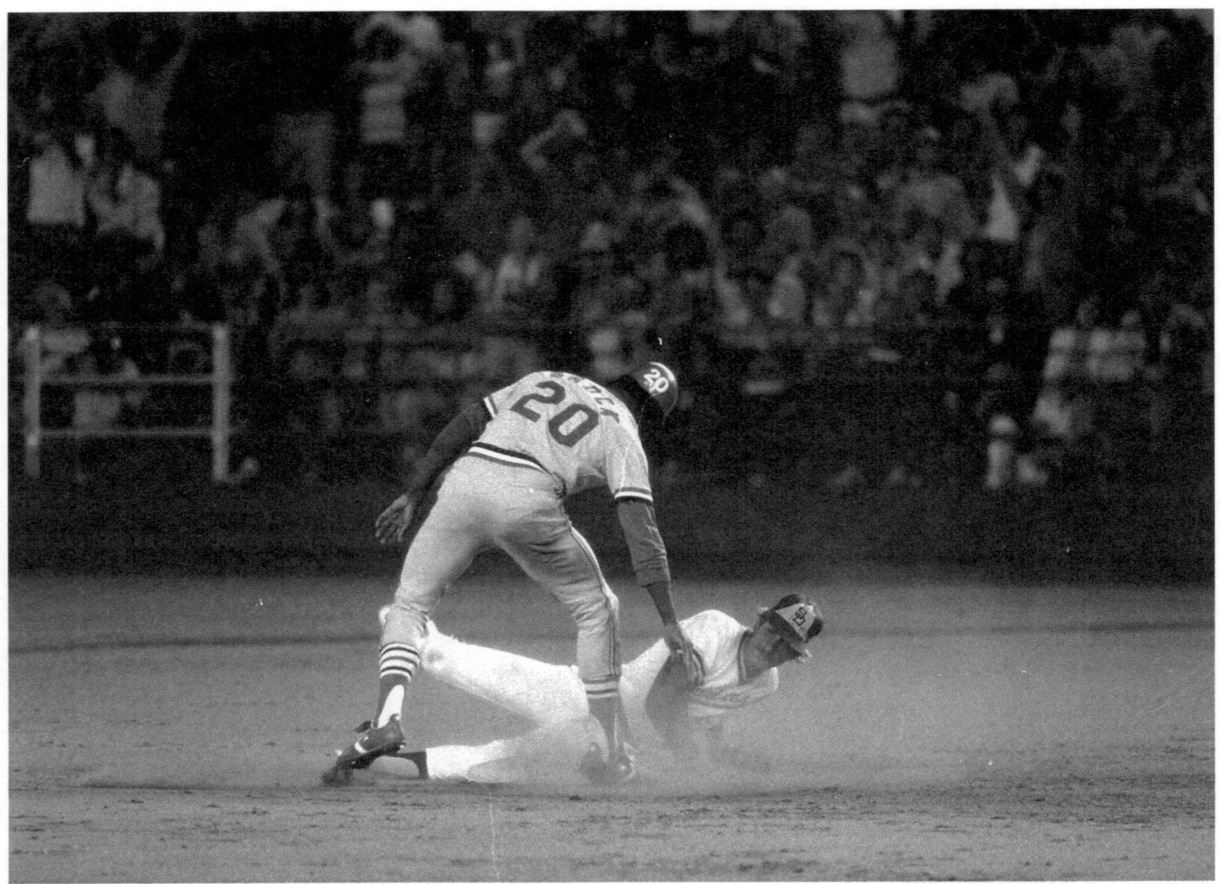

Lou Brock of the St. Louis Cardinals swept past Ty Cobb's career stolen base mark of 892, stealing second base in the seventh inning in a 4-3 loss to the Padres on August 29, 1977 at San Diego Stadium.

San Diego finished a disappointing fifth in the Western Division with a 69-93 record. The Padres drew 1,376,269 fans, surpassing one million in attendance for the fourth consecutive season. San Diego ranked eleventh in the league in pitching with a 4.43 ERA and struggled defensively with 189 errors, making six in each of several games. San Diego starting pitchers set a major-league record by completing only six games and went 74 consecutive games needing relief. Randy Jones came off a winter arm operation for nerve damage and lost 12 of 18 decisions with a 4.59 ERA. A sore arm landed him on the disabled list from June 18 to July 30. "When we lost Randy," Bavasi lamented, "we lost our stopper."

The Padres probably would have finished in last place without reliever Rollie Fingers. Fingers won the National League Fireman of the Year Award with an 8-9 record and a league-leading and club-record 35 saves. Three San Diego relievers unfortunately appeared in the three largest number of games in the major leagues. Fingers made 78 appearances to set a club record, while Dan Spillner and Dave Tomlin each recorded 76. The 44 combined team saves established a club mark.

Six rookies, including pitchers Bob Owchinko and Bob Shirley, became regulars during the season. Owchinko, *The Sporting News* National League Rookie Pitcher of the Year, won nine of 21 decisions, hurled three complete games, and tossed the club's only two complete-game shutouts. On September 5, he hurled a perfect game against the Los Angeles Dodgers for 7.1 innings until Steve Garvey laid a perfect bunt down the third base line. He allowed only two hits in the 1-0 home masterpiece. Shirley produced a 12-18 ledger with a 3.70 ERA.

The Padres finished eleventh in the National League with a .249 batting average, but set club season records with the highest batting average, 692 runs scored, 1,397 hits, 245 doubles, 49 triples, 653 RBIs,

602 walks, 133 stolen bases, and 71 pinch hits. Dave Winfield batted .275, paced the Padres in home runs (25) and RBIs (92), stole 16 bases, and set club records with 615 at bats and 104 runs scored. After the All-Star break, however, he hit just .249 with only eight homers and 32 RBIs. Center fielder George Hendrick enjoyed his finest season, leading the Padres with a .311 batting average, finishing second with 75 runs scored, 168 hits, 23 home runs, and 81 RBIs, and stealing 11 bases. Besides making four hits against the Philadelphia Phillies on May 14 at Veterans Stadium, he batted .368 with 12 RBIs against the Houston Astros and .344 with 12 RBIs against the Atlanta Braves.

Rookie Gene Richards became one of the best leadoff hitters in Padre history, batting .329 the second half of the season and .290 altogether. The fleet outfielder also established a club mark and a major-league record for most stolen bases by a rookie with 56. Nine times he stole two bases in one game. He and rookie shortstop Bill Almon set a club standard with 11 triples. Almon batted .261 with 43 RBIs and 20 stolen bases. Gene Tenace, who appeared as a catcher, first baseman, and third baseman, set Padre club records for being hit with 13 pitches and walking 125 times, including 10 intentional free passes. Outfielder Merv Rettenmund established a major league record by appearing in 86 games as a pinch-hitter and a National League record by walking 16 times. He batted .313 as a pinch hitter and delivered 21 pinch hits, just four short of the National League record.

Bobby Shirley pitched for the Padres from 1977 through 1980.

Bob Owchinko pitched for the Padres from 1976 through 1979.

Discontent, meanwhile, spread to the San Diego front office, leading to several key personnel changes. Buzzie Bavasi resigned as president in September after nine seasons reportedly following a disagreement with Joan Kroc, the owner's wife. He had co-owned the club with C. Arnholdt Smith from 1969 to 1974 and had managed daily operations for several years attempting to produce the elusive winning season. Owner Ray Kroc and vice president Ballard Smith promoted Bob Fontaine from player personnel director to general manager with instructions to make trades and sign young players. The club budget was increased, enabling the Padres to acquire more veterans, scout more talented players, and improve their farm system. Fontaine, on November 29, signed outfielder Oscar Gamble of the Chicago Cubs in the free agent draft to give the Padres a power-hitting left-hander in the regular lineup.

Part II

The Middle Years

[1978-1984]

6

The Padres Come of Age

[1978]

San Diego came of age in 1978, enjoying its best season yet as a major-league franchise. They installed a new scoreboard at San Diego Stadium and the Padres made several key personnel changes after their disappointing fifth-place finish in 1977. In January 1978, general manager Bob Fontaine lured star right-handed pitcher Gaylord Perry from the Texas Rangers for left-handed reliever Dave Tomlin and an estimated $125,000. Perry, a four-time All-Star and four-time 20-game winner, had compiled a 246-200 career mark in 16 major league seasons. San Diego on February 2 lured pitcher Mickey Lolich out of retirement and planned to use him in the bullpen to replace Tomlin. Lolich then ranked as the third-winningest major-league hurler behind Perry and Jim Kaat with 215 career victories. On February 28, the Padres sent temperamental infielder Mike Ivie, who had tied for the club lead with 29 doubles and ranked third in RBI with 66 in 1977, to the San Francisco Giants for infielder Derrel Thomas. Thomas had played with the Padres from 1972 through 1974 before spending three seasons in San Francisco. The Padres on March 14 released veteran shortstop Enzo Hernandez, who had batted .225 with 129 stolen bases in seven seasons.

San Diego made the earliest managerial change in major league history. The Padres dismissed manager Alvin Dark on March 21, just 17 days before the 1978 National League season. Dark, who had managed the 1977 Padres to only 65 victories, had served less than a full year on a three-year contract. No major-league manager had been fired during spring training since Phil Cavarretta of the Chicago Cubs in 1954. Several players had revolted against Dark's leadership.

Dark's failure to communicate with the front office and unwillingness to delegate authority to his coaches worsened the situation. "We were getting a lot of feedback from the players," owner Ray Kroc revealed, "and when you see something like that fomenting and feel it is festering, you have to do something.

Roger Craig managed the Padres in 1978 and 1979.

We decided to act quickly. We want relaxed, happy ballplayers." According to Kroc, Dark overmanaged and tended to run a one-man show. "He wanted to be the pitching coach, the batting coach, and the infield coach," Kroc recalled. Several players disliked the complex strategy and rigid discipline that the born-again Christian manager had imposed. Catcher Gene Tenace complained: "He put in so many trick plays and had so many signs that everyone was uptight. There were too many things to worry about." Tenace also objected to Dark calling the pitches from the dugout.

Roger Craig, a veteran Padre pitching coach, replaced Dark as manager. He had worked well with the young Padre pitchers from 1969 through 1972 and 1976 through 1977 and possessed the calm temperament that the team needed. Craig had pitched 12 years with six National League teams, sharing the National League lead in shutouts with the Los Angeles Dodgers in 1959 and winning two World Series games. He also had pitched in 1962 and 1963 for the fledgling New York Mets, becoming the first hurler to lead the National League two consecutive seasons in losses and tying a major-league record by dropping 18 consecutive decisions. The managerial change surprised Craig, who several days earlier had complained about being reduced to a "messenger boy." The appointment marked Craig's first major-league managerial assignment. Craig's managerial abilities bolstered Padre fortunes. Craig employed his motivational skills and calm personality to improve team performance and increased the confidence of his pitchers. "Craig," reserve infielder Tim Flannery observed, "believed in his players and won their respect as a manager of men." On March 28, the Padres released pitcher Brent Strom.

The 1978 season started well as San Diego defeated the San Francisco Giants, 3-2, on April 7 at Candlestick Park. Five starters—first baseman Gene Richards, third baseman Bill Almon, right fielder Dave Winfield, center fielder George Hendrick, and catcher Gene Tenace—returned from the 1977 Padre squad. The other starters were second baseman Derrel Thomas, shortstop Ozzie Smith, left fielder Oscar Gamble, and pitcher Gaylord Perry. The Padre roster carried several rookies during the year, including first baseman Broderick Perkins, third baseman Barry Evans, infielder Chuck Baker, outfielder Don Reynolds, catcher Rick Sweet, and reliever Mark Lee. Winfield was named team captain prior to the opening game and responded with three hits, including a home run, to key the Padre win. Dave Campbell, former Padre second baseman, replaced Bob Chandler in the broadcast booth.

Gaylord Perry pitched for the Padres in 1978 and 1979.

San Diego won only seven of 20 games in April. "We lost a lot of early season games," owner Ray Kroc recalled, "because we were experimenting at several positions." Nevertheless, the opening month produced several highlights. The Padres turned a triple play in a 3-2 victory over the Braves on April 11 at Atlanta-Fulton County Stadium. Atlanta pitcher Phil Niekro hit a high chopper to third baseman Bill Almon, who tagged out Rod Gilbreath going to third base and threw to Derrel Thomas at second base to force Pat Rockett. Thomas then relayed to Gene Richards at first base to retire Niekro. San Diego swept a four-game series at home with Atlanta from April 20 to April 23, winning 2-0, 9-3, 2-0, and 5-4.

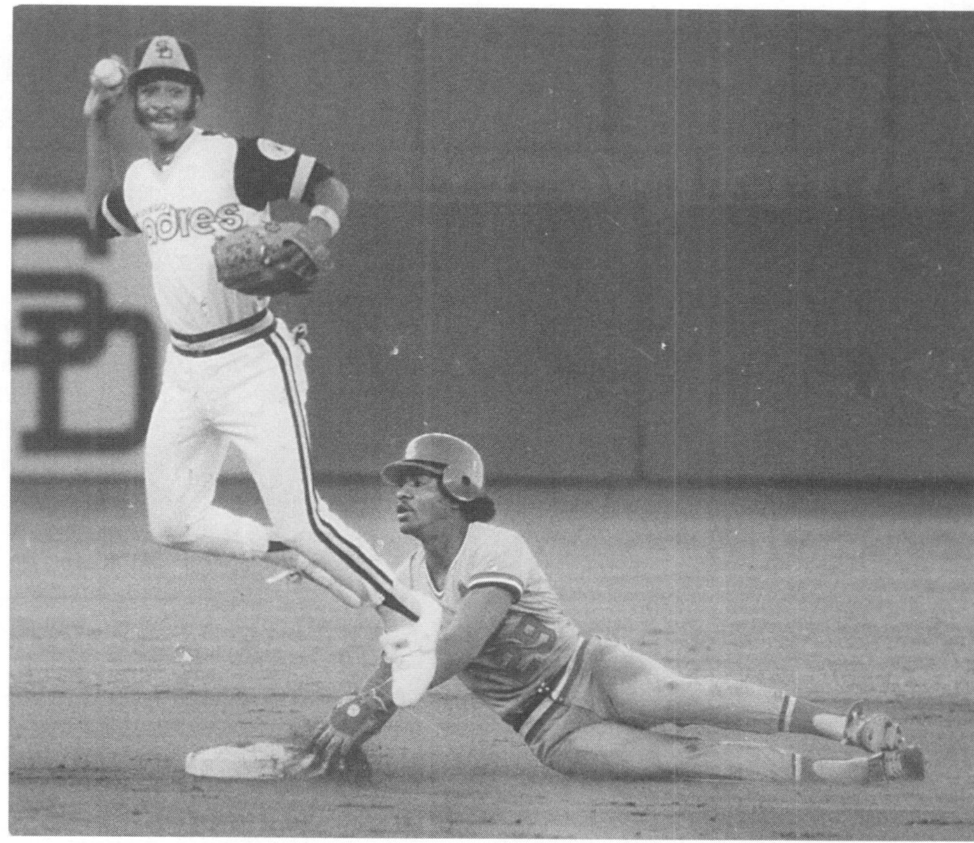
Ozzie Smith starred defensively at shortstop for the Padres from 1978 through 1981.

On April 20, Randy Jones blanked the Braves, 2-0, on three hits in the first game of the series. Rookie shortstop Ozzie Smith made perhaps the most spectacular defensive play in Padre history, robbing Jeff Burroughs of a base hit. He made a miraculous bare-handed grab of Burroughs' one-hop liner and threw him out at first base. Randy Jones recalled Smith "went to dive for it, and at least to save a run, and the next thing you know it takes a bad hop back over him. And all of a sudden, his hand popped up, he bare hands it, and jumps up and throws him out." Jones added: "You should have seen Burroughs's face. Burroughs is going, 'what do you have to do to get a hit around this place?'" Smith conceded, "It could have bounced off my finger, but the ball hit me and stuck in the palm of my hand. I was able to get up and throw him out."

San Diego split 28 games in May and still lacked consistency in early June. Ozzie Smith on May 5 hit triples in both the fifth and eighth innings, sparking a 2-1 victory over the St. Louis Cardinals at Busch Stadium. Gene Richards and Oscar Gamble also tripled in that game, tying the club record for most triples. The Padres swept all three games with the St. Louis Cardinals at home from May 15 through May 17. Jerry Turner on May 22 hit a dramatic two-run pinch-hit homer to help defeat the Pittsburgh Pirates 7-5 at San Diego Stadium. On June 9, Dennis Lamp of the Chicago Cubs blanked the Padres 5-0 at Wrigley Field, allowing only a two-out sixth-inning single by Gene Richards.

The inconsistent team performance prompted several roster changes. On May 26, San Diego traded outfielder George Hendrick to the St. Louis Cardinals for pitcher Eric Rasmussen. Rasmussen gave the Padres another effective starting pitcher to complement Perry, Randy Jones, and Bob Owchinko. The Padres stopped experimenting with Gene Richards at first base and returned him to the outfield. Mark Lee joined Rollie Fingers, John D'Acquisto, Mickey Lolich, and Bob Shirley in the bullpen. Fernando Gonzalez was acquired June 5 on waivers from the Pittsburgh Pirates and inserted at second base. Nine days later, San Diego sent starting pitcher Dan Spillner to the Cleveland Indians for reliever Dennis Kinney. On June 22, the Padres traded reliever Dave Freisleben to the Cleveland Indians for pitcher Bill Laxton. Despite these changes, the Padres still lacked consistency.

San Diego fortunes improved in late June. The Padres won 10 of 14 games from June 17 to June 30 and triumphed in six consecutive home games from June 22 to June 26, allowing opponents only 11 runs. Relievers were hardly used during that stretch. Bob Owchinko shut out the Atlanta Braves, 2-0, on June 22, while Gaylord Perry blanked the Houston Astros, 3-0, the following day. The Padres took the final three games with Houston and the first game with the San Francisco Giants before Vida Blue ended the winning streak. Dave Winfield enjoyed a sensational June, becoming the first Padre to garner National League Player of the Month honors. On June 10, he knocked in six runs with two homers in a 10-8 victory over the Chicago Cubs at Wrigley Field. Gene Richards batted safely in 11 consecutive games from June 17 through June 27.

San Diego carried the momentum into July, taking 17 of 30 contests. The Padres defeated the Astros and the Giants twice each at the beginning of the month. Dave Winfield celebrated Independence Day by clouting his third career grand slam in the first inning off John Montefusco of the Giants at Candlestick Park. In the second game of a July 8 doubleheader, Eric

Dave Winfield played outfield for the Padres from June 1973 through 1980.

Rasmussen blanked the Braves, 7-0, on a three-hitter at Atlanta-Fulton County Stadium.

San Diego hosted its first All-Star Game on July 11. Dave Winfield and Rollie Fingers represented the Padres on the National League roster, the former for the second consecutive year. Owner Ray Kroc threw out the ceremonial first pitch, aided by veteran Padre coach Whitey Weitelmann. A sellout crowd watched the National League stage a four-run eighth-inning rally to defeat the American League, 7-3. Winfield, singled to left center field in the eighth inning and eventually scored. Fingers exhibited his typical dazzling control, hurling two shutout innings in relief. Future Padre Steve Garvey earned All-Star Most Valuable Player accolades. The Padres opened the stadium gates for All-Star workouts the day before the game, with more than 30,000 fans in attendance. Over 15,000 San Diego area children came to an All-Star party hosted by Padres outfielder Dave Winfield for his All-Star friends.

San Diego played its best baseball after the All-Star break. Padre bats came alive on July 15 with nine extra-base hits and four home runs against the Chicago Cubs at Wrigley Field. Fernando Gonzalez belted his only two home runs of the season in that contest, while Dave Roberts and Gene Tenace also homered. Seven days later, Jerry Turner belted a dramatic three-run homer in the bottom of the ninth inning off of Bruce Sutter to defeat the Chicago Cubs, 4-2.

Pennant fever struck as the Padres won a season-high 10 consecutive games, including nine at home, from July 25 to August 4. San Diego swept three games each from the Pittsburgh Pirates, 2-1, 6-5, and 6-3, the St. Louis Cardinals, 8-3, 7-3, and 3-2, and the eventual National League champion Los Angeles Dodgers, 4-3, 1-0, and 2-1. The Padres outscored their opponents 39–20 during that homestand, with Bob Owchinko triumphing three times and Gaylord Perry, Bob Shirley, and Randy Jones twice each. Randy Jones outdueled Burt Hooton of the Los Angeles Dodgers on August 1, giving him his second 1-0 shutout victory. Manager Craig rarely used the relievers on that home stand, as San Diego climbed above a .500 winning percentage. The Padres defeated the Cincinnati Reds on August 4 at Riverfront Stadium but then suffered their longest losing streak of the season. San Diego dropped its remaining five games on that road trip to Cincinnati and Los Angeles.

During the remainder of August, San Diego prevailed in 13 of 21 games. The Padres returned home with three victories in four games against the Cincinnati Reds, scoring a season-high 15 runs and walking a club record 12 times in the first contest on August 10. San Diego batters set a franchise record by being walked intentionally four times, three to Fernando Gonzalez. The Padres embarked on a successful road trip, winning two of three from the New York Mets, sweeping a three-game series with the Montreal Expos, and conquering the Philadelphia Phillies in two of three contests. During that stretch, Padre hurlers seldom surrendered over three runs. On August 16, Bob Owchinko picked off John Stearns and Willie Montanez of the New York Mets at second base in the fourth inning of a 2-1 victory at Shea Stadium.

San Diego remained in pennant contention into late August. No previous Padre aggregate had stayed in pennant contention after the All-Star break. Jerry Koosman of the New York Mets held San Diego to just two hits on August 22, but the Padres still managed to win, 2-1. Outfielder Jerry Turner set a franchise record on August 23 by clouting his fifth pinch-hit home run of the season in the sixth inning with two runners on base, giving the Padres a 6-5 victory over the Philadelphia Phillies at Veterans Stadium. Turner's feat fell just one home run short of the major-league season record, set by pinch-hitter Johnny Frederick of the Brooklyn Dodgers in 1932. San Diego slumped the remainder of August, dropping five of eight home games.

The Padres, thanks largely to Gaylord Perry, split 26 games in September. Perry won nine of his last 10 decisions with a 1.74 ERA and triumphed in all six September starts, garnering National League Pitcher of the Month honors. He defeated the Atlanta Braves, 8-4, and 3-1, the Cincinnati Reds, 3-2, the Atlanta Braves, 3-1, the Houston Astros, 2-1, and the San Francisco Giants, 5-1, and 4-1. His 3,000th major-league strikeout came in the season finale, a 4-3 victory over the Los Angeles Dodgers on October 1. Perry, who became the then-oldest Padre to appear in a major-league game at 40 years and 16 days, fanned outfielder Joe Simpson late in the game to achieve that feat. Only Walter Johnson of the Washington Senators and Bob Gibson of the St. Louis Cardinals had reached the 3,000 strikeout pinnacle previously.

Dave Winfield and Gene Richards sparked the offense in September. Winfield had three hits in three consecutive games from September 12 through September 14, helping the Padres defeat the Atlanta

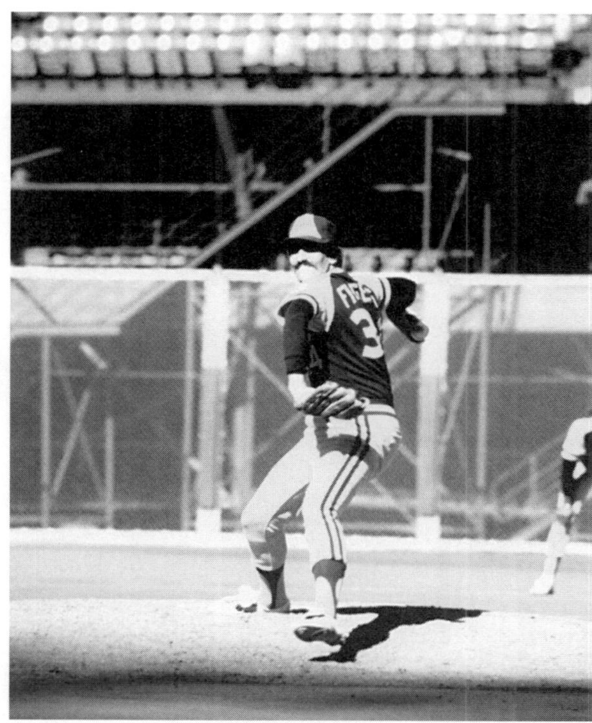

Rollie Fingers led National League relievers in saves twice.

Braves, 3-1, and the Cincinnati Reds, 6-2, and 8-1. Gene Richards feasted on San Francisco Giants pitching, making four hits in a 5-1 home triumph on September 21 and tripling in the first and third innings to spark a 4-1 win on September 26 at Candlestick Park. San Diego, on September 22, set a club record with 20 hits in a 12-3 romp over Los Angeles at Dodger Stadium. In the fifth inning, the Padres sent 12 batters to the plate.

In 1978, San Diego surpassed a .500 winning percentage for the first time in franchise history. The Padres set a club record with 84 victories while losing 78 contests. Their 50 home victories broke a club record, while their 34 road wins tied another. San Diego finished fourth in the Western Division, only 11 games behind the Los Angeles Dodgers. The Padres had ended the 1977 campaign 29 games behind first place. San Diego Stadium attendance rose nearly 18 percent to a record 1,670,107 people, an increase of nearly 300,000 spectators. San Diego drew over one million spectators for the fifth consecutive season. Over 40 percent of San Diego's victories came by one run, thanks to a solid relief corps. Fifteen of the 34 Padre one-run victories came on the road. San Diego fared best against the St.

Louis Cardinals, taking nine of 12 games. The Padres also won 10 of 18 contests from the Atlanta Braves and seven of 12 games from the New York Mets and Pittsburgh Pirates.

San Diego announcer Dave Campbell summed up the 1978 season by stating, "a lot of guys put together good years." For the first time, two Padre regulars batted over .300 in the same campaign. Dave Winfield enjoyed his finest season, ranking fifth in the National League with a .308 batting average and leading the club in home runs (24), RBIs (97), doubles (30), and hits (181). Winfield, along with Gene Tenace, supplied the power for the Padres and exhibited a strong defensive throwing arm. He produced 15 homers with 59 RBIs the first half of the season and batted .374 in his final 35 games. Besides producing eight three-hit games, he knocked in 15 runs against the Houston Astros and 13 against the San Francisco Giants. His honors included being named San Diego's Most Valuable Player for the first time. Leadoff batter Gene Richards finished sixth in the National League with a .308 batting average, tied for second in the senior circuit with 12 triples, and paced the club with 90 runs scored. He set club season marks for most singles (129), triples (12), and total bases (233) by a left-handed batter. Richards enjoyed 14 three-hit games and batted .331 after June 9 and a torrid .474 with 18 hits in his final nine games.

The Padres team batted .252, the best in club history. Oscar Gamble made four hits in three games, while Bill Almon, Ozzie Smith, and Derrel Thomas accomplished that feat twice. Gamble tied a club mark by hitting safely in seven consecutive plate appearances. The Padres set a club record with 152 stolen bases to rank third in the National League, paced by Ozzie Smith's 40 and Gene Richards's 37. Dave Winfield and Bill Almon combined for 38 stolen bases. Ozzie Smith and Jerry Turner added valuable dimensions to the offense. Smith batted .258, finishing runner-up to third baseman Bob Horner of the Atlanta Braves in the National League Rookie of the Year balloting. An excellent bunter, he established a franchise record with 28 sacrifice hits and finished fourth in the National League in stolen bases. Jerry Turner enjoyed a banner year, batting .400 with 19 RBIs as a pinch-hitter and ranking second on the Padres behind Winfield with seven game-winning RBIs. He had 20 pinch hits and his five pinch-hit home runs demolished old club records. The Padres made a team-record 55 pinch hits.

Jerry Turner played outfield for the Padres from 1975 through September 1981.

San Diego, however, experienced a major power shortage. The Padres placed tenth in home runs with just 75 and last in runs scored with only 591. San Diego barely averaged three runs per game and managed only one home run in 12 games against the Montreal Expos. Gene Tenace clouted two home runs in three different games, while Fernando Gonzalez and Dave Winfield accomplished the feat once.

The addition of acrobatic shortstop Ozzie Smith markedly improved the Padre defense. Manager Roger Craig boasted, "Ozzie is the best young infielder I've ever seen. Very soon, he's going to be one of the best shortstops in baseball." Frank Kern, San Diego Hall of Champions executive director, recalled, "Smith made hard plays look easy." Padre announcer Jerry Coleman termed Smith "a rookie with small frame, soft hands and a magic glove that put dazzle in the defense. Throughout the season, Ozzie Smith provided the unexpected and the spectacular." With Smith's wizardry, the Padres set a club record by converting 171 double plays.

San Diego pitchers boasted the National League's second best ERA at 3.28, surrendering 1.15 fewer runs per game than in 1977. The stingy Padre hurlers allowed just 598 runs and 522 earned runs, fewest in franchise history and fewer than any major-league team since 1968. No National League club since 1946 had surrendered fewer runs at home. San Diego hurlers yielded just 74 home runs, issued only 483 walks, and established a franchise record with nine shutouts at home. They demonstrated excellent control, hitting only 12 batters in 162 games. Gaylord Perry, Randy Jones, Eric Rasmussen, and Bob Owchinko formed an effective starting corps, combining for 56 wins.

The acquisition of Gaylord Perry paid big dividends for San Diego in 1978. Perry led National League pitchers with 21 victories, a club record for right-handers, and lost only six decisions, boasting an impressive 2.72 ERA and .778 winning percentage. The 1978 season marked Perry's fifth 20-win season. He paced Padre hurlers in innings pitched (260.2) and strikeouts (154), while his winning percentage established a club record. Perry showed remarkable consistency, finishing 9-3 with a 2.69 ERA the first half of the season and 12-3 with a 2.76 ERA the second half. He pitched superbly at home with an 11-2 mark and a 1.75 ERA in 18 starts. His 21 wins accounted for 25 percent of the 84 Padre victories, while his six defeats were less than eight percent of the 78 club losses.

Perry defeated every National League team at least once, recording four triumphs over the Houston Astros and three wins over the Atlanta Braves. He blanked opponents twice, outdueling the Montreal Expos, 1-0, on June 14 and the Houston Astros, 2-0, on June 23. Three of his losses were by scores of 1-0, 2-1, and 3-2. Perry was also involved in seven no-decisions when allowing under three runs. He easily outdistanced Burt Hooton of the Los Angeles Dodgers for the National League Cy Young Award, making him the first pitcher to receive the award in both leagues and the oldest hurler to win that coveted honor. *The Sporting News* named him to its All-National League team. Manager Roger Craig acknowledged, "I never saw a man who could get himself [psyched] up so consistently." Pitcher Steve Arlin reminisced, "Perry really knew the game and made people think."

Other starters contributed to the Padre success. Randy Jones won 13 of 27 decisions and led San Diego starters with seven complete games. He hurled two shutouts, both 1-0 masterpieces at home, over the Chicago Cubs on May 10 and Los Angeles Dodgers on August 1. Eric Rasmussen, secured from the St. Louis Cardinals for outfielder George Hendrick in late May, strengthened the Padre starting rotation with 12 victories in 22 decisions and won eight consecutive games from June 14 through July 31. Bob Owchinko produced a 10-13 ledger, contributing two shutouts.

Padre relievers established a club record with a National League best 55 saves. Rollie Fingers paced the senior circuit with 37 saves, repeating as Fireman of the Year. Clay Carroll of the Cincinnati Reds had set the National League record for most saves with 37 in 1972. Fingers struggled through the first part of the 1978 season, but then baffled opponents with his curve ball and did not surrender a run for over one month. He finished 12 games for Gaylord Perry, saving 10. "Never in my 17 seasons," Perry declared, "have I had the good fortune of having a pitcher like Fingers in my bullpen." Fingers revolutionized relief pitching as one of baseball's first great bullpen artists. "Relief pitching," Steve Arlin explained, "was not a very important thing until Fingers." Announcer Jerry Coleman recalled, "Veteran pitchers Gaylord Perry and Rollie Fingers continually slammed the door on opposing hitters." Relievers John D'Acquisto, Bob Shirley, Mark Lee, and Mickey Lolich combined for 19 victories and 23 saves.

Following the 1978 campaign, San Diego sought to strengthen the franchise at catcher, first base, second base, third base, and center field. The Padres on October 25 traded high-salaried outfielder Oscar Gamble, catcher Dave Roberts, and an estimated $300,000 cash to the Texas Rangers for first baseman Mike Hargrove, infielder Kurt Bevacqua, and catcher Bill Fahey. Hargrove, an excellent fielder, had batted over .300 lifetime until slumping in 1978. On November 14, San Diego lost outfielder-infielder Derrel Thomas to the Los Angeles Dodgers via free agency. The Padres sought infielder-outfielder Pete Rose of the Cincinnati Reds, but the free agent signed a $3.2 million contract on December 5 with the Philadelphia Phillies.

San Diego sports aficionados fondly remember the 1978 season. After the Padres had attained their first winning record, the San Diego Chargers tied for second pace in the Western Conference of the National Football League with a 9-7 mark. The Padres and Chargers have accomplished other winning seasons, but 1978 marked the only year until 1992 that both franchises surpassed a .500 winning percentage the same year.

7

The Years of Struggle [1979-81]

Optimism brimmed as San Diego opened the 1979 season. The Padres expected to challenge the Cincinnati Reds, Los Angeles Dodgers, and San Francisco Giants for the Western Division title. San Diego began the 1979 campaign with an effective starting rotation of Gaylord Perry, Randy Jones, Bob Owchinko, and Eric Rasmussen and a deep bullpen of right-handers Rollie Fingers, John D'Acquisto and Mark Lee and left-handers Mickey Lolich and Bob Shirley. The Padres also possessed excellent speed with Ozzie Smith and Gene Richards. San Diego expected outfielder Dave Winfield to provide the main offensive firepower, but the Padres suffered from weak hitting, leaky defense, and a weak bench.

Before the 1979 season, San Diego tried to augment its bench strength. On February 25, the Padres signed free agent catcher Fred Kendall of the Boston Red Sox, who had caught for San Diego from 1969 through 1976. On March 30, San Diego acquired first baseman-outfielder Dan Briggs from the Cleveland Indians for pitcher Mike Champion.

The Padres opened the season against the Los Angeles Dodgers on April 5. Gene Tenace handled catching duties, while Mike Hargrove played first base. San Diego shifted Bill Almon to second base to make room for third baseman Barry Evans. Ozzie Smith, runner-up in the National League Rookie of the Year balloting, started his second season at shortstop. Oscar Gamble's departure opened up the left field position for pinch-hitter Jerry Turner. Gene Richards moved from left field to center field, while team captain Dave Winfield converted from center field to right field.

San Diego played its first seven games on the road, losing five to the Los Angeles Dodgers and San Francisco Giants, and finished the month with just nine wins in 23 decisions. Shortstop Ozzie Smith symbolized the early season problems, going hitless in his first 34 official at-bats after leading the club in hitting and RBIs during spring training.

Starters Eric Rasmussen and Bob Shirley lost four consecutive decisions. San Diego split 30 games in May. Dick Ruthven of the Philadelphia Phillies on May 9 blanked the Padres, 2-0, on one hit. San Diego broke out of its slump, winning five straight games from May 28 through May 31, and scoring seven runs in the fifth inning in a 10-2 home victory on May 30 over the Atlanta Braves. The Padres experienced a June swoon, winning just 11 of 28 games. Bruce Kison of the Pittsburgh Pirates nearly no-hit the Padres in a 7-0 shutout on June 3 at Three Rivers Stadium. Third baseman Barry Evans doubled with two outs in the eighth inning for the lone San Diego hit. Two days later, the Padres tallied their highest run production of the season in an 11-3 victory over the Chicago Cubs at Wrigley Field. The normally erratic-fielding Padres did not commit an error for 93 straight innings from July 3 through July 12.

Outfielder Dave Winfield provided most of the first-half season highlights. He enjoyed six consecutive two-hit games from April 17 through April 22 and on April 30 took over the National League lead with a .394 batting average, tripling twice in a 4-3 loss to the New York Mets at Shea Stadium. Winfield on May 30 drove in a season-best five runs in a 10-2 home triumph over the Atlanta Braves. San Diego scored a season-high seven runs in the fifth inning. The National League Player of the Week from May 28 to June 3, Winfield batted .500 with 14 hits, 5 home runs, and 12 RBIs in eight games. He hit safely in 10 straight games from June 5 through June 15 and plated runs in six consecutive games from July 2 through July 8. On July 11, outfielder Jerry Turner, Winfield, and catcher Gene Tenace clouted consecutive home runs off of Randy Lerch in the first inning to spark a 7-3 victory over the Philadelphia Phillies at Veterans Stadium. Winfield had six hits, including two home runs, and five RBIs in a doubleheader split against the Montreal Expos at Olympic Stadium on July 13 and finished the four game series with 11 hits in 18 plate appearances.

During the first half of the season, manager Roger Craig juggled the Padre lineup frequently. San Diego recalled several pitchers from its Hawaii farm club, but the moves made little difference. The Padres on June 14 traded struggling first baseman Mike Hargrove to the Cleveland Indians for outfielder-third baseman Paul Dade. The next day, San Diego acquired veteran outfielder-first baseman Jay Johnstone from the New York Yankees for pitcher Dave Wehrmeister. Johnstone, who entertained teammates with his uninhibited clubhouse antics, batted .294 and knocked in 32 runs as an outfielder, first baseman, and pinch hitter. Rookie third baseman Barry Evans hit only .216 with 14 RBIs during the first two months of the season and quit baseball to play professional tennis rather than accept a June 22 demotion to Amarillo of the Texas League. The Padres on July 5 signed veteran outfielder Bobby Tolan.

San Diego struggled both on and off the field after the All-Star break. The Padres won only 14 games between July 19 and August 31, losing seven consecutive games from August 14 through August 20. San Diego on August 25 lost a heartbreaking 4-3, 19-inning, 6-hour, 12-minute contest to the Pittsburgh Pirates, leaving a club-record 26 runners on base. The game, which lasted from 7:08 p.m. to 1:20 a.m., marked the longest in club history. In mid-August, owner Ray Kroc announced that he would spend between $5 million and $10 million on star players to improve his team. In response to a reporter's question, he unfortunately vowed to pursue second baseman Joe Morgan of the Cincinnati Reds and third baseman Graig Nettles of the New York Yankees if they became free agents. When the story was published, the Cincinnati Reds and New York Yankees immediately brought charges of tampering. An apologetic Kroc said, "I'm sorry. There was no such intent." He declared, "I'm going to consider myself ineligible to bid for Morgan and Nettles, and the San Diego club won't draft them if they do become free agents."

Nevertheless, commissioner Bowie Kuhn on August 23 fined Kroc $100,000 for tampering, the largest penalty ever assessed a baseball owner. The decision incensed the Padre owner. "I couldn't believe it," he protested. "I had promised we would have nothing to do with either player. But [Kuhn] stuck it to me anyway." Kroc, the same day, stepped down as club president and named his son-in-law Ballard Smith, Jr. club president and director of team operations, authorizing him to invest heavily in the free agent market and to make trades. Smith, a 33-year-old former Pennsylvania district attorney and team executive vice president, tried to make the Padre organization a family unit. "Smith," announcer Dave Campbell observed, "created a family atmosphere and team harmony."

Outfielder Dave Winfield continued to provide the main San Diego offensive highlights. He became the first Padre chosen for the National League All-Star starting lineup, receiving over three million votes. Winfield enjoyed his most productive game on July 31 with a home run, double, three singles, four runs scored, and four RBIs against the Atlanta Braves at Atlanta-Fulton County Stadium. In the ninth inning, Kurt Bevacqua and Winfield clouted consecutive home runs off of Adrian Devine in the 10-2 San Diego victory. The Padres recorded a season-high 18 hits in that game. Winfield concluded that day with eight consecutive hits over a two-game span and stood atop the National League with a .345 batting average. On September 7, he became the first National League player to reach 100 RBIs in an 8-0 shutout of the Braves at Atlanta-Fulton County Stadium. Five days later, Winfield became just the second Padre to clout 30 home runs in a 5-2 loss to the Los Angeles Dodgers. On September 21, he passed Nate Colbert as the Padre single-season RBI leader with 113.

Other Padres provided late season highlights. Outfielder Paul Dade hit safely in 12 consecutive games from August 25 through September 8. At 40 years, 11 months, and 18 days, pitcher Gaylord Perry shut out the San Francisco Giants, 3-0, September 3, at San Diego Stadium. Infielder Tim Flannery made his major-league debut in the same game with a single and RBI. The intelligent, reliable, and popular infielder became a valuable utility player over the next decade. Two days later, catcher Bill Fahey singled five times in a 4-3, 10-inning loss to the Houston Astros at the Astrodome. San Diego, on September 8, tied a season-best with seven runs in the third inning of a 9-2 victory over the Atlanta Braves at Atlanta-Fulton County Stadium. On September 22, the Padres stole six bases, including three by Paul Dade and two by Dave Winfield, in a 10-8 home triumph over the Los Angeles Dodgers. On September 28, pitcher Eric Rasmussen blanked the San Francisco Giants, 2-0, on one hit at Candlestick Park. Third baseman Darrell Evans singled in the second frame for the lone Giant safety.

San Diego finished the campaign in fifth place in the Western Division with a disappointing 68-93 record, barely ahead of the last-place Atlanta Braves. The Padres struggled at the gate, in their bullpen, and at the plate. Fan interest diminished as the season progressed, with San Diego Stadium attendance declining by 213,140 to 1,456,967. Only 6,349 fans attended a September 19 contest against the Houston Astros. Padre pitchers slipped from second to fifth place in the National League, with the staff ERA rising from 3.28 to 3.69. Ineffective relief pitching contributed to the soaring club ERA. The San Diego bullpen attained only 25 saves, less than one-half the previous season. After developing elbow problems, Rollie Fingers missed two weeks in July and did not pitch after August 25. His 13 saves fell 24 short of his 1978 production. Relievers John D'Acquisto, Mark Lee, and rookie Steve Mura combined for only nine saves, while Bob Shirley and Mickey Lolich did not record a single save in 51 combined appearances. Mura split eight decisions, striking out 59 batters in 73 innings and boasting a 3.08 ERA.

San Diego starting pitchers lacked offensive support. Gaylord Perry led the Padre staff with a 12-11 mark, but walked out in early September of the last year of his contract because of personal problems. He wanted San Diego to trade him, but the Padres kept him until February. Randy Jones won 11 of 23 decisions with a 3.63 ERA, ranking fourth in the National League with 263 innings pitched and fifth with 36 starts. He finished 7-4 with a 3.07 ERA at San Diego Stadium and left games with a lead in the late innings that the bullpen blew. Starters Bob Owchinko, Eric Rasmussen, and Bob Shirley struggled with just 20 wins in 57 decisions. Owchinko and Rasmussen each won six games, while Shirley triumphed eight times.

San Diego plunged to last place in the National League with a .242 batting average, a 10-point decline from its 1978 production. The Padres languished in most other major offensive categories, placing tenth in runs scored (603) and home runs (93) and eleventh in slugging percentage (.348). San Diego did not even take advantage of its outstanding speed, finishing ninth with just 100 stolen bases.

Dave Winfield enjoyed his best season as a Padre. He furnished the bulk of the offensive firepower, single-handedly saving the club from last place with his 34 homers, .308 batting average, and league-leading and club-record 118 RBIs. Winfield led the National League in total bases (333), ranked third in home runs, shared third in game-winning RBIs (16), placed fourth in slugging percentage (.588), tied for fourth in games played (159) and seventh in triples (10), ranked eighth in batting average and hits (184), and finished tenth in runs scored (97). His postseason honors included being the first Padre Gold Glove Award winner and making *The Sporting News* All-National League team. Winfield placed third in the MVP balloting behind cowinners Willie Stargell and Keith Hernandez. He also received the most votes on both the AP and UPI National League All-Star teams. Manager Roger Craig observed, "He did it on his own; we had no one to hit behind him and the pitchers consistently pitched around him." Winfield also paced the senior circuit in intentional walks with 24 and stole 15 bases. Gene Tenace and newcomer Bill Fahey supplemented Winfield at the plate. Besides switching to first base in mid-August, Tenace raised his batting average 39 points to .263 while clouting 20 home runs and producing 67 RBIs. Fahey batted .286 for the season and .318 after assuming regular catching duties from Tenace in mid-August.

The other Padres, however, struggled at the plate. Craig tried both Bill Almon and Fernando Gonzalez at second base, but neither provided much offense. Shortstop Ozzie Smith struggled offensively the first half of the season and batted only .211, 47 points below his rookie average. Left fielder Jerry Turner set personal bests in several offensive categories, but batted only .248 and fielded erratically. Gene Richards struggled at the plate after switching to center field, as his batting average dropped from .308 to .279 and his stolen base production declined from 37 to 24.

In 1974, radio station KGB had hired Ted Giannoulas to don a chicken costume and attend sporting and entertainment events as the KGB Chicken. The identity of the KGB Chicken remained unknown to the public until 1976, when Giannoulas was arrested at an Aerosmith concert. The popularity of the KGB Chicken was such that Giannoulas began receiving offers to entertain outside of San Diego. During those events he wore his chicken suit but not his KGB vest, resulting in his firing from the radio station in 1979. After his firing from KGB, Ray Kroc hired Giannoulas and renamed him the San Diego Chicken.

The movie, *The Kid from Left Field,* filmed at the San Diego Stadium, was telecast nationally on September 30 and warmed the hearts of Padre fans. The film, starring Gary Coleman, featured a bat boy who guides the San Diego Padres from the cellar to the World Series. The bat boy uses strategies taught by his father, a former major-league journeyman reduced to a hot dog vendor. The movie, directed by Adell Aldrich, also starred Robert Guillaume, Tab Hunter, Tricia O'Neil, Gary Collins, and Ed McMahon and gave Padre fans hope that brighter days lay ahead.

San Diego also fired Craig, who had compiled a 152-171 record in two seasons as manager. The Padres surprised the baseball world the next day by naming Jerry Coleman, a New York Yankee second baseman from 1949 through 1957 and the Padres' radio announcer since 1972, as Craig's replacement. Coleman had batted .263 in nine major-league seasons with the New York Yankees and .275 in six World Series. His patented "Oh Doctor" and "Hang a Star on That One" calls had become trademarks of club broadcasts. Ballard Smith claimed, "Jerry Coleman had all the attributes to be a great baseball manager." Coleman, who held no previous managerial experience, accepted the job because of his tremendous respect for Kroc, Smith, and Bob Fontaine. Broadcasting colleague Dave Campbell initially was startled by Coleman's appointment. "Once I got over the shock of it and started looking at it," Campbell recalled, "I could see the possibilities." Upon accepting the managerial post, Coleman urged Smith to secure two starting pitchers, a center fielder, a second baseman, a third baseman, and a power hitter to follow Winfield in the lineup.

San Diego conducted wholesale housecleaning during the off season. Whitey Wietelmann, who had been associated with the San Diego Padres both in the

Jerry Coleman, longtime Padre announcer, managed the Padres in 1980.

minor and major leagues, retired as bullpen coach. Wietelmann, nicknamed "Mr. Indispensable," also was known for making chili and other culinary talents. Billy Herman retired as batting coach, and third base coach. Doug Rader was reassigned to manage the Hawaii farm club. Coleman retained Chuck Estrada and Don Williams as coaches and filled the remaining coaching vacancies with Dick Phillips and Al Heist. Frank Lane, who had attracted attention for trading players as general manager of the Chicago White Sox, St. Louis Cardinals, and Cleveland Indians, joined the Padres on October 1 as a consultant and special scout. On October 5, San Diego hired Bob Miller as pitching consultant and special assignment scout.

Several player transactions highlighted the off-season. The Padres released veteran pitcher Mickey Lolich on October 3 and veteran outfielder Bobby Tolan on October 25. Backed by owner Kroc's millions, general manager Bob Fontaine pursued two starting pitchers via the free agency. San Diego sought 13-year veteran Nolan Ryan of the California Angels, but the Houston Astros signed him on November 19. Fontaine also targeted pitcher Dave Goltz of the Minnesota Twins, who joined the Los Angeles Dodgers on November 15. Five days later, San Diego signed right-hander Rick Wise of the Cleveland Indians to a five-year $1.95 million contract. Wise had compiled a 178-165 career record and 3.68 ERA in 15 major-league seasons. On November 27, the Padres signed free agent left-hander John Curtis of the San Francisco Giants to a five-year $1.8 million contract. Curtis had logged a 77-80 lifetime mark and 3.87 ERA in 10 major-league campaigns.

Other transactions soon followed. San Diego on November 27 attempted to settle its second base problems by securing Dave Cash from the Montreal Expos for second baseman Bill Almon and first baseman-outfielder Dan Briggs. Cash, an experienced leadoff hitter, had batted .287 in 11 major-league seasons and had appeared in four National League Championship Series. San Diego and Los Angeles exchanged free agents on December 4, with reserve outfielder Von Joshua moving to the Padres and outfielder Jay Johnstone joining the Dodgers. In an attempt to solidify the infield defense, the Padres acquired third baseman Aurelio Rodriguez on December 7 from the Detroit Tigers. Although batting only .239 in 13 major league seasons, Rodriguez had fielded superbly.

Whitey Wietelmann served as bullpen coach for the Padres from 1969 to 1979.

San Diego made additional roster changes before spring training. The Padres on February 15 sent disgruntled pitcher Gaylord Perry, who had 279 lifetime victories, third baseman Tucker Ashford, and pitcher Joe Carroll to the Texas Rangers for first baseman Willie Montanez. A .277 lifetime batter with 132 home runs and 730 RBI in 11 major-league seasons, Montanez was acquired to provide left-handed firepower behind Dave Winfield in the lineup. The same day, San Diego released second baseman Fernando Gonzalez and dealt starting pitcher Bob Owchinko and outfielder Jim Wilhelm to the Cleveland Indians for outfielder Jerry Mumphrey. The Padres planned to use Mumphrey, who had batted .276 in six major-league campaigns, as a center fielder and return Gene Richards to left field. These transactions pleased Coleman. Barry Evans, an outstanding defensive third baseman, returned to the Padres. "If we don't move up in the standings and become competitive," manager Jerry Coleman told reporters, "I'll take the blame. I told the front office what I thought we had to have to compete and they got everything I asked for."

The 1980 campaign, however, marked the most disappointing yet in franchise history. San Diego's problems began at spring training when outfielder Dave Winfield attempted to renegotiate the four-year, $1.3

million agreement he had signed in 1977. Al Frohman, Winfield's agent, notified Kroc that Winfield wanted a 10-year, $13 million pact and a pledge by Kroc not to sell the club without Winfield's consent. President Ballard Smith offered the Padre slugger a long-term contract worth $700,000 annually, but contract negotiations broke down. The 1980 campaign marked Winfield's lame duck season. Padre fans booed Winfield the entire season as the latter's batting average, home run production, and RBIs dropped dramatically.

The season began well for San Diego, as Randy Jones defeated the San Francisco Giants, 6-4, in the April 10 home opener. The Padres also triumphed over the Giants, 5-3, and 4-2, in the next two games. San Diego, on April 15, stole six bases—two by first baseman Willie Montanez and one each by Ozzie Smith, Gene Richards, Dave Winfield, and Jerry Mumphrey—in a 9-5 home victory over the Los Angeles Dodgers. The Padres, however, lost 10 of 11 games between April 16 and April 27 and ended the month with a 7-11 record.

San Diego improved dramatically in May, winning 16 of 29 decisions. Rick Wise on May 2 blanked the New York Mets 1-0 at Shea Stadium, hurling 6.1 innings. Mumphrey recorded the only Padre hits, singling off Ray Burris in the second and seventh innings. Randy Jones set a club record by hurling three consecutive shutouts, blanking the Chicago Cubs, 4-0, at Wrigley Field on May 6, the Pittsburgh Pirates, 5-0, at home on May 11, and the Chicago Cubs, 3-0, at home on May 16. He hurled 30 straight scoreless innings during the streak but did not win another decision until July 29. Outfielder Jerry Turner on May 8 recorded a steal of home in the fourth inning of a 9-6 road victory over the Chicago Cubs. Third baseman Barry Evans on May 25 clouted San Diego's only grand slam of the season in the ninth inning off Pedro Borbon in an 11-5 romp over the St. Louis Cardinals at Busch Stadium. No Padre had connected with the bases loaded since Dave Winfield in July 1978.

Ten consecutive losses between June 3 and June 15 led to a dismal 10-18 record for the month. The Padres played their first tie game in franchise history on June 9 against the Cincinnati Reds at Riverfront Stadium. The contest was halted by rain after San Diego had batted in the top of eleventh inning with the score tied, 6-6, and was rescheduled as part of an August 4 doubleheader. Cincinnati won that doubleheader, 7-1, and 11-2. The Padres set a franchise record on June 11 with 16 singles, but still lost, 7-6, to the Montreal Expos at Olympic Stadium. Two days later, Padre pitchers yielded a club-record nine consecutive hits in the first inning to the Philadelphia Phillies in a 9-6 loss at Veterans Stadium. Speedster Jerry Turner on June 20 stole home in the fourth inning to spark a 4-2 victory over the Montreal Expos at San Diego Stadium. The theft marked the second time Turner had accomplished that remarkable feat in 1980. The Padres continued their swoon in July, losing five consecutive road games to the Los Angeles Dodgers and Atlanta Braves from July 2 through July 6 before the All-Star break. Dave Winfield on July 2 connected for five hits, including a home run, and knocked in four runs, but the Los Angeles Dodgers still prevailed, 10-7, at Dodger Stadium.

Bob Fontaine was fired on July 7, after serving less than three years as San Diego's general manager. Jack McKeon, Fontaine's assistant, held the post on an acting basis for the next two months. After interviewing nearly a dozen candidates, Padres president Ballard Smith on September 23 selected McKeon as general manager and director of baseball operations. Nicknamed "Trader Jack," the cigar-smoking McKeon had managed the Kansas City Royals and the Oakland Athletics. McKeon discussed with Kroc and Smith what direction the franchise should take and designed a plan to rebuild the club through trades, player development, and an improved scouting system. He realized the program would take several years to complete and expected the Padres to continue struggling in the interim. McKeon explained, "If we start making some strides toward improving this ball club by ridding some of the old, worn out players and bringing some fresh blood into the organization, I think we have a chance to win the pennant in four or five years."

McKeon's appointment signaled a major shakeup among Padre players. San Diego sold third baseman Aurelio Rodriguez to the New York Yankees on August 4 and the next day traded reserve infielder Kurt Bevacqua and a player to be named (pitcher Mark Lee) to the Pittsburgh Pirates for infielder Luis Salazar and outfielder Rick Lancellotti. On August 11, the Padres sent pitcher John D'Acquisto to the Montreal Expos for first baseman Randy Bass and cash and released both outfielder Von Joshua and catcher Fred Kendall. First baseman Willie Montanez on August 31 was sold to the Montreal Expos. During August, San Diego recalled infielder Barry Evans, pitcher Mike Armstrong, catcher Craig Stimac, first baseman Broderick Perkins, infielder Chuck Baker, and infielder-outfielder Luis Salazar from Hawaii. First baseman Randy Bass on September 7 joined the Padres from Denver of the American Association, and two days later pitchers Tom Tellman and George Stablein were recalled from Hawaii.

San Diego performed much better during the second half of the 1980 season, winning 34 of their final 66 games. The Padres split 20 decisions the remainder of July and won a season-high eight consecutive games from July 26 through August 3. On July 13, outfielder Gene Richards stole a club record four bases, including home in the first inning, in a 4-3 triumph over the Los Angeles Dodgers at Jack Murphy Stadium. Six days later, he enjoyed the first of three four-hit games and pilfered his 18th consecutive base in an 8-7 loss to the Chicago Cubs at Wrigley Field.

San Diego struggled in August, taking only 11 of 30 games and playing several marathons. Steve Mura on August 1 bested Jim Bibby, blanking the Pittsburgh Pirates, 1-0, on four hits at Three Rivers Stadium. The Padres on August 15 played their longest game in franchise history, a 6 hour, 17 minute, 20-inning, 3-1 loss at home to the Houston Astros. Six days later, the Padres lost a 17 inning road marathon, 9-8, to the Philadelphia Phillies in which Dennis Kinney set a club record by hurling 9.1 relief frames. First baseman Willie Montanez made five hits, including a double, in nine plate appearances. Outfielder Jerry Mumphrey's five hits on August 26 helped the Padres defeat the New York Mets, 8-6, in 18 innings at Shea Stadium. Besides knocking in two runs, Mumphrey doubled twice and clouted a home run.

San Diego tied a club record by winning ten consecutive home contests, including seven from September 3 through September 10 and another three from September 19 through September 21. The Padres finished the 1980 campaign by taking 16 of 27 decisions in September and splitting four games in October. The Padres walked to victory on September 7, tying a club record with 12 free passes in a 5-2 home triumph over the New York Mets. Ozzie Smith capped a sensational defensive season by setting a new major league single season record for assists by a shortstop. He established the mark in a 3-2 win over the Los Angeles Dodgers at San Diego Stadium on September 26, when he surpassed the 601 assists by shortstop Glenn Wright of the 1924 Pittsburgh Pirates. Smith finished the season with 621 assists.

Gene Richards played outfield for the Padres from 1977 through 1983.

Several rookies sparked the late season Padre drive to respectability. Third baseman Luis Salazar batted .337, drove in 25 runs, and stole 11 bases in just 44 games, reaching base safely in 32 contests and recording seven three-hit games. First baseman Randy Bass hit .286 with three homers and eight RBI in 19 games, clouting a 400-foot home run in his first official at-bat as a Padre on September 9 and producing three RBI in the 12-5 home victory over the San Francisco Giants. Bass homered twice against the Atlanta Braves, including one off knuckleballer Phil Niekro. First baseman-outfielder Broderick Perkins batted a sparkling .370 in 43 games and hit safely in 20 of his 25 starts, authoring a 13-game hitting streak from August 27 through September 10.

San Diego pitchers also performed well down the stretch. John Curtis, who overcame back problems, won his last six decisions and did not allow a home run in his last 90.1 innings. Rookie Tom Tellman defeated the Atlanta Braves, 3-1, on September 21 and won his other two decisions over the Los Angeles Dodgers and San Francisco Giants. Rookie reliever Gary Lucas boasted a 1.46 ERA in his final 25 appearances, being

Jerry Mumphrey played outfield for the Padres in 1980.

scored upon only twice. Bob Shirley, Steve Mura, and Juan Eichelberger also made impressive late season mound performances. "We finished last," John Curtis observed, "but a lot of very positive things happened to us."

Jack Murphy, sports editor and columnist for *The San Diego Union,* died on September 24 of cancer at age 57 in San Diego. Civic leaders credited him with playing a major role in luring major-league baseball and football to San Diego. After his death, the Padres and Chargers facility was renamed Jack Murphy Stadium.

San Diego finished in last place for the first time since Ray Kroc purchased the franchise in 1974, with 73 wins and 89 losses. The Padres' woes extended to the season's final series on October 3, when Dave Cash hit into a triple play in the fourth inning against the San Francisco Giants at Candlestick Park. He hit a line drive to second baseman Guy Sularz, who threw to shortstop Joe Pettini to double up Luis Salazar at second base. Pettini's relay to Eddie Murray at first base tripled up Gene Tenace. The Padres experienced a power shortage, clouting only 67 home runs in 162 games. Home attendance dropped 317,941 to 1,139,026, causing the Padres to lose around $2 million. The September 4 contest with the New York Mets drew only 2,635 fans, while the September 21 contest with the Atlanta Braves attracted just 2,846 people.

To compensate for the power shortage, manager Jerry Coleman made speed a valuable dimension of the offense. The Padres led the major leagues in stolen bases with a franchise-best 239. Coleman frequently gave runners the green light to pilfer bases. San Diego became the first major-league team to have three players with at least 50 stolen bases the same season. Gene Richards, Ozzie Smith, and Jerry Mumphrey established the major-league mark with 61, 57, and 52 thefts, respectively. Mumphrey pilfered 27 consecutive bases from June 3 to August 21. Padre runners swiped second base 221 times, third base 15 times, and home three times. "The Padre strength," pitcher Gary Lucas observed, "was speed."

San Diego set another club record by batting .255 as a team. Outfielder Dave Winfield led the Padres in home runs and RBIs, but his offensive production declined dramatically in his lame duck season. His batting average dropped from .308 to .276, home runs from 34 to 20, and RBIs from 118 to 87. Gene Richards, who batted .301, finished second in the National League with 193 hits and shared the senior circuit lead with 12 triples. He also ranked fifth in stolen bases, eighth in runs scored (91), twelfth in batting and set several club records, including most hits, singles (155), and total bases (247) by a left-handed batter. Outfielder Jerry Mumphrey batted .328 with 39 RBI and 35 stolen bases after the All-Star break to finish at .298 with 59 RBIs.

Defensively, San Diego established club records for best fielding percentage (.980) and fewest errors (132), averaging under one a game. The Padres also recorded the most putouts (4,399), assists (2,012), and chances (6,543) in franchise history. Ozzie Smith broke a 56-year-old major-league record for assists by a shortstop with 621 and along with outfielder Dave Winfield won Gold Glove awards for defensive excellence. Smith, whose .974 fielding percentage ranked third in the National League, paced shortstops playing on natural grass. Gene Richards led National League outfielders with 21 assists, edging Dave Winfield by one. Besides pacing National League left fielders with 335 total chances, he threw out two Montreal Expos runners on June 15 and two Houston Astros runners on September 15.

Padre pitchers finished seventh in the National League with a 3.65 ERA. Reliever Rollie Fingers became

Jack Murphy, *San Diego Union* sports editor and columnist for whom San Diego Stadium was renamed, played a major role in luring major league baseball to San Diego.

the first major-league pitcher to garner three Rolaids and *The Sporting News'* Fireman of the Year awards, compiling an 11-9 record with a 2.80 ERA and 23 saves. Bob Shirley won 11 games with seven saves and a 3.55 ERA, while Steve Mura and Juan Eichelberger compiled 8-7 and 4-2 ledgers, respectively. Injuries diminished the effectiveness of veterans Randy Jones and Rick Wise. Jones won only five of 18 decisions, while Wise took just six of 14 decisions.

Despite the late season surge, San Diego on October 4 dismissed Jerry Coleman as manager. Coleman, criticized by several prominent veteran players, returned to the broadcast booth after just one year as field manager. President Ballard Smith recalled, "We had a bunch of disgruntled veterans who were no longer productive, who were going to blame their shortcomings and the end of their careers on whoever was the manager. And Jerry did not get support from the veterans on the club." The Padres also released coaches Dick Phillips, Al Heist, and Don Williams.

Six-foot, seven-inch, 280-pound Frank Howard, former Washington Senators slugger and Milwaukee Brewers first base coach, replaced Coleman on October 6. He batted .269 with 382 home runs and 1,119 RBIs in 15 major-league seasons and managed Spokane of the Pacific Coast League, but like Coleman, he did not have any previous major-league managerial experience. Eddie Brinkman, Jack Krol, and Bobby Tolan joined the Padre coaching staff, and Chuck Estrada remained as pitching coach.

San Diego soon lost its first quality free agent. Star right fielder Dave Winfield, who had batted .284 with 154 home runs and 626 RBIs in eight years as a Padre, left for greener pastures. Shortly after the World Series, New York Yankees owner George Steinbrenner launched an all-out effort to land Winfield. He tried to arrange a trade with San Diego, but the deal fell through when Winfield refused to sign a new contract. Winfield wrote letters to 17 major-league clubs declaring that he did not want to play for them and advising them not to draft his negotiating rights.

All major-league teams except the Boston Red Sox, California Angels, New York Yankees, Atlanta Braves, Houston Astros, Los Angeles Dodgers, Montreal Expos, New York Mets, and Philadelphia Phillies received the letters. "I am determined," Winfield wrote, "to sign with a club that clearly will provide the opportunity for me to . . . contribute to the winning of a pennant. A metropolitan area where programs of the Winfield Foundation can be the most productive is a requirement." The Padre slugger had formed the David M. Winfield Foundation in 1977 to help underprivileged children. Cleveland Indians president Gabe Paul termed the letter a ploy to discourage other teams from drafting Winfield and thus guarantee the New York Yankees an opportunity to sign him. Under the reentry draft rules, the New York Yankees were scheduled to pick last among the 26 major-league clubs. According to Paul, Winfield feared that 13 major league teams, the maximum permitted, might choose him before the New York Yankees received a chance.

The New York Yankees, New York Mets, and Cleveland Indians ultimately vied for Winfield's services. Winfield told the media on December 15 that he had signed a 10-year contract with the New York Yankees. The Yankees awarded him baseball's most lucrative salary, paying the star $1.3 million in 1981 and giving him annual cost of living increases up to 10

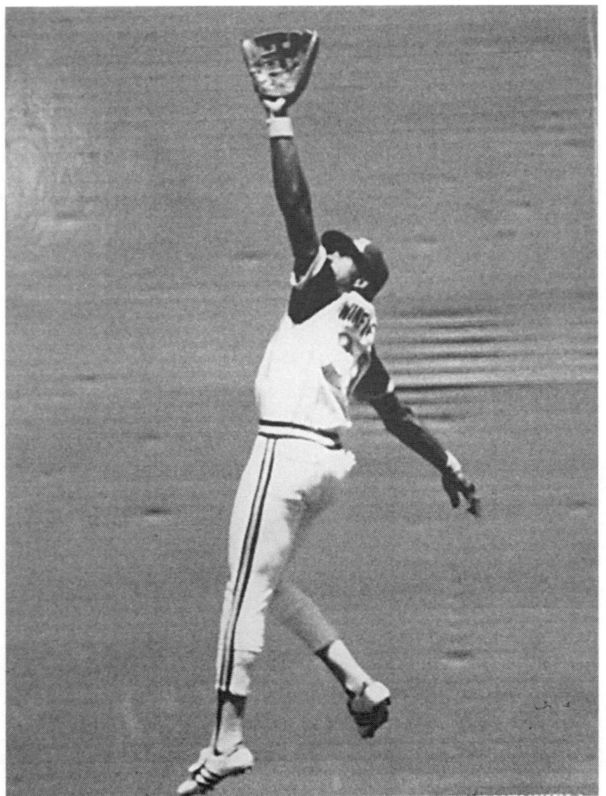

Outfielder Dave Winfield won consecutive Gold Glove awards in 1979 and 1980 for his defensive excellence.

percent per year. Winfield's contract was worth between $15 million and $23 million over the 10-year period. The New York Mets and Cleveland Indians allegedly offered Winfield higher amounts, but the star selected the New York Yankees because of their tradition, considerable talent, and ability to aid the Winfield Foundation. San Diego sportswriters, meanwhile, disclosed that the Padres had paid Winfield $100,000 above his salary to help his foundation purchase tickets to Padres games for underprivileged kids. The San Diego management claimed that the foundation owed the club over $62,000 from the arrangement. Winfield's agent, however, replied that the foundation had experienced difficulty finding children who wanted to attend Padres games.

At the Dallas, Texas, winter meetings, vice president Jack McKeon on December 8 engineered a blockbuster trade with general manager Whitey Herzog of the St. Louis Cardinals. Pitchers Rollie Fingers and Bob Shirley, catcher-first baseman Gene Tenace, and catcher Bob Geren were sent to the St. Louis Cardinals for catchers Terry Kennedy and Steve Swisher, infielder Mike Phillips, and pitchers John Littlefield, John Urrea, Kim Seaman, and Al Olmsted. The Padres unloaded Fingers, who sought $2 million for a three-year extension of his pact. Kennedy, the 24-year-old son of former major-league outfielder Bob Kennedy, possessed a strong throwing arm that San Diego hoped would deter other National League clubs from stealing so many bases. Al Olmsted, who shut out the Philadelphia Phillies for 9.2 innings in his major-league debut on September 12, gave the Padres another starting pitcher.

Other transactions soon followed. San Diego on December 8 traded infielder Chuck Baker to the Minnesota Twins for outfielder Dave Edwards and released infielder Paul Dade. The Padres the next day drafted infielder Mario Ramirez from the New York Mets and speedy second baseman Alan Wiggins from the Los Angeles Dodgers, hoping to use the latter as a leadoff hitter. San Diego the same day acquired outfielder Dave Stegman from the Detroit Tigers for pitcher Dennis Kinney. The Padres on December 15 traded veteran pitcher Randy Jones to the New York Mets for pitcher John Pacella and infielder Jose Moreno. Jones, who had lost 13 of 18 decisions in 1980, accepted a $200,000 buy-out to waive his no-trade clause.

Between August and December 1980, McKeon had traded 14 players and acquired 14 others. The departures of Fingers, Tenace, and Jones reduced the player payroll significantly and the club's average age from 29 years to 26 years. "The Padres went with age and experience last season," pitcher John Curtis observed, "and it didn't pay off." The transactions, however, left the Padres without hitters who had clouted 47 of 67 homers and plated 234 of 546 runs, pitchers who had gained 32 of 73 victories, and relievers who had accounted for 31 of 37 saves. The three biggest home run producers, three of the top four-run producers, and the two winningest pitchers had departed.

During spring training, McKeon exchanged several other players. San Diego on March 24 sold catcher Bill Fahey to the Detroit Tigers. Three days later, the Padres released pitcher Eric Rasmussen and acquired pitchers Bob Lacey and Roy Moretti from the Oakland Athletics for pitcher Eric Mustad and infielders Kevin Bell and Tony Phillips. San Diego on April 1 traded pitcher Lacey to the Cleveland Indians for second baseman Juan Bonilla. Later that day, McKeon sent center fielder Jerry Mumphrey and pitcher John Pacella to the New York Yankees for outfielders Ruppert Jones and Joe Lefebvre and pitchers Tim Lollar and Chris Welsh. The New York Yankees preferred trading outfielder Bobby Brown rather than Jones, but McKeon insisted on the latter. On April 4, San Diego released second baseman Dave Cash and the next day traded outfielder Bobby Mitchell to the Pittsburgh Pirates for pitcher Dave Dravecky.

In 1981, the Padres fielded one of the youngest, least experienced major-league teams. The opening night lineup on April 9 against the San Francisco Giants included only four returning players: shortstop Ozzie Smith, third baseman Luis Salazar, first baseman Randy Bass, and left fielder Gene Richards. Salazar and Bass had spent most of the previous season in the minor leagues. The newcomers included second baseman Juan Bonilla, center fielder Ruppert Jones, right fielder Dave Edwards, and catcher Terry Kennedy. The Padres also planned to use versatile Tim Flannery at second base. Veterans John Curtis and Rick Wise anchored an otherwise young starting pitching staff. Steve Mura, Juan Eichelberger, Tom Tellman, and Al Olmsted contended for the remaining spots in the starting rotation. In an attempt to fill the void left by the departure of Fingers, youthful Kim Seaman, Gary Lucas, John Urrea, and John Littlefield were counted on as relievers. McKeon believed that the team could become a contender in two or three years.

San Diego played 21 of its first 30 games on the road, winning just 10. On April 9, the Padres defeated the San Francisco Giants, 4-1, in 10 innings on opening night at Candlestick Park. San Diego triumphed over the Giants, 4-2, the next night but then dropped eight of its next nine contests. Between April 11 and April 20, four opponents blanked the Padres. Bruce Berenyi of the Cincinnati Reds shut out San Diego, 4-0, on April 14, at Jack Murphy Stadium, limiting San Diego to singles by Terry Kennedy in the third inning and Luis Salazar in the seventh frame. Doyle Alexander of the San Francisco Giants, Mario Soto of the Cincinnati Reds, and Fernando Valenzuela of the Los Angeles Dodgers also blanked the Padres. San Diego ended the month with five consecutive losses to the Los Angeles Dodgers and Cincinnati Reds.

The few Padre highlights came in losses. Randy Bass on April 12, clouted the first grand slam of the 1981 major-league season in the third inning of a 7-6, 14-inning loss to the San Francisco Giants at Candlestick Park. Sixteen days later, pitcher Tim Lollar belted a solo home run in the fifth inning off Tom Seaver for his first major-league hit in an 11-2 trouncing by the Cincinnati Reds at Riverfront Stadium. Outfielder Joe Lefebvre clouted two home runs on April 30, but the Cincinnati Reds edged the Padres, 4-3. During April, Ruppert Jones, Joe Lefebvre, Ozzie Smith, Luis Salazar, Gene Richards, and Randy Bass experienced batting slumps.

San Diego improved in May, winning 13 of 28 decisions. First baseman Broderick Perkins hit safely in 15 consecutive games from May 1 to May 16 and knocked in five runs against the Montreal Expos on May 6. The Padres scored season highs for both runs and hits that day in a 13-5, 19-hit victory at Olympic Stadium. In the bottom of the ninth frame, Mike Gates, Tim Raines, and Tim Wallach belted consecutive triples for Montreal. In the first inning of the first game of a May 8 doubleheader, San Diego made six consecutive hits in an 11-7 setback to the Philadelphia Phillies at Veterans Stadium. Second baseman Juan Bonilla doubled three times off Steve Carlton the next day, but the Phillies prevailed again, 9-6. Buoyed by Bonilla's performance, the Padres on May 10 sold infielder Mike Phillips to the Montreal Expos.

San Diego won four consecutive games from May 10 to May 14, sweeping the New York Mets in a three-game home series. Juan Eichelberger and Chris Welsh blanked the Mets, 3-0, and 5-0, in consecutive starts on May 12 and May 13. Eichelberger and Welsh suffered heartbreaking losses in succession to the Houston Astros on May 26 and May 27 at the Astrodome. Third baseman Luis Salazar, who enjoyed an 11-game hitting streak from May 22 through June 4, tripled, doubled, and singled twice in a 5-1 victory on May 31 over the Atlanta Braves at Jack Murphy Stadium.

June brought the player strike and free agent draft. San Diego split eight decisions that month before the strike to finish in last place with a 22-33 record. Just prior to the June 12 strike, the Padres won three straight road games against the St. Louis Cardinals and Pittsburgh Pirates. The June 8 free agent draft, meanwhile, signaled a brighter future for the franchise. San Diego drafted outfielder Kevin McReynolds, who held the University of Arkansas record for most career home runs, in the first round and Tony Gwynn, who starred in both baseball and basketball at San Diego State University, in the third round.

Frank Howard managed the Padres in 1981.

The June 12 strike gave the Padres a welcome respite. Major-league players engaged in the first mid-season walkout in the annals of professional sports in the United States and Canada. Owners provoked the strike with demands for a ceiling on salaries and for compensation in kind for players lost by teams in annual reentry drafts. The players rejected such compensation and struck for 50 days. The strike completely halted major-league baseball for almost two months, canceling one-third of the schedule and threatening the remainder of the season. The walkout aroused hostility between management and players, between hard-line and moderate club owners, and among the fans, who were deprived of the national pastime.

The strike hurt both sides financially and was settled on July 31. The owners lost their demand for a salary cap but won compensation for lost free agents by receiving a minor-league player or a major-leaguer chosen from a pool among all clubs. The two sides devised a confusing split season format in hopes of salvaging the playing season. Jack Murphy Stadium, meanwhile, hosted one minor-league baseball game during the strike. The Reno, Nevada Padres farm club played the Redwood Angels in a California League game on July 3, drawing 37,665 people.

San Diego fared even worse after the strike ended, triumphing in only 18 of 54 games. Owner Ray Kroc charged no admission when play resumed at home on August 10 after a 52-game interruption. Over 52,600 fans saw the Atlanta Braves edge the Padres, 3-2. Joe Niekro of the Houston Astros on August 16 blanked the Padres, 3-0. Pitcher Steve Mura singled in the third inning and outfielder Ruppert Jones doubled in the sixth frame for the lone San Diego hits. The Padres won only three of their first 20 games after the strike and endured a seven-game losing streak from August 23 to August 29. In the second game of an August 29 doubleheader, Juan Eichelberger set a club record by walking five St. Louis Cardinals in the second inning of a 6-5 loss at Busch Stadium.

San Diego's woes extended into early September. Padre outfielders set a club record with three assists on September 5 in a 2-1 home loss to the Pittsburgh Pirates. Left fielder Gene Richards threw out two runners, while right fielder Joe Lefebvre nabbed a third. San Diego two days later scored six runs in the seventh inning, but still lost, 8-7, to the Cincinnati Reds at Riverfront Stadium. The struggling Padres on September 9 sold outfielder-pinch hitter Jerry Turner to the Chicago White Sox. Catcher Terry Kennedy's four hits, including three doubles, on September 14 could not avert a 10-5 home setback to the Los Angeles Dodgers. He doubled twice and singled the next day,

Gene Tenace played catcher and first base for the Padres from 1977 through 1980.

Randy Jones won 20 games in 1975 and 22 games in 1976, earning the National League Cy Young Award.

extending his consecutive hit streak to seven and helping the Padres defeat the Los Angeles Dodgers, 8-2. In that contest, Juan Eichelberger struck out a season-high 10 batters. Tim Lollar on September 16 lost his eighth consecutive decision, 5-2, to the Houston Astros at home. Outfielder Alan Wiggins made his first major-league steal, nabbing second base on his first attempt. San Diego the next night drew only 2,428 fans in a 9-0 loss to the Houston Astros. The Padres played their worst game of the season on September 18, when Larry McWilliams of the Atlanta Braves limited them to second-inning singles by Ruppert Jones and Terry Kennedy in a 3-0 setback.

On September 21, San Diego broke out of the season-long slump with a 6-0 home triumph over the Cincinnati Reds, scoring all six runs in the sixth inning. The Padres' longest winning streak of the season came on the road the last week from September 29 through October 3, when they took five straight contests against the Houston Astros, Los Angeles Dodgers, and San Francisco Giants. Dan Boone and Fred Kuhaulua blanked the Los Angeles Dodgers, 2-0, and 1-0, in consecutive starts on September 30 and October 1 at Dodger Stadium. In the latter contest, Kuhaulua outdueled Dodger ace Fernando Valenzuela.

San Diego finished in last place in 1981 with a 41-69 record for its lowest winning percentage (.374) since 1974. The 1981 campaign ranked among the most disappointing in franchise history. The Padres fell far short of fulfilling manager Frank Howard's spring training predictions that the club would win half of its games and score 100 more runs than in 1980. The departure of sluggers Dave Winfield, Gene Tenace, and Jerry Mumphrey dramatically weakened the Padres' power production. Team home runs dropped by 35 to just 32 in 110 games, lowest in the major leagues. Outfielder Joe Lefebvre, who usually batted eighth, led San Diego with just eight home runs. Despite the shortened season, outfielder Gene Richards's tied his club record with 12 triples. The Padres also deserted the running game, stealing 156 fewer bases. Catchers caught San Diego runners trying to steal 62 times, nearly 43 percent of their 145 attempts. Ozzie Smith's stolen base output plunged from 57 to 22, while Gene Richards' total plummeted from 61 to 20.

Juan Eichelberger pitched for the Padres from 1978 through 1982.

Dave Winfield signed with the New York Yankees as a free agent after the 1980 season.

Defensively, San Diego fared little better. Padre pitchers ranked ninth in the National League with a 3.72 ERA, relying on starters Chris Welsh, Tim Lollar, Dan Boone, and John Littlefield. San Diego relievers struggled except for Gary Lucas and John Urrea. Lucas fashioned a 7-7 record and 2.00 ERA with 13 of the club's 23 saves and set a franchise record for most saves by a left-hander. Urrea established a Padre mark for right-handers by hurling 20 consecutive scoreless innings in his first 12 appearances and yielded just one run with a 0.32 ERA in 27.1 innings the first half of the season. The Padres gave their pitchers little defensive support, ranking tenth in errors with 102. Only the Chicago Cubs and New York Mets committed more miscues. Catcher Terry Kennedy made 20 errors in 100 games for a .964 fielding average and the worst errors/game ratio for a major-league catcher since 1915. Center fielder Ruppert Jones, however, fielded .993, the highest percentage by a Padre outfielder in team history.

The 1981 season, on the other hand, also brought a few glimmers of hope. San Diego batted .256, seventh best in the National League and the highest in franchise history. Terry Kennedy, Joe Lefebvre, and Luis Salazar made four or more hits in different games. Shortstop Ozzie Smith, who won his second straight Rawlings Gold Glove Award, and second baseman Juan Bonilla teamed effectively to help San Diego pace the senior circuit with 117 double plays. Bonilla and first baseman Randy Bass made the Topps All-Rookie team.

San Diego again made several personnel changes following the season. The Padres on October 13 fired rookie manager Frank Howard with a year remaining on his contract. Howard's refusal to communicate with the San Diego front office played a crucial role in president Ballard Smith's decision. Coaches Eddie Brinkman, Chuck Estrada, Jack Krol, and Bobby Tolan also were dismissed. Dick Williams, who possessed 14 years of major-league managerial experience, filled the vacancy on November 18. He had developed the Montreal Expos into a pennant contender and vowed to replicate that experience with San Diego. Williams observed, "The Padres are set up to do the same thing we did in Montreal; they're going to build from within." He added, "We could certainly use a right-handed power hitter, and I think we need to make better use of our speed." San Diego rehired Jack Krol and Bobby Tolan as coaches and named Norm Sherry and Ozzie Virgil as the other coaches. The Padres on December 10 acquired powerful outfielder Sixto Lezcano from the St. Louis Cardinals for pitcher Steve Mura.

8

The .500 Years

[1982-83]

San Diego enjoyed its first major field success as a franchise under manager Dick Williams, the Padres' fifth pilot in five seasons. Williams, former Brooklyn Dodgers' outfielder-infielder and the 11th winningest all-time skipper with over 1,000 major league victories, had signed a three-year contract. He had guided the Boston Red Sox to the 1967 American League pennant, the Oakland Athletics to the 1972 and 1973 World Series titles, and the Montreal Expos into National League contention. The tough, no-nonsense manager stressed consistency and sound fundamentals, featuring solid pitching, speed, and defense. Doug Rader, who had piloted the Hawaii Pacific Coast League farm club for three seasons, was unhappy at being snubbed for the Padres managerial position and became the Texas Rangers' manager on November 1.

Williams's managerial style quickly impressed San Diego players. Pitcher Ed Whitson classified him as "a very strict manager, who expected 110 percent from his players." "Players paid the price for mental mistakes and would sit on the bench," infielder Luis Salazar recalled. Williams, an aloof, intense, demanding skipper, possessed a keen knowledge of baseball. He relied heavily on percentages, form charts, and statistics in making decisions and instilled the importance of teamwork and a winning attitude in his players. "Williams," according to pitcher Eric Show, "always played the percentages." Players quickly discovered with Williams that "team play was in and excuses were out."

General Manager Jack McKeon, already nicknamed "Trader Jack," negotiated several more deals and signed two free agents before the 1982 season. The Padres on January 27, sold catcher Craig Stimac to the Cleveland Indians and on February 11 made a blockbuster trade with the St. Louis Cardinals involving premier shortstops. San Diego sent light-hitting Ozzie Smith to St. Louis for Garry Templeton. Although having won Rawlings Gold Glove Awards in 1980 and 1981, Smith had batted only .231 in four seasons with the Padres. San

Diego dealt Smith, the fifth leading base stealer in franchise history with 147 thefts, because it anticipated losing him to free agency after the 1983 season. Smith's agent wanted $35 million for his client over a 25-year period. "Smith and the Padres," club executive Elten Schiller recalled, "were miles apart financially."

San Diego did not want a repetition of the Dave Winfield case, where a star player had been lost without receiving any compensation. Pitcher Gary Lucas remarked, "the Padres wanted compensation this time if they were going to lose someone." The exchange pleased Jack McKeon, who explained, "the Padres traded an All-Star shortstop for an All-Star shortstop." Templeton, whom San Diego announcer Jerry Coleman termed "a remarkable athlete," possessed excellent range at shortstop, a great throwing arm, and a fine .305 batting average with 125 doubles and 69 triples during his first five major league seasons.

San Diego made several more transactions. Eight days later, the Padres sent pitcher Al Olmsted to the St. Louis Cardinals for pitcher Luis DeLeon to complete the earlier December 10, 1981 deal. San Diego planned to have DeLeon, a promising 23-year old Puerto Rican right-hander, share late-inning relief duties with left-hander Gary Lucas. The Padres on February 22 sold third baseman Barry Evans to the New York Yankees and on February 25, released relief pitcher John Littlefield. San Diego on March 6 entered the free agent market and signed starting pitcher John Montefusco of the Atlanta Braves, who had won 61 games and lost 65 contests with a 3.47 ERA in seven major-league seasons. The Padres wanted Montefusco to steady their inexperienced starting rotation. San Diego on March 26 released pitcher John Urrea and, on April 4 sold pitcher Mike Armstrong to the Kansas City Royals. Journeyman infielder Kurt Bevacqua of the Pittsburgh Pirates rejoined San Diego on April 2 as a free agent.

In an effort to energize their offense, San Diego changed the outfield dimensions at Jack Murphy Stadium. The Padres in 1981 had finished last in the major leagues with only 32 home runs and ranked tenth in the National League in scoring, averaging slightly under 3.5 runs per game. San Diego hoped to boost its team home run production by adding an inner fence in center field, shortening the distance from 420 feet to 405 feet. The dimensions remained 330 feet to both left field and right field.

Despite the numerous transactions and stadium alterations, the media expected San Diego to finish last in the National League Western Division for the third consecutive year. The 1982 season started in typical fashion, as the Padres lost four of their first six road games to the Atlanta Braves, Los Angeles Dodgers, and San Francisco Giants. San Diego played seven straight games and 15 of the next 17 contests at home, setting a club record with 11 consecutive victories. The winning streak started on April 14 when left-hander Tim Lollar bested Dan Schatzeder of the San Francisco Giants, 3-2, at Candlestick Park. A four-game sweep of the Los Angeles Dodgers at home followed. Juan Eichelberger set the tone for the Los Angeles series on April 15, the same day the Padres released veteran pitcher Rick Wise, besting sensational Fernando Valenzuela, 2-0. San Diego surrendered only three runs in each of the remaining contests of the Dodgers series, winning 8-3, 4-3, and 9-3. Pitchers John Curtis, Eric Show, and Luis DeLeon picked up those victories.

San Diego swept a three-game series with the San Francisco Giants at home. The Padres on April 19 trounced the San Francisco Giants, 13-6, in the series opener, setting a club record with 24 hits, including 18 singles and five doubles. In the fifth inning, San Diego tied franchise marks with eight straight hits and seven consecutive singles. Catcher Terry Kennedy clouted three doubles and knocked in four runs, while

Tim Lollar pitched for the Padres from 1981 through 1984.

starter Juan Eichelberger allowed the Giants four home runs and 11 hits. The Padres also took the second game, 8-4, and edged San Francisco, 7-6, in the series finale.

San Diego flew to Atlanta and swept two contests on April 23 and April 24 from the torrid Atlanta Braves at Atlanta-Fulton County Stadium. Atlanta just had established a National League record for most consecutive victories at the start of a season with 13. In the 12-inning, 6-3 Padre victory on April 23, Tim Lollar struck out 10 batters and outfielder Sixto Lezcano clouted two home runs. Lezcano won National League Player of the Week honors for April 19 through April 25, batting .571 with two triples, two homers, and nine RBI.

San Diego returned home on April 27 with an 8-5 triumph by Eric Show over the New York Mets, giving the Padres a share of the National League Western Division lead for one day with the Atlanta Braves. The 11-game winning streak abruptly ended with a heart-breaking, 5-4, 15-inning loss to the New York Mets the following night. Tim Lollar pitched his first major-league shutout on April 29, blanking the New York Mets, 6-0. The Padres finished April with a 13-6 record.

Although slumping to a 12-15 slate in May, San Diego still occupied second place behind the Atlanta Braves. Reliever Eric Show on May 2 struck out five consecutive Philadelphia Phillies over three innings in a 3-0 loss at home. Juan Eichelberger and Padre relievers on May 6 surrendered 16 hits in a 12-7 loss to the Philadelphia Phillies at Veterans Stadium. Three days later, shortstop Garry Templeton's three doubles backed Tim Lollar's 6-0 shutout of the Phillies. The Padres on May 16 rallied with seven runs in the ninth inning to rout the Montreal Expos, 8-2, at Olympic Stadium. Three days later, Juan Bonilla suffered a compound fracture of his left wrist when he collided with Willie McGee of the St. Louis Cardinals at first base, and he was sidelined for four months. The Padres that day tied a club record with six stolen bases—three by Alan Wiggins, two by Luis Salazar, and one by Garry Templeton—to spark a 5-4, 10-inning home victory. San Diego on May 22 exploded for 12 runs to trounce the Pittsburgh Pirates by nine runs at home. Three days later, Ferguson Jenkins of the Chicago Cubs recorded his 3,000th career strikeout when he fanned Templeton in the third inning. Nevertheless, the Padres won that home contest, 2-1.

At this juncture, San Diego made several player transactions. The Padres on May 17 sold first baseman-outfielder Randy Bass to the Texas Rangers and five days later traded pitcher Kim Seaman to the Montreal Expos for infielder Jerry Manuel. On June 8, San Diego traded pitcher Dan Boone to the Houston Astros for infielder Joe Pittman and returned Manuel to the Montreal Expos for a player to be named. The Padres acquired pitcher Mike Griffin to complete that deal on August 30.

San Diego returned to winning ways in June with a 17-11 record. Juan Eichelberger on June 2 hurled a one-hitter, defeating the Chicago Cubs, 3-1, at Wrigley Field. Scot Thompson reached base on an infield single with one out in the second inning for the lone Cubs safety. The Padres on June 14 drew their second-largest crowd in team history with 49,973 fans in a 4-3, 11-inning setback to the Los Angeles Dodgers. Tim Lollar on June 26 fanned 10 San Francisco Giants in a 7-6 triumph at Candlestick Park.

In July, San Diego won eight of 12 decisions before the All-Star break. Outfielder Ruppert Jones on July 3 made four hits, but the San Francisco Giants edged the Padres, 4-3, in 15 innings in San Diego. In the first inning of the first game of a July 9 doubleheader, Gene Richards stole two bases and Garry Templeton stole one to spark a 5-3 triumph over the New York Mets at Shea Stadium. Outfielder Gene Richards the following day clouted an inside-the-park home run and four singles, but New York still prevailed, 9-7. In the series finale, pitcher Tim Lollar's fourth-inning solo home run off Mike Scott keyed a 6-2 win over the Mets.

San Diego stood 50-36 at All-Star break in mid-July, just two games behind the Atlanta Braves. Lollar anchored the starting pitchers, winning his first five decisions and 10 of 12 by the All-Star break and clouting three home runs. Center fielder Ruppert Jones, the lone Padre representative on the All-Star team, ignited the Padre offense with a .312 batting average, 11 home runs, and 50 RBIs through mid-July. Besides enjoying a 13-game hitting streak from May 10 through May 24, he led the National League in batting from May 24 through June 14. Jones bruised his right heel on July 28 at Atlanta, jumping to avoid a collision with Braves pitcher Phil Niekro, and was ineffective thereafter.

Drug abuse problems also slowed the Padres after the All-Star break. Rookie outfielder Alan Wiggins, who had stolen 33 bases, was arrested at 2:30 a.m. on July 21 by San Diego police for possessing one gram of cocaine. After conferring with president Ballard Smith, the speedster checked into an Orange County drug and alcohol rehabilitation center for a 30-day treatment program. Upon Wiggins's release, Commissioner Bowie Kuhn suspended him for 30 days, through September 19. Second baseman Juan Bonilla met with Smith a few days after Wiggins's arrest and voluntarily joined his teammate at the same treatment facility.

Outfielder Tony Gwynn, meanwhile, joined the Padres and made an auspicious major-league debut on July 19 at home with two hits against the Philadelphia Phillies. He had starred in basketball and baseball at San Diego State University. The San Diego Clippers of the National Basketball Association had drafted Gwynn in the tenth round in June 1981, the same month the Padres had selected him in the third round. Most major-league baseball scouts considered his bat too slow and his fielding deficient. The Padres sent him to Walla Walla, Washington, where his .331 batting average led the Northwest League and earned him MVP honors. He hit .328 for Hawaii of the Pacific Coast League before Jack McKeon promoted him July 19 to the Padres. Manager Dick Williams inserted Gwynn in left field and saw him hit safely in a team-high 15 consecutive games from July 21 through August 4. Gwynn broke his wrist while diving for a fly ball on August 25 against the Pittsburgh Pirates at Three Rivers Stadium and missed three weeks.

Padre officials raved about Gwynn, who batted .289 in 54 games. "McKeon's promotion of Tony to the big leagues in my first year," manager Dick Williams recalled, "proved to be the nicest thing anybody has ever done for me. I don't think I've ever had a player who worked harder and cared more and was more deserving of his awards." The dedicated, conscientious, hard working, personable Gwynn studied videotape to refine his hitting skills and diligently practiced his fielding and throwing skills to become a more complete player. He demonstrated an excellent attitude and tremendous work ethic, frequently being the first player on the field for practice before games. "He can hit well for any manager," Jack McKeon observed. "If we had nine Tony Gwynns, we would always do very well." Shortstop Garry Templeton praised Gwynn as "a great player, great individual, and true professional, who loves to play baseball," while announcer Jerry Coleman called Gwynn "the single most dedicated Padre. He is the greatest player they have ever had, with such incredible dedication and work habits."

Dick Williams managed the Padres from 1982 through February 1986.

Gwynn's presence, however, did not deter San Diego from slumping to a 31-45 mark after the All-Star break. The final 11 weeks shattered any illusion that the Padres had become a legitimate Western Division contender. Injuries to Ruppert Jones, Garry Templeton, Tony Gwynn, and Sixto Lezcano, along with the drug problems of Wiggins and Bonilla, compounded San Diego's second-half woes. Williams was forced to shuffle the starting lineup constantly and insert three rookies in the pitching rotation. The club's problems worsened in August. Four Padres— Gwynn, Terry Kennedy, Joe Pittman, and Joe Lefebvre— grounded into double plays, a team record, in a 4-2 loss on August 5 to the Cincinnati Reds at Riverfront Stadium. Six days later, Nolan Ryan of the Houston Astros blanked the Padres at home, 3-0, with his eighth one-hitter. Catcher Terry Kennedy singled with one out in the fifth inning for the lone Padre hit. Outfielder Dave Edwards on August 23 hit into a triple play in the first inning against the Pittsburgh Pirates at Three Rivers Stadium. Edwards lined to shortstop Dale Berra for the first out. Berra threw to second baseman Johnny Ray to double up Gene Richards. Ray threw to first baseman Jason Thompson to nab Garry Templeton. The Padres on August 31 sold pitcher John Curtis to the California Angels.

San Diego's woes compounded in September. The Houston Astros on September 7 fanned 13 Padres, defeating San Diego 4-3. The sudden death of 65-year old bullpen coach Clyde McCullough, who had joined the club the previous spring, further diminished the team morale. McCullough, a National League catcher for 15 seasons, suffered a fatal heart attack on September 18 while traveling with the Padres in San Francisco. San Diego pitchers the next day surrendered four home runs and walked 11 Giants in an 11-inning, 4-3 loss at Candlestick Park. The Atlanta Braves routed the Padres, 11-6, on September 24 and 12-6 on September 25 at Atlanta-Fulton County Stadium, recording 16 hits in the first contest. In the latter contest, Juan Eichelberger set a club record by allowing 10 runs, eight earned, in just seven innings.

Nevertheless, the second half of the 1982 season produced a few San Diego highlights. Outfielder Sixto Lezcano earned National League Player of the Week honors for the second time for July 26 through August 1, batting .519 with four doubles, five homers, and 12 RBIs. In a July 31 doubleheader against the Cincinnati Reds at Riverfront Stadium, he recorded two doubles, two home runs, five RBIs, and 12 total bases in the first game and two hits with two RBIs in the nightcap. The Padres swept the twin bill, 5-4, and 6-2. Eric Show on August 6 blanked the Cincinnati Reds, 2-0, in the first complete game of his major-league career. Tim Lollar and Luis DeLeon on August 21 two-hit the Chicago Cubs, 2-0, at Wrigley Field. San Diego battered Cubs pitching the next day for seven extra-base hits, but still lost, 8-7. Ten days later, Dave Dravecky hurled 11 innings to key a 2-1, 13-inning victory over the Pittsburgh Pirates.

September brought several memorable San Diego performances. Terry Kennedy on September 4 clouted two home runs off Ferguson Jenkins, lifting the Padres to a 4-1 home triumph over the Chicago Cubs. Nine days later, Joe Lefebvre tied a franchise record by making six hits, including a home run and a double, in a heartbreaking 16-inning, 4-3 loss to the Los Angeles Dodgers at Dodger Stadium. During the same contest, Gene Richards registered his second five-hit performance of the season. Lefebvre and Richards each made eight plate appearances. In a 12-6 loss to the Atlanta Braves on September 25 at Atlanta-Fulton County Stadium, Kennedy clouted two home runs with four RBIs. Richards the next day belted an inside-the-park home run in the third inning off Rick Camp to help defeat Atlanta, 3-2. The Houston Astros knocked the Padres out of pennant contention on September 27, the then-latest elimination date in club history. San Diego celebrated Ray Kroc's eightieth birthday with a party attended by 43,077 fans at an October 2 game with the Atlanta Braves. The Padres triumphed over the Atlanta Braves, 5-1, the next day in the season finale to even the club record.

San Diego exceeded almost everyone's expectations, finishing 81-81. The Padres enjoyed just their second season with a .500 winning percentage and their second best record in franchise history, edging the Houston Astros for fourth place in the Western Division. Besides vacating last place for the first time since 1979, San Diego tied a club record with its fourth place finish and set club records for highest batting average (.257) and hits (1,435). From the outset, manager Dick Williams exuded optimism. "I said in April I thought we were capable of winning more than half of our games. I would have been disappointed if we had finished under .500." The 1,607,566 home attendance approached the club record of 1,670,107, established in 1978.

McKeon's trades and youth movement paid dividends. Under new pitching coach Norm Sherry, San Diego fielded one of the National League's best staffs. Padre pitchers set franchise records for innings pitched (1,476) and fewest hits allowed (1,348). Tim Lollar, one of the best left-handers in the National League, led San Diego with a 16-9 record and 3.13 ERA. Besides setting a club record for highest winning percentage (.640) by a left-hander, he finished seventh in the National League in victories, eleventh in ERA and strikeouts (150), and twelfth in innings pitched (233). Opposing batters hit only .225 against him. Lollar finished 8-6 at home and 8-3 on the road and did not lose a game until June 6. He also belted three home runs and shared the club lead among pitchers with 11 RBIs.

Other Padre pitchers performed well, too. Veteran John Montefusco recorded 10 triumphs, providing invaluable leadership for the young staff. Rookie starters Eric Show (10-6), Dave Dravecky (5-3), and Floyd Chiffer (4-3) surrendered under three earned runs per nine innings, while rookie reliever Luis DeLeon won nine of 14 decisions, compiled 15 saves, and boasted a sterling 2.03 ERA. Show's 2.64 ERA set a club record for a right-handed pitcher. The Padres, however, needed another starting pitcher capable of attaining 12 to 15 victories and additional effective relievers. Juan Eichelberger, the opening day starter, struggled with a 7-14 mark and 4.20 ERA. Reliever Gary Lucas set club records for most games finished (39) and most saves (16) by a left-hander, but lost 10 of 11 decisions. His

10 consecutive losses tied a franchise record for left-handers.

Catcher Terry Kennedy led the San Diego offense with a .295 batting average and 21 home runs, establishing club marks with 42 doubles and for left-handed batters with 97 RBIs, 273 total bases, and 91 strikeouts. He clouted just 11 fewer home runs than the entire 1981 Padre team and almost led the National League in doubles. Sixto Lezcano supplied the right-handed power San Diego had sought since Dave Winfield's departure, with 16 home runs, 84 RBIs, and a .289 batting average. The Padres ranked second in the National League with 165 stolen bases. Alan Wiggins, Luis Salazar, and Gene Richards each swiped at least 30 bases, while Garry Templeton and Ruppert Jones accounted for 45 thefts. San Diego runners, however, were caught stealing a record 77 times. The Padres still needed more leaders, another right-handed power hitter, an established first baseman, and more consistent defensive infielders.

During the fall, McKeon made several transactions. San Diego on October 7 purchased pitcher Elias Sosa from the Detroit Tigers and sold outfielder Rick Lancellotti to the Montreal Expos. The Padres on October 15 traded pitcher Tom Tellman to the Milwaukee Brewers for pitchers Weldon Swift and Tim Cook and on November 3 released outfielder Dave Edwards. In a major November 18 exchange, San Diego acquired pitcher Ed Whitson from the Cleveland Indians for pitcher Juan Eichelberger and first baseman-outfielder Broderick Perkins. The Padres planned to use Whitson, who had compiled a 34-41 mark with seven saves in six major-league seasons, as Eichelberger's replacement in the starting rotation. The departure of Perkins, San Diego's best pinch-hitter, depleted the bench strength.

San Diego attained legitimate title contender status on December 21, signing free agent first baseman Steve Garvey of the Los Angeles Dodgers to a five-year, $6.5 million contract. "This should show San Diego fans," president Ballard Smith explained, "that the front office is determined to field a winner here." Garvey provided the additional right-handed power, defensive stability, credibility, and professionalism that the Padres had needed to become a quality baseball club. "Now other teams will know it when we come to town," reserve infielder Kurt Bevacqua remarked. "This will cause some nervousness on other pitching staffs."

During 14 seasons with the Los Angeles Dodgers, Garvey had batted .301 with 1,968 hits, 992 RBIs, and 211 home runs, had appeared in four World Series, and had averaged 21 home runs and 98 RBIs over a nine-season span. Williams planned to insert Garvey in the middle of the batting order, relieving some of the pressure from Terry Kennedy and Sixto Lezcano. Garvey, Kennedy, and Lezcano represented the best trio of Padre power hitters since Dave Winfield, George Hendrick, and Gene Tenace had combined for 63 home runs in 1977. His acquisition gave San Diego five players, including Gene Richards, Terry Kennedy, Garry Templeton, and Luis Salazar, who had hit .300 or better at least once as major-leaguers. "Garvey," Jack McKeon remarked, "put the club close to where it wanted to be." According to Ed Whitson, "Garvey gave leadership like Reggie Jackson. He was the center of attention and took the pressure off younger players."

Garvey's acquisition paid immediate dividends. Ticket sales increased dramatically and raised hopes that 1983 home attendance might surpass two million people. "Garvey," announcer Dave Campbell stated, "gave the franchise legitimacy as a true superstar and integrated the team in the community." President Dick Freeman observed, "Garvey made a huge impact as a huge personality and enhanced the image of the Padres." Manager Dick Williams added, "He worked hard, influenced the kids, and made it easier for us to get rid of more veterans who weren't producing and not caring as much." Williams, however, downplayed Garvey's leadership and power and claimed that his defensive mobility had declined. San Diego on February 27 signed catcher Bruce Bochy and outfielder Jerry Turner and on March 27 released pitcher Tom Griffin.

The Padres, meanwhile, moved two of their minor-league teams for the 1983 season. The Hawaii club shifted from Honolulu to Las Vegas, Nevada, and finished second in the Southern Division of the Pacific Coast League under manager Harry Dunlop with an 83-60 record, two games out of first place. In the playoffs, Albuquerque edged the Las Vegas Stars, three games to two. The Amarillo, Texas team moved to Beaumont, Texas, and finished second in the Western Division of the Texas League under manager Harry Maloof with a 68-68 mark, six games out of first place. Beaumont defeated El Paso, two games to one, and Jackson in all three games to capture the Texas League title.

The media expected the San Diego Padres to finish third behind the Los Angeles Dodgers and San Francisco Giants. Left fielder Gene Richards led off for the Padres, followed by second baseman Juan Bonilla. First baseman Steve Garvey, catcher Terry Kennedy, and right fielder Sixto Lezcano supplied considerable power in the middle of the lineup. Center fielder Ruppert Jones survived a stern challenge from Alan Wiggins, while third baseman Luis Salazar edged out Joe Lefebvre. Tim Lollar, Ed Whitson, Eric Show, John Montefusco, and Dave Dravecky provided a formidable starting rotation, with Luis DeLeon and Gary Lucas heading the relief corps.

San Diego on April 5 defeated the San Francisco Giants, 16-13, at Candlestick Park in the highest scoring opening game and the then-longest nine-inning game (3 hours, 39 minutes) in franchise history. The eight runs and seven hits in the fifth inning and 16 runs and 17 hits for the contest marked Padre season highs. Dave Dravecky pitched his first complete major-league game in a 5-3 triumph over the Giants the next day, but the Padres then dropped five consecutive games from April 8 through April 12. The Padres drew their then-third-largest crowd in franchise history at 43,399 for the April 12 home opener, a 6-5 loss to the Giants.

From the outset, injuries stymied the Padres. Pitcher Tim Lollar hurt his elbow in the season opener and missed three weeks. Newly acquired pitcher Ed Whitson in mid-April underwent arthroscopic surgery for an injured knee that sidelined him for nearly six weeks. Shortstop Garry Templeton's injured left knee did not respond to treatment after identical surgery, landing him on the disabled list until mid-May. Left fielder Tony Gwynn did not join the starting lineup until mid-June because of a broken wrist suffered the previous December in the Puerto Rican Winter League.

Nevertheless, San Diego won 10 of 22 decisions in April. First baseman Steve Garvey on April 16 broke the National League record for most consecutive games with 1,118. The milestone ironically came in an 8-5 setback to the Los Angeles Dodgers, his former team, at Dodger Stadium. The Padres on April 26 matched a season high with 17 hits in a 10-8 victory over the Chicago Cubs at Wrigley Field. Garvey recorded his 1,000th career RBI on a home run off Craig Lefferts with one aboard. Catcher Terry Kennedy and infielder Tim Flannery also clouted home runs, the latter connecting on his first as a major-leaguer. Kennedy won National League Player of the Month honors for April, batting .390 with 21 RBIs.

An April 30 incident troubled the Padres. Reliever Chris Welsh defied manager Dick Williams's instructions against the Pittsburgh Pirates at Three Rivers Stadium. The Pirates had a runner on first base. Williams anticipated that the Pittsburgh runner might attempt to steal second base and consequently ordered Welsh to throw a pitchout. Welsh was supposed to pitch the ball outside so that catcher Terry Kennedy would have a better chance to throw out the Pirate baserunner. Welsh, however, ignored Williams's directive and threw the ball over to first baseman Steve Garvey to keep the Pittsburgh runner from getting a big lead. Williams was infuriated with Welsh's mental mistake because he wanted the Pirate baserunner to attempt a steal. Pitching coach Norm Sherry ran out to the mound to remind Welsh of his mistake.

From the dugout, Williams noticed Welsh talking back to Sherry. When Sherry returned to the dugout, Williams asked what Welsh had said. Sherry responded, "You sure you want to know? Well, he said if you didn't like the way he did it, you should get someone else." Williams ordered Sherry to have another Padre reliever warm up in the bullpen and informed Welsh at the end of the inning that he was being taken out of the game. In the clubhouse following the game, Williams asked Welsh if Sherry had reported his comments accurately. When Welsh replied affirmatively, Williams told him, "You've pitched your last game for me." San Diego sold Welsh to the Montreal Expos four days later. The incident dominated Padre clubhouse talk for several days and provoked some team dissension. Williams even admitted, "It united the slouchers in their hate for me, which meant they'd play harder, if only out of spite . . . And the reasonable folks became united with me in my love for winning." The Padres also signed outfielder Bobby Brown on April 19 and acquired reliever Sid Monge from the Philadelphia Phillies for third baseman-outfielder Joe Lefebvre on May 22.

The Padres struggled with an 11-13 mark in May. Eric Show on May 4 blanked the St. Louis Cardinals, 10-0, at home, benefiting from a 17-hit attack. Steve Garvey three days later singled in the fourth inning at home off Willie Hernandez for his 2,000th career hit, but the Chicago Cubs won, 6-4. The Beach Boys performed a concert after the Padres defeated the

Chicago Cubs, 5-3, the next day. Andy Hawkins on May 10 hurled a three-hit, 4-1 triumph at home over the Pittsburgh Pirates. Four days later, TV's *Game of the Week* covered the Padres' 4-1 home loss to the Los Angeles Dodgers. San Diego on May 26 even lost to their Las Vegas Stars farm club, as first baseman Joe Lansford and catcher Bruce Bochy homered. Eric Show, the following day, bested Tom Seaver of the New York Mets, 4-0, on a two-hitter.

San Diego improved to a 17-12 mark for June. Outfielder Kevin McReynolds on June 2 homered off Ron Reed in his first major-league game, sparking a 4-1 home victory over the Philadelphia Phillies. The next day, John Montefusco recorded his 1,000th career strikeout by fanning Mike Schmidt in the seventh inning, as the Padres defeated the Phillies 8-5. San Diego enjoyed its longest winning streak of the season, taking six straight from June 18 through June 23. Dave Dravecky started the steak at home on June 18, besting the Houston Astros, 2-1, to become the first major-league pitcher to win 10 games. Garry Templeton the next day hit three doubles with three RBIs, lifting San Diego to a 6-4 triumph over the Houston Astros.

For the first time, San Diego swept a four-game series against the Los Angeles Dodgers at Dodger Stadium. Tim Lollar and Luis DeLeon on June 21 combined on a two-hitter, blanking Los Angeles, 2-0. Dave Dravecky decisioned Dodger ace Fernando Valenzuela, 7-5, two days later to give the Padres the four-game sweep. Tim Lollar on June 26 no-hit the San Francisco Giants for six innings, but the latter defeated San Diego, 2-0, on just two hits. Three days later, Mark Thurmond recorded a complete game victory in his first major-league start. Steve Garvey, Kurt Bevacqua, and Luis Salazar homered in the 13-2 romp over the Los Angeles Dodgers at home. Sixto Lezcano on June 30 knocked in five runs, enabling the Padres to edge Los Angeles, 7-6. Four days later, Steve Garvey clouted his fifth career grand slam in a 4-1 triumph at home against the San Francisco Giants.

Dave Dravecky performed brilliantly the first half of the 1983 season with a 12-5 mark, 3.07 ERA, and eight complete games, making the National League All-Star team. He won five straight decisions from April 17 to May 13 and pitched 31.1 innings from April 22 to May 13 without issuing a walk. Dravecky hurled two shutout innings in the 13-3 loss to the American League in the All-Star Game, striking out George Brett and Fred Lynn.

San Diego, meanwhile, slumped to 41-44 after the All-Star break. The Padres reached one million in attendance against the St. Louis Cardinals in their 82nd game on July 10, the then-earliest date in franchise history. San Diego the next day scored six runs in the first inning and hung on for a 6-5 victory over the Chicago Cubs. Tim Flannery belted a grand slam, his first homer at Jack Murphy Stadium. The Padres defeated the Cubs, 5-3, on July 12, as Dick Williams recorded his 1,200th career managerial win and Sixto Lezcano made his 1,000th major league hit. The Padres then lost five consecutive games from July 14 through July 19. Kurt Bevacqua on July 14 belted his first grand slam off Rod Scurry in a five-run seventh inning, but the Pittsburgh Pirates prevailed, 8-6. No pinch-hit grand slam had previously been hit at Jack Murphy Stadium.

The slump ended on July 20, when outfielder Ruppert Jones clouted a three-run homer off Bruce Sutter in the ninth inning to give the Padres a come-from-behind, 5-4 victory over the Chicago Cubs at Wrigley Field. Two days later, second baseman Alan Wiggins doubled three times in a 7-3 loss to Chicago. Jones on July 26 registered four hits and six RBIs in a doubleheader split with the Pittsburgh Pirates at Three Rivers Stadium. The season defensive gem came in the fourth inning five days later when a San Diego triple play sparked a 5-2 home victory over the Atlanta Braves. Glenn Hubbard lined to shortstop Garry Templeton. Templeton tossed to second baseman Tim Flannery to double up Chris Chambliss. Flannery then relayed to first baseman Kurt Bevacqua to retire Terry Harper. Bobby Brown made a spectacular major-league return with a single, home run, two RBIs, and a stolen base.

San Diego won 15 of 32 decisions in August. Bobby Brown on August 1 clouted a three-run homer with two outs in the tenth inning, giving the Padres a 7-4 home win over the Houston Astros. Nolan Ryan of Houston two days later blanked the Padres, 1-0, on one hit. Tim Flannery lined a single to right field with one out in the third inning for the lone San Diego safety. The Padres on August 6 exploded for eight runs in the eighth inning in the first game of a doubleheader to key an 11-4 romp over the Cincinnati Reds at home. Brown clouted his first career grand slam off Tom Hume to spark the eight-run outburst.

Pitcher Tim Lollar on August 14 clouted a third-inning solo home run, helping San Diego defeat the Cincinnati Reds, 10-9, at Riverfront Stadium. Dave

Dravecky the next day hurled his first major-league shutout, blanking the Atlanta Braves, 4-0, at Atlanta-Fulton County Stadium. Brown tied Dave Winfield's 1977 club record by hitting safely in his 16th straight game in a 3-2 home victory over the New York Mets and broke the mark the next day in a 10-4 loss to the Montreal Expos at Olympic Stadium. Brown's streak ended at 21 games in the first game of an August 30 doubleheader against the Philadelphia Phillies at Veterans Stadium. Brown, Mario Ramirez, and Luis Salazar tripled to give the Padres a 7-5 triumph in the nightcap.

Jack McKeon, meanwhile, made three transactions after the All-Star break. After releasing outfielder Jerry Turner on July 26, San Diego a month later sent pitcher John Montefusco to the New York Yankees. The Padres acquired pitcher Dennis Rasmussen and infielder Edwin Rodriguez on September 12 to complete the deal. San Diego traded outfielder Sixto Lezcano to the Philadelphia Phillies on August 31 and received pitchers Lance McCullers, Ed Wojna, hard-thrower Marty Decker, and Darren Burroughs on September 20. The Phillies acquired pitcher Steve Fireovid on October 11 to complete the deal.

During September, San Diego improved to a 14-11 mark. Catcher Terry Kennedy homered in four straight games, helping the Padres on September 7 rally from a 7-0 deficit at home against Nolan Ryan to defeat the Houston Astros, 8-7. Six days later, Tony Gwynn hit safely in his 21st consecutive game to tie Bobby Brown's short-lived club record and help San Diego defeat the San Francisco Giants, 4-3, at home. He broke the record the next day in a 7-4 win over the Giants, while Brown contributed three stolen bases. Gwynn on September 18 extended his hitting streak to that season's major-league best 25 games. Ruppert Jones clouted a two-run homer in the 13th inning to defeat the Atlanta Braves, 4-2, at Atlanta-Fulton County Stadium that day. The San Francisco Giants stopped Gwynn's streak the following night at Candlestick Park. During the streak, he batted .361 with 35 hits and 12 RBIs.

The last two weeks featured more fine San Diego performances. Tim Lollar on September 21 struck out 12 San Francisco batters in a 5-4 setback. Two days later, Ruppert Jones knocked in five runs to give the Padres an 11-8 victory over the Cincinnati Reds at Riverfront Stadium. Alan Wiggins on September 25 stole two bases to give him a club-record 62 in a 5-2 loss to the Cincinnati Reds. Four days later, Andy Hawkins fanned 10 Los Angeles Dodgers in a 4-1 home triumph. Third baseman George Hinshaw on October 1 plated the winning run in the tenth inning with his fourth hit to defeat the Atlanta Braves, 4-3, at home.

San Diego again finished fourth in the Western Division with an identical 81-81 record. Steve Garvey provided the right-handed power that Williams sorely needed, batting .294 with 22 doubles, 14 home runs, and 59 RBIs through midseason. He missed the final 62 games of the 1983 campaign with a dislocated left thumb suffered in a collision at home plate on July 29 in a 2-1 loss at home to the Atlanta Braves. His consecutive-game playing streak, highest in National League history and third on the all-time major-league list, ended at 1,207 games.

Garvey's absence made it easier for opponents to pitch around slugging catcher Terry Kennedy. Kennedy still led the Padres in about every offensive category and made *The Sporting News* Silver Slugger Team. Besides batting .284, he paced San Diego in home runs (17), RBIs (98), game-winning RBIs (14), doubles (27), and sacrifice flies (9). His RBIs, sacrifice flies, and 15 intentional walks set club marks for a left-handed batter. Dave Dravecky, who had won 12 decisions before the All-Star Game break, missed the final five weeks with a shoulder problem.

The injuries enabled several younger Padres to gain valuable playing experience. The Lollar and Whitson injuries opened a spot in the starting rotation for left-hander Mark Thurmond, who was summoned from the Las Vegas farm club in late June. Thurmond filled the vacuum nicely with a 7-3 record and 2.65 ERA. The Padres recalled Bobby Brown, former New York Yankee outfielder, from Las Vegas when Garvey was injured. Brown, a leadoff switch hitter, batted .267 with 40 runs and 27 stolen bases in 57 games. Alan Wiggins replaced Garvey at first base, hitting .276, setting a club record with 66 stolen bases, and leading the Padres with 83 runs.

Williams trained replacements for veteran outfielders Gene Richards and Ruppert Jones, both eligible for free agency following the 1983 season. The Padres planned to use Kevin McReynolds in left field, Wiggins in center field, and Gwynn in right field. McReynolds, a right-handed power hitter who batted .377 with 32 home runs and 116 RBIs at Las Vegas in 1983, hit .269 with two home runs after being recalled in September. Gwynn batted .333 in the final 62 games and led the Padres with a .309 season average, hitting safely in 39 of 41 contests from August 11 to September 26.

Other Padre infielders picked up the slack following Steve Garvey's injury. After recovering from knee surgery, Garry Templeton attained the highest batting average (.263) ever by a San Diego shortstop. He evoked memories of his St. Louis Cardinals days, batting over .300 the final seven weeks and hitting safely in 19 of his last 21 games. Error-prone third baseman Luis Salazar hit 14 home runs and stole 24 bases.

Scholarly Eric Show led an improved starting rotation with 15 victories and hurling two May home shutouts. Dave Dravecky recorded 14 triumphs in an injury-shortened season. Mark Thurmond supplied seven late-season victories, while Andy Hawkins and Dennis Rasmussen showed considerable promise. The 6-foot 7-inch left-handed Rasmussen made his first major-league start on October 1 in a 4-3 win over the Atlanta Braves, retiring the first 14 batters and fanning seven altogether. San Diego starters hurled a franchise-low five shutouts, while the bullpen saved 44 games. Veteran Gary Lucas, who combined five victories with 17 saves, set a franchise record for most saves by a left-hander. His performance improved after the Padres secured left-handed reliever Sid Monge from the Philadelphia Phillies on May 22. Monge saved seven contests and won seven of 10 decisions, while Luis DeLeon contributed 13 saves. Hard-throwing right-hander Marty Decker performed well in four late season relief appearances, surrendering only two runs and striking out nine batters in 8.2 innings.

Statistically, the 1983 season brought mixed team results. Base stealing figured prominently in San Diego's offense. The Padres pilfered 125 bases after the All-Star break and swiped 179 bases altogether. San Diego also set a franchise record for fewest errors with just 129. The Padres enjoyed tremendous success against the Western Division-winning Los Angeles Dodgers, taking 12 of 18 contests. San Diego prevailed in 10 of its last 11 meetings with Los Angeles, including the final seven games at Dodger Stadium. The Padres also triumphed in seven of 12 contests against the National League champion Philadelphia Phillies.

San Diego home attendance dropped from 1,607,516 in 1982 to 1,539,819 in 1983. The Padres never generated much offense to excite fans, averaging only four runs per game and finishing next to last in the National League with 93 home runs. Garvey's season-ending injury in late July may have contributed to the diminished gate. Nevertheless, Williams reflected, "You had to be blind not to see that our team's future was bright."

At the December winter meetings, Jack McKeon built San Diego into Western Division contenders. San Diego on December 5 sent second baseman Joe Pittman and outfielder Tommy Francis to the San Francisco Giants for reserve outfielder-first baseman Champ Summers. Summers strengthened San Diego's pinch-hitting capabilities. Two days later, the Padres participated in a major three-way transaction with the Montreal Expos and Chicago Cubs. The Padres sent pitcher Gary Lucas to the Montreal Expos for pitcher Scott Sanderson. Sanderson was traded to the Chicago Cubs for left-handed pitcher Craig Lefferts, outfielder Carmelo Martinez, and third baseman Fritz Connally. San Diego planned to use Lefferts as a set-up bullpen reliever and Martinez, who had batted .258 with six home runs and 16 RBIs in 29 games, as the starting left fielder.

9

The Glorious Season

[1984]

The Padres dedicated their 1984 season to beloved owner Ray Kroc, who died of a heart attack on January 14 at age 81 in San Diego. Throughout the campaign, team members wore the initials "RAK" on the left sleeve of their uniforms. Under Kroc's benevolent ownership from 1974 to 1984, the franchise had remained in San Diego, gained financial stability, and improved from a struggling last-place squad to a respectable fourth-place club. "Kroc," pitcher Gary Lucas explained, "came in at a time when the Padres had an identity problem and made the organization more credible."

From the outset, Kroc had taken a keen interest in the team. "Kroc," pitcher Steve Arlin recalled, "was a great baseball fan." The McDonald's magnate had possessed the monetary resources to acquire free agents and to market the club more effectively. "His financial support," first baseman Steve Garvey reminisced, "gave the team money to change things." According to General Manager Jack McKeon, "The Padres have lost a great guy who was always interested in baseball and a genuine human being, revering people who produced."

Joan Kroc replaced her husband as the Padres' owner. The St. Paul, Minnesota native, "a bubbling matriarch with a heart of golden arches," had worked as a professional musician and music teacher for many years and served as music director of KSTP-TV before marrying Ray Kroc in 1969. An active philanthropist, she gave generously to substance abuse, world hunger, international peace, animal rights, hospice, AIDS research, flood relief, and other humanitarian concerns. She named Ballard Smith, her son-in-law, as club president in charge of daily operations.

Jack McKeon, meanwhile, continued building San Diego into Western Division contenders. On January 6, he signed ace free agent reliever Goose Gossage of the New York Yankees to a five-year $6.5 million contract, a then-record salary for a pitcher. Gossage, whose legendary fastball made him the sport's most intimidating reliever, gave the

Tony Gwynn, eight-time National League batting champion, played outfield for the Padres from 1982 through 2001.

Padres their best bullpen closer since Rollie Fingers. Besides compiling 206 career saves, he led the American League three times in saves and performed on three World Series teams.

San Diego solved its perennial third base problem on March 30 by securing San Diego native Graig Nettles from the New York Yankees for pitcher Dennis Rasmussen. Although past his prime at 39 years old, Nettles solidified the Padres infield defensively and supplied much needed offensive spark. Nettles had won two Gold Glove awards, clouted 333 home runs, plated over 1,000 runs, and appeared in four World Series. "Gossage," Jack McKeon asserted, "made the club a contender, and Nettles provided the last piece in the puzzle with steady third base play." Outfielder Tony Gwynn added, "These veterans knew how to win, taught the younger guys what it took to be successful, and supplied leadership through example." Rasmussen's departure still left the Padres with three left-handed starting pitching prospects: Mark Thurmond, Tim Lollar, and Dave Dravecky.

The Padres still faced many question marks. The national media predicted another fourth-place finish for San Diego. The Padres started an inexperienced outfield trio of 24-year-olds Carmelo Martinez in left field, Kevin McReynolds in centerfield, and Tony Gwynn in rightfield. The Padres carried too many outfielders and did not sign two veterans. Veteran outfielder Gene Richards left San Diego to sign as a free agent with the San Francisco Giants on March 28. Richards, unhappy with manager Dick Williams, ranked first among Padres in career stolen bases (242), second in batting average (.291), third in runs scored (484), and fourth in hits (994). Outfielder Ruppert Jones, whose batting average had dropped 50 points to .233 in 1983, also left the Padres after three seasons and signed on April 18 with the Detroit Tigers.

San Diego took its biggest gamble at second base, releasing drug offender Juan Bonilla on March 26 and moving fleet-footed outfielder Alan Wiggins there. Wiggins had not played second base regularly in six years. Williams settled on a relatively inexperienced five-man starting pitching rotation: with right-handers Eric Show, Andy Hawkins, and Ed Whitson and left-handers Mark Thurmond and Tim Lollar. Left-hander Dave Dravecky made spot starts and assisted Gossage in the bullpen. First baseman Steve Garvey and catcher Terry Kennedy recovered from a dislocated thumb and knee surgery in time to start opening day, relieving Williams of two other potential problems.

The schedule benefited the Padres, who began the season with 11 games at Jack Murphy Stadium. The successful quest for the Western Division title began on April 3, when San Diego defeated the Pittsburgh Pirates, 5-1, in what at the time was the earliest home opener in franchise history. Before the game, the 44,553 spectators witnessed a moving tribute to Ray Kroc. Eric Show allowed only three hits and fanned four batters in the first seven innings, while Goose Gossage pitched masterfully in the ninth inning to preserve the victory. Kevin McReynolds and Carmelo Martinez, nicknamed "the M&M Boys," clouted towering home runs off Rick Rhoden. The opening game marked an auspicious start for Pay Per View, which started that day for Padre home games.

San Diego enjoyed its best start ever with a 9-2 record in its first homestand. The Padres played their first seven games against Eastern Division clubs and won their first four contests, defeating the Pittsburgh Pirates, 8-6, on April 5 and the Chicago Cubs, 3-2, on April 6 and 7-6, on April 7. The first San Diego loss came on April 8 in an 8-5, 10-inning setback to the Chicago Cubs, but the Padres won their next four home games. Pinch hitter Champ Summers on April 10 belted a grand slam in the fifth inning off Bob Forsch, giving San Diego a 7-3 victory over the St. Louis Cardinals. San Diego also defeated the St. Louis Cardinals, 7-5, on April 11 and the Atlanta Braves, 6-1, on April 12 and, 5-2, on April 13. The Padres split their last two games with Atlanta on the homestand. San Diego on April 22 established a club record with 11 extra-base hits against the Los Angeles Dodgers at Dodger Stadium.

The Padres finished April with 15 wins against only eight losses. Eric Show and Andy Hawkins both won three starts in April, while reliever Goose Gossage saved seven games. Tony Gwynn hit a torrid .434 in April to take National League Player of the Month honors, raising hopes that he might win his first batting title. Kevin McReynolds supplied both average and power, while Carmelo Martinez made a smooth transition from first base to left field. Utility players also contributed significantly to San Diego's fast start.

San Diego stumbled in May and relinquished first place for nearly a month. From May 10 to May 16, the Padres lost seven consecutive games, including three each at home to the Philadelphia Phillies, 6-4, 3-2, and 8-3, and the Montreal Expos, 7-6, 6-4, and 3-2. San Diego's win-loss record dropped to 18-18. The Padres ended the losing streak on May 17, rallying in the ninth inning against ace reliever Jeff Reardon to defeat the Montreal Expos, 5-4. In that contest, San Diego set a club record with seven stolen bases and even pilfered three bases in one inning. Fleet-footed Alan Wiggins tied a modern National League record and established a franchise mark by stealing five bases. Three days later, pitcher Tim Lollar established a team record by striking out eight consecutive New York Mets at Jack Murphy Stadium. The Padres won six of their final nine games in May to move within 1.5 games of first place. They regained first place on May 25 with a 7-3 triumph over the Philadelphia Phillies at Veterans Stadium and finished the month with six victories in their final nine games.

San Diego selected two members of the initial U.S. Olympic team in the first round of the June 1984 free agent draft. Speedy outfielder Shane Mack, who starred on the diamond at the University of California at Los Angeles and made *The Sporting News'* 1984 College Baseball All-American team, was chosen eleventh overall. The Padres selected shortstop Gary Green, the son of former major-league pitcher Freddie Green, as the twenty-sixth overall selection. Green had starred as a shortstop for Oklahoma State University and appeared in several College World Series. Mack and Green played with the U. S. Olympic team in 1984 and joined the Beaumont, Texas farm club the next spring.

San Diego seized command of the West Division race in June with a 19-10 record. After dropping 1.5 games out of first place with a June 1 road loss to the San Francisco Giants, the Padres won six consecutive games and 11 of their next 12 contests. Tony Gwynn assumed the National League batting lead with three consecutive three-hit games from June 1 through June 3 against the Giants. Tim Lollar on June 8 struck out a club season-high 12 batters, blanking the Cincinnati Reds, 6-0, at home. The Padres never surrendered first place after thrashing Cincinnati, 12-2, with seven extra-base hits the next day. On June 10, San Diego clouted a season-high four home runs, including two by third baseman Graig Nettles, in a 7-5 victory over the Reds. Steve Garvey recorded his seventeenth consecutive game with a base hit, dating back to May 22. The same day, the Padres sold relief pitcher Sid Monge to the Detroit Tigers. Eric Show on June 19 pitched the best game of the month for the Padres and stymied the Houston Astros with a two-hit, 2-0 masterpiece. Six days later, San Diego blitzed Los Angeles Dodgers pitchers for a season-high 19 hits and left 12 men on base in a 9-4 triumph at Dodger Stadium.

The entire team contributed to San Diego's success. The Padres won games consistently, brilliantly executing fundamentals. "It was an excellent period for us," vice president Jack McKeon recalled. "We learned how to win, how to put a club away. We always won the games we really needed." "The veterans," manager Dick Williams added, "showed the young players never to get too high after a win and never too low after a loss. The youngsters watched the veterans after a rough day and saw they should handle it in the same manner." The younger Padres blossomed quickly. Carmelo Martinez led San Diego with 34 RBIs during June and July and performed well defensively in his new left field position. Second baseman Alan Wiggins improved defensively and sparked the San Diego offense with

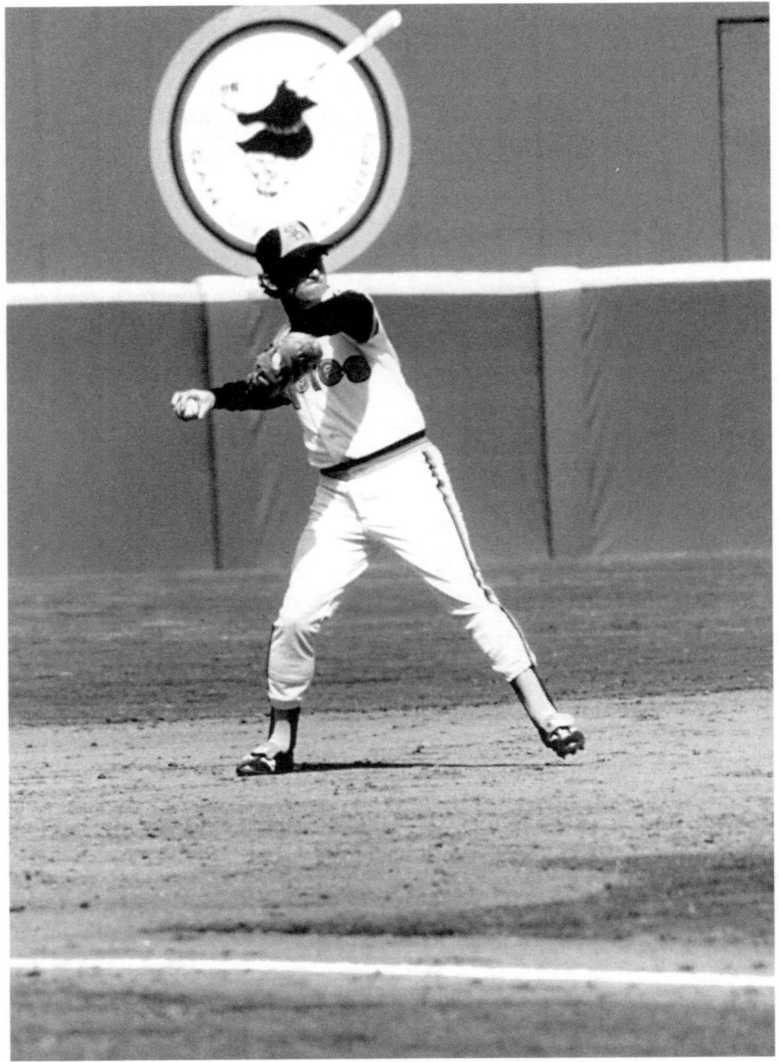

Graig Nettles played third base for the Padres from 1984 through 1986.

San Diego pitchers limited opponents to just 2.28 earned runs per game. Ed Whitson, who had never won more than 11 games in six major-league seasons, capitalized on his newly developed palm-ball to notch his twelfth season victory. Show blossomed into a consistent winner with his slider, while Mark Thurmond and Dave Dravecky each hurled 1-0 masterpieces that month. Reliever Craig Lefferts baffled hitters with his screwball pitch as an effective set-up man for Goose Gossage, who closed games with his blazing fastball. "If it wasn't for Lefferts," Gossage confided, "we wouldn't have been where we were."

San Diego pitchers finished July with four consecutive home shutouts, two each against the Houston Astros and the Los Angeles Dodgers. The Padres defeated the Houston Astros, 7-3, on July 27, the night of the Goose Honker Night promotion, when outfielder Kevin McReynolds clouted a seventh-inning home run into the second deck in left field off Dave Smith. No Padre had reached the second deck since Dave Kingman in 1977. The incredible shutout streak began in the second game of a doubleheader on July 28, when Eric Show and Gossage outdueled Nolan Ryan of Houston, 1-0. Tim Lollar, the beneficiary of Garry Templeton's sixth-inning grand slam off Mike LaCoss, spun

his speed on the basepaths. Tony Gwynn continued to lead the National League in batting average and base hits. Gwynn, Steve Garvey, and Graig Nettles combined to drive in 89 runs during June and July, while Kevin McReynolds and Terry Kennedy supplied offensive spark.

San Diego took advantage of the other injury-riddled West Division teams, widening its lead to nearly 10 games in July. The club won 21 of 30 contests that month, removing any suspense from the West Division race. "The Padres started great," Jack McKeon declared, "and had the division title won before the All-Star break." The quiet intellectual Eric Show conceded, "The Padres won that year by default." Tony Gwynn batted a sizzling .398 with 15 RBIs during July, while

a two-hit, 9-0 shutout against the Astros the next afternoon. On July 30, Dave Dravecky followed with a brilliant one-hit masterpiece against the Los Angeles Dodgers. The Padres blitzed Los Angeles, 12-0, as Dravecky surrendered only a seventh-inning double to Bill Russell with one out. Mark Thurmond and Goose Gossage finished the month combining on a 1-0 shutout over the Dodgers. "By then," vice president Jack McKeon stated, "we knew we had a fine staff." San Diego pitchers finally surrendered a run against Los Angeles in the second inning on August 1, the first in 40.2 innings dating back to the sixth inning of the first game July 28. Thurmond recorded a club-best 22 consecutive scoreless innings from July 26 to August 1.

Alan Wiggins played outfield and second base for the Padres from 1982 through June 1985.

During July, a major controversy brewed off the diamond. Padre pitchers Eric Show, Dave Dravecky, and Mark Thurmond revealed that they were members of the John Birch Society, an ultra-conservative organization formed to combat alleged Communist activities in the United States. Newspaper reporters learned that the trio distributed John Birch Society literature at the San Diego County Fair. The trio's political affiliation did not disturb their teammates, but the incident distracted from the team focus. The San Diego media embellished the story, provoking prompt negative fan reaction. After hearing fan complaints, the Padre management told the three pitchers to comment less about the subject.

Eric Show, whose varied interests included religion, philosophy, and jazz, had joined the John Birch Society in 1981 after earlier sojourns with Roman Catholicism, Eastern culture, and Mormonism. He had recruited the soft-spoken, deeply religious Dravecky and Thurmond as John Birch Society members and hoped to influence teammates by keeping controversial organization literature on his clubhouse chair. "It is a personal belief that I have," Show acknowledged, "and I firmly believe that I'm not doing anything wrong at all." Throughout the affair, he denied allegations that the John Birch Society was racist. The controversy subsided by the time the Padres returned on July 28 from an eastern road trip to St. Louis, Chicago, and Pittsburgh.

The Padres continued to record impressive feats in August. Second baseman Alan Wiggins on August 4 stole home in the third inning in a 6-2 triumph over the Houston Astros at the Astrodome, marking his second steal of home that season. Outfielder Kevin McReynolds on August 8 belted a pinch-hit home run off Mario Soto with one aboard in the ninth inning in a 4-2 loss to the Cincinnati Reds at Riverfront Stadium. Third baseman Graig Nettles recorded consecutive two-home run games on August 16-17 in home losses to the Philadelphia Phillies and Montreal Expos.

Two brawls marred a Sunday afternoon contest on August 12 with the second-place Atlanta Braves at Atlanta-Fulton County Stadium. Atlanta pitcher Pascual Perez opened the game by hitting Alan Wiggins with his first pitch. Padre hurlers retaliated by throwing at Perez in each of his four plate appearances. Umpire Larry McSherry ejected San Diego starting pitcher Ed Whitson and manager Dick Williams in the third inning. The first fight erupted in the eighth inning when Padre reliever Craig Lefferts beaned Perez. In the next frame, Atlanta reliever Donnie Moore provoked an even worse brawl by hitting Graig Nettles.

Altogether, McSherry ejected 14 Braves and Padres from that single contest. Both benches and bullpens were cleared, while police surrounded each dugout for the remainder of the game, won, 5-3, by Atlanta. National League President Chub Feeney fined Williams $10,000 and suspended the San Diego skipper 10 days. Seven Padres players and two Padres coaches, also were assessed fines. The incident, however, solidified team unity. "The brawl in Atlanta," announcer Dave Campbell claimed, "woke up the Padres out of their doldrums."

San Diego coasted the rest of the season as average attendance at Jack Murphy Stadium fell below 15,000 fans by mid-September. Outfielder Carmelo Martinez on September 2 belted an inside-the-park home run in the second inning off Walt Terrell in a 3-2, 12-inning loss to the New York Mets at Shea Stadium. Three days later, outfielder Kevin McReynolds set a franchise record with five singles in a 15-11 slugfest over the Cincinnati Reds at Jack Murphy Stadium. The Padres made one of the biggest comebacks in franchise history that game, rallying from a 7-0 deficit after two innings. Their seven runs in the seventh inning and 15 runs for the game both marked season highs.

San Diego clinched the West Division title on September 20, having led the Houston Astros by 9.5 games with 10 contests left. A Padre victory over the San Francisco Giants, coupled with a Houston Astros loss to the Los Angeles Dodgers, would give the franchise its first West Division crown. Pitcher Tim Lollar clouted a three-run homer off Mike Krukow in the second inning, helping vault San Diego to a 5-0 lead. The Padres held on to win, 5-4, clinching at least a tie for the title. San Diego players listened on their home radios as the Los Angeles Dodgers downed the Houston Astros, 6-2, at the Astrodome to give the Padres the West Division title.

San Diego set a club record for victories with a 92-70 mark. The Padres surpassed a .500 winning percentage for just the second time in franchise history, finishing 12 games ahead of the Houston Astros and Atlanta Braves. San Diego demonstrated remarkable resiliency throughout the 1984 dream season, using only 31 different players. Although injuries wreaked havoc on other West Division clubs, only two Padres appeared on the disabled list the entire regular season. No regular San Diego position player or starting pitcher spent a single day in 1984 on the disabled list, perhaps setting a modern record. Injuries sidelined reliever Luis DeLeon from May 6 to September 1 and reserve infielder Luis Salazar from May 15 to June 11.

Vice president Jack McKeon and manager Dick Williams helped orchestrate the West Division title. McKeon, the fast-talking, cigar-chomping executive nicknamed "Trader Jack," built the Padres into a premier club through key trades, shrewd free agent signings, and fine draft selections. He revamped the entire team over four seasons, keeping only popular reserve infielder Tim Flannery throughout that span. Manager Dick Williams rebuilt yet another faltering franchise, reaching the pinnacle in his third year this time. The strict disciplinarian stressed consistency and sound fundamental baseball, featuring solid pitching, speed, and defense. First baseman Steve Garvey, who had played under managers Walter Alston and Tommy Lasorda, called Williams "as good a baseball mind as I've ever played for." Outfielder Tony Gwynn lauded Williams as "a winner who taught his players how to play the game, how to win, and how to be mentally tough."

Manager Dick Williams effectively blended youth with veterans to produce a West Division title. "The Padres," Steve Garvey acknowledged, "were a well-balanced team with veterans and rookies. Everyone did what they had to do. The veterans set the examples not with words, but with actions. And the kids came through. We never lost a game we had to win." Outfielders Tony Gwynn, Kevin McReynolds, and Carmelo Martinez enjoyed excellent campaigns. Tony Gwynn, who waltzed to the major-league batting title with a .351 mark, became the first Padre to win a National League hitting crown and the first to attain 200 hits in a season. No other San Diego starter even reached .300 at the plate. Gwynn finished third in the Most Valuable Player Award balloting, topping the National League in both hits (213) and on-base percentage (.410) and pacing the Padres in triples (10) and total bases (269). His baserunning and defensive skills also improved. He stole 33 bases and struck out only 23 times in 606 at-bats, making *The Sporting News'* All-League and Silver Slugger teams. Kevin McReynolds shared the club lead in home runs (20) while batting .278 and knocking in 75 runs. Carmelo Martinez produced 66 RBIs and handled left field capably.

Padre infielders contributed substantially to the West Division title. Steve Garvey, who played in 160 games, set a major-league record for first basemen by playing an entire season without committing an error. "I take great pride in my fielding," he acknowledged. Although curiously not earning a Gold Glove Award, he led the Padres with 86 RBIs and drove in many crucial runs. Second baseman Alan Wiggins ignited the San Diego offense as leadoff hitter, setting team records for most stolen bases (70 in 91 attempts) and runs scored (106) and pacing the Padres in walks (75). The switch hitter combined with Gwynn to give San Diego the most potent one-two punch in franchise history. Defensively, he committed a club-high 32 errors while adjusting his new position but improved steadily as the season progressed. "Wiggins," pitcher Ed Whitson claimed, "made all the difference in the world."

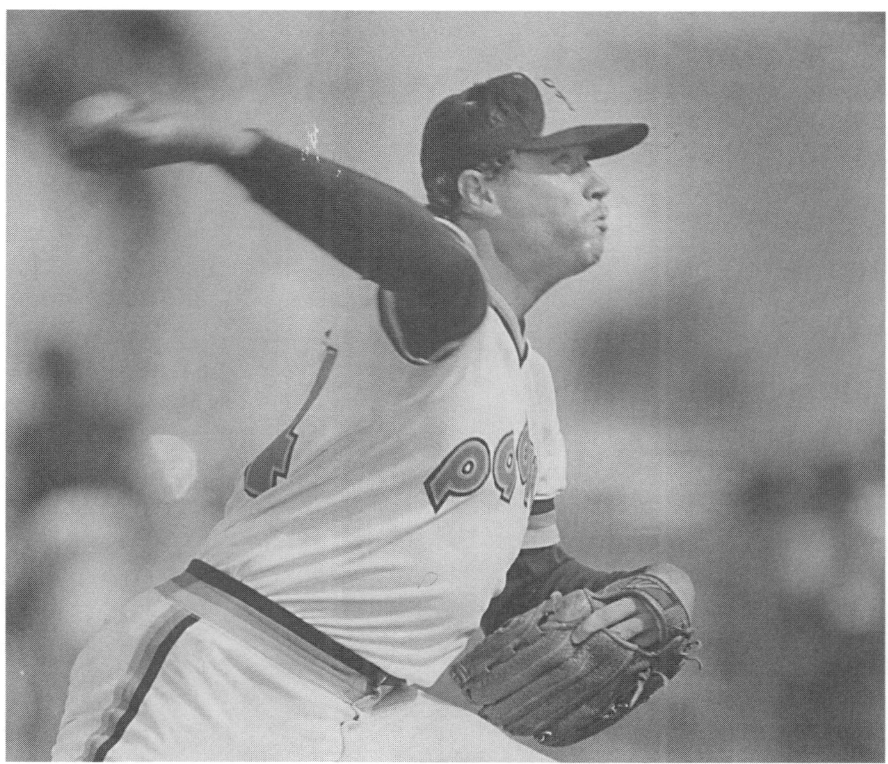

Goose Gossage pitched for the Padres from 1984 through 1987.

Third baseman Graig Nettles contributed 20 home runs and 65 RBIs in just under 400 at-bats. For most of the season, he boasted the National League's best home run per at-bat ratio. Nettles delighted his hometown fans by clouting seven home runs in one six-game stretch from August 11 to August 22 and solidifying the Padre infield defensively. Nettles, along with relief pitcher Goose Gossage, provided leadership and stability for a predominantly young ball club. "Nettles," reserve infielder Tim Flannery observed, "amazes me. He has played so long so well . . . he's just a true professional." Garry Templeton remained healthy throughout the season, playing in more games (148) than any other National League shortstop. He demonstrated the vitality he had shown with the St. Louis Cardinals, making *The Sporting News'* Silver Slugger team. Catcher Terry Kennedy struggled offensively, but worked well with the young starting pitchers.

San Diego's pitching corps performed splendidly in 1984. Five San Diego pitchers, including starters Mark Thurmond, Eric Show, Ed Whitson, and Tim Lollar, reached double figures in victories. Show led Padre hurlers with a 15-9 record and 3.40 ERA, utilizing his sinker effectively for the second consecutive year. Thurmond, who made *The Sporting News'* All-League team, and palmball specialist Whitson both logged 14-8 records with 2.97 and 3.24 ERAs, respectively. Lollar pitched brilliantly at times, while Dave Dravecky ably combined starting and relief roles. Lollar and Show also contributed three home runs apiece. Reliever Craig Lefferts, who replaced the injured Luis DeLeon, preserved many leads through the middle innings before giving way to Gossage. Lefferts, the most underrated Padres hurler, carried an ERA below 1.00 into June and collaborated with Dravecky for 12 victories and 18 saves. Goose Gossage, the bullpen mainstay, inspired memories of Rollie Fingers, posting 10 triumphs, 25 saves, and a 2.90 ERA. He provided San Diego its badly needed stopper, intimidating opposing batters with his blazing fastball.

Consistency and balance epitomized the Padres' dream season. According to shortstop Garry Templeton, "speed, power, pitching, and defense

Garry Templeton played shortstop for the Padres from 1982 through 1991.

produced the first-place finish." San Diego improved its team batting average from .250 to .259 and its home run production from 93 to 109. Six Padres knocked in at least 57 runs, helping the club average over four runs per game. San Diego pitchers lowered their team ERA from 3.62 to 3.48 while dramatically raising their shutouts from five to a league-leading 17. Announcer Dave Campbell concluded, "Lots of players performed up to their ability and even a few above their ability." "Everyone," Eric Show agreed, "had a good year. The team consistently executed the fundamentals." Tony Gwynn added, "The team had a lot of heart and spunk. Nobody expected anything at the start."

San Diego met the Chicago Cubs, the East Division titlist, in the National League Championship Series to decide the pennant. If the Padres could prevail, they would fulfill their ultimate dream of reaching their first World Series.

10

The Miraculous Comeback

[1984] postseason

The National League Championship Series with the Chicago Cubs gave the San Diego Padres one of the most exciting and memorable moments in their franchise history. The Chicago Cubs had astonished the baseball world with their meteoric rise from fifth place in 1983 to first place in the National League East Division in 1984. Chicago had finished the 1984 regular season with a 96-65 win-loss record, six and one-half games ahead of the New York Mets. Over 2.1 million people had attended the Cubs games at Wrigley Field, breaking the club home attendance record by nearly 430,000.

Chicago Cubs general manager Dallas Green had made several astute trades in 1984, while manager Jim Frey had become the first pilot to win divisional titles in his first season in each league. The Philadelphia Phillies in late March had sent center fielder Bob Dernier and left fielder Gary Matthews, Sr. to the Chicago Cubs. Dernier gave Chicago an effective leadoff hitter and outstanding center fielder, while Matthews supplied valuable leadership. The acquisitions of starters Dennis Eckersley from the Boston Red Sox in May and Rick Sutcliffe from the Cleveland Indians in June had made the Cubs a legitimate National League East Division contender. Eckersley finished 1984 with a 10-8 record and 3.03 ERA, while Sutcliffe triumphed 16 of 17 times after joining Chicago. Besides registering victories in all three of his decisions against the New York Mets, Sutcliffe became only the fourth major-league pitcher to win 20 games the same season with clubs in different leagues. His impressive 2.69 ERA helped earn him the coveted National League Cy Young Award. Lee Smith led the Cubs' relief corps with 33 saves, second best in the National League.

Second baseman Ryne Sandberg paced the Chicago Cubs offensively, garnering National League Most Valuable Player honors. Sandberg, who batted .314 and led the National League in scoring, fell just one triple short of becoming the first major-league player to collect 200 hits, 20 doubles, 20 triples,

20 home runs, and 20 stolen bases in the same year. Defensively, he had sparkled with 62 consecutive errorless games. Third baseman Ron Cey had led Chicago in round trippers and RBIs, while Bob Dernier, Gary Matthews, first baseman Leon Durham, catcher Jody Davis, and right fielder Keith Moreland augmented the offense.

The 1984 campaign gave both the Chicago Cubs and San Diego Padres recognition and respect. Chicago had not won a National League pennant since 1945 or a World Series since 1908. Long-suffering, loyal Cubs fans across the United States celebrated wildly when their favorites captured the National League East Division. San Diego had not finished higher than fourth place before 1984.

Chicago dominated the Padres in the first two afternoon games of the National League Championship Series at Wrigley Field, seeming destined to break their 39-year World Series famine. San Diego pitching disintegrated in the October 2 opening game as the Cubs overwhelmed the Padres, 13-0. Rick Sutcliffe hurled a masterpiece against Eric Show in Game 1. A 20 mile per hour wind blowing out at Wrigley Field spelled disaster for the Padres. Chicago batters set National League Championship Series records with 16 hits, five home runs, 34 total bases, and 13 runs off Show and reliever Greg Harris. Rick Sutcliffe surrendered just a bunt single to Steve Garvey and a bloop single to Garry Templeton while striking out eight Padres in seven innings.

Chicago Cubs leadoff batter Bob Dernier took advantage of the powerful wind, depositing Eric Show's second pitch of the game into the leftfield bleachers. No player ever had led off a National League Championship Series game with a home run. After second baseman Ryne Sandberg struck out, left fielder Gary Matthews also belted a round-tripper to left field. In the third inning, Sutcliffe clouted a tape-measure home run that cleared the rightfield bleachers and landed on Sheffield Avenue. The Cubs tallied twice more that frame on a run-scoring single by first baseman Leon Durham and a sacrifice fly by right fielder Keith Moreland, leaving Show "in shock."

The Padres loaded the bases with two outs in the fourth inning. Moreland then made the defensive play of the game, snaring Carmelo Martinez's sinking liner to right field. "Moreland's play," Rick Sutcliffe acknowledged, "turned what could have been a close game into a runaway." Chicago exploded for six runs, including Matthews's second homer of the game, a three-run round-tripper off reliever Greg Harris in the fifth inning. San Diego surrendered two more scores, including Ron Cey's solo home run, the next inning. Every Cubs starter recorded at least one hit and one RBI. "They just did everything right," manager Dick Williams lamented. "We'll come back and get them tomorrow."

The next afternoon, Chicago combined speed and daring strategy to defeat the Padres, 4-2. Bob Dernier and Ryne Sandberg spearheaded Chicago's triumph over San Diego. In the first inning, Dernier singled off Mark Thurmond and scampered to third base on Sandberg's grounder to third baseman Luis Salazar. First baseman Steve Garvey, caught off guard by Dernier's move, made a weak throw to third base. Dernier then scored on a Gary Matthews grounder to shortstop Garry Templeton. Chicago added two runs in the third frame. Keith Moreland singled and scampered home on Ron Cey's double to left center field. Shortstop Templeton's relay throw to the plate skipped away from Padres catcher Terry Kennedy, allowing Cey to take third base. Cey scored on a sacrifice fly by catcher Jody Davis.

The Padres finally produced their first run of the National League Championship Series in the fourth inning, as Tony Gwynn doubled and crossed home plate on Kevin McReynolds's sacrifice fly. The Cubs struck back the same frame against Thurmond with their final run of the game. Starting pitcher Steve Trout singled with one out. Dernier reached first base on a fielder's choice, stole second, and scored on Sandberg's double, knocking Thurmond out of the game. In the sixth inning, Alan Wiggins singled and tallied on Steve Garvey's base hit. Chicago left-hander Steve Trout pitched until one out in the ninth inning, allowing the Padres just five hits. Lee Smith relieved Trout and recorded the final two outs for the save. "We just can't get anything going," moaned manager Dick Williams.

The Cubs needed just one more victory to take the National League pennant. Only one major-league club, the 1982 Milwaukee Brewers, had overcome a two-game deficit to win a Championship Series. The Padres' plane left three hours late from O'Hare Airport in Chicago on October 3 and did not land at San Diego International Airport until late that night. According to sportscaster Dave Campbell, "The players already had given up and were talking about what they were going to do during the off season." Around 3,000 fans, however, awaited the Padres at the Jack Murphy Stadium parking lot. San Diego players and coaches alike were amazed that the throng had waited half the evening to welcome them home.

The crowd enthusiasm resurrected the spirits of the downtrodden Padres. The Padres truly had captured the hearts of a city often maligned for indifference. "The players weren't expecting anybody," Garry Templeton admitted, "when thousands of screaming and hollering fans showed up. The fans were a tenth man, motivating the team and getting their hearts pumping." The Padres soon caught the contagious zeal of their fans. Utility outfielder Bobby Brown, who had not played in the first two games, stormed around the parking lot shouting through a bull horn, "Three in a row." "Afterwards," Templeton explained, "the Padre players sensed that they could defeat the Cubs." "The fans," infielder Luis Salazar added, "turned things around."

San Diego indeed staged a miraculous comeback, termed "four magical days" by reserve infielder Tim Flannery, to reach the World Series. Over 58,000 boisterous fans jammed Jack Murphy Stadium for each of the three remaining games. Team captain Templeton stirred the crowd during player introductions before the third game on October 4. The normally low-key Templeton drew a tumultuous response while waving his hat wildly to the crowd. "I wanted to get everybody fired up," he declared. "Templeton's action," vice president Jack McKeon recalled, "fired up the team further. You could probably hear the crowd all the way to Tijuana."

Padre fans, however, had little to cheer about until the fifth inning. San Diego starter Ed Whitson struggled the first three frames, surrendering a double by Keith Moreland and a run-scoring single by Ron Cey in the second inning. In the fifth frame, Terry Kennedy and Kevin McReynolds singled off Dennis Eckersley. Both scored on Garry Templeton's crucial double to the left center-field wall, putting San Diego ahead, 2-1. "Templeton's hit," Tony Gwynn recalled, "gave the Padres the lead for the first time and confidence that they could come from behind." Templeton then scampered home on Alan Wiggins's single.

In the next inning, the Padres erupted for four more runs. Tony Gwynn singled and scored on Graig Nettles's base hit. After replacing Chicago starter Dennis Eckersley, George Frazier gave up a single to Terry Kennedy and a towering three-run homer to Kevin McReynolds. Ed Whitson, meanwhile, baffled the Cubs with his palmball and fastball after the third inning, allowing only one run and five hits. Reliever Goose Gossage struck out two batters in the ninth inning to preserve the victory. "This was the biggest game of my life," Whitson admitted. "I just went as hard as I could as long as I could." Steve Garvey acknowledged, "The cheering crowd won the game for us that night." Templeton predicted, "We will play hard Saturday. I know it will be a tough, hard-fought game but we're ready."

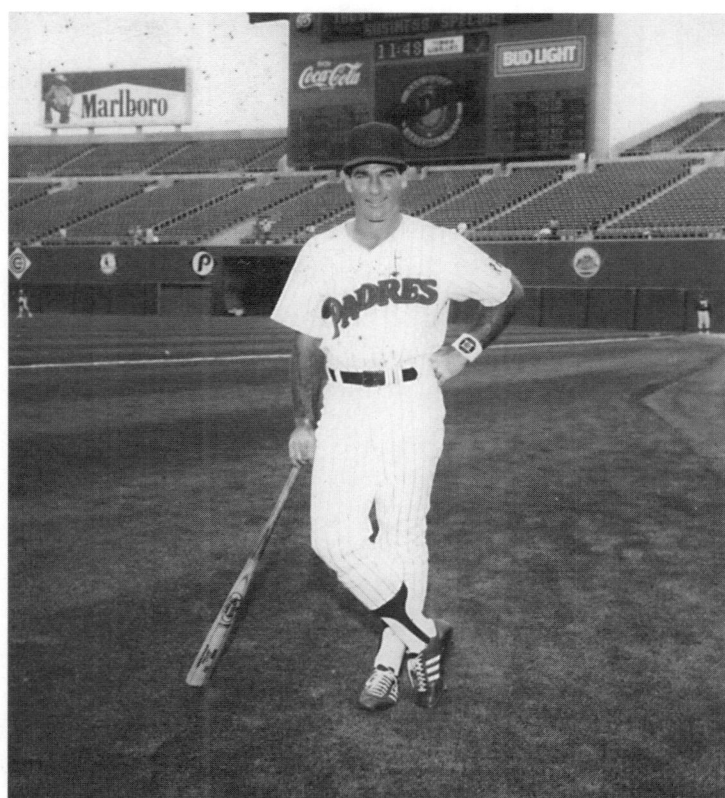

Steve Garvey played first base for the Padres from 1983 through 1987.

Thrilling Game 4 ranks among the most memorable in Championship Series history. San Diego fans still reminisce about the Padres' dramatic 7-5 victory on October 6. Steve Garvey enjoyed the most legendary game of his illustrious major league career with four hits and five RBI. For the initial time in the series, San Diego tallied first with two runs off Scott Sanderson in the third inning. Garry Templeton

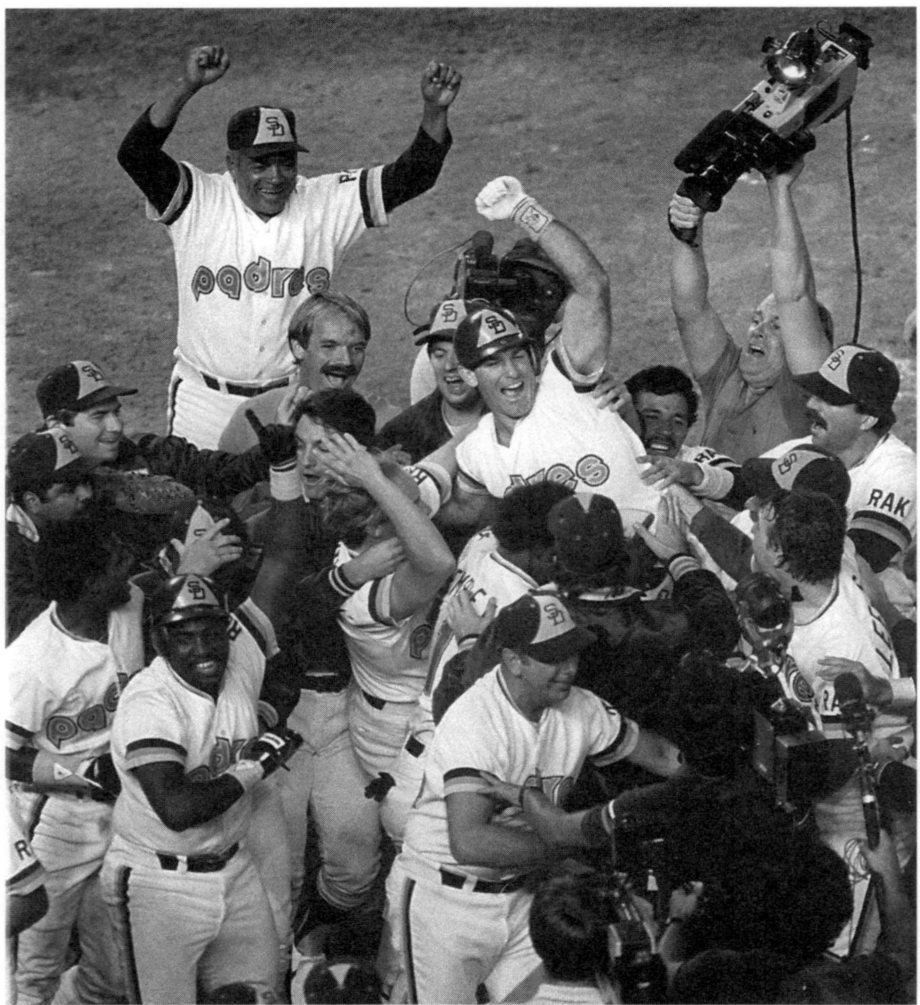

Steve Garvey, center, is carried triumphantly off the field by his teammates after hitting a game-winning home run in the ninth inning to beat the Chicago Cubs, 7-5, in Game 4 of the National League Playoffs, October 6, 1984, in San Diego.

singled, stole second base, and advanced to third base on Alan Wiggins' single. Tony Gwynn's sacrifice fly brought home Templeton, while Garvey's double scored Wiggins.

The Cubs responded with three runs against Tim Lollar in the fourth frame. After Gary Matthews walked, Jody Davis and Leon Durham clouted consecutive home runs with two outs to put Chicago ahead, 3-2. In the next inning, the Padres knotted the score. Pinch-hitter Tim Flannery singled, advanced to third base on a bunt and groundout, and came home on Steve Garvey's single up the middle. San Diego regained the lead in the seventh inning when pinch-hitter Bobby Brown walked with one out and stole second base. Reliever Tim Stoddard walked Tony Gwynn intentionally. Garvey singled to left field, scoring Brown and moving Gwynn to third base. Gwynn scored on a passed ball by Jody Davis.

The Cubs tied the score, 5-5, in the eighth inning off normally reliable reliever Goose Gossage. Ryne Sandberg reached first base on an infield hit, stole second base as Gary Matthews struck out, and scored on Keith Moreland's base hit. With two outs, Jody Davis plated Moreland with a double off the center field wall for his third hit of the game. Chicago loaded the bases with two out in the ninth frame. After Dernier doubled, Matthews was walked intentionally. Craig Lefferts hit Henry Cotto with a pitch, loading the bases. Ron Cey grounded weakly to second base to thwart the rally.

Wiggins struck out to open the bottom half of the same inning. Tony Gwynn singled off reliever Lee Smith. Steve Garvey, who already had driven in three runs, clouted a Lee Smith fastball toward the right center-field bleachers. "Time stood still," Garvey observed. "It was as if all sound stopped." As the ball propelled upward, the crowd noise rose. Cubs right fielder Henry Cotto leaped high, but the ball struck the permanent wall five feet above him. Garvey's two-run blast gave the Padres an historic victory, as pandemonium broke loose in the stands and at home plate. "That was the most exciting game I've ever been a part of," Tim Flannery shouted. "Unbelievable," a teammate yelled. Garvey knew "the Padres now had the home field advantage and, if they could stay close, they could win." Garvey's five RBIs that game gave him 20 for his National League Championship Series career, breaking slugger Reggie

Jackson's major league record for a league championship series.

Steve Garvey's heroics knotted the National League Championship Series at two games apiece. The normally restrained San Diego fans bubbled with excitement in anticipation of the decisive fifth game. The Padres faced Rick Sutcliffe, who had logged 15 consecutive victories and had defeated San Diego three straight times. Sutcliffe pitched superbly the first five innings, allowing just singles to Terry Kennedy in the second inning and Garry Templeton in the fifth frame. Padre starter Eric Show did not fare as well, surrendering a two-run homer to Leon Durham in the first frame and a solo leadoff blast by Jody Davis in the second inning. Andy Hawkins replaced Show with one out in the second inning. San Diego relievers Hawkins, Dave Dravecky, Craig Lefferts, and Goose Gossage, however, prevented further damage.

The Padres rallied for two runs in the sixth frame. After Alan Wiggins reached safely on a bunt, Tony Gwynn singled to left field. "I knew we could get to him," remarked Gwynn, "because he was getting his pitches up. He was wilting, and you could see it happening." Rick Sutcliffe walked Garvey to load the bases. Graig Nettles's sacrifice fly to center field scored Wiggins. Gary Matthews made a diving catch of Terry Kennedy's line drive to left field. Gwynn tagged up at third and crossed the plate with the second run.

San Diego exploded for four more runs the next inning. Carmelo Martinez walked on four consecutive pitches and moved to second base on Garry Templeton's sacrifice. Pinch-hitter Tim Flannery hit a ground ball between the legs of first baseman Leon Durham, permitting Martinez to score the tying run. After Alan Wiggins sliced a check-swing single into short left field, Tony Gwynn lined a one-hopper toward second baseman Ryne Sandberg. The ball took a bad hop and bounced over Sandberg's shoulder into right center field for a double, plating Flannery and Wiggins. Gwynn took third on the throw home and scored on Steve Garvey's single off Rick Sutcliffe, putting the Padres ahead, 6-3. Gossage shut out the Cubs the final two frames to give San Diego its first National League pennant. "Once the fifth game was tied," Jack McKeon declared, "there was no way we would lose the game." "I was crying during the last two innings," Tim Flannery confessed. "I was looking around, asking guys not to kid me, but I was just so overwhelmed."

Craig Lefferts pitched for the Padres from 1984 through July 1987 and 1990 through August 1992.

Bedlam reigned as the city and its team celebrated. Padre teammates mobbed Goose Gossage, while the normally taciturn San Diego fans poured onto the playing field and partied long into the Sunday night. Ray Kroc unfortunately had not lived long enough to witness this great moment in Padres history. Owner Joan Kroc gladly accepted the Championship Series trophy, beaming, "We just want to dedicate this victory to Ray." The National League pennant marked the culmination of a long elusive dream for the beleaguered Padres. The Padres, an expansion team in 1969, never had finished higher than fourth in the National League West before 1984. San Diego batters and relievers had performed brilliantly in the historic National League Championship Series comeback.

"The Padres," general manager Jack McKeon boasted, "played the greatest baseball in franchise history." Steve Garvey earned National League Championship Series Most Valuable Player accolades, batting .400 with eight hits and seven RBIs. Tony Gwynn finished closely behind at .368, hitting three doubles and four singles. Garry Templeton, Alan Wiggins, and Kevin McReynolds, who missed the final game with a broken wrist, all batted at least .300 while combining for 14 hits. Reliever Craig Lefferts hurled four shutout innings and earned two victories, while reliever Dave Dravecky allowed only two hits in six innings. "Everyone," Gwynn recalled, "did his share. Confidence was the big key."

San Diego's magic did not extend to the World Series, which the Detroit Tigers captured four games to one. The Tigers had quickly broken out of the starting gate like the Padres, winning their first nine games. Detroit dominated the American League East Division race from the outset, posting an amazing 35-5 mark for the best 40-game start in major league history. The Tigers had finished their dream campaign with an 104-58 regular season mark, 15 games ahead of the second-place Toronto Blue Jays. Starting pitchers Jack Morris, Dan Petry, and Milt Wilcox had combined for 54 victories, while reliever Willie Hernandez enjoyed an American League Cy Young Award season. Right fielder Kirk Gibson and catcher Lance Parrish had supplied considerable offensive power. Shortstop Alan Trammell and second baseman Lou Whitaker starred both offensively and defensively. Detroit had swept the Kansas City Royals in the American League Championship Series and entered the World Series as the favorite.

A record 57,908 fans packed Jack Murphy Stadium on October 9 for Game 1, which the Padres lost, 3-2. Detroit scored once in the first inning off Mark Thurmond. Lou Whitaker led off with a double and came home on Alan Trammell's single. San Diego seized the lead with two runs off Jack Morris in the same frame. Steve Garvey and Graig Nettles both singled and scampered home on Terry Kennedy's double into the rightfield corner. The Padres put two runners aboard in the third frame without scoring and clung to a 2-1 lead until the fifth inning. After Lance Parrish doubled down the leftfield line, left fielder Larry Herndon clouted a two-run homer on a 3-1 pitch into the right-field stands.

Nettles and Kennedy opened the sixth inning with singles, but Morris then struck out Bobby Brown, Carmelo Martinez, and Garry Templeton in succession. Designated hitter Kurt Bevacqua lined a ball into the rightfield corner to begin the seventh frame, but stumbled rounding second base and was thrown out trying to stretch the double into a triple. "Everyone has peaks and valleys in his life," Bevacqua stated. "I sure as hell didn't stumble on purpose in the first game. And I don't think I stumbled because I was running too quick. It was just one of those things." Morris fanned nine San Diego batters while going the distance for the Tigers victory. The Detroit right-hander became the first starter ever to complete a World Series game spanning 24 contests for manager Sparky Anderson.

The Padres rebounded the next night to take Game 2, 5-3. Detroit scored three times in the first inning, knocking out starter Ed Whitson. Consecutive singles by Lou Whitaker, Alan Trammell, and Kirk Gibson on Whitson's first three pitches produced the first run. Trammell crossed the plate on Lance Parrish's sacrifice fly. Third baseman Darrell Evans plated Gibson with a looping single. The Padres countered the same frame with one tally off Dan Petry. Alan Wiggins bunted for a single and eventually scored on Graig Nettles's sacrifice fly. The Padres added a run in the fourth inning on singles by Kurt Bevacqua and Garry Templeton and Bobby Brown's groundout.

San Diego rallied for three runs the next frame. After Nettles walked, Terry Kennedy reached base on an infield hit. His one-hop grounder took a bad hop and bounced off the chest of second baseman Lou Whitaker. Bevacqua atoned for his baserunning blunder the previous night by delivering a three-run homer on Petry's 0-1 pitch into the leftfield bleachers. The .200 hitter, with only one round-tripper during the regular season, declared, "I knew I wasn't going to be thrown out at third on that one." He turned a pirouette when the ball left the park, pumping his fist skyward, and then blew kisses to the fans on his magical sojourn around the bases. Reliever Andy Hawkins entered with

Kurt Bevacqua played infield and outfield for the Padres from 1979 through August 1980 and 1982 through 1985.

two outs in the first inning and allowed Detroit only one hit in 5.1 innings to earn the Padre victory, while Craig Lefferts preserved the lead by striking out five Tigers in the final three frames.

Detroit swept the final three World Series games at Tiger Stadium. San Diego pitchers set a dubious record by walking 11 Tigers in the Padres' 5-2 loss in Game 3 on October 12. Detroit ignited for four runs in the second inning. Chet Lemon singled off Tim Lollar and advanced to second base on a wild pitch. Third baseman Marty Castillo, who batted only .234 with four homers in 1984, belted a two-run homer on a 1-2 pitch into the left-field upper deck. Lou Whitaker walked and scored on Alan Trammell's double into the left-field corner. Lollar walked two more batters, giving him four in just 1.2 innings, to load the bases before Greg Booker relieved him. Booker promptly walked Larry Herndon, allowing Trammell to tally the fourth Tigers run. Each team scored once in the third frame. After Alan Wiggins and Tony Gwynn singled, Steve Garvey grounded out to produce the first San Diego run. In the bottom of the same inning, Padres reliever Greg Booker walked three Tigers to load the bases. Greg Harris replaced Booker and struck Kirk Gibson on the foot, scoring Darrell Evans.

Milt Wilcox pitched the first six innings for Detroit, surrendering only one run on seven hits. San Diego tallied one run off Tigers reliever Bill Scherrer in the seventh inning, when Tony Gwynn reached on an infield single. Steve Garvey doubled when left fielder Larry Herndon just missed making a shoestring catch and Graig Nettles hit a sacrifice fly to center field. Closer Willie Hernandez relieved Scherrer with two outs in the seventh inning. Center fielder Chet Lemon made a twisting, turning catch with his back to the plate on a line drive by Terry Kennedy to deep center field to end the inning. Hernandez retired six of the last seven batters to insure Detroit's victory. The Tigers managed only three hits after the second inning. The 14 baserunners stranded by the Tigers tied a single-game World Series mark, while the 24 baserunners left by both clubs shattered the previous record.

Game 4, won the next afternoon by Detroit, 4-2, featured the Alan Trammell and Jack Morris show. In the first inning, the Tigers quickly jumped to a 2-0 lead. After Lou Whitaker reached base on Alan Wiggins's wide throw to first, Trammell clouted a home run off Eric Show high into the left-field bleachers. Terry Kennedy's second-inning round-tripper into the right-field upper deck bleachers against Morris halved Detroit's lead. The Tigers widened the margin to 4-1 with two insurance runs off Show in the third frame. Whitaker singled to right field and scored on Trammell's second home run of the contest, a towering drive on a 1-1 pitch into the left field upper deck. Morris's split-fingered fastball stymied San Diego hitters with just four hits the first eight innings, but the Padres nicked him for one run in the final frame. Steve Garvey doubled into the left-field corner with one out, advanced to third on a Nettles' grounder, and scored when Morris uncorked a wild pitch. Kennedy lined to right fielder Kirk Gibson to end the game. Morris became the first pitcher since Mike Torrez of the 1977 New York Yankees to hurl two complete games in the same World Series. San Diego wasted fine relief performances by Dave Dravecky, Craig Lefferts, and Goose Gossage, who blanked the Tigers the final five innings.

Detroit captured the World Series finale, 8-4, to take its first title since 1968. The Tigers blitzed to a three-run lead off Mark Thurmond in the first inning. After Lou Whitaker lined a single to right field, Trammell forced Whitaker at second base on a grounder to shortstop Templeton. Kirk Gibson, a former All-American wide receiver in football at Michigan State University, clouted a towering two-run homer into the right centerfield upper deck. After Lance Parrish lined a single to left field, Larry Herndon blooped a single to center field. Chet Lemon smashed a single through the hole into left field, scoring Parrish before reliever Andy Hawkins shut the door. In the third inning, the Padres manufactured a run against Dan Petry. Bobby Brown reached base on an infield chop single behind second base. Brown advanced to second base on Alan Wiggins's bouncer to Whitaker and to third base on Gwynn's grounder to Trammell. Trammell knocked down Steve Garvey's smash to deep short but could not make a play, and Brown scored. In the next frame, Kurt Bevacqua walked. Garry Templeton was credited with a double when Herndon fell down after fielding his hit to left field, moving Bevacqua to third base. Bevacqua scored on Bobby Brown's hard liner to center fielder Chet Lemon, while Templeton crossed the plate on Alan Wiggins's loop single to center field to deadlock the game, 3-3.

Detroit regained the lead, 4-3, in the fifth inning. Kirk Gibson lined a single off Graig Nettles's glove into short left field and advanced to second on Lance

Parrish's towering fly to left fielder Carmelo Martinez. After Herndon walked, Craig Lefferts replaced Hawkins and walked Lemon to load the bases. Gibson scampered home on pinch-hitter Rusty Kuntz's sacrifice fly to short right field. Tony Gwynn lost sight of the ball in the clouds, forcing second baseman Alan Wiggins to catch it with his back to the infield. The Tigers added an insurance run with one out in the seventh frame when Lance Parrish drove a Goose Gossage 0-1 fastball into the left-field bleachers for a home run. In the eighth inning, Kurt Bevacqua clouted a solo round-tripper on an 0-1 pitch off Willie Hernandez into the left-field upper deck for his second World Series homer, reducing Detroit's lead to 5-4. The Tigers, however, ignited for three runs off Gossage in their half of the eighth frame. After Marty Castillo walked, Lou Whitaker reached base on a sacrifice bunt when Templeton was not on the bag to take Nettles's throw to second base. With one out, Gibson delivered a towering three-run homer deep into the right-field upper deck. The slugger's second round-tripper of the contest gave Detroit an insurmountable 8-4 lead. Hernandez preserved the 8-4 victory, giving the Tigers the World Series title.

Detroit culminated its dream season in convincing fashion, demonstrating in the World Series why it had been the best major-league baseball team in 1984. The Tigers entered the World Series well rested and brimming with confidence, having swept the Kansas City Royals in the American League Championship Series. Alan Trammell, the World Series Most Valuable Player, led Detroit with nine hits and a .450 batting average, homered twice, and recorded six RBIs. Slugger Kirk Gibson batted .333, added two home runs, and paced the Tigers with seven RBIs. Jack Morris won both of his starts, fanning 13 Padres. Tigers skipper Sparky Anderson became the first major-league manager to direct both National League and American League clubs to World Series titles. "Detroit," Ed Whitson concluded, "had been consistent all year." Garry Templeton concurred, "Detroit had an outstanding year. They had everything."

Dave Dravecky pitched for the Padres from 1982 through July 1987.

San Diego batted a respectable .265 in the World Series and especially fared well against Dan Petry, but abysmal starting pitching doomed the Padres. Kurt Bevacqua unexpectedly starred for San Diego, batting .412 with seven hits, two home runs, and four RBIs. "Bevacqua," announcer Dave Campbell observed, "thrived on pressure and enjoyed five days of fame." Alan Wiggins led the Padres with eight hits and batted .364, while Garry Templeton also hit over .300. By contrast, Tony Gwynn, Terry Kennedy, Steve Garvey, Carmelo Martinez, and Bobby Brown struggled at the plate. San Diego also did not match Detroit ace pitcher Jack Morris. Padre starters Mark Thurmond, Eric Show, Tim Lollar, and Ed Whitson all performed poorly, allowing nearly two earned runs per inning. Tigers batters shelled the starting quartet for 17 earned runs in only 10.1 innings. "The San Diego starting pitchers," Dave Campbell lamented, "could not survive the first three innings and always left the Padres behind." Relievers Andy Hawkins, Craig Lefferts, Greg Harris, and Dave Dravecky pitched superbly, limiting the Tigers to just one run and nine hits in 28 innings. Reserve infielder Luis Salazar observed, "We got amazing help from our bullpen."

Other factors influenced the World Series outcome. The National League Championship Series had drained the San Diego players both physically and emotionally. The Padres lacked the same degree of intensity in the World Series. Steve Garvey acknowledged, "The Padres had an emotional letdown against Detroit." Slugger Kevin McReynolds missed the entire World Series with a broken wrist, leaving a major power vacuum. In four National League Championship Series games against the Chicago Cubs, McReynolds had batted .300 with four RBI. "McReynolds's injury," Ed Whitson moaned, "killed us. It took power away from us." On the positive side, the National League Championship Series and World

Series had given the Padres valuable playoff experience. Garvey, Goose Gossage, Bruce Bochy, and Graig Nettles were the only San Diego players with previous post season experience. "Our young players," manager Dick Williams observed, "matured in the playoffs; there are no unseasoned players on this team anymore."

Williams made winning the World Series San Diego's main goal for the 1985 season. Vice president Jack McKeon, disappointed with the deplorable postseason performance by Padre starting hurlers, hired Galen Cisco to replace Norm Sherry as pitching coach and sought to improve the Padres' starting rotation during the off season. Cisco, formerly pitching coach under McKeon with the Kansas City Royals, had tutored major-league hurlers for 14 years. McKeon hoped to land Chicago Cubs free agent Rick Sutcliffe, but the ace starter remained in the Windy City. San Diego on December 6 acquired LaMarr Hoyt, 1983 American League Cy Young Award winner, from the Chicago White Sox to strengthen its starting rotation. The Padres dealt pitchers Tim Lollar and Bill Long, third baseman Luis Salazar, and shortstop Ozzie Guillen to the White Sox and also acquired pitchers Kevin Kristan and Todd Simmons, who were assigned to the minor leagues. Hoyt had slumped from a 24-10 record in 1983 to a disappointing 13-18 mark in 1984, but still ranked among the major leagues' premier hurlers. "It was a good trade," McKeon claimed. "It was not Hoyt's fault that the team slumped in 1985."

The New York Yankees, however, signed free agent Ed Whitson on December 27, leaving a vacuum in the San Diego starting rotation. Whitson had enjoyed his best season in 1984 with a 14-8 mark and 3.24 ERA and had won the crucial third game of the National League Championship Series. The Padres on January 3 signed utility infielder-outfielder Jerry Royster of the Atlanta Braves as a free agent, giving them a late-inning replacement for the aging Graig Nettles. Five days later, reliever Tim Stoddard, who had won or saved 17 games for the Chicago Cubs in 1984, joined the San Diego bullpen as a free agent. San Diego fans hoped that the Padres might be on the verge of a dynasty. The Padres' front office possessed seemingly unlimited financial resources to secure veteran players. "With everything we had going for us, we could have become one of the great franchises in baseball," Goose Gossage claimed.

Part III

The Rollercoaster Years

[1985-2001]

11

The Declining Years

[1985-1987]

The Padres were one step away from the World Championship in 1984. With the exception of Steve Garvey and Graig Nettles, they were a young team which had the potential to be together for years to come.

The Padres also gave a five-year contract to one of their 1984 players. Tony Gwynn signed the contract worth $4 million, which also included an option for the 1990 season.

Confidence in the Padres was high. The stadium had dodged one noticeable change and undergone another. On November 6, voters of the City of San Diego rejected Proposition D, which would have changed the name of Jack Murphy Stadium back to San Diego Stadium. In early December, the Padres announced plans for a larger scoreboard for 1985— a $5.5 million piece of equipment with instant replays, close-ups, animation, and highlights of other games. The DiamondVision display screen measured 26 feet by 35 feet, while the scoreboard itself measured 60 feet by 100 feet, somewhat larger than the previous 34 foot by 82 foot scoreboard.

The visual enhancements came at a good time, since the Padres' increased popularity meant more fans sitting in the more remote seats. The Padres' 1985 schedule was announced on November 28, 1994, and the April 15 home opener was sold out by December 12.

The Padres also introduced a new team logo and unveiled new uniforms in January. Pinstripes replaced the solid brown jerseys, which had caused complaints from team members. The Padres played their final home game in their old uniforms in an April 7 exhibition game against Minnesota in Jack Murphy Stadium which ended in a 2-2 tie after 13 innings.

Not only did the Padres have an optimistic view of their 1985 season, but so did the gambling industry. Harrah's selected the Padres and Cubs as cofavorites to win the National League pennant, giving each 4-1 odds.

Take out the word "favorites," and that translates into a 20 percent chance.

The first unpleasant surprise of spring training came March 3, when Carmelo Martinez left for the trainer's room. Martinez had injured his left hand during the off season and hadn't disclosed it to the team. On April 1, Martinez was placed on the 15-day disabled list.

On March 10, a record crowd for an intrasquad game came to Desert Sun Stadium in Yuma, Arizona. The 4,720 in attendance saw Jerry Royster's willingness to hustle when he dove for a ground ball. An X-ray the following day showed a chip fracture in Royster's left index finger from the contact with the ground.

Kurt Bevacqua and Bruce Bochy escaped injury March 25, when a tire on Bevacqua's car blew east of Gila Bend, Arizona. A knee injury to Alan Wiggins at the end of March created the possibility of his lack of availability for ten days.

The Padres opened their 1985 season in San Francisco April 9. Hoyt pitched seven innings, receiving no decision in the game the Giants won, 4-3, on a single in the bottom of the ninth. Although the Padres lost, a major goal was fulfilled as Hoyt did not issue a walk during his work.

The Padres evened their record at 1-1 the following day when Show pitched a four-hitter. He struck out 11 Giants, walked none, and threw first-pitch strikes to 26 of 30 batters.

Andy Hawkins won the Padres' next game at Atlanta, retiring the first twelve Braves batters and getting out of a bases-loaded, one-out jam in the fifth.

Hoyt's second start of the year did not bring him any better luck. In four innings, he allowed three Braves runs and five hits. Padres hitters did not help much in the 3-1 loss, but Braves second baseman Glenn Hubbard tied a major-league record with 12 assists.

The Padres entered their April 15 home opener with a 2-3 record. Martinez and Wiggins had not played in any of the first five games, but Martinez came off the disabled list for the home opener and Wiggins made his debut in the lineup. Before what was at the time the largest regular season crowd ever, the Padres defeated the San Francisco Giants, 8-3. Martinez homered twice, including a grand slam in the seventh, and Show improved his record to 2-0. On the negative side, Garvey's record of 193 consecutive games at first base without an error ended in the ninth inning when he dropped a foul popup off the bat of Bob Brenly.

Hawkins pitched the following day's game on three days' rest, but managed a victory in the 2-1 win. He did not pitch again until April 22, when Hawkins allowed four hits in the 5-3 win, and he and three relievers retired the final 24 Atlanta Braves.

On April 25, Wiggins did not show up for the team's practice. He had not notified the team of his absence, nor did he contact the team afterwards. Wiggins had been slumping at the plate; he was hitless in his last 22 at-bats and had one hit in his last 31 at-bats. Two days later, Wiggins checked into a drug treatment center. On May 4, the Padres suspended him for the rest of the season. Wiggins, having undergone treatment at the Hazelden Foundation in Center City, Minnesota, returned to San Diego May 29, and on June 10 he was cleared by the major league panel on drug abuse. On June 18, he agreed to a 20-day rehabilitation assignment. Since he was a two-time offender, Padres owner Joan Kroc and Padres president Ballard Smith had no desire to let him return to the team. On June 27, Wiggins was traded to the Baltimore Orioles for pitcher Roy Lee Jackson and a player to be named later.

Los Angeles Dodgers' pitching was another problem facing the Padres in April. On April 18, Fernando Valenzuela threw a two-hitter in a 5-0 Dodgers win in San Diego. Three days later, Orel Hershiser had a no-hitter until Gwynn's seventh-inning double and ended up with a two-hit shutout. In Los Angeles on April 26, Hershiser allowed only a single and a walk to Gwynn, who was erased both times to allow Hershiser to face only 27 batters.

On April 28, the Padres had a somewhat better result. Valenzuela threw eight shutout innings, and his strikeout of reliever Craig Lefferts to end the eighth was not only his 10th strikeout of the game, but also extended his streak at the start of the season to 41 innings without an earned run, breaking the 1912 record of 40.2 innings by Hooks Wiltse. Valenzuela extended his streak to 41.1 innings before Gwynn's one-out home run in the ninth gave the Padres a 1-0 win.

Hawkins had better luck. On April 27 against Los Angeles, he left for pinch hitter Kurt Bevacqua, who broke a 2-2 tie with a two-run double. On May 3, the Padres returned to Wrigley Field in Chicago for the first time since the 1984 playoffs, and Hawkins outdueled Sutcliffe for the win. On May 8, a day after a 12-2 win in St. Louis coupled with a Dodgers loss put the Padres in first place by half a game, Hawkins took the mound in another Padres 12-2 win, this time against Pittsburgh in San Diego, and did not walk a batter in eight innings pitched. A 6-2 win in St. Louis May 14, in which the Padres tied a club record with 22 assists, gave Hawkins his seventh straight win.

The Padres racked up 17 hits, including the 2,000th career hit of Graig Nettles, in an 8-3 road win May 19 over the Montreal Expos to give Hawkins an 8-0 record. On May 25, he took a shutout into the ninth in a win in Philadelphia.

The Padres also won the following day against the Phillies, giving them wins in seven straight games, 10 of their last 12, and 13 of their last 16. The streak ended the next day with a 10-9 loss, and the Padres went on a three-game losing streak. But on May 30, Hawkins snapped the streak with the help of Martinez, who hit two home runs. The home win over Montreal gave Hawkins a 10-0 record in his first ten games of the year.

On June 4, Hawkins fell behind 3-0 at home before retiring 14 of the next 15 Phillies batters. A two-out, two-run double by McReynolds gave the Padres a 6-5 win, but Hawkins had his first no-decision of the year.

The following day, Hawkins became the first Padre to earn National League Pitcher of the Month honors since Gaylord Perry in September 1978. Hawkins was 6-0 in May with a 2.72 earned run average in 43 innings pitched.

Hawkins improved to 11-0 on June 9 in Cincinnati, relegating Mario Soto to an 8-4 record by allowing one run in seven innings pitched. Hawkins exited the June 14 game at San Francisco with a lead, but Goose Gossage was unable to hold a ninth-inning lead and the Giants ended up with an 11-inning win.

On June 19 at Los Angeles, Hawkins's streak came to an end. Pedro Guerrero led off the bottom of the seventh with a home run to break a 1-1 tie, and the Dodgers scored three more runs in the seventh en route to a 5-1 win.

By that time, LaMarr Hoyt had a win streak of his own. Hoyt had been shelled during a 14-4 St. Louis Cardinals win May 15, but on May 20, he pitched a four-hit shutout in Shea Stadium against Dwight Gooden of the New York Mets. He then posted wins in his next seven starts before a no-decision against Houston July 1. Hoyt won his next three, giving him 11 consecutive wins over 12 starts. The streak came to an end July 28 against St. Louis, as Darrell Porter touched up Hoyt for a two-run double in the first and a solo home run in the fourth.

Hoyt's 11-game winning streak tied Hawkins for the team record, but Hoyt actually won 12 games in a row. As the manager who won the previous year's National League pennant, Dick Williams managed the National League in the 1985 All-Star game. That gave Williams the right to select pitchers, reserves, and substitutes for injured players. The fans selected the starters, and Garvey, Nettles, and Gwynn were voted to play at least the first three innings. Williams named Hoyt and Gossage to the squad; Hawkins was nursing an injured finger and was given the full break. Deacon Jones, Jack Krol, and Ozzie Virgil were named as the batting practice battery. Williams added Garry Templeton as a reserve, and, when planned starter Gary Carter was injured, Williams selected Terry Kennedy as Carter's replacement.

Hoyt started the game for the National League, holding the American League to two hits in three innings and allowing only one unearned run, on Kennedy's error. He was named the game's Most Valuable Player in the 6-1 win.

Kennedy tied the game in the second with an RBI single off Jack Morris, and Garvey drove in a run with a single against Morris in the third. Templeton added a pinch-hit single in the fourth, while Nettles and Gwynn were hitless. Gossage was effective in relief as the National League pitchers allowed a total of only five hits throughout the nine innings.

Williams seemed to be in good position to manage in the 1986 All-Star game. On July 4, the Padres had a five-game lead over the Los Angeles Dodgers. On July 7, the lead was four games. Then the Chicago Cubs won three of four against the Padres, including the completion of a May 5 suspended game, while the Dodgers swept Pittsburgh. On July 11, John Tudor of the St. Louis Cardinals shut out the Padres while the Dodgers defeated the Cubs to move to within half a game.

Hoyt's win on July 12 kept the Padres in first, but a Dodgers win over the Cubs on July 13, coupled with a Cardinals win over San Diego, moved the Padres into second place. The Padres and Dodgers both lost the following day to maintain the half-game margin going into the All-Star break.

Williams, anticipating an August 6 strike date set by the players and aiming to be in first by the date the season might end, dropped Ed Wojna from the rotation

Dick Williams managed the Padres to their first National League pennant in 1984.

after the All-Star break to return to a four-man rotation. The Padres won their first three games in the second half of the season, but so did the Dodgers. A six-game losing streak then left the Padres 4 1/2 games behind the Dodgers and only one game ahead of Cincinnati.

On July 31, Gossage, who had 21 saves at the time, was flown home because of a badly swollen knee. The diagnosis came back as ligament damage requiring arthroscopic surgery. A 12 millimeter by 6 millimeter piece of cartilage had pulled away from his femur.

On August 2, a Padres loss and a Cincinnati Reds doubleheader split placed both teams five games behind the Dodgers. Both teams lost the following day, but, on August 4, Houston defeated San Diego while the Reds defeated Los Angeles, putting Cincinnati in sole possession of second place.

On August 5, the Reds defeated the Padres in the last prestrike game. The loss gave the Padres a 3-11 record in their last 14 games and a 9-19 record since July 4, along with a 55-51 record for the season.

With Gossage on the disabled list, the Padres called up pitcher Gene Walter from Las Vegas. They also demoted outfielder Jerry Davis and called up pitcher Lance McCullers. Both impressed management and fans during their 1985 stays in San Diego and remained on the roster for the rest of the year.

The strike was settled shortly after it began, and San Diego won its next three games to move into a tie for second place with the Reds. Then the Padres split four games with the Reds in San Diego. They took two of three from Atlanta and swept the Expos in Montreal. A doubleheader sweep of the New York Mets on August 23 gave the Padres five straight wins and 12 wins in their last 16 games—a 2 1/2 game cushion over the Reds.

The Padres lost six of their next eight games, allowing the Reds to move into second place September 2. San Diego lost two more to the Mets, as Gary Carter became the 13th player in major-league history to hit five home runs in two games.

The Padres closed out a 2-7 homestand to play four games in Cincinnati on September 9-12. The Reds started the series one game ahead of San Diego, and Reds player-manager Pete Rose started the series tied for the all-time career record for base hits. Rose sat out the first game, but the Reds earned a 2-1 victory with a ninth-inning run. Hoyt, who had missed a handful of starts with tendonitis in his right shoulder and had not pitched since August 18, won the second game with the help of Gossage, who earned his first save since the surgery, and Rose was held hitless in four at-bats.

At 8:01 p.m. Eastern Daylight Time on September 11, 1985, Pete Rose singled off Eric Show for his 4,192nd career hit. Rose also had his 4,193rd hit and scored both Reds runs in the 2-1 win.

The Reds closed out the series with another 2-1 win, securing their hold on second place. San Diego then played Houston, which entered the series two games behind the Padres for third.

The Houston Astros swept the three games, putting them a game ahead of the Padres at the end of the series. The sweep also reduced the Padres' record to 71-71, their first time at .500 since they were 8-8 on April 26.

The Padres hovered around .500 for the next several games and were mathematically eliminated from the division title on September 23. The Padres won their next four games, lost to Atlanta, and won their next three to secure a winning record for 1985.

The season ended with three home games against the Astros, who were one game behind the Padres. The

Padres won the first game, 4-3, but the Astros earned 9-3 and 6-4 wins in the final two games to share third place with the Padres.

The 1984 Padres were the second expansion team to win a pennant without having previously finished first in the division. The other such team was the 1969 New York Mets. In 1970 the Mets slumped to third place with a record of 83-79. In 1985 the Padres also ended up with an 83-79 record.

"We had some guys that did a pretty good job pitching, but we didn't live up to the expectations of the '84 team," pitching coach Galen Cisco said years later. "You win with pitching and defense, and we had some holes that we didn't cover and it showed up at the end of the year."

Hawkins ended the season with an 18-8 record and a 3.15 ERA. Hoyt was 16-8 with a 3.47 ERA, and Dave Dravecky was 13-11 with a 2.93 ERA. Gwynn led the offense with a .317 batting average, fourth in the National League. The absence of Wiggins was felt on the base paths. The entire team only had 59 steals in 1985.

Garvey became the first Padre to play every game in a season, and the team set a major-league record for most 1-0 victories without a 1-0 loss, taking seven of the one-run shutouts during the year.

In November, the Padres fired third base coach Ozzie Virgil. The following month, Joan Kroc said that Williams would be retained as the manager despite the desire of Smith and general manager Jack McKeon to replace Williams. Kroc also offered Virgil his job back. Harry Dunlop, the bullpen coach in 1985, was reassigned as a roving minor-league instructor.

The Padres opened camp on February 23, and Williams and Virgil did not arrive prior to that day. The following day, Williams announced that he would not return as the team's manager. Williams left the team with a 337-311 record in four years.

Virgil joined Williams in resigning. Steve Boros, who in 1985 was the team's coordinator of minor-league instruction, was named manager. Dunlop was brought back to work the dugout with Boros, Krol was moved from first base to third base, and Sandy Alomar, a coach with the Charleston, South Carolina farm club in 1985, was named first base coach.

The winter meetings were held in San Diego for the first time since 1963, but McKeon failed to make a trade for the first time in six years as the Padres' general manager. The Padres selected second baseman "Bip" Roberts from Pittsburgh in the Rule V draft, hoping that the player who stole 128 bases in four minor-league seasons would solve their speed problem as well as their second base vacancy.

Free agent pickings were slim, so the Padres saved their money. They were able to pick up pinch hitter Dane Iorg, and they made no effort to re-sign Bevacqua, Al Bumbry, or Miguel Dilone. The Padres, along with several other National League teams, decided to use a 24-man roster for 1986, eliminating a spot taken by pinch-hitting specialists. Bevacqua went to camp as a non-roster player, but was cut March 24.

Another off-season action made Willie McCovey the first former Padres player to be elected to the National Baseball Hall of Fame. McCovey received 346 votes from the 425 ballots, more than the 319 needed to be placed in Cooperstown.

Spring training looked optimistic. McKeon called the team's rookies "the deepest crop of rookies we've had in my six springs here." But the Padres were soon to lose a veteran.

On February 10, U.S. Customs officials detained LaMarr Hoyt at the U.S.-Mexico border after finding three grams of marijuana, 79 Valium tablets, and 46 Quaaludes. He received a $200 fine and surrendered the drugs. On February 18, Hoyt was stopped for running a red light. The police officer smelled marijuana on his clothing and searched the pitcher, finding marijuana and a switchblade. On February 27, Hoyt entered a treatment facility to evaluate a possible problem. Hoyt completed rehabilitation March 27 and rejoined the team. On April 24, Hoyt pleaded guilty to a misdemeanor public nuisance charge and received a $375 fine and three years' probation. The District Attorney's office dropped the marijuana and switchblade possession charges.

The Los Angeles Dodgers won the first game of 1986, 2-1, and the two clubs split the first four games. San Diego then won two of three against Cincinnati and swept the Dodgers in three games. All ten of those games were one-run games, setting a record for the start of a season which was matched by the Dodgers, who had been involved in seven of the games with San Diego. The Padres' 7-3 start put them in first place.

The streak of one-run games ended with a 4-1 loss in San Francisco, and a four-game sweep by the Giants took San Diego out of first place.

Roberts was hitless for the month of April, and on May 3 an infield single gave him his first major-

Steve Boros managed the Padres in 1986.

league hit in his 21st at-bat. On May 20, Roberts pulled a groin muscle after fielding a ground ball, and six days later he was placed on the disabled list.

On June 5 against Atlanta, the Padres hit into a triple play in which Roberts broke from third on a double-play grounder. Home plate umpire Charlie Williams made no call, so Atlanta catcher Ozzie Virgil Jr. tagged Roberts and Williams called the out. Garvey, who was on deck, encouraged Williams to examine the marks through the dust where Roberts touched home plate. When Garvey said, "We've got to bear down," Williams ejected Garvey, his first ejection in 2,201 major-league, minor-league, and college games. During the lineup exchange the following day, Boros handed Williams a videotape of the play, and Williams ejected Boros. Williams also ejected Nettles in the seventh inning of that game.

A longer-lasting June 5 incident involved the ban of beer in the Padres' clubhouse. A memo signed by Ballard Smith said that the decision was made after consultation with the club's legal advisor and mentioned that liability insurance premiums had risen from $15,000 to $500,000 in the decade Smith had been with the club. The beer ban did not go over well with the players.

On June 12, the Padres acquired infielder Randy Ready from Milwaukee for a player to be named later. Four days later, Ready went home to Tucson, Arizona, where his wife was critically ill. Dorene Ready was diagnosed as having suffered an aneurysm and was in a coma. Ready did not return to the Padres for the rest of 1986.

Roberts was struggling in the big leagues, and Carmel Martinez's play caused Boros to utilize rookie John Kruk and off-season trade acquisition Marvell Wynne in the outfield in Martinez's place. A more excusable disappointment was Dane Iorg's job on the mound. With the Padres down, 14-1, on June 23, Iorg became the first field player in the Padres' history to pitch. He gave two Giants batters, including pitcher Mike LaCoss, their first major-league homers, and allowed four runs in one inning.

On July 9, the Padres made a pair of trades, both involving pitchers. Tim Stoddard was sent to the New York Yankees for Ed Whitson and Mark Thurmond was sent to the Detroit Tigers for Dave LaPoint.

The Padres took a 45-43 record into the All-Star game, but after winning their first contest in the second half, a five-game losing streak dropped them below .500.

Kruk did well as a regular, and on August 18 he was named one of two National League Players of the Week with Buddy Bell. Kruk had batted .433 with 13 hits in 30 at-bats, had homered twice, had scored three times, and had driven in five runs.

The following week, Kevin McReynolds earned that honor with 10 hits in 24 at-bats, including two doubles and three homers. He drove in 13 runs and had three game-winning RBI.

On August 29, Goose Gossage was suspended for 30 days without pay for his criticism of club management. He had called Smith and Kroc, "gutless, spineless people" in June, and in August he was quoted as saying that Smith "doesn't know anything and doesn't care." He also accused Kroc of "poisoning" the world with her cheeseburgers. The players called for Gossage's reinstatement, and the two sides agreed to arbitration. Less than 24 hours before arbiter George Nicolau was to hear the case, Gossage offered an apology and a

$25,000 donation to charity and was welcomed back to the team.

The Padres moved into last place after a loss to the Mets on September 6. The following day, the Mets swept a doubleheader. Steve Garvey sat out both games to rest a hamstring injury, ending his club record for consecutive games at 305.

On September 12, Las Vegas won the Pacific Coast League championship. The Padres called up nine players: pitchers Ray Hayward, Ed Vosberg, Jimmy Jones, and Greg Booker; catchers Benito Santiago and Mark Parent; first baseman Tim Pyznarski; shortstop Gary Green; and third baseman Randy Asadoor.

On September 20, Tony Gwynn tied a National League record with five steals in a game, becoming the fifth player since 1900 and the first since Wiggins to accomplish that feat. Although Gwynn had four hits in five at-bats, the Astros earned a 10-6 win.

The following day, Jimmy Jones threw a one-hitter in his major-league debut. He allowed a third-inning triple to Houston Astros pitcher Bob Knepper, who had been batting .093, but did not walk a batter. Jones had a hit in four trips to the plate and scored a run in the Padres' 5-0 victory, which moved the club into a tie for fifth place.

The Padres, Atlanta Braves, and Los Angeles Dodgers battled to stay out of the cellar during the final days of the season, and, after a 2-1 win over Cincinnati to close out the season, the Padres were 74-88, one game ahead of Los Angeles and 1 1/2 ahead of the Braves.

Gwynn, who finished third in the batting race, had 19 assists and earned a Gold Glove Award at the end of the season.

On October 28, Boros was reassigned to his previous position as a minor-league instructor and Larry Bowa, who posted a record of 80-62 with Las Vegas, was selected to manage the Padres.

That same day Hoyt tried to cross the San Ysidro border. An inspector noticed a large bulge in his crotch, and a pat-down search revealed 490 pills. Hoyt was released the following day after pleading not guilty to a charge of trying to import drugs. On November 13, he pleaded guilty to two federal drug charges in a plea bargain, and, on January 5, 1987, he began a 45-day prison sentence at Eglin Air Force Base, Florida.

Two days after the start of the prison sentence the Padres waived Hoyt, citing breach of contract. In February, the Major League Baseball Players Association filed a protest over his release, or more specifically over the Padres' intention not to pay the $3.2 million remaining on his contract over the next three years.

Benito Santiago's performance had made Terry Kennedy expendable, and, on October 30, Kennedy and minor-league reliever Mark Williamson were traded to Baltimore for pitcher Storm Davis. The following day, Royster, Iorg, and Bob Stoddard were released, and Roberts was dropped from the 40-man roster. On December 18, the Padres announced that Nettles and LaPoint would not be offered 1987 contracts.

On November 20, Joan Kroc went public with her decision to sell the Padres. She gave Ballard Smith the first opportunity to buy, but Smith said he was no longer interested. Steve Garvey said that he had been approached by some interested potential owners and had thought of ownership himself.

The Padres negotiated with free agents Tim Raines and Bob Horner, but were not able to come to terms with either. On December 11, they successfully negotiated an eight-player trade with the New York Mets which sent McReynolds, Walter, and minor-league infielder Adam Ging to New York, while bringing third baseman Kevin Mitchell, outfielders Stan Jefferson and Shawn Abner, and minor-league pitchers Kevin Brown and Kevin Armstrong to the Padres.

During spring training, Templeton was named the second team captain in club history and the first since Dave Winfield. Another off-field highlight in spring training was an agreement to sell the Padres to George Argyros, the owner of the Seattle Mariners. Argyros, who lived in neighboring Orange County, would buy the Padres after selling the Mariners.

The Padres opened the 1987 season with a 4-3 loss in San Francisco. They lost their first five games before a win in Cincinnati gave them a 1-5 record going into their home opener.

In the Padres' home opener on April 13, the San Francisco Giants scored two runs in the top of the first. Roger Mason then threw a full-count slider, which Marvell Wynne hit out of the park. Mason threw a fastball to Tony Gwynn on a 1-1 count which resulted in the second home run for the Padres. On a 1-1 count to Kruk, Mason threw a splitter which became the Padres' third consecutive home run to start the game, making the team the first ever to hit three home runs to lead off a game. The three hitters sent their bats to the National Baseball Hall of Fame later that week.

Marvell Wynne, Tony Gwynn, and John Kruk clouted consecutive home runs off pitcher Roger Mason in the first inning of the home opener in a 13-6 loss to the San Francisco Giants on April 13, 1987, setting a major league record for most consecutive home runs to start a game.

Jefferson was placed on the disabled list with an ankle sprain on April 15 and the Padres called up Luis Salazar, who had come to camp as a non-roster player. This time Salazar made himself useful as a utility player, including two pitching appearances in blowouts.

On May 12, Argyros rejected a $37 million offer from Oregon's Bruce Engel to buy the Mariners. On May 29, Kroc terminated negotiations with Argyros and announced that the team would not be put back on the market. Smith did not rescind his resignation as club president, and, on June 10, Chub Feeney, the 65-year-old former National League president, was named president of the Padres.

The Padres' first third of the season was dismal. They won 12 and lost 42. On May 26, Steve Garvey was placed on the disabled list for a shoulder injury, which turned out to be a ruptured tendon. He underwent surgery on May 30 and did not return for the rest of the season. He filed for free agency on November 5, after the team failed to offer him a new contract. He announced his retirement on January 13, 1988.

On May 27, Greg Gross of the Philadelphia Phillies homered off Lance McCullers for Gross's first home run since 1978, covering 1,618 at-bats. The Padres game drew 8,164 fans that night. The Major Indoor Soccer League playoff game at the San Diego Sports Arena that night drew 9,704 fans.

After their 12-42 start, the Padres won their next two games. They looked like they would win their third straight game on June 7, when they had an 11-2 lead in Atlanta after 3 1/2 innings. They held the Braves scoreless in the fourth, while scoring eight times, but the Braves scored ten runs in the sixth and seventh. The Padres tied the game in the top of the ninth, but the Braves scored a run in the bottom of the ninth for a 13-12 victory.

One player who helped the Padres break out of their slump was Gwynn, who was named the National League Player of the Week on June 8 after a .577 (15 for 26) performance in six games with six runs, six runs

Chub Feeney served as president of the Padres in the late 1980s.

batted in, and four stolen bases. Gwynn was also named the National League's Player of the Month for June after batting .473 (44 for 93) with five doubles, five triples, a home run, 16 runs batted in, and 12 stolen bases.

On June 15, Nicolau's arbitration ruling found the release of Hoyt invalid. The Padres released him again two days later, but with a commitment to pay his contract.

On July 4, the Padres and Giants made a seven-player trade. Kevin Mitchell, Dave Dravecky, and Craig Lefferts went to San Francisco while the Padres received third baseman Chris Brown and pitchers Mark Grant, Mark Davis, and Keith Comstock. The principals in the trade never reached their potential. Brown earned a reputation as a malingerer, while a cancerous node curtailed Dravecky's career and eventually led to the amputation of his left arm. Two years later, however, Mitchell would be the National League's Most Valuable Player and Davis would win the Cy Young Award.

On July 8, the Padres lost a seven-run lead to Chicago, and entering the All-Star break the Padres had a 30-58 record.

On July 30, Andy Hawkins was placed on the disabled list after a tendonitis exam. Eric Nolte, who had started the season with Class A Reno, Nevada and had been promoted to Class AA Wichita, Kansas in June, was called up to the Padres. In his first start on August 1, he pitched seven scoreless innings, allowing five hits and three walks and striking out seven in a 6-0 win against Houston.

On August 8, Kruk had three hits in five at-bats, placing him second behind Gwynn in the race for the National League batting title. He would end up fourth, with a .318 average in his first full season.

The Padres put together a seven-game winning streak in August, with Gwynn capping the seventh game with a five-hit performance. After an August 13 win over Atlanta, the Padres had won 11 of 14, and their 19-15 record since July 4 was the best in the National League.

On August 23, Benito Santiago was hitless in three at-bats to drop his average to .284. The Padres had August 24 off, but on August 25, Santiago hit a three-run homer in a 5-1 win over Montreal. That began a 34-game hitting streak which eclipsed the record for the longest hitting streak by a rookie, by a catcher, and by a Latin American player. On four occasions he extended the streak in his final at-bat.

The streak was extended to 34 games with an October 2 double in the first inning, but on October 3 Santiago struck out against Orel Hershiser of the Los Angeles Dodgers in the first, grounded out in the fourth, and flied out to right in the sixth. The Padres won the home game, 1-0, but without a need to play the bottom of the ninth, the Padres only sent 27 men to the plate and Santiago only came up to bat three times.

During the streak, Santiago hit .346 (47 for 136) with 12 doubles, two triples, five home runs, 18 RBIs, and one walk, which was intentional. The Padres were 13-23 during the streak and Santiago only sat out two games.

Santiago got hits in his first two at-bats in the season's final game October 4, giving him a .300 average to end 1987. Gwynn batted .370 for the season, and Ready finished the season at .309 in 400 plate appearances.

The Padres finished 65-97. On October 9, Dunlop and Cisco were notified that their contracts would not be renewed for 1988. Batting coach Deacon Jones announced his resignation to seek an administrative position. On October 30, Pat Dobson was named as the Padres' pitching coach, Amos Otis was selected as the hitting instructor, and Denny Sommers became the bullpen coach.

Santiago, who had 18 home runs, 79 RBIs, and 21 stolen bases to go with his .300 average, was the unanimous choice for the National League's Rookie of the Year.

Gwynn and Santiago were named to the Silver Slugger team and Gwynn, who was also eighth in Most Valuable Player voting, received his second consecutive Gold Glove.

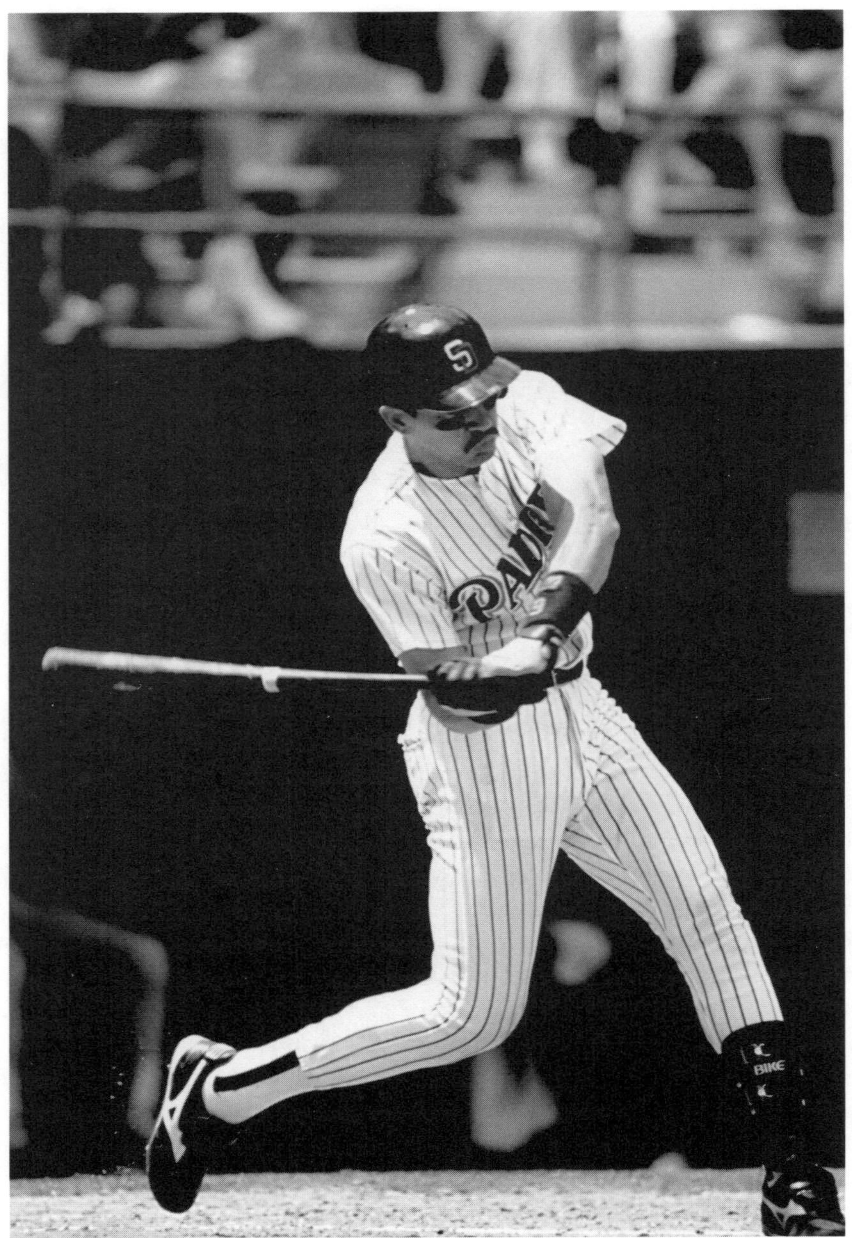

Benito Santiago caught for the Padres from 1986 through 1992.

12

The Resurgent Years

[1988-1989]

Although the Padres finished in last place in 1987, the team showed promise. The Padres did not make any trades at the winter meetings, and it looked like the most notable transaction during the off season would be the move of the team's California League affiliate from Reno to Riverside.

The Padres tried to sign Kirk Gibson, who was declared a "new look" free agent in the collusion ruling. They offered Gibson $4.2 million over three years, but the Dodgers bettered that offer with a contract for $4.5 million over three years and Gibson signed with Los Angeles.

The Padres' free agent transactions focused on reserve infielders. Luis Salazar left San Diego to sign with the Detroit Tigers, while shortstop Dickie Thon signed a one-year contract with the Padres in an effort to make a comeback from his 1984 beaning.

On February 12, a major trade was finally consummated. Pitchers Goose Gossage and Ray Hayward were sent to the Chicago Cubs for infielder-outfielder Keith Moreland and infielder Mike Brumley.

The Padres also renegotiated Tony Gwynn's contract, adding $500,000 to the 1988 and 1989 portions to increase his 1988 salary to $1.09 million and his 1989 salary to $1.19 million. The Padres also agreed to negotiate an extension at the end of the season. Gwynn was also forced into further negotiation of his bat deal. When he received his first shipment of Louisville Slugger bats in spring training, nine of the twelve bats were larger than his specifications and without the handle knob he preferred. Bat suppliers Louisville Slugger, Rawlings, Cooper, and Worth said that they could not make the old style with the new electronic lathes.

In February, Benito Santiago picked up another award. The Sports Committee of Puerto Rico's Federal Affairs Administration named him the most outstanding Puerto Rican athlete in the U.S. for 1987. In March, he agreed to a one-year, $175,000 contract.

The Padres opened camp with 17 pitchers. Manager Larry Bowa said that only three had "no way" of making the team. Two of those were Candy Sierra and Greg Harris. Sierra won a spot on the opening day's roster after a spring training 0.95 ERA, while Harris earned a callup when the rosters were expanded in September.

On March 10, Gwynn underwent surgery to repair tendon damage in his left index finger. The stitches were removed nine days later, and he returned to the exhibition games on March 25.

The Padres began the season with 11 players on the active roster who were not on the 24-man roster when the team opened the 1987 season. Moreland, at 33 years old, was the oldest player on the team.

The Padres also opened, for the second year in a row, with five straight losses. Moreland's two-run double in the opener gave the Padres a 3-1 lead going into the bottom of the eighth, but the Houston Astros came back for a 6-3 victory. The following day Thon, who had played with the Astros before his beaning, made his debut as a pinch hitter. Although he grounded out, he received a standing ovation from the Houston crowd.

The Padres broke a 14-game road losing streak on April 10 with a win in San Francisco, giving them a 1-5 record going into the home opener on April 12. The first six games of the season produced the same results as 1987, but in 1988, the Padres won their home opener, taking a 5-3 match over the Los Angeles Dodgers in which John Kruk hit the team's first grand slam since 1986 and Mark Davis struck out seven in 3.2 innings of relief.

On April 16, the Padres retired Steve Garvey's uniform, the first in club history to receive such honors. The retirement of uniform number 6 caused Moreland to switch to number 7, while Marvell Wynne changed from number 7 to number 16. John Kruk, who had replaced Garvey at first base, hit a pinch-hit home run in the bottom of the ninth for a 2-1 victory over San Francisco.

The following day also made history, but for another reason. Tony Gwynn disputed a called strike in the third inning against San Francisco and told umpire Joe West, "If you don't like what I'm saying, you can kick me out of here." West took Gwynn up on the offer, giving Gwynn his first major-league ejection in his 781-game career.

On April 19, Stanley Jefferson was placed on the disabled list. Roberto Alomar, the Class AA second baseman in 1987, was given a chance. After the struggles of Bip Roberts in 1986 and Joey Cora in 1987, the Padres were reluctant to promote another second baseman from Class AA, but Alomar (who started 1988 at Class AAA Las Vegas) was up to the task. His first hit, an infield single in the first inning April 22, followed Tony Gwynn's 1,000th career hit. The Padres ended up with a 3-1 win over Houston. Two days later, Alomar had the game-winning RBI in a 3-0 victory over the Astros in which Andy Hawkins pitched a one-hitter.

The Padres threw three straight shutouts against Houston, but the team's shutout streak and four-game winning streak was stopped when St. Louis Cardinals batter Tom Brunansky led off the fifth inning on April 27 with a home run. The 2-1 Cardinal win gave Alomar his first loss as a Padre.

Gwynn was batting .275 through May 8 when a sprained ligament in his thumb placed him on the 21-day disabled list. The Padres, who started with a 9-11 record, lost 11 of their next 12 to fall into fifth place.

The May 24 game was an ugly one for Padres fans. The Padres had four leads and three save opportunities, and Wynne hit two home runs, but the Montreal Expos ended up with a 7-6 victory in the bottom of the 13th inning. The Padres had one-run leads going into the bottom of the ninth, eleventh, and twelfth innings and a two-run lead going into the bottom of the thirteenth.

On May 28, Bowa was fired as field manager. General manager Jack McKeon replaced Bowa as field manager. Bowa blamed club president Chub Feeney for his troubles, calling Feeney "a joke."

The Padres lost to the New York Mets, 5-1, in McKeon's debut May 29, but the following day a five-run seventh gave the Padres a 6-3 win in New York. Gwynn came off the disabled list that day, and on May 31 he drove in three runs in the Padres' 8-0 win over Philadelphia.

San Diego concluded that road trip with a 3-6 record, having blown nine leads. A 9-7 loss to the Philadelphia Phillies in the final game, coupled with an Atlanta Braves win, put the Padres in sixth place. The Padres returned home, facing the Braves in a battle for fifth. San Diego took two of three.

The Braves moved back into a tie for fifth after Cincinnati's Tom Browning threw a one-hitter against the Padres on June 6, taking a no-hitter into the ninth before Gwynn singled with one out. Two days later, the Padres and Reds traded players as well as lineup cards; Sierra was sent to Cincinnati for pitcher Dennis Rasmussen, who was 2-6 with a 5.75 ERA in his eleven starts that year before the trade.

Rasmussen made his Padres debut on June 11 and struck out 10 Dodgers while walking only one in a five-hitter which gave the Padres their third straight win, 2-1 over Los Angeles. The Padres completed a sweep of the Dodgers the following day, and the winning streak reached six before a loss to the San Francisco Giants.

On June 27, a pregame fight between Chris Brown, who had missed 32 of the club's 76 games, and Wynne took place in the locker room. The fight left a lump over Wynne's eye, but X-rays were negative and the two players apologized to each other the following day.

San Diego ended June with a 34-45 record, two games out of fourth place. By the All-Star break, the Padres were 39-49.

Gwynn's batting average had dropped to .246 on July 2, but a hitting streak of 18 games, including 15 multi-hit games during that streak and eight consecutive multi-hit games, raised his average to .313. Gwynn batted .513 (39 for 76) during that streak. During July, Gwynn had 16 multi-hit games and batted .406, raising his average from .249 to .300. His performance earned Gwynn the National League's Player of the Month honors.

Rasmussen was also hot for the Padres, resuming his San Diego career (he played briefly in 1983 before his trade to the New York Yankees for Graig Nettles) with four straight wins, a no-decision, and five wins before his first Padres loss. The Padres concluded July with a 48-57 record.

McKeon was successful, but Feeney did not want McKeon serving as both general manager and field manager in 1989. "I think it's too hard to hold both jobs," Feeney was quoted as saying. "There are too many conflicts involved between signing players and managing them."

The Padres played a 16-inning game in Atlanta on August 10, overcoming a 3-1 Braves deficit in the ninth. Benito Santiago opened the top of the 16th inning with a home run, and shortly after, Dave Leiper's first at-bat in the majors produced an RBI single. The Padres survived an Atlanta run in the bottom of the 16th to win, 5-4.

Rasmussen improved his record with the Padres to 10-1 against Montreal on August 17, but after 6.2 innings he left the game with a strained right hamstring. He next pitched on August 30, earning the loss in a 1-0 New York Mets win, despite seven innings of six-hit ball.

The Padres ended August with a 65-67 record. Gwynn batted .370 during August, while Carmelo Martinez led the National League that month with seven home runs. The Padres moved above .500 on September 5 during a six-game win streak.

The future was looking up for the Padres. Four of their five farm clubs (not including the Arizona State League rookie club) posted the best overall records in their leagues with the remaining club posting the fourth-best record. The Padres would be honored by the Topps Company as their baseball organization of the year. Mark Davis had gone 27.2 innings without allowing a run until a three-run eighth inning on September 9 against Atlanta. Rasmussen's tenth win gave the Padres four pitchers with at least 10 wins.

The Padres were moved back to .500 after a September 14 loss to the San Francisco Giants. Losing two of three to Atlanta put the Padres below .500.

In a doubleheader split with the Braves on September 17, Gwynn became the Padres' all-time hit leader, matching Dave Winfield's total of 1,134 in Gwynn's 3,427th at-bat and concluding the night with 1,136. Gwynn was also in a battle with Rafael Palmiero and Gerald Perry for the National League batting title.

The Padres defeated Houston on September 23, giving them a 9-0 record in homestand openers for the season. They returned to .500 with their third straight win on September 24. Many in the crowd of 21,252 expressed their displeasure with Chub Feeney by cheering a "Scrub Chub" banner. During the seventh-inning stretch, the banner was paraded in front of Feeney's box. Feeney responded with his middle finger, earning the boos of the fans. While Feeney denied the incident, Cable Sports Network televised the game, showing Feeney on video. Announcer Ted Leitner responded, "And Chub says we're No. 1."

The following day Feeney resigned, effective the final day of the season. Joan Kroc hired Tal Smith Enterprises to find a successor for Feeney. Gwynn went to the stadium's security office to retrieve the "Scrub

Tony Gwynn receives the Silver Slugger Award for winning the 1989 National League batting championship.

Chub" banner. On October 4, Dick Freeman, an accountant from Iowa who had joined the team in June 1980 after a savings and loan career and had been serving as the team's executive vice president, was named the interim club president. The "interim" was removed on March 14, 1989. In February 1989, Tal Smith was hired to oversee day-to-day operations.

The Padres swept Houston, and, on September 25, Greg Harris struck out 11 in his first major-league start. Two days later, Eric Show earned a career-high 16th win with his tenth complete game in his last 14 starts, bringing the Padres to 79-78.

In the Padres' final home game on September 28, Orel Hershiser set a major-league record with 59 consecutive scoreless innings, breaking Don Drysdale's 1968 record of 58 innings. Hershiser and Hawkins both pitched 10 innings of shutout ball, each allowing four hits before giving way to relievers. Hershiser set the record in the tenth inning. Wynne had struck out, but the ball was in the dirt and Wynne reached first. Santiago sacrificed, making Wynne the only runner to reach second against Hershiser for the game. Wynne advanced to third as Randy Ready grounded out to shortstop, and after an intentional walk to Garry Templeton, Moreland pinch hit for Hawkins and flied to right on a 1-2 pitch.

Los Angeles scored a run in the top of the 16th on a throwing error. In the bottom of the 16th, catcher Mark Parent came up with a runner on and two outs. Parent became the second catcher of the year to hit a home run in the 16th inning for the Padres and San Diego closed out its home season with a 2-1 win.

With two games to go, Gwynn was batting .311 and Palmiero was batting .306. Gwynn rested September 30, but said, "I want to play tomorrow." He also said, "I'm going to play if I have to choke Jack."

Gwynn singled in his first two at-bats on October 1. He was pulled in the sixth inning after a third at-bat. Palmiero went two for three, giving him a .308 batting average and forcing him to go 5-for-5 in the season's final game to catch Gwynn. Gwynn, who had batted .367 since his low of .246 on July 2, finished the season at .313, the lowest average ever by a National League batting champion. The win over Houston, coupled with a Dodgers win over San Francisco, put the Padres in third place, half a game ahead of the Giants and the Astros.

Santiago was named to the Associated Press All-Star team. He also earned a Gold Glove for the 1988 season in which he committed only 12 errors while throwing out 35 of the 77 runners who opted to steal against him.

Gwynn got the final day off, but Rasmussen won his 14th game in 18 decisions as a Padre. The Padres closed out their season with five straight wins and nine wins in their final 10 games. The team finished 83-78, including 67-48 with McKeon managing.

Two days after the final game, announcer Dave Campbell was let go after 11 years with the team when the club chose not to pick up the option on his three-year contract. On January 6, 1989, the Padres hired Rick Monday, who had been with Channel 11 in Los Angeles.

The Padres did not wait until the 1988 winter meetings to start trading. On October 24, Stan Jefferson and pitchers Jimmy Jones and Lance McCullers were traded to the New York Yankees for first baseman Jack Clark and pitcher Pat Clements. The addition of Clark, who hit 27 home runs in 1988, was expected to shore up an offensive power performance whose 94 home runs in 1988 ranked eleventh in the National League. On October 28, Chris Brown, who missed 81 games in 1988 without a trip to the disabled list, and Keith Moreland were sent to the Detroit Tigers for pitcher Walt Terrell.

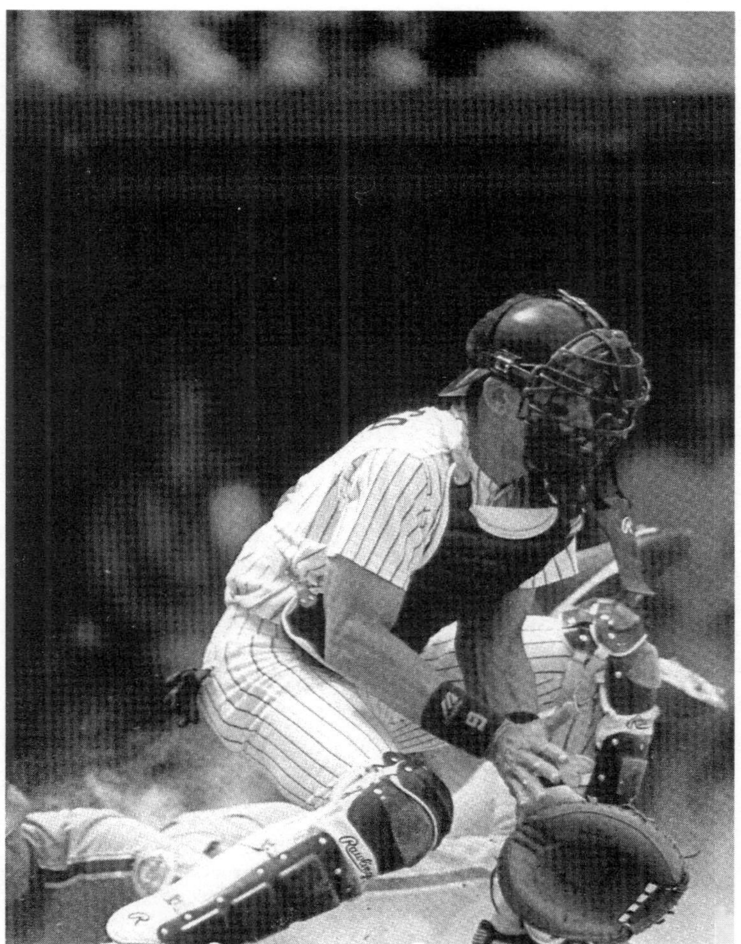

Benito Santiago

Dickie Thon asked to be traded if he could not play regularly, a request which was fulfilled on January 27 when he was sold to the Philadelphia Phillies.

The Padres set their sights on free agent pitcher Bruce Hurst, who had been 18-6 with the Boston Red Sox in 1988. The St. Louis Cardinals offered Hurst $5.1 million over three years, but the Mormon pitcher was not interested in being on a team linked closely with a beer company. The Padres offered Hurst $5.25 million for three years while the California Angels and Red Sox upped the ante to $5.5 million. Hurst chose intangibles over the extra $83,333 a year and signed with the Padres on December 8.

The Padres were unsuccessful in keeping Hawkins, who was 14-11 in 1988. They offered him $1.7 million for two years, but the Yankees provided an offer of $3.6 million for three years. Hawkins signed with New York the day Hurst signed with San Diego.

Even without Hawkins, the Padres had a strong pitching staff. The signing of Hurst and the trade for Terrell made the Padres the only team with five pitchers who had thrown at least 200 innings in 1988. The addition of Hurst gave the Padres a second left-hander in the rotation to join Rasmussen.

The increase in salaries caused the Padres to extend Gwynn's contract, giving him a guaranteed $2 million in 1991, an option for 1992 at $2 million, and incentive clauses. Rasmussen was signed for two years at $1.75 million. Santiago was given a one-year contract for $350,000.

The Padres also looked to their future with the addition of a seventh farm club. The Waterloo, Iowa

Diamonds of the Midwest League would be shared with the Baltimore Orioles and a few Japanese players were expected to be contributed to the squad.

The Padres reacquired Luis Salazar by sending Mike Brumley to Detroit in a March 23 trade. The club set a spring training record with 18 wins (against seven losses and a tie) entering their game against the Las Vegas, Nevada farm club.

The off season saw the renovation of the Padres' clubhouse and the addition of an indoor batting cage. The Padres opened the 1989 season at home for the first time since 1984, but the Giants spoiled the opener with a 5-3 win. The following day, the Giants touched up Hurst for 10 hits and eight runs in five innings. The Padres won the final game of the series and then took two of three in a short trip to Houston. The final game of the series was the first career loss to San Diego in the Astrodome for Mike Scott, who had been 12-0 against the Padres in Houston. San Diego committed five errors, and Ken Caminiti, who would go into the Padres' record books for his San Diego performances years later, hit into a triple play in the eighth inning.

The Padres returned home on April 10 to face Atlanta. Hurst retired the first eight batters, issued a walk to pitcher Pete Smith, allowed a home run to Lonnie Smith, and retired the next 19 batters for a one-hit victory in which he struck out 13. The following day, a 3-2 win over the Braves gave San Diego first place for the first time since April 1986.

The Padres shored up their front office staff April 14 when Tony Siegle, who had been the Phillies' vice president of baseball administration, became San Diego's vice president of player personnel. The team still had no general manager officially, but McKeon was given the authority to make major-league trades while Siegle would be overseeing minor-league and scouting duties and handling contract negotiations and administration.

Hurst retired his first nine batters against Cincinnati on April 15, bringing his streak to 28, but the Reds prevailed in 10 innings. A Reds win the following day brought the Padres to one game under .500.

The Padres then took two of three in San Francisco, and by the end of April the team was 14-12 and in second place. Mark Davis had saved 11 games in 11 appearances, and after winning the first Saturday night game ever at Wrigley Field over the Chicago Cubs on April 29, the Padres shared first place with the Reds.

The Padres fell back to .500 after a loss to Chicago on May 4, but a more serious concern was John Kruk. He tried to catch Andre Dawson's second-inning triple, but the ball fell out of Kruk's glove when he hit the warning track. He suffered a hip pointer and strained his right shoulder. He was placed on the disabled list, and the team did not return to above .500 until May 19.

Third strikes were notably eluding Santiago. On May 15, he set a club record for a catcher with seven assists, but five of them were on dropped third strikes. On June 6, the Padres had already given the Houston Astros a pair of two-out runs in the ninth inning after a 7-4 San Diego lead. After a strikeout pitch eluded Santiago, Caminiti scored the tying run in a game the Astros would win 8-7 in 10 innings. Santiago's dropped third strike also gave Mark Davis his first blown save of the year.

Kruk was activated on May 21, the same day Philadelphia's Steve Jeltz hit his first home run since 1984 to end a streak of 1,357 at-bats without a four-bagger. But some good things were occurring. Ed Whitson won seven games in a row between April 27 and June 5, including his 100th career win against Philadelphia May 30. The Padres ended May with a 29-25 record.

The Padres, who had benefitted in the past from players who valued loyalty more than additional money, sent a similar message on May 31 when they renewed their radio contract with KFMB for five more years. XTRA, which at the time was a talk radio station and which would become a sports talk station in 1991, claimed that they had offered more money, but the Padres selected KFMB in a contract which for the first time had the radio station paying the Padres instead of the ballclub paying the radio station and selling its own advertising.

The Padres' first game of June did not go well, with the Cincinnati Reds earning a 9-4 victory on June 2. Eric Davis drove in six runs and became the first Red to hit for the cycle since Frank Robinson in 1959. The Padres also made a trade with Philadelphia that day, sending Kruk and Ready to the Phillies for third baseman Chris James.

On May 29, Phillies third baseman Mike Schmidt announced his retirement in San Diego. The Padres spoiled the retirement announcement with a 1-0 win, and James, who replaced Schmidt, ended the game by grounding out to third. When James was traded to the

Padres, he was hitless in his last 31 at-bats. He was hitless in his first seven Padres at-bats, but in 87 games for the Padres he batted .264.

The Padres played a three-game series with the Giants in San Francisco June 9-11. The Giants swept all three games. They took the first game, 12-2, then ended Whitson's seven-game winning streak with a 1-0 win despite only getting two hits off Whitson and none off Harris in relief. The Giants took 12 innings to win the third game, in which Jack Clark struck out five times. The Padres returned home after the 1-9 road trip, and on June 13, they lost their seventh straight game. Jack Clark struck out four times to set a major-league record with nine whiffs in two consecutive games and tie a major-league record with 10 strikeouts in three consecutive games.

The losing streak ended against Cincinnati the following day. Show set a team record with his 93rd career win, while Davis earned his first save in June after recording 17 in April and May.

The Padres faced the San Francisco Giants in San Diego June 23-25. They lost the first two games, but held on to win the final game and split the 12-game homestand. Despite the win, they had lost 15 games of their last 22, and McKeon called a workout for what was to have been an off day on June 26.

The Padres swept their next three games in Los Angeles, and, at the end of June, the club was 39-41 and in fourth place. Gwynn batted .448 in June with 47 hits and 16 RBIs. By the All-Star break, Gwynn was batting .353.

The Padres moved into third place on July 18 with a 17-4 win over Pittsburgh. The Padres, who banged out 22 hits, set a team record for most runs in a nine-inning game. Jack Clark had his first three-hit game of the year and James and Santiago each had four hits. One of James's hits was a grand slam. Clark would compile a 14-game hitting streak before it was ended by former Cardinals teammate Joe Magrane on July 20.

On July 23, the Padres traded Walt Terrell, who had been 5-13 with a 4.01 ERA, to the Yankees for third baseman Mike Pagliarulo and right-handed pitcher Don Schulze. Whitson won his 14th game against six losses three days later. On July 29, Schulze made his debut as a Padres' starting pitcher, allowing two runs in six innings in a 9-4 win over Los Angeles. The following day, the Padres had another pitching problem when Whitson left the game after two innings due to a blister on the tip of his middle finger. At the end of July, the Padres were 10 games out of first place with a 51-54 record.

The Padres opened August with a three-game sweep of the Atlanta Braves to move back to .500, where they hovered for most of August. On August 8, the Padres brought up pitcher Andy Benes from Class AAA Las Vegas. Benes, the team's first draft pick in 1988, began 1989 with Class AA Wichita, Kansas and struck out 115 batters in 108 1/3 innings. He had a record of 8-4 with Wichita, along with a 2.16 ERA, before being called up to Las Vegas. Benes was 2-1 in five starts with Las Vegas before his callup to the Padres.

Benes lost his first game on August 11 against Atlanta. He threw six innings and gave up six runs on six hits, walking four and striking out seven. In his second game on August 18, the day after Hurst's 100th major-league win, Benes gave up four runs on six hits over 6.1 innings in a loss to the Expos. He only walked one while striking out seven, and while only six of his 30 breaking pitches in his first game were strikes, 21 of his 30 breaking balls in his second outing were strikes.

Hurst left the August 22 game in the fourth inning with a strained groin, and the Philadelphia Phillies obtained a 4-2 win in that contest to put the Padres ten games out of first place. But the Padres won their next six games to go back to over .500, this time for the rest of the season.

During the win streak, the Padres made a trade with the Cubs, giving Chicago Wynne and Salazar in exchange for right-handed pitcher Calvin Schiraldi, outfielder Darrin Jackson, and a player to be named later (Phil Stephenson).

The Padres posted an 18-11 record in August, although they only gained 3 1/2 games on the Giants. After the end of their first six-game winning sreak, the Padres posted another six-game win streak. After losing the final series game to the Houston Astros, the Padres were met at the airport at 2:00 a.m. by 1,500 fans. Upon returning home, the Padres took five of seven from Los Angeles, Houston, and Atlanta. The two-game sweep of Houston put the Padres in second place, ahead of the Astros.

On September 12, Mark Davis was named the National League's Player of the Week. Davis had recorded saves in all five Padre wins, including his 37th save on September 6 to tie Rollie Fingers's club record and his 38th save against Los Angeles on September 8.

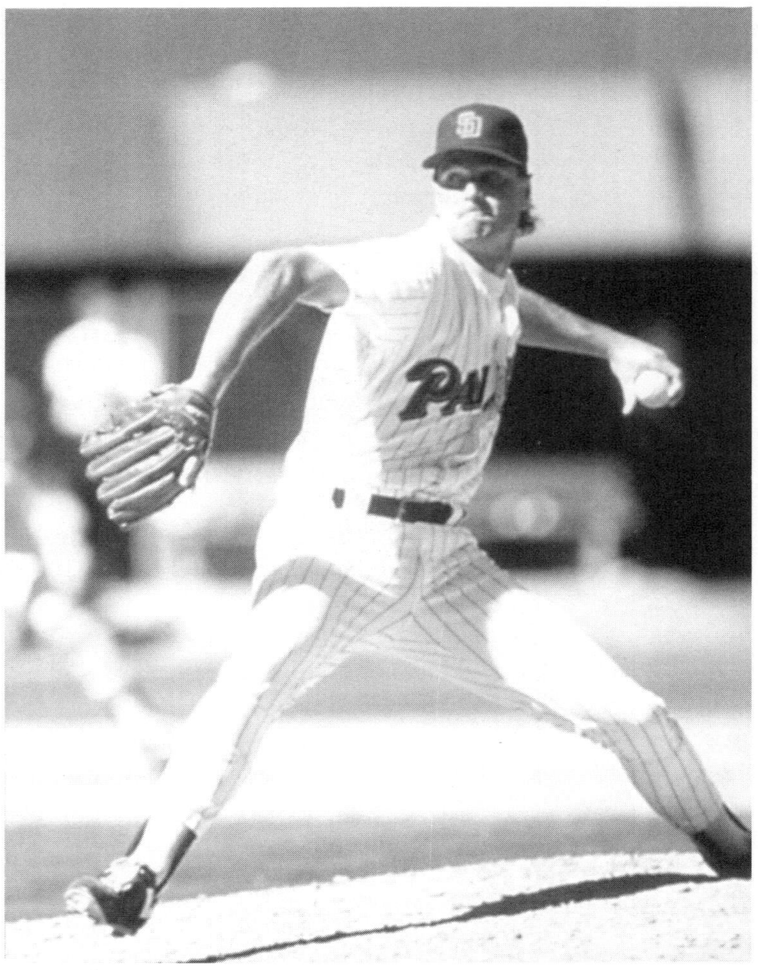

Mark Davis relieved for the Padres from 1987 through 1989 and in 1993 and 1994.

The San Francisco Giants were not helping the Padres catch up. On September 4, they trailed Cincinnati by a score of 8-0 before winning a 9-8 ballgame. On September 13, the Giants scored three times in the bottom of the 13th inning to defeat the Reds, 8-7.

In San Francisco on September 15, the Padres and Giants met for the first time since June 25. The Padres had won 44 games and lost 28 since then. The Padres won the first game of the series, 5-3, to move the club five games behind the Giants. The following day's game was rained out, and, on September 17, the two clubs split the doubleheader.

Then the Padres came away with their first-ever three-game sweep in Cincinnati and won two of three in Los Angeles, but they did not pick up a game on the Giants at any time. Los Angeles had a 7-0 lead after five innings against San Francisco on September 20, but the Giants scored five times in the bottom of the ninth to win, 8-7. Benes, who won his first game on August 23, won his sixth straight on September 24 against Hershiser and the Dodgers with a 1-0 win.

San Diego won 24 of its last 30 games going into the season's final homestand and was 17-5 in September to that point. Since the Padres and Giants closed the season with three games in San Diego, the Padres had a chance to win the division if they were no more than three games behind after the Cincinnati series.

The Los Angeles Dodgers defeated the Giants, 5-2, on September 25, but the Padres could not hold a 3-1 lead and the Reds scored the winning run in the eighth inning on a bases-loaded, two-out error by Robbie Alomar. The following day, the Padres defeated Cincinnati, 3-1, while the Dodgers' win over San Francisco moved the Padres to four games behind.

The Dodgers defeated the Giants, 1-0, on September 27. If the Padres won their game, the three-game series against San Francisco would be for the division championship. The Reds took a 1-0 lead, but the Padres tied the game in the bottom of the ninth inning on a one-out grounder. The Padres stranded the runners in the ninth, and they also left the bases loaded in the 11th inning after the first two men reached base. In the 12th inning, a drive off Darrin Jackson's bat was caught against the 370-foot sign in left center. In the 13th inning, Herm Winningham led off with a single for the Reds and stole second. Norm Charlton popped out to Calvin Schiraldi on a bunt attempt, and Schiraldi struck out Luis Quinones. With two outs and first base open, McKeon chose to pitch to Eric Davis. Davis doubled in the run which gave the Reds a 2-1 lead.

San Diego had a chance to tie the game in the bottom of the 13th inning, but Templeton struck out with Gwynn on third. After 159 games, the Padres were eliminated.

The Giants won the first game of the final series, 7-2, but a 4-3 Reds win over Houston clinched second for the Padres. As he had promised earlier in the season,

Tim Flannery signed his retirement papers on that day, his 32nd birthday, and the following night the Padres honored Flannery in a 30-minute pregame ceremony.

One race remained: the batting race between Gwynn and the Giants' Will Clark. In the first game, Clark had two hits in four at-bats to bring his average up to .334 while Gwynn was 1-for-5 to drop to .331. In the Padres' 11-5 win of the following night game, Gwynn had three hits, bringing his total for the season to 200. His 3-for-4 performance brought his average to .333 while Clark's 1-for-4 performance rounded up to .334.

The Padres won the final game of the season, 3-0, to finish with an 89-73 record. Gwynn had three hits in four at-bats to finish at .336, while Clark had one hit in four tries to finish second in the batting race at .333.

Tim Flannery received congratulations from San Diego native Ray Boone, a former major leaguer, upon his retirement as a player in 1989.

Tim Flannery played infield for the Padres from 1979 through 1989.

Benes finished the season with a 6-3 record, striking out 66 batters in 66.1 innings pitched. Whitson was 16-11 with a 2.66 ERA and Hurst was 15-11 with a 2.69 ERA. Clark had 26 home runs and 94 RBIs, and Gwynn stole 40 bases.

Mark Davis recorded his 44th save in the final game, one short of the National League record. His saves came in 48 save opportunities, and he was given the National League's Rolaids Relief Man Award. He also captured the Cy Young Award.

13

The Transitional Years [1990-1992]

The Padres had high expectations for 1990, but trouble struck almost immediately after the 1989 season. On October 17, Joan Kroc announced that the Padres were back on the selling block. Jerry Buss, who owned the Los Angeles Lakers as well as a home in northern San Diego County, immediately expressed interest. Kroc had an apparent deal with Sid and Jenny Craig, who made their fortune in the diet business, but Kroc was not happy with the Craigs' publicity over the upcoming sale and refused to sell. Steve Garvey was no longer an option after a pair of paternity claims in 1989.

Kroc even offered the ballclub to the City of San Diego, although that option never came to fruition.

The Padres had not extended Mark Davis's contract past the 1989 season, planning to work on a contract after the year was over. Davis's performance, along with the increases in top salaries, made that an expensive gamble for the Padres. After the season, they offered $7 million over three years. The Royals offered $12 million over four years, costing the Padres their top reliever and Cy Young Award winner when Davis signed with Kansas City on December 11.

Carmelo Martinez was also lost to free agency, although he had been dropped from the team's long-term plans.

When Marvell Wynne was with the Padres, the joke was that the team would acquire Fred Lynn so that they could have a rhyming outfield. The team missed having Tony Gwynn, Marvell Wynne, and Fred Lynn on the roster together by only 29 games. The club signed Fred Lynn as a free agent for the 1990 season, giving him a one-year contract on December 6. The following day, they signed Craig Lefferts to a three-year contract. Lefferts had been a middle reliever in his first stint with the Padres, but the team planned to use him as the closer in 1990. By the time he was traded in August 1992, he was in the Padres' starting rotation.

Jack McKeon, whose big trade after the 1987 season came two months after the winter meetings and whose big trades after 1988 came prior to the winter meetings, made a big trade at the 1989 winter meetings on December 6. Outfielder-third baseman Chris James, minor-league third baseman Carlos Baerga, and catcher Sandy Alomar Jr. were sent to the Cleveland Indians. In exchange, the Padres received outfielder Joe Carter.

The Padres also acquired pitcher Mike Dunne from Seattle in the Rule V draft. Dunne had been the runner-up to Benito Santiago in the 1987 Rookie of the Year voting, but off-season arm surgery made the Mariners unwilling to protect him. The Padres took a gamble on Dunne, who would begin the 1990 season on the disabled list.

One issue which had complicated negotiations for contracts past 1989 was whether players would be paid in the event of a lockout. When players and owners were not able to come to terms for a collective bargaining agreement, a lockout occurred. The lockout wiped out nearly a month of spring training, although the regular season was delayed by only a few days and all games lost at the beginning of the season were made up.

The Padres did well in the short spring training period, compiling a 12-2 record in exhibition games.

On April 2, Kroc reached an agreement with a group of 15 individuals, headed by television producer Tom Werner, for the sale of the Padres for an estimated $90 million. The National League owners unanimously approved the sale on June 13, and the deal closed June 15.

The Padres started their season with a loss at Los Angeles on April 9. The following day, they played their home opener against the Dodgers and fell to 0-2. The Padres won their next five games, but never climbed higher than second place. By the end of April, the club was 9-10.

Club discord was rampant. Both Jack Clark and Mike Pagliarulo accused Tony Gwynn of selfishness and caring more about statistics than the team. Gwynn received the sympathy of the Padres fans, although before one game a Tony Gwynn voodoo doll was found hanging from the top of the dugout.

Later in the season, the two announcers from the Spanish-language radio station which carried the Padres games got into a fight with each other during a Padres road trip.

The Padres were 30-27 going into the June 14 game against San Francisco. Santiago had been batting .317 with nine home runs and 33 RBIs. A pitch by Giants pitcher Jeff Brantley broke Santiago's arm, putting him on the disabled list for the first time in his career and costing him a starting berth in the All-Star game.

The Padres purchased the contract of Ronn Reynolds from Las Vegas to back up Mark Parent. On July 11, they traded outfielder Alex Cole, who had been with the Las Vegas farm club, to Cleveland for catcher Tom Lampkin. Cole turned out to be a sensation for Cleveland.

The injury to Santiago took place the night before the deal closed. Several years later, minority owner Michael Monk said he believed it was a bad omen. Santiago accused his teammates of not standing up for him after Brantley's pitch.

On June 10, the Padres were 30-25, five games above .500 and in second place. The team lost 29 of its next 37 games, falling to fifth place and 21 games out of first after a July 23 loss to Cincinnati.

On July 11, during the All-Star break, McKeon resigned as field manager. McKeon ended his Padres managerial career with 193 wins and 164 losses, including a 37-43 record in 1990. The Padres had gone 3-12 in McKeon's final 15 games as manager.

Dugout coach Greg Riddoch was selected as the team's new manager, with Spokane manager Rob Picciolo earning the position as the team's new first base coach. The Padres lost 11 of their first 12 games under Riddoch.

Riddoch was not exempt from team turmoil. During his first year with San Diego, Jack Clark called him a "snake."

The day after Riddoch took over, McKeon made another trade, sending Mark Grant to Atlanta for left-handed pitcher Derek Lilliquist.

Bruce Hurst broke the team's eight-game losing streak with a 10-0 win over Cincinnati on July 24. The win put the Padres back in fourth place after two days in fifth, but the Padres' slump would not be over until the fat lady sang.

The cancellation of the season's first week forced the opening series against Cincinnati to be rescheduled throughout the season. On July 25, the Padres, who experimented with a handful of Wednesday afternoon games for the 1990 season, hosted a doubleheader against the Reds.

Greg Riddoch managed the Padres from July 1990 through 1992.

For years the Padres had called their weekday afternoon games "businessman's specials." The July 25 doubleheader, which was changed to an evening start, was designated as Working Women's Night. Padres president Dick Freeman, aware that owner Werner was the producer of the Roseanne television show, thought that Roseanne Barr would be a match and asked if Barr could sing.

"If we had gone with 'Take me out to the ball game', it would have been a whole lot better deal," Michael Monk noted.

Monk listened to the game on radio, and Jerry Coleman did not make a significant issue out of Barr's singing of the National Anthem. Monk was not aware of what happened until the following morning, when close friends called him to complain about Barr's desecration of the Star-Spangled Banner. "The minute that thing broke apart, I knew that this was going to label us," Monk said. "It was a horrible beginning."

Reds announcer Marty Brennaman was much more critical of Barr than Coleman was. So was the national media the following day.

But the Padres played better than Roseanne Barr sang. They swept the doubleheader and won their next two games against Houston. At the end of July, the Padres were 45-56.

The Padres spent the entire month of August in fourth place. They won 15 games and lost 13 during that month. On August 9, Garry Templeton got his 2,000th career hit. He also broke the record for career games played for San Diego, ending the season with 1,254. Santiago returned from a rehabilitation assignment on August 10.

Losses in four of their first five September games dropped the Padres into fifth place, but two wins over Houston moved them back into fourth. Although the Padres shared fourth place on three more occasions and finished the season tied for fourth, they did not drop to fifth for the rest of the year.

Following an eight-game losing streak, the Padres won four of their last six games to finish with a 75-87 record and tied for fourth place with Houston. The season's final game, a 7-3 win in Los Angeles, was Eric Show's first victory since September 9 and the 100th of his Padres career.

The season cost McKeon his job as general manager. He was fired on September 21, and, on October 2, Joe McIlvane, formerly the Mets' vice president for baseball operations, took over as general manager.

Gwynn fractured his right index finger in Atlanta while trying to make a catch against the wall on September 15. He missed the season's last 19 games and ended up with a .309 batting average, tied for sixth in the National League. He also drove in a career-high 72 runs.

Ed Whitson won 14 games against nine losses, and his 2.60 ERA was the lowest for a Padres starter since Randy Jones's 2.24 ERA in 1975. Santiago finished the season with a .270 batting average and won a Silver Slugger award for the third time, as well as the Gold Glove for the third consecutive year.

Jack Clark led the team with 25 home runs but batted .266. Joe Carter had 24 home runs and led the team with 115 RBIs, but he batted .232 for the year with an on-base percentage of .290. Pagliarulo batted .254 with just seven home runs. Show finished the season with a 6-8 record and an a 5.76 ERA.

When free agency came around, Pagliarulo and Show were encouraged to seek deals elsewhere. A collusion ruling had made Clark a new look free agent, and the Padres used that opportunity to rid themselves of him. Lynn's one-year contract was also not renewed.

During the winter meetings, the Padres traded quality for quality. Carter and Roberto Alomar were traded to Toronto, and the Blue Jays gave up first baseman Fred McGriff and shortstop Tony Fernandez. The move was intended to improve the Padres' .257 batting average they compiled in 1990.

A week later, the Padres traded Mark Parent to Texas for third baseman Scott Coolbaugh. In their free agent acquisitions, the Padres signed right-handed relief pitcher Larry Andersen and third baseman Jim Presley, and second baseman Marty Barrett was invited to spring training as a non-roster player.

The Padres changed uniforms for the 1991 season, replacing the brown colors, which they had used since 1969, with the blue colors used by the Pacific Coast League Padres. Navy blue and orange replaced the brown and gold of the Padres' first 22 seasons.

A pair of Padres figures were voted into the National Baseball Hall of Fame for 1991. Gaylord Perry was elected by the Baseball Writers Association of America. When he was inducted, he wore a jersey representing all eight of the teams for which he played. *San Diego Union* writer Phil Collier received the J.G. Taylor Spink Award, earning him a spot in the Writers and Broadcasters wing of the Hall of Fame.

Riddoch filled out his coaching staff with former St. Louis Cardinals pitching coach Mike Roarke, bench coach Jim Snyder, third base coach Bruce Kimm, and batting coach Merv Rettenmund.

Santiago lost his arbitration case and threatened to leave the club when he could after the 1992 season. The arbitration hearing brought out animosity between Santiago and the club ownership. "When we bought the team I loved the guy. I ended up where I can't stand the guy," recalled Monk, who is a labor lawyer and sat in on arbitrations during his ownership period.

The Padres were also in the process of negotiating a new lease with the city of Yuma, Arizona for spring training facilities—a task which would not be resolved to Werner's satisfaction. During the off season, the club's California League affiliate was moved from Riverside to Adelanto, where they became known as the High Desert Mavericks.

The Padres released Dunne and Calvin Schiraldi during spring training. Nine days before the start of the season, they traded second baseman Joey Cora to the Chicago White Sox for pitchers Adam Peterson and Steve Rosenberg, both of whom started the season in Las Vegas.

The Padres won their first opener since 1984, defeating the San Francisco Giants by a 7-4 score. Jim Presley came off the bench and had a bases-loaded single in his first at-bat.

Marty Barrett also made an impact in his first at-bat, belting a home run. But both were released in June after poor performances. Barrett had three hits in 16 at-bats for a .188 batting average, and Presley had eight hits in 59 at-bats for a .136 average.

They lasted longer than Mike Aldrete, who was hitless in 15 at-bats before his May 10 release. During the season, the Padres set a record by using 48 players. The figure included 22 actual pitchers (Darrin Jackson also made an appearance on the mound).

The Padres also released a pair of pitchers during May. Eric Nolte was 3-2 in six starts but had an ERA of 11.05, and Wes Gardner had an ERA of 7.08 in 14 relief appearances. Nolte had started the season with a 3-0 record.

The Padres won six of their first seven games, including a three-game sweep in Los Angeles. They took over first place April 12 and stayed in first through April 28. An April 29 loss in Philadelphia left them tied for first but behind on percentage points, and a loss in New York the following day put them clearly in second place.

The Padres moved back into a first-place tie May 5 and held either first place or a share of first through May 10. At the end of May, the Padres were 24-25 and in fourth place.

Fred McGriff had a huge part in the Padres' move back to first place. He was named the National League's Player of the Week for April 29 to May 5 after hitting three home runs, driving in eight runs, and batting .423 with a slugging percentage of .885.

On May 31, the Padres traded shortstop Garry Templeton, who had become expendable with the Fernandez acquisition, for New York Mets infielder Tim Teufel. As had Barrett in his first at-bat, Teufel's offensive debut for the Padres was a home run. Teufel fared slightly better at the plate than Barrett, batting .228 with 11 home runs in 97 Padres games.

Second basemen Paul Faries and Jose Mota had not fared well, and the acquisition of Teufel allowed Bip Roberts to be moved to third. Scott Coolbaugh, who batted .217 before he was sent down, was not panning out as the Padres' third baseman, and, on July 30, San Diego gained another option when Shawn Abner was traded to the California Angels for Jack Howell.

The scoreboard videos at San Diego Jack Murphy Stadium were becoming unpopular. "Fungo" had fans guessing at what three clues had in common, and the answers didn't necessarily have anything to do with baseball. "Fungo" was dropped early in the season. "Surf the Murph" involved three video surfers racing around the stadium. That was also booed, but "Surf the Murph" stayed as an off-field function for the entire year before being dropped in 1992.

A six-game win streak moved the Padres to within two games on June 4, but the team was not able to clear .500 on a permanent basis, and at the end of June the Padres were 38-39.

Tony Gwynn picked up another Player of the Week accolade for his June 4-9 performance in which he batted .522, or 12 for 23. Gwynn also had a multi-hit All-Star game for the first time in his career, getting two hits in four at-bats on July 9.

The Padres struggled in July, and Andy Benes's record fell to 4-10 with a July 15 loss. On July 28, Benes defeated the New York Mets in San Diego. In his next start on August 3, he carried a no-hitter through six innings but left because of a sore left foot. Three relievers preserved the Padres' win, although not the no-hitter, and Benes did not miss any scheduled starts. He won 10 in a row before an October 1 loss in Los Angeles, and, on August 29, he pitched his first major-league shutout, throwing a two-hitter against St. Louis.

The Padres fell to fifth place after a July 30 loss, but a three-game winning streak moved them into fourth place as of August 11. The Padres spent the rest of August moving between third, fourth, and fifth. They completed the month in fourth place with a 63-67 record.

On August 13, Fred McGriff hit a grand slam off Houston's Mark Portugal. The following day, he hit a another off the Astros' Jim Deshaies, becoming the fourth player in National League history to hit grand slams in consecutive games.

A seven-game winning streak, which began September 3, moved the Padres back over .500 and into third place. That streak ended on September 11 in Atlanta. Pitchers Kent Mercker, Alejandro Pena, and Mark Wohlers accounted for the first combined no-hitter in National League history. Terry Pendleton hit a home run for the only score of the game. The Atlanta scorer made a dubious call on a Darrin Jackson drive which was ruled an error. With two out in the ninth inning, Tony Gwynn made the final out, giving Chris and Tony Gwynn the distinction of both brothers making the final out of a no-hitter in the same season.

Fred McGriff played first base with the Padres from 1991 through July 1993.

A 10-inning loss to the Braves in San Diego on September 19 put the Padres back at .500 with 74 wins and 74 losses. But the Padres won 10 of their last 14 games, including their last four, to stay above .500 for the rest of the season. The team finished in third place with a record of 84-78, the third best in club history to that point.

Benes started the final game of the season on October 6, but was removed after being hit by a batted ball. He was awarded the win in the 3-1 game over Cincinnati, giving him a 15-11 record and a 3.03 ERA. Benes led the team with 223 innings pitched and 167 strikeouts. Close behind was Bruce Hurst, who pitched 221.2 innings and struck out 141 while winning 15 games against only 8 losses and allowing 3.29 earned runs for every nine innings. Greg Harris, who spent two months on the disabled list, was 9-5 in 20 starts with an ERA of 2.23 over 133 innings.

Gwynn finished third in the National League batting race with a .317 batting average in 530 at-bats. He also struck out only 19 times in those 530 at-bats. McGriff and Fernandez batted .278 and .272

respectively, while Santiago batted .287 to help overcome the team's .244 batting average.

McGriff led the team with 31 home runs and 106 RBIs. His ratio of one home run per 17.0 at-bats placed him third in the National League among hitters with at least 350 at-bats. Fourth was Darrin Jackson, who hit 21 home runs for the Padres in 359 at-bats while driving in 49 runs.

Of McGriff's home runs, 14 were off southpaw pitchers, while 17 were against right-handers. Entering the 1991 season, only 19 of his 125 major-league home runs had been off lefties.

During the winter meetings, Bip Roberts was traded to the Cincinnati Reds for relief pitcher Randy Myers. The Padres lost another third baseman when Jack Howell signed a contract with the Yakult Swallows of the Japanese League.

On February 17, the Padres traded right-handed pitcher Jim Lewis to Baltimore for third baseman Craig Worthington. Tim Teufel's ability to play third base allowed the Padres additional breathing room when they signed free agent second baseman Kurt Stillwell. Worthington did not last through the end of spring training. On March 27, the Padres sent right-handed pitcher Ricky Bones, minor-league infielder Jose Valentin, and 1991 California League Most Valuable Player Matt Mieske (an outfielder) to Milwaukee for third baseman Gary Sheffield and minor-league pitcher Geoff Kellogg. On March 31 Worthington was released. The Padres made another roster cut that day when Ed Whitson was placed on the 60-day disabled list with arm problems. He never returned to baseball as an active player.

Santiago won his arbitration case and was awarded \$3.3 million, but he asked to be traded. On May 31, he went on the disabled list after breaking a finger, and the Padres called up catcher Dan Walters from Las Vegas, who then batted .251 in 57 games during the season.

Bip Roberts played infield with the Padres in 1986, 1988 through 1991, and 1994 through 1995.

The Padres got off to a 7-2 start in 1992. An Eric Karros home run spoiled the Padres' home opener with Los Angeles on April 9, but the following day pitcher Dave Eiland became the first Padre to hit a home run in his first major-league at-bat. Eiland, who made his major-league debut in 1988 and allowed a home run to Paul Molitor, also became the only pitcher to hit a homer in his first big-league at-bat and to give one up to the first big-league batter he faced.

Because Eiland left after four innings, he did not receive a decision in the 8-3 win. He made four more starts, none earning him a win, before going on the disabled list on May 8 with back spasms. He returned June 26 after a rehabilitation assignment, but in his second start back he slid into Montreal's Darrin Fletcher during a play at the plate and left after three innings. He was placed on the disabled list again and assigned to Las Vegas after activation.

In the first five games of the season, McGriff had four home runs, including a grand slam on April 10, and batted .348 with nine RBIs, earning him shared Player of the Week honors along with Tom Glavine.

A loss on the last day of April put the Padres half a game out of first place with a record of 12-11.

Tony Gwynn missed four games early in the season after closing a car door on his hand, fracturing the tip of his middle finger. He also sprained a ligament in his left knee on September 8, curtailing him for the rest of the season.

During the season, the Padres had several instances in which they fell to one game above .500. But after falling to 17-17 in a May 13 game at New York, the Padres won four straight and stayed above .500 for the rest of the year.

A 10-0 win on May 31 left the Padres tied for first place at the end of May with a 28-22 record. Gwynn, McGriff, Sheffield, and Fernandez were all batting above .300 during the first half of the season. May highlights included Bruce Hurst throwing two consecutive shutouts, both against the Mets with the second shutout a one-hit gem. Hurst would also shut out the Mets on July 26, and in his final appearance against New York on August 22 he took a shutout into the seventh inning before a leadoff home run ended his streak. Hurst still earned the victory against the Mets, and he shut out San Francisco on June 25.

The Padres slipped to third place in June. They shared third after the games of June 12 and June 13, but held sole possession of third for the remainder of the season. The Padres closed out June with a 41-36 record and were 47-42 at the All-Star break.

Joe McIlvane served as general manager of the Padres from October 1990 through June 1993.

McGriff earned Player of the Week honors for June 29 through July 5 with home runs in four straight games, a .474 batting average (9 hits in 19 at-bats), and a 1.105 slugging percentage.

The 1992 All-Star game was held at San Diego's Jack Murphy Stadium on July 14, and five Padres participated. Gwynn tied an All-Star game record with two outfield assists, and McGriff was 2-for-3 with an RBI. Santiago also started, with Fernandez and Sheffield being selected as reserves. Trainer Bob Day was also selected for the 1992 All-Star game.

The Padres ended July with a 56-48 record, 4 1/2 games out of first place. Four and a half games behind was the closest the Padres came to first place for the rest of the year.

On August 6, McGriff and Sheffield hit back-to-back home runs in the first inning against Houston. In the second inning, they once again hit back-to-back home runs, becoming the first players in major league history to accomplish the feat in consecutive innings.

On August 11, the Padres peaked at 12 games over .500 with a 63-51 record. On August 28, the Padres were six games out of first place. They proceeded

Gary Sheffield played third base with the Padres from 1992 through June 1993.

to lose their next four games, and at the end of August the team was 69-61 and 8 1/2 games behind.

On August 31, the Padres traded Craig Lefferts to Baltimore for pitcher Erik Schullstrom and shortstop Ricky Gutierrez.

On September 23, Riddoch was fired and Jim Riggleman became the National League's youngest manager at the age of 39. Riggleman managed the Padres' final twelve games of 1992, winning four of them.

Coaches Rob Picciolo, Merv Rettenmund, and Mike Roarke were retained for 1993. Bruce Bochy, who won the Texas League championship as Wichita's manager in 1992, became the new third base coach, while Albany Yankees manager Dan Radison became the new first base coach. Dave Bialas became the new bullpen coach.

Hurst compiled a 14-9 record in 1992, his tenth consecutive year with at least 10 wins. But he missed his last two starts with an inflamed rotator cuff in his left shoulder and underwent offseason surgery to repair the rotator cuff and a cartilage tear. Lefferts won 13 games and lost nine before he was traded, and Benes won 13 games while losing 14 despite a 3.35 ERA.

Sheffield threatened to become the first National League player since 1937 to win the Triple Crown, but missing the final six games with a fractured index finger cost him the chance to win the home run and RBI titles. Sheffield led the National League with a .330 batting average while hitting 30 homers and driving in 100 runs.

Sheffield was third in the Most Valuable Player voting, but *The Sporting News* named him Player of the Year.

The National League leader in RBIs was Darren Daulton with 109. The leader in home runs was McGriff with 35. He became the first player in the modern era to lead both the American League and National League in home runs and the first Padre to have at least 30 homers in consecutive seasons.

Gwynn finished with another .317 season and struck out only 16 times in 520 at-bats. Fernandez closed out at .275, and the team upped its average to .255.

The team finished at 82-80, one game ahead of the fourth-place Houston Astros.

14

The Bargain Basement Years

[1993-1994]

During the 1992 season, some of the minority owners expressed a desire to sell the team. After the season, Tom Werner said that if he was going to lose money, he would rather spend it on charity than on a shortstop who did not produce. Tony Fernandez was traded to the New York Mets for pitcher Wally Whitehurst, minor-league outfielder D.J. Dozier, and minor-league catcher Raul Cassanova. Pitcher Mike Maddux was traded to the Mets for pitcher Roger Mason. Pitcher Jose Melendez was traded to Boston for outfielder Phil Plantier.

Benito Santiago, Jim Deshaies, Randy Myers, and Larry Andersen all became free agents and signed elsewhere.

Other cuts included broadcaster Rick Monday. The Padres also eliminated mini-season ticket plans for field level seats, requiring full season purchases for that section of the stadium although grandfathering existing mini-season plans.

The 1993 season also saw the beginning of play for the Colorado Rockies and the Florida Marlins. Outfielder Jerald Clark was lost to the Rockies, as were two minor-league pitchers.

Dick Freeman promised that the nucleus of the team would remain intact. In a renewal request letter to season ticket holders, he named specific players, including Gary Sheffield, Fred McGriff, and Darrin Jackson.

On March 30, the Padres traded Jackson to Toronto for outfielder Derek Bell. Fans threatened to sue for breach of contract, citing the letter.

During the 1992 season, Werner had made arrangements to move the Padres to a new spring training facility in Peoria, Arizona. The Padres played their final spring training game in Yuma on March 31, 1993. (The Padres would later schedule exhibition matches in Desert Sun Stadium, but at the time there were no plans for exhibition home games in Yuma.) The Padres won their final game,

Desert Sun Stadium in Yuma, Arizona, served as the spring training facility for the Padres from 1970 through 1993.

but the bottom of the ninth inning was played anyway. After three Padres were retired in the bottom of the ninth inning, Mickey Myers, the Padres' spring training batboy, threw out the last ball.

The Padres never reached .500 in 1993. They were 11-12 after a May 1 win, but they lost eight of their next 10 games. They settled into sixth place on May 18, and after the May 1 win they did not win two games in a row until June 11. The Padres did not have consecutive wins again until after the All-Star break.

Rather than trade more players, Joe McIlvane resigned as general manager. On June 9, he was replaced by Randy Smith, who had been the club's director of scouting. Smith, at the age of 29, was the youngest general manager in major-league history.

Dan Walters was not faring well as Santiago's replacement, and, on May 25, he was sent down to Las Vegas when Bruce Hurst came off the disabled list. Hurst returned to the disabled list on June 5, and the Padres purchased the contract of right-handed pitcher Mark Ettles from Las Vegas.

In 1991, the Padres had called up infielder Craig Shipley, who five years earlier had become the second Australian-born player in the majors. Shipley, who was born in Sydney, would finish 1993 as the player with the third longest consecutive seniority on the Padres, behind Tony Gwynn and Andy Benes. The callup of Ettles, who was born in Perth, made the Padres the first team ever with two native Australians. Ettles was sent back to the minors on July 10 when the Padres picked up Mark Davis, who had been released by the Philadelphia Phillies.

On June 23, the Padres traded right-handed pitcher Tim Scott to Montreal for third baseman Archi Cianfrocco. The following day, they traded Sheffield and left-handed reliever Rich Rodriguez to the Florida Marlins for reliever Trevor Hoffman and minor-league pitchers Jose Martinez and Andres Berumen.

The Padres ended June with a 29-49 record, 22 1/2 games out of first place. On July 2, they played at Philadelphia in a doubleheader. The first game was supposed to start at 4:35 p.m. eastern time, but a rain delay postponed the start of the game by one hour and 10 minutes. The game got under way, but two additional rain delays caused the first game to end at 1:03 a.m. after the Padres secured a 5-2 victory. The game lasted 2 hours and 34 minutes, not including 5 hours and 54 minutes of rain delays. Ettles won his first major-league decision in that contest.

The second game started at 1:28 a.m., breaking the 12:01 a.m. record for latest start set at San Diego Stadium on September 25, 1971. (The first game of a September 24 doubleheader between the Padres and Houston Astros lasted 21 innings, delaying the start of the second game until the following day.) The Phillies won the second game, 6-5, in 10 innings. The winning run crossed the plate at 4:40 a.m., breaking the major-league record for the latest game set by a 1985 contest which concluded at 3:55 a.m.

In the 1993 All-Star game, Andy Benes became the second Padres pitcher in the team's history to give up an earned run in the summer classic. In previous games, eight different pitchers had made 10 appearances for San Diego, and only Gaylord Perry, in 1979, had given up an earned run in All-Star competition.

Benes, who allowed only one run in two All-Star innings, was named the National League's Player of the Week for July 26 through August 1 after winning both starts and allowing nine hits and only one unearned run in 16 innings while striking out 13.

By the end of the 1993 season, the Padres' owners were forced to pay capital calls. The capital calls cost the owners about a million dollars a month.

On July 18, the Padres traded McGriff to Atlanta for pitcher Donnie Elliott and outfielders Vince Moore and Melvin Nieves, none of whom were on the Braves' roster at the time. Eight days later, they traded pitchers Greg Harris and Bruce Hurst to Colorado for pitchers Andy Ashby and Doug Bochtler and catcher Brad Ausmus. The extra players caused the Padres to release Kurt Stillwell, leaving the team with just three players who began the 1992 season on the club's roster.

This time a class action lawsuit was filed against the Padres, who had stipulated specific players in their season ticket renewal notices. The Padres agreed to provide refunds for the remainder of the season's games for ticketholders wishing to exercise that option.

Also released was Bob Geren. Geren, who graduated from Clairemont High School in San Diego, had been drafted by the Padres in 1979 but traded to St. Louis after the 1980 season in the 11-player trade between the Padres and Cardinals. He had returned to the Padres as a free agent in 1993 and made the club's roster as the backup catcher.

Tony Gwynn had two five-hit games in April. His third five-hit game of the season came at Chicago on July 27, when he also broke Dave Winfield's club record of 626 RBIs. In a 12-inning game against San Francisco on August 4, Gwynn hit safely six times, becoming only the fourth player in major-league history to have four games in a season with at least five hits.

Two days later, Gwynn became the 193rd player in history to collect 2,000 hits. Gwynn earned Player

Trevor Hoffman has relieved for the Padres since June 1993.

of the Week honors for August 2 through August 8 and earned Player of the Month recognition for August after a .448 (47-for-105) month.

Gwynn played his last 1993 game on September 5 and had knee surgery on September 12. He finished with a .358 batting average, which ended up as the second best figure in the National League.

The Padres fell to seventh place the day before the All-Star break. They climbed back to sixth place but returned to the cellar August 22 after a seven-game losing streak.

The Padres moved back into a tie for sixth on August 24, when they set a club record with 13 runs in an inning against visiting St. Louis. The 13 first-inning runs allowed the club to tie the team record of 17 runs in a nine-inning game, and the 17-4 win gave San Diego a 48-78 record.

Phil Plantier was the National League's Player of the Week for August 23-29, hitting five home runs while batting .409 (9-for-22) and driving in 18 runs. Plantier provided one of the team's highlights, belting 34 home runs and driving in exactly 100 runs for the season.

The Padres did not return to the cellar until a 13-1 loss to Atlanta on September 11. Two subsequent wins put them in sixth, but a four-game losing streak moved them back into seventh, this time for the rest of the season. The Padres lost nine of their last 11 games and finished 61-101, putting them in triple figures for losses for the first time since 1974.

Attendance at Padres games did not match that of the international soccer exhibitions preparing for the 1994 World Cup. After one such exhibition, Werner asked for a new stadium, citing too many empty seats. The solution agreed to by Werner and the City of San Diego was to provide a tarp over most of the upper deck, which lasted until new ownership removed the tarp.

Tony Gwynn

The Padres changed pitching coaches for the 1994 season, replacing Mike Roarke with Sonny Siebert.

The Padres made only minor trades in the off season. They also signed free agent Bip Roberts, who became the second baseman for 1994.

The Padres were 11-18 in their first exhibition season based out of Peoria. The regular season did not go well for the Padres, either. They lost their first four games, all at home, and after defeating Florida on April 8 they lost their next six games. Divisional realignment had reduced the National League West to four teams, and the Padres were tied for third after a July 6 win. The rest of the season was spent in fourth place.

The Padres lost 14 of their first 17 games before a four-game win streak put them at .333. They then lost five more games in a row. They won their next three to give them a 10-19 record as of May 7.

Their next win was May 22. The Padres lost 13 games in a row against Colorado, Cincinnati, Los Angeles, Chicago, and Houston to set a club record. They were 10-32 before a three-game win streak followed the losing skid.

Andy Ashby started the season 0-5 in 10 starts, but he had an 2.85 ERA during that time. He finished the season with a 6-11 record and a 3.40 ERA.

The Padres managed to put together a six-game win streak, giving them a 19-34 record as of June 1. The club stabilized somewhat from there, earning a 35-54 record at the All-Star break.

The club's May 31 home win against the Pittsburgh Pirates tied the record for runs scored in an inning, as the Padres scored 13 in the second inning during their 15-5 win.

When the players went on strike on August 12, the Padres had a 47-70 record. They were 12 1/2 games out of first place, one game better than when they had completed their record losing streak.

Andy Benes became the first Padres pitcher to lead the National League in strikeouts, fanning 189 batters in 25 starts and 172.1 innings. Benes had the league's three highest single-game totals, fanning 14 New York Mets in a two-hitter on July 15, 13 Mets in a one-hitter on July 3, and 12 San Francisco Giants on June 12.

Tony Gwynn batted .394 to win his fifth National League batting title. He played the entire All-Star game and scored the winning run in the bottom of the tenth inning. Gwynn also led the majors with 165 hits and struck out fewer than 20 times for the fourth season in a row. He also paced the team with 64 RBIs.

Joey Hamilton was called up May 24. He won his first two starts and was 3-0 with a no-decision in his first four starts, posting a 2.36 ERA to that point. After losing his next two decisions, he shut out Cincinnati on six hits on June 25. In seven of his 16 starts, he issued one earned run or less, and he finished the season with a 9-6 record and a 2.96 ERA in 108.2 innings.

Outfielder Phil Plantier played outfield with the Padres from 1993 through 1995 and in 1997.

Joey Hamilton pitched for the Padres from May 1994 through 1998.

Rookie Luis Lopez batted .277. He hit a grand slam on May 23 against San Francisco for his first major-league home run, becoming the second Padre to hit a grand slam for his big league homer debut. The other player was Mike Corkins, who hit his first homer on September 4, 1970, the day Lopez was born.

Another rookie, Scott Sanders, struck out 109 batters in 111 innings pitched.

Bip Roberts had a 23-game hitting streak, which began May 26 and was snapped on June 21. The hitting streak was the longest in the National League in the 1990s to that point. Roberts batted .320, eighth in the National League.

Dave Staton and Archi Cianfrocco were disappointments at first and third base, and both were demoted to Las Vegas by the end of June. Eddie Williams was called up to the team on June 14. In 49 games with San Diego, he had 11 homers, 11 doubles, and 42 RBIs. He scored 32 runs and batted .331. He also secured for himself the incumbent's position at first base for the 1995 season.

Phil Plantier's batting average dropped to .220, but he still led the team with 18 home runs.

The team batted .275 while holding opponents to a .252 average.

In the minors, pitcher Kerry Taylor led the Pacific Coast League in strikeouts while Marc Kroon was second in the California League.

After the season, Jim Riggleman accepted an offer to manage the Chicago Cubs. On October 21, the Padres named Bruce Bochy as the club's next manager. Graig Nettles and Davey Lopes were added as base coaches and Tye Waller became the new bullpen coach.

The team showed promise, even if their record did not reflect it. That, and a low payroll, would make the Padres attractive to a potential new owner.

15

The Restoration Years [1995-1997]

The players' strike of 1994 meant that none of the teams were receiving any revenue. While the players were no longer being paid, the front office staff was. The Padres laid off several members of their front office, but even the necessary personnel cost more money than the owners were making.

Tom Werner and his minority owners entertained potential buyers. After negotiations with two potential new owners failed to produce a sale, Werner entered negotiations with John Moores and Larry Lucchino.

Moores owned a software company in northern San Diego County. Lucchino was the former president and CEO of the Baltimore Orioles.

The sale of the team to the Moores/ Lucchino partnership was finalized on December 21, 1994. Moores took the title of chairman of the board while Lucchino became the chief executive officer.

Randy Smith remained as general manager, and his next trade actually brought higher salaries to San Diego. On December 28, the Padres traded outfielders Derek Bell and Phil Plantier, infielders Craig Shipley and Ricky Gutierrez, and pitchers Doug Brocail and Pedro A. Martinez to Houston. In return, the Padres received third baseman Ken Caminiti, shortstop Andujar Cedeno, first baseman Roberto Petagine, outfielder Steve Finley, pitcher Brian Williams, and a player to be named later. The 12-player deal was the largest in the Padres' history and the largest in baseball since 1957.

The players themselves were still on strike. The Padres, as did the other 27 teams in the majors, began the 1995 exhibition season with replacement players. When a settlement was reached, the season was rescheduled and the regular players began spring training. The Padres posted a 3-8-1 record in the exhibition games.

The resumption of regular preparation and play also brought the Padres some players who were free to try out with any team they desired. Those players included second baseman Jody Reed and pitchers Willie Blair and Fernando Valenzuela, all of whom made the club.

The Padres opened the season with a 10-2 loss against Houston on April 26, but won their next four games. Their fifth game was Valenzuela's first start. He would have earned the win, but Trevor Hoffman failed to hold a three-run lead in the ninth inning. Cincinnati tied the game before the Padres scored the winning run in the bottom of the ninth inning.

The Padres lost their next seven games to fall into fourth place, but after winning seven of their next 11 they were back in third. They spent much of May and June in fourth place, but a four-game winning streak gave them a 25-24 record by June 19.

On June 24, the Padres were only half a game out of first place and the team was 28-26, putting them two games above .500 for the first time since the beginning of the season. The team was 30-28 four games later, the last time until 1996 that the team would be more than one game above .500.

A more lasting legacy that month was the establishment of the Padres Scholars program. The program gives $5,000 college scholarships to 25 local middle school children if they continue to be successful in school.

At the All-Star break, the Padres were 33-36 and tied for third. They lost their next three games to Atlanta to move them into fourth place, but they moved into a tie for third on July 17 and into sole possession on July 21. The Padres stayed in third place through September 8, spent three days the following week in fourth or tied for third, and spent the rest of the season in third place.

In Philadelphia on May 28, the Padres set a post-1900 National League record by scoring nine runs in the tenth inning of a 13-5 victory.

On July 15, the team had a roster spot available after Bip Roberts was placed on the disabled list. The organization thought about calling up Ira Smith, who was nearly hitting .400 in the Pacific Coast League, but Smith was a replacement player. Club management asked the players about calling up a replacement player. The existing players were uncomfortable, and the Padres called up Archi Cianfrocco instead. Six days later at Atlanta, Cianfrocco hit a pinch-hit grand slam and added a two-run single, becoming the first Padre since 1992 to drive in six runs in one game.

Andy Benes lost his first five decisions of 1995, but rebounded to a 4-7 mark after 19 starts, striking out 126 batters in 118.2 innings. On July 31, Benes, a 1988 Olympian, was traded to Seattle for pitcher Ron Villone, a 1992 Olympian, and outfielder Marc Newfield.

Larry Lucchino served as president and chief executive officer of the Padres from December 1994 to October 2001.

John Moores has co-owned and served as chairman of the Padres since December 1994.

Willie Blair took Benes's place in the rotation and made the most of it. He was 3-1 with a 1.00 ERA in his first four starts and finished the season with a 7-5 record. In his four losses as a starter, the Padres only scored a total of eight runs.

On August 26, Melvin Nieves hit a bases-loaded home run at New York in the ninth inning, allowing the Padres to tie a National League record during 1995 with nine grand slams in a single season.

The Padres moved to within two games of first place on August 20 after winning 11 of 14 games. A two-game win streak brought them to within 2 1/2 games of first on September 2. At no time during the season were the Padres more than 8 1/2 games out.

In the Padres' previous 26 seasons, no player had homered from both sides of the plate in the same game. On September 16 against Chicago, Caminiti homered left-handed in the first and from the right side of the plate in the seventh. The following day against the Cubs, he became the first National League player to clout switch-hit homers in consecutive games, hitting one right-handed in the fifth and another left-handed in the seventh.

On September 18, Caminiti was hitless in four at-bats with two strikeouts. On September 19, he batted left-handed in the second inning and hit a solo home run off Armando Reynoso of Colorado. Caminiti had already batted in five runs when he stepped to the plate in the seventh inning to attempt his fourth hit of the ballgame.

Steve Finley played outfield for the Padres from 1995 through 1998.

Caminiti, batting right-handed against Bryan Hickerson, hit a three-run homer. It made him the second player in Padres history to drive in eight runs in a game and the first player in major-league history to homer from both sides of the plate three times in a season.

The 15-4 win over the Rockies was attended by 10,321 fans. The same fan caught both of Caminiti's home run balls.

Caminiti finished the season with a .302 batting average, 26 home runs, and 94 RBIs. He also led National League third basemen with 295 assists, 28 double plays, and 424 total chances and earned his first career Gold Glove Award.

Finley also earned a Gold Glove for his play in center field. At the plate, he batted .297, scored 104 runs, and stole 36 bases.

Andy Ashby entered the season's final game with a 2.99 ERA. Ashby risked the sub-3.00 stat and allowed only one earned run in six innings before being pulled for a pinch hitter, giving him a 2.94 ERA which was third lowest in the league. Ashby's 12 wins, against 10 losses, led Padres pitchers, and he struck out 150 batters in 192.2 innings.

Another player acquired in the 1993 trade with Ashby, Brad Ausmus, batted .293, including a National League best .339 when eighth in the batting order. His 63 assists tied for the lead among National League catchers, and his 16 stolen bases were a major-league high for catchers.

Tony Gwynn won his sixth batting title with a .368 performance. He led the National League with 197 hits and 154 singles and struck out only 15 times in 577 at-bats.

Joey Hamilton was 6-9 for 1995 but posted a 3.08 ERA for 204.1 innings. His figure, combined with his 1994 ERA of 2.98, gave him the second best ERA in the National League over that two-year period. Ashby, with a 3.15 ERA in 1994 and 1995, was third.

Valenzuela did not get his first victory until June 6, when he allowed three hits in six innings and drove in the game's only run. Although he started the season 0-2, he finished it with an 8-3 record, including six wins in a row to close out the season.

The Padres finished the 1995 season with a 70-74 record. The team's improvement from a .402 winning percentage in 1994 to a .486 mark was the best in the National League.

After the season, Randy Smith accepted a position as general manager of the Detroit Tigers. The Padres sought someone with scouting experience and experience with the club. On November 17, they selected Kevin Towers, previously the Padres' director of scouting.

Smith ended up with several former Padres for 1996, including free agent Eddie Williams.

The Padres began seeking free agents who could help improve the club. On December 21, they signed pitcher Bob Tewksbury. On December 29, they came to terms with outfielder Rickey Henderson. The team sent Bip Roberts to Kansas City to acquire first baseman Wally Joyner.

The Padres also signed Tony Gwynn's brother, Chris, and invited him, as a non-roster player, to camp.

Tim Flannery took over as third base coach for 1996, Grady Little joined the club as the bullpen coach, and Dan Warthen became the new pitching coach.

The Padres also hired Enrique Morones as the Director of Hispanic/Multicultural Marketing. The issues of border crossing, economics, and travel arrangements were identified as the biggest obstacles to bringing Mexican fans to Padres games. The Padres established a merchandise store in Tijuana which also sold tickets to the games and created "Domingos Padres con Tecate," which included tickets for Sunday games and bus rides from Mexico in a single package.

The 1996 season started off with a 5-4 loss to the Cubs at Wrigley Field in Chicago, but the Padres won the final four games of their first road trip. They closed out their first set of away games with a 17-2 win over Houston on Easter Sunday, April 7, setting a club record for the largest margin of victory.

The Padres opened in San Diego on April 8 with a 9-2 win over Florida. The Padres won five of their first six home games before closing the home stand with a loss to Atlanta.

The Padres closed their next road trip with four straight victories to go 5-3 on that set of visits. They returned home on April 24 and extended their winning streak to seven. The club closed out April with a 17-10 record.

The club followed the 6-5 home stand by splitting a six-game road trip. The Padres returned home on May 13 and won seven of 10 games on that stay in San Diego.

The Padres won six of their first eight games on the ensuing nine-game road trip. Their win over Philadelphia on June 1 gave them a 35-20 record and put them in first place by 6 1/2 games.

In the final game of the road trip June 2 at Philadelphia, Wally Joyner, who was batting .321 at the time and led the majors at the end of April with a .407 average, tried to break up a double play. He fractured his left thumb, putting him out of action through the All-Star break. He returned for the second half of the season and his average dropped to .277, but he would finish the season leading all National League first baseman with a .997 fielding percentage.

The Padres lost that game, 9-8, to the Phillies in 12 innings. They returned home and lost the first two games to the St. Louis Cardinals. A three-run home run by Tony Gwynn with two outs in the bottom of the ninth inning on June 5 gave the Padres a 6-4 victory and averted a sweep, but then the Pittsburgh Pirates came into town and took all three games, two of which were shutouts. The Cincinnati Reds completed the home stand with a three-game sweep of the Padres.

On June 12, Ashby, who had a 7-2 record at the time, was put on the disabled list with a right shoulder strain. He returned for two starts, winning his only decision, before returning to the disabled list with tendonitis in that shoulder on July 5. He made three more starts, without any decisions, before another trip to the disabled list on August 1.

San Diego took to the road, losing the first game to the Chicago Cubs in 14 innings. Chicago extended the Padres' losing streak to eight the following day. The Padres broke the losing streak on June 15, but a loss in Chicago next day put the Padres into a tie for first place. The Padres lost all three games in Atlanta, putting them two games behind and in fourth place for the first time all year.

On June 18, the Padres exchanged catchers and shortstops with the Detroit Tigers. Brad Ausmus and Andujar Cedeno went to Detroit for catcher John Flaherty and shortstop Chris Gomez.

On June 21, Flaherty hit safely for the Padres. It started the second longest hitting streak in club history and the second longest hitting streak in major-league history by a catcher, trailing only Benito Santiago's 1987 performance. Flaherty's 27th and final game of the streak, on July 27, included a grand slam. During the streak, Flaherty was 42-for-112 (.375) with seven home runs and 24 runs batted in.

The Padres returned home on June 20 and lost a 3-2 game to the Chicago Cubs. They posted a 10-

inning win on June 21 but fell in a 16-inning game the following day. The Padres defeated Chicago in the final match of the four-game series, but then the Astros came to San Diego and took both contests. The June 26 loss, closing out the home stand, evened the Padres' record at 39-39, the first time since the second game of the season that the club was not over .500.

Losing 19 of 23 games might have been devastating in the old six-team divisions, but the Padres were still only two games down. They also had their next 22 games against divisional opponents. The Padres went to San Francisco and swept four games from the Giants, putting themselves back into first place and giving the team a 43-39 record at the end of June.

The Padres then returned for a seven-game home stand. They lost the first two games to the Los Angeles Dodgers, but won the third game and swept four more games from the Giants to give them a 48-41 record at the All-Star break.

Ken Caminiti was a late addition to the All-Star roster. Tony Gwynn was voted to the team, but did not play due to injury. When third baseman Matt Williams was unable to play because of an injury, National League manager Bobby Cox brought in Caminiti as a replacement. In the sixth inning, he hit the first-ever home run by a Padre in All-Star play, driving a Roger Pavlik pitch over the right center-field fence of Veterans Stadium in Philadelphia.

Gwynn was placed on the disabled list July 3, retroactive to the day before, with a frayed Achilles tendon. He did not return to action until August 6, 30 days later.

When Gwynn was placed on the disabled list, the Padres called up Rob Deer from Las Vegas. In 25 games, Deer batted .180 with nine hits, seven of which were for extra bases. Deer and Jody Reed also gave the Padres the first two teammates in major-league history whose last names mirrored each other.

The Padres opened the second half of 1996 at Colorado, where the Rockies swept them in four games. The Dodgers extended San Diego's losing streak to five before the Padres won the next two games in Los Angeles.

Then the Padres returned home for a four-game series with Colorado. They took three of the four games to move back into first. The 22-game swing against divisional opponents had produced a 14-8 record.

The Padres then traveled to Houston. They lost two of three to the Astros to fall back into second place.

John Flaherty caught for the Padres in 1996 and 1997.

But a 10-inning, 3-0 win against the Florida Marlins in Miami on July 26 put the Padres back in first place. The following day, the Padres set a club record with 20 runs scored in a 20-12 win over Florida. San Diego split its final two games with the Marlins to return home with a 57-50 record.

The acquisition of Marc Newfield and Ron Villone for Andy Benes was intended to bring the Padres long-term dividends. With the team in contention in 1996, the trade brought short-term dividends. Newfield, Villone, and pitcher Bryce Florie were sent to Milwaukee on July 31 for outfielder Greg Vaughn.

Vaughn's acquisition gave the Padres four solid outfielders. With Tony Gwynn on the disabled list there was no conflict, but when Gwynn returned Vaughn and Henderson had to share time on the bench. Vaughn's .206 batting average with San Diego in 1996 made the decision somewhat easier on Bruce Bochy, but he still hit 10 home runs in his two months with the Padres to bring his season total to 41.

The Padres split six games against Atlanta and Florida on the home stand. The club then embarked on a 10-game road trip and split those matches, ending with three losses which moved the Padres back into a tie for first place.

The Republican National Convention was held in San Diego in 1996. The Republican Party had contemplated the idea of holding the convention at Jack Murphy Stadium. The logistics, including preparation and teardown, would have required the Padres to move their August 16-18 series against the New York Mets elsewhere.

The Padres saw an opportunity. They began to work out arrangements to play their three games against the Mets in Monterrey, Mexico. When the Republicans abandoned their plans to use the stadium, the Padres continued their plans to play three home games in Mexico.

The Padres sent Mexican hero Fernando Valenzuela to the mound August 16. He picked up the win in the 15-10 victory. Steve Finley earned the distinction of hitting the first home run in a regular season game in Mexico, while Greg Vaughn hit the first grand slam in Mexico.

In 1998, Greg Vaughn became the first Padre to clout 50 home runs in a season.

The Mets won the second game, 7-3, but the Padres won the third game, 8-0. Ken Caminiti was dehydrated prior to the game and had to be given IV fluids. He also had a craving for a Snickers bar, which was provided for him. Caminiti hit two home runs in that game, and after Wally Joyner was subsequently retired he returned to the bench and asked for an IV and a Snickers.

Caminiti had 17 home runs entering August. On August 1 against Atlanta, he switch-hit home runs for the fourth time as a Padre. He also switch-hit home runs on August 21 and August 28 against Montreal and New York, respectively. He finished August with 14 more home runs and 38 more RBI than when he started. He also began receiving bags of Snickers bars in the locker room.

After the Padres went back to the United States for the remainder of their home stand, they swept Montreal and took two of three from Philadelphia to move back into first place.

The Padres won the first four games on their ensuing road trip, but lost five of the final eight games on the trip to move back into a tie for first.

The Padres hosted Pittsburgh September 9 through 11 and won all three games with two outs in the bottom of the ninth inning. A September 12 off-day and a September 13 loss to Cincinnati put the Padres half a game behind of the Los Angeles Dodgers, and two subsequent wins against the Reds were negated by Dodgers wins.

The Padres went to San Francisco for three games, taking two out of three but not gaining any ground on Los Angeles. The Padres still trailed by half a game with nine games left—seven against the Dodgers.

The Dodgers began the four-game series in San Diego with a 7-0 win on September 19. The Padres stayed in contention the following day with a 4-2 win. Los Angeles countered with a 9-2 victory, and San Diego salvaged a split of the series with a 3-2 win in the finale on September 22.

The Padres and Dodgers both had an off day on September 23. The Padres and Colorado Rockies then faced off for the final two regular season games in San Diego. The Rockies earned a 5-4 victory in 11 innings in the first game, despite Caminiti's 39th home run of the season to break a Padres team record, and a 5-3 win in the second match. The losses, combined with two Dodgers wins, put San Diego 2 1/2 games back with three games to play.

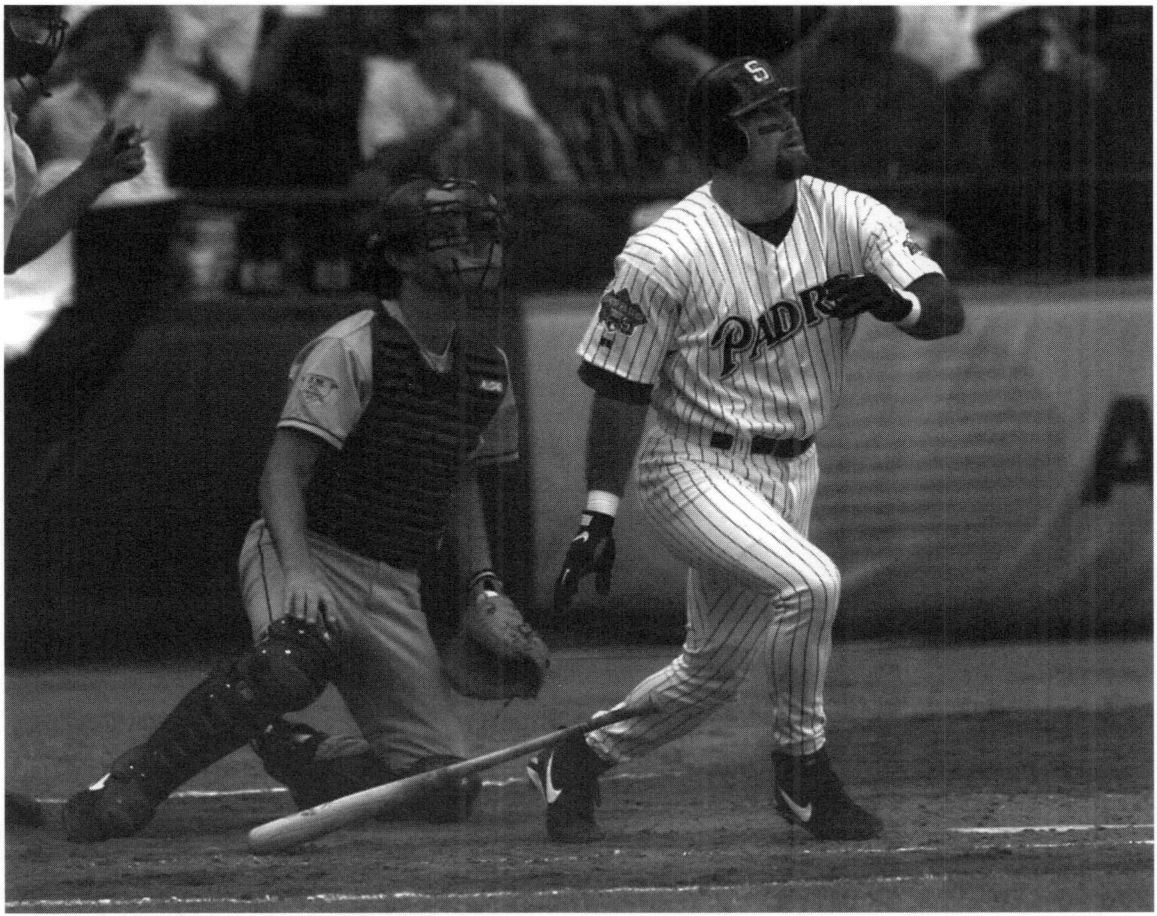

Ken Caminiti, right, and Brent Mayne of the New York Mets watch a three-run homer hit by Caminiti fly over the fence Sunday, August 18, 1996, at the Monterrey Baseball Stadium in Monterrey, Mexico.

The Padres had September 26 off, and the San Francisco Giants defeated the Dodgers to move the Padres to two games back with three games to play, all in Los Angeles.

The Padres and Dodgers battled for nine innings on September 27, with each team scoring two runs in regulation. In the top of the tenth, Caminiti hit a double to break the tie, and the Padres scored three times in the inning to move to within one game of Los Angeles after the 5-2 win.

The following day, the score was tied 2-2 going into the eighth, when Tony Gwynn hit a two-out double to score two runs. The Padres held on for the 4-2 win, giving both teams a 90-71 record going into the final game of the regular season.

The 162nd game for both teams, and the first game since 1908 where two teams had entered the final game of the season against each other tied for first place, was also close. Again the Padres and Dodgers battled for nine innings, with neither team giving up a run. The Dodgers and Padres held each other scoreless in the tenth inning. In the 11th inning, a two-run pinch-hit double by Chris Gwynn scored two runs, and the Padres held on in the bottom of the inning for the victory and the division title.

The Padres had spent 142 days in first place during the season and were never more than 2 1/2 games out of first.

The rules of baseball require that a player have 3.1 plate appearances per scheduled game for the team in order to qualify for the batting title. For a 162-game season, this equates to 502 plate appearances. However, a subsection of the rule states that if a player has enough of a lead that he could go hitless for enough plate appearances to total 502, but would still be ahead of his nearest competitor, he could win the batting title with fewer than 502 plate appearances. Prior to the 1996 season, the rule had never been used in the majors.

Gwynn's final game of the season gave him 498 plate appearances and a .353 batting average. The extra four at-bats would have given him a .349 batting average. Ellis Burks had a .344 average. The rule gave Gwynn his seventh career batting title and his third in a row.

Gwynn's winning batting average went into the books as .353. He also earned the "hardest to fan" title, striking out only 17 times.

The team's 91-71 record was only one game behind their previous best in 1984, but their 46-35 road record was an all-time best. They also set club records with 771 runs scored, 456 extra-base hits, 285 doubles, and 2,273 total bases.

Caminiti earned National League Player of the Month awards for both August and September, as well as a pair of Player of the Week awards during that span. In addition to his 40 home runs, his 130 RBIs and his .621 slugging percentage were also team records. He also batted .326, scored 109 runs, had 37 doubles, and tied for the National League lead with 10 sacrifice flies.

Caminiti earned his second Gold Glove award. He also earned the National League's Most Valuable Player award, being selected as the first choice by all 28 writers voting.

He won the "second-half triple crown" by leading National League hitters after the All-Star break with a .360 batting average, 28 home runs, and 81 RBIs.

Steve Finley set club records with 348 total bases, 84 extra-base hits, 45 doubles, and 126 runs scored. Finley also hit 30 home runs, giving the Padres two players with 30 home runs in a season for the first time in club history. Eighteen of his home runs either put the Padres ahead or tied the score, including a September 10 blast against the Pittsburgh Pirates in which the Padres were down by one run with two outs and Joe Boever had an 0-2 count on Finley.

Trevor Hoffman had 42 saves and led all National League relief pitchers throwing at least 60 innings by limiting opposing batters to a .161 batting average. Opponents were held to .122 when Hoffman got ahead in the count, and he led the majors by limiting opponents with two strikes to a .089 batting average. He saved all of the final three games of the season in Los Angeles, and *The Sporting News* gave him the N.L. Fireman of the Year award.

The pitchers set a Padre record with 1,194 strikeouts. They also tied a club record by using only seven different starting pitchers throughout the season. Hamilton posted a 15-9 record with 184 strikeouts while Valenzuela was 13-8 with a 3.62 ERA. In 150 innings, Ashby had a 3.23 ERA and a 9-5 record.

The first-place finish put the Padres in the National League playoffs against St. Louis. Hamilton was selected to pitch the first game in St. Louis on October 1. He allowed only five hits and struck out six in six innings, but gave up a three-run home run to Gary Gaetti in the first inning. The Cardinals never trailed, allowing only a sixth-inning home run to Rickey Henderson.

In the second game, October 3, the Cardinals took a 1-0 lead in the bottom of the third inning. The Padres tied the game in the top of the fifth, but St. Louis scored

Trevor Hoffman led National League relievers with nine victories and 111 strikeouts in 1996, helping the Padres win the National League West.

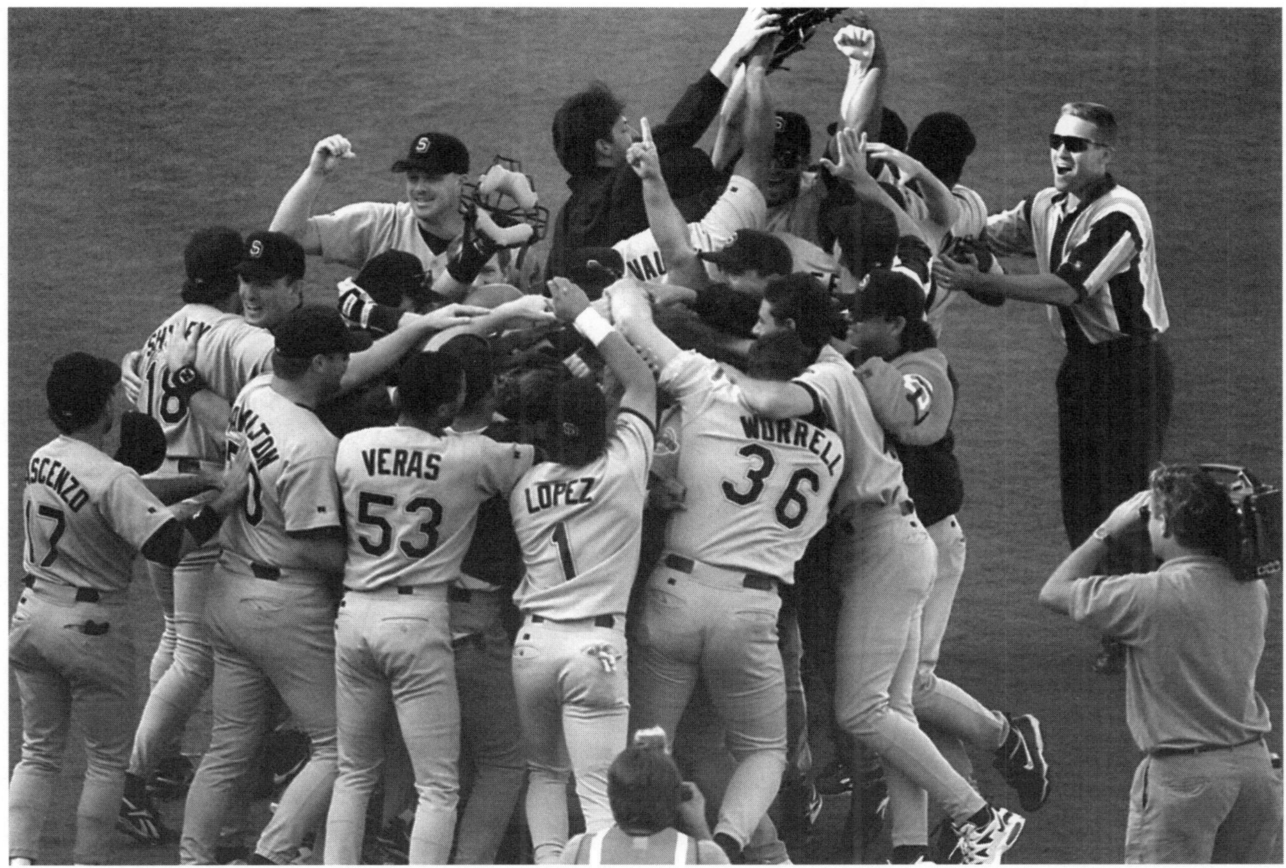

Members of the San Diego Padres celebrate on the pitchers mound after defeating the Los Angeles Dodgers, 2-0, to win the National League West Division Sunday, Sept. 29, 1996, in Los Angeles.

three times in the bottom of the fifth. The Padres scored twice in the sixth and once in the eighth to tie the game again. The Cardinals scored in the bottom of the eighth to win, 5-4, and take a 2-0 lead into San Diego.

In the third game of the series on October 5, the Cardinals scored in the top of the first inning, but the Padres scored twice in the second and Ken Caminiti homered in the third. The Padres scored again in the fourth to take a 4-1 lead, but the Cardinals tied the game with three runs in the sixth and went ahead with a run in the seventh.

In the eighth inning, Caminiti hit his second home run of the game and third of the series, tying the score at five runs apiece in the process. In the top of the ninth inning, Brian Jordan hit a two-run home run to win the game and the division series for the Cardinals.

Bruce Bochy became the first Padres manager to earn Manager of the Year awards, being selected by both the Baseball Writers Association of America and by his peers. Bochy outdistanced Felipe Alou by two points, 76 to 74, for the BBWAA award, but had 8 1/2 votes for *The Sporting News* award selected by managers compared to 2 1/2 for Atlanta's Bobby Cox, the closest challenger.

The Padres sought to shore up a couple of positions. They traded pitcher Dustin Hermanson to Florida for second baseman Quilvio Veras, who was injured for part of 1996 but led the National League with 56 stolen bases in 1995. They sent right-handed pitcher Scott Sanders to Seattle for left-hander Sterling Hitchcock. A four-player transaction with Detroit brought them middle reliever Joey Eischen, who was subsequently traded during spring training.

On September 20, 1996, John Moores and Larry Lucchino announced the Little Padres Parks program in which the club would build or refurbish 60 youth parks in the area. The first of those parks, at the Jackie

Bruce Bochy, the winningest manager in Padre history, piloted the Padres to the National League West title in 1996.

Robinson YMCA in southeast San Diego, was dedicated on January 31, 1997.

On January 12, 1997, the Padres reached an agreement with the Chiba Lotte Marines of the Japanese Pacific League. The agreement included having San Diego farm clubs host two or three Chiba Lotte prospects in their farm system and having a Chiba Lotte coach study baseball as a member of the Padres organization coaching staff. The clubs also agreed to exchange scouting information and to attempt to promote eventual world play.

The Padres also ended up with negotiating rights to right-handed Japanese pitcher Hideki Irabu. Baseball's executive council upheld the Padres' rights to Irabu, but Irabu expressed his desire to play for the New York Yankees instead.

On April 22, the Padres sent the rights to Irabu, along with three minor-league players, to the Yankees for outfielder Ruben Rivera and pitcher Rafael Medina. Rivera spent most of 1997 on the disabled list or in the minors. Medina spent all of 1997 in the minors.

The Padres' 1996 success came two years after the San Diego Chargers' Super Bowl appearance. In 1995, the Chargers requested an expansion of the stadium. The City of San Diego was receptive, but political battles over financing lasted until a judge's ruling in February 1997, and the stadium was under construction during the 1997 baseball season. Part of the financing involved Qualcomm paying $18 million for the stadium naming rights, and in May 1997 the giant "Q" was erected at the ballpark. The Padres added a pitcher's board on the left field wall for ball and strike count and pitch speed, and in August the Chargers added a second giant scoreboard which gave football fans a scoreboard for each end zone and for baseball purposes was behind third base.

The Padres opened their 1997 season on April 1. They trailed the New York Mets in the sixth inning, but Chris Gomez led off the bottom of the inning with a home run. Then Rickey Henderson, pinch hitting for Joey Hamilton, homered. And Quilvio Veras homered. The three consecutive home runs were joined by eight additional runs in the inning, giving the Padres a 20th-century record for most runs in an inning on opening day.

On April 4, the Padres defeated Philadelphia, 13-3. Vaughn hit two home runs, one measuring 415 feet and one traveling 475 feet into the second deck. Bochy's decision to play Vaughn worked. His decision to sit the left-handed hitting Finley, instead of right-handed batters Vaughn or Henderson, against a right-handed starter was a sign of trouble. Finley was bothered by elbow problems and ended April on the disabled list.

During the season, 18 different players went on the disabled list. The list was used 20 times, including 19 after the regular season opened.

Wally Joyner and Joey Hamilton also ended April on the disabled list. Henderson, Caminiti, and Ashby were among those placed on the list in May.

During the first home stand, the Padres created the Cindy Matters fund. Cindy Matters, a lifelong Padres fan, had passed away from cancer in January at the age of 28. The purpose of the fund was to raise money for pediatric cancer research and also to honor scientists working on fighting the disease. Ken Caminiti donated a motorcycle for a raffle, which raised over $34,000, and corporate pledges helped bring the first-year contributions to over $100,000.

The Padres also agreed to a contract extension with Tony Gwynn during the first week of the season, keeping Gwynn in San Diego through 2000.

The Padres spent the first week of the season in first place or tied for first, winning five of their first

Wally Joyner played first base for the Padres from 1996 through 1999.

seven. A week later, they were in fourth place although only one game out of first and with a 7-4 record.

The success of the series in Mexico, along with the approval of the visiting team, caused the Padres to schedule a three-game series with St. Louis in Hawaii. The Paradise Series in Honolulu involved a doubleheader on April 19, swept by the Cardinals, and a single game on April 20, won by the Padres.

The Padres ended April with an eight-game losing streak, giving them a 9-15 record for the month. They ended May in the middle of a six-game winning streak, which gave them a record of 26-30 as of June 4, the final win of that streak.

On May 19, Steve Finley became the first Padre since 1972 to hit three home runs in a game. In the 13-6 win in Cincinnati, Finley homered in the third, fourth, and ninth innings. On June 23, he became the sixth player in National League history to homer three times in a game twice in a season, connecting in the first, seventh, and ninth innings against San Francisco. Finley also added a single against the Giants to break Nate Colbert's team record of 12 total bases in a game. Five days after his feat against the Giants, Finley faced Los Angeles and hit two home runs in the game.

The 1997 season was the debut of interleague play, and on June 12 the Padres went to Anaheim to play their first interleague game. The Angels earned an 8-4 victory in the interleague opener. Rickey Henderson, the first Padres batter against a regular season American League opponent, struck out against Matt Perisho. In the third inning, Flaherty's home run off Perisho gave the Padres their first interleague run.

The Padres won their first interleague game the following day, an 8-7 win over the Angels in 14 innings. The Padres then went to Texas, but lost both games to conclude their first interleague road trip with a win and three losses.

On June 17, the Padres hosted the Oakland Athletics for their first interleague home game. The A's took a 10-3 win in the first game and a 11-9 win the next day to sweep the Padres' first interleague home series.

Another trade with the New York Yankees was underway, this one solving the outfielder surplus by sending Vaughn to New York for pitcher Kenny Rogers. But when Vaughn failed a Yankees physical, the trade was called off.

The Padres entered the All-Star game with a 38-49 record. They won 12 of their next 15 to move back into third place.

The Padres held on to third place through August 10, spent time in both third and fourth between then and August 26, and fell to fourth place for the rest of the season after their August 26 loss in Philadelphia.

On August 12, Rickey Henderson hit his 250th career home run. After the game, reporters in the Padres' locker room sought to ask him questions. He asked them to wait and walked into Bochy's office. The door was closed for several minutes. The following day, Henderson was traded to Anaheim for third baseman George Arias and two minor-league pitchers.

Vaughn set out to prove the Padres right in keeping him. On August 15 against Chicago, he became the first player to hit two career home runs into the second deck of Qualcomm Stadium. He lifted his batting average to .216 by the end of the season and gave the Padres 18 home runs in 361 at-bats for 1997.

On September 5, Ashby accomplished something which had not been done since 1972. In the Padres' fourth season, Steve Arlin had taken a no-hitter into

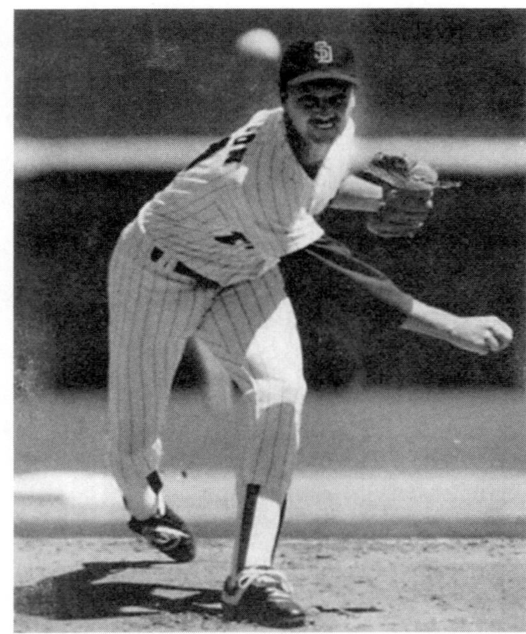

Andy Ashby pitched for the Padres from July 1993 through 1999.

the ninth inning before allowing two Philadelphia hits with two outs. Ashby held the Atlanta Braves hitless for eight innings, but Kenny Lofton led off the top of the ninth with a single, and with two outs a Fred McGriff home run spoiled the shutout.

The Padres closed the season with a 76-86 record, 14 games behind the first-place San Francisco Giants. They ended the season with an 8-8 record against American League opposition.

Gwynn's .372 batting average tied him with Honus Wagner for the all-time record for most National League batting championships won. His 220 hits and 49 doubles set club records. He also earned National League Player of the Month honors for May after batting .447, and he was batting over .400 as late as July 14. Fifth in the batting race, with a .327 mark was Wally Joyner.

The team set club records with 795 runs scored, 1,519 hits, 761 RBIs, 2,282 total bases, and 604 walks received.

The team also had the highest ERA in club history, with a 4.99 ERA, and allowed a club-record 1,581 hits. They also broke their club record for fewest shutouts, blanking opponents only twice.

Middle relief pitching was sought, and in November the Padres made four trades in one week, including sending Flaherty to Tampa Bay for right-hander Brian Boehringer and sending Tim Worrell to Detroit in a five-player deal which brought the Padres right-handers Donne Wall and Dan Miceli.

The Padres also fired their trainer, replacing him with assistant trainer Todd Hutcheson.

16

The Dream Season

[1998]

In August 1997, a task force concluded that the Padres would need a baseball-only ballpark to ensure long-term financial stability. Mayor Susan Golding convened a committee for a new ballpark site and financing, and in January 1998 they recommended a ballpark in the South Embarcadero area of downtown San Diego.

The battle of the stadium expansion for the Chargers convinced the city that a public vote would be needed. The concept of a downtown ballpark seemed nice in theory, but the higher cost of land and the longer travel distances for a greater population, especially the 59 percent of Padres fans, according to the task force, who lived outside city limits made a downtown ballpark a tough sell. The threat of losing the team would be most effective if the team was worth keeping.

Dan Warthen was not retained as pitching coach. Dave Stewart, who had served as a special assistant to general manager Kevin Towers in 1997, was named as the new pitching coach.

On December 15, 1997, the Padres sent first baseman Derek Lee, pitcher Rafael Medina, and pitching prospect Steve Hoff to Florida for pitcher Kevin Brown, who had a 33-19 record with the Marlins the past two years and led the National League with a 1.89 ERA in 1996.

Left-handed pitcher Mark Langston and catcher Greg Myers were signed as free agents.

The Padres won the Cactus League with a 19-10 record, and Kevin Brown led the majors with an 0.75 ERA in five starts, striking out 15 in 24 innings. Spring training included a return to Yuma, Arizona, for the first time since the Padres trained there in 1993.

The Padres opened their regular season in Cincinnati with a 10-2 win, making Brown victorious in his Padres debut. The Padres split their remaining two with Cincinnati and then won two out of three in St. Louis to enter their first home stand tied for first.

The Padres trailed the Cincinnati Reds in the ninth inning of their home

Dave Stewart served as a pitching coach for the Padres in 1998.

opener on April 7, but Carlos Hernandez homered with two outs in that inning and the Padres won in the tenth on a sacrifice fly. The Padres swept the Reds in three games, bringing in the Arizona Diamondbacks for their first-ever game against the Padres.

The Diamondbacks had a 4-2 lead going into the ninth inning on April 10, but a ninth-inning two-out grand slam by Steve Finley gave the Padres a 6-4 win. The Padres won their remaining three games with Arizona to sweep the homestand and extend their winning streak to eight.

A loss to San Francisco ended the winning streak, but the Padres won five of the remaining six games on the visits. They returned home to lose three of five against Pittsburgh and Chicago and went 5-6 on their next road trip.

The Padres won their first game of the home stand against the New York Mets on May 11. The following day was greeted with the Padres' first home rainout in 15 years, and the Padres lost to the Mets on May 13. The Padres won the remaining five games of the homestand to give them a 29-14 record.

The Padres returned to the road, this time winning four and losing six. Kevin Brown took the loss in Pittsburgh on May 21 to even his record at 3-3. He won a 12-2 decision in Arizona five days later, and did not lose again until August 10, matching the club record with 11 straight wins.

The Padres returned home for a four-game series against St. Louis from May 29 through June 1. The fans went away pleased. They saw the Padres win three of the four games and Mark McGwire hit two home runs. Chris Gomez also homered twice in the series, both in the final game.

Houston won two of the three games in that series to close out the homestand, bringing up the first interleague games of the year. The Padres lost the first two at Texas, with the first loss putting them into a tie for first and the second loss relegating them to second place, before a 17-8 win on June 7.

The Padres opened the homestand by sweeping the Cincinnati Reds in three games, but the Giants won their first two games to stay one game ahead of San Diego before a June 10 Giants loss evened the division. The Padres and Giants squared off in a three-game series June 12-14. San Diego won the first game, 10-3, and won the next two games to take a three-game lead. The Padres closed out their homestand with an 8-0 record after taking two from the Los Angeles Dodgers.

The Padres won their first two games in San Francisco to extend their winning streak to 11 straight, matching the 1982 club record. The Giants won the third game of the four-game series, but the Padres took the final game to leave San Francisco with a 5 1/2 game lead.

On June 21, the Padres swung a five-player trade with the Boston Red Sox which brought catcher-first baseman Jim Leyritz to the Padres.

The Padres split a pair in Seattle, returned home to split two more with Seattle, and took two of three from Anaheim in San Diego. The Padres then traveled to Oakland, losing two of three to give them a 54-31 record as of July 2.

The Padres played their final three games before the All-Star break in San Diego and swept the Colorado Rockies. The final game, July 5, marked Ashby's 50th win as a Padre. He needed only 75 pitches to throw nine innings and only 43 for the first six innings of work. The win gave the Padres a 57-31 record and a 5 1/2 game lead at the All-Star break.

Fans voted Tony Gwynn onto the National League All-Star team, and manager Jim Leyland added

Greg Vaughn, Kevin Brown, Trevor Hoffman, and Ashby. Vaughn was the first Padre and the 23rd player in major-league history to have 30 home runs by the All-Star break.

The Padres started the second half of the season with a four-game split in Los Angeles. On July 12, Ken Caminiti hit three home runs in the 6-3 win over the Dodgers. He also homered from each side of the plate for the eighth time in his Padres career. The Padres lost their first game in Colorado, but they won the next two against the Rockies and then swept the Reds in three Cincinnati games.

A 13-1 loss to the St. Louis Cardinals in the homestand opener snapped the Padres' winning streak, but the Padres won the second game with St. Louis and then won four of five from Arizona and Houston to move 13 games in front.

The final game against Houston saw the end of Trevor Hoffman's streak of 41 consecutive saves. Hoffman entered the game with a 4-3 lead in the ninth, but the first batter, Moises Alou, homered to give Hoffman his first blown save since 1997. The Padres recovered to win in 10 innings, 5-4, which preserved the streak of not losing in a game they led after eight innings. Throughout the year, the Padres were 85-0 in games they led after eight innings, the second straight year they were undefeated with a lead going into the ninth.

San Diego won three of seven on a road trip to New York and Montreal, but started the next home stand by winning four of six from Philadelphia and Florida. Brown's winning streak was snapped on August 10 in a 3-2 loss to Florida's Livan Hernandez.

The three-game series against the Atlanta Braves August 11-13 now had implications for home field playoff advantage. In the first game, Joey Hamilton outdueled Denny Neagle for a 3-1 Padres win. In the second game, Ashby improved his record to 16-9 while Greg Maddux fell to 15-6 as the Padres prevailed, 5-1. Atlanta took the third game by a 5-0 score, but the Padres closed out their homestand by taking two of three from Milwaukee, including a one-hitter by Brown in the first game of an August 16 doubleheader.

The Padres split two games on the road at Florida and split two more in Atlanta. They lost to Milwaukee before winning their final five games of the road trip.

A win against Montreal on August 28 extended the winning streak to six and put them 16 games ahead of their nearest rival. The Padres were also 41 games above .500 with an 88-47 record. Four games later, the Padres were 90-49.

Greg Vaughn played outfield for the Padres from 1996 through 1998.

Although Sterling Hitchcock was the losing pitcher in a 3-1 game against Montreal on August 29, he tied a club record by striking out 15 batters in a game. Hitchcock, who did not walk a batter, only threw eight frames. Two strikeouts by reliever Scott Sanders set a club record for a nine-inning game with 17.

The Padres had won one game in March, 18 in April, 16 in May, 18 in June, 18 in July, and 18 in August. They were poised to win 100 games for the first time in their history.

A 9-15 record in September spoiled their plans. The Padres lost their final game against the New York Mets, lost two of three at Colorado, and opened a 14-game homestand by losing the first two to the Giants. They defeated San Francisco to avert a sweep and lost the first match of a four-game series to the Los Angeles Dodgers.

On September 11, Joey Hamilton earned his 13th victory in a 1-0 win over the Dodgers. The following day, before a sellout crowd of 60,623, the Padres defeated Los Angeles, 8-7, to clinch the National League West.

Third baseman Ken Caminiti played for the Padres from 1995 through 1998.

San Diego lost the final game of the series to the Dodgers, bringing up the Chicago Cubs and Sammy Sosa. On September 14, the Padres kept the products of Sosa's swings in the ballpark in a 4-3 win. They lost the second game of the four-game series, but also kept Sosa from matching or overtaking Mark McGwire for the home run record.

On September 16, the Padres and Cubs were tied at two runs apiece when Sosa came to the plate with the bases loaded in the eighth inning. He placed Brian Boehringer's pitch into the second deck of left field for his 63rd home run of the year, tying McGwire and breaking the tie game. The Padres lost the final game against Chicago, although they kept Sosa from hitting a home run.

A 4-1 loss to Colorado gave the Padres four straight losses for the first time in 1998. The Padres split the remaining two games with the Rockies, closing out home attendance at 2,555,901 for 79 games and giving the Padres a home record of 54-27.

After two losses to Arizona in the final series of the year, the Padres earned a 3-2 victory in the regular season's final game on September 27. In his last at-bat, Greg Vaughn became the tenth player in National League history to hit 50 home runs in a season, and Trevor Hoffman tied Randy Myers's National League record with 53 saves in a season.

The club's 98-64 record was the best in its history. The Padres were alone or tied for first place for 175 days out of the 181-day regular season. They swept 11 of the 66 series they played, but were not swept once in 1998.

The Padres had only used the disabled list 10 times. One of those trips was a season-long stay by pitcher Ed Vosberg. Another sidelined Heath Murray in September.

The team lowered its ERA to 3.63, and the pitching staff set a record with 1,217 strikeouts. Brown posted a 2.38 ERA, and Ashby's 3.34 ERA was the 11th best in the National League. Brown also set a club record with 257 strikeouts, while Brown and Ashby compiled 18-7 and 17-9 records, respectively.

Hoffman converted 53 out of 54 save opportunities, earning him second place in the Cy Young Award behind Tom Glavine and a plurality of first-place votes in the Cy Young Award balloting. In 66 appearances, he had a 4-2 record with a 1.48 ERA and he struck out 86 in 73 innings.

"Trevor Time" became one of the more popular routines in San Diego. When Hoffman went in for a save opportunity, the stadium speakers played the AC/DC song "Hell's Bells." The tradition began on July 25, 1998, when Hoffman saved his 41st consecutive game to tie Rod Beck's record. In San Diego, that song became associated with Hoffman. In March 1999, Hoffman signed a contract extension to remain in San Diego through at least 2003.

Gwynn's .321 batting average was the eighth best in the National League—the first time in his career he finished lower than sixth.

Wally Joyner only batted .298, but his .412 average with runners in scoring position was second in the National League.

The Padres set team records with 292 doubles, 489 extra-base hits, 604 walks drawn, and a .409 slugging percentage. They also set a record with home

The San Diego Padres pose on Turner Field in Atlanta after winning the National League Championship Series by downing the Atlanta Braves 5-0 in Game Six October 14, 1998. The Padres faced the New York Yankees in the World Series.

runs in 14 consecutive games, covering July 14 through July 29.

The team also set records for best fielding percentage in a season, with .983 and fewest errors with 104.

The Padres opened the playoffs in Houston on September 29. Kevin Brown struck out 16 Astros in eight innings, allowing only two hits in his stint. Hoffman added another strikeout in the ninth, although he gave up an unearned run as the Padres came away with a 2-1 victory. The Astros tied the series in the second game on October 1 with a 5-4 win after the Padres came back in the top of the ninth inning to tie the score. On October 3, the Padres took the first game in San Diego, 2-1. They took the series with a 6-1 win the following afternoon as Hitchcock allowed only three hits in six innings while striking out 11.

The Padres took a 3-0 lead against Atlanta in the National League Championship Series with 3-2, 3-0, and 4-1 wins, the middle of which was a complete-game gem by Brown with 11 strikeouts and only three Braves hits. But the Braves came back with an 8-3 win in the fourth game and sent the series back to Atlanta after a 7-6 win in Game 5. The Padres rectified that situation on October 14 with a 5-0 win, as Hitchcock struck out eight in five innings of two-hit ball. Hitchcock's 0.90 ERA, 14 strikeouts in 10 innings, and 2-0 record earned him MVP honors for the League Championship Series.

Leyritz, who homered four times for San Diego in 143 regular season at-bats, homered three times in the division series and once in the League Championship Series.

For the third time in the post-season, the Padres faced a team which had won at least 100 games in the regular season. The New York Yankees had set an American League record with 114 wins before disposing of their playoff opposition.

The 1998 World Series opened in New York on October 17. The Padres had a 5-2 lead after 4 1/2 innings, but the Yankees scored seven runs in the bottom of the seventh for a 9-6 win. In the second game on October 18, the Yankees took a 7-0 lead after three innings on the way to a 9-3 victory. The teams came to San Diego for Game 3 on October 20. The Padres scored three runs in the bottom of the sixth to open the scoring, but the Yankees scored twice in the seventh and three times in the eighth, and the Padres' single run in the eighth did not prevent a 5-4 Yankees triumph. The following day, the Yankees sealed the series with a 3-0 defeat of the Padres, scoring once in the sixth and twice in the eighth.

The Padres did not defeat the Yankees in their final quest on the diamond. But they had one more victory. On November 3, 1998, approximately 60 percent of the city of San Diego's voters approved Proposition C, allowing the city and the Padres to enter into negotiations for a downtown ballpark.

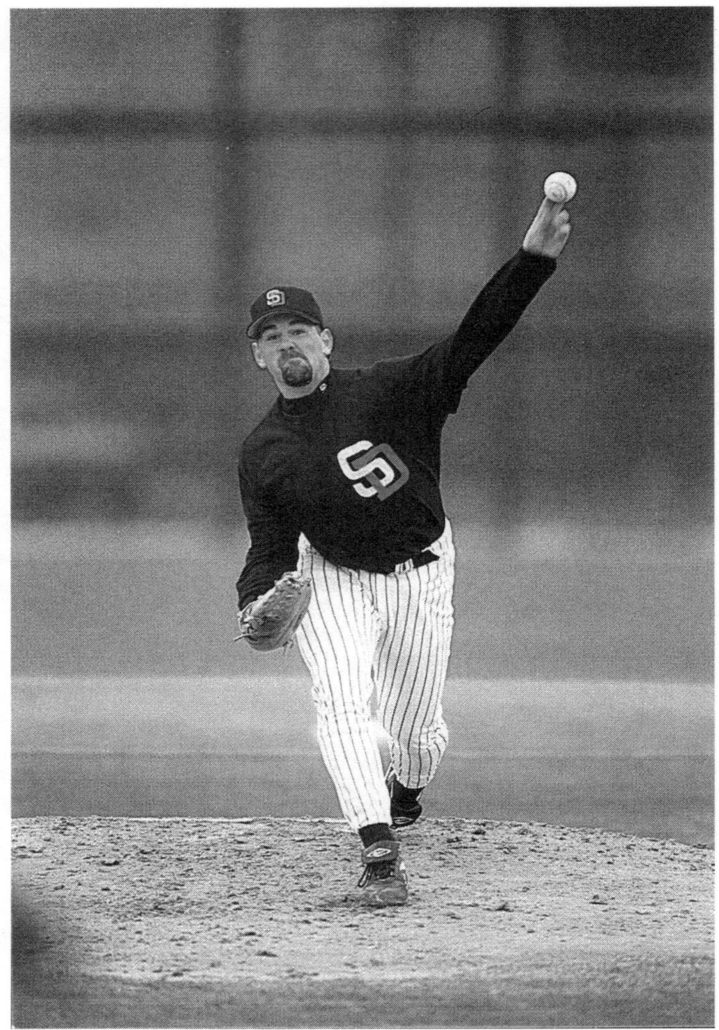

Sterling Hitchcock pitched for the Padres from 1997 through July 2001.

17

The End of an Era

[1999-2001]

The debate over the downtown ballpark vote focused on two main subjects. The first was the appropriateness of using public funds for the stadium. That was settled with the passage of Proposition C. The second issue was whether a downtown ballpark would really attract fans in San Diego. That will be settled at the turnstiles when the new stadium opens. The fans in the suburbs get to vote on that one.

The concept of condemning the Padres and 26 blocks of downtown San Diego to abandonment is not a pleasant one. San Diego State University's basketball program has proven that a new facility will not necessarily attract fans in San Diego. The Padres have spent their entire history competing against other recreation opportunities in the greater San Diego area, and the travel logistics of a downtown location must be overcome by a superior product.

The Padres did not retain some veteran players and planned to rebuild the team around the opening of the new stadium. The Padres' personnel moves after the 1998 season reflected this plan.

Ken Caminiti, who hit 29 home runs in 1998 but whose batting average fell to .252, was allowed to become a free agent. He negotiated with the Padres, who were not willing to provide a guaranteed contract. He signed with the Houston Astros. Steve Finley, who batted .249 in 1998, took the Arizona Diamondbacks' offer. Kevin Brown got seven guaranteed years, totaling $105 million, from the Los Angeles Dodgers.

The Padres hit 167 home runs and stole 79 bases in 1998. In a trade of more power for more speed, they sent Greg Vaughn to Cincinnati for outfielder Reggie Sanders and infielder Damian Jackson. Joey Hamilton, who had a 13-13 record with a 4.27 ERA in 1998, was traded to Toronto.

Dave Stewart left for other opportunities, so Dave Smith was named as the Padres' new pitching coach.

In January 1999, country music star Garth Brooks called a press conference at the Hotel Del Coronado to announce the Touch 'Em All Foundation, in which athletes pledged various amounts to charities for their accomplishments. On

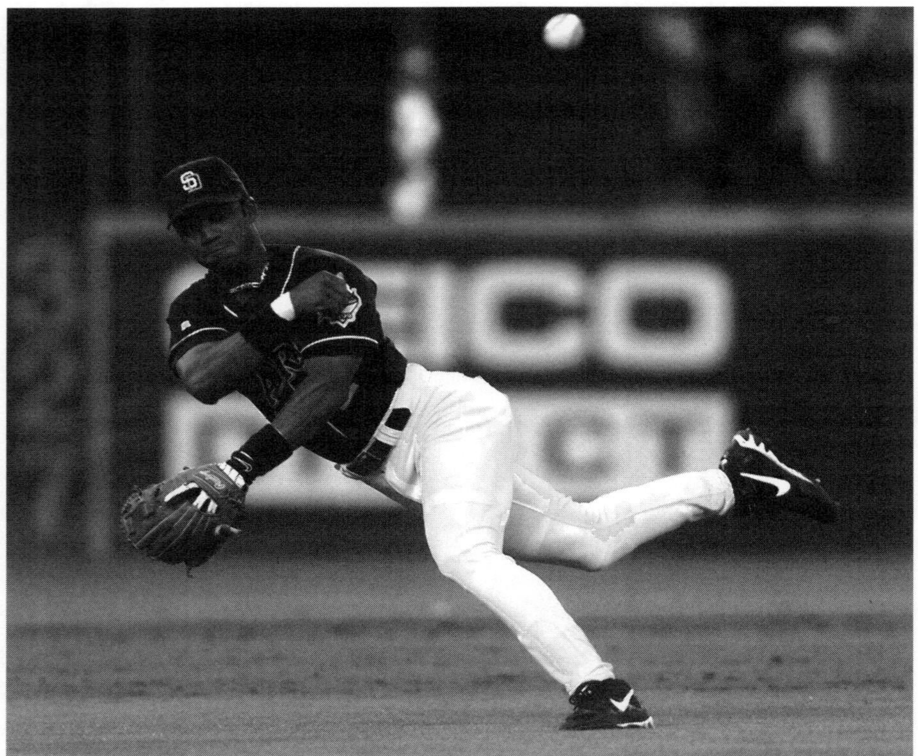

Shortstop Damian Jackson makes an off-balance throw on a slow roller hit by Pittsburgh Pirates' Abraham Nunez in the second inning Saturday, June 19, 1999, in San Diego.

The teams returned to San Diego two days later, and the Padres took both contests. But the Padres lost four of six on their first official road trip.

The Padres started 1999 with a streak of 174 consecutive wins when leading after eight innings. They had not been defeated after an eight-inning lead since a July 24, 1996 loss in the Astrodome which Houston won in ten innings. But on April 28, 1999, a single in the bottom of the ninth by the New York Mets' Jon Olerud and a home run by Mike Piazza ended that streak at 181. The streak was still the longest in baseball in the 20th century.

A five-game losing streak gave the club a 9-15 record as of May 2 as well as a spot in fifth place in the National League West. Except for one night when the team shared fourth place, the Padres did not escape the cellar until June 27.

On May 22, Tony Gwynn was placed on the disabled list with a strained right calf. He was activated June 12, but on June 24 he returned to the disabled list, this time with a strained left calf. He stayed on the disabled list until July 19.

February 12, Brooks announced that he would like to spend the season in the Padres' minor leagues. He joined the club for spring training and had one hit in 22 at-bats before retiring after 15 games. The team was also high on the charts with a 20-12-1 record in exhibition play.

The 1999 Padres were not done in by the players they knew they lost. They were hampered by the players they thought they had. In 1999, 15 different Padres made 16 trips to the disabled list. Eight of the nine opening day starters were on the disabled list at one time during the season, and the ninth, Ruben Rivera, was day-to-day at one point during the season. Eric Owens, who played six different positions during the year, led the team with 149 games played, 98 of which he started.

The 1996 Mexico trip was a success in terms of public relations. The team tried it again in 1999, opening their season against the Colorado Rockies in Monterrey. This time they only played one game, which the Rockies won, 8-2.

Owens made the most of his playing time. On May 21, 1999, against Cincinnati, he became the second Padre in history to execute a straight steal of home, beating Brett Tomko's delivery to the plate. Three other Padres also stole home in 1999, setting a club record for steals of home in a season. Owens also had the team's longest hitting streak of the year, batting safely in 18 consecutive games between June 19 and July 6. He batted .431 in 51 interleague at-bats, an average which trailed only the Kansas City Royals' Joe Randa.

A loss to Philadelphia on June 17 gave the Padres a 25-38 record and put them 13 1/2 games out of first place. The Padres completed their homestand with three games against Pittsburgh. On June 18, the Padres defeated the Pirates, 4-2, and the Padres swept the remaining two games.

The Padres went on the road for three games at Los Angeles. They won all three, holding the Dodgers to a total of four runs.

The Padres returned to Qualcomm Stadium on June 25, cruising to a 10-1 win over the Rockies. The following day, they took a 13-6 game from Colorado, and two days later they completed a four-game sweep.

On June 29, the Padres required 12 innings to defeat the Dodgers, but the 4-3 win tied the club record for consecutive wins. The following day, the Padres went for their record 12th consecutive win and touched Kevin Brown early and often in an 11-2 victory. The Padres closed the homestand with a 6-3 win over the Dodgers on July 1, evening their record at 38-38.

The winning streak was extended to 14 on July 2, as the Padres defeated Colorado by a 15-3 score. The streak ended the following day with a 12-10 Rockies win, but the Padres had moved into third place.

The club went into the All-Star break with a 43-43 record. They went on the road for 12 games, including the completion of a suspended game with Houston. They won six of their first eight games on the trip to move to within two games of first place.

The July 23 completion of the suspended game, which had stopped on June 13 with the Astros leading 4-1 in the eighth, gave the Padres another loss for their record after two runs were not enough to overcome the deficit. The Astros took the second game of the

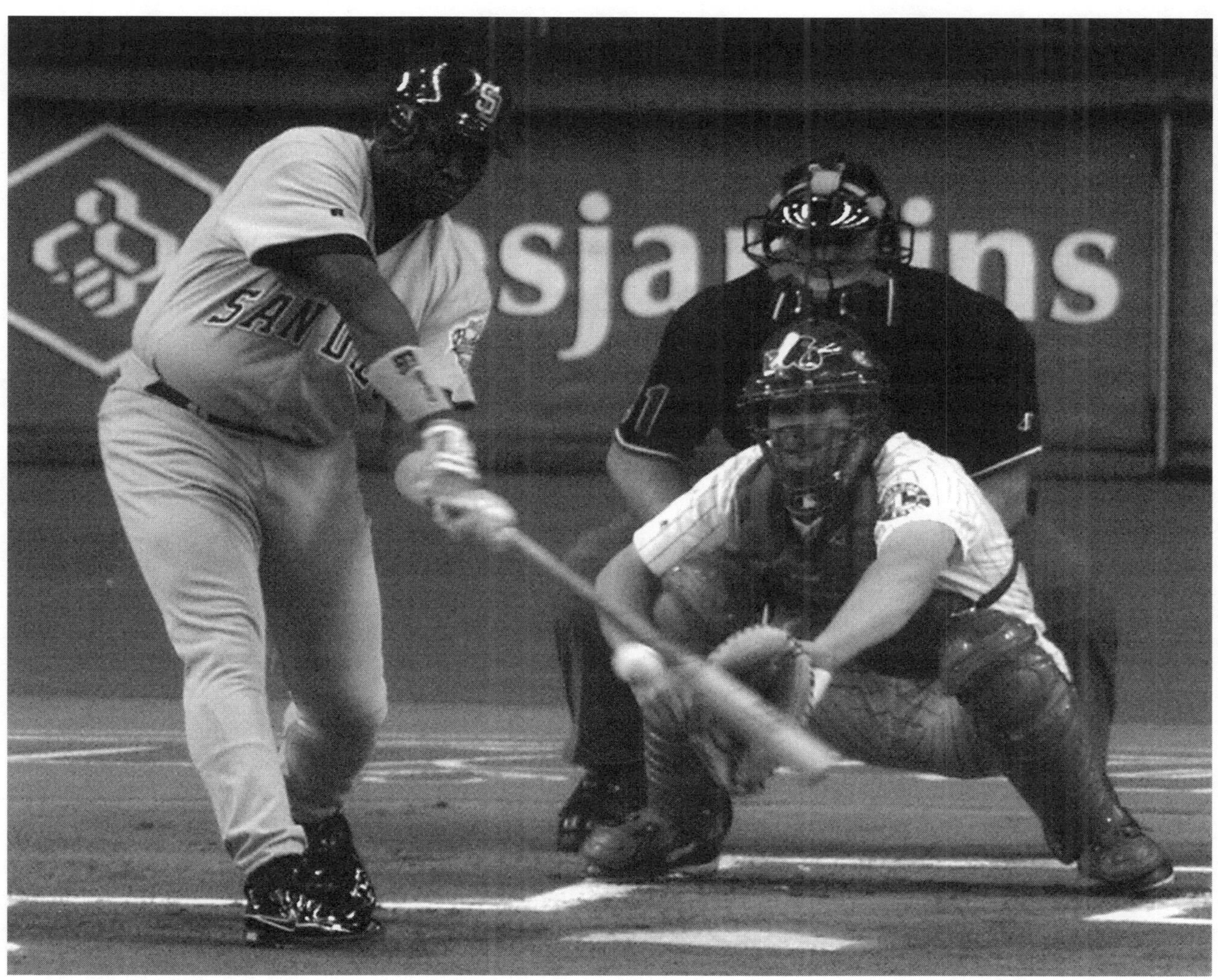

San Diego Padres' Tony Gwynn hits his 3,000th career hit in the first inning against the Montreal Expos, Friday, Aug. 6, 1999, in Montreal. Catching for Montreal is Chris Widger. Umpire is Bob Davidson.

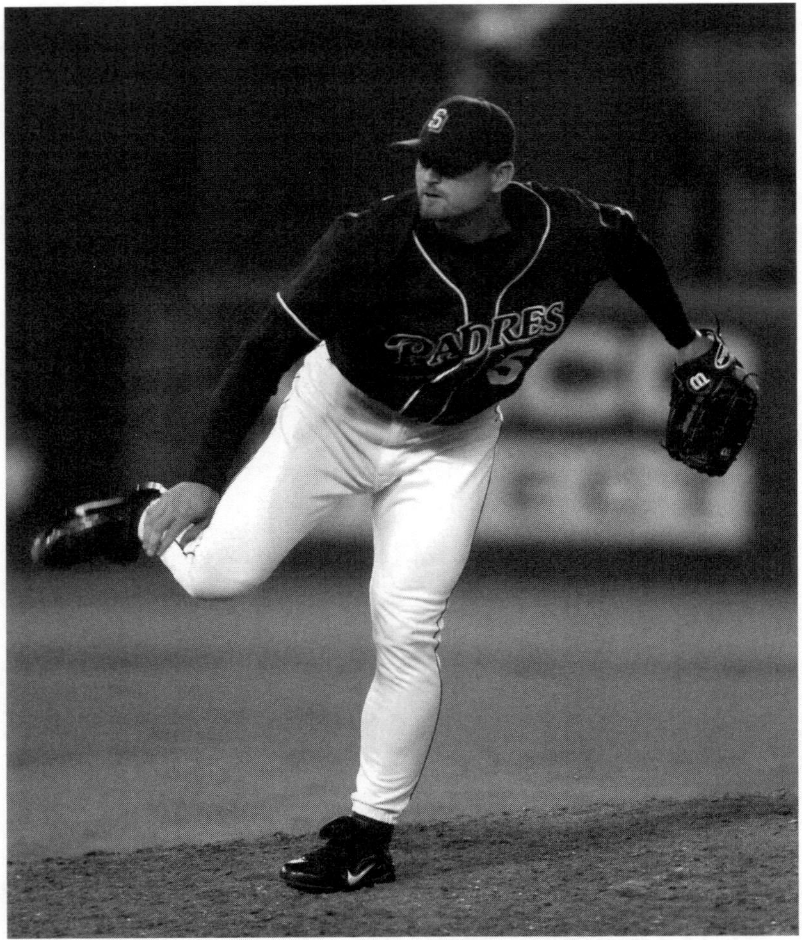

Trevor Hoffman follows through with a pitch while earning his 300th career save in the Padres' 2-1 victory over the New York Mets Wednesday, August 15, 2001, in San Diego.

doubleheader, and the Padres did not win another game for the rest of July.

The Padres lost the first five games of a six-game homestand, extending the losing streak to nine and giving the Padres a 49-54 record as of July 31.

The Padres ended the streak on August 1 with a win over Houston. Next they traveled to St. Louis for four games. They lost the first three, but they won the finale on August 5.

The following day, the Padres traveled to Montreal. In the first inning of the August 6 game, Tony Gwynn faced Expos pitcher Dan Smith. Smith worked Gwynn to a 1-2 count. Then Gwynn lined a ball into right center, giving Gwynn his 3,000th career hit. He finished the night with four hits in five at-bats, and the Padres won, 12-10.

A seven-game losing streak began August 7. The streak covered the rest of the road trip and included the first game of the ensuing homestand, in which 48,743 fans showed up to see the Padres honor Gwynn for his 3,000th hit.

By the end of August, the Padres were 61-72 and in fourth place. They moved into third place on September 9, but fell back into fourth after a September 26 loss.

The Padres closed the century with six losses in their final seven games to finish with a record of 74 wins and 88 losses, 26 games behind the Arizona Diamondbacks.

The Padres had the worst road record in the majors, winning 28 games away from Qualcomm Stadium and losing 53.

On the other hand, their 11-4 record against interleague opposition was the second best mark in the majors, and their 2.78 ERA against the American League easily topped the second highest interleague average of 3.52.

For the first time in their team's history, four players stole at least 30 bases for the Padres. Two of them came in the trade for Greg Vaughn; Reggie Sanders had 36 steals, while Damian Jackson led all major-league rookies with 34 steals. Eric Owens stole 33 bases, while Quilvio Veras pilfered 30 bags during the year.

The Padres also set a club record with 12 sets of back-to-back home runs.

Rivera batted .195 with 23 home runs, becoming only the second player in major-league history to hit at least 20 home runs while batting under .200. Gwynn batted .339 and struck out only 14 times in 411 at-bats. He was honored with the 1999 Roberto Clemente Man of the Year Award for his community service work.

Gwynn, who batted above .300 for his 17th consecutive season, also tied Honus Wagner for the National League record for most consecutive seasons batting over .300.

Phil Nevin had been acquired in the last week of spring training as a backup catcher after Carlos Hernandez tore his Achilles tendon. Nevin spent the beginning of 1999 on the disabled list. When George

Arias faltered at third base, Nevin took over. He ended the season with 24 home runs in 383 at-bats, 85 RBIs, a .269 average, and a secure job as the team's third baseman in 2000.

Three pitchers gave the club at least 200 innings. Andy Ashby was 14-10 with a 3.80 ERA in 206 innings. Sterling Hitchcock struck out 194 in 205.2 innings and posted a 12-14 mark. Woody Williams was 12-12 and threw 208 innings.

On October 10, the Padres traded Ashby to Philadelphia for three pitchers. One of them, Carlton Loewer, broke his leg in an off-season hunting accident and missed the start of the 2000 season.

On December 22, the Padres traded Wally Joyner, Quilvio Veras, and Reggie Sanders to the Atlanta Braves for Bret Boone, Ryan Klesko, and a minor-league pitcher. The trade left Gwynn, Gomez, and Hernandez as the only starters from the 1998 team still on the roster.

Rickey Henderson hits a looper down the right field line that falls in for a double and his 3,000th career hit during the first inning of the Padres' game against the Colorado Rockies Sunday, October 7, 2001 in San Diego.

The Padres also replaced a couple of coaches. Alan Trammell replaced first base coach Davey Lopes, who accepted the managerial job with Milwaukee, and Ben Ogilvie took over for hitting coach Merv Rettenmund, who took a position instructing the Braves after nine years with San Diego.

The Padres also hired Ted Simmons as the Vice-President of Scouting and Player Development. On January 1, 2000, former Braves international scouting director Bill Clark began work with the Padres. On January 11 the Padres signed their first high school prospect from Japan, 18-year-old left-handed pitcher Nobuaki Yoshida.

The Padres also returned to KOGO, the radio station which had broadcasted the club's games from 1970 to 1977, after 22 years with KFMB.

Another significant off season transaction was an agreement with the Sycuan Band of Mission Indians. The tribe paid the Padres $1.5 million for a sponsorship package which included marketing the team as "Padres 2000 presented by Sycuan". No reference was made to the Sycuan Casino in the marketing package, avoiding any promotion of gambling in the arrangement.

Work on the new ballpark seemed to be going well. On January 14, 2000, a "project-labor" agreement for the new ballpark was announced, in which prevailing wages would be paid in exchange for a no-strike clause. On March 7 Judge Judith McConnell dismissed two lawsuits which claimed that the California Environmental Quality Act had not been properly followed when construction of the ballpark was authorized.

The new ballpark suffered a couple of minor setbacks during the first months of 2000. On February 21 the Padres announced that the downtown stadium was scheduled to open in May 2002, a month later than expected. On March 7 the voters of San Diego cast ballots to elect a new mayor. Of the six major candidates, the three current members of the San Diego City Council finished fourth, fifth, and sixth. County Supervisor Ron Roberts and Judge Dick Murphy, both former members of the San Diego City Council, earned positions in the November runoff. Murphy had criticized the ballpark deal during the primary, although he later pledged to fulfill the city's obligations.

Contract signings were also part of the off-season. The January 17 agreements with Donne Wall, Rivera, and Brian Boehringer signed the only three Padres eligible for arbitration.

Matt Clement was signed to a five-year contract, with $8 million provided for the first four years and a club option for $6 million in the fifth year. General manager Kevin Towers' contract was extended to the end of 2003, paying Towers an average of $650,000 a year.

One contract negotiation still to be handled was that of Tony Gwynn, whose contract expired at the end of the 2000 season. Gwynn had asked for a contract extension and a raise prior to the start of the season April 3. Gwynn, who had missed 168 games over the previous four years but who had batted .365 in his final 208 at-bats during the 1999 season, said that it would take more than the "low 5's" to sign him for 2001.

On March 2 the Padres and Gwynn reached a short-term compromise. Gwynn was given an extra $2 million in salary for 2000, and the agreement called for a $6 million option in 2001. The option would be automatic if Gwynn had 502 plate appearances in 2000, and if Gwynn fell short of that total the club had the option of picking up his contract for 2001 or buying that year out for $2 million.

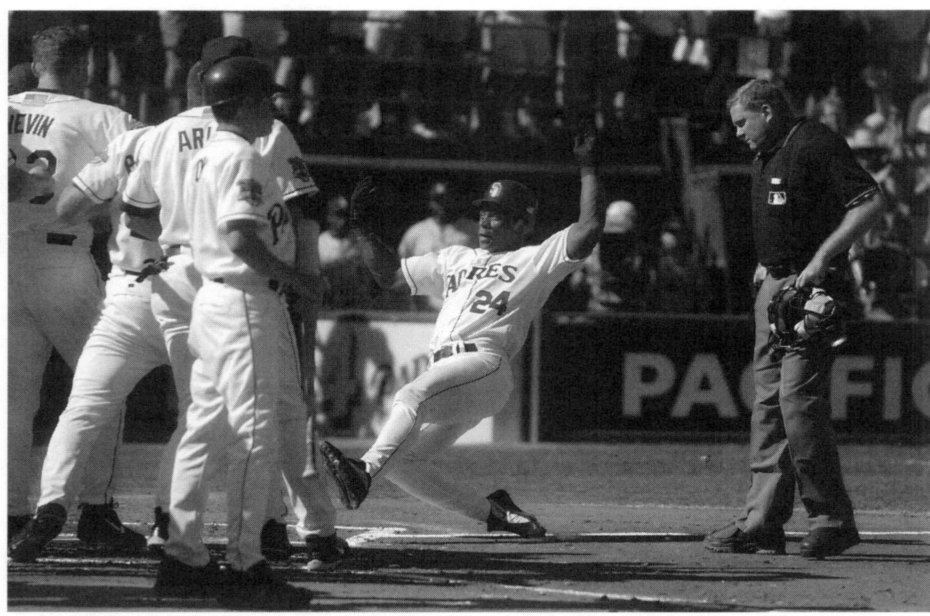

Rickey Henderson slides into home under the watch of home plate umpire Mike Everitt as he scores his 2,246th career run to break the all-time record held by Ty Cobb Thursday, October 4, 2001 in San Diego. Henderson homered to score the run in the third innng against the Los Angeles Dodgers.

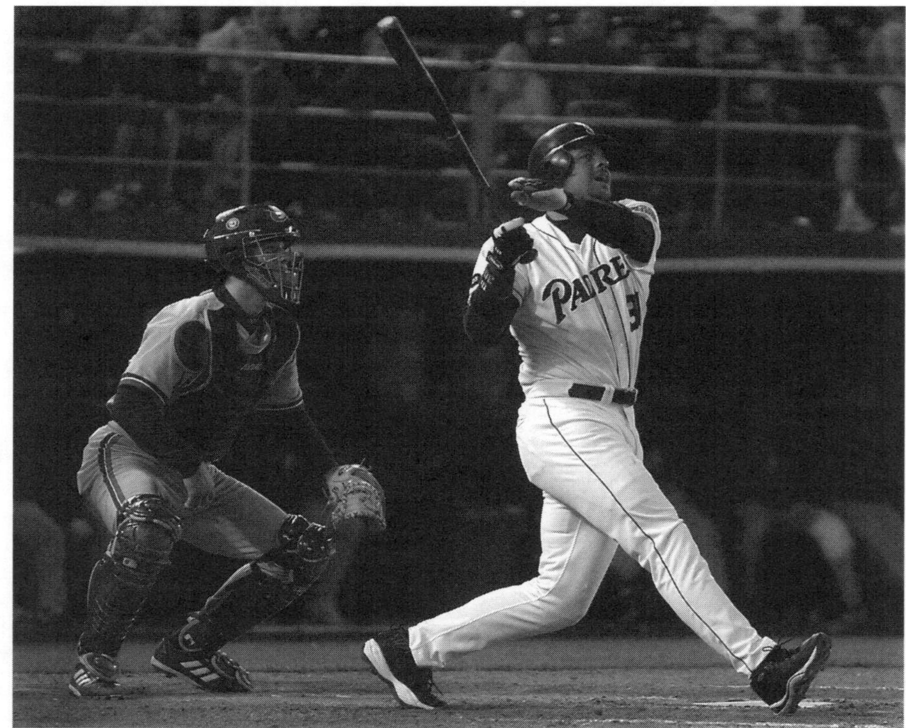

Ryan Klesko, right, and Montreal Expos catcher Michael Barrett watch Klesko's game-winning single off the scoreboard on the right-field wall in the 14th inning Wednesday, May 15, 2002, in San Diego.

The Padres opened Spring Training with a 10-5 win over the Mariners in a charity game March 2. The team posted an 18-14 record in Cactus League play, fourth among the ten Arizona-based teams. Carlos Hernandez batted .469 in 49 at-bats and Gwynn batted .457 in 46 at-bats. Although John Roskos started the season with Class AAA Las Vegas, he batted .458 with 22 hits in 48 at-bats; in his first 12 at-bats he had 10 hits, including two home runs and five doubles. Klesko batted .444 in 54 at-bats, and Rivera batted .352 and led the team with 16 runs batted in.

If 1993 was a fire sale, 2000 was a fire. In reality the fire was more the sterilization of surgical needles rather than a structural inferno, but injuries did to the 2000 team what payroll cuts did to the 1993 club. At one time the players on the disabled list had a higher payroll than the players on the active roster. The presence of 11 players on the disabled list at the same time, including nine pitchers, took its toll on the club. By the end of the season, 18 different players had made a total of 23 trips to the disabled list and missed a cumulative 1,408 games while on the 15-day or 60-day disabled list.

"We had a rough year. We faced a lot of adversities," manager Bruce Bochy noted.

The Padres utilized 17 rookies during the 2000 season, including eight pitchers. When Xavier Nady pinch-hit for the Padres September 30, he became the 56th player to appear in a game for the Padres during the season, tying the Major League record set by the Philadelphia Athletics of 1915. "One record I don't want to ever see is the one we broke this year as far as the number of players used," Bochy remarked.

Those 56 players do not include Randy Myers or Carlton Loewer, who were on the disabled list all season. The Padres also used 29 pitchers, establishing a National League record.

On January 2, Loewer was deer hunting near his Louisiana home and fell from a blind in a tree, resulting in a compound fracture to his left leg. Nevin suffered a preseason injury March 7, spraining his right ankle trying to avoid stepping on a runner, and missed part of the exhibition season.

Loewer was not the only off-season acquisition to start the season on the disabled list. Four days after acquiring Rodney Myers, the Padres learned that he had a partial rotator cuff tear which would require surgery. Rule V acquisition Kory DeHaan began the season on the disabled list with a left knee contusion, and a right shoulder strain kept Montgomery from beginning the season on the active roster.

Newcomer Al Martin also had preseason trouble. On March 21 he was arrested in Scottsdale, Arizona, for a domestic violence assault. The woman noted that she and Martin had been married in Las Vegas in December 1998, which also created a potential bigamy charge against Martin.

Hitchcock was hit in the knee during batting practice March 31, but it didn't prevent him from making the Opening Day start April 3 in New York. Nevin's home run in the second inning gave the Padres a 1-0 lead, but the Mets tied the game in the seventh and went ahead on Derek Bell's eighth-inning home run off Wall. The Mets won the 2-1 pitchers' duel, which saw New York limited to four hits and Nevin collecting three of the Padres' five hits in his first-ever Major League opener. The baserunners also included Tony Gwynn, who was hit in the elbow by an Al Leiter fastball. Gwynn missed the next three games due to a bruised right elbow.

The Padres and Mets had the next day off, allowing the team to sign Bochy to a contract extension through 2004 at an average annual salary of over $1 million. The teams returned to action April 5 with the Padres earning a 4-0 win in which they held the Mets hitless in ten at-bats with runners in scoring position. The Padres took a 7-0 lead in the rubber game and held on for an 8-5 win, and they improved their record to 3-1 with a 10-5 win in Montreal, putting the club into a tie for the division lead.

The Expos won the next two games, and the Padres entered their home opener April 10 with a 3-3 record. The Padres unveiled a new public address announcer; Tom Roberts had beaten out nearly 1,400 other applicants for the job held for 14 years by Bruce Binkowski, who had resigned to become the executive director of the Culligan Holiday Bowl. The Arizona Diamondbacks spoiled the home opener with five home runs and took an 8-4 win from the Padres.

Dave Magadan was placed on the disabled list with an elbow strain the following day, and Roskos was called up to take his place. Roskos started the April 11 game in left field and was hitless in four at-bats, but he became the 500th player to appear in a Padres uniform during the regular season. Ed Sprague, who tied the game with a home run in the bottom of the ninth, also homered in the 13th to give San Diego the 3-2 win over Arizona. A two-run pinch-hit single by

Sprague the following night gave the Padres a 4-2 win over the Diamondbacks and a winning record.

The Diamondbacks won a 5-4 game the following day, which also saw left-handed reliever Kevin Walker promoted to San Diego and reliever Dan Serafini sent to Las Vegas. On April 14 Jeff Bagwell hit a grand slam against Walker in the pitcher's first Major League appearance during the Astros' 10-4 victory. The Padres returned to .500 April 15 with a 5-3 win over Houston, a day which also saw Rivera placed on the disabled list and Mike Darr called up to San Diego.

On April 16 Martin led off the bottom of the first with a walk. He stole second and scored on Klesko's double. Nevin then hit his sixth home run to take the National League lead. Martin led off the third inning with a single and scored the first of San Diego's four runs that inning. As the first batter in the bottom of the fourth, Martin was safe on an error and scored one of three Padre runs in the frame. With a runner on first and no outs, Martin homered in the fifth.

Martin, who had scored four runs against Montreal on April 7, came to the plate with one out in the seventh inning. He singled off pitcher Jose Cabrera and advanced to second on a walk. After Klesko popped out, Sprague was hit by a pitch. Owens followed with an infield single, his fourth hit of the game, and Martin crossed the plate to become the first Padre ever to score five runs in a game. The run closed out the scoring in the Padres' 13-3 victory.

The win put the Padres into a tie for third place, but they fell to fourth after their off-day April 17, and starting their road trip by being swept in a three-game series with St. Louis kept them in fourth. A sweep in Houston returned the Padres to third and gave them their final winning mark, at 10-9, for the season. After two losses in Pittsburgh the Padres closed out the road trip April 27 with a 12-4 win to give the Padres an 11-11 record, the last time the team would be at .500 in 2000.

The news got worse for Rivera; a form of arthritis was found in his left wrist and his right ankle. On April 28 Boehringer went on the disabled list with shoulder tendinitis. News also took a turn for the worse on the ballpark after an April 21 revelation that San Diego City Councilwoman Valerie Stallings had made a profit on an initial public offering of stock in Neon Systems, a company controlled by San Diego Padres owner John Moores. Stallings had purchased stock on March 5, 1999 and had sold 275 shares for a profit of $9,391 on March 31, 1999, two months before the City Council voted to proceed with redevelopment and the ballpark project. The potential conflict of interest forced a delay in the sale of the municipal bonds needed for the city's contribution to the ballpark.

The Padres' position in the standings also worsened at the end of April. The Atlanta Braves, on their way to a 15-game winning streak, took games 11 through 13 in San Diego to open the Padres' six-game homestand. The Padres ended all three nights tied for third in the standings and ended April five games out of first place with a 11-14 record. The third-place tie became sole possession of fifth place after a 5-2 loss to Florida May 1, and the Padres spent the remainder of the 2000 season in the division cellar.

On April 30, Gwynn was placed on the disabled list with a sore left knee. Left knee soreness had kept him out of six games between April 11 and April 17 and fluid had been drained from the knee, for the fifth time since February, on April 27. When he was placed on the disabled list, Gwynn had 8 hits in 43 at-bats for a .186 average.

Woody Williams, who had thrown 101 pitches in 8 1/3 innings May 1, had reported numbness on the fingers and wrist of his right hand. An April 30 MRI showed a small clot, but a May 3 angiogram revealed an aneurysm, or a distorted blood vessel, in Williams' right armpit. Although the May 4 operation to remove the aneurysm was successful, Williams was expected to miss 10 to 12 weeks of the season. Williams joined Boehringer, Gwynn, Loewer, Magadan, Randy Myers, Rodney Myers, and Rivera on the disabled list.

Rodney Myers was activated May 5, but after winning the final two games of the homestand against Florida the Padres were swept in a six-game road trip to Arizona and Cincinnati. Clement, who had started the season 4-0, lost in Arizona May 7, and the 2-0 loss in Cincinnati May 10 was the only shutout of the Padres prior to the All-Star break.

The May 11 game, which gave the Padres their third 0-6 road trip in the club's history and the first since 1975, was notable for two other reasons. Bret Boone homered twice, including an inside-the-park home run down the left field line, and Aaron Boone hit the winning homer in the bottom of the ninth inning. It was the eighth time in history that brothers on opposing teams had both hit home runs.

The other item of note was a season-ending knee injury to Rodney Myers, who tore the tendon in his left knee. Myers finished the 2000 season with two innings pitched and three strikeouts in three appearances.

The Padres extended their losing streak to eight after two losses against Arizona, which also allowed the Diamondbacks to set a club record with nine consecutive wins. Meadows broke both streaks on May 14 by allowing two hits in eight innings, including a leadoff home run to Tony Womack, in the Padres' 3-1 win. The Padres also sent Roskos to Las Vegas and activated Gwynn that day.

After the three-game homestand, the Padres split six games in Florida and Atlanta. On May 18 Stan Spencer earned his first win since August 1998 despite Florida stealing ten bases off Spencer. The 11-7 win in Atlanta May 19 was the Padres' first double-figure run total against the Braves dating back to June 1993. Gwynn was three-for-three in the May 19 game before his left knee gave out trying to avoid a rundown.

During the road trip Nevin batted .667 with 14 hits in 21 at-bats. He had an on-base percentage of .720 and a slugging average of 1.476. He also had three doubles, one triple, and four home runs, along with 14 runs batted in, and he crossed the plate seven times. The performance earned Nevin the National League's Player of the Week honors for May 15-21.

The Padres returned home to win seven of nine games against New York, Montreal, and Milwaukee. During the May 26 win against Montreal, Hitchcock felt a pop in his left elbow while delivering a fifth-inning pitch. He threw two more pitches before taking himself out of the game, and MRI and X-ray examinations the following day revealed a mild sprain of the ulnar collateral ligament in his left elbow. The MRI also revealed a small bone chip in the joint. Tendon replacement surgery was performed June 6, along with the removal of the bone chip, and Hitchcock's season was ended. The Padres' top three starting pitchers in December - Hitchcock, Williams, and Loewer - were all now on the disabled list.

Adam Eaton, the third pitcher the Padres received in exchange for Ashby, made his Major League debut May 30. In 5 1/3 innings he allowed three runs, and shutout relief gave the Padres a 6-3 victory. Eaton earned the win and also drove in a run. The Padres made a coaching change that day, naming Las Vegas manager Duane Espy as the hitting coach while offering Ogilvie a job with the Padres' Peoria operation. Ogilvie's low-key style had drawn complaints from some players, while Espy, the Padres' minor league batting instructor for five years before taking the managerial job in Las Vegas, shared Rettenmund's hands-on approach.

The Padres closed out the homestand May 31 with a 9-5 win against Milwaukee, tying a team record with 12 walks in the game.

Late May brought good news for Martin. On May 19 the Maricopa County (Arizona) District Attorney forwarded the bigamy case to the District Attorney of Clark County, Nevada, where Martin had been married. On May 25 the District Attorney of Clark County said he doubted he would file charges, since Nevada case history indicates that a marriage is not valid if one party is already married at the time. The domestic violence charge was continued until the off-season, and on November 2 Martin plea-bargained to a sentence which gave him one day in jail, 24 hours of community service, $734 in fines and costs, and two years unsupervised probation.

After finishing the homestand - and the month of May - with a 24-28 overall record, the Padres went on the road for six interleague games in Seattle and Oakland. They lost five of the six games, with the sole win coming in Seattle June 3 when Spencer threw 8 2/3 innings, the most to date by a Padres pitcher in 2000. That day also saw Wall go to the disabled list with right shoulder tendinitis, and during his second rehabilitation outing Loewer reported shoulder stiffness, which scrapped his planned June 6 start in Oakland. Three days later Boehringer returned to the disabled list with right shoulder tendinitis and remained on the disabled list for the remainder of the season.

The June draft took place during that road trip. In the first round the Padres took left-handed pitcher Mark Phillips, an 18-year-old from Hanover, Pennsylvania. In the second round the club took Xavier Nady, a third baseman from Cal. Poway High School's Anthony Gwynn, whose father had been undrafted out of high school in 72 rounds of the 1978 draft despite a .780 batting average for Long Beach Poly, was the 1,000th overall player taken when the Braves selected the younger Gwynn in the 33rd round. Gwynn opted instead to play at San Diego State as his father had done 22 years earlier. The Padres also made history June 9 when 17-year-old Wilmer Villatoro, a right-handed pitcher, signed with the Padres and became the first player from El Salvador to sign a pro baseball contract.

The nine-game homestand following the American League trip resulted in four Padres wins and five losses, including a sweep by St. Louis and a sweep of Cincinnati. In the 13-3 win over Houston June 10, Boone drove in six runs in the first two innings, including a grand slam in the first. That night Dave Winfield was inducted into the Padres' Hall of Fame. The Padres had an off-day during that homestand June 15, and Tony Gwynn took that opportunity to announce some of his future plans. Tony and Alicia Gwynn announced that they would become involved in the Church's Fried Chicken chain and would open up 100 franchises in Southern California, providing economic development and employment for community members. Gwynn had a pinch-hit single in the eighth inning June 17 to break a 1-1 tie against Cincinnati, but the following day his left knee was drained for the seventh time in 2000. It was also announced that day that Gomez would have surgery on his left knee. The Padres opened a ten-game road trip June 19 in Arizona with Spencer reporting a sharp pain after throwing a slider in the fifth inning. The following day Spencer was diagnosed with a flexor strain, and on June 26 he became the ninth pitcher on the disabled list.

The Padres' only win in the three-game Arizona series came June 20, when Brian Tollberg made his Major League debut. In seven innings he allowed only one hit - a fourth-inning single to Steve Finley - and three walks. The Padres' next win came at Cincinnati June 23, in which Boone had three home runs and six RBI in the first nine innings. Boone was intentionally walked in the tenth to bring up Rivera, who hit a three-run home run to give the Padres a 10-7 lead which held up through the end of the tenth inning. Gwynn had a pinch-hit double in the tenth but then returned to San Diego for a knee examination, and Gomez was placed on the disabled list. Gomez' spot on the active roster was filled by Kevin Nicholson, a 1997 draft pick who went hitless in three at-bats in his Major League debut June 23 but who became the first Canadian-born player selected in the first round of the draft to play in the majors.

The Padres announced the dimensions for the new ballpark June 22, with the right-field foul pole 322 feet from home plate, the left-field foul line 334 feet away, and dead center at 396 feet. The right-center field gap would have a maximum 411 foot distance and the left-center power alley would have a maximum distance of 402 feet. The right-field fence would be at 323 feet ten feet inside the foul line but would jut to 358 feet when it reached 25 feet away from the foul pole. The Padres' plans to sell naming rights to the new stadium were hampered by Commissioner Bud Selig, who sent a letter saying that he would reject any name linked to casinos. Although Selig's communication didn't affect the sponsorship of Sycuan, the letter indicated that a reservation name which was also a casino name would not be acceptable for a ballpark.

On June 26 Boone set a team single-inning record with five runs batted in during the Padres' 9-5 victory in Los Angeles. He had a two-run home run and a three-run double off Orel Hershiser in the second inning, in which San Diego scored eight runs. Tollberg, who had taken a shutout into the eighth inning the previous day, was named the National League's Player of the Week for his 14 1/3 innings in which he allowed two earned runs and four walks while striking out 14. He became the first Padres pitcher since Andy Benes in 1993 to earn Player of the Week honors. June 26 also saw Tony Gwynn undergo arthroscopic surgery on his left knee. He became the 11th Padre on the disabled list, where he remained for the rest of 2000. The following day Montgomery was activated from the disabled list, but the ten players on the disabled list still had a higher total salary than the 25 players on the active roster, with the disabled list accounting for $28,730,000 of the payroll and the active players receiving $27,033,000.

After the 4-6 road trip, the Padres lost to Colorado June 30 to end the month with a 35-43 record. Owens finished June with a .338 average, and Tollberg's home debut June 30 resulted in no decision for the pitcher. June 30 also saw the Padres trade Sprague to Boston for two minor league prospects.

The Padres won two of seven games during their final homestand before the All-Star break, but they gained two players from the disabled list. Wall was activated July 1, and on July 2 Williams returned ahead of schedule, throwing 113 pitches over eight innings in a 3-2, ten-inning loss to Colorado.

The final three games before the All-Star break were played in Texas, and the Padres lost two of three against the Rangers. In the July 7 loss Boone's two-run homer gave him 61 RBI for the year, breaking the team record for a second baseman set by Roberto Alomar in 1990. In the seventh inning of that game Jeff Zimmerman struck out Nicholson in the first matchup ever between a pitcher and a catcher both born in

British Columbia. The following day Eaton, who had six consecutive no-decisions after his win, suffered his first Major League loss after allowing six runs in six innings.

The Padres won the final game of the series to enter the All-Star break with a 38-49 record. Nicholson, who was batting ninth, tied a club record with three doubles. Jackson was inserted into left field as a defensive replacement and ended the 4-3 game by catching a line drive hit by Chad Curtis. That catch also gave Trevor Hoffman his 250th career save and his 22nd of the season. Hoffman didn't do as well at the All-Star game two days later, entering the game with the National League trailing 3-2 and allowing three earned runs on three hits.

In the week after the All-Star game, the Padres reacquired both of the players they lost in the 1998 expansion draft. Pitcher Todd Erdos was claimed off waivers from the Yankees July 12, and outfielder Dusty Allen was traded to Detroit five days later for third baseman Gabe Alvarez. Erdos joined the big league roster immediately, while Alvarez started his second Padres tenure in the minors.

The Padres split the six-game homestand which followed the All-Star break. Against Anaheim July 16-18, they handed Angels closer Troy Percival two blown saves. On July 16 Hoffman also blew a save, giving up four runs in the ninth, but the Padres tied the game against Percival before winning in the tenth. On July 18, the Angels had a 2-1 lead with two outs in the ninth before Rivera hit an inside-the-park home run. Hoffman entered the game in the 11th and allowed the winning Angel run to score on a triple and wild pitch. That day also saw both Boehringer and Loewer undergo shoulder surgery, ending the season for both. In the Padres' 7-3 loss in San Francisco July 20, Williams had three hits in three at-bats, including a double and a two-run home run, while the rest of the team had two hits in 28 at-bats. The pitcher hitting streak continued the following day, when Eaton went three-for-three against Colorado and stole a base in the 5-1 win.

The streak was extended July 22, when Clement's only plate appearance was a sacrifice bunt. Clement also tied Steve Arlin's single-season record with his 15th wild pitch in the 9-4 loss. Tollberg ended the pitcher hit streak with two hitless at-bats, but the Padres won in ten innings July 23 to take three of the five games on the road trip, giving San Diego its first winning road trip of 2000.

In Williams' next game he had a hit and a sacrifice fly in two plate appearances July 25, earning the only win in a three-game homestand against San Francisco. Hoffman closed out the game for his 250th career save as a Padre, retiring Russ Davis on a pop-up for the final out. In the final game of the series July 26 Eaton took a perfect game into the sixth before a pair of home runs in that inning gave the Padres a 3-1 loss. Williams was retired that night as a pinch-hitter. The Padres spent three days in Pittsburgh, losing two of the three games, before returning home July 31. Tollberg, who had been 6-0 with Las Vegas, received his first loss of the year July 29 in the 10-2 Pirates win, but the following day the Padres overcame an 8-3 Pirate lead after six innings to win 9-8.

The July 31 trading deadline ended with Hernandez and minor league infielder Nate Tibbs being sent to St. Louis for reliever Heathcliff Slocumb and minor league outfielder Ben Johnson, Martin going to Seattle for outfielder John Mabry and pitcher Tom Davey, and Meadows headed for Kansas City for pitcher Jay Witasick. July also ended with the club's first complete game of the year, as Williams took a shutout against Philadelphia into the ninth inning July 31 before settling for a 4-1 victory.

Mabry began his Padres career August 1 by homering in his first Padres' at-bat - on the first pitch to him. When Slocumb relieved Eaton in the seventh inning, he became the 48th player to appear in a Padres uniform in 2000, tying the club record. On August 4 Witasick pitched five innings in his Padres debut, becoming the 49th Padre to play in 2000 and setting a club record. Witasick received no decision, but the Padres won their sixth consecutive game, and two days later they closed out a 6-1 homestand.

Boone, who had started the Padres' first 111 games, was relegated to pinch-hitting duty August 7 due to a sore knee and a slump, but the Padres won the opening game of their ten-game road trip. They split those ten games, including a sweep of Florida and a sweep by Atlanta.

The Padres returned home for six games with Montreal and New York and won the middle four of those. On August 22 a 16-1 win over New York tied a club record for the largest margin of victory. Boone missed a game for the first time all year, but Jackson started at second and hit a grand slam in the second inning, the 141st of the season in the majors to tie the 1996 record for most grand slams in a year. In the third inning a second-deck home run by Nevin was followed by a loge-level shot from Mabry, which was not only the first-ever loge-level shot into right field but also completed the first-ever back-to-back home runs into the second deck.

After four wins in a seven-game road trip to Milwaukee and Chicago, the Padres ended August with a 65-69 record. The 18-11 record in August gave the Padres their first winning month since June 1999. The road trip also saw Boone go on the disabled list with a bruised knee, and the August 30 loss to Chicago ended Nevin's streak of reaching base in 49 consecutive games.

The ensuing six-game homestand saw the Pirates sweep the Padres and the Padres sweep Milwaukee. On September 4 Davey appeared in relief to become the 28th different pitcher used by the Padres during the season, which broke the National League record of 27 shared by the 1967 New York Mets and the 1995 Florida Marlins.

While splitting a four-game road trip in San Francisco, the Padres tied the National League record of 54 players used in a season set by the 1967 Mets and the 1996 Phillies. In the seventh inning of a 13-0 loss September 7 in San Francisco, Alvarez entered the game to become the 54th player used in 2000. The following day the Padres ended San Francisco's nine-game winning streak, overcoming a 7-1 deficit with two runs in the seventh and seven runs in the eighth. Clement broke a 26-year-old club record September 12 with his 13th hit batter of the season, and the Padres lost four of six on the homestand.

Hoffman recorded his 40th save September 15, retiring Barry Bonds on a grounder to second with a runner on base, to become the third player ever to record four 40-save seasons and the third to have three consecutive 40-save seasons.

The Padres came to terms with Nady on September 17 and placed him on the 40-man roster. The Padres split six games on their final road trip, and when Buddy Carlyle pitched in relief September 20 the Padres set a National League record with their 55th different player.

The final road loss September 24 gave the club a 35-46 road record for 2000, which was still an improvement over the 28-53 mark of 1999. The team, which won five road series and split four in 1999, won nine series and split five in 2000.

The Padres lost the first five games of their final homestand before an October 1 win over Los Angeles closed out the season. On September 30, Nady pinch-hit in the seventh inning and singled off Onan Masaoka. He became the third Padre draft pick to start his professional career in the majors and the 56th Padre of the season, tying the Major League record. That night Clement set another team record; his four walks allowed gave him 125 for the season and broke Arlin's 1972 standard of 122.

The 4-0 win in the season finale gave the Padres a final record of 76-86. The club batted .254 but led the majors with 141 errors. Nevin batted .303 with 31 homers and 107 runs batted in, and despite Owens' second-half struggles he still finished the season with a .293 average. Walker led all National League rookie pitchers with 70 appearances and finished the season with a 7-1 record, and Clement led the team with 13 wins, although he also led the team with 17 losses and set club records with 23 wild pitches, 16 hit batters, and 125 walks.

Finances were still an issue for the Padres. On September 9 the Padres issued a $20 million cash call for expenses for the 2001 season. On September 19 the club announced that ballpark construction would cease as of October 2, and with two weekend days preceding that date the last work on the ballpark for the year took place on September 29.

At the end of the season Towers said that the team would offer Gwynn a contract for 2001. The club announced that it would exercise its $2 million buyout on October 3, and on October 27 the club formally notified the labor relations office that it wouldn't pick up Gwynn's $6 million option. The Padres also exercised a $250,000 buyout of Boone's contract October 30 rather than paying him a $4 million option for 2001.

Gwynn's agent, John Boggs, filed for free agency October 31. The Detroit Tigers and Cleveland Indians expressed interest, and the Padres announced plans to make an incentive-laden offer to Gwynn and Boggs. The first proposal was offered November 8, providing Gwynn with a $1 million guaranteed salary and approximately $250,000 for each 100 plate appearances. Gwynn rejected the offer, the Kansas City Royals announced interest in Gwynn, and Boggs offered a counterproposal November 27. The sides continued negotiations, agreeing on certain portions of the contract, and on December 7 Gwynn signed a contract for 2001. His guaranteed salary would be $2 million, including $1 million which would be deferred and paid between 2003 and 2007, and a graduated plate appearance incentive provision would pay Gwynn $5.7 million for the year if he went to bat 600 times. Other contract negotiations weren't as successful. The plan to trade Nevin to Milwaukee for outfielder Jeromy Burnitz fell through when Burnitz rejected the Padres' offer of three years for $19 million. Ashby, now a free agent, was offered $32 million over four years by the Padres but signed with the Dodgers for $27.5 million over three years.

In December the Padres sent Wall to the Mets for outfielder Bubba Trammell. Free agent signings included another former Met, pitcher Bobby Jones, and Phillies shortstop Alex Arias.

On January 16, 2001, voting for the Hall of Fame was announced. Dave Winfield received 435 votes out of 515 cast, making him the first player who started his career with the Padres to be elected to the Hall of Fame.

On January 29, Valerie Stallings resigned from the City Council and pled guilty to two misdemeanors. The resignation cleared the way for subsequent votes to confirm the ballpark agreements, which would take place in March. The investigation noted that Stallings had accepted undisclosed gifts from John Moores as early as 1996 but cleared Moores of any wrongdoing. Dick Murphy had won the election for Mayor of San Diego, and in February he unveiled a revised ballpark financing plan which included an increased up-front contribution by the Center City Development Corporation.

On February 20 pitching coach Dave Smith took a leave of absence for personal reasons. The Padres named bullpen coach Greg Booker as the interim pitching coach and brought up Class AAA pitching coach Darrel Akerfelds as the interim bullpen coach. The following day the club confirmed that Smith was being treated for an alcohol-related problem.

On February 27, Gwynn batted in an intrasquad game, his first game since June 23 of the previous season. He grounded into a double play and singled. In the Padres' first exhibition game, a 4-3 win over Seattle, Gwynn was the designated hitter and was hitless in two at-bats. He started in right field March 3, but on March 12 he was scratched with a sore left knee and the following day he said he doubted he'd play many nine-inning games during the season.

The Padres waived Rivera March 14, and four days later the team signed Rickey Henderson to a minor league contract. On March 28 the Padres sent Clement and Owens, along with a minor league pitcher, to Florida for outfielder Mark Kotsay and utility player Cesar Crespo.

The Padres concluded Cactus League play with a 17-11 record, and on March 30 the club played an exhibition in Lake Elsinore, which had switched parent club affiliations and would be the Padres' California League farm team in 2001. The crowd of 7,569 saw the Padres defeat the minor league team, 8-2, although a motorcycle accident earlier in the day caused Bochy to miss the game with an ankle injury.

Henderson began the season at Portland, the Padres' new Class AAA affiliate, and Gwynn began the season batting fifth in the order. The Padres opened the 2001 season April 3 in San Francisco, with nine players from the 2000 Opening Day roster still on the 2001 team. Gwynn struck out in his first at-bat but finished the day with two hits in four at-bats in the 3-2 loss. By the end of the season, Barry Bonds would make history with 73 home runs for the season; Williams allowed the first home run during the opener.

Gwynn was scratched from the following game April 5 with a stiff left knee, and the Giants took that game and the following contest for a three-game sweep. The Padres rebounded with their first-ever three-game sweep in Colorado, outscoring the Rockies 35-19. The Giants spoiled the Padres' home opener April 10 with an 11-6 win. Gwynn had a hit in three at-bats. The Giants also won the following day, but the Padres captured the final game of the series despite Bonds' second home run of the season, which broke the slugger's 0-for-21 slump.

The Padres then took two of three from the Dodgers, and on April 13 Winfield announced that he would enter the Hall of Fame in a Padres uniform. During the 10-inning Padres win that night, Dodgers outfielder Gary Sheffield homered into the second deck, becoming the first player to hit loge-level shots both as a Padre and as a visiting player. The following night the Padres retired Winfield's uniform number, and their win gave them a record of 6-5, their first mark over .500 since April 2000. During the game fan Jim Esterbrooks had criticized Sheffield in the presence of

Dodgers general manager Kevin Malone. Malone allegedly responded with an offer to fight, and five days later Malone resigned his position.

The Padres lost their next six games, and on April 17 Kotsay was placed on the disabled list. Henderson was called up to fill the roster spot. One day later Darr, who on April 12 was batting .452 to lead the National League, returned to the lineup after a groin strain. On April 21 Gwynn and Henderson became the first pair of teammates over 40 to appear in the same outfield since Doc Cramer and Chuck Hostetler of the 1945 Detroit Tigers, but Gwynn suffered a hamstring strain in the loss to Los Angeles and was placed on the 15-day disabled list the following day. On April 24 Walker was placed on the disabled list with tendinitis of the flexor tendon. On April 24 Henderson drew a pinch-hit walk from Chris Brock, tying Babe Ruth for the record of 2,062 career walks. On April 25 Henderson drew a ninth-inning walk off Jose Mesa to break Ruth's record with 2,063 career walks, although the Phillies earned a 3-1 victory. "The record's over with. Now I can bear down," Henderson said after the game.

The Padres did just that over the next month. After their 7-14 start, they won 19 of their next 26 games. The path wasn't entirely smooth; Darr aggravated a rib cage strain May 1 and was placed on the disabled list, Gwynn felt cramping in his right hamstring on his 41st birthday May 9 and returned to the disabled list two days later and only three days after his activation, Tollberg fractured a finger while fielding a drive May 6 and was placed on the disabled list, and the Padres were no-hit at home May 12 by Florida's A.J. Burnett, whose nine walks were the most in a nine-inning no-hitter since 1900. Burnett, who coaxed Nevin to pop up for the final out, also hit Damian Jackson in the right thumb, which put Jackson on the disabled list after the digit was determined to have been broken. Santiago Perez joined the disabled list May 18, and Rodney Myers was placed on the disabled list May 24.

Highlights included an 11-5 win in Cincinnati May 5 in which all nine starters had at least one hit. Eaton's stolen base that day, the third of his career, broke the career club record for pitchers. The 8-2 win against Cincinnati May 7 was Bochy's 500th career win as a manager in 985 games and also saw Henderson hit a leadoff double to reach base for the 5,000th time in his career. On May 8 the club stole eight bases, including one by Gwynn, in the 7-1 win over Atlanta which evened the club's record at 16-16, and Dave Smith returned to the club that day.

Although Burnett's no-hitter started a three-game losing streak which put the Padres into fifth place May 13, a May 16 win in New York put them into a tie for fourth. The following day four Padres homered in the third inning in the 15-3 win over the Mets, and a 20-7 victory over Montreal May 19 moved the Padres into sole possession of fourth as well as tied a club record for runs in a game.

On May 23 the Padres were tied with Arizona for the division lead after a 7-6 win in Houston which closed out a 7-2 road trip, and one day later the Padres began a homestand with their sixth consecutive win, a 3-1 victory against Arizona, to take sole possession of first place for the first time since 1998.

The Diamondbacks took the second game of that series with a 7-1 win May 25, giving both teams a 26-22 record and a share of first place. The following night Curt Schilling had a perfect game until Ben Davis beat out a bunt single with one out in the eighth inning. The hit sent the tying run to the plate, but Arizona manager Bob Brenly expressed his displeasure about Davis bunting to break up a no-hitter and Padres players accused several Diamondbacks of cursing at Davis. Trammell followed with a walk to put the tying run on base, but Schilling retired the next two hitters. Each team scored in the ninth, and the Diamondbacks took first place with a 3-1 victory. The Diamondbacks scored four runs in the ninth inning to win the fourth and final game of the series and take a two-game lead.

The Padres beat the Astros May 29, but an eight-game losing streak followed which put the team back into last place. Another struggling local baseball team, the San Diego State University Aztecs, made an announcement May 29 after discussions between baseball coach Jim Dietz and athletic director Rick Bay. Dietz would return for his 31st season in 2002 and then retire. Gwynn expressed a desire to become Dietz's replacement.

The losing streak ended June 7 with a 10-7 win in San Francisco. Cesar Crespo, who had been called up May 29, hit his first Padres home run in the top of the seventh. That blast made the game the ninth in which brothers homered for opposing teams; Felipe Crespo had homered in the second and sixth for the Giants. The Padres concluded that road trip with three games in Seattle, giving the Mariners their 15th consecutive victory June 8 before breaking that streak with a 6-3 win June 9. On June 10 Loewer finally made his Padres debut but allowed six runs in 2 2/3 innings. Loewer made one more start before being optioned back to the minors June 17. On June 17 Dave Smith resigned as pitching coach with Booker taking over the duties. Booker's pitchers soon entered the record books; on June 19 the Padres won a 15-inning, 4-3 game over the Giants in which the two teams combined for 40 strikeouts to set a National League record. The Padres struck out 20, including 10 by Eaton, although Giants pitchers also struck out 20 batters.

After closing out a 3-6 homestand with an 8-3 loss to the Giants June 21, the Padres activated Jackson and released Gomez, making Gwynn the last starting field player from the 1998 team still on the roster. Two days later Witasick was traded to the Yankees for shortstop D'Angelo Jimenez.

The Padres won the first five games of their six-game road trip, moving into a tie for fourth, before Colorado overcame 6-1 and 8-3 deficits for a 10-9 win June 27.

On June 28 Gwynn announced that he would retire at the end of the season. The Padres lost the game that night and lost the next two games to conclude June and the first half of the season with a 37-44 record. On July 1 the Dodgers completed their first four-game sweep of the Padres in San Diego since 1977. After a day off, Gwynn was activated July 3 and struck out in a pinch-hit appearance, but the Padres ended their five-game losing streak with a win over Colorado. The following day Hitchcock made his return and pitched seven innings to gain the win as the Padres took over fourth place from the Rockies, but Colorado won the July 5 game to reclaim fourth place. Eaton fell to 8-5 with the loss that day despite allowing only four runs in eight innings, but on July 6 an MRI revealed a strained flexor tendon which put Eaton on the disabled list.

An 8-3 win against Texas July 6 put the Padres back into fourth place, and splitting the remaining two games against Texas kept the club in fourth going into the All-Star break. Gwynn was named as an honorary member of the National League team, and Klesko and Nevin earned berths on the squad. Klesko's sacrifice fly drove in the circuit's only run in the 4-1 loss while Nevin flew out in his only at-bat.

The Padres split the six-game road trip following the All-Star break and returned home for a two-game series against Arizona. On July 18 Gwynn started his first game in right field since May 9, flying out to center in his first at-bat. Arizona had a 1-0 lead in the top of the third inning with Schilling at the plate. A blown circuit breaker caused the game to be suspended and continued as the first game of a doubleheader the next day, although the circuit breaker saved the stadium's transformer from damage.

Johnson replaced Schilling, and the tandem carried a perfect game into the sixth inning. This time the other Padres' catcher, Wiki Gonzalez, broke up the perfect game with a walk. In the eighth inning Gonzalez singled for the Padres' only hit, and Johnson closed out the game by striking out Davis. That was Johnson's 16th strikeout of the game, setting a Major League record for a relief pitcher. Johnson also set a single-game record for relief pitchers with seven consecutive strikeouts. Although Gwynn was removed from the first game when play resumed, he started the second game in right field and had one hit in three at-bats on the 19th anniversary of his Major League debut.

On July 20 Larry Lucchino announced that he would be stepping down as the Padres' President and Chief Executive Officer as of October 31, although he would remain with the club in an advisory capacity to direct planning and design for the new stadium. Bob Vizas, the club's general counsel, was named as Lucchino's replacement.

A three-game sweep of Milwaukee July 20-22 gave San Diego its first winning homestand of the season. The six-game road trip to Arizona and Milwaukee resulted in controversy, although not with the expected team. The Padres were one-hit in Arizona July 24, with Trammell obtaining a first-inning single off Johnson, but harsh words were avoided in Phoenix. In Milwaukee the Padres had a 12-5 lead July 29 when Rickey Henderson took off for second base. The play was ruled as fielder's indifference, not as a stolen base, and Lopes shouted threats at Henderson. Two days later Lopes was fined and given a two-game suspension for those remarks, and Henderson called the suspension too strict.

The Padres were able to eliminate Hitchcock's salary prior to the July 31 trade deadline, sending him to the Yankees July 30 for two minor league players. Although the trade of Williams to St. Louis for outfielder Ray Lankford wasn't completed by the deadline, both players cleared waivers, allowing the trade to be made August 2.

The Padres split a six-game homestand which began July 31 and ended August 5 with a 10-9 loss to the Reds. Prior to the August 5 game Winfield was inducted into the Hall of Fame, making a 23-minute acceptance speech in which he thanked 1973 Padres scout Don Williams for encouraging him to play professional baseball.

The Padres then split six games on the road. During the road trip an MRI showed damage to Eaton's elbow ligament, and like Walker he was through for 2001 and likely for all of the 2002 season. The trip included a 6-2 win in Pittsburgh August 11 which turned out to be Gwynn's final start in right field. Gwynn had two hits in three at-bats, including his final Major League home run, before being removed in the sixth inning. The road trip closed with the Padres blowing a three-run lead in the eighth inning and losing in the bottom of the ninth.

That blown lead, however, gave Hoffman a chance to earn his 300th career save at home. The Padres opened the homestand with a 6-0 win over the Mets August 14, not allowing for a save opportunity. The following night Jones allowed only two hits and one run in eight innings, giving the Padres a 2-1 lead. Hoffman retired Matt Lawton, Mike Piazza, and Todd Zeile to become the 14th player in history with 300 saves. The following day the Padres evened their record at 60-60 with their third straight win over the Mets and Hoffman obtained his 30th save of the season, becoming the first player ever with seven consecutive 30-save seasons. Although Montreal won the August 17 game, the following night Hoffman earned his 300th save as a member of the Padres.

A four-game winning streak during the ten-game road trip August 21-30 put the Padres above .500 for the first time since May, but two losses in St. Louis gave the Padres a 5-5 mark on the road trip and a 66-67 mark entering their upcoming homestand. A four-game series against the Diamondbacks brought three wins and another winning record, but on September 3 the Padres were no-hit at home for the second time in 2001 as Bud Smith, making his 11th Major League start, allowed only four walks. Nevin, who made the last out of Burnett's no-hitter while pinch-hitting, grounded out to Smith to end the Labor Day no-hitter. Prior to Smith's no-hitter, the Padres had only four hits, including a 13th-inning Klesko home run, in the 1-0 win over Arizona. The Padres had eight hits the day after Smith's no-hitter, but on September 5 Williams returned to face the Padres. He took a perfect game into the seventh before Jimenez singled. Jimenez was thrown out trying to extend that hit, and Ben Davis singled in the ninth inning but pinch-runner Henderson was erased on a double play, so Williams faced the minimum number of Padre batters in the two-hit, 2-0 shutout. September 5 was also the day Gwynn filed his formal application for the San Diego State University baseball coaching position, hand-delivering his resume to Bay.

The Padres lost two of three in Arizona and expected to return home September 11. But the terrorist attacks that day caused a six-day postponement of the baseball season. The postponed games were rescheduled to the end of the season, meaning that Gwynn would close out his playing career at home instead of in San Francisco. Play resumed September 17, with Padres pitcher Jason Middlebrook making his major league debut and allowing two infield hits in six innings. The Padres swept the three games in Los Angeles, evening their record at 73-73. Gwynn closed out his Dodger Stadium career September 19 with a pinch-hit single in the tenth, breaking an 0-for-13 slump.

On September 20 Gwynn was named as San Diego State University's next baseball coach.

A transition plan made the head coach position for Gwynn effective July 1, 2002, with Gwynn serving as a volunteer coach for the 2002 season. The Padres lost two of three on their homestand against San Francisco. In his second appearance in the majors, Middlebrook gave up two home runs to Bonds September 23. The Padres began their final road trip of the year with four games in Colorado. Henderson scored three times in the first game and twice in the second game, but he sat out the final two games in order to break the all-time record for runs scored in the Bay Area or in San Diego. The Padres won two of the four games, including the September 26 game which gave Hoffman his 40th save of 2001 to make him the only player ever with four consecutive or five overall 40-save seasons.

Henderson had two hits but didn't score in the three games in San Francisco. Bonds hit his 68th home run off Middlebrook September 28, making Middlebrook one of three pitchers to allow three home runs to Bonds during the 2001 season. Bonds broke a 1-1 tie with a home run of Chuck McElroy the following day, his 11th home run against the Padres in 2001. After two losses in San Francisco, the Padres closed out their road season with a 5-4 win September 30, giving the team a 44-37 road mark for the year. Henderson didn't score in the Padres' 5-2 loss to Los Angeles October 2, but the following day he led off the third inning with a walk and scored his 2,245th career run on Klesko's double, tying Ty Cobb's record for runs scored. The Dodgers took a 12-5 victory as Bobby Jones suffered his 19th loss of the year and gave up his 37th home run of the season, setting a new club record.

The October 4 game was tied 1-1 in the bottom of the third inning. With one out and a 1-0 count, Henderson swung at a 93 mph fastball offered by Luke Procopec. The drive hit the top of the left-field fence before bouncing off the back wall for a home run. As Henderson had previously promised, he slid across the plate when he scored his 2,246th career run which set the all-time record. The run also proved to be the winning tally as the Padres earned a 6-3 victory.

The Padres, who finished with a .500 record in each of Gwynn's first two seasons, were toying with .500 until an October 5 loss to Colorado clinched a losing season. The Rockies shut out the Padres, the 16th shutout of San Diego for the season and a club-record 13th shutout at home. Kevin Jarvis allowed his 37th home run of the season, tying Jones for the club record and tying Jones and Schilling for the National League lead. The Padres' final win of 2001, a 10-4 victory over Colorado October 6, saw Henderson double for his 2,999th career hit. The game also saw Nevin become the first Padre ever to hit three home runs at home in one game. In the first inning he hit his fourth grand slam of the season, in the sixth inning he hit a solo home run for his 40th blast of the season, and in the seventh inning Klesko and Nevin hit back-to-back home runs. Klesko's homer, his 30th of the year, was the second in team history to reach the second deck in right field.

Tollberg worked six innings, giving him his tenth win of the season against four losses. In the bottom of the sixth, Gwynn batted for Tollberg. The double turned out to be Gwynn's final Major League hit, and Kevin Witt then replaced Gwynn on the basepaths.

Henderson had said that he would sit out the season's final game October 7 so that he wouldn't upstage Gwynn. But Gwynn requested that Henderson participate in the game. Henderson led off the bottom of the first by swinging at John Thomson's first pitch. The blooper evaded Colorado's fielders and fell five feet inside the right-field foul line. Henderson stretched his 3,000th career hit into a double and scored the game's first run on Nevin's single. Henderson was removed from the game in the top of the second inning, but he and Gwynn had become the first National League teammates ever to have 3,000 hits apiece.

The Padres had a 3-0 lead before Colorado scored twice in the third and eight times in the fourth. The Rockies had a 14-5 lead in the bottom of the ninth when Gwynn pinch-hit for reliever Jeremy Fikac with one out. Gwynn swung at the first pitch from Jose Jimenez and grounded to shortstop Jose Uribe, who threw to first baseman Greg Norton for the out. Mike Colangelo then grounded to Jimenez for the final out.

The Padres closed out the season with a 79-83 record, good for fourth place in the National League West. Hoffman's 43 saves tied for second in the league, and Nevin's 41 home runs and 126 runs batted in were seventh-place figures. The 239 runs batted in by Nevin and Klesko set a club record for a tandem, and the Padres set a club record and led the majors by drawing 678 walks.

When the ballpark vote passed in 1998, the final game of 2001 was supposed to mark the end of an era. By the time the 2001 season ended, the Padres weren't scheduled to move to the downtown ballpark until 2004, but it still turned out to be the end of an era. Gwynn retired with 3,141 hits and a .338 lifetime batting average. He batted over .300 for 19 consecutive seasons, a National League record, and he tied the National League record with eight batting titles. In addition to his batting average and hits, he retired holding team records with 2,439 games played, 9,287 at-bats, 1,383 runs, 545 doubles, 85 triples, 1,138 runs batted in, 790 walks, 319 stolen bases, and an on-base percentage of .388. During the post-game ceremony October 7, many of Gwynn's former teammates and other historical Padres heroes were welcomed as Gwynn's career was remembered. Although Gwynn wouldn't be playing in the new ballpark, Mayor Dick Murphy announced that the new stadium's address would be 19 Tony Gwynn Drive.

18

All-Time All-Star Team

We selected a San Diego Padres All-Time All-Star team through 2001, designating one player for each of the starting positions, one utility infielder and outfielder, three starting pitchers, two relief pitchers, one manager, and one executive. The general criteria for selections included the on-field accomplishments and impact made by the team member.

Nate Colbert is our consensus choice as Padre first baseman. The 210-pound right-hander enjoyed his best seasons with San Diego from 1969 to 1974. The St. Louis native began his professional baseball career in the St. Louis Cardinals farm system and performed briefly with the Houston Astros in 1966 and 1968. The Padres selected him ninth in the 1968 expansion draft. Despite playing in a large home ballpark, Colbert belted 163 home runs in six seasons with San Diego and remains the Padres' all-time home run leader. He exhibited a strong, compact swing and excelled at hitting fastballs, ranking third in RBIs with 481, fourth in runs scored with 442, and sixth in hits and doubles with 780 and 130, respectively.

Nate Colbert remains the all-time Padre home run leader.

Colbert, elected a charter member of the San Diego Padres Hall of Fame in 1999, led the Padres in home runs five consecutive seasons, belting 24 the inaugural 1969 season, 38 in 1970, 27 in 1971, 38 in 1972, and 22 in 1973. He also paced San Diego four times in RBIs with 66 in 1969, 84 in 1971, 111 in 1972, and 80 in 1973. From 1971 to 1973, no other Padre recorded more runs scored, hits, and doubles. Colbert enjoyed his best season in 1972, driving in 111 of the club's 488 runs. He belted 38 home runs, over one-third of the team total. On August 1, 1972, at Atlanta, Colbert slugged five home runs in a doubleheader against the Atlanta Braves to tie the major-league record set by Stan Musial of the St. Louis Cardinals. Three home runs came in the second game. Altogether, Colbert drove in 13 runs and accumulated 22 total bases, both records for a twinbill. He tied a National League record for most home runs in one week with eight in nine games from July 30 through August 5, 1972.

Colbert, who made the National League All-Star team three consecutive years from 1971 through 1973, led National League first basemen in putouts and double plays in 1971 and assists in 1972 and 1973. The Padres traded him to the Detroit Tigers in November 1974. Back problems forced him to retire two years later after brief stints with the Montreal Expos and Oakland Athletics. In 1,004 major-league games,

Colbert batted .243 with 141 doubles, 173 home runs, 520 RBIs, and a .451 slugging percentage. Nearly 22 percent of his 788 hits resulted in home runs and over 40 percent involved extra bases.

Roberto Alomar is our choice as the best Padre second baseman. The 6 foot, 185-pound right-hander, son of former major-leaguer Sandy Alomar, Sr. and younger brother of major leaguer Sandy Alomar, Jr., starred for San Diego from 1988 through 1990.

In February 1985, the Padres signed the Ponce, Puerto Rico native as a nondrafted free agent. Alomar joined San Diego as the regular second baseman in 1988 as a 20-year-old, batting .266 with 24 stolen bases. He led the Padres with 84 runs scored and 24 doubles. Alomar struggled offensively through July, but hit safely in 46 of the remaining 55 games and batted .330 in September. He won the Clyde McCullough Award as San Diego Rookie of the Year and finished fifth in the National League Rookie of the Year balloting.

Alomar's best season with the Padres came in 1989, when he batted .295. Besides pacing the Padres with 42 stolen bases, he shared the club lead with 82 runs scored and 27 doubles and led the National League with 17 sacrifice hits. In 1990, Alomar batted .287 with 27 doubles, 60 RBIs, and 24 stolen bases. His 17 errors topped National League second basemen, but the miscues came mostly on errant throws after making difficult stops. The durable switch-hitter, who averaged nearly 150 games a season with the Padres, reached the major leagues at such an early age that he possessed enormous potential for growth. He recorded more base hits after his first four seasons than Joe Morgan or Rod Carew made at the same stage. Tony Gwynn helped Alomar perfect his swing. Alomar, primarily a singles hitter, quickly developed into one of the game's premier performers. He consistently makes good contact at the plate and exhibits considerable speed, stealing many bases. A smooth-fielding second baseman, Alomar displays exceptional range. He turns double plays masterfully and positions well against rival hitters. Former Detroit manager Sparky Anderson lauded him as the most complete major-league player.

A blockbuster December 1990 trade sent Alomar and outfielder Joe Carter to the Toronto Blue Jays for shortstop Tony Fernandez and first baseman Fred McGriff. Alomar starred with the Toronto Blue Jays from 1991 through 1995, the Baltimore Orioles from 1996 through 1998, and the Cleveland Indians from 1999 through 2001. The New York Mets acquired him in December 2001. Through 2001, Alomar has batted .306 with 446 doubles, 190 home runs, 1,018 RBIs, and 446 stolen bases. He has batted .284 in four American League Division Series, .316 in five American League Championship Series and .347 in two World Series. The 12-time All-Star has earned ten Gold Glove Awards and made *The Sporting News* American League All-Star and Silver Slugger Teams five times and four times, respectively. By his retirement, he may rank among the greatest second basemen of all time.

Ken Caminiti received unanimous support as the best Padre third baseman. He enjoyed a distinguished major-league career with the Houston Astros and San Diego Padres. The Houston Astros selected the Hanford, California native in the third round of the June 1984 free agent draft. The 6 foot, 200-pound switch-hitter started at third base for Houston from 1989 through 1994 and ranks among the top 10 career Astros leaders in doubles (191), home runs (88), and RBIs (501). In a December 1994 1-player transaction, the Houston Astros sent Caminiti to the San Diego Padres. Caminiti in 1995 batted .302 with 26 home runs and 94 RBIs and earned his first Gold Glove award, displaying good hands, fine range, and a powerful throwing arm. He led the Padres in slugging

Ken Caminiti remains the all-time Padre leader in slugging percentage.

percentage (.513), doubles (33), home runs, extra base hits (59), and RBIs. In a four-game span from September 16 through September 19, Caminiti became the first major-leaguer to homer from both sides of the plate in the same game three times in a season.

In 1996, Caminiti became the first Padre to win the National League Most Valuable Player Award. He batted a career-high .326 and led the Padres to the National League West title with a then club-record 40 home runs and a team-record 130 RBIs. Caminiti established career bests in batting average, runs (109), hits (178), total bases (339), doubles (37), home runs, RBIs, extra-base hits (79), slugging percentage (.621), on-base percentage (.408), and walks (78). Besides winning a second straight Gold Glove Award, he ranked third in the National League in RBIs and slugging percentage and fifth in home runs. Caminiti homered from both sides of the plate four times in a six-week span. His dramatic tenth-inning home run sparked the crucial three-game season-ending sweep of the Los Angeles Dodgers, giving the Padres the National League West crown. He batted .300 with two home runs in the National League Division Series against the St. Louis Cardinals.

In 1997, Caminiti batted .290 with 26 home runs and 90 RBIs. He helped the Padres capture the National League West in 1998 with a .252 batting average, 29 home runs, and 82 RBIs. Caminiti clouted three home runs against the Los Angeles Dodgers on July 12 and batted .273 with two home runs and four RBIs to help the Padres upset the Atlanta Braves in the National League Championship Series. He rejoined the Houston Astros as a free agent in November 1998, having ranked first as a Padre in slugging percentage (.477), third in batting average (.295), fourth in home runs (121), and sixth in RBIs (396). In December 2000, the Texas Rangers signed Caminiti as a free agent. He split the 2001 campaign between the Texas Rangers and Atlanta Braves and batted twice without a hit in the National League Division Series against the Houston Astros. In 15 major-league seasons through 2001, the three-time National League All-Star batted .272 with 1,710 hits, 348 doubles, 239 home runs, 983 RBIs, and a .951 fielding percentage.

Shortstop honors were garnered by Ozzie Smith, although Garry Templeton received some recognition. Smith spent his first four major-league seasons with the Padres from 1978 through 1981, demonstrating weak hitting and sterling defense.

Nicknamed "The Wizard of Oz," the 5 foot 10 inch, 155-pound Mobile, Alabama native was selected by the Padres in the fourth round of the 1977 draft and spent just one partial season in the minor leagues. In 1978, the acrobatic shortstop finished second to Bob Horner in the National League Rookie of the Year balloting. Manager Roger Craig predicted that Smith would become one of the best shortstops in baseball, "if not *the* best." As a rookie, Smith batted .258 and led the Padres with 40 stolen bases.

Smith slumped to .211 in 1979, but still made contact and seldom struck out. He led San Diego in stolen bases (28) and sacrifice hits (22) and finished second in runs scored (77) and games played (156). His fielding scintillated. Smith ranked just behind shortstops Larry Bowa and Tim Foli in fielding percentage and placed second in assists. Smith, "The Octopus," handled 150 more chances than either Bowa or Foli, performing unbelievable feats. In a 19-inning game on August 25, 1979, he tied a major-league record for converting the most double plays in an extra-inning game, with six. Smith batted .230 in 1980 and repeated as the National League leader with 23 sacrifice hits. He paced senior circuit shortstops in total chances, putouts, assists, and double plays. His 621 assists established a major-league record for most assists by a shortstop. Smith was awarded the first of 13 consecutive Gold Gloves at shortstop. His batting average slumped to .222 in 1981, but he ranked first among National League shortstops in fielding percentage, total chances, and assists.

In February 1982, San Diego dealt Smith to the St. Louis Cardinals for Garry Templeton. The Padres expected to lose Smith to free agency and did not want a repetition of the Dave Winfield case without receiving compensation. Smith enjoyed an outstanding career with the Cardinals from 1982 through 1996, appearing in 14 All-Star Games, four National League Championship Series, and three World Series. The 1985 National League Championship Series saw him earn Most Valuable Player honors with a .435 batting average, one home run, and three RBIs. *The Sporting News* named him to five National League All-Star teams and one Silver Slugger team. Smith improved his batting average markedly and led National League shortstops seven times in fielding percentage. His 2,573 games at shortstop set a senior circuit record. In 19 major-league seasons, he batted .262 with 2,460 hits,

793 RBIs, and 580 stolen bases. Smith holds major-league shortstop standards for most assists (8,375), double plays (1,590), and chances (12,624) and most seasons leading the National League in assists (8) and chances accepted (8). His eight errors in 1991 established a single-season mark for fewest miscues by a shortstop with at least 150 games. He still holds several other National League shortstop fielding records. In 2002, he was elected to the National Baseball Hall of Fame in his first year of eligibility.

Tim Flannery was named reserve infielder, with Bip Roberts receiving some mention. San Diego selected the 5 foot 11 inch, 180-pound Flannery from Tulsa, Oklahoma, in the sixth round of the June 1978 draft and promoted him to the parent roster toward the end of the 1979 season. Flannery spent parts of 11 seasons with the Padres, becoming a crowd favorite with his all-out style of play and hustle. His major-league debut came on September 3, 1979, when he singled against the San Francisco Giants to drive in a run. In his first full major-league season in 1982, he replaced the injured Juan Bonilla at second base and batted .264 in 122 games. The following year, Flannery platooned at third base with Luis Salazar and belted a grand slam off Ferguson Jenkins of the Chicago Cubs on July 11.

Flannery helped San Diego win its first National League pennant in 1984, pinch-hitting 48 times and playing three infield positions. He singled in the fifth inning in Game 4 of the National League Championship Series against the Chicago Cubs. His ground ball in the final game skipped by first baseman Leon Durham to ignite a four-run, seventh-inning rally, giving the Padres the National League pennant. He singled in Game 4 in his lone World Series appearance against the Detroit Tigers.

Tim Flannery played a valuable role as a reserve infielder for the Padres in the 1980s.

Flannery's best major-league season came in 1985, when he attained career major-league bests in batting average (.281), hits (108), RBIs (40), and walks (58). Flannery started 102 games at second base, platooning with Jerry Royster. He led the Padres in on-base percentage, even being hit by pitches nine times. In 1986, Flannery appeared in his most major-league games (134) and batted .280. He batted .311 in August and finished second to Ryne Sandberg in fielding percentage. His .993 fielding percentage remains a franchise record for second basemen. Flannery saw diminished playing time thereafter and retired following the 1989 season. After batting .255 in 972 games with San Diego, he managed in the Padre minor-league system from 1993 through 1995 and has served as third base coach for the Padres since 1996.

Tony Gwynn, the best hitter in San Diego history, occupies the first outfield post. The Padres chose the 5 foot 11 inch, 200-pound right fielder from Los Angeles in the third round of the 1981 free agent draft. The San Diego Clippers of the National Basketball Association drafted the versatile Gwynn, who had starred in basketball at San Diego State University the same day. Gwynn spent parts of the 1982 and 1983 seasons with the Padres and quickly blossomed into a National League star. He led the senior circuit in both batting average (.351) and hits (213) in 1984, his first full major-league campaign. In 1986, he paced the National League in at-bats (642), hits (218), and runs scored (107).

Gwynn enjoyed an outstanding 1987 season. His .370 batting average led both major leagues, while his 218 hits topped the National League. He slumped to .313 the next season but still repeated as National League batting champion. In 1989, Gwynn again paced the senior circuit in batting average (.336) and hits (203). He batted a superb .358 in 1993, trailing only Andres Galarraga of the Colorado Rockies. The strike-shortened 1994 season featured Gwynn setting a club record by batting a National League best and career-high .394 with 165 hits and 64 RBIs. In 1995, Gwynn hit a major-league best .368 to win another National

League batting title, becoming the first player to bat over .350 for three consecutive seasons since Joe Medwick in the 1930s. He shared the National League lead in hits with 197 and drove in 90 runs.

Gwynn batted .353 in 1996 to win his seventh career and third consecutive National League batting title. He became only the seventh major-leaguer to win three straight batting titles and joined Ty Cobb as the only players to have two separate streaks of three consecutive batting titles. Gwynn enjoyed the most spectacular season of his illustrious career in 1997 by winning his eighth batting title with a major-league best .372 to tie Honus Wagner for the most National League batting crowns. He became the only major-leaguer to win four batting titles in two separate decades, tied Wagner, Rod Carew, and Wade Boggs with four consecutive batting titles, and led the major leagues in batting for the fifth time. Gwynn established career highs with 17 home runs and 119 RBIs and shattered club records with 220 hits and 49 doubles. He posted personal bests with 68 extra-base hits and 324 total bases and paced the National League with 67 multihit games, including four four-hit contests.

Tony Gwynn, who made 3,141 career hits, leads the Padres in most career offensive categories.

The 1998 season ended Gwynn's remarkable streak of batting titles, as he finished eighth in the senior circuit with a .321 batting average. He hit over .300 for the 16th consecutive season, tying Stan Musial for the second longest streak in National League history. Gwynn also produced 16 home runs, 51 extra-base hits, and 69 RBIs to help San Diego record its best mark in franchise history and win the National League West for the second time in three years. In 1999, he batted .338 to tie Honus Wagner with 17 straight .300 seasons, best in National League history and second best in major-league history. On August 6, Gwynn became the 22nd major-leaguer to reach the 3,000 hit pinnacle with a first-inning single off Dan Smith of the Montreal Expos, making four hits in five plate appearances that night. In 2000, he batted .323 in just 36 games before undergoing season-ending arthroscopic surgery on his left knee in late June. San Diego declined in October to exercise its $6 million option on his contract, but re-signed him on December 7. Gwynn appeared in 71 games mainly as a pinch hitter in 2001, leading the Padres with a .324 batting average. During the 2001 All-Star Game at Safeco Field in Seattle, Commissioner Bud Selig presented Gwynn and Cal Ripken of the Baltimore Orioles the Commissioner's Historic Achievement Award in a surprise sixth-inning ceremony. He retired following the 2001 season, becoming the seventeenth player with at least 20 years of service with only one major-league club.

Gwynn's batting average did not fall below .300 between 1983 and 2001. Although using one of the smallest bats in the major leagues, he captured eight batting titles and consistently ranked among the top ten in the National League batting race. Gwynn ranks as the all-time Padre leader in batting average (.338), runs scored (1,383), hits (3,141), doubles (543), triples (85), RBIs (1,138), stolen bases (319), walks (790), and games played (2,440). He clouted 135 career home runs, trailing only Padres Nate Colbert and Dave Winfield, and remains second in on-base percentage (.388) and third in slugging percentage (.459). Upon his retirement, Gwynn led all active players in batting average and hits, ranked second in doubles, fourth in total bases, and fifth in runs. He paced the National League a record seven times in singles and shares the mark with Pete Rose for leading the senior circuit seven times in hits. In 9,288 at-bats, Gwynn struck out only 434 times. Gwynn, admired for his work ethic, combined video technology with hours of extra drills to augment his natural batting talent and markedly improve his suspect fielding ability. His honors include five Gold Glove awards and 15 National League All-Star team times.

Gwynn saw limited post-season action. In the 1984 National League Championship Series, he batted .368 and made key hits in the final two games to help San Diego defeat the Chicago Cubs. Gwynn hit .263 against the Detroit Tigers, as the Padres lost the World Series, four games to one. He then played 1,648 regular season games before appearing in another post-season game. In 1996, Gwynn batted .308 with one RBI against the St. Louis Cardinals in the National League Division Series. After struggling in the 1998 National League Division Series against the Houston Astros and in the National League Championship Series against the Atlanta Braves, he returned to the World Series for the first time since 1984. Although the New York Yankees swept the series, Gwynn batted a team-best .500 with eight hits, a home run, and three RBI.

Dave Winfield unanimously takes the second outfield position. The Minneapolis native starred in baseball, football, and basketball at the University of Minnesota, winning Most Valuable Player honors at the 1973 College World Series. San Diego signed the six foot six inch, 220 pounder to a $50,000 to $100,000 bonus and converted him from a pitcher to an outfielder. Winfield joined the Padres directly from the University of Minnesota campus without spending any time in the minor leagues and starred with the club from 1973 through 1980. He enjoyed a respectable rookie year, batting .277 in 56 games.

Winfield developed into the most prolific run producer in franchise history. He slugged 48 home runs from 1974 to 1976 and paced San Diego with 13 home runs in 1976, 75 RBIs in 1974, and 76 RBIs in 1975. In 1975, Winfield shared the National League lead in home runs and ranked near the top in RBI before hurting his wrist in July. His batting average soared 16 points the next year to .283. Winfield's 1977 season saw him pace the Padres in home runs (25) and RBIs (92). In 1978, he batted .308 and led the club in home runs (24), RBIs (97), doubles (30), and hits (181). Winfield singled in the eighth inning of the 1978 All-Star Game and in 1979 became the first Padre voted to start the Summer Classic. He enjoyed his best season as a Padre in 1979, saving the club from last place with 34 homers, a .308 batting average, and league-leading and club record 118 RBIs. Winfield led the senior circuit with 333 total bases and 24 intentional walks. His post-season honors included being the first San Diego player to win a Gold Glove Award and making *The Sporting News'* All-League team. The following year, he paced the Padres in home runs (20) and RBIs (87) and earned a second Gold Glove.

San Diego lost Winfield, its most consistent offensive weapon in the late 1970s, to free agency after the 1980 campaign. Besides leaving with the club career record for RBIs (626), Winfield still ranks second in runs scored (599), home runs (154), slugging percentage (.464), and walks (463), third in games (1,117), plate appearances (3,997), hits (1,134), doubles (179), and triples (39), fourth in strikeouts (585), fifth in on-base percentage (.357), and sixth in batting average (.286) and stolen bases (133). San Diego management negotiated a renewal of Winfield's contract, but he and his agent Al Frohman demanded considerably more money. After the San Diego management balked at the monetary terms, the New York Yankees signed the All-Star right fielder for $1 million. The Padres did not receive any compensation when Winfield left. The star outfielder wanted to perform in New York, where he could receive more publicity.

Winfield achieved even more stardom in the American League from 1981 through 1995. He in 1984 battled teammate Don Mattingly for the American League batting title until the last day of the season, finishing second with .340. The next season, Winfield ranked third in the junior circuit in RBI with 114. In September 1993, he became only the 17th major leaguer to attain 3,000 career hits when he singled in the ninth inning off Dennis Eckersley of the Oakland Athletics. Winfield appeared in two American League Division Series, two American League Championship Series, two World Series, and 12 All-Star Games. In 2,973 major-league games, he batted .283 with 3,110 hits, 465 home runs, and 1,833 RBI. The fine outfielder with bullet-like throws earned two National League and five American League Gold Glove awards. "Winfield," Padre coach Whitey Wietelmann claimed, "could do everything. He could run, field, throw, hit, hit with power." He was elected to the San Diego Padres Hall of Fame in 2000 and to the National Baseball Hall of Fame in 2001 in his first year of eligibility, becoming the fourth San Diego player so honored and the first to come in as a Padre. He has served on the Padres' board of directors since 2000 and

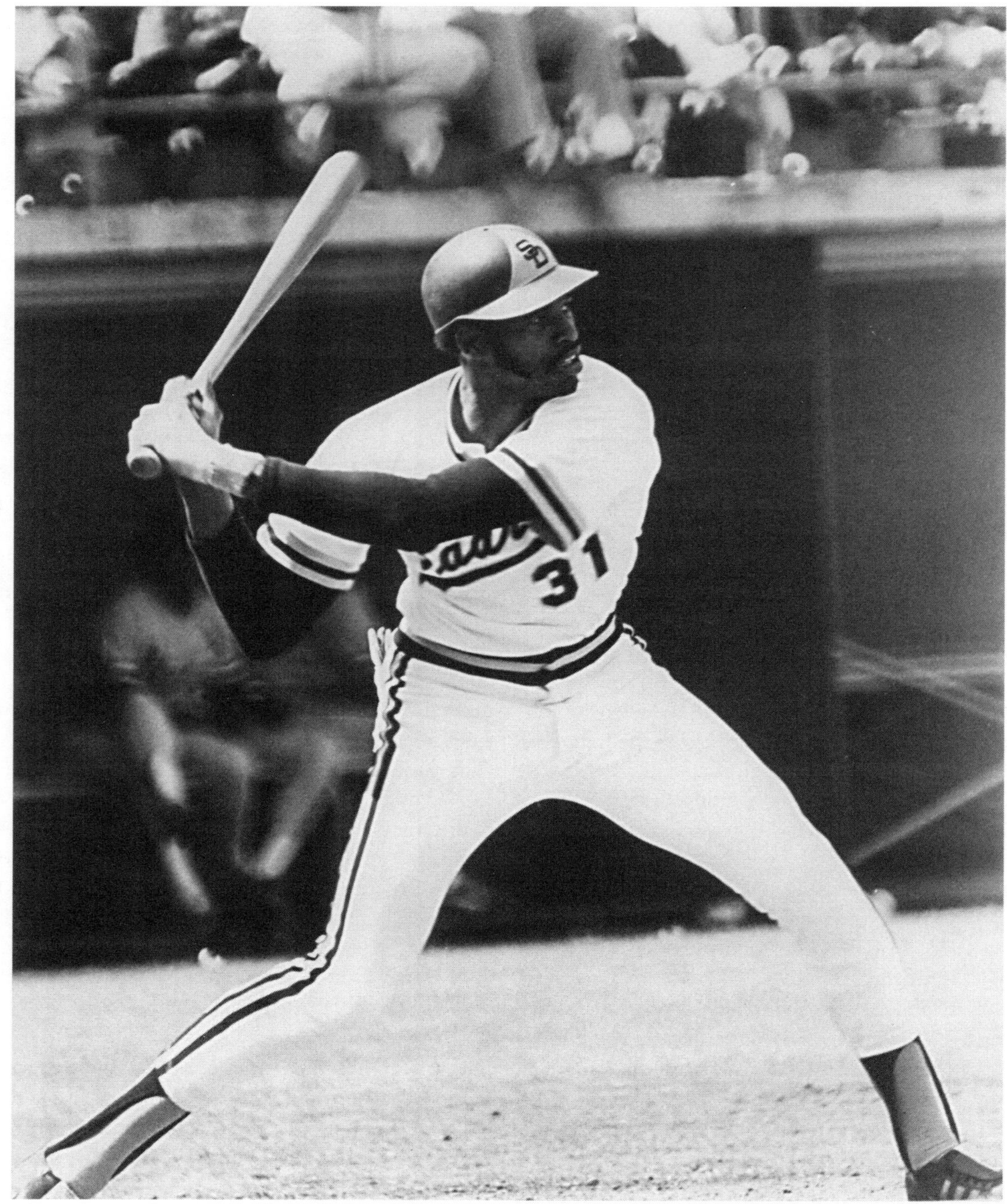

Dave Winfield, who made 3,110 career hits, and holds the Padre career record with 626 RBIs, was elected to the National Baseball Hall of Fame in 2001.

in February 2002 became a vice president and senior adviser for the club.

Steve Finley unanimously garners the remaining outfield spot. The Baltimore Orioles selected him in the thirteenth round of the June 1987 free agent draft after he had starred at Southern Illinois University. He spent most of 1989 and all of 1990 with the Baltimore Orioles. In January 1991, Baltimore traded Finley and Curt Schilling to the Houston Astros for Glenn Davis. Finley played outfield with the Astros from 1991 through 1994, recording a career-high 44 stolen bases in 1992 and pacing the National League with 13 triples in 1993. A blockbuster December 1994 12-player transaction sent 6 foot 2 inch, 195-pound Finley to the San Diego Padres. In 1995, Finley batted .297 with 23 doubles and 44 RBIs and became the only National Leaguer to combine 100 runs, 10 homers, and 35 steals in the same season. He ranked third in the National League in runs scored (104), tied for third in triples (8), and shared fourth in hits (167) and steals (35). He earned his first Gold Glove Award and batted .338 in the leadoff position, the best in the major leagues.

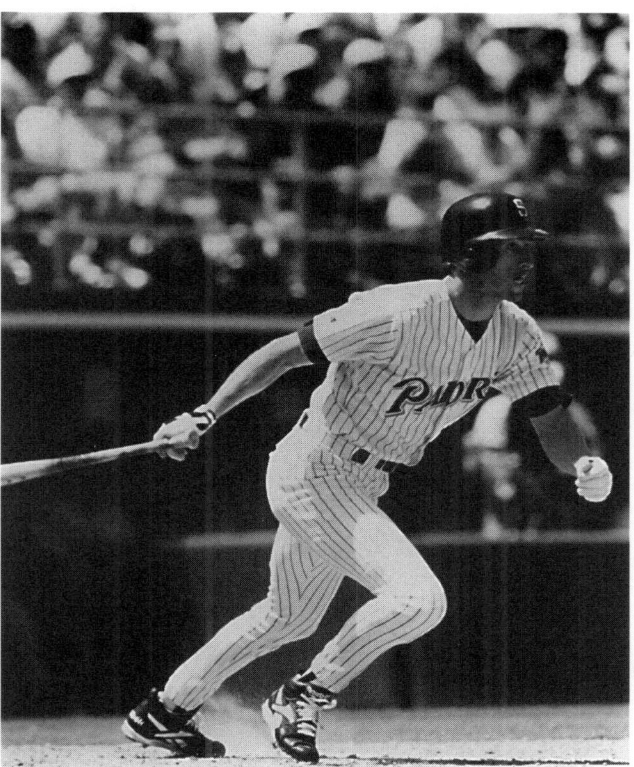

Steve Finley established several career highs in hitting categories in 1996, helping the Padres win the National League West.

In 1996, Finley established career-highs in batting average (.298), runs (126), hits (195), doubles (45), home runs (30), extra-base hits (84), total bases (348), RBI (95), slugging percentage (.531), and at bats (655), helping the Padres win the National League West. He set franchise single-season records for runs scored, doubles, extra-base hits, and total bases. Besides ranking second in the National League in runs scored and doubles, third in total bases and extra-base hits, and fourth in triples (9), he earned his second straight Gold Glove Award by tracking down balls with the best in the game. He tied a franchise record by homering in three consecutive plate appearances, but struggled in the National League Division Series against the St. Louis Cardinals.

In 1997, Finley batted .261 with 26 doubles, 92 RBIs, and two grand slam home runs, and made the National League All-Star team for the first time. He became the first club member to tally 100 runs in three consecutive seasons and led the Padres with 101 runs, five triples, and 28 home runs. Finley ranked second on the Padres in RBIs and extra-base hits (59) and became the eleventh major leaguer to clout three home runs twice in the same season. He played highlight reel defense, making several spectacular catches in center field. His offensive production declined dramatically in 1998 after surgery on a bunion. Finley batted just .249 with 14 home runs and 67 RBIs, but led the Padres with 40 doubles and six triples. After struggling in the National League Division Series against the Houston Astros, he hit .333 with one double and two RBIs in the National League Championship Series against the Atlanta Braves. The New York Yankees limited him to an .083 batting average in his first World Series.

In December 1998, the Arizona Diamondbacks signed Finley as a free agent. Upon his departure from the Padres, he ranked fifth in doubles (134), sixth in triples (28) and runs (423), seventh in batting average (.276) and home runs (82), and tenth in hits (662). Finley, in 1999, batted .264 with 34 home runs and 103 RBIs to help the Diamondbacks win the National League West and hit .385 with five RBIs in the National League Division Series against the New York Mets. In 2000, he hit .280 with 35 home runs and 96 RBIs. Finley batted .275 with 14 home runs and 73 RBIs in 2001 as Arizona captured the National League West. He paced the Diamondbacks with a .421 batting average and knocked in two runs in the National League Division Series against the St. Louis Cardinals and hit

.286 with four RBI in the National League Championship Series against the Atlanta Braves. Arizona won its first World Series title, as Finley batted .368 with two RBI and homered in Game 5 against the New York Yankees. Through 2001, he has batted .275 with 1,071 runs, 1,873 hits, 329 doubles, 94 triples, 202 home runs, 818 RBI, and a .987 fielding average.

Kevin McReynolds garners the reserve outfield spot, with Gene Richards close behind. San Diego selected the 6 foot 1 inch, 225-pound Little Rock, Arkansas, native, the all-time University of Arkansas home run leader, in the first round of the 1981 free agent draft and signed him in 1982. McReynolds moved rapidly through the Padre farm system and joined the Padres in June 1983, batting .221 in 39 games. In 1984, he played an instrumental role in helping San Diego win its first National League pennant. McReynolds shared the club lead in home runs with 20, batted .275, and knocked in 75 runs.

Kevin McReynolds emerged as the Padres' top slugger in 1986, leading the club in home runs, RBIs, and slugging percentage.

He sparked the Padres' dramatic comeback in the National League Championship Series against the Chicago Cubs. After Chicago had won the first two games, he slugged a three-run homer in the sixth inning to help San Diego take crucial Game 3. McReynolds batted .300 in the National League Championship Series before breaking his wrist in Game 4 and missed the World Series against the Detroit Tigers. Pitcher Ed Whitson lamented, "McReynolds' injury killed us. It took power away from us." McReynolds still knocked in 75 runs in 1985, but his batting average slumped to .234 and his home run production plunged to 15. McReynolds emerged as the Padres' top slugger in 1986, batting .286 and leading the club with 26 home runs, 96 RBI, and a .504 slugging percentage. In just over three seasons with San Diego, McReynolds batted .263 with 65 home runs and 260 RBI in 496 games. In December 1986, San Diego traded McReynolds and two other players to the New York Mets for infielder Kevin Mitchell and four other young prospects. McReynolds had just completed the fourth year of a six-year contract. His agent rejected the Padres' $4.5 million, five-year contract offer and made demands that the club could not meet. San Diego feared that McReynolds would probably file for free agency and wanted compensation. The trade ultimately disappointed San Diego, who could not fill the power vacuum left by McReynolds' departure. McReynolds played from 1987 through 1991 with the New York Mets, helping them reach the National League Championship Series in 1988. After performing for the Kansas City Royals in 1992 and 1993, he ended his major-league career in 1994 with the New York Mets. During 12 major-league seasons, McReynolds batted .265 with 211 home runs and 807 RBI in 1,502 games.

Benito Santiago wins honors as best Padre catcher, with Terry Kennedy finishing close behind. San Diego signed the 6 foot 1 inch, 182-pound Ponce, Puerto Rico, native as a free agent in September 1982. Santiago spent four seasons in the minor leagues and dramatically improved San Diego's fortunes in 1987 as a 22-year-old rookie, catching more games than any other major-league receiver. He earned National League Rookie of the Year honors, batting a career-high .300 with 18 home runs and 79 RBI. Santiago became only the second Padre catcher to hit .300. His 34-game hitting streak at the end of the season, the longest in the senior

Benito Santiago, whose 34-game hitting streak in 1987 marked the longest ever by a rookie, won three consecutive National League Gold Glove awards as a catcher between 1988 and 1990.

circuit in 10 years, marked the longest ever by a rookie. No major-league catcher had ever hit in even 30 consecutive games. *The Sporting News'* Silver Slugger and All-Star teams included the San Diego catcher.

Santiago caught for the Padres through the 1992 season. Although his batting average slumped to .248 in 1988, he made *The Sporting News'* Silver Slugger team and won his first Gold Glove Award. Eight runners were picked off base by the Padre catcher, who also threw out 45 percent of those trying to steal. Santiago led major-league catchers with 78 assists and hit safely in 14 of his first 15 games. The 1989 season featured him earning a second Gold Glove Award and being named to *The Sporting News'* National League All-Star team. He also appeared in the All-Star game. Santiago picked off 16 runners, but his batting average declined further. He homered 10 times in his final 33 games, giving him 16 round trippers and 62 RBI altogether.

Santiago enjoyed his best season in 1990 until breaking his arm in June, and earned a third Gold Glove Award. He batted .267 with 17 home runs and a career-high 87 RBI in 1991, leading National League catchers in assists. He hit .250 in 1992. Santiago made the National League All-Star team from 1989 through 1992. In six seasons with the Padres, he batted .264 with 85 home runs and 375 RBI. His exceptional throwing arm enabled him to pick runners off base, throw out runners attempting to steal, and prevent many runners on second base from scoring on singles. Jerry Coleman, who has followed major-league baseball since World War II, remarked, "Santiago has the best

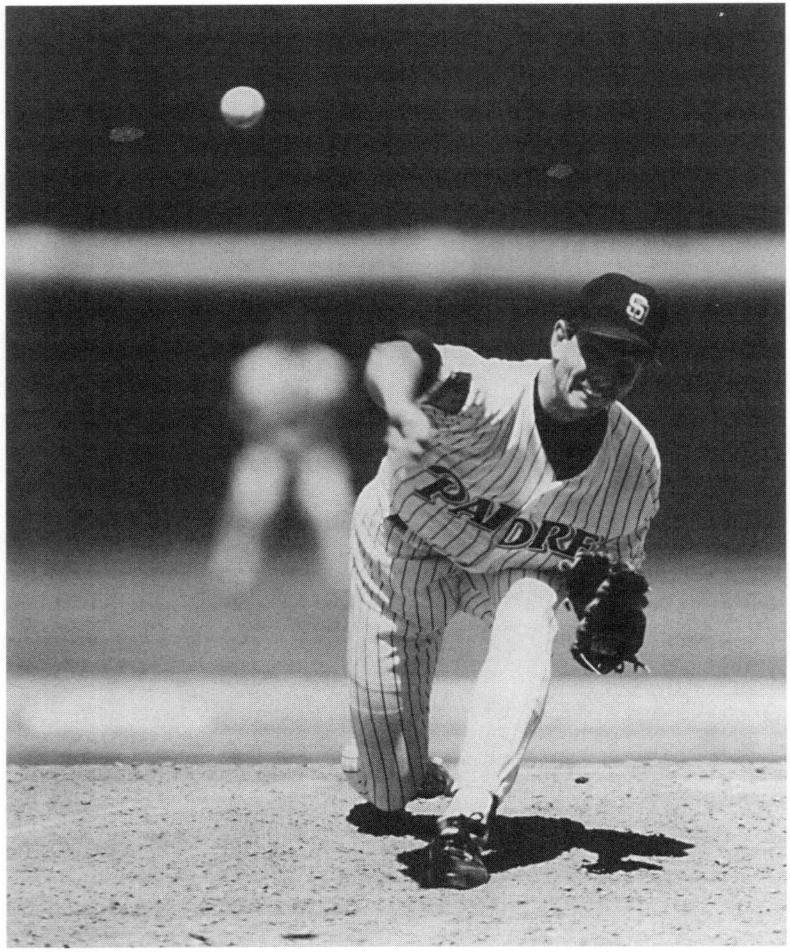

Andy Ashby won 70 games as a Padre and ranks among Padre leaders in virtually every pitching category.

throwing arm I've ever seen. He stops runners from stealing."

Santiago signed with the Florida Marlins for the next two seasons, pacing National League catchers in assists in 1994. He batted .286 with the Cincinnati Reds in 1995, but struggled in the National League Championship Series against the Atlanta Braves. Santiago clouted a career-best 30 home runs with 85 RBI for the Philadelphia Phillies in 1996 and spent the next two seasons with the Toronto Blue Jays, missing most of the latter campaign with injuries suffered in an automobile accident. After spending 1999 with the Chicago Cubs, he caught for the Cincinnati Reds in 2000 and the San Francisco Giants in 2001. Through 2001, he has batted .261 with 184 home runs and 767 RBI in 1,689 games. The four-time All-Star has appeared in one National League Division Series and one National League Championship Series.

Andy Ashby ranks among the three best Padre starting pitchers. The 6 foot 5 inch, 202-pound right-hander signed with the Philadelphia Phillies as a free agent in May 1986 and spent seven seasons in their minor league system. The Colorado Rockies selected the Kansas City, Missouri native in the November 1992 expansion draft. After Ashby lost all four decisions in 1993, the Colorado Rockies traded him on July 27 with catcher Brad Ausmus and pitcher Doug Bochtler to the Padres for pitchers Greg W. Harris and Bruce Hurst. Ashby immediately joined the Padre starting rotation, finishing with a 3-6 mark and 5.48 ERA in 1993. He improved in 1994 to a 6-11 ledger and a 3.40 ERA, ranking fourth in complete games. In 1995, Ashby compiled a 12-10 mark and a 2.94 ERA with 150 strikeouts to earn Padre Pitcher of the Year honors. He led San Diego in wins and posted the third best ERA in the National League. His 150 strikeouts placed eighth in the senior circuit.

Despite three trips to the disabled list in 1996, Ashby finished 9-5 and led Padre starters with a 3.23 ERA. He recorded a personal-best five consecutive victories from May 9 through June 28. In Game 3 of the National League Division Series, Ashby fanned five and allowed four earned runs in 5.1 innings in a 7-5 loss to the St. Louis Cardinals. Although struggling with a 9-11 mark in 1997, he led the Padres in starts (30), ERA (4.13), complete games (2), innings pitched (200.1), and strikeouts (144) and allowed the sixth fewest walks in the National League. His best start came on September 5, when he defeated the Atlanta Braves, 6-2, and came within three outs of hurling the first no-hitter in Padre history. Kenny Lofton led off the ninth inning with a looping single to right field on a 3-2 pitch to end the no-hit bid.

Ashby enjoyed his best season in 1998, helping the Padres win the National League West. He posted a 17-9 record and a 3.34 ERA, establishing career highs with 17 victories, 151 strikeouts, 226.2 innings, 33 starts, and five complete games. His 17 triumphs marked the sixth best in Padre history. Ashby developed a forkball, the perfect complementary pitch for his fastball. Kevin Brown's addition took some of the heat off him. The Padres scored only 12 runs in his nine losses. Ashby went the distance in three consecutive starts and set a career high with five straight victories from May 30 through June 19. He needed only 75 pitches in a 7-2 complete game victory over the Colorado Rockies on July 5 and made the National League All-Star team for the first time. After struggling in the National League Division Series against the Houston Astros, Ashby allowed only three earned runs in 13 innings in his two National League Championship Series starts against the Atlanta Braves. In his lone World Series start, he lasted less than three innings against the New York Yankees.

Ashby in 1999 logged a 14-10 mark with a 3.80 ERA, hurling four complete games and working 206 innings. The Padres dealt him to the Philadelphia Phillies in November 1999.

As a Padre, he authored a 70-62 mark with a 3.60 ERA, 827 strikeouts, and four shutouts. Ashby ranks among the Padre leaders in virtually every pitching category, standing third in strikeouts, fourth in victories, fifth in innings pitched, and sixth in ERA. His .530 winning percentage remains fourth best in Padre history.

Ashby pitched for Philadelphia until being traded in July 2000 to the Atlanta Braves. He finished 8-6 to help Atlanta win the National League East and relieved twice in the National League Division Series against the St. Louis Cardinals. In December 2000, the Los Angeles Dodgers signed Ashby to a $22 million, three-year contract. Ashby pitched just 11.2 innings in 2001 before undergoing elbow surgery in mid-April, winning both decisions with a 3.86 ERA. Through 2001, he has compiled an 86-87 record with a 4.10 ERA and struck out 1,023 batters in 1,554 innings.

Randy Jones was unanimously chosen as one of the three starting pitchers. The 6 foot, 178-pound left-hander from Fullerton, California, starred in baseball at Chapman College and was selected by San Diego in the fifth round of the June 1972 free agent draft. He joined the Padres in 1973, winning 7 of 13 decisions. Jones, in 1974, tied for the most losses in the National League with 22, but followed with two fine seasons. In 1975, he compiled a 20-12 record to earn *The Sporting News'* National League Comeback of the Year accolades. Jones, the first Padre-developed superstar, gave pride and respectability to the once-pathetic franchise. Under pitching coach Tom Morgan, he became the club's first 20-game winner and tied Fred Norman's club shutout record with six. The sinkerball specialist authored a sparkling career-best 2.24 ERA, finishing second to Tom Seaver in the National League Cy Young Award balloting. Besides tossing two one-hitters, two two-hitters, one three-hitter, and three four-hitters, he hurled a scoreless ninth inning in relief to record a save for the National League in the 1975 All-Star Game.

His banner season came in 1976, when Jones won the National League Cy Young Award. He finished with a 22-14 win-loss mark and recorded senior circuit highs and season club records for wins, starts (40), complete games (25), and innings pitched (315). Jones won an incredible 16 of 19 decisions before the All-Star break. From May 17 to June 22, he tied Christy Mathewson's National League record of 68 consecutive innings without surrendering a walk. No major-league pitcher since World War II had compiled 20 victories without striking out 100 batters. Half of his losses were by one run, including three shutouts. Jones also established a major-league record for most chances accepted by a pitcher (112) without making an error and tied the major-league mark for highest fielding percentage (1.000). He equaled a National League season record for most double plays with 12 and won the 1976 All-Star Game for the National Leaguers.

Arm surgery limited Jones' effectiveness in 1977, as he won only 6 of 18 decisions. He improved to a 13-14 mark and 2.88 ERA in 1978, but struggled thereafter. Jones finished 11-12 in 1979 and 5-13 in 1980, but established a Padre record by hurling three consecutive shutouts in May 1980. He pitched ineffectively after being traded to the New York Mets in December 1980. In eight seasons with the Padres, Jones compiled a 92-105 record with 677 strikeouts and a 3.30 ERA. He still holds franchise career records for most starts (253), innings pitched (1,766), complete games (71), and shutouts (18) and ranks second in victories (92), third in ERA, fifth in appearances (264), and sixth in strikeouts. Steve Arlin stressed, "Jones always kept his infielders in the game," while announcer Dave Campbell observed, "People reveled in his success. Jones drew 10,000 to 15,000 additional people to home games and received standing ovations when warming

Randy Jones still holds franchise career records for most starts, innings pitched, complete games, and shutouts.

up." He was elected to the San Diego Padres Hall of Fame as a charter member in 1999, when the Padres retired his uniform number 35. He remains an active ambassador for Padres baseball in the community and operates his popular Randy Jones Ballpark Barbecue at Qualcomm Stadium.

Eric Show earned the remaining starting post, followed closely by Clay Kirby. In June 1978, San Diego selected Show in the 18th round of the free agent draft. The 6 foot 1 inch, 180-pound right-hander from Riverside, California spent four seasons in the minor leagues before joining the Padres as a reliever in September 1981. He did not become a starter until late in the 1982 season. Show compiled a 10-6 record and produced a 2.64 ERA, fourth best in the National League. He in 1983 paced the young pitching staff with 15 victories and enjoyed several outstanding performances, including a two-hit 2-0 victory over the New York Mets. Show helped San Diego capture their first National League pennant in 1984 with a 15-9 record, 104 strikeouts, and a 3.40 ERA. He triumphed nine times on the road and won seven of his last 10 decisions. Poor performances followed in the National League Championship Series against the Chicago Cubs and in the World Series against the Detroit Tigers.

In 1985, Show won 12 of 23 decisions with a 3.09 ERA and led the Padre staff in innings (233) and strikeouts (141). He prevailed in three consecutive games in September, allowing only two earned runs in 25 innings. In a 3-2 loss to the Cincinnati Reds at Riverfront Stadium on September 11, Show surrendered Pete Rose's historic, record-breaking 4,192nd hit in the first inning. He boasted a 2.97 ERA in 1986 and fanned a career-high 13 San Francisco Giants in April, but injuries sidelined him much of the season. Although struggling with a 8-16 mark in 1987, he led the Padres in innings pitched (206.1) and shutouts (3).

Show, in 1988, enjoyed his best major-league season with a 16-11 record, a 3.26 ERA, and 13 complete games, striking out 144 batters in 234.2 innings. Besides producing the most complete games by a Padre pitcher since Randy Jones, he won nine of his last 10 decisions and capped the season with a career-best five game winning streak. The Padres scored over two runs in only one of his 11 losses. Show in 1989 won eight games before suffering a season-ending back injury in July and struggled in 1990 to a 6-8 mark before joining the Oakland Athletics as a free agent that November. With the Padres, he compiled a 100-87 mark and a 3.59 ERA and ranks first among San Diego hurlers in victories (100), innings pitched (1,603.1), complete games (35), and strikeouts (951), shares second in shutouts (11) and ranks third in appearances (309).

Rollie Fingers was unanimously chosen as one of the two best Padre relief pitchers. The 6 foot 4 inch, 190-pound right-handed Steubenville, Ohio native starred from 1977 through 1980 with San Diego. In 1976, the Padres dramatically strengthened their bullpen by signing Fingers to a six-year contract worth $1.6 million. Between 1971 and 1975, he had appeared in five American League Championship Series and three World Series with the Oakland Athletics. His addition boosted San Diego attendance and paid immediate

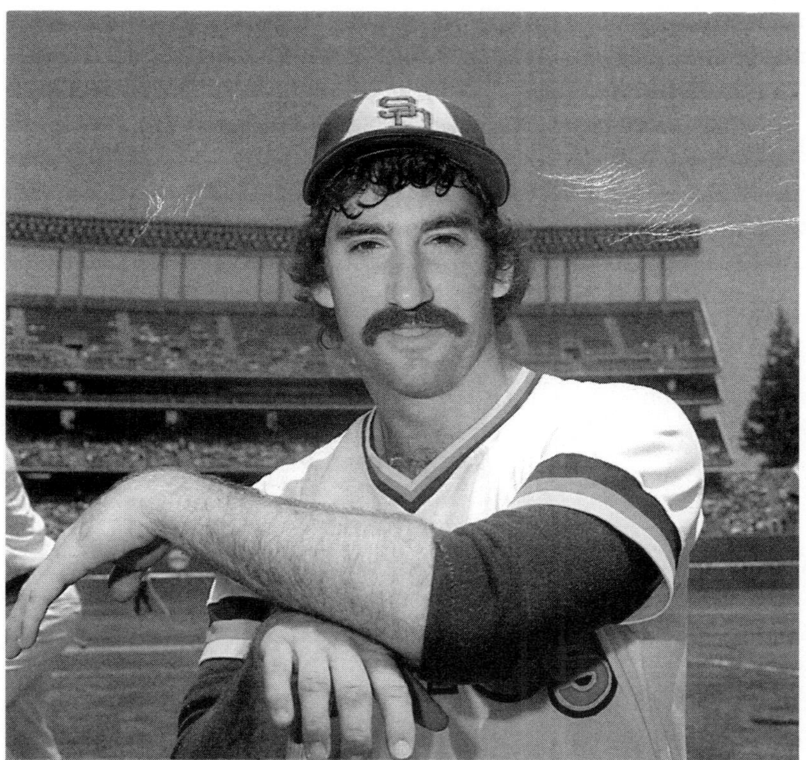

Eric Show holds the franchise record for most career wins.

Between 1977 and 1980, Fingers won 34 games, paced the National League twice in saves, and established then San Diego career (108) and season (37) records for saves. He ranks fourth in career club pitching appearances with 265. During his 17 year major-league career, Fingers logged a 114-118 mark with a 2.90 ERA, struck out 1,299 batters in 1,701 innings, and boasted a then major-league record 341 saves. He appeared in one American League Division Playoff Series, five American League Championship Series, and three World Series. He revolutionized relief pitching and provided incredible consistency as one of baseball's first great bullpen artists. "Relief pitching," Steve Arlin remembered, "was not a very important thing until Fingers." In 1992, the National Baseball Hall of Fame enshrined him.

dividends. In 1977, Fingers was named *The Sporting News'* National League Fireman of the Year with an 8-9 slate, a 3.00 ERA, and senior circuit leading 78 appearances and 35 saves. He struck out 113 batters in just 132 innings.

Fingers in 1978 posted a 2.52 ERA, repeating as the National League's Fireman of the Year. His league-best 37 saves tied the then major-league record. Although ineffective the first part of the 1978 season, the fierce competitor pitched scoreless baseball for over one month with his curves, sliders, and fastballs. Fingers saved 10 victories for 21-game winner Gaylord Perry. "Never in my 17 seasons," Perry declared, "have I had the good fortune of having a pitcher like Fingers in my bullpen." Fingers exhibited pin-point control in the 1978 All-Star Game at San Diego, hurling two shutout innings in relief. He in 1979 compiled a 9-9 record, but his ERA ballooned to 4.50 and his saves plummeted to 13. Fingers developed a forkball to supplement his sinker and slider and rebounded in 1980 with an 11-9 mark, a 2.80 ERA, and 23 saves. San Diego traded the 34-year-old to the St. Louis Cardinals in December 1980.

Trevor Hoffman earned the other relief spot, with Goose Gossage receiving honorable mention. The 6 foot, 205-pound right-hander from Bellflower, California is the younger brother of former major-league player and manager Glenn Hoffman. The Cincinnati Reds selected the University of Arizona shortstop in the eleventh round of the June 1989 free agent draft. Hoffman spent four seasons in the Reds minor league system, during which time he switched to relief pitching. The Florida Marlins selected him as the eighth overall pick of the November 1992 expansion draft. After splitting two decisions with two saves and a 3.28 ERA, Hoffman was traded to the San Diego Padres in June 1993. He finished 1993 with a 2-4 mark, 4.31 ERA, and three saves, fanning 53 batters in 54.1 innings and allowing only one of 29 inherited runners to score against him.

In 1994, Hoffman split eight decisions with a 2.57 ERA and 20 saves in 23 opportunities. He fanned 68 batters in 56 innings, earning Padre Pitcher of the Year honors. Hoffman in 1995 won seven of 11 decisions with a 3.88 ERA and 31 saves, sixth best in the National League. He recorded the most saves by a San Diego reliever since Rollie Fingers in 1978, failing to convert only seven save opportunities and fanning 52 batters in 53.1 innings.

Hoffman in 1996 continued his emergence as one of the game's dominating closers, combining a 9-5 record with a 2.25 ERA and 42 saves. He led National League relievers with nine victories and 111 strikeouts in 88 innings, helping the Padres win the National League West. Hoffman's wins, strikeouts, and 70 appearances marked career highs. His 42 saves ranked third in the senior circuit, as he won National League Fireman of the Year honors. Hoffman converted 86 percent of his save opportunities and did not allow a run in 56 appearances. The St. Louis Cardinals, however, hit him well in the National League Division Series. In 1997, Hoffman enjoyed another spectacular season with a 6-4 mark, 2.66 ERA, and 37 saves and earned a win or save in 57 percent of the 76 Padre victories. Besides appearing in 70 games for the second consecutive year, he ranked second in the National League in saves and again garnered Padre Pitcher of the Year honors. Hoffman converted 84 percent of his save opportunities and fanned 111 batters in just 81.1 innings and passed Rollie Fingers as the all-time Padre save leader.

Hoffman emerged as the premier major-league closer in 1998, when the Padres captured the National League West. Besides compiling a 4-2 record, he established career-bests with a 1.48 ERA and 53 saves and fanned 86 batters in only 73 innings. Hoffman tied a National League record with his major-league leading 53 saves and failed in only one save opportunity. His 98 percent conversion rate marked the best in history by a closer with at least 30 saves. Hoffman blanked opponents in 57 of his 66 appearances and earned the save or win in 57 of San Diego's 98 wins. He made his first National League All-Star team, won his first National League Rolaids Relief Man of the Year Award, and finished second in the Cy Young Award balloting.

His 53 saves marked the second highest in a major-league season and shattered the previous club mark of 44. Hoffman converted his first 33 save opportunities to tie Rod Beck's major-league record of 41 straight saves without a miss. After posting two saves in the National League Division Series against the Houston Astros, he won his lone decision with one save in the National League Championship Series against the Atlanta Braves and took the loss in Game 3 of the World Series against the New York Yankees.

Hoffman in 1999 finished 2-3 with a 2.14 ERA and 40 saves in 64 appearances and struck out 73 in 67.1 innings. He led the major leagues for the second consecutive season in save percentage, converting 40 of 43 save opportunities. Hoffman ranked second in saves and made the National League All-Star team for the second straight year. He won or saved 57 percent of the Padres' 74 victories and garnered his fifth Clyde McCullough Award as Padres Pitcher of the Year.

Hoffman in 2000 finished 4-7 with a 2.99 ERA and ranked second in the National League with 43 saves. He blew only seven save opportunities, striking out 85 batters in just 72.1 innings. Hoffman again made the National League All-Star team and earned his 250th career save. He became one of only three closers to post 40 or more saves in three consecutive seasons and to have four 40-save seasons. Hoffman in 2001 compiled a 3-4 slate with a 3.43 ERA and shared second in the National League with 43 saves. He failed to convert on just three save opportunities, fanning 63 batters in 60.1 innings. Hoffman became the second-fastest and third-youngest to attain 300 career saves and the first major-league reliever to record seven straight 30-save seasons. He also became the first major-league reliever to notch four straight 40-save seasons and to attain five overall. In nine major-league seasons through 2001, Hoffman owns a 43-39 record with a 2.79 ERA and 728 strikeouts in 641.2 innings. He also holds Padre career records for most saves (312) and appearances (543) and ranks seventh with 639 strikeouts.

Bruce Bochy was unanimously designated best field manager, with Dick Williams as runner-up. The Houston Astros signed the 6 foot 4 inch, 225-pound Bochy, who was born in Landes de Boussac, France, out of Florida State University in the secondary phase of the June 1975 draft. Bochy served as a reserve catcher for the Astros from 1978 through 1980 and was traded to the New York Mets in February 1981. He spent nearly two years in the minor leagues, appearing briefly with the New York Mets in 1982. He served as a reserve catcher for the San Diego Padres between June 1983 and 1987 and singled as a pinch hitter in Game 5 of the 1984 World Series against the Detroit Tigers. His best major-league seasons came in 1985, when he batted .268 with six home runs and 13 RBI in 48 games, and in 1986, when he batted .252 in 63 games and set personal highs with eight home runs and 22 RBI. During nine major-league seasons, he hit .239 with 26 home runs and 93 RBI in 358 games.

After spending 1988 as a player-coach with Las Vegas, Bochy managed the next four seasons in the San Diego Padre organization. He rejoined the Padres as a third base coach in 1993 and replaced Jim Riggleman as manager in October 1994, making him the youngest National League pilot. Under Bochy in 1995, San Diego made the biggest improvement among National League clubs. The Padres finished third in the National League West with a 70-74 mark, the best by a first-year San Diego manager since 1988.

San Diego enjoyed its second-best season in franchise history under Bochy in 1996, capturing the National League West with a 91-71 mark. The Padres vaulted into first place with a franchise-record 17 victories in April and remained there for over two months. Bochy's club struggled during the summer, but won its division by sweeping the Los Angeles Dodgers in the final three-game series at Dodger Stadium. The St. Louis Cardinals eliminated San Diego in the National League Division Series. The Padres dropped to fourth in the National League West with a 76-86 record in 1997. Injuries forced Bochy to use 45 players, three short of the 1991 club record.

Bochy in 1998 guided San Diego to its best record (98-64) in franchise history and another National League West crown. The Padres held first place until June 6 and regained it four days later. Bochy's club clinched its second National League West title in three years, rallying from a 7-0 deficit on September 12 to defeat the Los Angeles Dodgers, 8-7. San Diego defeated the Houston Astros, 3-1, in the National League Division Series and the Atlanta Braves, 4-2, in the National League Championship Series. The New York Yankees, however, swept San Diego in the World Series.

The Padres slipped to fourth in the National League West with a 74-88 record in 1999 and to last place with a 76-86 mark in 2000. The injury-riddled Padres used 56 different players, tying the major-league record set by the Philadelphia Athletics in 1915. San Diego players made 23 trips to the disabled list. Ten Padres underwent surgery, including four of them twice. San Diego improved to a 79-83 mark and fourth place National League West finish in 2001, faring much better on the road than at home. The Padres clouted ten grand slam home runs, including four by third baseman Phil Nevin, but fell victim to two no-hitters at home.

Bruce Bochy was named National League Manager of the Year in 1996 and 1998.

Under Bochy, San Diego has compiled a 564-552 regular season record and .505 winning percentage with two National League West titles and one National League pennant. Although Jack McKeon and Dick Williams have better winning percentages as Padre skippers, Bochy has earned more victories and remains the only Padre pilot to win Manager of the Year accolades. He was named *The Sporting News'* National League Manager of the Year in 1996 and 1998 and Baseball Writers Association of America's National League Manager of the Year in 1996 and runner-up in 1998.

Popular owner Ray Kroc was named unanimously as top Padre executive. In 1974, the 72-year-old Chicagoan and chairman and largest stockholder of the McDonald's restaurant chain rescued the staggering San Diego franchise when it appeared headed for a move to Washington, D.C. He had already built the McDonald's hamburger operation into the nation's largest fast-food chain and had amassed a personal fortune estimated at $500 million. Kroc, who loved the Chicago Cubs and had always wanted to own that franchise, bought the Padres for $12 million in cash and saved major-league baseball for San Diego. Padre players, management, and fans alike welcomed Kroc's action.

Kroc's involvement soon turned the franchise around. Kroc vowed to build a contender quickly, letting baseball authorities handle the front office and field manager operations. As a baseball fan, he took a much keener interest in the Padres than previous club owners. Kroc possessed the financial resources to make San Diego more competitive on the field and to market the club more effectively. During his tenure, Padre attendance increased dramatically. Before his arrival, San Diego had never drawn more than 644,000 fans in five years of existence. By 1978, 1,670,107 visited San Diego Stadium to watch the Padres finish above .500 for the first time. The same year, Kroc threw out the ceremonial first pitch at the All-Star Game in San Diego. During Kroc's tenure as owner, attendance failed to reach one million paying customers only in the strike-shortened 1981 season.

Kroc built the franchise into a contender before his death in 1984. He contemplated selling the Padres in 1979 after being fined $100,000 for tampering with free agents Joe Morgan and Graig Nettles. Kroc instead turned the Padre presidency and team operations over to his son-in-law Ballard Smith, authorizing him to invest heavily in the free-agent market and make trades. In September 1980, Jack McKeon became vice-president of baseball operations and built the Padres into a contender. During the early 1980s, McKeon hired Dick Williams as manager, acquired catcher Terry Kennedy, shortstop Garry Templeton, and pitcher Ed Whitson in trades, and signed free agents Steve Garvey and Rich Gossage. San Diego finished with identical 81-81 records in 1982 and 1983 before Kroc's death at age 81 in January 1984. As Jack McKeon eulogized, "The Padres had lost a great guy who was always interested in baseball and a genuine human being revering people who produced." Kroc unfortunately did not live long enough to witness the miracle 1984 season. The Padres dedicated the 1984 campaign to him, winning their first National League pennant and making their initial World Series appearance. He was elected to the San Diego Padres Hall of Fame as a charter member in 1999.

Ray Kroc rescued the San Diego franchise in 1974, and built it into a contender.

19

Executives

BUZZIE BAVASI

Buzzie Bavasi owned one-third of the San Diego Padres during the first years of the major-league franchise from 1968 through January 1974 and served as club president until September 1977. He was born in New York City in 1915 and joined the Brooklyn Dodgers' National League organization following graduation from DePauw University in 1938. In 1951, Bavasi became vice president and general manager of the Brooklyn Dodgers. He moved with the Dodgers to Los Angeles in 1958 and remained with the club until 1968. During Bavasi's tenure, the Dodgers won six National League pennants and four World Series.

Bavasi, an expert in internal baseball operations, and C. Arnholdt Smith led the campaign for San Diego to acquire a major-league baseball team. The San Diego Padres had played in the Pacific Coast League from 1936 through 1968. Bavasi's connections with Los Angeles Dodgers' owner Walter O'Malley helped San Diego secure a major-league franchise for the 1969 season. Bavasi convinced National League owners that San Diego could support a major-league franchise with its growing population exceeding one million people and believed that the team could draw one million fans in 1969. Bavasi recruited Los Angeles Dodgers personnel to fill key administrative positions, hiring Preston Gomez as manager, Roger Craig and Wally Moon as coaches, and Duke Snider as scout and announcer. He filled the remaining coaching positions with Sparky Anderson and San Diego personality Whitey Wietelmann.

At the October 14 expansion draft, Bavasi selected 10 veterans and 20 younger players. First baseman Nate Colbert, outfielders Ollie Brown and Cito Gaston, and pitchers Clay Kirby and Dave Roberts formed the nucleus of the new club. Bavasi gambled that the younger talent would make San Diego a contender within four years and expected the Padres to win only 60 to 65 games their inaugural campaign. San Diego, however, struggled longer than anticipated, finishing last its first six major-league seasons. The Padres consistently ranked last in National League attendance with under 650,000 fans, well short of the 800,000 needed to make the franchise profitable. Bavasi often was forced to sell or trade players for financial reasons.

Nevertheless, Bavasi hoped to keep the Padres in San Diego. In November 1972, however, Washington, D.C. grocer Joseph Danzansky offered to purchase the Padres from Bavasi and Smith for $11,750,00 and to move the struggling team to Washington, D. C. Bavasi told San Diego mayor Pete Wilson that the Padres were considering leaving because of the lack of community support and consulted lawyers to explore the legal ramifications.

Unbeknownst to Bavasi, C. Arnholdt Smith on May 5, 1973, sold the Padres to Danzansky's Washington, D.C., group for $12 million. Bavasi opposed the sale and remarked, "I don't see how they can move the franchise in the middle of the season." Smith on June 8 officially informed the city that the Padres planned to move the franchise to Washington, D.C. before the 1974 season. City officials, however, did not let the Padres sever their 20-year lease agreement on San Diego Stadium and filed suit against the Padres, the National League, Smith, Bavasi, and Danzansky. The city demanded $12 million from the Padres for terminating the San Diego Stadium lease. The National League in December conditionally approved the sale to Danzansky's Washington, D.C., group, but later rescinded its action because the latter failed to protect the National League from damage suits by the city.

Chicagoan Ray Kroc, 72-year-old chairman and largest stockholder of the McDonald's restaurant chain, bought the Padres for $12 million in January 1974 and retained Bavasi as president. Kroc, who brought financial stability and vowed to build a contender, let

Buzzie Bavasi, left, and Ray Kroc previously owned the Padres.

through 1984. He and announcer Jerry Coleman were inducted into the Padres Hall of Fame in 2001.

DICK FREEMAN

Dick Freeman served as president of the San Diego Padres from March 1989 through January 1995. The Oskaloosa, Iowa, native graduated in 1962 from Oskaloosa High School, where he participated in basketball and tennis. He earned a B.A. degree in business administration from the University of Iowa in 1966 and spent two years in the U.S. Navy, being stationed at the Naval Air Station North Island in San Diego in 1969 and 1970. After serving as treasurer of a San Diego area savings and loan, Freeman worked as a certified accountant with Peat, Marwick, Mitchell & Company in Los Angeles from 1970 to 1977 and San Diego from 1977 through 1981.

In 1981 Freeman joined the San Diego Padres as chief financial officer. He became vice president of administration in 1983 and executive vice president and chief operating officer in 1986. Freeman handled all non-player personnel functions, including finances, marketing, broadcasting, stadium operations, and ticket sales. In March 1989, he replaced Chub Feeney as president of the Padres. Feeney the previous September had made an obscene gesture to San Diego fans who were carrying "Scrub Chub" signs. Freeman served as a member of the executive committee of the National League and attended league meetings.

"My job with the Padres," Freeman reflected, "has given us the opportunity to meet many interesting people, travel to interesting places, and attend many exciting events. No doubt the highlight was 1984, when the Padres defeated the Cubs for the National League pennant but lost to the Detroit Tigers in the World Series. The excitement in San Diego during those two weeks, the trips to Chicago and Detroit and the overall interest of the San Diego fans was something we'll never forget."

Freeman also participated in community affairs, serving on the board of directors for the San Diego YMCA and San Diego and Imperial County Chapters of the March of Dimes and on the Board of Trustees of

Bavasi handle the front office operations. Bavasi finally possessed the financial resources to strengthen the Padres. In June 1973, he drafted University of Minnesota star outfielder-pitcher Dave Winfield, who became the club's primary offensive threat, and acquired veteran slugger Willie McCovey that October.

Although San Diego finished last in 1974, the Padres profited for the first time. San Diego drew over 1 million spectators to obliterate the franchise record by 431,127. Bavasi's rebuilding efforts enabled the Padres in 1975 to escape the cellar for the first time and draw nearly 1,300,000 fans. Dave Winfield's clutch hitting and Randy Jones's timely pitching lifted San Diego to fourth place. The Padres slipped one notch in 1976, but Jones won the National League Cy Young Award. Bavasi's acquisitions of outfielder George Hendrick, pitcher Rollie Fingers, and catcher-first baseman Gene Tenace strengthened San Diego following the 1976 season.

Despite Bavasi's acquisitions, the Padres finished a disappointing fifth in 1977. Discontent spread to the front office after Alvin Dark replaced John McNamara as manager. Bavasi resigned as president in that September after nine seasons without attaining the elusive winning season. Kroc promoted Bob Fontaine from player personnel director to general manager. Bavasi, who resides in La Jolla, California, served the California Angels as executive vice president from 1978 the national March of Dimes. He belonged to the La Jolla Rotary Club.

When John Moores assumed ownership of the Padres, Larry Lucchino replaced Freeman as club president in January 1995. Freeman has served as chief operating officer of the Pittsburgh Pirates since February 1996 and oversaw the construction of PNC Park, which opened in April 2001.

Freeman and his wife, Judi, have a daughter, Heather, and reside in the Pittsburgh, Pennsylvania, area.

JOAN KROC

Joan Kroc served as owner and chairwoman of the Board of Directors for the San Diego Padres from January 1984 through June 1990. The St. Paul, Minnesota native, the daughter of a railroad telegrapher and concert violinist, worked as a professional musician and music teacher for many years. Her strong midwestern values influenced her life. She married Ray Kroc, founder of the McDonald's Corporation, in 1969 and moved from Chicago, Illinois to the San Diego area in 1976. Her husband purchased the San Diego Padres for $12 million in January 1974 when they appeared headed to Washington, D.C. and built them into a pennant contender. She replaced her husband as Padres owner when he died in January 1984.

Joan Kroc, pictured with John Moores, served as owner and chairwoman of the board of directors of the Padres from January 1984 through June 1990.

The San Diego Padres dedicated their 1984 season to Ray Kroc, winning their first National League pennant and appearing in their first World Series. Joan Kroc left the daily baseball operations to Jack McKeon and other front office executives. In October 1989, she put the club up for sale to devote more time to her family. On April 2, 1990, Hollywood producer Tom Werner agreed to buy the Padres for $90 million. Werner enlisted nine partners, mostly influential San Diego area business leaders. The group had expanded to 15 investors by June 13 when the other major-league owners unanimously approved the sale.

Kroc, a major stockholder in the McDonald's Corporation, supplied significant support to local, national, and international social issues. In 1976, she founded Operation Cork to build awareness of chemical dependence and its negative impact on the family. Seven years later, she formed the Joan B. Kroc Foundation to address substance abuse, world peace, care for the terminally ill, and other social concerns. In 1985, she started giving $18 million in installments to the San Diego Hospice, an inpatient facility for the terminally ill, and contributed $3.1 million to house and permanently endow the International Institute of Peace Studies at the University of Notre Dame.

The following year, Kroc gave $3 million to the St. Vincent de Paul Center in downtown San Diego. She also donated over $5 million to support AIDS research and provide care for victims of the deadly disease. In 1989, Kroc contributed $1 million to San Diego's Soviet Arts Festival and purchased a rare $2.8 million Faberge egg to exhibit at the largest cultural exchange ever held between the United States and the Soviet Union.

Kroc serves as honorary chairwoman of Ronald McDonald Children's Charities, established in memory of Ray Kroc in 1984 to benefit needy children. In 1986, she gave her 200-acre ranch near Solvang, California to Ronald McDonald Children's Charities. Two years later, Kroc sent nearly $250,000 to the school district of a 12-year-old who was about to lose his private tutor. In 1989, Kroc contributed $5 million to the Ronald McDonald Children's Charities.

During the 1990s, Kroc continued generous philanthropy to groups working to prevent nuclear war, world famine, and drug and alcohol abuse. She gave $60 million in stock to 121 Ronald McDonald Houses in 1993 and $50 million to Ronald McDonald Children's Charities in 1995. In 1996, Kroc donated $500,000 to the St. Vincent de Paul Center in San Diego to keep its kitchen and medical clinic open. *Fortune* magazine estimated her 1996 donations at $33 million. In 1997, she anonymously gave an unprecedented $15 million to Grand Forks, North Dakota, flood victims. Kroc also contributed $3.5 million to the San Diego Zoo, $1 million to the Betty Ford Center, and $1 million to the Special Olympics.

Kroc has received honorary doctorates from the Universities of Notre Dame and San Diego, the Gold Key Award from the National Council on Alcoholism, the Medal of Honor of the Daughters of the American Revolution, the Carrie Chapman Catt Award from the California League of Women Voters, a Bronze Medal from the Society for the Family of Man, the St. Jude Hospital's Woman of the Year Award, and the Neil Jacoby Award from UCLA.

Kroc, who is in her seventies, resides in Rancho Santa Fe, California. She enjoys traveling around the United States in a 36-foot motor home with her four granddaughters. Neil Morgan, a friend and columnist at *The San Diego Union-Tribune*, says, "She has a big heart and a sort of Cinderella sense." He added, "She gives with great spontaneity and generosity."

Owner Ray Kroc built the Padres into a respectable franchise from 1974 through 1983.

RAY KROC

Owner Ray Kroc built the San Diego Padres into a respectable franchise from 1974 through 1983. He was born in Oak Park, Illinois on October 5, 1902, and grew up a Chicago Cubs fan. After dropping out of Oak Park High School, Kroc joined the Red Cross Ambulance Corps in World War I. He served as musical director for WGES in Chicago and played double piano with a Harry Sosnick band. Kroc worked 17 years as Midwest Sales Manager for Lily-Tulip Cup and became exclusive salesman for a new invention, a milkshake multimixer machine. A small hamburger restaurant in San Bernardino, California, owned by the McDonald Brothers, purchased eight of his machines. Kroc realized that a chain of similar restaurants would use a lot of his multimixers and started his own hamburger restaurants under a royalty agreement with the two brothers. In 1955, he used the concept of licensing independent owners and helped create the modern fast-food industry. McDonald's restaurants began appearing nationwide.

Kroc served as chairman and largest stockholder of the McDonald's restaurant chain, built the hamburger operation into the nation's largest fast-food chain and amassed a $500 million personal fortune. The number of McDonald's restaurants steadily increased from 228 in 1960 to over 7,000 by 1982, located in all 50 states and around the world. The sales of all McDonald's Corporation licensed and company-owned restaurants jumped from $37 million in 1960 to $587 million in 1970 to over $1 billion in 1972. The same year marked the sale of the 10 billionth McDonald's hamburger.

Kroc had always wanted to own the Chicago Cubs, but Philip Wrigley refused to sell that franchise. On January 25, 1974, he rescued the staggering San Diego Padres franchise just before the vans were ready to move the team to Washington, D.C. He bought the Padres for $12 million in cash, saving major-league baseball in San Diego. Padre players, management, and fans alike welcomed Kroc with open arms.

The enthusiastic, dynamic Kroc vowed to build the Padres into a National League pennant contender quickly, letting baseball authorities handle the front office and field manager operations. Kroc took a much keener interest in the Padres than previous club owners. In April 1974, he grabbed the microphone of the public address system at San Diego Stadium and chastised the Padre players for ineptness. Kroc pledged to make his baseball team a winner, becoming an instant hero to his fellow fans. He possessed the financial resources to make San Diego more competitive on the field and to market the club more effectively. Kroc declared, "A winning team, a fighting team, a personality team will draw, just like a great show will be a success."

San Diego, however, still struggled in the standings, but club attendance increased dramatically. The Padres had never drawn more than 644,000 fans before Kroc's arrival. By 1978, 1,670,107 watched San Diego finish with a winning record for the first time. Kroc threw out the ceremonial first pitch for the 1978 All-Star Game at San Diego Stadium. During Kroc's ownership, attendance failed to reach one million paying customers only in the strike-shortened 1981 season. The Padres in 1982 drew their then second largest attendance of 1,607,516 fans and reached the .500 level for just the second time.

Kroc built San Diego into a contender by 1984. He contemplated selling the Padres in 1979 after being fined $100,000 for tampering with free agents Joe Morgan and Graig Nettles. Kroc instead turned over the Padre presidency and team operations to his son-in-law Ballard Smith, authorizing him to invest heavily in the free agent market and make trades. In September 1980, Jack McKeon became vice president of baseball operations and began improving the Padres. During the early 1980s, McKeon hired Dick Williams as manager, acquired catcher Terry Kennedy, shortstop Garry Templeton, and pitcher Ed Whitson in trades and signed free agents Steve Garvey and Rich Gossage.

San Diego on October 2 honored Kroc with a huge baseball party at Jack Murphy Stadium to celebrate his eightieth birthday. Nearly 46,300 fans witnessed the celebration. One scribe wrote, "Nowhere else would something like this happen for a team owner." Kroc was treated to some very exciting seasons. San Diego finished with identical 81-81 win-loss records in 1982 and 1983 before Kroc's death at age 81 in January 1984. Jack McKeon eulogized, "The Padres lost a great guy who was always interested in baseball and a genuine human being, revering people who produced." The Padres dedicated the 1984 campaign to Kroc. Padres president Ballard Smith predicted Kroc's spirit would permeate the stadium. "If we do win the title," he stated, ". . . and I think that day is not far away, I think he'll know about it." The Padres won their first National League pennant and made their only World Series appearance until 1998.

In 1983, Kroc was inducted into the Hall of Fame for U. S. Business Leadership. *Fortune* called him "one of the great marketers of modern times. Kroc served up an unbeatable combination of quality, speed, lower prices and cleanliness." Dartmouth College awarded him an honorary degree in 1977. His Kroc Foundation in Santa Barbara, California benefited diabetes, arthritis, and multiple sclerosis work. Kroc supported the Boy Scouts of America through Project SOAR, a national program to beautify America. In 1972, he donated $75 million to hospitals and museums. In August 1999, he was inducted into the San Diego Padres Hall of Fame as a charter member.

LARRY LUCCHINO

Larry Lucchino served as president and chief executive officer of the San Diego Padres from December 1994 to October 2001. He was born on September 6, 1945, in Pittsburgh, Pennsylvania and starred in basketball and baseball at Taylor Allerdice High School. Lucchino graduated with honors in 1967 from Princeton University, where he played basketball for two Ivy League championship teams. A graduate from Yale University Law School in 1972, he specialized in business, sports law, and litigation as a law partner at Williams and Connolly. Besides serving as counsel and member of the board of directors for the Washington Redskins, Lucchino in August 1979 became vice president/general counsel of the Baltimore Orioles. He assumed the presidency of the Orioles in May 1988 and part ownership of the club in 1989. His vision of the traditional, old-fashioned ballpark with modern amenities became a reality with Oriole Park in Camden Yards. The Orioles were sold following the 1993 season.

After joining San Diego in December 1994, Lucchino vowed to revitalize the Padres. First, he pledged to field a team worthy of the fans' support. He helped elevate the Padres from the worst major-league record in 1994 to a National League pennant winner in 1998. The Padres were the most improved National

League team in 1995 and won the National League West in 1996. Two years later, the Padres recaptured the National League West and won the National League Championship Series. Second, Lucchino created a new, warm, friendly environment at Jack Murphy Stadium. The Padres have increased season ticket sales each year since 1994 and drew a record 2,555,901 people in 1998. Lucchino installed palm trees in 1995 and made the Padres the first team to display the speed of every pitch on the scoreboard. In 1996, he added a Jumbo Tron video board and right-field scoreboard.

Lucchino aggressively marketed San Diego regionally and abroad. Under Lucchino, the Padres held their first press conference in Tijuana, Mexico, in January 1995, opened their first merchandise store and ticket outlet in Tijuana in December 1996, and began providing rides and special ticket prices for Mexican fans each Sunday in April 1997. The Padres played a three-game series with the New York Mets from August 16 through August 18, 1996, in Monterrey, Mexico, the first regular season major-league games outside the United States or Canada. In January 1997, San Diego made an agreement with the Chiba Lotte Marines of the Japanese Pacific League to exchange players, coaches, and baseball information and gained exclusive rights to negotiate with pitcher Hideki Irabu. In April 1997, the Padres hosted the St. Louis Cardinals in the first regular-season major-league games in Hawaii. Tony Gwynn in March 1998 conducted a batting clinic for children in Culiacan, Mexico. Lucchino also directed an aggressive marketing campaign in northern San Diego County and Orange and Riverside counties.

Lucchino increased Padre involvement in education, recreation, and health programs. In 1995, he helped initiate the Padres Scholars program, which has provided a $5,000 college scholarship each year to 25 deserving students who might not otherwise have been able to attend. Lucchino the next year helped establish the Little Padres Park program, which has built several youth baseball fields in the region. In 1997, he helped create the Cindy Matters Fund, which provides money for children's cancer research and improves the quality of life for young patients at the University of California San Diego Medical Center. His efforts also increased home attendance dramatically. The Padres doubled their attendance in 1996, drew two million fans for the second consecutive season in 1997, and set a single- season attendance mark in 1998.

Lucchino found 1998 especially rewarding. The Padres won the National League pennant and reached the World Series for the second time. Lucchino also headed the campaign for the ballpark redevelopment project that won decisive approval from San Diego voters with the November passage of Proposition C. Construction of the city's new downtown ballpark was halted in October 2000 when temporary funds ran out. Stadium construction resumed in February 2002 when Merrill Lynch purchased $169 million in bonds. The stadium is scheduled to open in 2004.

Lucchino created a short-term and long-term reorganization plan designed to build a perennial winning franchise. The club added Ted Simmons, Bill Bryk, and Bill Clark, three highly regarded baseball evaluators, augmented its scouting and player development programs, and focused on acquiring young talent, especially pitchers.

Besides attending Major-league Baseball ownership meetings, Lucchino served on Major-league Baseball's Restructuring Committee and the American League's Cable Television Committee and chaired the Baseball Operations and Player Development Contract Negotiations committees. He also belongs to the Realignment and Expansion Committee and the Commissioner's Blue Ribbon Task Force on Baseball Economics. Lucchino resigned as Padre president in October 2001 and became part owner and head of baseball operations for the Boston Red Sox in January 2002.

JOHN MOORES

John Moores has co-owned and served as chairman of the San Diego Padres since December 1994. He was born on July 9, 1944, in southeastern Texas. He and his wife Becky both graduated from the University of Houston and the University of Houston Law School and were married in 1963. Moores built his fortune in the computer software business while living in Houston. He spent eight years with IBM and four years with Shell Oil before founding BMC Software with a $1,000 investment in 1980. Moores generated most of his net worth from BMC Software and currently chairs two publicly-held software companies, Peregrine Systems, Inc., of San Diego and NEON Systems of Sugar Land, Texas. He resides in Rancho Sante Fe, California, and has become a San Diego civic leader and generous benefactor.

John Moores has become a major contributor to San Diego sports, cultural, and philanthropic institutions.

Moores joined Larry Lucchino, president and chief executive officer, in purchasing the San Diego Padres on December 21, 1994. He bought the franchise under difficult circumstances. It was in the middle of the worst labor dispute in baseball history, and the previous owners had alienated many fans with unpopular, salary-slashing trades. Moores and Lucchino made a major financial commitment to rebuild the Padres. Within one week, they negotiated a blockbuster trade with the Houston Astros for third baseman Ken Caminiti and center fielder Steve Finley. Caminiti and Finley, along with Tony Gwynn, sparked the Padres to the best improvement in the National League in 1995 and a National League West title in 1996.

San Diego did not live up to Moores's expectations in 1997 but reached the World Series in 1998. After winning the National League West crown for the second time in three years and claiming the franchise's second National League pennant, San Diego lost to the New York Yankees in the World Series. To Moores's delight, the Padres established a club attendance record by drawing over 2.5 million fans in 1998.

In November 1998, San Diego voters decisively approved Proposition C for the construction of a new stadium in downtown San Diego. Moores has taken many steps toward the stadium's completion, including entering JMI Real Estate into a joint venture with John Burnham & Company, one of San Diego's largest and oldest commercial real estate firms. Stadium construction of the Padres' downtown ballpark, however, was halted for 16 months when temporary funding ran out in October 2000.

The Padres struggled for another year to assemble a financing plan for the new ballpark. In November 2001, the San Diego city council voted 8-1 to approve a $166 million bond issue to fund it, but San Diego lawyer Bruce Henderson filed several lawsuits to stall stadium construction and a downtown redevelopment project. In January 2002, the Padres filed a lawsuit in San Diego Superior Court accusing Henderson of malicious prosecution.

On February 15, 2002, the same day Padre outfielder Mike Darr was killed in an automobile crash, Merrill Lynch purchased $169 million in bonds to finance construction of the Padres' new downtown ballpark. A check for $130 million, the proceeds from the sale after closing fees, insurance, and other expenses, was given to San Diego mayor Dick Murphy, financing the new ballpark. Ballpark construction resumed three days later and should be completed for the 2004 season.

Moores envisioned a perennial winner in San Diego, improving the front office infrastructure with the hiring of Ted Simmons, Bill Bryk, and Bill Clark, highly regarded baseball evaluators, and augmenting the scouting and player development programs.

Since his arrival in San Diego, Moores has become a major contributor to San Diego sports as well as cultural and philanthropic institutions. He has donated more than $17 million to the San Diego State University athletic department, funding the modern Tony Gwynn Stadium, a new athletic administration building, a championship tennis complex, and a women's softball field.

The Padres have been much more involved in educational, recreational, and youth relations since Moores became club chairman. Moores in 1995 established the Padres Foundation, which funds the Padres Scholars Program. Each year, the program has provided $5,000 college scholarships to 25 deserving students who might not otherwise have been able to attend college. The contributions of Padres players, owners, and corporate partners through 2000 totaled over $900,000. In 1996, Moores initiated the Little Padres Parks program, which has built seven baseball

C. Arnholdt Smith co-owned the San Diego Padres from 1969 through January 1974.

fields in the region. In 1997, he helped create the Cindy Matters Fund, which supports children's cancer research and strives to improve the quality of life for young patients at the University of California San Diego Medical Center. The Padres Foundation has donated $550,000 to the Cindy Matters Fund since 1997.

Moores has contributed to several other San Diego and Houston facilities. He donated around $5 million to the new San Diego Hall of Champions sports museum in Balboa Park, $6.6 million to the Zoological Society of San Diego, $17 million to the Scripps Research Institute, and $1 million to the new Preuss School at the University of California San Diego. He also has given over $75 million to the University of Houston and around $44 million to the Carter Center of Emory University in Atlanta.

Moores serves as a trustee of the Carter Center of Emory University and of the Scripps Research Institute, belongs to the advisory board of the San Diego Hall of Champions, chairs JMI Services, Inc., for family investments, and belongs to the University of California Board of Regents. He and his wife, Becky, have one son, John, Jr., and a daughter, Jennifer.

C. ARNHOLDT SMITH

C. Arnholdt Smith co-owned the San Diego Padres during the first years of the franchise from 1969 through January 1974. He was born in Walla Walla, Washington in 1899 and moved to San Diego with his parents in 1906. Smith worked as a grocery store clerk after leaving San Diego High School at age 15 and joined the Bank of Italy (later Bank of America) at age 17. After rising to division vice president in 1932, he and his brother purchased the U.S. National Bank of San Diego in 1933. Smith built a $1 billion financial empire by 1973. The Westgate-California Tuna Packing Corporation, created in 1960, formed the nucleus of his enterprise. The $200 million conglomerate encompassed seafood, ground transportation (Yellow Cabs), aviation (Air California), insurance, and hotels (Westgate Plaza Hotel).

In 1956, Smith purchased the San Diego Padres of the Pacific Coast League from Bill Starr and his associates for $350,000. Two years later, he moved the Padres from the termite-ridden Lane Field to beautiful Westgate Park. Westgate Park, which seated about 8,200 people, was built on Smith's property with his money. San Diego captured Pacific Coast League pennants in 1962, 1964, and 1967, the last year Westgate Park was used.

Smith played a crucial role in securing a major-league baseball franchise for San Diego. He paid a then record $10.2 million franchise fee, borrowing over 90 percent of the money. Smith, who owned two-thirds of the club, secured approval of the National League owners on May 27, 1968, for the Padres to join the National League. The Padre organization on August 13 arranged a 20-year lease with the San Diego City Council to use San Diego Stadium for major-league games. The Padres selected a 30-player roster at the October 14 expansion draft and entered the National League in 1969. San Diego finished in last place its first five years as a major-league franchise and consistently ranked last in attendance with under 650,000 fans, well short of the 800,000 needed to make it profitable.

In May 1973, *San Diego Union* sports editor Jack Murphy disclosed that Smith was struggling financially and wanted to sell the Padres. Smith lacked the money to pay the annual $700,000 interest on the $10 million he had borrowed to buy the Padres. He had secretly juggled millions of dollars to keep his massive financial empire afloat. The Securities and Exchange Commission suspended trading in stock of Westgate-California, the parent company of Smith's empire, and Air California, the airline controlled by Westgate-

California. Smith resigned as president, board chairman, and chief executive officer of the U.S. National Bank. The Padres did not have the financial resources to make the team competitive.

On May 5, Smith sold the Padres to Joseph Danzansky's Washington, D.C. group for $12 million. Danzansky handed Smith a $100,000 check as a downpayment and was given 45 days to finish financial arrangements, obtain a lease from Robert F. Kennedy Stadium, and secure approval from National League owners. The Padres on June 8 officially informed the city they planned to move the franchise to Washington, D.C., before the 1974 season. City officials, however, did not allow the Padres to sever their 20-year lease agreement on San Diego Stadium and threatened legal action. The city demanded $12 million from the Padres for terminating the San Diego Stadium lease agreement.

Smith's financial and legal problems worsened in October. The United States Comptroller of the Currency declared his U. S. National Bank of San Diego insolvent because it had made numerous unwise loans. The Internal Revenue Service claimed that Smith owed $22.8 million in back taxes and interest for 1969 and placed temporary liens on his properties in nine California counties. The Securities and Exchange Commission sued Smith and other Westgate Corporation executives for trying to defraud stockholders of Westgate and the U.S. National Bank.

Smith on November 23 sold the Padres to Marjorie Everett and several other California investors for around $10 million. National League owners rejected Everett's bid, 8-3, on December 6 perhaps because of her involvement in a race track scandal, and conditionally approved the sale of the Padres to Danzansky's Washington, D.C. group. The National League owners rescinded the sale on December 21 because the Danzansky group failed to raise the $5 million to protect the senior circuit from damage suits by the City of San Diego. On January 9, 1974, they again rejected the sale to the Everett group, 9-3.

Smith sold the Padres to Chicagoan Ray Kroc, 72-year-old chairman and largest stockholder of the McDonald's restaurant chain. Kroc paid Smith $12 million in cash for the Padres on January 25 and accepted a new lease with the city, committing the Padres to stay in San Diego through 1980. The National League owners on January 31 unanimously approved Kroc's acquisition of the Padres. Smith died on June 8, 1996, in Del Mar, California, at age 97.

Randy Smith served as vice president of baseball operations/general manager for the Padres from June 1993 through November 1995.

RANDY SMITH

Randy Smith served the San Diego Padres in several capacities, including director of scouting and vice president of baseball operations/general manager between 1984 and 1996. He was born on June 15, 1963, in Houston, Texas, and attended Southwest Texas State University in San Marcos. His father, Tal, served many years as a baseball executive with the Houston Astros, New York Yankees, and Cincinnati Reds. Smith began his professional baseball career in 1984 with the San Diego Padres organization as an administrative assistant for Beaumont, Texas, of the Texas League. That September, he assisted the Padres in preparing for their first postseason appearance in franchise history. Smith worked as assistant director of scouting and minor leagues from 1985 through 1987 and as director of scouting from 1988 through September 1991. He inherited the smallest scouting staff in major-league baseball and expanded operations to include the Dominican Republic, Venezuela, and Australia. *Baseball America* named him one of 10 people most likely to influence baseball in the 1990s.

From September 1991 through June 1993, Smith served as assistant general manager of the expansion Colorado Rockies. He scouted talent for both the June free agent draft and the Major-league baseball expansion draft. His responsibilities included negotiating player contracts and assisting in scouting and player development.

In June 1993, Smith replaced Joe McIlvaine as the San Diego Padres' vice president/baseball operations and general manager. At 29 years old, he became the youngest general manager in major-league history. The Padres finished last with a 61-101 record in 1993 and struggled with a 47-70 mark for the worst major-league record in the strike-shortened 1994 season. In December 1994, Smith negotiated the biggest trade in team history and the largest deal in major-league baseball since 1957. In the 12-player transaction, the Padres acquired third baseman Ken Caminiti and outfielder Steve Finley from the Houston Astros. The trade helped the Padres improve dramatically to a 70-74 mark in Smith's final season. Kevin Towers replaced him as general manager in November 1995. Smith worked as vice president of baseball operations/general manager of the Detroit Tigers from 1996 to 2002.

Kevin Towers has served as Padres vice-president and general manager since Novermber 1995.

KEVIN TOWERS

Kevin Towers rose rapidly through the San Diego Padre organization as player, scout, and executive and has served as Padre vice president and general manager since November 1995. Towers was born on November 11, 1961, in Medford, Oregon, and earned All-Western Athletic Conference honors as a right-handed pitcher for Brigham Young University. The San Diego Padres selected Towers in the first round of the June 1982 draft. Towers pitched seven years in the Padres' minor-league organization before arm injuries ended his playing career in 1988 with Las Vegas of the Pacific Coast League.

Towers scouted for the Padres in Texas and Louisiana from 1989 through 1991 and was pitching coach for Spokane of the Northwest League in 1989 and 1990. After spending two years as a regional and national cross-checker for the Pittsburgh Pirates, he returned to the Padres as director of scouting in August 1993. The Padres signed each of their first 14 selections in the 1995 draft and eight of their top 10 choices in the 1996 draft. *Baseball America* considered the 1995 and 1996 Padre drafts to be the strongest in the National League.

Towers helped the Padres reach the post-season in 1996 for just the second time, securing veterans Wally Joyner, Rickey Henderson, Bob Tewksbury, and Greg Vaughn. The Padres struggled in 1997, prompting other major changes. Towers named Dave Stewart as pitching coach and special assistant to the general manager and made several trades following the expansion draft. In December 1997, he landed ace pitcher Kevin Brown from the Florida Marlins for three minor-leaguers.

San Diego posted the best record in franchise history in 1998. During the season, Towers acquired veterans Jim Leyritz, Scott Sanders, Randy Myers, and John Vander Wal. The Padres won their second National League West title in three years under Towers's leadership and defeated the Houston Astros in the National League Division Series. The Padres captured the National League pennant by upsetting the Atlanta Braves, but lost to the formidable New York Yankees in the World Series.

Towers sought to keep the Padres competitive after losing stars Kevin Brown, Steve Finley, and Ken Caminiti to free agency. In December 1998, Towers sent Joey Hamilton to the Toronto Blue Jays for Woody Williams and two other players and in February 1999 he traded Greg Vaughn to the Cincinnati Reds for Reggie Sanders and Damian Jackson.

In March 1999, San Diego acquired third baseman Phil Nevin and pitcher Keith Volkman from the Anaheim Angels for infielder Andy Sheets and outfielder Gus Kennedy. The same month, the Padres signed closer Trevor Hoffman to the most lucratrive contract in club history and largest deal ever for a relief pitcher. In the June 1999 draft, San Diego selected six of the first 51 picks, including first rounders Vince Faison, Gerik Baxter, and Omar Ortiz.

In September 1999, Towers established a new structure in the baseball operations department. He hired veteran talent evaluators Ted Simmons as vice president of scouting and player development, Bill Bryk as special assistant to the general manager and minor-league field coordinator, and Bill Clark as international scouting supervisor. After struggling in 1999, the Padres in October acquired Carlton Loewer, Adam Eaton, and Steve Montgomery from the Philadelphia Phillies for veteran Andy Ashby. In December, they secured Ryan Klesko, Bret Boone, and Jason Shiell from the Atlanta Braves for Quilvio Veras, Reggie Sanders, and Wally Joyner.

Since that time, Towers has engineered several other trades. In July 2000, he acquired pitcher Heathcliff Slocumb and outfielder Ben Johnson from the St. Louis Cardinals for catcher Carlos Hernandez and infielder Nate Tibbs, pitcher Jay Witasick from the Kansas City Royals for pitcher Brian Meadows, and outfielder John Mabry and pitcher Tom Davey from the Seattle Mariners for outfielder Al Martin. In December 2000, San Diego traded pitcher Donne Wall to the New York Mets for outfielder Bubba Trammell. In March 2001, the Padres signed veteran outfielder Rickey Henderson and traded pitchers Matt Clement and Omar Ortiz and outfielder Eric Owens to the Florida Marlins for outfielder Mark Kotsay and infielder Cesar Crespo. From the New York Yankees, Towers in June 2001 acquired shortstop D'Angelo Jimenez for pitcher Jay Witasick and the following month pitcher Brett Jodie and outfielder Darren Blakely for pitcher Sterling Hitchcock. In August 2001, San Diego sent veteran pitcher Woody Williams to the St. Louis Cardinals for outfielder Ray Lankford. In December 2001, Towers traded catcher Ben Davis, pitcher Wascar Serrano, and shortstop Alex Arias to the Seattle Mariners for shortstop Ramon Vasquez, pitcher Brett Tomko, and catcher Tom Lampkin.

San Diego's commitment to player development and scouting has begun yielding positive results. Several players from the farm system have reached the Padres over the last three years. *Baseball America* has ranked some San Diego minor leaguers among its top 10 prospects and considers the Padre farm system among the best in baseball.

In March 2002, Towers agreed to a contract extension through the 2007 season, with a team option for an additional year. During his tenure since 1996, the Padres have compiled a 494-478 record, won the National League West division in 1996 and 1998, and captured National League pennant in 1998.

Towers and his wife, Kelley, reside in San Diego with their bulldogs, Dutch Henry and Fiona.

20
Managers

BRUCE BOCHY

Bruce Bochy caught for the San Diego Padres between June 1983 and 1987 and has managed them since 1995. The 6-foot 4-inch, 225-pound Bochy, who batted and threw right-handed, was born on April 16, 1955 in Landes de Boussac, France. After graduating from Melbourne, Florida High School, he attended Brevard Community College and Florida State University. The Houston Astros selected him in the secondary phase of the June 1975 draft. His brother, Joe, caught for the Minnesota Twins organization from 1969 through 1972. Bochy spent nearly four seasons in the minor leagues and caught with the Astros from 1978 through 1980. In February 1981, the Houston Astros traded him to the New York Mets. He spent nearly two seasons in the minor leagues, batting .306 in 17 games for the Mets in 1982.

In February 1983, Las Vegas of the Pacific Coast League signed Bochy as a free agent. After batting .303 in 42 games, Bochy joined the San Diego Padres in June 1983. He appeared in 23 games for San Diego, starting eight. In a 5-4, 10-inning victory over the San Francisco Giants on July 2, Bochy threw out two runners attempting to steal, singled, and hit a sacrifice fly. He doubled home a run against the Pittsburgh Pirates on July 14, made two hits in a 7-5 conquest of the Philadelphia Phillies on August 30, and tripled against the Houston Astros on September 8. Besides batting .333 with four hits as a pinch-hitter, he handled 56 chances without an error.

After Bochy hit .264 in 34 games at Las Vegas in 1984, San Diego recalled him on May 18. Bochy batted .228 with four home runs and 15 RBIs in 37 games. Two days after being recalled, he singled home a run against the New York Mets. Bochy filled in for catcher Terry Kennedy in August, hitting .300 with two home runs and five RBIs in seven games. He plated three runs in a 10-4 triumph over the Atlanta Braves on August 10. His second home run lifted the Padres to a 2-1 victory over the Montreal Expos on August 26. He singled as a pinch-hitter in Game 5 of the World Series against the Detroit Tigers.

Bochy enjoyed his best major-league season in 1985, batting .268 with six home runs, 16 runs scored, and 13 RBIs in 48 games. He batted .307 in his last 29 games, closing out the season with a five-game hitting streak. Two of his home runs came off 20-game winner Tom Browning of the Cincinnati Reds. Bochy's first home run came off Steve Carlton of the Philadelphia Phillies on May 26 in a 7-2 victory. On July 1, his tenth-inning home run off Nolan Ryan of the Houston Astros gave the Padres a 6-5 victory. He hit .313 with four home runs and eight RBIs at Jack Murphy Stadium.

Bruce Bochy managed the Padres to their second World Series in 1998.

In 1986, Bochy batted .252 with career bests of eight home runs and 22 RBIs. He appeared in more major-league games (63) and started more (29) than in any other season. His eight home runs all came against left-handed pitchers. Bochy clouted two game-winning home runs in pinch-hit situations. His first round-tripper on April 14 off Ed Vande Berg helped the Padres edge the Los Angeles Dodgers, 4-3. On July 4, he clouted a two-out, ninth-inning home run off Ray Fontenot to defeat the Chicago Cubs, 2-1. Bochy batted .350 with seven hits and six RBIs as a pinch-hitter. Defensively, he threw out 43 percent of the 28 runners attempting to steal. Bochy underwent arthroscopic knee surgery in November. His batting average slipped to just .160 with two home runs and 11 RBIs in his final major-league season in 1987. During nine major-league seasons, he hit .239 with 26 home runs and 93 RBIs in 358 games.

After serving as a player-coach with Las Vegas in 1988, Bochy managed Spokane, Washington to the Northwest League title in 1989. He piloted Riverside, California of the California League in 1990 and guided High Desert to the California League crown in 1991. In 1992, he managed Wichita to the Texas League title. Bochy rejoined the San Diego Padres as a third base coach in 1993 and replaced Jim Riggleman as manager in October 1994, making him the youngest National League and second youngest major-league pilot.

In 1995, San Diego made the biggest improvement among National League clubs. The Padres finished third in the National League West with a 70-74 mark, eight games behind the Los Angeles Dodgers, in an abbreviated 144-game schedule. Bochy recorded the best mark by a first-year San Diego manager since Jack McKeon in 1988 and used 40 different players. Bochy's club remained in contention through early September. Tony Gwynn, Steve Finley, and Ken Caminiti sparked the offense, while Andy Ashby and Trevor Hoffman anchored the pitching.

San Diego enjoyed the second best season in franchise history under Bochy in 1996, capturing the National League West with a 91-71 mark. The Padres vaulted into first place by winning a franchise record 17 games in April and remained in first place through June 9, their longest stretch atop the division since 1985. Bochy earned his 100th major-league managerial victory on May 24 against the New York Mets. Only Jack McKeon reached the century mark sooner among Padre managers. The Padres struggled after Wally Joyner broke his thumb in early June, but regained first place from the Los Angeles Dodgers in late August. Although temporarily relinquishing first place during the final week of the season, San Diego captured the National League West by sweeping the Los Angeles Dodgers in the three-game series finale at Dodger Stadium. The St. Louis Cardinals swept the Padres in the National League Division Series.

San Diego finished fourth in the National League West with a 76-86 record in 1997. After routing the New York Mets, 12-5, on opening day, the Padres suffered numerous injuries. Starting pitchers Andy Ashby, Joey Hamilton, and Sterling Hitchcock, third baseman Ken Caminiti, and center fielder Steve Finley spent time on the disabled list. Bochy used 45 players, three shy of the club record. He notched his 200th major-league managerial victory on July 10 against the Colorado Rockies and coached for manager Bobby Cox at the All-Star game in Cleveland. A four-game sweep by the Philadelphia Phillies at Veterans Stadium in late August doomed the Padres to the cellar.

Bochy guided San Diego to a franchise-best 98-64 and a National League West crown in 1998. The Padres held first place until June 6 and regained it four days later. A June 12-14 sweep of the San Francisco Giants during an 11-game winning streak ignited the division title run, as the Padres set a franchise record for home attendance in a three-game series. His 300th major-league managerial victory came on July 18 against the Cincinnati Reds. On September 12, Bochy's club clinched its second National League West title in three years, overcoming a 7-0 deficit to defeat the Los Angeles Dodgers, 8-7. Greg Vaughn sparked the offense, while starter Kevin Brown and reliever Trevor Hoffman anchored the pitchers. The Padres defeated the Houston Astros, 3-1, in the National League Division Series and upset the Atlanta Braves, 4-2, in the National League Championship Series. The New York Yankees, however, swept San Diego in the World Series.

In 1999, the Padres slipped to fourth in the National League West with a 74-88 mark. Bochy's team won a franchise record 14 consecutive games, the longest streak in the major leagues, from June 18 through July 2, garnering 11 victories against division rivals Los Angeles Dodgers and Colorado Rockies. After closing within two games of first place, San Diego lost nine straight contests in late July. Injuries to Carlos Hernandez, Tony Gwynn, Quilvio Veras, and Chris

Gomez devastated the club. Although faring well at home, the Padres won only 28 of 81 road games.

San Diego finished last in the National League West with a 76-86 mark in 2000, as Bochy suffered his fourth losing season. The injury-riddled Padres used 56 different players, tying the major-league record set by the Philadelphia Athletics in 1915. San Diego players made 23 trips to the disabled list. Ten Padres underwent surgery, including four of them twice. Tony Gwynn and Sterling Hitchcock missed most of the season. Rookie pitchers fared relatively well, but the club performed poorly offensively and committed the most errors in the major leagues.

In 2001, Bochy guided the Padres to a 79-83 mark and a fourth-place finish in the National League West. His club fared much better on the road than at home, performed very well in May, and clouted 10 grand slam home runs, but fell victim to two no-hitters at home. The season featured outfielder Rickey Henderson setting major-league records for career walks and runs and for becoming the 25th major leaguer to reach the 3,000-hit plateau, third baseman Phil Nevin clouting four grand slams, and legendary outfielder Tony Gwynn's swan song.

Under Bochy, the Padres have compiled a 564-552 win-loss mark and a .505 winning percentage with two National League West titles and one National League pennant. Bochy has posted a 7-10 record in two postseason appearances. During his tenure, the Padres rank sixth in the National League in winning percentage. Although Jack McKeon and Dick Williams own better winning percentages as Padre skippers, Bochy has earned more victories and remains the only Padre pilot to earn Manager of the Year accolades. Bochy was named *The Sporting News'* National League Manager of the Year in 1996 and 1998 and Baseball Writers Association of America National League Manager of the Year in 1996. He and his wife, Kim, reside in Poway, California, with their two sons, Greg and Brett.

STEVE BOROS

Steve Boros managed the San Diego Padres in 1986. The 6-foot, 185-pound Boros, who batted and threw right-handed, was born on September 3, 1936 in Flint, Michigan, and earned a B.A. degree in literature from the University of Michigan. The Detroit Tigers signed him to a $25,000 bonus contract in 1957 after his junior year. Between 1957 and 1965, Boros played mainly third base in seven major-league seasons with the Detroit Tigers, Chicago Cubs, and Cincinnati Reds. After earning American Association Most Valuable Player honors with Denver, Colorado in 1960, he enjoyed an excellent season with the Detroit Tigers in 1961 until sidelined with a broken collarbone. In 422 major-league games, he batted .245 with 26 home runs and 149 RBIs. Boros retired after the 1969 season with Omaha, Nebraska in the American Association. He managed Waterloo, Iowa, of the Midwest League from 1970 through 1972 and San Jose, California of the California League in 1973 and 1974.

Boros joined the Kansas City Royals coaching staff at third base under Jack McKeon in 1975 and at first base under Whitey Herzog from 1976 through 1979. He excelled at teaching base running. After managing Calgary, Canada of the Pioneer League in 1980, he coached at first base for the Montreal Expos in 1982 and 1983. Boros piloted the Oakland A's to a 74-88 record and a fourth- place finish in 1984 and to a 20-24 mark in 1985 before his dismissal. The low-key computer whiz joined the San Diego Padres in January 1986 as coordinator of minor-league instruction and replaced Dick Williams as manager during spring training the next month at Yuma, Arizona.

Little time remained for Boros to plan strategy or player personnel moves. Boros knew baseball well, lacked Williams's strictness, and gave younger players more action. Under Boros, the Padres struggled to a fourth-place finish with their worst mark (74-88) since 1980. Club attendance dropped dramatically. Veterans exhibited declining skills, while Tony Gwynn, Kevin McReynolds, John Kruk, and other younger players demonstrated considerable promise. Boros shouldered the blame for the team's sub-par performance and was replaced in late October by Larry Bowa. "Boros," Jack McKeon explained, "got caught up in a transition period. The players did not perform what they were capable of that year."

Boros, who coached for the Kansas City Royals in 1993 and 1994 and the Baltimore Orioles in 1995, has scouted for the New York Yankees since 2000. He enjoys reading, attending the theater, and playing tennis. He and his wife, Sharla, reside in Tampa, Florida and have one daughter, Sasha, and one son, Stephen. He also has a daughter, Renee, by a previous marriage.

LARRY BOWA

Larry Bowa managed the San Diego Padres from October 1986 through May 1988. The 5-foot 10-inch, 155-pound Bowa, who switch hit and threw right-handed, was born on December 6, 1945 in Sacramento, California. After starring in baseball and basketball at McClatchy High School in Sacramento, he attended Sacramento City College for two years. His father, Paul, played and managed in the minor leagues.

Bowa played shortstop with the Philadelphia Phillies from 1970 through 1981 and Chicago Cubs from 1982 through August 1985, ending his major-league career with the New York Mets in 1985. Although batting .260 with 2,191 hits and hitting a career-high .305 in 1975, he was known primarily for his defensive skills. Bowa holds the major-league record for highest lifetime fielding percentage by a shortstop with a .980 mark and won Rawlings Gold Glove awards in 1972 and 1978. He set the National League record by leading shortstops in fielding six times. His .987 fielding percentages in both 1971 and 1972 remain the best single-season marks for a National League shortstop. In 1972, Bowa committed a National League record low nine errors in 150 games. He also holds the major-league standard for highest fielding percentage by a shortstop in over 100 contests, fielding .991 in 146 games in 1979. Only Ozzie Smith played more than his 2,222 National League games at shortstop. Bowa, who ranks fourth in career major-league games at shortstop, made the National League All-Star team five times and appeared in five National League Championship Series. In the 1980 World Series, his .375 batting average and record-setting seven double plays helped the Phillies defeat the Kansas City Royals in six games.

In November 1985, Jack McKeon hired Bowa to manage the Las Vegas, Nevada Stars of the Pacific Coast League. Bowa piloted the Stars to the Pacific Coast League title. After posting a 36-34 first half record, Las Vegas finished 44-28 in the second stanza to run away with the Southern Division crown and defeated Phoenix and Vancouver in the playoffs to take the title.

In October 1986, Bowa replaced Steve Boros as manager of the San Diego Padres. The dedicated, diminutive, fiery Bowa was more vocal, intense, and emotional than Boros, an overachiever who expected others to demonstrate his work ethic. Although possessing a wealth of baseball knowledge and having mastered baseball strategy, he finished 1987 with a disappointing 65-97 ledger. The Padres started slowly with a 12-42 slate through June 4. Bowa was too intense, took losses too personally, and vented his frustration on Padre players in team clubhouse meetings. Between June 5 and September 23, the Padres produced one of the most remarkable turnabouts in franchise history. Bowa made several major lineup changes, improving the club both offensively and defensively. San Diego played the best of the Western Division clubs from June through August, winning 52 of 97 games from June 6 through September 23. Tony Gwynn went on a batting surge, while Benito Santiago hit in 34 consecutive games. San Diego, however, lost 10 of 11 games from September 24 through October 4 to end in sixth place.

San Diego opened 1988 with five consecutive losses and struggled to a 16-30 mark through May 27. Bowa grew more agitated with the disenchanted players and pressured them too much. The pitchers frequently lost leads, while the batters could not seem to score runners from second base. Tony Gwynn was mired in one of his worst batting slumps. President Chub Feeney fired Bowa on May 28. Bowa had compiled an 81-127 mark as Padre manager. John Kruk declared, "Even God couldn't manage this team."

Bowa coached for the Philadelphia Phillies from 1988 through 1996, the Anaheim Angels from 1997 through 1999, and the Seattle Mariners in 2000. In November 2000, the Philadelphia Phillies appointed him as manager. The Phillies fared much better than expected in 2001, occupying first place in the National League East for much of the season and finishing second, just two games behind the Atlanta Braves, with an 86-76 record. As a major-league pilot, he has compiled a 167-203 record for a .451 winning percentage. He and his wife, Sheena, reside in Radnor, Pennsylvania, and have one daughter, Victoria.

JERRY COLEMAN

Jerry Coleman has broadcast San Diego Padres games for 29 years and managed the club during 1980. The 6-foot, 165-pound Coleman, who batted and threw right-handed, was born on September 14, 1924 in San Jose, California, and attended the University of San Francisco. He entered professional baseball in 1942 with the New York Yankees organization and spent the next three years serving in World War II.

After three minor-league seasons, Coleman played infield for the New York Yankees from 1949 through

1957. In 1949, he led American League second basemen in fielding and was named Associated Press Rookie of the Year. His best major-league season came in 1950, when he batted .287, made the American League All-Star team, and garnered World Series Most Valuable Player honors in the sweep of the Philadelphia Phillies. Coleman appeared in six World Series, missing the 1952 and 1953 fall classics because of Korean War military service. He flew a combined 120 missions and received two Distinguished Flying Crosses, 13 Air Medals, and three navy citations. In nine major-league seasons, he batted .263 with 217 RBIs.

Coleman spent 1958 and 1959 as personnel director of the New York Yankees, supervising 10 farm clubs. He broadcast New York Yankees' games from 1963 through 1969 and worked sports events for CBS television and World Series special assignments for both ABC and NBC. Coleman announced for the California Angels in 1970 and 1971, joining the San Diego Padres broadcasting team in 1972.

In October 1979, the San Diego Padres replaced manager Roger Craig with Coleman. Coleman had no previous managerial experience. The Padres plummeted to last place in the National League West Division with a 73-89 record in 1980, but ironically they led the major leagues with 239 stolen bases. San Diego became the first major-league team to have three players, including Gene Richards, Ozzie Smith, and Jerry Mumphrey, break the 50-stolen-base barrier. Richards finished second in the National League in hits, Smith and Dave Winfield won Rawlings Gold Glove awards, and Rollie Fingers was named Fireman of the Year.

Coleman, however, returned to the broadcast booth in October 1980. He has covered San Diego Padre games since then on KFMB and KOGO radio and still stirs fans with his patented "Oh Doctor" and "Hang a Star on That One" calls. For 22 seasons, Coleman called the CBS Radio Network's Game of the Week. To commemorate his fiftieth year in baseball, the Padres in 1999 retired his jersey. In 2001, Coleman was inducted into the San Diego Padres Hall of Fame. He and his wife, Maggie, and their daughter, Chelsea, reside in La Jolla, California. Coleman and his first wife, Louise, had two children, Jerry and Diane.

ROGER CRAIG

Roger Craig served the San Diego Padres as a pitching coach from 1969 to 1972, 1976, and 1977, and as manager in 1978 and 1979, achieving the first winning record in franchise history. The 6-foot, 4-inch, 192-pound Craig was born on February 17, 1931 in Durham, North Carolina and attended North Carolina State University. The Brooklyn Dodgers signed the right-handed pitcher in 1950. He spent slightly over three seasons in the minor leagues and two years in military service.

Craig pitched for the Brooklyn Dodgers from 1955 through 1957, Los Angeles Dodgers from 1958 through 1961, New York Mets in 1962 and 1963, St. Louis Cardinals in 1964, Cincinnati Reds in 1965, and Philadelphia Phillies in 1966, compiling 74 wins, 98 losses, and a 3.83 ERA and appearing in four World Series. He scouted for the Los Angeles Dodgers in 1967 and managed at Albuquerque, New Mexico in 1968 before joining the San Diego Padres as pitching coach in September 1968.

Craig patiently guided the expansion Padres staff. The young pitchers quickly identified with him, while the veterans respected him. Craig carefully developed Al Santorini, Clay Kirby, and other promising pitchers. Three San Diego hurlers won at least 10 games in 1970, with Danny Coombs compiling the third best ERA among senior circuit left-handers.

Under Craig's direction, the Padre staff recorded the third best ERA in the National League in 1971. Clay Kirby won 15 games, while Steve Arlin contributed nine victories. Kirby, Arlin, and Fred Norman combined for 29 victories in 1972. Craig returned to the Padres as pitching coach in 1976 and 1977. He tutored National League Cy Young Award winner Randy Jones, who led the senior circuit in 1976 with 22 victories, 25 complete games, and 315 innings pitched, and worked with National League Rookie Pitchers of the Year Butch Metzger in 1976 and Bob Owchinko in 1977. Craig taught Padre hurlers the split-finger fastball and pioneered calling pitches from the dugout.

The San Diego Padres appointed Craig as manager in mid-March 1978, when Alvin Dark was fired. Craig guided the Padres to an 84-78 record for the best mark in the first decade of the franchise. His stellar performers included National League Cy Young Award winner Gaylord Perry, who led the National League with 21 victories and a 2.72 ERA, reliever Rollie Fingers, who paced the senior circuit with 37 saves, and slugger Dave Winfield. When the Padres slumped

Roger Craig served as pitching coach for the Padres from 1969 to 1972 and in 1976 and 1977.

to 68-93 in 1979, Jerry Coleman replaced Craig as Padre manager.

Craig served as pitching coach for the Detroit Tigers from 1980 to 1984, when Detroit won the American League pennant and World Series. After scouting for the Tigers in 1985, he managed the San Francisco Giants from September 1985 through 1992 and piloted them to the 1989 National League pennant. Craig compiled a 738-737 record in 10 seasons as a major-league manager. He and his wife, Carolyn, reside in Warner Springs, California and have four children, Sherri, Roger, Jr., Teresa, and Vicki.

ALVIN DARK

Alvin Dark managed the San Diego Padres from May 1977 to March 1978. The 5-foot 11-inch, 185-pound Dark, who batted and threw right-handed, was born on January 7, 1922 in Comanche, Oklahoma and attended Louisiana State University, where he made the 1942 and 1943 All-American football teams. He played shortstop in the major leagues in 1946 and from 1948 through 1960 with the Boston Braves, New York Giants, St. Louis Cardinals, Chicago Cubs, Philadelphia Phillies, and Milwaukee Braves. Dark won National League Rookie of the Year honors in 1948, when he batted .322 to help the Braves reach the World Series. With the New York Giants, he batted over .300 in three consecutive seasons from 1951 through 1953 and played in the 1951 and 1954 World Series. The three-time National League All-Star batted .289 with 2,089 hits, 358 doubles, 126 home runs, and 757 RBIs in 14 major-league seasons.

Dark managed the San Francisco Giants from 1961 through 1964. The Giants won the 1962 National League pennant with a 103-62 record, defeating the Los Angeles Dodgers in a three-game playoff and losing the World Series in seven games to the New York Yankees. He piloted the Kansas City Athletics in 1966 and 1967 and Cleveland Indians from 1968 through 1971. Dark piloted the Oakland A's to an American League pennant in 1974 with a 90-72 record and the Western Division title in 1975 with a 98-64 mark. The A's defeated the Los Angeles Dodgers in the 1974 World Series, but lost to the Boston Red Sox in the 1975 American League Championship Series. Through 1975, he had compiled 946 wins and 889 losses in 12 seasons as a major-league manager.

After beginning 1977 as first base coach for the Chicago Cubs, Dark replaced John McNamara as manager of the San Diego Padres on May 30. Padres president Buzzie Bavasi stated, "We have always respected Alvin's abilities over the years and have always felt he was one of the best managers in the game." Upon accepting the assignment, Dark said, "There's still a lot of games left to play, and I've seen and experienced many situations where big leads have disappeared. No task is impossible." Dark guided the Padres to a doubleheader sweep over the San Francisco Giants on May 30 and finished his first series with three wins in four attempts. The Padres, however, ended 1977 mired in fifth place with a disappointing 48-65 mark under Dark.

In March 1978, the Padres fired Dark 17 days before the National League season opened. Dark, the victim of the earliest managerial change in major-league history at that time, was dismissed because of a player revolt, his failure to communicate with the front office, and his unwillingness to delegate authority to his coaches. "We were getting a lot of feedback from players," owner Ray Kroc revealed. Several players disliked the complex strategy and rigid discipline that the born-again Christian had imposed. Catcher Gene

Tenace complained, "He put in so many trick plays and had so many signs that everyone was uptight." Roger Craig, Padre pitching coach for six years, replaced Dark as manager. Dark's managerial career ended at 994 wins and 954 losses in 13 major-league seasons. His autobiography, *When in Doubt, Fire the Manager*, written with John Underwood, was published in 1980. He and his first wife, Adrienne, had four children before their divorce. He and his second wife, Jackie, reside in Easley, South Carolina. She has two children by an earlier marriage.

Preston Gomez was the first manager of the San Diego Padres.

PRESTON GOMEZ

Preston Gomez managed the San Diego Padres during the first years of the franchise from 1969 through April 1972. The 5-foot 11-inch, 185-pound Gomez, who threw and batted right-handed, was born on April 20, 1923 in Central Preston, Cuba and attended Belen College. He signed with the Washington Senators in 1944 as a shortstop and batted .286 in eight games. Gomez spent the next decade in the minor leagues with Buffalo, New York, Vicksburg, Mississippi, New London, Connecticut, Florence, Alabama, Saginaw, Michigan, Three Rivers, Canada, Toledo, Ohio, Charleston, West Virginia, Havana, Cuba, and Yakima, Washington.

Gomez piloted Fresnillo, Mexico and Mexico City, Mexico in 1957 and 1958. In 1959, he guided Havana, Cuba to third place in the International League and the Junior World Series crown over Minneapolis of the American Association. Gomez managed Spokane, Washington to the Pacific Coast League title in 1960, but struggled the next two seasons there and with Richmond, Virginia of the International League in 1963 and 1964. He coached for the Los Angeles Dodgers from 1965 through 1968 and was lauded by manager Water Alston as the "best coach I ever had."

Gomez, known for developing young talent, was named manager of the expansion San Diego Padres on August 29, 1968. From 1969 to 1971, the Padres finished sixth in the West Division. The dismal 1969 season ended just 52-110 with numerous lopsided defeats and only 99 home runs. The Padres improved markedly to 63-99 in 1970, but lost a near National League record 37 games by just one run. Gomez remarked: "We were not only representative but also competitive. That means we had a good chance to win just about every game. And I consider that a big step forward." San Diego clouted 172 home runs, third best in the National League. Eight players belted at least 11 home runs, topped by Nate Colbert's 38. Three pitchers won at least 10 games. The Padres defeated the Cincinnati Reds in 10 of 18 games and split season series with the Pittsburgh Pirates and New York Mets.

San Diego, however, dropped to 61-100 in 1971. Gomez was fired after the Padres started 4-7 in April 1972, giving him a composite record of 180 wins and 316 losses. He demonstrated patience and understanding in the development of young players, including pitchers Clay Kirby and Steve Arlin, first baseman Nate Colbert, and outfielder Cito Gaston. He arrived at the ballpark first, left last, and gave his players a quiet dignity, an abundance of knowledge, and a wonderful patience through difficult times. Gomez managed the Houston Astros in 1974 and 1975 and the Chicago Cubs in 1980. He coached for the Houston Astros in 1973, St. Louis Cardinals in 1976, Los Angeles Dodgers from 1977 through 1979, and California Angels from 1981 through 1984. His seven-year major-league managerial career featured 346 wins, 529 losses, and a .395 winning percentage. He resides in Chino Hills, California.

FRANK HOWARD

Frank Howard managed the San Diego Padres in 1981. The 6-foot 7-inch, 255-pound Howard, who batted and threw right-handed, was born on August 8, 1936 in Columbus, Ohio and attended Ohio State University, where he made the All-Big Ten Conference basketball team and starred in baseball. The Los Angeles Dodgers signed Howard for a $108,000 bonus in 1958. After two minor league seasons, Howard joined the Los Angeles Dodgers in 1960 and earned National League Rookie of the Year honors. He played outfield for the Los Angeles Dodgers from 1960 through 1964, appearing in the 1963 World Series. Howard starred for the Washington Senators from 1965 through 1971, leading the American League in home runs twice and in RBIs once and making the American League All-Star team from 1968 through 1971. From May 3 through May 18, 1968, he belted 12 home runs. The streak included setting major-league records for most home runs in six consecutive games (10) and five straight games (8) and tying American League records for most home runs in four consecutive games (7) and most straight games with home runs (6). Howard spent the remainder of his playing career with the Texas Rangers and Detroit Tigers. During 16 major-league seasons, he batted .273 with 382 home runs, 1,119 RBIs, and a .499 slugging percentage.

After playing baseball in Japan in 1974, Howard managed Spokane, Washington of the Pacific Coast League in 1976 and coached for the Milwaukee Brewers from 1977 through 1980. He replaced Jerry Coleman as pilot of the San Diego Padres in October 1980. In the strike-shortened 1981 season, the Padres lost 20 of their first 30 games and struggled to their worst record (41-69) since 1974. Ozzie Smith won his second consecutive Gold Glove, but defensive and bullpen problems plagued San Diego. Howard was fired as manager that October.

Howard coached for the New York Mets from 1982 through 1984, piloting them to a 52-64 slate in late 1983. He coached for the Milwaukee Brewers in 1985 and 1986, Seattle Mariners in 1987 and 1988, New York Yankees in 1989, 1991, and 1992, New York Mets from 1994 through 1996, and Tampa Bay Devil Rays in 1998 and 1999. Howard managed the Gulf Coast Braves of the Gulf Coast League in 1997 and served as senior adviser for baseball operations for the Tampa Bay Devil Rays in 2000 and 2001. In June 2002, he was named manager of Columbus, Ohio of the International League. He and his wife, Cecelia, reside in Sterling, Virginia and have six children, Tim, Cathy, Dan, Mitchell, Mary, and Becky.

JACK McKEON

Jack McKeon served as vice president of baseball operations and manager of the San Diego Padres in the 1980s. The 5-foot, 8-inch, 205-pound McKeon, who batted and threw right-handed, was born on November 23, 1930 in South Amboy, New Jersey and attended Holy Cross College and Seton Hall University. He graduated with a Bachelor's degree in physical education and science from Elon College in North Carolina. He signed with the Pittsburgh Pirates and caught for 11 minor- league seasons from 1949 through 1959. His brother, Bill, also caught in the minor leagues between 1952 and 1957 and scouted for the Kansas City Royals and San Diego Padres.

McKeon managed six minor-league clubs from 1955 to 1964, guiding Wilson, North Carolina of the Carolina League to first place in 1961. After scouting for the Minnesota Twins from 1965 through 1967, he piloted High Point-Thomasville, North Carolina of the Carolina League in 1968 and Omaha, Nebraska of the American Association from 1968 through 1972. Omaha finished first in the Eastern Division in 1970. McKeon managed the Kansas City Royals from 1973 through 1975, finishing second in the American League West with an 88-74 record in 1973. After piloting Richmond, Virginia of the International League in 1976, he returned to the major leagues as manager of the Oakland Athletics in 1977. He guided the Athletics to a 26-27 record in 1977 and 45-78 mark in 1978.

The San Diego Padres recruited McKeon as a scout and assistant to the general manager in 1980. In September 1980, he became vice president of baseball operations. The cigar-smoking McKeon, nicknamed "Trader Jack," developed a youth movement and solidified the club through trades and free agent acquisitions. Following the 1980 season, he unloaded 14 veterans. In December 1980, pitcher Rollie Fingers and catcher Gene Tenace were sent to the St. Louis Cardinals. The Padres traded popular pitcher Randy Jones to the New York Mets the same month and outfielder Jerry Mumphrey to the New York Yankees in April 1981. McKeon planned "to secure players at each position who could help his club win at least 50 percent of the games." He astutely judged player talent and planned well for both the immediate season and the future.

McKeon made several pivotal moves in the early 1980s. He secured catcher Terry Kennedy in the 11-player trade with the St. Louis Cardinals in December 1980. In November 1981, he lured Dick Williams as manager. Under Williams, the Padres escaped the cellar with consecutive .500 seasons in 1982 and 1983 and won their first National League pennant in 1984. McKeon made three trades with the St. Louis Cardinals before the 1982 season, securing outfielder Sixto Lezcano, trading light-hitting shortstop Ozzie Smith for shortstop Garry Templeton, and acquiring pitcher Luis DeLeon. San Diego dealt Smith because it feared losing him to free agency after the 1983 season. Templeton possessed excellent range and a fine throwing arm at shortstop and hit better than Smith.

McKeon continued building the Padres through trades. In November 1982, he acquired starting pitcher Ed Whitson from the Cleveland Indians. The Padres became a legitimate contender in December 1982, signing free agent first baseman Steve Garvey of the Los Angeles Dodgers. Garvey provided the right-handed power and defensive stability that San Diego needed to become a quality team. Ticket sales increased dramatically after Garvey's signing. Garvey provided leadership for Tony Gwynn, Kevin McReynolds, Carmelo Martinez, Eric Show, Ed Whitson, Alan Wiggins, and the other young players. Three major moves before the 1984 season made the Padres National League pennant contenders. In a three-way December 1983 transaction, San Diego secured relief pitcher Craig Lefferts and outfielder Carmelo Martinez from the Chicago Cubs. Free agent Rich Gossage, the intimidating New York Yankees reliever, joined the Padres in January. Gossage gave San Diego the bullpen stopper it had lacked since Rollie Fingers departed. The Padres solved their perennial third base problem by acquiring San Diego native Graig Nettles from the New York Yankees in March. Although 40 years old, Nettles remained an explosive hitter and provided invaluable clubhouse leadership. McKeon stated, "Gossage made the club a contender and Nettles provided the last piece in the puzzle with his steady third base play." The Padres captured the Western Division title with an impressive 92-70 mark in 1984 for the best record in franchise history at that time and swept the last three games of the National League Championship Series against the Chicago Cubs to reach their first World Series.

Jack McKeon made many trades as vice president of baseball operations for the San Diego Padres during the 1980s.

San Diego made winning the World Series its goal for the 1985 season. McKeon strengthened the pitching staff in December by acquiring LaMarr Hoyt, an American League Cy Young Award winner, from the Chicago White Sox and signed reliever Tim Stoddard of the Chicago Cubs. San Diego played well until July, but nosedived after the All-Star break. Manager Dick Williams wanted McKeon either to grant him a one-year contract extension or let him resign with pay for the 1986 season. In February 1986, the Padres announced that Williams would not return as manager.

The Padres entered another rebuilding phase with managers Steve Boros and Larry Bowa. McKeon traded catcher Terry Kennedy to the Baltimore Orioles in October 1986 for pitcher Storm Davis and outfielder Kevin McReynolds to the New York Mets in December 1986 for infielder Kevin Mitchell and four other prospects. The Padres did not fill the power vacuum left by the departures of Kennedy and McReynolds and dropped to last place in 1987.

McKeon helped engineer one of the most remarkable turnabouts in franchise history. When San Diego fell 30 games below .500 in June, Bowa and McKeon made several changes. The Padres inserted John Kruk at first base, moved Carmelo Martinez to left field, and recalled pitcher Jimmy Jones from Las Vegas. Kruk, Martinez, and Jones enjoyed very productive seasons, while catcher Benito Santiago compiled a 34-game hitting streak. San Diego paced the Western Division with a 42-38 record from June through August.

McKeon made a blockbuster trade in July with the San Francisco Giants, exchanging pitchers Dave Dravecky and Craig Lefferts and third baseman Kevin Mitchell for third baseman Chris Brown and pitchers Mark Davis, Mark Grant, and Keith Comstock. McKeon knew the power potential of Mitchell, but disliked his erratic off-the field behavior. Brown did not fulfill expectations, but Davis blossomed into one of the best relievers in Padres history and Grant became an effective set-up man.

Club president Chub Feeney fired manager Larry Bowa in May 1988 after a disappointing 16-30 start and selected McKeon, who had two years remaining as vice president of baseball operations, as field manager. McKeon, who relished returning to the field 10 years after being fired as Oakland Athletics manager, encouraged the players to relax and enjoy baseball. "My motto," McKeon stressed, "is that the players should have fun. Fun is winning." He implored the players to concentrate less on individual statistics and execute baseball fundamentals better. The fatherly McKeon talked to his players calmly and soothed their tempers. Garry Templeton explained, "McKeon changed the attitude of the players and made baseball more fun to play."

McKeon's approach transformed the 1988 Padres into a winner. San Diego won its first six games and compiled an excellent 67-48 mark under him. McKeon guided the once-floundering club to a respectable 83-78 third-place finish. He lamented, "I only wish we had 30 more days in the season. I didn't think we'd turn it around this quickly."

"What a comeback," Tony Gwynn exclaimed. "Finishing in third place, it was like us winning the pennant. We learned how to win."

McKeon handled the team personnel shrewdly in 1988. Gwynn was switched from right field to center field and hit a torrid .367 in his final 73 games to win his third National League batting title. Carmelo Martinez moved from first base to left field, clouting 11 home runs and driving in 34 runs in his last 38 games. McKeon converted John Kruk to a right fielder and encouraged rookie second baseman Roberto Alomar, who fielded brilliantly and finished second in club hitting, and catcher Benito Santiago, who threw out 45 percent of the runners trying to steal. McKeon also instilled confidence in his starting pitchers, keeping them in games longer. Eric Show enjoyed his best season, winning nine of his final 10 decisions, while Andy Hawkins and Ed Whitson combined for 27 victories. In June, McKeon secured left-hander Dennis Rasmussen from the Cincinnati Reds for Candy Sierra. Rasmussen, who won 14 of 18 decisions for the Padres, asserted, "I always knew I could pitch like this. It was a matter of the Padres and Jack giving me the confidence to do it." Mark Davis became the dominant bullpen closer the Padres needed with 28 saves.

Off the field, club president Chub Feeney engaged in a power struggle with McKeon. Feeney did not want McKeon to continue serving as both vice president of baseball operations and field manager. McKeon, however, insisted that he could hold both posts simultaneously as Whitey Herzog had done with the St. Louis Cardinals. He relinquished his vice presidency in September 1988 and signed a three-year, $1.3 million contract to remain as a manager, being assured that he would still handle most player personnel decisions.

Several McKeon transactions improved San Diego's prospects following the 1988 season. In late October, McKeon lured first baseman Jack Clark and a pitcher from the New York Yankees for three players. He hoped that Clark would provide the power the Padres had lacked since the departure of Kevin McReynolds. When San Diego lost pitcher Andy Hawkins to free agency, McKeon signed pitcher Bruce Hurst of the Boston Red Sox to give them a quality left-handed starter.

Under McKeon, the Padres ended 1989 with an 89-73 record, only three games behind the San Francisco Giants. Inconsistent hitting, low run production, and lack of speed hurt the Padres through midseason. San Diego showed signs of ending the slump on July 17, setting a club record with a 17-4, 19-hit shellacking of the Pittsburgh Pirates. The Padres played superlative baseball from early August to mid-September. Tony Gwynn, Jack Clark, Roberto Alomar, Benito Santiago, Mark Davis, Ed Whitson, Bruce Hurst, Eric Show, and newcomer Andy Benes performed well. Gwynn became the first National Leaguer since Stan Musial to win three consecutive batting titles. Davis won the National League Cy Young Award, saving 44 games and winning or saving 48 of the club's 89 victories. Outfielder Chris James, obtained in June from the Philadelphia Phillies for John Kruk, belted two grand slams.

McKeon encountered mixed results following the 1989 season. He engineered the biggest off-season deal in acquiring outfielder Joe Carter from the Cleveland Indians for catcher Sandy Alomar, Jr., infielder Carlos Baerga, and third baseman-outfielder Chris James but the Padres lost Mark Davis to free agency. The Padres struggled the first half of 1990 with a 37-43 mark and replaced McKeon as manager in mid-July. McKeon served as senior adviser of player personnel with the Cincinnati Reds from January 1993 through July 1997, when he replaced Ray Knight as manager. He guided Cincinnati to a 33-30 record and a third-place finish in 1997 and a 77-85 mark in 1998. In 1999, the Reds placed second in the National League Central with a 96-67 record. On October 4, the New York Mets blanked Cincinnati, 5-0, in a one-game playoff for the wild card. Cincinnati again finished second in the National League Central with an 85-77 record in 2000, leading to McKeon's dismissal that October. In 12 seasons as a major-league manager, McKeon compiled a 770-733 record for a .512 winning percentage.

JOHN McNAMARA

John McNamara managed the San Diego Padres from 1974 through 1977. The 5-foot 10-inch, 175-pound catcher, who batted and threw right-handed, was born on June 4, 1932 in Sacramento, California. After graduating from Sacramento High School in 1951, he spent two years in the U.S. Army and attended Sacramento State College. The St. Louis Cardinals signed McNamara in 1951. The smooth-fielding, light-hitting catcher played minor-league baseball for 14 seasons with Houston, Texas, Lynchburg, Virginia, Lewiston, Idaho, Sacramento, California, Tulsa, Oklahoma, Binghamton, New York, Dallas, Texas, Mobile, Alabama, and Birmingham, Alabama.

McNamara managed in the minor leagues from 1959 through 1967, guiding Lewiston to the Northwest League title in 1961. His clubs won consecutive Southern League pennants at Mobile in 1966 and Birmingham in 1967. The Oakland A's appointed him third base coach in 1969 and manager that September. After piloting the Oakland A's to second place in 1970, McNamara coached third base with the San Francisco Giants from 1971 to 1973.

The San Diego Padres named McNamara manager in February 1974. Although never finishing above .500, San Diego improved its record each year under McNamara. The personable pilot taught baseball fundamentals and handled pitchers well. In 1974, he produced 60 victories, then the most for a Padre first-year manager. Nevertheless, San Diego finished last in the National League West Division. The Padres improved in 1975 with 71 triumphs and finished fourth, escaping the cellar for the first time. The power of Willie McCovey and Dave Winfield, coupled with the 20-victory season of pitcher Randy Jones, sparked the progress. The Padres recorded 73 victories in 1976, but slipped to fifth place in the National League West Division. Winfield supplied the offensive power, 22-game winner Randy Jones became the first Padre to garner the National League Cy Young Award, and reliever Butch Metzger shared National League Rookie of the Year. Alvin Dark replaced McNamara on May 30, 1977 after the latter had guided the Padres to a 20-28 record. McNamara had become the then winningest manager in franchise history with a 224-310 record in slightly over three seasons at the helm.

McNamara coached for the California Angels in 1978 and piloted the Cincinnati Reds from 1979 through 1982, winning the National League West Division in 1979. He managed the California Angels in 1983 and 1984 and Boston Red Sox from 1985 through mid-1988. The Red Sox won the American League pennant in 1986, but lost the World Series to the New York Mets. After scouting for the Seattle Mariners in 1988 and 1989, McNamara managed the Cleveland Indians in 1990. He instructed catchers for the California Angels for the next five seasons and was interim manager in late 1996. In 19 major-league seasons, his clubs won 1,167 games and lost 1,242 contests for a .484 winning percentage. He and his first wife, Kathleen, had four children before their divorce. He and his second wife, Ellen, live in Brentwood, Tennessee.

GREG RIDDOCH

Greg Riddoch managed the San Diego Padres from July 1990 through late September 1992. The 5-foot 11-inch, 175-pound Riddoch, who batted and threw right-handed, was born on July 17, 1945 in Greeley, Colorado and graduated from Garden Grove High School in California. He earned a Bachelor's degree in business administration and a master's degree

John McNamara managed the Padres to improving records each year from 1974 through 1976.

in education administration from Northern Colorado University. Riddoch made the College All-America team as a shortstop in 1967, when he led the NCAA with 17 home runs in 26 games. The Cincinnati Reds selected Riddoch in the secondary phase of the June 1967 free agent draft. He played shortstop and third base in the Cincinnati Reds' minor-league system from 1967 through 1971 but struggled offensively.

Riddoch managed eight seasons from 1974 through 1981 in the Cincinnati Reds organization. He guided Eugene, Oregon to Northwest League titles in 1975, 1977, and 1980 and also piloted Seattle, Washington of the Northwest League and Billings, Montana of the Pioneer League. Riddoch served the Cincinnati Reds as scouting supervisor in 1982 and 1983, assistant director of player development in 1984, and director of minor-league clubs in 1985. He joined the San Diego Padres as the associate director of minor leagues and scouting in January 1986. When Steve Boros became manager in February 1986, Riddoch was promoted to director of minor leagues and scouting. From October 1986 to July 1990, he coached in the dugout and at first base for the San Diego Padres.

In July 1990, Riddoch replaced Jack McKeon as the San Diego Padres' manager. San Diego triumphed only once in its first dozen games under Riddoch, but played above .500 the rest of the season. With Riddoch at the helm, the Padres finished 38-44 in 1990 and shared fifth in the Western Division. In 1991, San Diego improved to 84-78 and ended third in the Western Division. The Padres won six of their first seven games and shared first place on May 10, but slumped disastrously before the All-Star break. San Diego won seven consecutive games in early September and boasted one of the best records in franchise history. Tony Gwynn and Fred McGriff supplied the main offensive spark, while Andy Benes anchored the pitchers.

In 1992, San Diego performed 78-72 under Riddoch through September 23. After winning seven of their first nine games, the Padres occupied second place through much of May. Riddoch's club won 21 of 29 games from July 9 through August 11 and remained in contention until trading 13-game-winner Craig Lefferts to the Baltimore Orioles in late August. Gary Sheffield and Fred McGriff enjoyed spectacular seasons. On September 23, San Diego fired Riddoch, who had compiled a 200-194 record in nearly three seasons. Jim Riggleman, pilot of the Las Vegas farm club, replaced him.

Riddoch coached for the expansion Tampa Bay Devil Rays from 1997 through 1999 and has served as director of player development for the Milwaukee Brewers since 2000. He and his wife, Linda, reside in Estes Park, Colorado and have two sons, Rory and Raleigh. Riddoch has taught psychology and coached baseball, football, and basketball at the high school level and has done substitute teaching. Riddoch, who enjoys hunting and fishing, also spent three years as athletic director of District 6 in Greeley, Colorado.

JIM RIGGLEMAN

Jim Riggleman managed the San Diego Padres from September 1992 through 1994. The 5-foot 11-inch, 175-pound Riggleman, who batted and threw right-handed, was born on December 9, 1952 in Fort Dix, New Jersey and graduated from Richard Montgomery High School in Rockville, Maryland. Riggleman earned a Bachelor's degree in physical education in 1974 from Frostburg State College, where he earned NAIA All-America honors in baseball in 1974. He was inducted into the Frostburg State Hall of Fame.

The Los Angeles Dodgers selected Riggleman in the fourth round of the June 1974 free agent draft. Riggleman played third base and second base with Waterbury, Connecticut of the Eastern League from 1974 through July 1976, when he was traded to the St. Louis Cardinals organization. He performed in the

Cardinals system through May 1981. His best season came in 1980, when he batted .295 with 21 home runs and 90 RBIs for Arkansas of the Texas League.

After coaching for Arkansas in 1981 and Louisville, Kentucky of the American Association in early 1982, Riggleman managed seven years in the St. Louis Cardinals organization. He piloted St. Petersburg, Florida of the Florida State League from 1982 through 1984 and Arkansas of the Texas League from 1985 through June 1988, attaining first place in the first half of 1985. He served as director of player development for the Cardinals in latter 1988 and coached for the St. Louis Cardinals in 1989 and 1990.

Riggleman joined the San Diego Padres organization as manager at Las Vegas, Nevada of the Pacific Coast League in 1991 and 1992, guiding the Stars to first place the first half of 1992. Riggleman replaced Greg Riddoch as the San Diego Padres manager in September 1992, posting a 4-8 record. He was the youngest National League pilot and third youngest major-league pilot.

In 1993 the Padres unloaded Gary Sheffield, Fred McGriff, Bruce Hurst, and several other high-salaried players. San Diego struggled with a 61-101 record for seventh place in 1993, using 46 different players. The Padres lost seven of their first nine contests and suffered over 100 losses for the first time since 1974. "The players," Riggleman explained, "were preoccupied so much with what was happening off the field that it affected them on the field. They were upset by all of the players that left and kept thinking they were next." Despite sharply slashing player salaries, the Padres lost $3.7 million in 1993 and closed the upper deck at Jack Murphy Stadium.

During the strike-shortened 1994 season, San Diego compiled the worst record in the major leagues with a 47-70 mark and was the only club drawing under one million fans. The Padres won only 10 of their first 42 games and set a team record with 13 consecutive losses in May. Tony Gwynn's National League-best .394 batting average and Trevor Hoffman's 20 saves brightened an otherwise dismal season. After compiling a 112-179 overall mark as Padres manager, Riggleman in October 1994 became manager of the Chicago Cubs.

Riggleman managed the Chicago Cubs from 1995 through 1999. In 1998, Chicago finished 90-73 for second place in the National League Central and earned a wild card spot in the playoffs. Through 1999, Riggleman compiled a 486-598 record for a .448 winning percentage as a major-league manager. He served as bench coach for the Cleveland Indians in 2000 and for the Los Angeles Dodgers since 2001. An avid runner and reader, he resides in Madiera Beach, Florida and has a son, Jon.

DICK WILLIAMS

The San Diego Padres enjoyed success as a franchise under manager Dick Williams from 1982 through 1985. The 6-foot, 190-pound Williams, who batted and threw right-handed, was born on May 7, 1929 in St. Louis, Missouri and attended Pasadena Junior College. He batted .260 with 70 home runs and 331 RBIs as an outfielder in 14 major-league seasons from 1951 through 1964 with the Brooklyn Dodgers, Baltimore Orioles, Cleveland Indians, Kansas City Athletics, Houston Astros, and Boston Red Sox. Williams managed the Boston Red Sox to the 1967 American League pennant, the Oakland A's to the 1972 and 1973 World Series titles, and the Montreal Expos into contention.

In November 1981, the San Diego Padres signed Williams to a three-year contract. His tough, no-nonsense approach stressed consistency and sound, fundamental baseball, featuring solid pitching, speed, and defense. Williams, an intense, demanding pilot, possessed great baseball knowledge. He relied heavily on percentages, form charts, and statistics, and instilled a winning attitude and the importance of teamwork in his players.

San Diego fortunes improved dramatically under Williams to an 81-81 record in 1982, eight games behind the Atlanta Braves in the National League West. The Padres escaped the cellar for the first time in three seasons, placing fourth with the second best record in franchise history at that time. San Diego set a then club mark by winning 11 consecutive games in April and trailed the first place Atlanta Braves by just two games at the All-Star break. The Padres retained second place until early August when injuries and drug problems intervened. Williams observed, "We have a solid nucleus of hungry young ballplayers. And they seemed to mesh as a unit." General manager Jack McKeon concurred, "Dick has to be given credit for turning the ballclub around. He instilled a bit of discipline as well as aggressiveness into the club which they didn't have before. He made them believe they can win."

San Diego again finished fourth with an identical 81-81 record in 1983, 10 games behind the Los Angeles Dodgers. Injuries sidelined Tony Gwynn, Steve Garvey, Garry Templeton, Ed Whitson, Tim Lollar, and Dave Dravecky in 1983, forcing Williams to develop Andy Hawkins, Kevin McReynolds, Mark Thurmond, Alan Wiggins, and other younger players. After starting slowly, the Padres won 17 of 29 games in June and swept a four-game series from the Los Angeles Dodgers at Dodger Stadium between June 20 and June 23. San Diego finished strong in September, triumphing in 14 of 25 games. Base stealing became a major component of the Padre offense, with 179 stolen bases in 246 attempts for a 73 percent success rate.

With Williams at the helm, San Diego captured its first Western Division crown with a 92-70 mark in 1984. The Padres surpassed the .500 mark for only the second time with a .568 winning percentage, the second best performance in franchise history, finishing 12 games ahead of the Atlanta Braves and Houston Astros. After winning nine of 11 games in its first homestand, San Diego moved into first place by half a game on June 9 and never relinquished the lead thereafter.

Youth and veterans blended well to produce the superb 1984 season. Tony Gwynn won his first batting title, while Kevin McReynolds, Carmelo Martinez, and Graig Nettles supplied considerable power. Young starting pitchers Eric Show, Ed Whitson, Mark Thurmond, and Andy Hawkins hurled better than anticipated, while Goose Gossage supplied brilliant relief. The Padres reached their first National League Championship Series and World Series, making a dramatic comeback against the Chicago Cubs to take the National League pennant.

San Diego finished in third place in 1985 with a disappointing 83-79 record, 12 games behind the Los Angeles Dodgers. The Padres fared well through July 4 with a 46-31 record, leading the Western Division by five games. Williams managed the National League All-Stars, including seven Padres. The Padres fared only 10-17 in July, falling five games behind the Los Angeles Dodgers. Williams unfortunately switched from a five-man to four-man rotation after the All-Star break. Padre players and the media increasingly grew disenchanted with Williams, a stern, demanding taskmaster.

Williams asked general manager Jack McKeon to grant him a contract extension or let him resign with one year's pay. In February 1986, San Diego replaced Williams with Steve Boros. Williams, the first Padre mentor to leave with a winning record, boasted a 337-311 mark in four seasons with San Diego and joined Bill McKechnie as the only managers to win pennants with three different teams. He piloted the struggling Seattle Mariners from 1986 through May 1988 and has served as an adviser and consultant with the New York Yankees since 1996. His career managerial record in 21 major-league seasons included 1,571 wins and 1,451 losses for a .520 winning percentage. He and his wife, Norma, reside in Henderson, Nevada and have three children, Kathi, Ricky, and Marc.

DON ZIMMER

Don Zimmer managed the San Diego Padres in 1972 and 1973. The 5-foot 9-inch, 188-pound Zimmer, who batted and threw right handed, was born on January 17, 1931 in Cincinnati, Ohio and graduated from Western Hills High School in 1949. He signed with the Brooklyn Dodgers and spent nearly six years as a minor-league infielder. In July 1953, the injury-prone Zimmer was almost killed when a pitch fractured his skull while playing for St. Paul, Minnesota of the American Association. He lay unconscious for 13 days and was hospitalized for a month. In 1956, a fastball broke his cheek and nearly blinded him.

Zimmer spent 12 years in the major leagues as a utility infielder with the Brooklyn Dodgers from 1954 through 1957, Los Angeles Dodgers in 1958, 1959, and 1963, Chicago Cubs in 1960 and 1961, New York Mets and Cincinnati Reds in 1962, and Washington Senators from 1963 through 1965, batting .235 with 91 home runs and 352 RBIs. He played in the 1955 and 1959 World Series and 1961 All-Star game.

Zimmer managed Knoxville, Tennessee of the Southern League and Buffalo, New York of the International League in 1967 and Indianapolis, Indiana of the Pacific Coast League in 1968. When the San Diego Padres were formed, he joined their organization as pilot at Key West, Florida of the Florida State League in 1969 and Salt Lake City, Utah of the Pacific Coast League in 1970. After serving as third base coach for the Montreal Expos in 1971, he joined the San Diego Padres as a coach in October 1971.

On April 27, 1972, San Diego fired manager Preston Gomez and put Zimmer at the helm. In 1972, Zimmer guided San Diego to a 54-88 win-loss record and sixth place in the West Division. The very young team posted winning records against the Cincinnati Reds and Atlanta Braves. Zimmer expected his players to hustle, think baseball all the time, master the fundamentals, and eliminate mistakes. The young players gave Zimmer his source of enthusiasm. The spirited, active Zimmer constantly talked on the bench and did anything that it took to win. President Buzzie Bavasi expected San Diego to reach the .500 level for the first time in 1973. The Padres, however, finished in last place with a 60-102 record. John McNamara replaced Zimmer as manager in February 1974.

Zimmer managed the Boston Red Sox from 1976 through 1980, Texas Rangers in 1981 and 1982, and Chicago Cubs from 1988 through 1991, guiding the Cubs to an East Division title in 1989 and earning National League Manager of the Year honors. When New York Yankees manager Joe Torre underwent prostate cancer surgery in 1999, Zimmer piloted the club to a 21-15 record. His major-league clubs compiled a 906-873 win-loss record for a .509 winning percentage. Zimmer also coached for the Boston Red Sox from 1974 through 1976 and in 1992, New York Yankees in 1983, 1986, and since 1996, Chicago Cubs from 1984 through 1986, San Francisco Giants in 1987, and Colorado Rockies from 1993 through 1995. He and his wife, Jean, were married at home plate in Elmira, New York in August 1951 and reside in Rye Brook, New York. They have two children, Thomas and Donna. Thomas played and managed in the minor

22

Players

ROBERTO ALOMAR

Roberto Alomar, the best second baseman in San Diego history, starred for the Padres from 1988 through 1990. The 6-foot, 185-pounder, who switch hits and throws right-handed, is the son of former major-leaguer Sandy Alomar, Sr. and younger brother of major-leaguer Sandy Alomar, Jr. He was born in Ponce, Puerto Rico on February 5, 1968 and attended Luis Munoz Rivera High School in Salinas, Puerto Rico. In February 1985, the Padres signed him as a nondrafted free agent for $80,000. Alomar played slightly more than three seasons in the minor leagues, leading the California League with a .346 batting average for Reno, Nevada in 1986. In April 1988, the San Diego Padres summoned him from Las Vegas, Nevada of the Pacific Coast League.

Alomar became San Diego's regular second baseman as a 20-year-old in 1988, batting .266 with 24 stolen bases as the National League's youngest player. He made his major-league debut at home on April 22, singling to the hole at shortstop off Nolan Ryan in a 3-1 victory over the Houston Astros. Besides leading the Padres with 84 runs scored and 24 doubles, Alomar finished second in hits (145), triples (6), and stolen bases (24) and paced the senior circuit in sacrifice hits (19). He hit safely in 46 of the last 55 games and batted .330 in September with a 13-game hitting streak. Defensively, Alomar helped the Padres lead the National League in double plays. He won the Clyde McCullough Award as San Diego's Rookie of the Year and finished fifth in the National League Rookie of the Year balloting.

Alomar's best season with the Padres came in 1989, when he batted .295 for sixth best in the National League. He batted .326 in July, .321 in August, and .365 in September, hitting safely in 31 of his final 33 games. He recorded a career-best 17-game hitting streak and a 12-game hitting streak at the end of the season. Alomar led the Padres with 42 stolen bases, sharing second best in the National League. Alomar finished second in the senior circuit with 54 multiple-hit games, ranked third with 184 hits, and authored four-hit contests in a 6-2 home loss to the Los Angeles Dodgers on June 21 and in a 6-2 win over the New York Mets at Shea Stadium on August 17. Ten days later, Alomar drove in a career-best five runs in a 13-7 home triumph over the New York Mets. He shared the club lead with 82 runs scored and 27 doubles and paced the National League with 17 sacrifice hits. Alomar batted .329 at home and .313 from the left side. Defensively, he led the National League with 28 errors at second base.

In 1990, Alomar batted .287 with 168 hits, 27 doubles, 60 RBIs, and 24 stolen bases and made the National League All-Star team. His 43 multi-hit games included four hit efforts on May 6 in an 8-3 victory over the Chicago Cubs at Wrigley Field and May 10 in a 9-1 victory over the St. Louis Cardinals at Busch Stadium. He scored four runs in a 9-0 romp over the Atlanta Braves at home on June 2. His 17 errors topped National League second basemen, but his miscues occurred mostly on errant throws after making difficult stops.

Alomar bats well from both sides of the plate and compiles excellent on-base and slugging percentages. He recorded more base hits after his first four seasons than either Joe Morgan or Rod Carew. Tony Gwynn helped Alomar perfect his swing. A singles hitter, Alomar quickly developed into one of the game's premier performers. He consistently makes contact at the plate, exhibits considerable speed on the bases, and displays exceptional range defensively. Alomar turns double plays masterfully and positions himself well against rival hitters.

A blockbuster December 1990 trade sent Alomar and outfielder Joe Carter to the Toronto Blue Jays for shortstop Tony Fernandez and first baseman Fred

McGriff. Alomar starred with Toronto from 1991 through 1995, the Baltimore Orioles from 1996 through 1998, and the Cleveland Indians from 1999 to 2001. The New York Mets in December 2001 acquired Alomar, pitcher Mike Bacsik, Jr., and outfielder Danny Peoples from the Indians for outfielders Matt Lawton and Alex Escobar, pitchers Jerrod Riggan and Bill Traber, and first baseman Earl Snyder. Through 2001, he has batted .306 with 446 doubles, 190 home runs, 1,018 RBIs, and 446 stolen bases. Alomar has appeared in 12 All-Star games, earned 10 Rawlings Gold Glove awards, made *The Sporting News'* American League All-Star Team five times, and made *The Sporting News'* American League Silver Slugger Team four times. He has batted .284 with 19 hits, one home run, and 12 RBIs in four American League Division Series, .316 with 36 hits, three home runs, and 15 RBI in five American League Championship Series, and .347 with 17 hits and six RBIs in two World Series. Alomar, who remains single, resides in Salinas, Puerto Rico.

Steve Arlin

STEVE ARLIN

Steve Arlin pitched for the San Diego Padres from June 1969 through June 1974. The 6-foot 3-inch, 195-pound right-hander was born on September 25, 1945 in Seattle, Washington and graduated from Ohio State University, where he made All-America as a junior and senior. In 1965, he compiled a 13-2 win-loss record with a 2.23 ERA and led NCAA pitchers with 165 strikeouts to help Ohio State attain second in the 1965 College World Series. Arlin finished 11-1 with a 1.58 ERA to lead the Buckeyes to the 1966 College World Series Championship and blanked Oklahoma State University, 1-0, in the NCAA finals. He completed dental studies at Ohio State in June 1970. His grandfather, Harold Arlin, is credited with being the first announcer to broadcast a baseball game in 1921, when the Pittsburgh Pirates played the Philadelphia Phillies at Forbes Field in Pittsburgh.

The Philadelphia Phillies selected Arlin in the special phase of the June 1966 draft and signed him for a reported $108,000 bonus. Arlin pitched three years in the Phillies' farm system and hurled a 9-2 seven-inning no-hitter for Reading, Pennsylvania of the Eastern League against York on July 25, 1967. San Diego selected him in the October 1968 expansion draft. Arlin spent the next two seasons mostly in the minor leagues, splitting two decisions with the Padres. Dental studies forced him to miss spring training until 1971. His first major-league victory came on September 23, 1970 in a seven-hit shutout against the Atlanta Braves at Atlanta-Fulton County Stadium.

In his rookie 1971 season, Arlin won only nine decisions and led the National League with 19 losses. He finished with a 3.47 ERA, completing 10 of 34 starts and fanning 156 batters in 228 innings. Arlin blanked the Cincinnati Reds, 10-0, on May 8, the Philadelphia Phillies, 6-0, on June 2, the Pittsburgh Pirates, 2-0, on July 25, and the New York Mets, 3-0, on August 12. The Padres scored two runs or less in 13 of his 19 defeats, including his 3-2, two-hit loss on May 14 to the Chicago Cubs. Although finishing 10-21 with a 3.60 ERA in 1972, Arlin pitched several brilliant games. On July 18 at home, he came within one strike of hurling a no-hitter in a 5-1 victory over the Philadelphia Phillies. Denny Doyle singled with two outs in the ninth inning, and Tommy Hutton followed with another single. He hurled two other two-hitters in a 1-0 triumph over the Pittsburgh Pirates on June 18 and a 3-2 loss to the New York Mets on July 14 and one-hitters in 1-0 triumphs over the San Francisco Giants on June 23 and in 10 innings over the New York Mets on July 6. In a nine-game stretch from June 8 to July 23, he allowed only 40 hits in 79 innings and yet won only three games.

His record improved to 11-14 in 1973, but his ERA soared to 5.14. Arlin led the Padre staff in victories and hurled three road shutouts in four starts from June 30 to July 17. He threw consecutive shutouts of 3-0 over the Houston Astros on June 30 and 4-0 over the Los Angeles Dodgers on July 5 and blanked the Chicago Cubs, 1-0, on July 17. He also tied a National League record by surrendering three grand slams.

After slipping to 1-7 in 1974, Arlin was traded to the Cleveland Indians on June 15 and finished his major-league career that season there. His major-league record included 34 wins, 67 losses, a 4.33 ERA, and 463 strikeouts in 788.2 innings. He and his wife, Susan, have two sons, Steve and Scott. He practices dentistry in San Diego.

Andy Ashby

ANDY ASHBY

Andy Ashby starred as a pitcher for the San Diego Padres from 1993 through 1999. The 6-foot 5-inch, 190-pound Ashby, who bats and throws right-handed, was born on July 11, 1967 in Kansas City, Missouri and graduated from Park Hill, Missouri High School. He attended Crowder Junior College in Missouri and signed with the Philadelphia Phillies as a free agent in May 1986. Ashby spent seven seasons in the minor leagues, pitching briefly with Philadelphia in 1991 and 1992. The Colorado Rockies selected him in the November 1992 expansion draft. After Ashby lost all four decisions in 1993, the Colorado Rockies traded him on July 27 to the San Diego Padres.

Ashby immediately joined the Padre starting rotation, finishing with a 3-6 mark and 5.48 ERA in 1993. On August 10, he struck out 10 Houston Astros in a 7-2 win. His second win came on August 24 against the St. Louis Cardinals, as the Padres scored 13 first, inning runs in a 17-4 triumph. Ashby improved considerably in 1994 with a 6-11 ledger and 3.40 ERA. In his first full major-league season, he shared fourth among league leaders with four complete games and ranked ninth with 164.1 innings pitched. He allowed less than three runs in seven of his first 10 starts.

In 1995, Ashby compiled a 12-10 mark with a 2.94 ERA and 150 strikeouts to earn the Clyde McCullough Award as Padre Pitcher of the Year. He led the Padres with 12 wins, posting the third best ERA in the National League. His 150 strikeouts ranked eighth in the senior circuit, while his 31 starts shared fourth best. No Padre had finished with a lower ERA since Ed Whitson's 2.60 in 1990. Ashby enjoyed two three-game winning streaks. His first career shutout came on June 18 at Three Rivers Stadium, where he fanned 10 Pittsburgh Pirates and allowed just four hits in a 2-0 victory. Ashby blanked the St. Louis Cardinals, 3-0, on August 11, striking out 11 and surrendering five hits. He hurled 19 consecutive scoreless innings from August 5 through August 21 and won his final four decisions. Ashby did not yield an earned run in six of his last 14 starts and allowed fewer than three runs in 10 of his last 20 starts.

Despite three trips to the disabled list in 1996, Ashby finished 9-5 and led Padre starters with a 3.23 ERA. The consistent Ashby posted excellent ERAs of 2.51 in May, 2.61 in June, and 2.08 in July. He walked slightly over two batters per nine innings and made his first opening day start on April 1 against the Chicago Cubs at Wrigley Field. Ashby won three consecutive starts from April 11 through April 22, outdueling Greg Maddux of the Atlanta Braves on April 11. The Cy Young Award winner had won a major-league record 18 consecutive road victories. Ashby became just the third pitcher in the 1990s to make four hits in a game, singling and doubling twice each against the Colorado Rockies on April 16. He posted a 4-1 record in May and recorded a personal-best five consecutive victories from May 9 through June 28 with a 2.16 ERA. Ashby struck out eight New York Mets on May 14 and eight Philadelphia Phillies on May 31. He ranked second in the major leagues with 17 sacrifice bunts and led Padre hurlers with a .244 batting average. In Game 3 of the National League Division Series, he allowed four earned runs in 5.1 innings and fanned five in a 7-5 loss to the St. Louis Cardinals.

Ashby struggled with a 9-11 mark in 1997, but led the Padres in starts (30), ERA (4.13), complete games (2), innings pitched (200.1), and strikeouts (144). He completed at least seven innings in 60 percent of his starts. Ashby issued the sixth fewest walks in the National League. He earned his initial victory on April 20, defeating the St. Louis Cardinals, 8-2, in the final game of the Paradise Series in Honolulu, Hawaii. Ashby allowed two runs on seven hits over 7.0 innings, walking two and fanning six. He pitched the club's first complete game of 1997 on May 1, defeating the New York Mets, 7-3, to snap a season-high eight-game Padre losing streak.

Ashby finished 3-1 with a 3.40 ERA in his final six starts. He fanned 23 hitters and walked only two in 22.0 innings in his final three starts. His best start came on September 5, when he defeated the Atlanta Braves, 6-2. He came within three outs of hurling the first no-hitter in Padre history. Kenny Lofton led off the ninth inning with a looping single to right field on a 3-2 pitch to end the no-hit bid. Fred McGriff spoiled Ashby's shutout with a towering two-run homer. Ashby finished with his first two-hitter, walking three and fanning eight. He matched his career best and set a Padre season high with 11 strikeouts in 8.0 innings in a four-hit, 5-4 win over the Colorado Rockies on September 17.

Ashby enjoyed his best major-league season in 1998, helping the Padres take the National League West. He posted a 17-9 record and 3.34 ERA, establishing career highs with 17 victories, 151 strikeouts, 226.2 innings, 33 starts, and five complete games. His 17 triumphs marked the sixth best in Padre history. Ashby developed a forkball, the perfect complementary pitch for his fastball. Kevin Brown's addition also took some pressure off him. The Padres scored only 12 runs in Ashby's nine losses. Ashby pitched at least seven innings in 19 of his starts, normally inducing batters to hit ground balls.

Ashby threw a 112-pitch complete game four-hit shutout to defeat the Arizona Diamondbacks, 1-0, as the Padres finished the first 1998 home stand with a 7-0 record. He did not allow a hit or walk after two outs in the sixth inning. No Padre had hurled a complete game shutout in nearly two years. Ashby completed three consecutive starts against the Arizona Diamondbacks, St. Louis Cardinals, and Houston Astros from May 25 through June 4, becoming the first major-league pitcher in 1998 and the first Padre in a decade to accomplish that feat. During that streak, he fared 2-1 with a 1.73 ERA. His five straight victories from May 30 to June 19 marked a career high. Ashby needed only 75 pitches in a 7-2 complete game victory over the Colorado Rockies on July 5 in his final start before the All-Star break to attain his 50th victory as a Padre. He threw 55 strikes and only 20 balls in that contest, allowing two solo home runs and just five hits in the two-hour, one-minute game. No major-league hurler had thrown that few pitches in a nine-inning complete game in over a decade. Ashby entered the All-Star break with 11 victories and made the National League All-Star team for the first time, surrendering a home run to Alex Rodriguez of the Seattle Mariners in his lone inning. On August 12 he became the first National League pitcher to attain 16 victories, outdueling Greg Maddux of the Atlanta Braves, 5-1. He never regained his top form, however, after developing buttocks tendonitis.

Ashby authored a 10-4 record with four complete games and a 2.85 ERA at home. After struggling with a 6.75 ERA in his lone National League Division Series start against the Houston Astros, Ashby allowed only three earned runs in 13 innings in his two National League Championship Series starts against the Atlanta Braves. In his lone World Series start, he lasted less than three innings in Game 2 against the New York Yankees.

Ashby in 1999 compiled a 14-10 record and 3.80 ERA and struck out 132 batters in 206 innings. He led the Padres in victories, ERA, complete games, and shutouts, hurling half of their six shutouts and four of their five complete games. His 14 victories marked the second highest of his major-league career. Ashby blanked the Los Angeles Dodgers, 3-0, at home on April 16, the Pittsburgh Pirates, 2-0, at home on April 21, and the Colorado Rockies, 11-0, at Coors Field on July 4 and hurled a six-inning 1-0 shutout over the Chicago

Cubs at Wrigley Field on June 1. Although losing the season opener, 8-2, to the Colorado Rockies at Monterrey, Mexico, Ashby fared 8-4 before the All-Star break. His final victory came on September 6 against the Pittsburgh Pirates at Three Rivers Stadium.

The San Diego Padres on November 10 traded Ashby to the Philadelphia Phillies for pitchers Carlton Loewer, Steve Montgomery, and Adam Eaton. Ashby pitched for Philadelphia until being traded in July 2000 to the Atlanta Braves. He finished 8-6 to help Atlanta win the National League East and relieved twice in the National League Division Series against the St. Louis Cardinals. In December 2000, the Los Angeles Dodgers signed Ashby to a $22.5 million, three-year contract. Ashby pitched just 11.2 innings in 2001 before undergoing elbow surgery in mid-April, winning both decisions with a 3.86 ERA. As a Padre, Ashby authored a 70-62 mark with a 3.60 ERA, 827 strikeouts, and six shutouts. He ranks among the Padre leaders in virtually every major pitching category, standing third in strikeouts, fourth in victories, fifth in games started (185) and innings (1,210), sixth in ERA and losses, eighth in shutouts, and ninth in complete games (18). His .530 winning percentage remains third best in Padre history. Through the 2001 season, Ashby has compiled a 86-87 record with a 4.10 ERA and struck out 1,023 batters in 1,554 innings. He and his wife, Tracy, reside in Pittston, Pennsylvania with their three daughters, Eastin, Madison, and Taryn.

ANDY BENES

Andy Benes starred as a pitcher for the San Diego Padres from August 1989 through July 1995. The 6-foot 6-inch, 235-pound right-hander was born on August 20, 1967 in Evansville, Indiana and attended Evansville University, where he finished 16-3 with a 1.42 ERA, led the nation in strikeouts, and made the All-America baseball team as a junior. He pitched for the U.S. Olympic team in 1988, winning his only start at the Seoul, South Korea games. His brother, Alan, pitches for the Chicago Cubs organization. The San Diego Padres selected Benes as the first overall pick in the June 1988 draft. He spent just half a season in the minor leagues with Wichita, Kansas of the Texas League and Las Vegas, Nevada of the Pacific Coast League.

The San Diego Padres summoned Benes to the major leagues in August 1989. Benes finished 6-3 with a 3.51 ERA. He struggled in his major-league debut on August 11, giving up six runs and three home runs while fanning seven Atlanta Braves in a 6-5 loss. After another setback, Benes won six consecutive games. His initial triumph came against the Philadelphia Phillies at Veterans Stadium on August 23, when he allowed three hits over seven innings in a 7-3 victory. He hurled two 1-0 victories over Orel Hershiser of the Los Angeles Dodgers, fanning 13 batters and allowing only six hits in 15 innings. Benes won Padres Pitcher of the Month honors in September with a 4-1 slate and a 2.21 ERA. He struck out nine batters in consecutive starts on September 13 against the Atlanta Braves and September 19 against the Cincinnati Reds. *The Sporting News* voted him Rookie Pitcher of the Year.

Benes fared 10-11 with a 3.60 ERA in 1990 and shared seventh best in the National League with 149 strikeouts. He hurled a two-hitter in his first major-league complete game on May 14, fanning five in a 5-1 victory over the Philadelphia Phillies. Benes won three consecutive games from May 24 through June 4 and took four of five decisions from July 27 through August 24, allowing only one run in a 7-2 victory over Tom Glavine of the Atlanta Braves on August 7. He prevailed in all three starts against the Philadelphia Phillies and was nicknamed "Rainman" because he pitched or was scheduled to appear seven times when the Padres experienced rain delays or postponements.

In 1991, Benes finished 15-11 with a career-best 3.03 ERA, ninth lowest in the National League. He struggled with a 4-10 ledger in his first 18 starts, as the Padres scored two runs or less nine times and were blanked four times. Benes posted an 11-1 slate with a 1.77 ERA in his final 15 starts. He established then career highs in wins, innings (223), and strikeouts (167), sixth best in the senior circuit. Benes fanned 13 Cincinnati Reds on April 13 and averaged nearly seven strikeouts per nine innings. On July 28 he hurled a five-hitter over eight innings in a 2-0 victory over the New York Mets, starting a career-best 10-game winning streak that lasted until October 1. The streak marked the longest in the National League since Dennis Martinez won 11 straight in 1989 and the longest for a Padre since Andy Hawkins and LaMarr Hoyt won 11 consecutive contests in 1985. During the span, Benes allowed just seven earned runs in 73.2 innings. He hurled his first major-league shutout in a two-hit, 1-0 victory over the St. Louis Cardinals on August 29.

In 1992, Benes dropped to 13-14 with a 3.35 ERA. His 169 strikeouts and career-high 231.1 innings pitched fared seventh in the National League. The

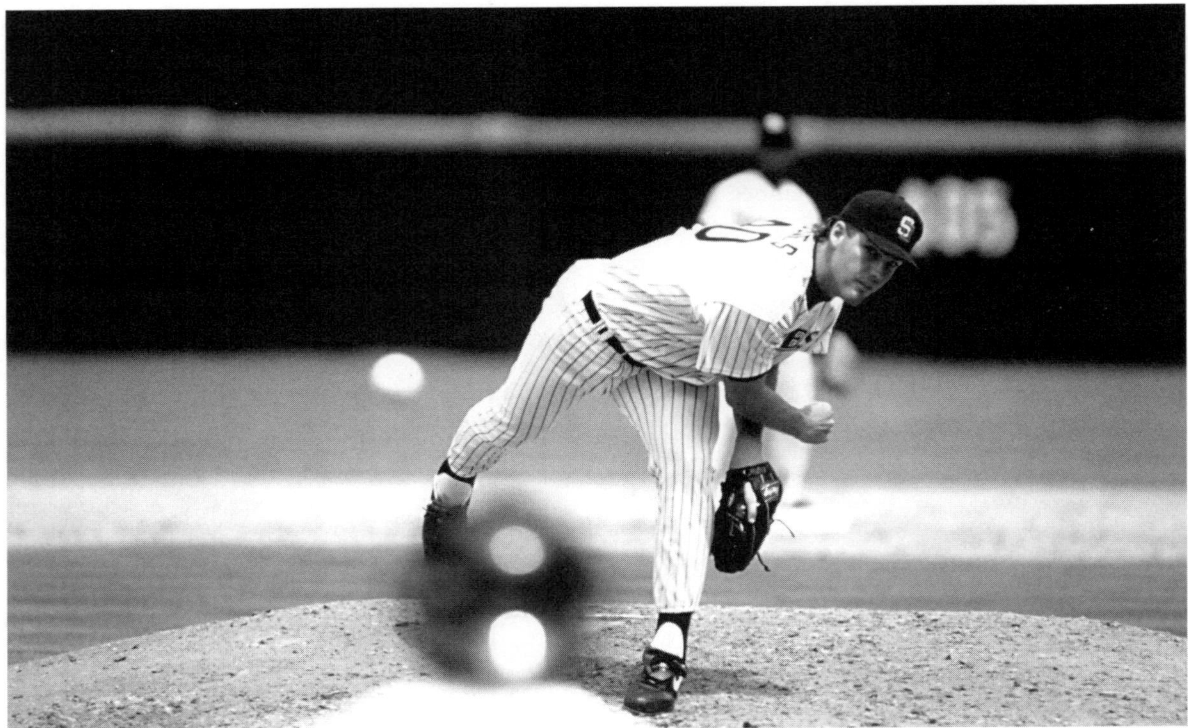

Andy Benes

Padres scored two runs or less in 18 of his 34 starts. He went 2-0 with a 0.39 ERA in his first three starts and yielded just five hits and struck out 11 in nine shutout innings against the Houston Astros on April 19 in an 11-inning 1-0 loss. Benes hurled a three-hit, eight-strikeout, 2-0 performance against the Chicago Cubs on May 22. His other shutout came on June 17 in a 5-0 four-hitter at Houston, where he also fanned eight Astros. In his final eight starts, he finished 4-3 with a 1.96 ERA. His other 11-strikeout masterpiece game came against the San Francisco Giants on September 22. In 10 daytime starts, Benes posted a 6-1 mark and a 2.34 ERA.

In 1993, Benes split 30 decisions with a 3.78 ERA. He fanned 179 batters, tying Bruce Hurst for second highest in club history and finishing sixth best in the National League. His 230.2 innings ranked ninth best in the senior circuit. Twelve of his 15 wins followed Padre losses. After losing the opening game to the Pittsburgh Pirates, he was one of the most dominant National League pitchers in his next 22 games with a 12-6 record. During the streak, Benes won his first four starts, allowed two runs or less in 15 starts, and did not surrender any earned runs in six contests. He hurled a three-hit shutout on May 17 against the Colorado Rockies. In a seven-inning outing against the Cincinnati Reds on June 27, Benes allowed just a third-inning single by Jeff Branson. In his final start before the All-Star game, he threw 105 pitches over eight innings in 97-degree heat against the New York Mets at Shea Stadium. He allowed just an infield single in the second inning by Jeff Kent in the 2-0 victory.

In the All-Star game at Camden Yards in Baltimore on July 13, Benes gave up one run with two strikeouts in two innings. He won National League Player of the Week honors from July 26 through August 1. After blanking the Chicago Cubs on a five-hitter with eight strikeouts on July 27, Benes surrendered one unearned run over seven innings in defeating the Cincinnati Reds, 3-1, on August 1. He finished 13-7 with a 2.62 ERA in his first 24 starts, but struggled in his last 10 starts. He clouted his fourth career home run on May 12 off Jose Rijo of the Cincinnati Reds, leaving him four behind Tim Lollar's club record.

His record plunged to 6-14 with a 3.86 ERA in 1994, but Benes led the National League with 189 strikeouts. No Padre hurler had accomplished that feat. In franchise history, only Clay Kirby had fanned more batters in a season. Benes shared fourth in the senior circuit with 172.1 innings and third with two shutouts. He lost on opening day to the Atlanta Braves, 4-1, and started the season with four setbacks. He hurled a four-hit 8-0 shutout with 10 strikeouts against the Colorado Rockies on May 6 and enjoyed a four-game winning streak from May 31 through July 3.

Benes compiled the top three strikeout performances in the senior circuit, fanning 12 San Francisco Giants on June 12. The best game of his major-league career came in a 7-0 victory on July 3 at Shea Stadium. Benes allowed just one hit and walked only one in a 13-strikeout performance against the New York Mets, knocking in three runs with a bases-loaded double. His masterpiece marked the seventeenth one-hitter in Padre history and one of only two in the National League in 1994. In his first start after the All-Star break, Benes fanned a career-best 14 New York Mets and allowed just two hits in eight innings in a July 15 duel with Bret Saberhagen at Shea Stadium. His 14 strikeouts missed the Padre record by one.

In 1995, Benes compiled a 4-7 mark with a 4.17 ERA and struck out 126 batters in 118.2 innings. He lost five consecutive games from April 26 through May 26 and was traded to the Seattle Mariners for two players on July 31. Upon his departure, Benes ranked first among Padre pitchers in strikeouts (1,036), fourth in wins (69) and innings pitched (1235), and fifth in ERA (3.51) and shutouts (8). He compiled a 7-2 record with Seattle in 1995 and 18-10 mark with the St. Louis Cardinals in 1996. After hurling for St. Louis in 1997, Benes joined the expansion Arizona Diamondbacks in 1998. He helped Arizona win the National League West with a 13-12 mark in 1999, but was dropped from the starting rotation for the National League Division Series. In January 2000, Benes returned to the St. Louis Cardinals as a free agent. He compiled a 12-9 record to help St. Louis win the National League Central Division in 2000 and picked up the lone Cardinal victory in the National League Championship Series against the New York Mets. He split 14 decisions in 2001 for the wild card club, but did not pitch in the National League Division Series against Arizona. Through 2001, Benes has authored a 150-135 win-loss mark with a 4.02 ERA, 1,936 strikeouts in 2,408.1 innings, and nine shutouts. He and his wife, Jennifer, reside in Evansville, Indiana and have one son, Andrew II, and two daughters, Brynn, and Bailey.

KEVIN BROWN

Kevin Brown set several single-season franchise records as a pitcher for the San Diego Padres in 1998. The 6-foot 4-inch, 193-pound Brown, who bats and throws right-handed, was born on March 14, 1965 in McIntyre, Georgia and graduated from Wilkinson County High School in Irwinton, Georgia in 1983. He majored in chemical engineering at Georgia Tech University, where he compiled a school-record 28 victories and 249 strikeouts in three seasons. *The Sporting News* named Brown a first team All-American in 1986 after he set single-season school records with 11 victories and 122 strikeouts. The Texas Rangers selected him in the first round of the June 1986 free agent draft. Brown pitched only six minor-league games before winning his first start for the Texas Rangers in September 1986. He hurled two more minor-league seasons before rejoining the Texas Rangers in September 1988.

Brown pitched for the Texas Rangers through the 1994 season. With a four-seam fastball in the mid 90s, a sinking fastball, an outstanding hard slider, and a good change-up, Brown quickly improved in the Texas

Kevin Brown

starting rotation. His best season came in 1992, when he led American League pitchers with 21 victories and 265.2 innings, threw 11 complete games, and struck out 173 batters. After spending 1995 with the Baltimore Orioles, he joined the Florida Marlins in 1996. Brown compiled a 17-11 mark and the lowest National League ERA (1.89) since 1985, finishing second to John Smoltz in the National League Cy Young Award voting. In 1997, he finished 16-8 with a 2.69 ERA and 205 strikeouts. Besides hurling a 9-0 no-hitter against the San Francisco Giants on June 10, Brown performed brilliantly during the final two months of the season. He surrendered just one run in his only National League Division Series start against the San Francisco Giants. His two victories helped the Marlins upset the Atlanta Braves in the National League Championship Series, but he lost both World Series starts to the Cleveland Indians.

In December 1997, the Florida Marlins traded Brown to the San Diego Padres. Brown finished with an 18-7 ledger and 2.38 ERA in 1998, hurling seven complete games and three shutouts and fanning 257 batters in 257 innings. He led Padre hurlers in victories, ERA, complete games, shutouts, strikeouts, and innings pitched. Besides making the National League All-Star team for the third consecutive season, Brown shared the Clyde McCullough Award with Trevor Hoffman as Padre Pitchers of the Year. After hurling a 1-0 four-hit shutout against the San Francisco Giants on April 15, he tied a Padre record by winning 11 consecutive games from May 26 through August 5. Brown won four games in June, finished 4-0 in July, and triumphed in four of six starts in August, boasting three complete games and two shutouts. He hurled a 4-0 one-hitter against the Milwaukee Brewers in Game 1 on August 16, allowing just a seventh-inning single to Jeremy Burnitz. Brown broke the single-season club strikeout record of 231 by fanning Trenidad Hubbard of the Los Angeles Dodgers in the fourth inning on September 10. He ended the season with 257 strikeouts, 26 more than Clay Kirby in 1971. He finished second to Tom Glavine in the National League Cy Young Award balloting and earned *The Sporting News'* National League Pitcher of the Year and National League All-Star team honors.

Brown started two games in the National League Championship Series against the Houston Astros, fanning 21 batters and boasting a 0.61 ERA. He outdueled Randy Johnson in Game 1, striking out a Division Series record 16 batters and allowing only two hits in eight shutout innings. The Padres won the contest, 2-1. The right-hander limited the Astros to one run and three hits over 6.2 innings in Game 3 on just three days' rest and authored a 3-0, three-hit complete game victory over the Atlanta Braves at Atlanta-Fulton County Stadium in Game 2 of the National League Championship Series, fanning 11 batters. Michael Tucker clouted a three-run, eighth-inning home run in Game 5 at Qualcomm Stadium off Brown, who had come in from the bullpen to try to protect a 4-2 lead. Brown ended up with the loss, ending the Championship Series with a 1-1 record and 2.61 ERA. Despite fanning 13 New York Yankees in 14.1 innings, he lost his only World Series decision with a 4.40 ERA. Brown surrendered four runs in 6.1 innings without a decision in Game 1 at Yankee Stadium and allowed all three runs in a 3-0 loss to the New York Yankees in decisive Game 4 at Qualcomm Stadium.

In December 1998, Brown signed a record seven-year, $105 million contract with the Los Angeles Dodgers. He finished 18-9 with a 3.00 ERA in 1999, 13-6 with a league-best 2.57 ERA in 2000, and 10-4 with a 2.65 ERA in 2001 for the Dodgers. Through the 2001 season, Brown has compiled a 180-121 record with a 3.18 ERA, completed 72 of 399 starts, hurled 17 shutouts, and fanned 2,021 batters in 2,776.1 innings. He and his wife, Candace, reside in Macon, Georgia with their two children, Ridge and Grayson.

OLLIE BROWN

Ollie Brown played outfield for the San Diego Padres from 1969 through 1972. The 6-foot 3-inch, 200-pound Brown, who batted and threw right-handed, was born on February 11, 1944 in Tuscaloosa, Alabama and attended Long Beach City College. His older brother, Oscar, played outfield for the Atlanta Braves. Another older brother, Willie, starred as a running back with the University of Southern California, Los Angeles Rams, and Philadelphia Eagles. In 1962, the San Francisco Giants signed Brown as a pitcher because of his strong arm. He spent four seasons in the Giants' farm system, pitching a no-run, no-hit game for Decatur, Illinois of the Midwest League against the Wisconsin Rapids on August 23, 1963. Brown earned the nickname "Downtown" by clouting 40 home runs for Fresno, California of the California League in 1964. He spent the entire 1967 campaign and parts of the 1965, 1966, and 1968 seasons with the San Francisco Giants, but never lived up to expectations.

The San Diego Padres made Brown their first selection in the November 1968 expansion draft. In 1969, Brown led San Diego with a .264 batting average and finished second on the Padres with 20 home runs. On May 3, he belted a grand slam off Tony Cloninger of the Cincinnati Reds. Brown made four hits against the Atlanta Braves on July 10 and clouted a home run against every National League club except the St. Louis Cardinals. Blessed with an outstanding throwing arm, he ranked third in the National League with 14 assists. His best major-league season came in 1970, when he batted .292, led San Diego with 34 doubles, and set personal highs in practically every offensive department. His 89 RBIs and 156 hits ranked second on the Padres, while his 23 home runs fared third. During July, Brown enjoyed a 12-game hitting streak and clouted eight home runs. He homered twice with six RBIs against the San Francisco Giants on July 1 and drove in five runs against the Cincinnati Reds on August 3. He also recorded 12 assists and participated in three double plays.

In 1971, Brown batted .273 with 59 RBIs and made nine game-winning hits. He broke up two no-hitters, making the only hit off Larry Dierker of the Houston Astros on May 26 and off Juan Pizarro of the Atlanta Braves on August 5. Brown hit safely in 12 of his last 14 games and feasted on Cincinnati Reds pitching with a .377 batting average. His offensive production declined in 1972, when he was traded to the Oakland A's. He spent 1972 through 1977 with the Milwaukee Brewers, Houston Astros, and Philadelphia Phillies. During 13 major-league seasons, he batted .265 with 102 home runs and 454 RBIs. He and his wife, Sandra, live in Buena Park, California and have one child, Troy.

KEN CAMINITI

Ken Caminiti starred as a third baseman for the San Diego Padres from 1995 through 1998. The 6-foot, 220-pound Caminiti, who switch hit and threw right-handed, was born on April 21, 1963 in Hanford, California and graduated from Leigh High School in San Jose, California. He attended San Jose State University, batting .347 as a junior in 1984 and making *The Sporting News'* College All-America second team. The Houston Astros selected Caminiti in the third round of the June 1984 free agent draft. He spent four seasons in the minor leagues and clouted a triple and a home run in his major-league debut in July 1987. Caminiti, who overcame a drinking problem, started at third base for the Houston Astros from 1989 through 1994 and made the 1994 National League All-Star team. He ranks among the top 10 career Astros leaders in doubles (191), home runs (88) and RBIs (501).

Ken Caminiti

In a December 1994 blockbuster 12-player transaction, the Houston Astros sent Caminiti to the San Diego Padres. Caminiti batted .302 with 26 home runs and 94 RBIs in 1995 and earned his first Rawlings Gold Glove award with his good hands, fine range, and powerful throwing arm. He established then career-highs in batting average, hits (159), home runs, RBIs, and stolen bases (12) and led the Padres in games (143), slugging percentage (.513), doubles (33), home runs, extra base hits (59), total bases (270), RBIs, and walks (69). Caminiti became the first Padre third baseman to lead the club in RBIs since Graig Nettles in 1995. He ranked among the top 10 National Leaguers in hits, doubles, extra-base hits, RBIs, total bases, and walks and paced National League third basemen in assists (295), double plays (28), and chances (424).

In a four-game span from September 16 through September 19, Caminiti became the first major-leaguer to homer from both sides of the plate in the same game three times in a season. On September 16, he became the first Padre to homer from both sides of the plate in the same game against the Chicago Cubs and he became the first National Leaguer to accomplish that feat in consecutive games the next day against Chicago. Eddie Murray of the Baltimore Orioles was the only other major-leaguer to duplicate that feat. On September 19, Caminiti tied a franchise record with a career-high eight RBIs against the Colorado Rockies.

In 1995, Caminiti started 142 of the 144 Padre games at third base. On June 28, he equaled then career highs with a four-hit, two-homer, five-RBI game against the Los Angeles Dodgers. Caminiti was named National League Co-Player of the Week from June 26 through July 2, batting .400 with three homers and 11 RBIs. His consecutive two-homer games earned him National League Player of the Week honors from September 11 through September 17. During that span, Caminiti batted .542 with four homers, eight RBI, and an incredible 1.125 slugging percentage. He hit .331 right-handed with 10 home runs and .289 left-handed with 16 home runs.

In 1996, Caminiti became the first Padre to win the National League Most Valuable Player Award, receiving all 28 first-place votes. He was just the fourth unanimous selection in the 66-year history of the award, dating back to 1931. Caminiti batted a career-high .326 and led the Padres to the National League West title with club records of 40 home runs and 130 RBIs. He established career bests in batting average, runs (109), hits (178), total bases (339), doubles (37), home runs, RBI, extra-base hits (79), slugging percentage (.621), on-base percentage (.408), and walks (78). Caminiti ranked third in the National League in RBIs and slugging percentage, fifth in home runs, total bases, and extra-base hits, and sixth in batting average. After the All-Star break, he led the senior circuit with a .360 batting average, 28 home runs, and 81 RBIs and had .760 slugging and .443 on-base percentages. He also won his second consecutive Rawlings Gold Glove Award, ranking second among major-league third basemen with 433 total chances and 310 assists and second among National League third basemen with 130 putouts and 28 double plays.

Caminiti earned ESPY awards as Baseball Player of the Year and for making the Baseball Play of the Year against the Florida Marlins on April 22. After making a diving back-handed stab on a grounder down the line, he threw from a sitting, near-prone position to get Greg Colbrunn at first base. The Major-League Baseball Players Association named him Player of the Year, while *The Sporting News* selected him to its Silver Slugger team as the top offensive National League third baseman. He earned the Padres Most Valuable Player Award, National League Player of the Month awards for both August and September, and Player of the Week Awards for July 29 through August 4 and August 19 through August 25.

Caminiti rewrote the Padres' record book, setting a single-season Padre mark with a .621 slugging percentage. He surpassed Nate Colbert's home run record with his 39th round-tripper against the Colorado Rockies on September 24 and established a team mark with 20 home runs at home. Caminiti broke Dave Winfield's RBI record with his 119th RBI against the San Francisco Giants on September 17 and Gary Sheffield's slugging percentage record of .580. He also eclipsed the previous Padre standard for most total bases with 339 and matched Winfield's mark with 79 extra-base hits. He equaled Mickey Mantle's major-league record for most RBIs in a season by a switch hitter with 130 and became just the third switch hitter to clout 40 round-trippers in a season.

Caminiti joined Al Rosen and Eddie Mathews as the only major-league third basemen to hit .300 with 40 home runs and 130 RBIs. His 40 home runs shared eighth best all-time for a third baseman. He and Vinny Castilla became just the sixth and seventh third basemen to clout 40 home runs in a season. In August, Caminiti enjoyed the best offensive month in Padre history. Besides hitting .344, he broke team monthly records with 14 home runs and 38 RBIs and earned his first National League Player of the Month Award. His 14 round-trippers set a National League record for homers in a month by a switch hitter and came within three of Willie Mays's senior circuit record for a month. He averaged more than one homer every seven at bats and had four multihomer games.

Minutes before the San Diego Padres-New York Mets game on August 18 in Monterrey, Mexico, Caminiti lay dehydrated on the clubhouse floor with food poisoning. He took two liters of intravenous fluids, ran a wind sprint, and started the contest at third base. After the top of the first inning, Caminiti ate a Snickers bar and clouted home runs in each of his first two at-bats off Paul Wilson. The first came with the bases empty, while the second was a three-run blast. He hit a grand slam in his first plate appearance the following day. Caminiti earned National League Player of the Month honors in September, when he batted .375 with nine homers and 23 RBIs. His dramatic tenth-inning home run on September 27 sparked the crucial three-game season ending sweep of the Los Angeles Dodgers to give the Padres the National League West title.

Caminiti broke his own single-season major-league record by homering from both sides of the plate four times in six weeks. The four came on August 1 against the Atlanta Braves, August 21 against the Montreal Expos, August 28 against the New York Giants, and September 11 against the Pittsburgh Pirates. He enjoyed seven multi-homer games, slugging two right-handed against the Pittsburgh Pirates on May 8, two left-handed against the New York Mets on August 18, and two left-handed against the San Francisco Giants on September 17. Several home runs were monumental. His 461-foot blast off Steve Reed of the Colorado Rockies on July 11 became just the third to reach the third deck at Coors Field. Caminiti also clouted two of the longest home runs at Jack Murphy Stadium, a 449-foot clout off Pedro Martinez of the Montreal Expos on August 19 and a 447-foot homer off Donne Wall of the Houston Astros on June 26. In his second All-Star appearance, he became the first Padre to homer in the summer classic. His deep right center-field clout came off Roger Pavlick of the Texas Rangers in the sixth inning.

Caminiti enjoyed other landmark games. He drove in six runs against the Montreal Expos on August 19 and knocked in four runs seven different times. In four games from August 18 through August 21, Caminiti clouted five home runs and drove in 14 runs in just 14 at bats. He homered in five consecutive contests, including the All-Star Game, from July 7 through July 13 and scored four runs against the Colorado Rockies on July 12.

His three hits in the National League Division Series against the St.Louis Cardinals were home runs. He batted .300 and clouted two home runs, including a dramatic game-tying clout off Rick Honeycutt in the eighth inning in Game 3 at Jack Murphy Stadium. Caminiti surpassed Kurt Bevacqua as the club's all-time post-season home run leader with three and tied Marquis Grissom and Vinny Castilla as the National League Division Series leaders with most round-trippers in a single series.

Caminiti played 146 games despite extensive injuries. He tore a rotator cuff after falling on his shoulder leaping for a ball on April 6 against the Houston Astros and missed 10 games in May with a severe lower abdominal strain.

In 1997, Caminiti batted .290 with 26 home runs and 90 RBIs. He tied his own National League record for most home runs by a switch hitter in two consecutive seasons with 66 and tied Fred McGriff's record for the most home runs by a Padre in successive campaigns. Caminiti ranked second among Padres in home runs and third in batting average and RBIs. He needed the first half of the 1997 season to recover from his October reconstructive shoulder injury. Caminiti suffered various ailments, hitting only .247 with just six home runs and 35 RBIs in 64 games before the All-Star break.

After the summer classic, Caminiti batted .331 with 20 home runs and 55 RBIs in 73 games and ranked third in the senior circuit in batting, tied for fourth in home runs, and shared eighth in RBIs. Caminiti ranked third on the club with 23 multiple-RBI games and knocked in six runs with two three-run homers against the Colorado Rockies on July 10. His first-inning 465-foot blast off John Burke was only the fourth homer to reach the third deck in right field at Coors Field. Caminiti's .508 slugging percentage was surpassed on the club only by Tony Gwynn.

Caminiti's 1997 season featured other milestones. He homered on August 15 and 16 against the Chicago Cubs and on September 17 and 18 against the Colorado Rockies. Besides recording three consecutive three-hit games from August 26 through August 28, he became just the twelfth player to homer into the upper deck in right field at Veterans Stadium. His monumental round-tripper came off Curt Schilling of the Philadelphia Phillies in the sixth inning on August 27. Caminiti also drove in runs in seven consecutive games from September 16 through September 22. He clouted consecutive home runs with Chris Jones in the ninth inning on May 4 against the Montreal Expos and Craig Shipley in the first inning on July 24 against the Pittsburgh Pirates.

Besides making the National League All-Star team for the third time and his first All-Star game start, Caminiti became the first National League third baseman since Mike Schmidt to win three consecutive Rawlings Gold Glove Awards. He fielded .941, committing only 24 errors in 405 total chances and participating in 20 double plays.

Caminiti helped the San Diego Padres win the National League West in 1998 with a .252 batting average, 29 home runs, and 82 RBIs, enjoying 30 multi-hit and 19 multi-RBI games. During April, he clouted seven home runs, knocked in 21 runs in 25 games, and belted a 457-foot home run into the second deck in left field at Qualcomm Stadium in the seventh inning off Ricardo Jordan of the Cincinnati Reds on April 9. A strained leg muscle landed him on the disabled list in May.

Caminiti clouted home runs from both sides of the plate as part of a three-homer effort against the Los Angeles Dodgers on July 12, extending his National League record to nine. Only two other Padres had homered three times in a game. In August, he clouted eight home runs with 18 RBIs. Caminiti collaborated with Greg Vaughn on consecutive home runs off Carl Pavano of the Montreal Expos in the first inning on July 31 and homered twice against the Philadelphia Phillies on August 25. Caminiti hit only .143 in the National League Division Series against the Houston Astros, but he batted .273 with two home runs and four RBIs to help the Padres upset the Atlanta Braves in the National League Championship Series. His tenth-inning round-tripper gave the Padres a 3-2 series opening victory at Turner Field. He also belted a first-inning, two-run homer in San Diego's 7-6 loss in Game 5 at Qualcomm Stadium. In his only World Series, he hit just .143 with a sacrifice fly in Game 3 and made errors in Games 2 and 3 against the New York Yankees.

In November 1998, Caminiti rejoined the Houston Astros as a free agent. Upon his departure from the Padres, he ranked first in slugging percentage (.477), third in batting average (.295), fourth in home runs (121), sixth in RBIs (396), seventh in doubles (127), walks (298), and strikeouts (419), eighth in runs (362), fourteenth in hits (592), and twentieth in games (557). His .256 batting average, 13 home runs, and 56 RBIs helped Houston win the National League Central Division in 1999. Caminiti batted .471 with three home runs and eight RBIs against the Atlanta Braves in the National League Division Series. Injuries limited him to 59 games in 2000, but he still hit .303 with 15 home runs and 45 RBIs. In December 2000, the Texas Rangers signed Caminiti to a $3 million, one-year contract. He split the 2001 campaign between the Texas Rangers and Atlanta Braves and batted twice without a hit in the National League Division Series against the Houston Astros. Caminiti retired following the 2001 season. He was arrested in October 2001 after Harris County, Texas sheriff's department deputies said they found him in a southwest Houston-area motel room with unspecified drugs and drug paraphernalia. Caminiti pleaded guilty to cocaine possession and was sentenced to three years probation. Besides being fined $2,000, he was ordered to receive counseling three times a week, speak to students about drugs, continue attending Alcoholics Anonymous meetings, and submit to periodic urinalysis.

In 15 major-league seasons, Caminiti batted .272 with 1,710 hits, 348 doubles, 239 home runs, 983 RBIs, and a .951 fielding percentage. He and his wife, Nancy, reside in Richmond, Texas with their three daughters, Kendall, Lindsey, and Nicole. Caminiti enjoys drag racing and owns a motorcycle, a 1973 Chevrolet, a 1955 Post 250, and a 1963 Impala. He restores and rebuilds cars and in 1996 won a National Rookie of the Year award.

DAVE CAMPBELL

Dave Campbell played infield with the San Diego Padres from 1970 through June 1973 and broadcast their games from 1978 through 1988. The 6-foot 1-

Dave Campbell

inch, 180-pound Campbell, who batted and threw right-handed, was born on January 14, 1942 in Manistee, Michigan. His father coached high school baseball at Lansing. Campbell earned a B.S. degree from the University of Michigan, starring in baseball on the 1962 NCAA Championship squad and captaining the 1964 aggregate. The Detroit Tigers signed him to a bonus contract in 1964. He spent nearly six seasons as a minor league infielder and batted just .102 in 43 games with the Tigers between 1967 and 1969.

In December 1969, the San Diego Padres acquired Campbell and pitcher Pat Dobson for pitcher Joe Niekro. Campbell started at second base for San Diego in 1970, hitting .219 in 154 games. As the leadoff hitter, he paced the Padres with 18 stolen bases and hit 28 doubles and 12 home runs. Campbell enjoyed eight- and nine-game hitting streaks and produced four game winning RBI. In 1971, he batted .227 and played every infield position, the outfield, and even third-string catcher. Campbell hit .364 against the Los Angeles Dodgers, including three hits and the game-winning RBI in a 5-4 victory on June 25. His home run on July 28 sparked a 4-2 triumph over the Cincinnati Reds. He batted .240 in 1972 before rupturing an Achilles tendon in his left ankle while running to first base on June 2. The Padres traded him to the St. Louis Cardinals in June 1973. The Cardinals sold Campbell that August to the Houston Astros, where he finished his major-league career in 1974. In eight major-league seasons, he batted .213 with 89 RBI.

Campbell broadcast for both KCST-TV and KSDO radio in San Diego before managing Amarillo, Texas of the Texas League in 1977. He announced baseball games for the Padres from 1978 through 1988 and for the Colorado Rockies from 1993 through 1997. Campbell serves as a baseball analyst for the ESPN network. He and his wife, Diane, live in Post Falls, Idaho with their two daughters, Courtney and Shelby.

JACK CLARK

Jack Clark played first base for the San Diego Padres in 1989 and 1990. The 6-foot 3-inch, 200-pound Clark, who batted and threw right-handed, was born on November 10, 1955 in New Brighton, Pennsylvania and attended Gladstone High School in Azusa, California. The San Francisco Giants selected Clark as a pitcher in the June 1973 free agent draft and converted him to an outfielder in the minor leagues. Clark spent nearly four seasons in the minor leagues, having two brief trials with San Francisco. He excelled with the Giants from 1977 through 1984, averaging over 20 home runs per season and setting a club record with a 26-game hitting streak in 1978. In February 1985, San Francisco traded him to the St. Louis Cardinals for four players. Clark starred with the Cardinals from 1985 through 1987, clouting a memorable two-out, three-run homer in the ninth inning of the sixth game to clinch the National League Championship Series against the Los Angeles Dodgers. In 1987, he attained career highs with 35 home runs and 106 RBI while leading the National League with a .597 slugging percentage.

After being a designated hitter with the New York Yankees in 1988, Clark was traded to the San Diego Padres that October. In 1989, he batted .242 with 26 home runs and 94 RBI and led the National League with 132 walks. Twenty-two of his homers came against left-handers. Clark sharply reduced his strikeouts and broke Gene Tenace's club record for walks by seven. Besides finishing second in the National League with a .410 on base percentage and sixth in RBI, Clark shared seventh in home runs. He established a career best by driving in seven runs against the Atlanta Braves on September 4. Clark clouted a grand slam home run off Mark Eichorn and added a three-run homer. His other multiple-homer game came against the Montreal Expos on August 28, when he clouted a pair of two-run homers off Kevin Gross and knocked in six runs. In July, Clark enjoyed a 14-game hitting streak. He homered four times with 12 RBI in Atlanta Fulton County Stadium.

In 1990, Clark batted .266 with 62 RBI and again paced the senior circuit with 104 walks. He led the Padres with 25 home runs and recorded his 1,000th career RBI the last week of the season. Clark produced 17 multiple-hit games, including five three-hit games. In December 1990, he joined the Boston Red Sox as a free agent. He finished his major-league career with Boston in 1991 and 1992, joining Bobby Bonds as the only major leaguers to hit 25 home runs with five different clubs.

During 18 major-league seasons, Clark batted .267 with 340 home runs and 1,180 RBI. He walked 1,262 times, but struck out 1,441 times. He and his wife, Tammy, live in Scottsdale, Arizona with their three daughters, Danika, Rebekah, and Ericka, and one son,

Anthony. Clark, who enjoys collecting automobiles, has served as hitting coach for the Los Angeles Dodgers since 2001.

NATE COLBERT

Nate Colbert starred as a first baseman with the San Diego Padres from 1969 through 1974. The 6-foot 1-inch, 210-pound Colbert, who batted and threw right-handed, was born in St. Louis, Missouri on April 9, 1946 and attended St. Louis Baptist College. The St. Louis Cardinals signed him as a free agent in June 1964. He spent five seasons in the minor leagues, performing briefly with the Houston Astros in 1966 and 1968.

The San Diego Padres selected him in the October 1968 expansion draft. Colbert, who possessed a strong, compact swing and excelled at hitting fastballs, batted .255 with 24 home runs and 66 RBI in 1969. Despite missing 17 days for military training in June, he led San Diego in home runs and RBI and hit at least one home run against every team except the New York Mets. Colbert clouted a grand slam home run against Don Nottebart in a 10-2 home victory over the Chicago Cubs on May 25 and belted five round-trippers against the Houston Astros. His five RBI on October 1 against the San Francisco Giants at Candlestick Park set a Padre record.

Colbert in 1970 hit .259 with 86 RBI and established a San Diego mark with 38 home runs, including 11 in May and two in five different games. His best offensive production came in September, when he batted .358 with nine home runs. Colbert hit .383 against the Philadelphia Phillies and homered against every club except the Pittsburgh Pirates, belting seven against the Los Angeles Dodgers and six against the Atlanta Braves. He reached base safely in all five at-bats in a 15-inning game against the San Francisco Giants at Candlestick Park on May 23 and twice made hits in all four plate appearances.

In 1971, Colbert batted .264 and led the Padres with 27 home runs, 149 hits, and 84 RBI. He began the season with a 12-game hitting streak and clouted consecutive home runs off Gaylord Perry of the San Francisco Giants at home on April 7. Colbert knocked in six runs on April 11 in a 9-7 triumph over the Los Angeles Dodgers at Dodger Stadium and clouted a grand slam home run off John Strohmayer in an 8-4 win over the Montreal Expos on June 6. He homered against every club except the Cincinnati Reds and

Nate Colbert

feasted on New York Mets pitching with a .436 batting average, five home runs, and 10 RBI.

Colbert enjoyed his best major-league season in 1972, leading the Padres in nearly every offensive category. He drove in 111 of San Diego's 488 runs for fourth best in the National League and belted 38 home runs, over one-third of the Padre total and second best in the senior circuit. Twenty-two of his home runs came on the road. Colbert also paced the Padres with 87 runs, 141 hits, 27 doubles, and 286 total bases, ranking sixth in slugging percentage. Besides exhibiting unusual speed with 15 stolen bases, he batted .391 against the Philadelphia Phillies and tied a club record by hitting safely in his final 15 games. Colbert homered for the third time into the second deck in left field to edge the St. Louis Cardinals, 3-2, at home on August 17 and belted a grand slam home run off Jack Billingham in a 5-1 home win over the Cincinnati Reds on September 7. He won National League Player of the Week honors twice and the Eddie Dyer Award for Slugger of the Year from the Houston Sports Association.

In an August 1, 1972 doubleheader at Atlanta, Colbert clouted five home runs, made seven hits in nine at bats, scored seven times, and drove in 13 runs against the Atlanta Braves. His home runs in the 9-0 first game romp came off Ron Schueler in the first inning with two runners aboard and in the seventh inning off Mike McQueen with the bases empty. In the 11-7 second game win, he clouted a grand slam home run off Pat Jarvis in the second inning and two-run homers off Jim Hardin in the seventh inning and Cecil Upshaw in the ninth inning. His 13 RBI and 22 total bases set major-league records for a twinbill, while his five home runs tied a doubleheader mark set by Stan Musial of the St. Louis Cardinals on May 2, 1954. He tied a National League standard for most home runs in one week with eight from July 30 through August 5.

Although slowed by back spasms and bronchitis, Colbert in 1973 hit a career-high .270 and paced the Padres with 73 runs, 143 hits, 25 doubles, 22 home runs, and 80 RBI. Chicago Cubs pitchers allowed him a .409 batting average. Colbert's production fell dramatically in 1974, when he batted only .207 with 14 home runs and 54 RBI. In November 1974, the Padres traded him to the Detroit Tigers for Eddie Brinkman, Dick Sharon, and Bob Strampe.

Colbert made the National League All-Star team three consecutive years from 1971 through 1973 and scored the winning run in the 1972 classic. His 866 games played, 3,080 at bats, 441 runs scored, 780 hits, 130 doubles, 29 triples, 163 home runs, and 481 RBI ranked first in Padre history upon his departure, while his 48 stolen bases stood second. Despite playing in a larger home ballpark, he remains the Padres' all-time home run leader and ranks third in RBI and extra base hits (315), fourth in runs scored, sixth in doubles, hits, and games, and ninth in triples (22). Colbert led the Padres in home runs five times and RBI four times. From 1971 to 1973, no Padre recorded more runs scored, hits, or doubles. His 127 major-league home runs between 1969 and 1972 trailed only Willie Mays and Frank Robinson. He also led National League first baseman in putouts and double plays in 1971 and in assists in 1972 and 1973.

Back problems forced Colbert to retire in 1976 after brief stints with the Montreal Expos and Oakland Athletics. In 1,000 major-league games, Colbert batted .243 with 173 home runs and 520 RBI. Nearly 22 percent of his 788 hits resulted in home runs, while over 40 percent of his hits involved extra bases. Colbert, who coached for the Wichita, Kansas, Pilots of the Texas League in 1987 and 1988, has been an ordained minister of the Branch of the Lord Church in Escondido, California since 1981. He in 1990 founded the Traveling School of Baseball, which gives baseball instruction to youngsters. In August 1999, he was inducted into the San Diego Padres Hall of Fame as a charter member. He and his wife, Carol Ann, have one son, Nathan, and two daughters, Dana and Donia.

MARK DAVIS

Mark Davis starred with the San Diego Padres as a relief pitcher from July 1987 through 1989. The 6-foot 200-pound left-hander was born on October 19, 1960 in Livermore, California and excelled in baseball at Granada High School. After pitching for Chabot College in Hayward, California, he was selected by the Philadelphia Phillies as their first choice in the secondary phase of the January 1979 draft. Davis pitched four years in the minor leagues and started a few games for the Philadelphia Phillies in 1980 and 1981. His first major-league victory came on September 24, 1981 over the St. Louis Cardinals.

In December 1982, the Philadelphia Phillies traded Davis and Mike Krukow to the San Francisco Giants for Joe Morgan and Al Holland. After beginning

Mark Davis

1983 with Phoenix, Arizona of the Pacific Coast League, Davis compiled a 6-4 record and 3.49 ERA as a starter with San Francisco. He won only five of 22 decisions in 1984 and moved to the bullpen in late August. Davis spent the next two seasons as a reliever, logging a 5-7 ledger and 2.99 ERA in 1986. The Giants used him both as a starter and reliever in 1987 and traded Davis, Mark Grant, Keith Comstock, and Chris Brown that July to the San Diego Padres for Dave Dravecky, Craig Lefferts, and Kevin Mitchell.

Davis blossomed as a reliever with the Padres during the last half of 1987, boasting a 5-3 mark, a 3.18 ERA, and two saves in 43 appearances. He enjoyed a three-game winning streak in August and allowed only nine earned runs in 38.2 innings with a 2.09 ERA in his final 25 games. His nine victories, including four with San Francisco, established a career best. In 21 games at Jack Murphy Stadium, he won all three decisions with a save and allowed only three runs in 31.2 innings for a sparkling 0.85 ERA. Two of his victories came against the Los Angeles Dodgers.

In 1988, Davis worked exclusively out of the bullpen for the first time in his major-league career and was the lone Padre All-Star selection. As a closer for the first time, he compiled a 5-10 record with a 2.01 ERA and 28 saves in 34 opportunities. Davis fanned 102 batters in 98.1 innings and seven Los Angeles Dodgers in 3.2 innings on April 14 to earn his first save of the season. He made saves in all 12 opportunities through June 20 and entered the All-Star break sharing the league lead in saves (16) with Todd Worrell. After the All-Star break, he surrendered only six earned runs in 45.1 innings for a 1.19 ERA.

Davis established a club record for consecutive scoreless innings in relief with 27.2 between July 22 and September 7, breaking Goose Gossage's 1985 record by 7.1 innings. He surpassed Gossage's record in a 2.1-inning stint on August 26 against the Montreal Expos. During the streak, he earned a win and 11 saves in 16 appearances. After July 21, Davis allowed only three earned runs in nearly 40 innings for an 0.68 ERA. He yielded only two home runs and did not give up one after June 3. Davis earned a save against every National League club, making five against the Cincinnati Reds. At Jack Murphy Stadium, he finished 4-2 with 14 saves and a 0.94 ERA. Only 16 of his 51 inherited base runners scored.

In 1989, Davis converted a career-high 44 of 48 save opportunities and won the National League Rolaids Relief Man-of-the-Year and Padres MVP awards. He became only the fourth reliever and third Padre to win the National League Cy Young Award. Davis finished 4-3 with a career-best 1.85 ERA in 70 appearances and struck out 92 batters in 92.1 innings. His 44 saves marked the then most for a Padre in a season and second best in National League history, trailing Bruce Sutter by one. Davis registered a win or save in 48 of San Diego's 89 victories, including his first 17 opportunities, and did not allow a run in his final 24 innings. Padre President Dick Freeman recalled, "Davis made a dramatic impact. I don't know where we would have been without him." Bruce Hurst responded, "We would have been down near the cellar."

In December 1989, the Kansas City Royals signed Davis as a free agent. Davis slipped to a 2-7 mark with a 5.11 ERA and only six saves. He remained with the Royals until being traded to the Atlanta Braves in July 1992 and spent the first half of 1993 with the Philadelphia Phillies. The San Diego Padres signed him as a free agent in July. After rejoining the Padres, Davis lost all three decisions with a 3.52 ERA and converted four of six save opportunities. He saved consecutive games against the Philadelphia Phillies on July 15 and July 16 and recorded 15 scoreless innings in 13 appearances between August 25 and September 24. In 1994, he lost one decision with an 8.82 ERA in 20 appearances before being released.

During his major-league career, Davis compiled a 51-84 win-loss record with 96 saves, a 4.15 ERA, and 993 strikeouts in 1,128.2 innings. He held the single-season Padre record for saves with 44 until 1998 and ranks fourth in franchise history with 78 career saves. Davis serves as a pitching coach in the Arizona Diamondbacks organization. He and his wife, Candy, reside in Marietta, Georgia and have two daughters, Taylor and Madison, and one son, Logan.

DAVE DRAVECKY

Dave Dravecky starred as a pitcher for the San Diego Padres from 1982 through 1987. The 6-foot 1-inch, 200-pound Dravecky, who batted right-handed and threw left-handed, was born on February 14, 1956 in Youngstown, Ohio and attended Youngstown State University. The Pittsburgh Pirates selected him in the 21st round of the June 1978 draft. Dravecky toiled for three minor league seasons in the Pirate organization until being traded to the San Diego Padres in April 1981. He pitched for Amarillo, Texas of the Texas

League in 1981 and started 1982 at Hawaii of the Pacific Coast League.

After joining the Padres in June 1982, Dravecky relieved in 19 games and joined the starting rotation for the final 10 contests. He logged a 5-3 record with a 2.57 ERA, including a 4-2 ledger with a 2.91 ERA as a starter and a 1-1 slate with a 1.95 ERA and two saves as a reliever. Dravecky pitched one shutout inning and picked a runner off first base in his major-league debut against the Los Angeles Dodgers on June 15. He recorded his first major-league victory on July 4 with 3.2 hitless innings in a 4-3 victory over the San Francisco Giants and saved his first game on July 31 with 2.1 hitless innings in a 5-4 triumph over the Cincinnati Reds. In his first start on August 8, Dravecky allowed only one run in six innings to defeat the Cincinnati Reds, 3-1. He also won his next two starts over the Atlanta Braves, 7-4, on August 13 and the St. Louis Cardinals, 4-3, on August 19. Dravecky on August 30 pitched the longest start of any National League pitcher in 1982, surrendering one run and five hits in 11 innings against the Pittsburgh Pirates. The Pirates won that game, 2-1, in 13 innings.

In 1983, Dravecky finished 14-10 with a 3.58 ERA as a starter. Only four National League left-handers won more games. His nine complete games ranked fourth best in the senior circuit. He led the Padres in complete games and finished second in innings pitched (183.2), third in starts (28), and fifth in strikeouts (74). He walked only 44 batters. Dravecky ranked among the National League's top pitchers for the first half of 1983 with a 12-5 record, 3.07 ERA, and eight complete games and made the National League All-Star team. He pitched his first complete major-league game in his initial 1983 start, defeating the San Francisco Giants, 5-3, on April 6 at Candlestick Park. Dravecky won five consecutive starts from April 17 to May 13 and rarely issued a walk. His 11-inning home stint against the Houston Astros on June 18 equaled the longest in the senior circuit in 1983. In the All-Star game, he hurled two shutout innings and struck out George Brett and Fred Lynn. Dravecky pitched his first major-league shutout on August 15, blanking the Atlanta Braves, 4-0, on a five-hitter at Atlanta-Fulton County Stadium.

Dravecky boasted a 9-8 record and a 2.93 ERA in 1984, starting 14 games and relieving in 36 contests. He opened the 1984 season in the bullpen, making 31 consecutive relief appearances. Dravecky fashioned a 4-3 record with seven saves and a 2.52 ERA as a reliever. He made 10 relief appearances with a 0.55 ERA and four saves in June. Manager Dick Williams shifted him to the starting rotation on June 27 in the heat of the pennant race. After dropping his first start, Dravecky won three consecutive starts and hurled a 6-1 six-hitter over the St. Louis Cardinals on July 15 at Busch Stadium. He limited the Los Angeles Dodgers to just one hit and four walks at home on July 30, the third of four consecutive shutouts by the Padre staff. Bill Russell doubled in the seventh inning for the lone Dodger safety in the 12-0 Padre victory. Dravecky blanked the Cincinnati Reds, 2-0, on three hits at Riverfront Stadium on September 18 and rejoined the relief corps two days later when the Padres clinched the Western Division title. He relieved nearly three innings against the San Francisco Giants that day to preserve the game for Tim Lollar. Dravecky's relief pitching sparkled during the post-season when he blanked the Chicago Cubs for six innings in the National League Championship Series. In the final two games against Chicago, he retired 12 of 13 batters in four innings. Dravecky allowed one hit while fanning four in middle relief. He blanked the Detroit Tigers for nearly five innings in the World Series, retiring 14 of 16 batters.

The 1985 campaign saw Dravecky match his 2.93 ERA with a 13-11 ledger. He added a forkball to his pitching repertoire. His 2.93 ERA ranked fourth best in the National League. In 31 starts, he posted a 13-10 record with a 2.77 ERA. During the opening week, Dravecky lost his first two starts when Orel Hershiser of the Los Angeles Dodgers shut out the Padres. Five of his defeats came by one run. Dravecky won four consecutive games over the St. Louis Cardinals, 12-2, on May 7, the Chicago Cubs, 5-3, on May 12, the Montreal Expos, 8-2, on May 18, and Philadelphia Phillies, 1-0, on May 24. Following two setbacks, he hurled two complete game shutouts and a team-high 24 consecutive scoreless innings. After pitching seven shutout innings in a 3-0 win over the San Francisco Giants at Candlestick Park on June 13, Dravecky threw a 4-0, three-hitter over the Los Angeles Dodgers at Dodger Stadium on June 18, defeated the San Francisco Giants, 6-1, with nine strikeouts at home on June 23, and tossed a 3-0, eight-hitter against the Cincinnati Reds at home on June 29. In that four-game span, he allowed just one earned run and 26 hits in 34 innings. Dravecky hurled an eight inning, one-hitter against the Pittsburgh Pirates at Three Rivers Stadium in his next outing, but was not involved in the decision. He won all four starts against the San Francisco Giants.

Dravecky slipped to 9-11 with a 3.11 ERA in 1986. He posted a 2-1 ledger with a National League-best 0.55 ERA in five April starts, being selected Padre Pitcher of the Month. Dravecky on April 8 hurled a 1-0, three-hitter over Orel Hershiser of the Los Angeles Dodgers at Dodger Stadium in his initial start. He hurled 19.2 consecutive scoreless innings from April 8 through April 19 and recorded three straight triumphs in mid-May, fanning 11 Philadelphia Phillies on May 21 in a 7-2 victory. Shoulder soreness limited him to eight appearances in the second half. Dravecky defeated the Montreal Expos twice with a 0.64 ERA.

Dravecky struggled with a 3-7 mark and 3.76 ERA in 1987 before being traded to the San Francisco Giants on July 4. Upon leaving the Padres, he ranked third in wins (53) and ERA (3.12), fourth in innings (980.1), strikeouts (456), and complete games (23), and fifth in shutouts (6) and losses (50). Dravecky's record with San Francisco was 7-5 in 1987, 2-2 in 1988, and 2-0 in 1989. He blanked the St. Louis Cardinals on two hits in Game 2 of 1987 National League Championship Series, but missed nearly all of the 1988 season because of a life-threatening cancerous tumor in his pitching arm. Doctors removed the tumor and the muscle from his pitching arm in October 1988 and gave him hardly any chance of ever pitching again. Dravecky defied the odds by winning two games in August 1989 before his weakened arm broke as he threw a pitch. He rebroke it on the field during the Giants' National League Championship Series victory celebration and never pitched again. During eight major-league seasons, Dravecky compiled a 64-57 win-loss record with a 3.13 ERA, nine shutouts, and 558 strikeouts in 1,062.2 innings. He and his wife, Jan, live in Colorado Springs, Colorado with their two children, Tiffany and Jonathan. He wrote two books about his baseball career and his battle with cancer, which included the amputation of his left arm in 1991.

JUAN EICHELBERGER

Juan Eichelberger pitched for the San Diego Padres between 1978 and 1982. The 6-foot 3-inch, 205-pound Eichelberger, who batted and threw right-handed, was born on October 21, 1953 in St. Louis, Missouri and starred in baseball for the University of California at Berkeley. The San Diego Padres selected Eichelberger, who possessed a strong arm and good fastball, in the first round of the secondary phase of the January 1975 free agent draft. After pitching nearly four full minor-league seasons, Eichelberger joined the Padres in September 1978 and performed well in two of three relief appearances. He hurled for Hawaii of the Pacific Coast League in 1979 and split two decisions with a 3.43 ERA for the Padres. His first major-league victory came on September 21, when he defeated the Los Angeles Dodgers, 3-1, in a four-hitter at home. He also allowed only two runs on five hits in seven innings in a 6-5 loss to the San Francisco Giants on September 29 at Candlestick Park.

Eichelberger, who began 1980 at Hawaii, logged a 4-2 record with a 3.65 ERA after rejoining San Diego in June. The Padres won nine of the 13 games he started. Eichelberger won his first four decisions and allowed only one earned run in 10 innings on July 13 in a 4-3, 15 inning victory over the Los Angeles Dodgers. One loss came in a 2-1 decision to the Los Angeles Dodgers at Dodger Stadium on September 17.

Eichelberger enjoyed his best major-league season in 1981. He split 16 decisions with a 3.50 ERA, leading the Padre staff in victories (8), starts (24), innings pitched (141.1), and strikeouts (81). Eichelberger received strong consideration for the National League All-Star team after finishing the first half of the season with a 6-3 record and a 2.81 ERA. He pitched his first major-league shutout on May 12, blanking the New York Mets 3-0 on a seven-hitter at home.

In his first start after the strike, Eichelberger donated his pay to charity since owner Ray Kroc invited the fans to attend free. He gave up two runs in eight innings to the Atlanta Braves, but was not involved in the decision. Eichelberger surrendered only eight runs in his final 39 innings and did not allow a home run in his last 50 innings. However, he set a Padre record by issuing five walks in one inning at home against the St. Louis Cardinals on August 29. Eichelberger defeated the Cincinnati Reds, 6-1, on a six-hitter on September 8 at Riverfront Stadium and fanned a career-high 10 Los Angeles Dodgers in an 8-2 victory one week later at home. Four of his losses came by margins of 1-0 and 2-1 to the Houston Astros, 2-0 to the San Francisco Giants, and 3-2 to the Cincinnati Reds.

Eichelberger struggled with a 7-14 record and a 4.20 ERA in his final season with San Diego, while he led the Padres with eight complete games. At Atlanta-Fulton County Stadium on September 25, he set Padre records for the most runs and earned runs allowed in a nine-inning game. He gave up 10 runs and eight earned runs in just seven innings against the Atlanta Braves. In November 1982, San Diego traded Eichelberger and Broderick Perkins to the Cleveland Indians for pitcher Ed Whitson. As a Padre, Eichelberger compiled a 20-25 ledger with 12 complete games, one shutout, and a 3.87 ERA. He struck out 209 batters in 432 innings.

After winning just four of 15 decisions for the Cleveland Indians in 1983, Eichelberger spent the next four and half seasons in the Milwaukee Brewers, Pittsburgh Pirates and Atlanta Braves minor-league organizations. He finished his major-league career with a 2-0 record and a 3.86 ERA for the Atlanta Braves in 1988. In seven major-league seasons, he logged a 26-36 mark with a 4.10 ERA. The hard thrower with unusual short-arm delivery suffered from control problems, walking 273 batters while striking out 268.

He and his wife, Juliette, reside in Poway, California.

TONY FERNANDEZ

Tony Fernandez played shortstop for the San Diego Padres in 1991 and 1992. The 6-foot 2-inch, 195-pound Fernandez, who switch hit and threw right-handed, was born on June 30, 1962 in San Pedro de Macoris, Dominican Republic and attended Gasto Fernando de Ligne High School. The Toronto Blue Jays signed him at age 16 in April 1979. His twin brother, Jose, also signed with the Toronto Blue Jays, but Jose never played in the major leagues. Fernandez spent a little over four seasons in the minor leagues, debuting with the Toronto Blue Jays in 1983. He became the starting shortstop for Toronto in 1985 and remained with the Blue Jays through 1990. Defensively, Fernandez exhibited exceptional range, a powerful, accurate arm, and tremendous anticipation. Besides earning four Rawlings Gold Glove awards from 1986 through 1989, he recorded 65 consecutive errorless games in 1988 and set a major-league record for shortstops with a .992 fielding average in 1989. Solid hitting performances of .310 in 1986 and .322 in 1987 won him spots on the American League All-Star team both years. In 1986, Fernandez became the first Blue Jay to record 200 hits in a season and made the AP All-Major-League team. He made the American League All-Star team in 1989 and holds the Toronto records for career hits (1,406), doubles (246), and triples (72).

In a blockbuster December 1990 trade, the San Diego Padres acquired Fernandez and first baseman Fred McGriff from the Toronto Blue Jays for Roberto Alomar and Joe Carter. In 1991, Fernandez batted .272 with 152 hits, four home runs, 64 RBIs, and a .972 fielding percentage and led the Padres with 27 doubles. A four-hit game highlighted his season. In 1992, his batting average improved to .275 and his fielding percentage to .983 while he had 171 hits, 32 doubles, four home runs, and 37 RBIs. As a member of the National League All-Star team, Fernandez singled in the Summer Classic. He led the Padres with 20 stolen bases, but tied a major-league record by being caught twice trying to steal in the fifth inning at home against the San Francisco Giants on June 26. He shared the second longest National League hitting streak, reaching safely in 19 consecutive games from September 14 through October 4.

San Diego traded Fernandez to the New York Mets in December 1992. In June 1993, New York sent him to the Toronto Blue Jays. He batted .333 in the 1993 World Series victory over the Philadelphia Phillies, leading both clubs with nine RBIs. After spending 1994 with the Cincinnati Reds, he joined the New York Yankees in December 1994 and hit for the cycle against the Oakland A's on September 3, 1995. Injuries sidelined him for the entire 1996 season. The Cleveland Indians signed him as a free agent in December 1996. Fernandez starred in the 1997 American League Championship Series against the Baltimore Orioles, clouting a dramatic eleventh-inning home run in Game 6 to clinch the American League pennant. He hit .471 in the 1997 World Series against the Florida Marlins, but made a crucial error in the 11-inning loss in decisive Game 7. Fernandez rejoined the Toronto Blue Jays for the third time in December 1997 and spent the 1998 and 1999 seasons there. He played in the Japanese Central League in 2000 and returned to the Toronto Blue Jays as a pinch-hitter and designated hitter for his final major-league season in 2001. In 17 major-league seasons through 2001, he batted .288 with 414 doubles, 92 triples, 93 home runs, 841 RBIs, 245 stolen bases, and a .979 fielding percentage.

He and his wife, Clara, reside in San Pedro de Macoris, Dominican Republic and have three children, Joel, Jonathan, and Abraham.

ROLLIE FINGERS

Rollie Fingers ranked among the best relievers in San Diego Padres history from 1977 through 1980. The 6-foot 4-inch, 190-pound right-hander was born on August 25, 1946 in Steubenville, Ohio and attended Chaffey Junior College in California. His father, George, and brother, Gordon, both played minor-league baseball. Fingers starred as a reliever with the Oakland A's from 1969 to 1976, finishing among American League leaders in saves. He appeared in five American League Championship Series and three World Series.

In December 1976, the San Diego Padres dramatically improved their bullpen by signing Fingers to a six-year $1.6 million contract. His addition boosted club attendance and paid immediate dividends. In 1977, Fingers was named *The Sporting News'* National League Fireman of the Year and Rolaids' National League Relief Man of the Year with an 8-9 win-loss slate and a 3.00 ERA. He led the senior circuit with 78 appearances and 35 saves. His 35 saves set club single-season and career records. Opponents did not score in 52 of his 78 appearances. He relieved 5.2 innings against the Montreal Expos at Olympic Stadium on May 21, but was not involved in the decision. Fingers struck out 113 batters in just 132 innings, fanning a season-best five Chicago Cubs at home on June 14. He recorded saves against each National League club, securing five against the Houston Astros and four each against the Cincinnati Reds, San Francisco Giants, New York Mets, and St. Louis Cardinals. Fingers registered saves in four consecutive appearances from May 29 through May 31 and five straight outings from July 30 through August 10.

In 1978, Fingers finished with a 6-13 mark and a 2.52 ERA, repeating as the Rolaids Fireman of the Year. His National League-best 37 saves tied the senior circuit record. The fierce competitor with a handlebar moustache pitched brilliantly during the second half of the season. He did not allow a run in 14 consecutive games covering 20.1 innings and surrendered only one run in 21 games spanning 35 innings. Fingers registered saves in six straight appearances from July 26 through August 4, challenging opponents with his curves, sliders, and fastballs. In his final 26 games, he finished 2-2 with 17 saves and a 0.92 ERA. Fingers compiled a 4-3 record and a 1.29 ERA in 34 games at San Diego Stadium and saved 10 victories for 21-game winner Gaylord Perry. "Never in my 17 seasons," Perry declared, "have I had the good fortune of having a pitcher like Fingers in my bullpen." Fingers exhibited pinpoint control in the 1978 All-Star game at San Diego, hurling two shutout innings in relief.

Rollie Fingers

Elbow problems caused Fingers's production to drop in 1979. Fingers split 18 decisions, but his ERA soared to 4.50 and save production slumped to 13. Nevertheless, he led Padre pitchers in appearances (54) and saves and finished 6-0 with a 2.09 ERA and eight saves at home. Through June 22, Fingers fashioned a 6-3 record and a 2.73 ERA with 10 saves and surrendered only one home run. He recorded three consecutive saves from May 1 through May 5 and from May 28 through May 31. Fingers developed a forkball in 1980 to supplement his sinker and slider, rebounding with an 11-9 mark, 2.80 ERA, and 23 saves. He shared the Padre lead in victories with Bob Shirley and paced the Padres again in saves.

San Diego considered the 34-year old Fingers expendable and traded him to the St. Louis Cardinals in December 1980. From 1977 to 1980, Fingers established Padre records for career (108) and season

(37) saves, had paced the National League twice in saves, and had won 34 games. His 265 relief appearances rank fourth among club pitchers. Fingers later starred with the Milwaukee Brewers, winning the American League Most Valuable Player and Cy Young awards in 1981.

Fingers revolutionized relief pitching as one of the first great major-league bullpen artists. During his 17-year major-league career, he compiled a 114-118 record with a 2.90 ERA and a then record 341 saves. No major-league pitcher saved more games during the 1970s. His saves still rank sixth in major-league history. He demonstrated remarkable control, striking out 1,299 batters and walking only 492 in 1,701 innings. "Relief pitching," Steve Arlin remembered, "was not a very important thing until Fingers." In 1992, the National Baseball Hall of Fame enshrined Fingers, making him just the third Padre to accomplish that feat. The San Diego resident and his former wife, Jill, have three children.

STEVE FINLEY

Steve Finley starred as a center fielder with the San Diego Padres from 1995 through 1998. The 6-foot 2-inch, 185-pound Finley, who bats and throws left-handed, was born on March 12, 1965 in Union City, Tennessee and graduated from Tilghmann High School in Paducah, Kentucky. His father served as a middle school dean in Paducah, where his mother teaches middle school. Finley earned a Bachelor's degree in physiology from Southern Illinois University, making the All-Missouri Valley Conference baseball team twice and helping the Salukis win Missouri Valley Conference titles in 1984 and 1986. The Baltimore Orioles selected him in the thirteenth round of the June 1987 free agent draft. He spent two full seasons in the minor leagues, leading the International League with a .314 batting average for Rochester, New York in 1988.

Finley spent most of 1989 and all of 1990 with the Baltimore Orioles. In January 1991, he was traded with Curt Schilling to the Houston Astros for Glenn Davis. He played outfield with the Houston Astros from 1991 through 1994 and paced the National League with 13 triples in 1993. His best season there came in 1992, when he batted .292 with 29 doubles, 55 RBIs, and a career-high 44 stolen bases. A blockbuster December 1994 12-player transaction sent Finley and third baseman Ken Caminiti to the San Diego Padres.

Steve Finley

In 1995, Finley batted .297 with 23 doubles, 10 home runs, and 44 RBIs. He ranked third in the National League in runs scored (104), tied for third in triples (8), and shared fourth in hits (167) and stolen bases (36). Besides becoming the only National Leaguer to combine 100 runs, 10 homers, and 36 steals in the same season, Finley earned his first Rawlings Gold Glove Award. Finley batted .338 in the leadoff position, best in the major leagues, and scored 62 runs with 15 doubles, six triples, six home runs, 28 RBIs, and 25 stolen bases while leading off. He stole 36 bases, the most by a Padre since Bip Roberts in 1990. Finley batted .381 during a 10-game hitting streak from May 5 through May 12 and enjoyed four-hit games against the Montreal Expos on May 25, Houston Astros on July 7, Colorado Rockies on August 4, and St. Louis Cardinals on August 11. Finley preserved a June 21 1-0 victory with a leaping catch over the center-field wall to rob Rick Wilkins of the Chicago Cubs of the potential game-tying, ninth-inning homer. He stole four bases on August 12 in a 6-5 home triumph over the St. Louis Cardinals and batted .440 against the San Francisco Giants. He compiled a .997 fielding percentage, ranking sixth among senior circuit outfielders with 291 putouts and sharing the team lead with eight assists.

In 1996, Finley established career highs in batting average (.298), runs (126), hits (195), doubles (45), home runs (30), extra-base hits (84), total bases (348), RBIs (95), slugging percentage (.531), and at-bats (655), helping the Padres win the National League West. He set franchise single-season records for runs scored, doubles, extra-base hits, and total bases and stole 22 bases, becoming just the fourth Padre to combine 20 stolen bases with 20 home runs in a season. After batting either first or second through June 21, Finley batted .329 with 15 home runs and 49 RBIs mostly in the third spot. The fleet-footed Finley won his second straight Rawlings Gold Glove Award and finished tenth in the Most Valuable Player voting. He jumped high over the wall in center field to rob Ron Gant of the St. Louis Cardinals of a home run on May 4 and nearly tripled his previous best home run output.

Finley ranked second in the National League in runs scored and doubles, third in total bases and extra-base hits, fourth in triples (9), and sixth in hits. His 21-game hitting streak from June 20 to July 14 marked his personal best and the year's fourth highest in the senior circuit. During that span, Finley batted .419 with 10 doubles, seven home runs and 17 RBIs. He homered twice against the Pittsburgh Pirates on May 8, San Francisco Giants on June 29, and Los Angeles Dodgers on September 20. His home runs won games against the Philadelphia Phillies on May 3, Chicago Cubs on June 15, New York Mets on August 27, and Pittsburgh Pirates on September 10. In September, Finley shared the team lead with nine home runs. He and Ken Caminiti (40 home runs, 130 RBIs) combined for more home runs (70) and RBIs (225) than any previous tandem in Padre history.

Finley batted .388 with seven home runs and 15 RBIs against the San Francisco Giants, tying a franchise mark by homering in three consecutive plate appearances on June 29 and June 30. He also homered against the Los Angeles Dodgers on July 1, setting a career high with round-trippers in three consecutive games. In a 7-5 victory over the Philadelphia Phillies at home on May 23, Finley singled three times, doubled, and homered with two RBIs for his first five-hit game. He clouted a grand slam off Dave Leiper in an 8-3 triumph over the Philadelphia Phillies at Veterans Stadium on June 1 and scored four runs in a 20-12 victory over the Florida Marlins at Joe Robbie Stadium on July 27. Finley earned his first National League Player of the Week Award, batting .483 with two homers and seven RBIs from July 1 through July 7. He struggled in the National League Division Series against the St. Louis Cardinals.

In 1997, Finley batted .261 with 26 doubles and 92 RBIs and made the National League All-Star team for the first time. He led the Padres with 101 runs scored, five triples, and 28 home runs and became the first club member to tally 100 runs in three consecutive seasons. Finley ranked second on the Padres in RBIs and extra-base hits (59) and third in hits (146) and stolen bases (15). He knocked in 15 runs in interleague games. He batted .303 with 23 home runs and 62 RBIs in 71 road games.

Finley became just the eleventh major-leaguer to clout three home runs twice in the same season, first connecting in a 13-6 romp over the Cincinnati Reds on May 19. He hit solo home runs off Pete Schourek in the third and fourth innings and against Stan Belinda in the ninth inning at Riverfront Stadium. On June 23, Finley made four hits with three homers, four runs scored, and four RBIs in an 11-6 rout over the San Francisco Giants at Candlestick Park. He clouted home runs with the bases empty off Mark Gardner in the first inning and Rich Rodriguez in the fourth inning before belting a two-run homer off Joe Roa in the ninth inning. Finley, who added a single in the fifth inning, finished with a club-record 13 total bases, one more than Nate Colbert made in his three-home-run game against the Atlanta Braves in August 1972. No other Padres had homered three times in a contest.

Finley won National League Player of the Week honors from June 23 through June 29, batting .520 with six homers and nine RBIs. He tied a Padre single-season record by belting two grand slams: including a first-inning shot off Derek Lowe in a 10-8 home win over the Seattle Mariners on July 3 and a ninth-inning blow off Bobby Ayala on September 1 at the Seattle Kingdome. Finley scored four runs on June 23 against the San Francisco Giants and September 9 in a 13-inning contest against the Florida Marlins. He tied the latter game with a solo home run off Rob Nen in the ninth inning and scored the game-winner in the thirteenth inning in the 7-6 victory. Finley led the major leagues by scoring a run over half the time he reached base.

Although not receiving a third consecutive Rawlings Gold Glove Award in 1997, Finley led the Padres with 10 outfield assists, participated in three double plays, posted a .989 fielding percentage, and made only four errors. He caught a sinking line drive hit by Dante Bichette with the tying runners on base to preserve a 6-4 win over the Colorado Rockies on June 4 at Coors Field. He leaped over the center-field fence at home to rob Lance Johnson of a fifth-inning home run in a 5-3 victory over the New York Mets on July 27. Finley clouted 23 home runs off right-handed pitching and enjoyed 15 three-hit games. He matched a career high with five RBIs in a 10-8 triumph over the Seattle Mariners on July 3 and clouted eight home runs with 14 RBIs from June 23 through July 3.

Following the 1997 season, Finley underwent surgery on a bunion. In 1998, he batted just .249 with 14 home runs and 67 RBIs. Nevertheless, he led the Padres with 40 doubles and six triples and finished second with 92 runs scored, 154 hits, and 248 total bases. Although striking out a career-high 103 times, Finley shared the National League lead in double plays by an outfielder with six. He recorded 38 multiple-hit games with two four-hit contests.

On April 10, his two-out grand slam off Felix Rodriguez in the bottom of the ninth inning lifted the Padres to a 6-4 home victory over the Arizona Diamondbacks. He clouted four grand slams as a Padre, trailing only Nate Colbert. Finley doubled three times and knocked in five runs in a 17-8 romp over the Texas Rangers at the Ballpark in Arlington on June 7. Finley and Carlos Hernandez belted consecutive home runs off Jamey Wright in the fifth inning in a 4-2 victory over the Colorado Rockies on July 3. He batted just .100 with one double and one RBI in the National League Division Series against the Houston Astros, but hit .333 with one double and two RBIs against the Atlanta Braves in the National League Championship Series. The New York Yankees limited him to one double and an .083 batting average in his first World Series.

Finley remained very active in the San Diego community. He formed the Steve Finley Charitable Youth Fund to encourage youngsters to stay in school, earn a degree, and live drug-free. Besides helping inspire the Padres Scholars program, Finley participated in the Padres' Community Relations Department.

In December 1998, the Arizona Diamondbacks signed Finley as a free agent. Upon his departure from the Padres, he ranked fifth in doubles (134), sixth in triples (28) and runs (423), seventh in batting average (.276) and home runs (82), tenth in hits (662), and eleventh in RBIs (298) and stolen bases (85). In 1999 Finley batted .264 with 34 home runs and 103 RBIs to help the Diamondbacks win the National League West and hit .385 with five RBIs in the National League Division Series against the New York Mets. In 2000, Finley hit .280 with 35 home runs and 96 RBIs. Finley batted .275 with 14 home runs and 73 RBI in 2001, helping Arizona capture the National League West. He paced the Diamondbacks with a .421 batting average and knocked in two runs in the National League Division Series against the St. Louis Cardinals and hit .286 with four RBIs in the National League Championship Series against the Atlanta Braves. Arizona won its first World Series title as Finley batted .368 with two RBIs and homered in Game 5 against the New York Yankees. Through 2001, Finley has batted .275 with 1,071 runs, 1,873 hits, 329 doubles, 94 triples, 202 home runs, 818 RBIs, and a .987 fielding percentage. He and his wife, Amy, reside in Del Mar, California and have three sons, Austin, Reed, and Blake.

TIM FLANNERY

Reserve infielder Tim Flannery was one of the most popular players in San Diego Padres history. The 5-foot 11-inch, 176-pound infielder, who batted left-handed and threw right-handed, was born on September 29, 1957 in Tulsa, Oklahoma and played baseball at Chapman College in Orange, California. The San Diego Padres selected him in the sixth round of the June 1978 draft. He was the runner-up for the batting title with Reno, Nevada of the California League in 1978 and Amarillo, Texas of the Texas League in 1979.

Flannery spent all or part of 11 seasons with San Diego, becoming a crowd favorite with his all-out style of play and hustle. In 1979, he batted only .154 with four RBIs in 22 September games. His major-league debut came on September 3, when he singled against the San Francisco Giants to drive in a run. Flannery tripled against the Cincinnati Reds on September 19 for his first extra-base hit. He started 1980 at Hawaii of the Pacific Coast League, but rejoined the Padres on June 3 and collected a pinch-hit single that night to drive in a run against the Houston Astros. Flannery batted .240 with 25 RBI in 95 games. He enjoyed an 11-game hitting streak from June 7 through June 21 and hit safely in 10 consecutive games from September 10 through September 20, recording three hits against the Montreal Expos on June 11 and June 12 and the San Francisco Giants on June 26.

Flannery began 1981 at Hawaii, but was recalled May 12 and batted .254 with six RBIs in 37 games. He started 15 games, including 12 at third base, and reached safely twice against the Montreal Expos on May 19 and May 20. A .375 batter as a pinch-hitter, Flannery made four consecutive pinch hits in September. He played his first full major-league season in 1982, batting .264 with 30 RBIs in 122 games. Flannery became the regular second baseman after Juan Bonilla broke his wrist in May. He proved especially effective at scoring runners from third base with less than two out and fanned only twice in 379 at bats.

Flannery platooned at third base with Luis Salazar for the first half of 1983 and saw his batting average plunge to .234 with three home runs and 19 RBIs. He started 43 games at third base and 13 games at second base. Flannery belted a bases-loaded triple against the St. Louis Cardinals on April 23 and clouted his first major-league home run three days later off Chuck Rainey in a 10-8 win over the Chicago Cubs at Wrigley Field. He belted a grand slam off Ferguson Jenkins to edge the Chicago Cubs, 6-5, on July 11 for his first round-tripper at Jack Murphy Stadium. He collected three hits, including two doubles, against the Pittsburgh Pirates at home on July 17 and singled in the second inning for the only hit off Nolan Ryan in a 1-0 home loss to the Houston Astros on August 3.

Flannery helped San Diego win its first National League pennant in 1984, batting .273 with two home runs and 10 RBIs in 86 games. He pinch hit 48 times and batted .313 in 19 infield starts. On June 5 he clouted a home run to defeat the Houston Astros, 3-0, and batted .375 the last week of the regular season. Flannery hit an infield single and scored in the fifth inning of Game 4 of the National League Championship Series to tie the score, 3-3, against the Chicago Cubs. His ground ball in the deciding game skipped by first baseman Leon Durham for an error and ignited a four-run, seventh-inning rally, giving the Padres the National League pennant. Flannery scored the winning tally. He made only one World Series appearance, singling as a pinch-hitter in the eighth inning of Game 4 against the Detroit Tigers.

Flannery's best major-league season came in 1985, when he attained major-league bests in batting average (.281), runs (50), hits (108), RBIs (40), and walks (58). He started 102 games at second base, platooning with Jerry Royster, and shared the club lead with a .386 on-base percentage. During July and August, he authored eight-game and seven-game hitting streaks. His three-run homer to the opposite field off Orel Hershiser sparked a 10-4 home triumph over the Los Angeles Dodgers on June 26. Flannery enjoyed four three-hit contests, batting over .400 against the Philadelphia Phillies and Atlanta Braves.

Tim Flannery

In 1986, Flannery appeared in a career-high 134 games and started 83 contests at second base. He batted .280 with three home runs, 28 RBIs, and a .378 on-base percentage, hitting .304 against right-handed pitching. Flannery walked 54 times and led the Padres in being hit by pitches for the second consecutive year with five. On April 19, he recorded his first four-hit major-league game against the San Francisco Giants at Candlestick Park. Flannery clouted a dramatic three-run homer off Tom Niedenfuer of the Los Angeles Dodgers with two outs in the ninth inning on June 22 to give the Padres a 5-4 victory at Dodger Stadium. Flannery finished August with a career-best 11-game hitting streak and hit over .350 against the Philadelphia Phillies, Montreal Expos, Atlanta Braves, and Los Angeles Dodgers. Flannery finished second to Ryne

Sandberg in fielding percentage, making only three errors in 458 chances. His .993 fielding percentage remains a franchise record for second baseman.

In 1987, Flannery batted just .228 with 20 RBIs in 106 games. During batting practice in May, he stepped on a baseball that had rolled under the tarp in front of home plate and tore ligaments on both sides of his right ankle. The ankle hindered his performance for the rest of the campaign and especially in September, when he went hitless in 29 consecutive plate appearances. On June 24, he made four hits in a 12-7 home loss to the Houston Astros.

In December 1987, Flannery underwent arthroscopic surgery on his ankle. In 1988, he batted .265 with 19 RBIs in 79 games. Flannery hit .355 in August and made four hits in a 5-3 victory over the Montreal Expos at Olympic Stadium on August 28. He batted .308 as a pinch-hitter and matched a club record with five consecutive pinch hits from August 10 through September 6. In 1989, Flannery hit just .231 with five doubles and eight RBIs. He retired following the 1989 season with a .255 career batting average, nine home runs, and 209 RBIs in 972 games. After working as a television features reporter in San Diego from 1990 through 1992, he managed in the Padres' minor-league system from 1993 through 1995. Flannery has coached at third base for the Padres since 1996. He and his wife, Donna, reside in Leucadia, California and have one son, Daniel, and two daughters, Virginia and Kelly. Flannery enjoys surfing and playing guitar and has recorded three CDs. His Tim Flannery Band has performed concerts in southern California and Arizona.

DAVE FREISLEBEN

Dave Freisleben pitched for the San Diego Padres from 1974 through 1978. The 5-foot 11-inch, 200-pound right-hander was born on October 31, 1951 in Coraopolis, Pennsylvania and was selected in the fourth round of the June 1971 free agent draft by the San Diego Padres. He pitched for Tri-City of the Northwest League in 1971, Alexandria, Louisiana of the Texas League in 1972, and Hawaii of the Pacific Coast League in 1973.

Freisleben joined the San Diego Padres' starting rotation in 1974, compiling a 9-14 win-loss record and a 3.65 ERA. He tied Larry Hardy and Dan Spillner for most wins by a Padre rookie and ranked second on the staff with 212 innings pitched and 130 strikeouts.

Dave Freisleben

Freisleben set the rookie record for most strikeouts and won consecutive four-hit home games, 6-2 over the Philadelphia Phillies on April 26 and 5-1 over Montreal Expos on May 1. Besides blanking the St. Louis Cardinals, 1-0, at home on June 7, he hurled a 13-inning, 1-0 home shutout against the Cincinnati Reds on August 4 and a 3-0, three-hit shutout over the Montreal Expos at Jarry Park on August 20. His nine victories all came against National League East teams.

Control problems plagued Freisleben in 1975, when he finished with a 5-14 win-loss record and a 4.28 ERA. Three of his five victories came against the Chicago Cubs. On July 28, he hurled a 2-0 five-hit shutout over the Houston Astros at the Astrodome. The Padres scored two runs or less in 12 of his losses. Manager John McNamara moved him to the bullpen for the final five weeks. After starting 1976 at Hawaii, Freisleben rejoined San Diego in late May and compiled a 10-13 record with a 3.51 ERA. At home, he blanked the Los Angeles Dodgers, 2-0, on May 24, the San Francisco Giants, 4-0, on May 29, and the New York Mets, 3-0, on June 8. Freisleben triumphed in six of his first seven decisions, but opponents blanked San Diego in six of his 13 losses. Besides winning two games in relief with a save, he fanned eight San Francisco Giants on June 21 and Los Angeles Dodgers on September 7.

In 1977, Freisleben logged a 7-9 mark with a 4.60 ERA. He started the season with San Diego, was demoted to Hawaii, and rejoined the Padres in late June. Freisleben struck out eight San Francisco Giants on September 24 and defeated the Houston Astros and Montreal Expos twice. He lost all three decisions in 1978 before being traded that June to the Cleveland Indians. His major-league career ended with the Toronto Blue Jays in 1979.

During six major-league seasons, Freisleben compiled a 34-60 record with a 4.29 ERA. For San Diego, he logged a 31-53 ledger with a 3.80 ERA. Freisleben ranked fourth among Padres in innings pitched (730) and victories (31), fifth in strikeouts (376), and eighth in appearances (148). He resides in Pasadena, Texas and enjoys golf, hunting, and playing pool.

STEVE GARVEY

Steve Garvey starred as a first baseman for the San Diego Padres from 1983 through 1987. The 5-foot 10-inch, 190-pound Garvey, who batted and threw right-handed, was born on December 22, 1948 in Tampa, Florida and graduated in 1971 with a B.S. degree in education from Michigan State University, where he excelled as an All-American baseball player and starting defensive back in football. In June 1968, the Los Angeles Dodgers selected him as their first draft choice. He spent nearly three seasons as a minor-league third baseman, appearing briefly with the Los Angeles Dodgers in 1969. Garvey rejoined the Los Angeles Dodgers in 1970 and moved to first base in 1973, combining with Davey Lopes, Bill Russell, and Ron Cey in the remarkable Dodgers infield for nearly a decade. He was chosen as the National League's Most Valuable Player in 1974 and set a National League record in 1976 for fewest errors (3) by a first baseman handling at least 1,500 chances. His 33 round-trippers in 1977 established a record for Dodgers first basemen. On August 29, 1977, Garvey tied a National League mark with five extra-base hits, consisting of home runs and three doubles, against the St. Louis Cardinals. He played the entire Dodgers schedule for seven consecutive seasons from 1976 through 1982.

After 13 seasons with the Dodgers, Garvey signed a five-year, $6.6 million contract with the San Diego Padres. In 1983, he batted .294 with 14 home runs and 59 RBIs. In his Padre home debut on April 12, he homered and doubled in a 6-5 loss to the San Francisco Giants. Four days later against the Los Angeles Dodgers at Dodger Stadium, he surpassed Billy Williams for most consecutive games by a National League player with 1,118. Garvey knocked in his 1,000th career run in a 10-8 home win over the Chicago Cubs on April 26 and recorded his 2,000th major-league hit in the fourth inning against the Chicago Cubs at Wrigley Field on May 7. On July 3, he clouted a grand slam off Mark Davis to spark a 4-1 win at home over the San Francisco Giants. Owner Ray Kroc had never witnessed a Padre grand slam home run. Garvey's playing streak ended in 1983 at 1,207 games, the third longest in major-league history. He suffered a dislocated thumb in a collision at home plate at San Diego on July 29 against the Atlanta Braves. At the time, Garvey ranked second in the National League in runs scored (76), shared fourth in hits (114) and eighth in doubles (22), and stood ninth in RBIs. He was leading the Padres in runs scored, hits, home runs, and RBIs.

In 1984, Garvey batted .284 with 175 hits, eight home runs, and 86 RBIs to help the San Diego Padres

Steve Garvey

win their first National League pennant. He recorded a team-high 17-game hitting streak in May and batted .342 in June. During a 59-game span, he scored 34 runs and drove in 24 runs. Garvey received over 1.7 million popular votes for the All-Star game. He broke a National League record for first basemen by playing in 159 consecutive games without making an error and the major-league record by appearing in 179 straight contests without a miscue. Garvey batted .400 with seven RBIs and several clutch hits in the National League Championship Series against the Chicago Cubs. He nearly single-handedly defeated the Cubs in Game 4 with four hits, five RBIs, and the most memorable home run in Padres history. With the score tied, 5-5, and one out in the bottom of the ninth inning, he clouted a two-run homer to right field off reliever Lee Smith. In the decisive Game 5, he drove in the final insurance run in the four-run seventh inning to send the Padres to the World Series against the Detroit Tigers.

In 1985, Garvey hit .281 with six triples, 17 home runs and 81 RBIs. His offensive production increased by nine hits and 21 extra-base hits, while his slugging percentage soared to a team-leading .430 and his home run output more than doubled. He shared fifth in the National League with a team-high 34 doubles and batted .359 in the first month. Garvey homered twice in a 7-3 home triumph over the Atlanta Braves on April 12 and fashioned a 12-game hitting streak from April 30 through May 12. He enjoyed four-hit games in a 12-0 shellacking of the St. Louis Cardinals at Busch Stadium on May 7 and in a 6-0 romp over the Atlanta Braves at Atlanta-Fulton County Stadium on August 1 and batted .447 in his final nine games. Defensively, he made a miscue at first base against the San Francisco Giants on April 15 to end his errorless streak at 193 games. Fans again selected him to the All-Star team.

Garvey's offensive production declined in his final two years with the Padres, as he batted .255 with 21 home runs and 81 RBIs in 1986 and just .211 in 27 games in 1987. He retired following the 1987 season and still ranks eighth in batting average (.275), ninth in RBIs (316), and eleventh in runs (291), doubles (107), and hits (631) on the Padre career batting list.

During 19 major-league seasons, the steady, durable Garvey batted .294 with 2,599 hits, 440 doubles, 272 home runs, and 1,308 RBIs. Besides twice leading the National League in hits and having six 200-hit seasons, he surpassed 100 RBIs and 20 home runs five times. Garvey appeared in 11 All-Star games, five National League Championship Series and World Series, and earned two Rawlings Gold Glove awards. The Los Angeles resident and his wife, Cyndy, had two children before their divorce. He broadcast for XTRA in San Diego, served as an executive for *Sport*, founded Professional Athletes Career Enterprises, and operated a marketing management consultant company.

CITO GASTON

Cito Gaston starred as an outfielder with the San Diego Padres during the infant years from 1969 through 1974. The 6-foot 4-inch, 210-pound Gaston, who batted and threw right-handed, was born on March 17, 1944 in San Antonio, Texas and graduated from Holy Cross High School in Corpus Christi, Texas. The Milwaukee Braves signed Gaston in March 1964. He spent five seasons in the minor leagues, appearing briefly with the Atlanta Braves in September 1967.

The San Diego Padres selected Gaston as their final pick in the October 1968 expansion draft. He played six campaigns with San Diego, appearing in over 100 games each season. In 1969, Gaston participated in the second most double plays (4) among National League outfielders. He was the only Padre to make the National League All-Star team in 1970, when he batted

Cito Gaston

a career-high .318 and led San Diego in batting average, at-bats (584), runs (92), hits (186), total bases (317), and RBIs (93). His 29 home runs, second highest on the Padres, bettered his previous production by 27. He batted .358 with five triples and five home runs in May. Gaston homered against every National League club and clouted nine round-trippers against the Atlanta Braves. He feasted on Cincinnati Reds, Chicago Cubs, and Atlanta Braves pitching and made four hits against the Montreal Expos on May 9, the Cincinnati Reds on May 25, the Los Angeles Dodgers on October 1, and in two other games. Gaston homered in four consecutive games and ranked tenth in the National League with a .543 slugging average.

Gaston's 17 home runs and 61 RBIs in 1971 placed second on the Padres. He made at least three hits in five games. Gaston batted .269 with seven home runs and 44 RBIs in 1972. He belted a pinch-hit grand slam off Ferguson Jenkins of the Chicago Cubs at Wrigley Field on June 14 and tied a club record with a 15-game hitting streak from July 28 through August 9. Gaston hit .288 the first half of 1973 and ended the season with a .260 batting average, 16 home runs, and 57 RBIs. He compiled 16 assists, third best among National League outfielders. His offensive production declined dramatically in 1974, as he batted just .213 with six home runs and 33 RBIs.

The Atlanta Braves reacquired Gaston in November 1974. His major-league career ended with the Pittsburgh Pirates in 1978. In 11 major-league seasons, he batted .256 with 799 hits, 91 home runs, and 387 RBIs. After serving as a roving hitting instructor with the Atlanta Braves and Toronto Blue Jays, he managed the Toronto Blue Jays to a 681-635 record from May 1989 through September 1997. The Blue Jays won Eastern Division crowns in 1989 and 1991 and World Series titles over the Atlanta Braves in 1992 and Philadelphia Phillies in 1993. Gaston rejoined the Toronto Blue Jays as a coach in 2000. The Toronto, Canada resident and his wife, Denise, have two children, Adrian and Carly.

GOOSE GOSSAGE

Goose Gossage ranked among the best relievers in San Diego Padres history from 1984 through 1987. The 6-foot 3-inch, 180-pound right-hander was born on July 5, 1951 in Colorado Springs, Colorado and majored in forestry at Southern Colorado State College. After pitching for the Chicago White Sox and Pittsburgh Pirates, he reached his pinnacle with the New York Yankees from 1978 through 1983. Gossage had compiled an 81-71 record with a 2.85 ERA and 206 saves, appearing in three American League Championship Series and two World Series. In January 1984, Gossage signed a multiyear contract worth over $6 million with the San Diego Padres. His acquisition boosted San Diego's prospects as a National League pennant contender.

Gossage gave San Diego the bullpen stopper the franchise had lacked since the departure of Rollie Fingers. In 1984, he helped the Padres capture the Western Division title and National League pennant. Gossage provided brilliant bullpen relief for the youthful starters in 1984, compiling a 10-6 win-loss record with 25 saves, a 2.90 ERA, and 84 strikeouts in 102.1 innings. He earned saves in seven of his first nine appearances, including five consecutive saves from April 13 to April 25. After saving four games in May, he won two decisions and saved two contests in June. In July, Gossage saved seven games and allowed only one earned run in 13 innings, as San Diego increased its lead in the National League West from four to 8 1/2 games. Gossage fanned two batters in one inning at the All-Star game. He yielded two runs in four innings and appeared in all three Padres victories in the National

Goose Gossage

League Championship Series against the Chicago Cubs. In Game 3, Gossage preserved Ed Whitson's victory by retiring all three batters in the ninth inning. He relieved two innings to save decisive Game 5 for Craig Lefferts, but pitched ineffectively in two World Series appearances against the Detroit Tigers.

In 1985, Gossage saved 26 games, won five of eight decisions, and led the staff with a 1.82 ERA, the third best of his career. Gossage earned five saves in April and 13 saves in his first 15 games, allowing only a three-run homer to Leon Durham of the Chicago Cubs. No other National Leaguer homered off Gossage that year. Gossage joined six teammates at the All-Star game, striking out two in the ninth inning to preserve the National League victory. He earned 21 saves through July 30, when he required arthroscopic surgery to repair a torn articulating cartilage in his right knee. Gossage returned to the mound in late August, posting five saves and two wins in his final eight games. He pitched especially well against the Los Angeles Dodgers, San Francisco Giants, New York Mets, Philadelphia Phillies, and Pittsburgh Pirates.

His 1986 production declined to 21 saves, a 5-7 mark, and a 4.45 ERA. Gossage still led the Padres in saves, winning two and saving three in his first seven appearances. After dropping three consecutive decisions, he recorded 10 saves and two wins in his next 15 outings. Gossage boasted 15 saves prior to the All-Star break. In an eight-game span from July 19 to August 12, he collected five saves and a win and allowed only one run. In August 1986, Padre management suspended Gossage for 20 days without pay for critical remarks. Gossage paid a $25,000 fine to charity and apologized publicly. After winning five of nine decisions with only 11 saves in 1987, he was traded to the Chicago Cubs. In four seasons with the Padres, Gossage compiled a 25-20 win-loss mark with 83 saves, still third highest in club history. Between 1988 and 1994, he pitched with the Chicago Cubs, San Francisco Giants, New York Yankees, Texas Rangers, Oakland A's, and Seattle Mariners.

During 22 major-league seasons, Gossage appeared in 1,002 games and struck out 1,502 batters in 1,809 innings. He compiled 310 saves, a 124-107 win-loss record, and a 3.01 ERA. He ranks 11th in career saves and third in career relief victories. His greatest assets as a pitcher included fear and intimidation. He threw a baseball nearly 100 miles per hour, making him fully confident that he could get batters out. He and his wife, Cornelia, live in Colorado Springs, Colorado and have three sons, Jeff, Keith, and Todd.

JOHN GRUBB

John Grubb starred as an outfielder with the San Diego Padres from 1972 through 1976. The 6-foot 3-inch, 175-pound Grubb, who batted left-handed and threw right-handed, was born on August 4, 1948 in Richmond, Virginia and attended Manatee Junior College in West Bradenton, Florida. Grubb graduated from Florida State University and made the All-Tournament team at the 1970 College World Series. He exhibited a smooth, natural swing and learned to bat left-handed by imitating his idol, Mickey Mantle.

The San Diego Padres selected Grubb in the first round of the secondary phase of the January 1971 draft. Grubb spent less than two years in the minor leagues, batting .333 in seven games for the Padres in 1972. In 1973, he hit .311 with eight home runs and 37 RBIs as a rookie, setting a club record for the highest batting average by a left-handed batter and contending for National League Rookie of the Year honors. Besides

John Grubb

making at least three hits in nine different games, Grubb batted .583 with five RBIs as a pinch-hitter. He hit .286 with eight home runs and 42 RBIs in 1974 as the most consistent Padre batter and made the National League All-Star team. Grubb collected at least three hits nine times and made four in a 7-4 loss to the Montreal Expos at Jarry Park on August 19. He also hit safely in 22 of 26 games from late August to mid-September.

A hand injury caused his batting average to drop to .269 in 1975. Grubb clouted four home runs with 38 RBIs and led the National League with 36 doubles, setting a Padre record. He established a franchise record for left-handers with 149 hits. Grubb collected four hits against the Atlanta Braves on April 27 and St. Louis Cardinals on May 19, clouting a dramatic ninth-inning home run to defeat the Cardinals, 1-0. After batting .284 with five home runs and 27 RBIs in 1976, he was traded that December to the Cleveland Indians for George Hendrick. Upon his departure, Grubb ranked first among Padres in career batting average (.286), second in doubles (101), fourth in runs (235) and hits (513), and sixth in triples (11). His career batting average remains fifth best in Padre history.

Grubb played with the Cleveland Indians in 1977 and 1978, the Texas Rangers from 1978 to 1982, and the Detroit Tigers from 1983 to 1987. In 16 major-league seasons, he batted .278 with 99 home runs and 475 RBIs. His 21-game hitting streak in 1979 tied for the longest in the American League. He spent nine stints on the disabled list and had a rib removed in 1981 to relieve a circulatory problem. Grubb became a key designated hitter with the Tigers and won Game 2 of the 1984 American League Championship Series with a double. He and his wife, Linda, reside in Chesterfield, Virginia and have one son, Chris.

TONY GWYNN

Tony Gwynn

Tony Gwynn, the most popular player in San Diego history, starred as an outfielder with the Padres from July 1982 until his retirement in 2001 and holds most club batting records. The 5-foot 11-inch, 200-pound Gwynn, who batted and threw left-handed, was born into a baseball family on May 9, 1960 in Los Angeles, California. His two brothers, Charles, Jr. and Chris, played professional baseball. Charles, Jr. was drafted by the Cleveland Indians, while Chris performed for three different major-league clubs. Gwynn starred in both baseball and basketball at San Diego State University. He hit over .400 in baseball his junior and senior seasons and starred as a basketball point guard, being drafted by the San Diego Clippers of the National Basketball Association.

The San Diego Padres selected Gwynn in the third round of the June 1981 draft. In 1981, Gwynn led the Northwest League with a .331 batting average for Walla Walla, Washington and hit .462 in 23 games for Amarillo, Texas of the Texas League. After batting .328 with Hawaii of the Pacific Coast League in 1982, he joined the San Diego Padres on July 19 and batted .289 with 12 doubles and 17 RBIs. In his major-league debut that night, Gwynn doubled, singled, and drove in a run in a 7-6 home loss to the Philadelphia Phillies. He hit safely in 15 consecutive games from July 21 through August 4, making four hits against the Atlanta Braves at Atlanta-Fulton County Stadium on July 27. His first major-league home run came off Bill Campbell of the Chicago Cubs at Wrigley Field on August 22. Gwynn broke his left wrist diving for a fly ball at Three Rivers Stadium against the Pittsburgh Pirates on August 27 and was sidelined until September 13. Upon his return, he batted .348 in his final 16 games.

Gwynn hit .368 in the Puerto Rican Winter League until fracturing his right wrist in December 1982, delaying his 1983 season until June. Gwynn rejoined the San Diego Padres on June 21. He hit .309, sixth best in the National League, with 37 RBIs in 86 games in 1983. After struggling through July, he hit .333 the remainder of the season. Gwynn, who batted consistently at home and on the road, set a club record with a 25-game consecutive hitting streak from August 21 through September 19. The streak, the longest in the major leagues in 1983, broke the Padre mark of 21, set in August by Bobby Brown. In a doubleheader home sweep of the Cincinnati Reds on August 6, Gwynn recorded a triple, a double, and two singles in the first game and singled twice in the nightcap.

In 1984, Gwynn led the National League with a .351 batting average, 213 hits, and 69 multiple-hit games and became the first Padre to collect over 200 hits in a season. His batting average marked the second best by a left-handed batter since Stan Musial in 1957. Gwynn helped the Padres capture the National League West Division, batting .434 in April, .361 in June, and .398 in July. He enjoyed three consecutive three-hit games from June 1 through June 3 against the San Francisco Giants at Candlestick Park and boasted three 12-game hitting streaks. Gwynn recorded his 194th hit on September 9 against the Houston Astros to break Gene Richards's franchise record and hit 177 singles, shattering the previous club mark by 22. He batted .443 against the San Francisco Giants and .422 against the Houston Astros and established a career best with 33 stolen bases. In the 1984 National League Championship Series, Gwynn hit .368 with three doubles and three RBIs to help the Padres defeat the Chicago Cubs. His ninth-inning single in Game 4 set the stage for Steve Garvey's dramatic, game-winning home run, while his two hits, including a game-winning double in the seventh inning of Game 5, sent the Padres to the World Series. He batted .263 in the World Series against the Detroit Tigers, but the Padres lost the fall classic four games to one. Besides starting the All-Star game, he made *The Sporting News'* National League All-Star team, won the Padres' Most Valuable Player honors, and finished third in the National League Most Valuable Player balloting.

Gwynn batted .317, fourth best in the National League, in 1985 with 90 runs, 29 doubles, and six home runs. His 197 hits placed third in the National League. He homered in the ninth inning on April 28 to defeat the Los Angeles Dodgers, 1-0, at Dodger Stadium, ending Fernando Valenzuela's consecutive streak of not allowing an earned run in 41.2 innings. In the second game of a June 7 doubleheader against the Cincinnati Reds at Riverfront Stadium, his eleventh-inning home run off Ted Power gave the Padres a 3-2 victory. After making the National League All-Star team for the second consecutive year, he batted .330 in August and .337 in September. Gwynn ended the season with a 12-game hitting streak and led the major leagues for the second straight campaign in multiple-hit games with 63.

Gwynn won his first Rawlings Gold Glove Award for defensive excellence in 1986, when his 19 assists ranked second in the major leagues. On August 27 at home against the New York Mets, he threw out one runner at the plate and two runners trying to stretch singles into doubles. Gwynn led National League outfielders in games (160), chances (360), and putouts (337) and batted .329, pacing the National League with 211 hits and striking out only 35 times in 701 plate appearances. Gwynn shared the National League lead in runs scored (107), finished third in total bases (300) and fifth in on-base percentage (.381), and tied for fifth in triples (7). Gwynn's 14 round-trippers surpassed his entire major-league output before 1985. He won Padre Most Valuable Player honors, made *The Sporting News'* Silver Slugger and National League All-Star teams, and earned the Padres Player of the Month Award in April, June, and July.

Gwynn homered twice on April 27 in a 6-4 home victory over the San Francisco Giants. He batted .361 in May with two four-hit games. His three-run homer with two outs in the bottom of the ninth inning off Jesse Orosco on May 23 gave the Padres a 7-4 triumph over the New York Mets. Gwynn helped the Padres sweep a three-game series against the Los Angeles Dodgers at Dodger Stadium from June 20 through June 22. During August, Gwynn authored five three-hit efforts in a six-game period. On September 20 against the Houston Astros at the Astrodome, he produced his fifth four-hit game and became just the fifth National Leaguer to steal five bases in a game. Gwynn hit over .400 against the St. Louis Cardinals and the New York Mets.

In 1987 Gwynn established several Padre records. His .370 batting average and 218 hits led both major leagues. He broke his own franchise records for batting average and hits and also set Padre standards for runs scored (119), triples (13) and intentional walks (26). His batting average was the highest in the National League since Stan Musial hit .376 in 1948. Gwynn became the first National Leaguer to bat .370 and steal 50 bases in the same season. He batted .390 at Jack Murphy Stadium and enjoyed 64 multiple-hit games, including his first five-hit games at home on April 16 in a 3-2, 10-inning victory over the Los Angeles Dodgers and on August 11 in a 7-6 triumph over the Atlanta Braves. He stole 56 bases, becoming the fifth Padre with 50 thefts in a season.

Marvell Wynne, Gwynn, and John Kruk hit consecutive home runs off Roger Mason in a 13-6 home loss to the San Francisco Giants on April 13, becoming the first major-leaguers to start a game with three straight round-trippers. Gwynn began June with a 12-game hitting streak and ended the month with an 11-game hitting streak. During June, he batted .473 with 16 RBIs and a .786 slugging percentage. Gwynn won the Padres Player of the Month awards in April and June and National League Player of the Month in June. He twice garnered National League Player of the Week honors in June, hitting .577 from June 1 through June 7 and .542 from June 22 through June 28. After batting .402 in August, Gwynn assumed the leadoff batting spot on September 4 and hit .380 thereafter. His best batting average of .466 came against the Atlanta Braves. He won his second Rawlings Gold Glove Award, was selected for his fourth consecutive All-Star game, and made *The Sporting News'* Silver Slugger team for the third time.

Nagging injuries caused Gwynn's batting average to slump to .313 in 1988, but he still repeated as National League batting champion. No National Leaguer had won a batting title with a lower average than Larry Doyle of the New York Giants with .320 in 1915. Gwynn led the Padres in hits (163), RBIs (70), and stolen bases (26), winning team Most Valuable Player honors for the fourth time, and seldom struck out. He underwent surgery on his left hand on March 11 to give the tendon unrestricted movement and was irritated by the scar tissue all season.

Gwynn's 1,000th major-league hit came on a first-inning single off Nolan Ryan of the Houston Astros at home on April 22. He missed 21 games in May after injuring his right thumb in a fall on artificial turf in Pittsburgh. His batting average plunged to just .246 on July 2. Gwynn won National League Player of the Month honors in July, batting .406 with 17 RBIs and an 18-game hitting streak. He knocked in a then career-best four runs on July 15 in a 7-3 triumph over the St. Louis Cardinals at Busch Stadium and batted .488 against them for the season. He became the Padres' career hit leader with 1,135 on September 17 against the Atlanta Braves, breaking Dave Winfield's record in 570 fewer at-bats.

Gwynn paced the senior circuit with a .336 batting average, 203 hits, and 62 multihit games in 1989 as a center fielder and right fielder. Six hits in head-to-head competition with Will Clark of the San Francisco Giants on the final weekend of the season ensured the title. Gwynn became the first National Leaguer since Stan Musial to win three consecutive batting titles. Clark led Gwynn by four percentage points on September 27, but the latter batted .429 in his final five games. Gwynn ranked sixth in stolen bases (40) and seventh in on-base percentage (.389). Besides pacing the senior circuit with a .345 batting average on the road and a .351 batting average against right-handed pitching, was the hardest National Leaguer to strike out, fanning once per 22.6 plate appearances.

Gwynn clouted two of his four home runs in the first nine games and enjoyed a 13-game hitting streak in June. He won National League Player of the Week honors, batting .516 with six multi-hit contests from June 5 through June 11. From June 16 to June 18, Gwynn tied a Padre mark by reaching base in nine consecutive plate appearances, combining seven hits and two walks. Defensively, he won his third Rawlings Gold Glove Award and finished third in outfield assists with 13. After a year's absence, he made the National League All-Star and *The Sporting News'* All-Star teams. He batted over .400 against the Houston Astros and the San Francisco Giants.

In 1990, Gwynn batted .309 with 177 hits and 72 RBIs, finishing sixth in the National League batting race and eighth in hits. He proved the toughest to strike out and clouted 10 triples, second best in the senior circuit. Gwynn boasted a 12-game hitting streak from May 9 through May 22 and won the Padres Player of the Month award in June. Two of his four home runs came in a series with the Pittsburgh Pirates at Three Rivers Stadium from July 12 through July 15. He missed the final 19 games of the season with a fractured right index finger after trying to make a catch against the wall in Atlanta-Fulton County Stadium on September 15. Besides batting .412 against the Philadelphia Phillies, Gwynn appeared in his sixth All-

Tony Gwynn

Star game and earned his fourth Rawlings Gold Glove Award. Defensively, he made only five errors with 11 outfield assists.

In 1991, Gwynn ranked third in batting with a .317 average and knocked in 62 runs. He hit .425 with 22 RBIs from May 11 through June 9 to raise his batting average to a season-high .373 and boasted hitting streaks of 12 and 15 games. Gwynn won National League Player of the Week honors from June 4 through June 9, batting .522 with four RBIs. After earning another All-Star game selection, however, he batted just .243 and missed the final 21 games because of arthroscopic surgery on his left knee. Despite the injury, Gwynn still ranked second in the senior circuit in road batting average (.325) and triples (11) and third in multiple-hit games (50). He again proved the toughest major-leaguer to fan and earned a fifth Rawlings Gold Glove Award.

Gwynn batted .317 with six home runs and 41 RBIs in 1992. From May 5 through May 31, he hit .416 with four home runs and 19 RBIs. Gwynn made four hits in a 9-2 romp over the Pittsburgh Pirates at Three Rivers Stadium on May 15. Although fracturing the tip of his right middle finger when he slammed a car door on it, Gwynn started in the All-Star game at San Diego. He made five hits in one game for just the third time in his major-league career against the San Francisco Giants at Candlestick Park on September 8, but sprained the medial collateral ligament in his left knee and missed the rest of the season. Gwynn, who underwent arthroscopic surgery in October, struck out just 16 times in 520 plate appearances, or once every 35.6 at-bats. No other major leaguer with over 500 at bats struck out fewer than 20 times. Gwynn ranked fourth in the senior circuit with a .326 road batting average and shared third with 53 multi-hit contests, batting .422 against the Atlanta Braves.

Gwynn experienced a resurgence in 1993, when he batted .358 and trailed only Andres Galarraga of the Colorado Rockies for the crown. The .358 mark represented the fifth-highest batting average of his career and third best in the major leagues that year. Despite playing only 122 games, he shared fourth place in the National League with 41 doubles, tied for fifth with 54 multi-hit games, and struck out only once every 28 plate appearances. Gwynn narrowly missed tying Terry Kennedy's club record for most doubles in a season, and on August 4 he collected six hits for the first time in a 12-inning, 11-10, home squeaker over the San Francisco Giants. The performance marked his fourth time that season with at least five hits, tying a major-league record shared by Wee Willie Keeler, Ty Cobb, and Stan Musial.

Gwynn's first five-hit game, on April 18, helped defeat the St. Louis Cardinals, 10-6, at home. His second five-hit game came on April 30 in a 7-6 triumph over the New York Mets. Gwynn made four hits the next night in a 5-3 victory over New York, finishing the three-game series with a .786 batting average. He matched a career best by driving in four runs in a 14-2 rout over the Los Angeles Dodgers at home on June 10 and drove in three runs with a bases-loaded double in the ninth inning the next day to give the Padres a 5-4 win over Los Angeles. Gwynn boasted five three-hit contests in nine games from July 4 through July 16 and made five hits on July 27 in an 8-0 triumph over the Chicago Cubs at Wrigley Field, breaking Dave Winfield's club mark of 626 RBIs with his second-inning RBI single. During August, he led the major leagues with a .448 batting average to garner National League Player of the Month honors. Gwynn recorded his 2,000th major-league hit on August 6 with a sixth-inning single off Bruce Ruffin of the Colorado Rockies in the second game of a home doubleheader. Among contemporary players, only Wade Boggs and Kirby Puckett had attained 2,000 hits quicker. Gwynn made the All-Star team for the ninth time and underwent arthroscopic surgery on his left knee in mid-September.

Gwynn enjoyed his best major-league campaign in the strike-shortened 1994 season, capturing his fifth National League batting title with a career-high .394 average. His batting average marked the highest in the senior circuit since Bill Terry of the New York Giants hit .401 in 1930 and the best in the major leagues since native San Diegan Ted Williams batted .406 in 1941. He also led the major leagues in hits (165), multi-hit games (54), and at bats to strikeout ratio (419-19). Gwynn paced the senior circuit with a .454 on-base percentage, while finishing third in doubles (35) and tenth in slugging percentage (.568). His 12 home runs and 64 RBIs were the second highest of his major-league career.

Gwynn batted .769 with 10 hits in a three-game home series against the Philadelphia Phillies between April 22 and April 24, tying Padre records by making eight straight hits and reaching base safely nine consecutive times. On April 23, he made hits in all five plate appearances for the eighth time in his major-league career to spark an 8-2 triumph. Gwynn drove in a career-high five runs on May 30 in a 10-2 home win over the Pittsburgh Pirates and also produced two four-hit games. During the season, he authored six hitting streaks of at least seven games. Gwynn batted .475 in August, .571 against the Philadelphia Phillies, .420 during day games, and .403 at Jack Murphy Stadium. Gwynn played the entire All-Star Game and scored the game-winning run in the bottom of the tenth inning in an 8-7 victory to give the National League its first win since 1987. Besides being selected the club's Most Valuable Player for the fifth time, he was voted to *The Sporting News'* Silver Slugger and National League All-Star teams.

Gwynn hit a major-league best .368 to win the National League batting title for the sixth time in 1995. He became the first major leaguer to bat over .350 three consecutive seasons since Joe Medwick of the St. Louis Cardinals between 1935 and 1937. Gwynn paced the major leagues in batting average against right-handers (.389), at home (.387), on grass (.381), and in day games (.431) and led the National League by hitting .394 with runners in scoring position. He exhibited more power with 90 RBIs and belted his first career grand slam after 6,991 major-league at-bats on August 22 to lift the Padres over the Philadelphia Phillies, 5-3, at Veterans Stadium. Besides leading the major leagues in multi-hit games (65), Gwynn shared first in the National League in hits (197) and ranked third in on-base percentage (.404). He led the senior circuit in singles (154) for a record sixth season and struck out only 15 times, once every 38.5 plate appearances. Gwynn also stole 17 bases, his most since 1990.

His 26th career four-hit game came on June 4 in an 8-4 home victory over the Montreal Expos. He compiled a team-high 15-game hitting streak from July 1 to July 17, batting .431 with five doubles and 15 RBIs. Gwynn also recorded hitting streaks of 13, 12, nine, and eight games and led the major leagues by hitting .405 in September and October. Gwynn started in his eighth All-Star Game and earned his sixth Silver Slugger and Padres Most Valuable Player awards.

Gwynn batted .353 in 1996 to win his seventh career and third consecutive batting title, helping the Padres capture the National League West. Gwynn, one of only seven major leaguers to win three straight batting titles, joined Ty Cobb as the only major leaguers to boast two distinct streaks of three consecutive batting titles. He hit .350 or better for the fourth straight season, the longest in the National League since Rogers Hornsby, who had six in a row from 1920 through 1925.

Gwynn opened the 1996 season by batting .462 in his first 14 games. He clouted his first home run of the season, a three-run round-tripper, with two outs in the bottom of the ninth inning off Tony Fossas of the St. Louis Cardinals on June 5 to give the Padres a 6-4 home victory. On August 14, he became just the 71st major leaguer to reach the 2,500 hit mark with an eleventh-inning, opposite-field single off Hector Carrasco of the Cincinnati Reds for his third hit that night at Riverfront Stadium. He hit safely in 11 consecutive games from September 4 to September 16. His hit on September 28 against the Los Angeles Dodgers at Dodger Stadium in the next-to-last game of the regular season drove in the two runs that clinched a post-season berth for the Padres. He hit a two-out, two-run single through the hole on the left side with the bases loaded in the eighth inning off Mark Guthrie to drive in Jody Reed and Greg Vaughn, giving San Diego a 4-2 win. Gwynn called the clutch single "the biggest hit" of his major-league career. The Padres completed the sweep of the Dodgers the next day to win the National League West title. Besides hitting .381 with runners in scoring position, Gwynn led the major leagues with a .471 batting average after the sixth inning, authored 48 multi-hit games, and struck out only 17 times in 498 plate appearances. The St. Louis Cardinals eliminated the Padres in the National League Division Series, but Gwynn batted .308 with one RBI. Gwynn, the only Padre remaining from the 1984 post-season, had played 1,648 regular season games between post-season appearances. He underwent surgery on his right heel in late October.

In 1997, Gwynn won his eighth batting title with a major-league best .372 to tie Honus Wagner for the most National League batting crowns and became the only major-leaguer to win four batting titles in two separate decades. Gwynn led the major leagues in batting for the fifth time. Gwynn flirted with a .400 batting average for part of the season and on July 14 singled, doubled, and tripled with three RBIs to key a 5-3 triumph over the San Francisco Giants at home.

Despite using just a 32.5-inch, 31-ounce bat, Gwynn demonstrated unusual power in 1997. He established career highs with 17 home runs and 119 RBIs and shattered Padre records with 220 hits and 49 doubles. Gwynn posted personal bests with 68 extra-base hits and 324 total bases and paced the National League with 67 multi-hit games, including four four-hit contests. He made the National League All-Star team for the thirteenth time and was voted to start for the tenth time. He finished sixth in the National League Most Valuable Player voting and was named Padres' Most Valuable Player for the seventh time. *The Sporting News* selected Gwynn to its National League Silver Slugger team for the seventh time and its National League All-Star team for the sixth time.

Gwynn achieved several other remarkable batting feats in 1997. He led the major leagues in hits and tied Pete Rose's mark for leading the senior circuit seven times in hits. Besides being the hardest National Leaguer to strike out, Gwynn ranked second in the senior circuit in doubles (49), tied for sixth in RBIs (119), and shared eighth in on-base percentage (.409) and slugging percentage (.547). On June 7, he slugged his 100th career home run off Donne Wall in a 5-4, 10-inning home triumph over the Houston Astros, becoming the third Padre to reach the century mark.

Gwynn's 119 RBIs established a career high and marked the second highest in club history. He became the oldest major-leaguer to drive in 100 runs in a season for the first time, taking 16 major-league seasons to reach the century mark. Besides batting a major-league best .459 with runners in scoring position, Gwynn hit .615 with four doubles and a homer with the bases loaded. His grand slam on June 26 triggered a 9-7 win over the Los Angeles Dodgers at Dodger Stadium and was the first inside-the-park grand slam in the major leagues since August 1991. Gwynn won National League Player of the Month honors for May, batting .447 with four homers, 20 RBIs, a .650 slugging percentage, and a .478 on-base percentage. He reached safely in 20 consecutive games from May 20 through June 10 and hit in 19 straight contests from June 21 through July 14.

The 1998 season ended Gwynn's streak of batting titles, but he again paced the Padres with a .321 batting average. He hit over .300 for the 16th consecutive season, tying Stan Musial for the second-longest streak in National League history and the third-longest streak in major-league history. Gwynn also produced 16 home runs, 51 extra-base hits, and 69 RBIs to help San Diego record its best winning percentage in franchise history and capture the National League West for the second time in three years. He was named to his 14th National League All-Star team and again was selected to start. He struck out only 18 times in 505 plate appearances, making him the toughest to fan.

Gwynn recorded 46 multi-hit games and made hits in all five plate appearances, homered, and knocked in two runs in a 7-3 home victory over the Chicago Cubs on April 28. He recorded two nine-game hitting streaks, batting .515 from July 28 through August 5.

Gwynn recorded his 1,000th career RBI on May 16 with a pinch-hit sacrifice fly off Curt Schilling in a 3-2 home win over the Philadelphia Phillies and collected his 2,900th career hit on August 3 with a third-inning single to right field off Dustin Hermanson of the Montreal Expos at Olympic Stadium. He clouted two home runs for the third time in his career to key a 13-3 rout over the Cincinnati Reds at Riverfront Stadium on July 17.

Gwynn made his third post-season and second World Series appearance, batting .298 with three doubles, a home run, and seven RBIs in 14 games. He hit safely in 11 post-season contests, including four two-hit-games and one three-hit effort. Gwynn struggled in the National League Division Series against the Houston Astros, batting just .200 with two doubles and two RBIs. He threw out Moises Alou trying to advance from first base to third base on a single to right field with no outs in the seventh inning of Game 3 and the Padres ahead, 1-0. Atlanta Braves pitchers limited Gwynn to a .231 batting average with one double and two RBIs in the National League Championship Series. Gwynn made two hits with an RBI in San Diego's 10-inning, 3-2 win in Game 1 and two hits in the pennant-clinching, 5-0 triumph in Game 6. He returned to the World Series for the first time since 1984. The New York Yankees swept the Padres in the Fall Classic, but Gwynn batted a team-best .500 with eight hits, a home run, and three RBIs. He recorded three hits with a fifth-inning two-run homer off David Wells in Game 1 at Yankee Stadium and two hits in both Games 3 and 4 at Qualcomm Stadium.

Although missing 44 games, Gwynn in 1999 led the Padres with a .338 batting average, 139 hits, and 41 multi-hit games. He batted over .300 for the 17th consecutive season, tying Honus Wagner's National League record. On August 6, Gwynn became the 22nd major-leaguer to collect 3,000 hits with a first-inning single to right center field on a 1-2 pitch off Dan Smith of the Montreal Expos at Olympic Stadium. His four hits sparked a 12-10 victory that night. On April 28, he belted his 500th career double at home off Armando Benitez of the New York Mets. On, August 14, clouted a two-run homer in the second inning off Ryan Dempster in a 6-4 win over the Florida Marlins in his 9,000th career at-bat. Gwynn made seven hits in a September 29 doubleheader sweep by the St. Louis Cardinals at Busch Stadium.

Gwynn suffered a chip fracture near his right elbow when hit by a pitch in the Padres' April 3, 2000 season opener against the New York Mets at Shea Stadium. He on April 23 collected his 2,331st career major-league single to move past Cap Anson into tenth place on the all-time list in an 11-10 triumph over the Houston Astros at Enron Field. His batting average rose to over .300 in June, but he needed to have his left knee drained several times and underwent season-ending arthroscopic surgery on June 27. Gwynn finished the 2000 season with a .323 batting average in just 36 games. San Diego in October declined to exercise its $6 million option on his contract, and the team re-signed him on December 7.

Gwynn finished his illustrious major-league career in 2001, becoming the seventeenth player with at least 20 years service to only one major-league club. He appeared in 71 games mainly as a pinch-hitter, leading the Padres with a .324 batting average. His pinch-hit single on April 4 against the San Francisco Giants at Pacific Bell Park moved him ahead of Dave Winfield for sixteenth on the career hit list with 3,111. On April 17, Gwynn tripled, doubled, and singled for the final three-hit game of his major-league career in a 9-5 home loss to the Colorado Rockies. On April 20 he started in right field and Rickey Henderson started in left field, marking the first time since 1945 that two players at least 40 years old started the same game in the outfield. Gwynn went on the disabled list May 11 with a strained right hamstring and announced on June 28 that he would retire following the 2001 season.

On July 10, Commissioner Bud Selig presented Gwynn and Cal Ripken of the Baltimore Orioles the Commissioner's Historical Achievement Award in a surprise sixth-inning ceremony during the All-Star Game at Safeco Field in Seattle. On August 11, Gwynn made his last appearance in right field and clouted his final round-tripper, a two-run homer off pitcher Joe Beimel in the sixth inning, in a 5-2 victory over the Pittsburgh Pirates at PNC Park. On September 19, he singled as a pinch hitter in the tenth inning for his final hit at Dodger Stadium, the park of his boyhood, to help the Padres edge the Los Angeles Dodgers, 4-3. San Diego had not swept a three-game series at Dodger Stadium since 1983. On October 6, Gwynn doubled in a run as a pinch-hitter for his 3,141st and final hit of his major-league career in a 10-4 victory over the visiting Colorado Rockies. The next day, he grounded out as a pinch-hitter for pitcher Jeremy Fikac in the ninth-inning against the Colorado Rockies in his final plate appearance. The Padres honored him before and after the game, attended by a sellout crowd of 60,013 at Qualcomm Stadium.

Gwynn ranks as the Padre career leader in batting average (.338), runs scored (1,383), hits (3,141), doubles (543), triples (85), RBIs (1,138), stolen bases (319), walks (790), and games played (2,440). He clouted 135 career home runs, trailing only Nate Colbert and Dave Winfield, and is second in on-base percentage (.388) and third in slugging percentage (.459). Upon his retirement, Gwynn led all active major-leaguers in batting average and hits and ranked second in doubles, fourth in total bases, and fifth in runs. He paced the National League a record seven times in singles and shares with Pete Rose the mark for leading the senior circuit seven times in hits.

Gwynn captured eight batting titles and consistently ranked among the top 10 in the National League batting race. He owned 901 multi-hit games, including 36 four-hit games, eight five-hit games, and one six-hit contest, and trailed Pete Rose by one for most National League games with at least five hits. The 15-time All-Star started the Summer Classic 11 times. Besides earning five Rawlings Gold Glove awards for his defense, he made *The Sporting News'* National League Silver Slugger team seven times and the National League All-Star squad six times. Gwynn garnered National League Player of the Month honors five times and the Padres' Most Valuable Player award seven times. In 1995, he received the Branch Rickey Award for being the top community activist in major-league baseball and the Chairman's Award for best exemplifying the community spirit of the team owners. Four years later, he won the Roberto Clemente Man of the Year Award for combining sportsmanship and community involvement with excellence on the field and was inducted into the World Sports Humanitarian Hall of Fame.

Gwynn, admired for his work ethic, combined video technology with hours of extra drill to transform his natural batting talent into consistent efficiency at the plate and his once-suspect fielding ability into above-average skill. A model of consistency and stability, he ranked among the game's most complete players. Gwynn, whose one unfulfilled goal was not winning a World Series, served as volunteer batting and outfield coach at San Diego State University in 2002 and replaced Jim Dietz as head baseball coach in June 2002. In March, ESPN hired Gwynn as a baseball analyst. Gwynn lives in Poway, California with his wife, Alicia, and their two children, Anthony II and Anisha. Anthony II, a student at San Diego State University, was named the baseball program's top defensive player in 2001.

JOEY HAMILTON

Joey Hamilton pitched for the San Diego Padres from 1994 through 1998. The 6-foot 4-inch, 230-pound Hamilton, who bats and throws right-handed, was born on September 9, 1970 in Statesboro, Georgia, and attended Georgia Southern University. Hamilton compiled a 35-19 record in three seasons and paced NCAA Division I pitchers in victories with 18 in 1990, leading Georgia Southern to the College World Series. In 1991, *Baseball America* named him the top college pitching prospect. The San Diego Padres selected Hamilton in the first round of the June 1991 free agent draft. He spent 1992 and 1993 in the minor leagues and started 1994 with the Las Vegas, Nevada Stars of the Pacific Coast League.

In May 1994, the San Diego Padres promoted Hamilton. Hamilton finished 9-6 with a 2.98 ERA, one shutout, and 61 strikeouts in 108.2 innings. He paced the Padres in victories and shared the lead with

Joey Hamilton

Steve Trachsel for the most by a rookie. Hamilton induced batters to hit ground balls and hurled relatively short games. His major-league debut came at home on May 24, when he yielded three runs in six innings in a 6-3 triumph over the San Francisco Giants. The 23-year-old became the first Padre rookie to win his first two starts since Dave Freisleben in 1974 and boasted a 3-0 ledger with a 2.36 ERA in his first four starts, blanking the Cincinnati Reds, 6-0, on a six-hitter at Riverfront Stadium on June 25. He won three of his final four starts, fanning 18 batters. His honors included making the Topps 1994 Rookie All-Star team as a right-handed pitcher and ranking fifth in *Baseball America*'s Top 20 Rookies list.

Although slipping to a 6-9 mark in 1995, Hamilton boasted a 3.08 ERA with two shutouts and fanned 123 batters in 204.1 innings. In his first full major-league season, he ranked fifth in the National League in ERA and fourth in innings pitched. Hamilton and Andy Ashby were the first Padre duo to make the top five in ERA since Ed Whitson and Bruce Hurst in 1989.

Hamilton struggled until hurling nine shutout innings at home on June 3 against the Montreal Expos. Pedro Martinez posted nine perfect frames, triumphing, 1-0, in 10 innings. Hamilton blanked the St. Louis Cardinals, 3-0, on a two-hitter at Busch Stadium on June 14 and the Colorado Rockies, 2-0, at home on June 24, both contests lasting under two hours. He struck out eight Atlanta Braves at Atlanta-Fulton County Stadium on July 23, losing, 2-1, in 94-degree heat.

In 1996, Hamilton boasted a 15-9 mark with a 4.17 ERA and one shutout, fanning 184 batters in 211.2 innings. He led the Padres and established career highs in wins, strikeouts, and complete games (3), ranking eighth in the National League in winning percentage (.625) and ninth in strikeouts. Hamilton fared 12-2 with a 3.03 ERA in 18 home games. The New York Mets and Colorado Rockies were the only two teams to defeat him at Jack Murphy Stadium.

Hamilton logged a 5-1 ledger in April, becoming the first Padre hurler to record five victories that month. He blanked the Houston Astros, 2-0, at home on April 29, in just two hours and six minutes. Hamilton established career highs with 10 strikeouts in a 5-2 home triumph over the Philadelphia Phillies on May 22, in an 8-2 loss to the Florida Marlins at Joe Robbie Stadium on July 28, and in an 8-0 shutout over the New York Mets on August 18 at Monterrey, Mexico. Besides hurling a shutout for seven innings against the Mets, Hamilton clouted his first major-league home run off Paul Wilson in the fourth inning. No other major-league hurler has clouted a home run outside the United States or Canada.

After struggling at mid-season, Hamilton regained his form with a 3-1 mark in August and hurled consecutive home victories in September. He combined with Willie Blair for an 8-0 shutout of the Cincinnati Reds on September 15 and defeated the Los Angeles Dodgers, 4-2, five days later, fanning Dave Clark with the bases loaded to end the seventh frame. The Padres lost three Hamilton starts by 1-0 scores. He allowed first-inning runs and just three hits in eight innings in 1-0 losses to the Cincinnati Reds at Riverfront Stadium on May 11 and the Houston Astros at the Astrodome on July 22 and tossed a four-hit, eight-inning shutout without decision against the St. Louis Cardinals at Busch Stadium on August 7. In the three 1-0 setbacks, the hard-luck Hamilton allowed only two runs and 10 hits in 24 innings.

Hamilton became the first Padre to register 99 miles per hour on the Jack Murphy Stadium scoreboard radar gun in a July 6 relief appearance against the San Francisco Giants. He led San Diego with 14 wild pitches and nine hit batsmen. He lost his only start in the National League Division Series against the St. Louis Cardinals, posting a 4.50 ERA.

In 1997, Hamilton boasted a 12-7 mark, posted a 4.25 ERA, and fanned 124 batters in 192.2 innings. He led the Padres in victories and pitched very effectively with a 9-1 record and 3.90 ERA in 14 road games, but he struggled with a 3-6 mark and a 4.56 ERA in 17 games at Qualcomm Stadium. His only road loss came in a 9-6 setback at the Kingdome on September 1, when the Seattle Mariners knocked him out in the fourth inning. Although batting only .130, Hamilton led Padre pitchers with two solo home runs and six RBIs. He homered off Hideo Nomo of the Los Angeles Dodgers at home on May 22 in the fifth inning in a 4-1 win and off Chan Ho Park of the Los Angeles Dodgers at Dodger Stadium on June 27 in the third inning in a 7-5 victory.

Hamilton made his first career opening day start, triumphing over the New York Mets, 12-5, on April 1 and benefiting from an 11-run Padre sixth inning. Hamilton won three consecutive starts, defeating the Cincinnati Reds, 6-2, at Riverfront Stadium on May

17, the Los Angeles Dodgers, 4-1, at home on May 22 and the Houston Astros, 6-3, at the Astrodome on June 1. Hamilton posted a career-high six straight victories, defeating the Los Angeles Dodgers, 7-5, at Dodger Stadium on June 27, the Seattle Mariners, 8-5, at home on July 2, the Colorado Rockies, 11-7, at Coors Field on July 12, the St. Louis Cardinals, 3-1, at Busch Stadium on July 17, the Montreal Expos, 8-2, at Olympic Stadium on August 1, and the Cincinnati Reds, 6-3, at Riverfront Stadium on August 6. He needed only 82 pitches in the August 1 complete-game four-hitter over Montreal. His other triumphs came against the Los Angeles Dodgers on September 24 and in relief against the San Francisco Giants on September 28.

Hamilton split 26 decisions with a 4.27 ERA and 147 strikeouts in 1998, posting career highs with 34 starts, 106 walks, and 217.1 innings. Besides pacing the Padres in losses, earned runs allowed, and walks, he suffered a six-game losing streak from May 7 through June 3. He impressed pitching coach Dave Stewart by winning all four decisions in July and allowing the Atlanta Braves only one run on August 11. Hamilton made two brief appearances against the Houston Astros in the National League Division Series and lost one start in the National League Championship Series against the Atlanta Braves. He hurled just one inning in the World Series against the New York Yankees.

In December 1998, the San Diego Padres traded Hamilton to the Toronto Blue Jays for three players. As a Padre, Hamilton authored a 55-44 record with a 3.83 ERA and struck out 639 batters in 934.2 innings. He completed seven of 142 starts and hurled four shutouts. Upon his departure, Hamilton ranked second in winning percentage (.556), fifth in victories, seventh in strikeouts, eighth in innings and games started, and ninth in walks (343). He logged a 7-8 record and a 6.52 ERA for third-place Toronto in 1999 and finished 2-1 with a 3.55 ERA in just six starts in an injury-riddled 2000 campaign. In 2001, Hamilton struggled with a 5-8 mark and a 5.89 ERA for Toronto before being released that August. He won one of three decisions with a 6.37 ERA after joining the Cincinnati Reds. During eight major-league seasons, he has logged a 70-63 ledger with a 4.29 ERA, completed seven of 192 starts, fanned 802 batters in 1,205.1 innings, and spun four shutouts. He and his wife, Angie, have one child and reside in Statesboro, Georgia.

ANDY HAWKINS

Andy Hawkins pitched for the San Diego Padres from 1982 through 1988. The 6-foot 3-inch, 200-pound right-hander was born on January 21, 1960 in Waco, Texas and attended Waco schools. The San Diego Padres drafted him in the first round as the fifth overall pick in June 1978. Hawkins, a power pitcher with a good fastball and outstanding delivery, spent parts of six seasons in the minor leagues between 1978 and 1983.

Hawkins compiled a 2-5 mark with a 4.10 ERA in 1982 after joining the San Diego Padres from Hawaii of the Pacific Coast League on July 15. Two days later, he lost his major-league debut at home to the Montreal Expos, 4-1. His first major-league victory came at home on July 23, when he hurled a seven-hit, 11-4 complete game over the New York Mets. After struggling in his next two starts, Hawkins allowed just one run and five hits in a 4-1 home victory over the Cincinnati Reds on August 7 and only two runs in a 2-1 loss to the St. Louis Cardinals at Busch Stadium on August 18. He did not surrender a run in five relief appearances.

The Padres in 1983 recalled Hawkins from Las Vegas, Nevada on April 19. Hawkins won five of 12 decisions with a 2.93 ERA. He made seven consecutive strong starts in April and May, posting a 3-3 record and one shutout. His three heartbreaking losses were 2-0 to the St. Louis Cardinals at Busch Stadium on April 24, 3-2 to the Los Angeles Dodgers at home on May 15, and 2-0 to the Montreal Expos at Olympic Stadium on May 25. His first major-league shutout came on May 20, when he blanked Steve Carlton's Philadelphia Phillies on a 5-0, five-hitter at Veterans Stadium. Hawkins pitched two complete-game victories over the Pittsburgh Pirates, including a 4-1 three-hitter at home on May 10. After struggling in June, he was optioned to Las Vegas. Hawkins rejoined the Padres in late August and performed well in September. Hawkins defeated the Cincinnati Reds, 8-2, in a four-hitter at home on September 9 and struck out 10 Los Angeles Dodgers in a 4-1 triumph at home on September 29. Jose Morales' pinch-hit home run with two outs in the ninth inning denied Hawkins a shutout. In nine San Diego Stadium starts, he finished 3-1 with a 2.49 ERA.

Hawkins in 1984 split time between the starting rotation and the bullpen with an 8-9 record and 4.68 ERA. He opened 1984 with 14 consecutive starts, logging a 4-3 mark. Hawkins won all three April decisions over the St. Louis Cardinals, San Francisco Giants, and Los Angeles Dodgers, allowing the latter only one run and five hits. His best game came at home on June 5, when he blanked the Houston Astros, 3-0, on a three-hitter. Hawkins made five consecutive relief appearances at midseason with a 1.64 ERA in 11 innings. He won three of his next four starts, including a 3-2, four-hit victory over the Pittsburgh Pirates at Three Rivers Stadium on July 20.

His clutch work came to the forefront in the post-season. In 15.2 innings, Hawkins yielded just one run and four hits for a sparkling 0.57 ERA. In Game 2 of the National League Championship Series, he retired four of five Chicago Cubs at Wrigley Field. Although the Padres lost, Hawkins showed manager Dick Williams that he could relieve in clutch situations. With one out and two runners on base in the fifth inning of Game 4 at home, he induced Gary Matthews to ground into a double play. In the climactic Game 5 of the series, Hawkins entered in the second inning and retired all four Cubs he faced. In the World Series against the Detroit Tigers, he gave up only one run and four hits in 12 innings with an 0.75 ERA. He recorded the only win for the Padres with over five scoreless innings of one- hit pitching in a 5-3 triumph in Game 2 at home. He suffered the loss in Game 5, although allowing only one earned run and two hits in four relief innings.

Hawkins enjoyed his best major-league season in 1985 with an 18-8 record and a 3.15 ERA. His 18 victories placed the sixth best in the National League and were the most by a Padre since Gaylord Perry attained 21 in 1978. Eight victories and just two losses came on the road. Hawkins opened the season with a record-setting 11-0 mark, including wins in his first 10 starts. He became the first National League hurler to start a campaign 11-0 since Elroy Face of the Pittsburgh Pirates began 17-0 in 1959. No major-league pitcher had opened that well since Ron Guidry began 13-0 in 1978. Hawkins broke the Padre records for consecutive wins, including starter Tim Lollar's 5-0 in 1982 and reliever Butch Metzger's 10-0 in 1976. Teammate LaMarr Hoyt, likewise, recorded 11 consecutive wins later that season. Hawkins won National League Pitcher of the Month honors in May with a 6-0 record and a 2.72 ERA. At Veterans Stadium on May 25, he allowed the Philadelphia Phillies only one run and six hits in a 4-1 victory. The streak was snapped on June 19 in a 5-1 setback to the Los Angeles Dodgers at Dodger Stadium.

On July 19, Hawkins hurled seven scoreless innings in a 6-0 home victory over the Pittsburgh Pirates. During August, he won five of six decisions and hurled two complete-game road shutouts. He blanked the Atlanta Braves, 6-0, with a six-hitter at Atlanta-Fulton County Stadium on August 1 and the Montreal Expos, 3-0, with a four-hitter at Olympic Stadium on August 22. Hawkins won his seventeenth game on September 1 and defeated the Cincinnati Reds, 9-4, in the season finale on October 3.

Hawkins boasted a 10-8 record with a 4.30 ERA in 1986, faring 6-2 with a 3.07 ERA at home. He led the Padres in innings (209.1), starts (35), and strikeouts (117) and tied Lance McCullers in wins (10). Hawkins surrendered 21 home runs, but finished 3-0 against the Cincinnati Reds and 2-0 against the Chicago Cubs. He defeated the Cincinnati Reds, 7-4, at Riverfront Stadium on April 23 and knocked in a run with two hits. The Philadelphia Phillies walloped him, 16-5, at Veterans Stadium on June 1, temporarily relegating him to the bullpen. Hawkins blanked the San Francisco Giants, 4-0, in a seven-hitter at home on June 16. He won four of his final five decisions and hurled a three-hit, 2-1 victory over the Cincinnati Reds at Riverfront Stadium on October 5.

Hawkins missed two months of 1987 with an injured shoulder, struggling to a 3-10 record and a 5.05 ERA. He dropped five decisions before defeating the Philadelphia Phillies, 6-5, at Veterans Stadium on May 17. His only other triumphs came at home over the Montreal Expos on May 22 and over the San Francisco Giants at Candlestick Park on June 13. He did not have a complete game in 1987 and seldom pitched beyond six innings.

In 1988, Hawkins finished 14-11 with a 3.35 ERA. He led the Padres with two shutouts, including a 3-0 one-hit home victory on April 24 over the Houston Astros. Bill Doran broke up the no-hitter with a single in the seventh inning. Hawkins hurled seven seasons with the Padres and ranks sixth in victories (60) and shutouts (7), seventh in innings (1,002.2), and eleventh in strikeouts (489). For San Diego, he lost 58 decisions with a 3.84 ERA.

In December 1988, Hawkins joined the New York Yankees as a free agent. He pitched in 1989 and 1990 for the New York Yankees and ended his major-league career with the Oakland Athletics in 1991. On July 1, 1990, he pitched an eight-inning no-hitter against the Chicago White Sox but lost 4-0. During 10 major-league seasons, Hawkins won 84 games and lost 91 decisions with a 4.22 ERA, 706 strikeouts, and 10 shutouts. He serves as pitching coach for the Savannah, Georgia Sand Gnats of the South Atlantic League in the Texas Rangers organization. He and his wife, Jackie, reside in Waco, Texas and have two daughters, Kathryn and Elizabeth.

RICKEY HENDERSON

Rickey Henderson, the greatest leadoff hitter in major-league history, played outfield with the Padres in 1996, 1997, and 2001. The 5-foot 10-inch, 190-pound Henderson, who bats right-handed and throws left-handed, was born on December 25, 1958 in Chicago, Illinois and graduated in 1976 from Oakland Technical High School, where he starred in baseball and as an All-America running back in football. Several college football powers recruited him.

The Oakland Athletics selected Henderson in the fourth round in June 1976. Henderson spent minor-league seasons with Boise, Idaho of the Northwest League in 1976, Modesto, California of the California League in 1977, Jersey City, New Jersey of the Eastern League in 1978, and Ogden, Utah of the Pacific Coast League in 1979 and made his major-league debut with the Athletics in 1979, stealing 33 bases in his first 89 games.

Rickey Henderson

Henderson starred with the Oakland Athletics from 1980 through 1984 and was traded to the New York Yankees in December 1984. The Yankees returned him to the Oakland Athletics in June 1989. In July 1993, the Toronto Blue Jays acquired him in a trade. He returned to the Oakland Athletics for 1994 and 1995 and joined the San Diego Padres in December 1995 as a free agent.

Henderson displayed a rare combination of hitting ability, power, and speed. He led the American League in stolen bases 11 times, including seven consecutive seasons. In his first full major-league campaign in 1980, the speedster surpassed Ty Cobb's 65-year-old American League stolen base record by four with 100 thefts. His 130 stolen bases in 1982 erased Lou Brock's major-league single-season mark of 118. Henderson also led the American League in walks three times and runs five times and holds the major-league record for most career stolen bases and most home runs leading off a game. In 1989, he starred in the American League Championship Series and was named Most Valuable Player of the World Series with a .474 batting average. He won the American League Most Valuable Player Award in 1990, when he hit a career-high .325 and led the American League with 119 runs scored and 65 stolen bases.

In 1996, Henderson helped the Padres win the National League West Division, batting .241 with nine home runs, 29 RBIs, a career-high 125 walks, .410 on-base percentage, and 37 stolen bases. He scored 110 runs, third highest in franchise history. Henderson topped 30 stolen bases for the seventeenth time, scored 100 runs for the twelfth time, and reached the 100-walk plateau for the fourth time. He led off three games with home runs, extending his major-league record to 70 first-inning leadoff home runs. Henderson batted .333 in the National League Division Series against the St. Louis Cardinals and tied Tony Gwynn for the team lead in hits with four. He hit .274 with six home runs and 27 RBIs in 1997 before being traded to the Anaheim Angels that August.

Henderson rejoined the Oakland Athletics as a free agent in October 1997 and led the American League with 118 walks and 66 stolen bases in 1998. He signed with the New York Mets as a free agent in December 1998, hit .315 in 1999 to help them to the wild card, and starred in the National League Division

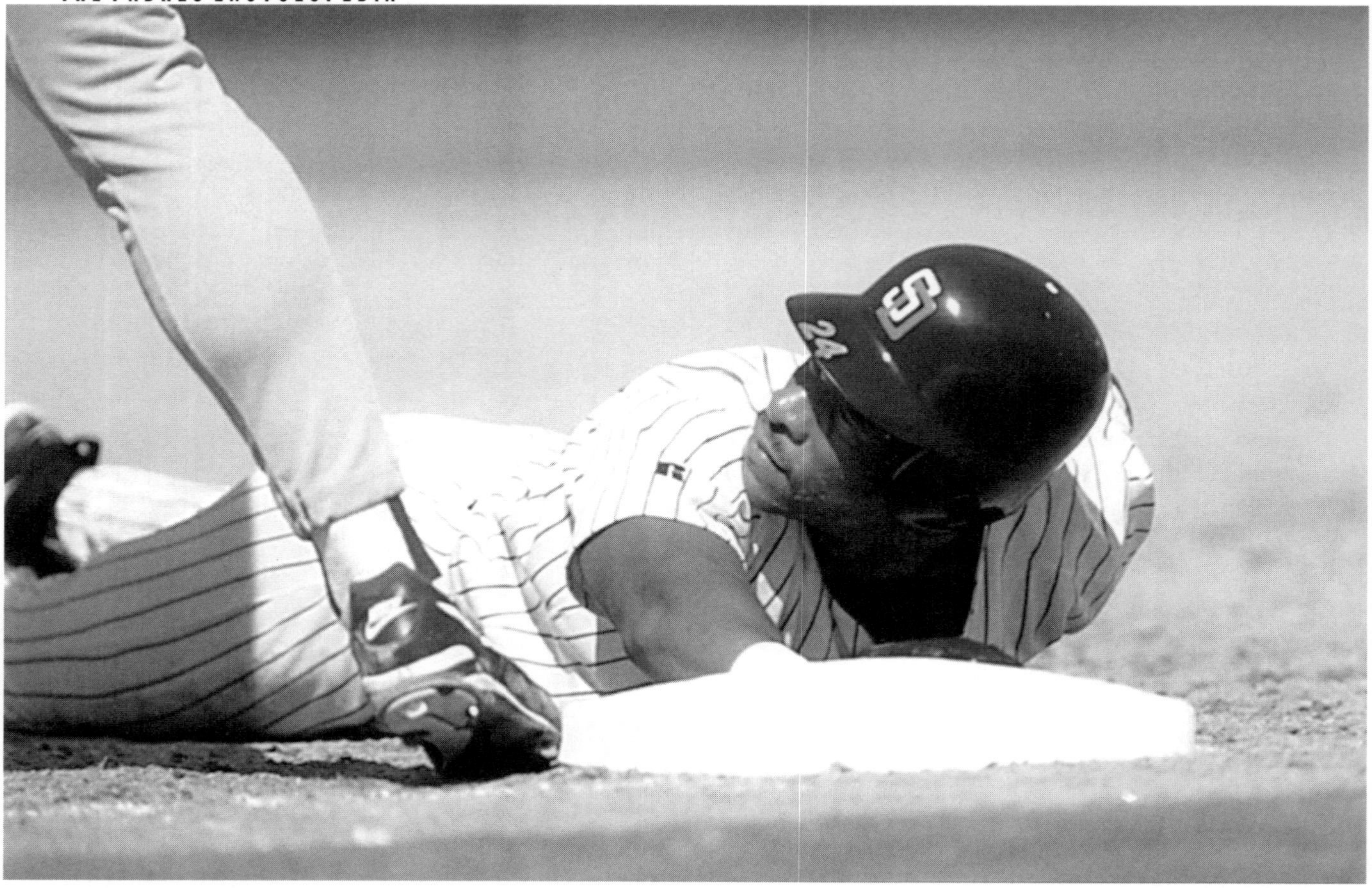

Rickey Henderson led the American League in stolen bases seven consecutive years.

Series. Henderson divided 2000 between the New York Mets and Seattle and rejoined the San Diego Padres as a free agent in March 2001.

In 2001, Henderson set the major-league records for most career runs (2,248) and walks (2,141) and recorded his 3,000th major-league hit. Although batting just .227, he clouted eight home runs with 42 RBIs, 81 walks, and 25 stolen bases. On April 20, Henderson started in left field, while Tony Gwynn played right field, marking the first time since 1945 that two players at least 40 years old had started in the same outfield. Four nights later, he walked in the sixth inning as a pinch-hitter for pitcher David Lee to tie Babe Ruth's career walk record of 2,062 in a 12-7 loss to the visiting Philadelphia Phillies. The following night, Henderson walked off reliever Jose Mesa in the ninth inning to break Ruth's career walk record in a 5-3 setback to the Philadelphia Phillies. He donated his jersey to the National Baseball Hall of Fame and the ball to the Babe Ruth Museum in Baltimore, Maryland.

Henderson attained other milestones in May and September 2001. On May 6, he doubled to reach base safely for the 5,000th time in an 8-2 triumph over the Cincinnati Reds at Cinergy Field, helping Bruce Bochy record his 500th career victory as Padre manager. On May 16, Henderson extended his major-league record of games led off with a home run to 79, ending pitcher Glendon Rusch's streak of 21 consecutive scoreless innings and igniting a four-run rally in a 5-2 triumph over the New York Mets at Shea Stadium. The next night, he and three other Padres tied a club record by homering off pitcher Steve Trachsel in a seven-run third-inning, sparking a 15-3 rout over the Mets. On May 19, he tallied twice to join Ty Cobb as the only major-league players to score 2,200 career runs. Henderson homered and singled with three RBIs in the 20-7 shellacking over the Montreal Expos at Olympic Stadium. On September 24, he recorded a season-high four hits, including a double, with two RBIs in a 15-11 marathon loss to the Colorado Rockies at Coors Field.

Henderson's most significant milestones came in October. On October 3, he walked off pitcher Eric Gagne in the third inning and scored on first baseman Ryan Klesko's double down the right-field line, matching Ty Cobb's major-league record of 2,245 runs in a 12-5 setback to the visiting Los Angeles Dodgers. The following day, he became major-league baseball's career run leader with a solo home run in the third inning off pitcher Luke Prokopec, passing Cobb with run number 2,246 and celebrating with a feet-first slide at the plate. His record-setting home run, off the top of the left-field fence, helped the Padres defeat the Los Angeles Dodgers, 6-3.

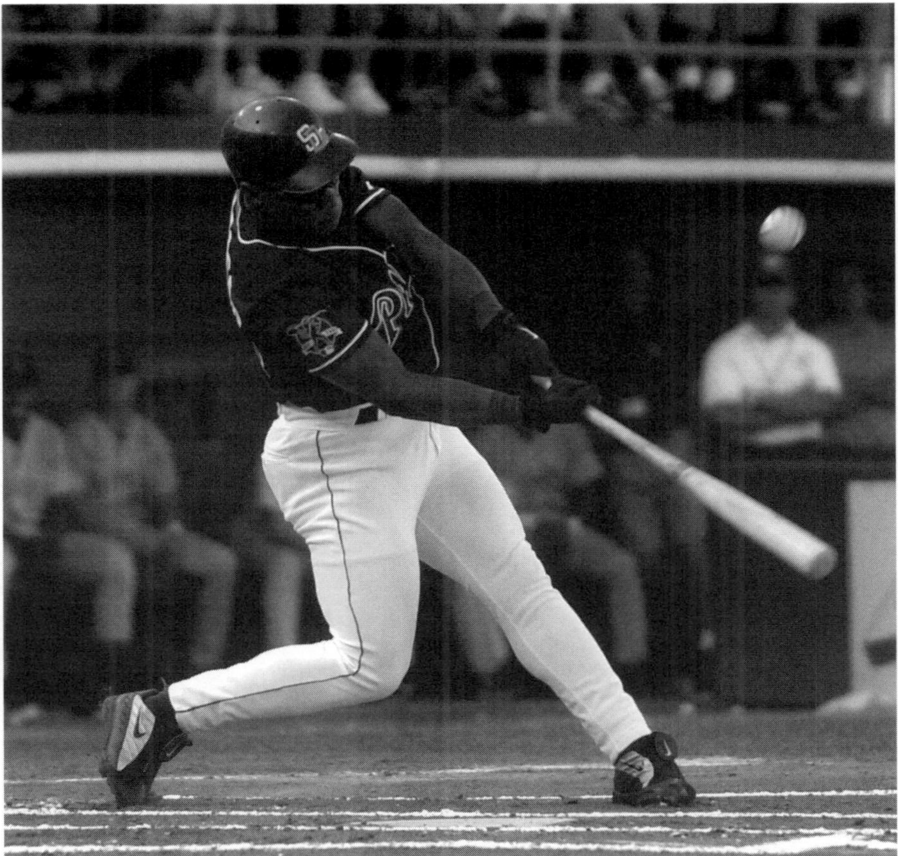

Rickey Henderson hits a looper down the right field line that falls in for a double and his 3,000th career hit during the first inning of the Padres' game against the Colorado Rockies Sunday October 7, 2001 in San Diego.

Henderson reached another career milestone in the season finale October 7 in a 14-5 setback to the Colorado Rockies at Qualcomm Stadium. He led off the home half of the first inning with a bloop double down the right-field line off pitcher John Thomson, becoming the twenty-fifth major-leaguer and the first player in October to reach 3,000. His teammates rushed to congratulate him at second base. He was presented with a plaque and given the ball by Rockies shortstop Juan Uribe. Henderson scored on a single by third baseman Phil Nevin to break his already established career runs record with 2,248. He joined outfielder Tony Gwynn as the only players to reach their 3,000th hit with the Padres. He became a free agent following the 2001 season and signed a minor-league contract with the Boston Red Sox organization in February 2002.

Through the 2001 season, Henderson has batted .280 with 3,000 hits, 2,248 runs, 503 doubles, 65 triples, 290 home runs, 1,094 RBIs, 2,141 walks, 1,631 strikeouts, and 1,395 stolen bases in 2,979 games. With the Padres, he has batted .245 with 277 hits, 45 doubles, 23 home runs, 98 RBIs, 277 walks, and 91 stolen bases in 359 games. Henderson holds the major-league records for most stolen bases, home runs by a leadoff batter in a game, and years leading his league in stolen bases. He holds the American League records for most stolen bases (1,262), home runs as a leadoff batter (72), and years with 50 or more stolen bases (7). The 10-time American League All-Star holds the Oakland Athletics' all-time marks for most runs (1,270) and most stolen bases (867) and the New York Yankees' record for most stolen bases (326). He batted .326 with nine stolen bases in four Division Series, .244 with 17 stolen bases in seven Championship Series, and .329 with seven stolen bases in three World Series.

Henderson and his wife, Pam, have three daughters, Angela, Alexis, and Adriann, and live in Phoenix, Arizona. He coauthored *Off Base: The Confessions of a Base Thief* following the 1991 season.

GEORGE HENDRICK

George Hendrick

George Hendrick played outfield for the San Diego Padres from April 1977 through May 1978. The 6-foot 3-inch, 195-pound Hendrick, who threw and batted right-handed, was born on October 18, 1949 in Los Angeles, California, and attended East Los Angeles Junior College. The Oakland Athletics selected him in the first round of the January 1968 free agent draft. After spending just over four seasons in the minor leagues, Hendrick played with the Oakland Athletics in 1971 and 1972. In 1972, he appeared in the American League Championship Series against the Detroit Tigers and in the World Series against the Cincinnati Reds. Hendrick excelled for the Cleveland Indians from 1973 through 1976, averaging 22 home runs and 74 RBIs and making the 1974 and 1975 All-Star teams. He knocked in 86 runs in 1975 and belted 25 home runs in 1976.

The San Diego Padres sought a power-hitting outfielder and acquired him in December 1976 for John Grubb, Fred Kendall, and Hector Torres. Hendrick's .311 batting average in 1977 tied Grubb for the second highest in franchise history and was sixth best in the National League. Hendrick was second best on the Padres with 75 runs scored, 168 hits, 23 home runs, and 81 RBIs. His 47 multi-hit games included a four-hit contest in a 9-5 loss to the Philadelphia Phillies at Veterans Stadium on May 14. He enjoyed an 11-game hitting streak from April 13 through April 23 and hit .484 with two doubles, three home runs, and 10 RBIs during an eight-game hitting streak from May 24 through May 30. In a 5-2, 15-inning home loss in the second game of a doubleheader against the Montreal Expos on July 26, he went hitless in five plate appearances and yet stole three bases. Hendrick clouted two home runs with four RBIs in a 7-5 triumph over the Montreal Expos on July 27 and knocked in five runs with two doubles and a home run in an 8-6 win over the New York Mets at Shea Stadium on July 30. He authored a seven-game hitting streak from August 28 through September 4 and ended the season with a 10-game hitting streak, belting two round-trippers with four RBIs in a 9-2 home romp over the San Francisco Giants on September 25. He batted .368 with 11 RBIs against the Houston Astros and .344 with 12 RBIs against the Atlanta Braves.

In 1978, Hendrick batted a disappointing .243 with just three home runs and eight RBIs in 36 games before being traded in May to the St. Louis Cardinals for pitcher Eric Rasmussen. Playing with the Padres slightly more than one season, he batted .299 with 195 hits, 26 home runs, and 89 RBIs. Hendrick starred for the St. Louis Cardinals from 1978 through 1984, hitting over .300 three times and knocking in over 100 runs twice. He made the National League All-Star teams in 1980 and 1983 and played in the 1982 World Series against the Milwaukee Brewers. Although refusing to talk with the press, Hendrick was well liked by both St. Louis players and fans. *The Sporting News* gave him Silver Slugger awards at both outfield and first base. He split the 1985 campaign between the Pittsburgh Pirates and California Angels and ended his major-league career with the Angels from 1986 through 1988. During 18 major-league seasons, Hendrick batted .278 with 1,980 hits, 267 home runs, and 1,111 RBIs. He served as hitting coach for the St. Louis Cardinals in

1996 and 1997 and first base coach for the Anaheim Angels in 1998 and 1999. Hendrick rejoined the San Diego Padres as a minor-league hitting instuctor in 2000. He and his wife, Carol, reside in Las Vegas, Nevada and have two sons, Brian and Damon.

Enzo Hernandez

ENZO HERNANDEZ

Enzo Hernandez played shortstop for the San Diego Padres from 1971 through 1977. The 5-foot 8-inch, 155- pound Hernandez, who batted and threw right-handed, was born on February 12, 1949 in Valle de Guanape, Venezuela and started his professional baseball career in the Houston Astros organization. He spent four seasons in the Houston and Baltimore Orioles minor-league systems. In February 1970, the San Diego Padres acquired Hernandez, Tom Phoebus, Fred Beene, and Al Severinsen from the Baltimore Orioles for Pat Dobson and Tom Dukes.

Hernandez performed steadily as the San Diego shortstop in his rookie 1971 season. Although suffering from a groin pull and batting only .222 with 12 RBIs, he established a Padre record with 21 stolen bases in 25 attempts. Hernandez hit about .250 the first half of 1971, but struggled the final seven weeks. He nearly always made contact at the plate, striking out only 35 times in almost 500 at-bats, and batted .306 against the Los Angeles Dodgers.

His batting average dropped to .195 with 15 RBIs in 1972, but he broke his club stolen base record with 24. He pilfered 11 bases in September and three in a 3-1 triumph over the Houston Astros at the Astrodome on October 1. Catchers threw him out only three times in stolen base attempts. Besides fanning only 25 times in 329 at-bats, Hernandez clouted his first major-league home run off Jim Willoughby of the San Francisco Giants and made three other hits. He also connected with three hits on May 11 against the Philadelphia Phillies at Veterans Stadium and on October 1 in a 3-1 win over the Houston Astros at the Astrodome.

Hernandez batted .223 with nine RBIs in 70 games in 1973 and whiffed only 14 times in 247 at-bats. He played well until ankle and hamstring injuries diminished his effectiveness. Hernandez stole 11 consecutive bases at the start of the season and pilfered three bases against the Atlanta Braves at Atlanta-Fulton County Stadium on May 13. Defensively, he made only seven errors and went 42 consecutive games without making an error.

In 1974, Hernandez batted .232 and recorded personal highs for doubles (19), RBIs (34), and stolen bases (37). He tied his own club stolen base record, swiping three bases in a 10-2 home romp over the New York Mets on April 23 and being caught only 10 times. Hernandez collected three hits in three separate games, grounded into the fewest double plays (4) for National League regulars, and sacrificed 12 times. He batted .340 against the New York Mets and .310 against the Pittsburgh Pirates. Defensively, he handled 120 consecutive chances spanning 22 games from April 19 through May 13 without making an error.

Hernandez struggled with a .218 batting average and 19 RBIs in 116 games in 1975, but made at least two hits in 17 contests. He led the National League with a club-record 24 sacrifices and stole three bases to spark a 5-3 home win over the Atlanta Braves on April 25. His stolen base production declined to 20, but he batted .371 against the Atlanta Braves and made four hits in an 8-3 home triumph over the Philadelphia Phillies on June 9.

His best season came in 1976, when he batted .256 with 24 RBIs and 12 stolen bases in 113 games. He batted over .300 until mid-June and connected with 20 multi-hit games, including five three-hit contests.

Hernandez authored a nine-game hitting streak from May 30 through June 9 and batted .400 from June 30 through July 9 with four consecutive two-hit games. In the first game of an August 2 doubleheader at Atlanta-Fulton County Stadium, he clouted his second career major-league home run in a 7-0 triumph over the Atlanta Braves. Hernandez swiped two bases in a 5-1 home victory over the New York Mets on June 7 and collected four RBIs in an 11-7 slugfest over the St. Louis Cardinals at Busch Stadium on August 16. He hit .381 against the New York Mets and .306 against the Los Angeles Dodgers.

Hernandez spent nearly all of 1977 on the disabled list with a back problem, appearing in only seven games, mostly as a late-inning defensive replacement. His most extensive action came on April 28, when he went hitless with a sacrifice bunt against the Los Angeles Dodgers. The Padres released him in March 1978. During his Padre career, he batted .225 with 522 hits, 66 doubles, 113 RBIs, and 129 stolen bases in 710 games and ranked first in stolen bases, third in games and at-bats (2,324), fourth in runs (241), hits, and triples (13), and seventh in doubles. His major-league career ended with the Los Angeles Dodgers in 1978. He and his wife, Ellys, reside in Guantra Puerta Lacruz Anz, Venezuela and have one daughter, Ellys.

STERLING HITCHCOCK

Sterling Hitchcock pitched for the San Diego Padres from 1997 through July 2001. The 6-foot, 205-pound Hitchcock, who bats and throws left-handed, was born on April 29, 1971 in Fayetteville, North Carolina and graduated in 1989 from Armwood High School in Seffner, Florida, where he earned all-conference and all-league honors as a senior. The New York Yankees selected him in the ninth round of the June 1989 free agent draft. He spent nearly four seasons in the minor leagues before starting three games for New York in 1992. He compiled an 11-10 record with a 4.70 ERA for the Yankees in 1995 and a 13-9 record with a 5.35 ERA for the Seattle Mariners in 1996. On December 6, 1996, the San Diego Padres acquired Hitchcock from the Seattle Mariners for pitcher Scott Sanders.

Hitchcock finished 10-11 with a 5.20 ERA in 1997, ranking second among Padres in wins, third in starts (28) and innings pitched (161) and fourth in strikeouts (106). San Diego scored only 21 runs in his 11 losses. In his Padre home debut on April 5, he hurled eight innings in a 4-1, one-hit win over the Philadelphia Phillies. Hitchcock pitched a perfect game until allowing a walk to Danny Tartabull and a double by Rico Brogna in the fifth inning. He faced only two batters over the minimum and threw 90 pitches, including 62 strikes. Hitchcock on May 20 allowed only one run on five hits in eight innings in a 7-3 victory over the Los Angeles Dodgers and on August 15 defeated the Chicago Cubs, 5-1, at home.

His best major-league season came in 1998, when he helped San Diego win the National League West with a 9-7 record and career-best 3.93 ERA. He joined the starting rotation permanently on May 4 and fanned 158 batters in 176.1 innings. The Padres tallied just 11 times in his seven losses. Hitchcock on June 27 became the eighth Padre in club history to take a no-hitter into the eighth inning, but Phil Nevin of the Anaheim Angels homered on the first pitch. He allowed just one run on two hits in the 5-1 victory at Qualcomm Stadium. On August 14, he blanked the Milwaukee Brewers, 7-0, at home on a five-hitter, fanning nine. In a 3-1 home loss to the Montreal Expos on August 29, he became just the third Padre to strike out 15 batters in a game. He did not walk a single batter, but he surrendered home runs to pitcher Dustin Hermanson and Vladimir Guerrero.

Hitchcock proved to be the Padres' most effective hurler in post-season play. He won his sole decision with a 1.50 ERA in the National League Division Series against the Houston Astros, clinching the series by outdueling Randy Johnson, 6-1, in Game 4. He allowed only three hits in six innings, striking out 11 and walking just one. He earned Most Valuable Player honors in the National League Championship Series upset victory over the Atlanta Braves with two wins and a 0.90 ERA. He started both Games 3 and 6, besting Greg Maddux and Tom Glavine. In a 4-1 Game 3 victory at home, he gave up one run on three hits, walked five, and fanned six in five innings. In Game 6 at Turner Field, he helped clinch San Diego's first National League pennant since 1984 by blanking the Braves on two hits over five innings with three walks and eight strikeouts. The Padres scored five times in the sixth inning to ice the victory. He made his only World Series start in Game 3 against the New York Yankees, allowing two runs and seven hits with seven strikeouts in six innings.

Hitchcock led San Diego with 33 starts in 1999, but slumped to a 12-14 slate and a 4.11 ERA. He ranked sixth in the National League with a career-high 194 strikeouts, third best in Padre history, and compiled a career-best 205.1 innings pitched. His 8.5 strikeouts per nine innings trailed only Randy Johnson of the Arizona Diamondbacks. The Padres scored just 33 runs in his 14 losses. Hitchcock on May 9 blanked the Atlanta Braves, 5-0, at home on four hits and eight strikeouts in eight innings and won five consecutive starts from June 22 to July 16 for the first time in his major-league career. On July 16, he blanked the Seattle Mariners on six hits in seven innings in a 2-1 victory at Safeco Field. On September 1, Hitchcock struck out nine Chicago Cubs in a 1-0 loss at home. He lost five of six decisions that month. The Arizona Diamondbacks defeated him all four times.

Hitchcock started just 11 games in 2000 before undergoing season-ending reconstructive Tommy John surgery on June 6 to repair a torn ligament in his left shoulder. He won only one of seven decisions with a 4.93 ERA. Hitchcock missed the first half of the 2001 season, triumphing on July 4 in his initial start over the Colorado Rockies, 8-3 at home. He compiled a 2-1 mark and 3.32 ERA for San Diego before being traded on July 30 to the New York Yankees for pitcher Brett Jodie and outfielder Darren Blakely. Hitchcock split eight decisions with a 6.49 ERA for the Yankees. He surrendered two home runs in three innings with a 6.00 ERA in the American League Division Series against the Oakland Athletics and did not appear in the American League Championship Series against the Seattle Mariners. He struck out six Arizona Diamondbacks in four scoreless innings in the World Series, winning dramatic Game 5.

During his major-league career, Hitchcock has authored a 61-62 mark with a 4.69 ERA, has fanned 841 batters in 1,067 innings, and has recorded three shutouts and three saves. As a Padre, Hitchcock finished 34-39 with a 4.40 ERA and 534 strikeouts in 627.2 innings. Upon his departure, he ranked tenth among Padre career leaders in strikeouts, fifteenth in games started (102), nineteenth in innings pitched, and shared seventeenth in victories and nineteenth in losses. He and his wife, Carrey, reside in Tampa, Florida.

TREVOR HOFFMAN

Trevor Hoffman has starred as a reliever for the San Diego Padres since 1993. The 6-foot 205-pound Hoffman, who bats and throws right-handed, was born on October 13, 1967 in Bellflower, California. His older brother, Glenn, played infield for three major-league clubs and managed and coached for the Los Angeles Dodgers. After graduating from Savanna High School in Anaheim, California, Hoffman played baseball at Cypress Junior College and the University of Arizona. The Cincinnati Reds selected him as a shortstop in the eleventh round of the June 1989 free agent draft. Hoffman spent four seasons in the minor leagues, two as a shortstop before converting to a relief pitcher. The Florida Marlins selected him as the eighth overall pick of the November 1992 expansion draft. After splitting four decisions with two saves and a 3.28 ERA, he was traded to the San Diego Padres in June 1993.

Hoffman finished 1993 with a 2-4 mark, a 4.31 ERA, and three saves for San Diego, fanning 53 batters in 54.1 innings. Only one of 29 inherited runners scored against him. His first Padre win came on July 30, when he hurled three innings in an 11-9 slugfest over the Cincinnati Reds at Riverfront Stadium. During a 15-game stretch from August 6 through September 15, Hoffman allowed just eight earned runs in 28 innings. He struck out four batters in losses to the Atlanta Braves on September 4 and September 9 and in an 11-7 triumph over the Colorado Rockies at Mile High Stadium on September 20.

In 1994, Hoffman improved to a 4-4 record with a 2.57 ERA and 20 saves in 23 opportunities. He fanned 68 batters in 56 innings and stranded 21 of 31 inherited runners, limiting opponents to a .193 batting average. Besides earning the Clyde McCullough Award as Padres' Pitcher of the Year, Hoffman ranked seventh in the National League in saves. In his first 13 games, he won two decisions with three saves and 21 strikeouts and allowed just one earned run in 17.1 innings. Hoffman, who did not surrender a home run in his first 33 games, fanned five Montreal Expos in 2.2 innings at Olympic Stadium on May 1. He earned saves in five straight appearances from May 22 through June 1 and recorded saves in all five stints on the final road trip of the season.

In 1995, Hoffman won seven of 11 decisions with a 3.88 ERA and 31 saves, sixth best in the National League. His seven wins shared third best on the staff, while his 31 saves marked the most by a Padre right-hander since Rollie Fingers in 1978. Hoffman failed to convert only seven save opportunities for an .816

save percentage. Besides leading San Diego with 55 appearances, he struck out 52 batters in 53.1 innings. Hoffman allowed 10 round-trippers, including four three-run homers. He recorded 12 consecutive saves and fanned 12 in just 13 innings from July 21 to August 2. He finished 1995 by posting a 3-0 record with six saves, a 0.75 ERA, and 13 strikeouts in 12 innings.

In 1996, Hoffman compiled a 9-5 record with a 2.25 ERA, 42 saves, and 111 strikeouts in 88 innings. He led National League relievers in victories and strikeouts, helping the Padres win the National League West. Hoffman's wins, strikeouts, and appearances (70) all marked career highs. His 42 saves ranked third in the National League and the best ever by a Padre right-hander, trailing left-hander Mark Davis. Hoffman struck out at least one batter in 58 of his 70 stints, winning the Clyde McCullough Award as Padres' Pitcher of the Year and earning *The Sporting News'* National League Fireman of the Year honors.

Hoffman blew just seven save opportunities, converting 86 percent of the time. Opponents batted only .161 against him, lowest in the National League. He authored three streaks of 10 or more appearances without allowing an earned run and did not surrender a run in 56 of his 70 appearances. In an 8-4, 13-inning triumph at the Astrodome on April 6, Hoffman fanned a career-high seven Houston Astros in three perfect innings to record his first triumph of the season. He yielded only two earned runs in 22 innings in his first 17 outings through May 24 and did not allow a run in 15 consecutive innings from June 3 through July 3. He earned three straight saves against the San Francisco Giants at Candlestick Park from June 28 through June 30, New York Mets at Shea Stadium from August 27 through August 29, and Los Angeles Dodgers at Dodger Stadium from September 27 through September 29. In August, Hoffman finished 1-0 with nine saves and fanned 12 batters in 14 scoreless innings. He closed the season with 18 consecutive saves and hurled three scoreless innings with four strikeouts in the final Los Angeles Dodgers series. Hoffman fanned Chad Curtis with a fastball on the last pitch of the regular season to clinch the National League West for the Padres. Altogether, he saved seven games against the Los Angeles Dodgers and allowed only 19 hits in 40 innings at home. He did not pitch well in the National League Division Series against the St. Louis Cardinals, losing his only decision with a 10.80 ERA in two innings.

Trevor Hoffman

In 1997, Hoffman posted another spectacular season with a 6-4 mark, a 2.66 ERA, and 37 saves. He earned a win or save in 43 of the Padres' 76 victories (57 percent). Only Jeff Shaw of the Cincinnati Reds won or preserved a higher percentage of his club's victories. Besides matching his career-high 70 games for the second consecutive season, Hoffman ranked second in the National League in saves and shared third in the Rolaids Relief Man standings. He won his second straight Clyde McCullough Award as Padres' Pitcher of the Year. Hoffman converted 37 of 44 save opportunities, including 27 of his last 28. His 84-percent saves ranked fifth in the major leagues. He finished with 22 saves in his last 36 outings and blanked opponents in 30 of his last 34 outings. Hoffman fanned 111 batters and walked only 24 in 81.1 innings, averaging a career-best 12.3 strikeouts per nine innings.

Hoffman reached several milestones. He attained his 100th major-league save on April 13 in a 3-1 win over the Philadelphia Phillies at Veterans Stadium and his 100th Padre save on May 3 in a 1-0 shutout over the Montreal Expos at home. On June 23 against the San Francisco Giants at 3 Com Park, Hoffman became the all-time Padres save leader with 109, surpassing Rollie Fingers. He set the record in just 241 Padre

Trevor Hoffman holds the Padres career record for most saves (312) and appearances (543).

outings, fanning J.T. Snow with the bases loaded to preserve an 11-6 win. Hoffman worked a career-long four innings on August 27 in an eventual 12-inning loss to the Philadelphia Phillies at Veterans Stadium, matching a career-high seven strikeouts and allowing only one hit.

Hoffman fared better at Qualcomm Stadium than on the road. He won all six decisions with 16 saves and a 2.85 ERA in 37 home games, but lost all four decisions with 21 saves and a 2.45 ERA in 33 road games. Hoffman fanned 63 batters and walked only seven in 41.0 innings at home while striking out 48 and walking 17 in 40.1 innings on the road. He finished 3-1 with 21 saves and a 1.44 ERA in 35 games after the All-Star break.

The Padres won the National League West in 1998, when Hoffman emerged as the premier major-league closer. Besides compiling a 4-2 record, he established career bests with a 1.48 ERA and 53 saves and fanned 86 batters in just 73 innings. Hoffman matched Randy Myers's 1993 National League save record and missed converting just one save, becoming just the fifth closer to reach the 50-save plateau in a single season. His 98.1 percent conversion rate marked the best in history by a closer with at least 30 saves. He blanked opponents in 57 of 66 appearances (86 percent) and earned the save or win in 58 of San Diego's 98 victories (59 percent). The Padres finished 62-4 in his appearances. Hoffman did not lose any game that he entered with a lead. He limited opponents to a .165 batting average, third best in the major leagues. In his final 32 appearances, he finished 1-1 with 29 saves and a brilliant 0.76 ERA.

Hoffman made his first Associated Press Major-League All-Star team and first National League All-Star team, surrendering a home run to Roberto Alomar in the, Summer Classic. He finished second to Tom Glavine of the Atlanta Braves in the National League Cy Young Award balloting despite receiving more first-place votes, and seventh in the National League Most Valuable Player vote. Hoffman won his first National League Rolaids Relief Man of the Year award and second National League Fireman of the Year Award from *The Sporting News* and shared the Clyde McCullough Award with Kevin Brown as Padre Pitcher of the Year.

On September 27, Hoffman hurled a perfect ninth inning to preserve a 3-2 win over the Arizona Diamondbacks at Bank One Ballpark in the season finale. His 53 saves demolished the club record of 44 set by Mark Davis in 1989. He led all major-league relievers in permitting only 7.8 base runners per nine innings and ranked second among major-league relievers with a 1.48 ERA, trailing only Ugueth Urbina of the Montreal Expos. Hoffman yielded only one run in 43 night games for a minuscule 0.18 ERA. He also recorded his 150th Padre save with a scoreless ninth inning in a 4-2 home win over the Cincinnati Reds on June 8.

Hoffman began 1998 by converting 33 straight saves to match Rod Beck's major-league record of 41 consecutive saves. His streak, later surpassed by Tom Gordon of the Boston Red Sox, ended when he inherited a 4-3 lead to start the ninth inning on July 26 at home against the Houston Astros and allowed a leadoff home run to Moises Alou. The Padres won that contest, 5-4, in 10 innings. Hoffman finished 2-2 with 27 saves and a 1.23 ERA at home and 2-0 with 26 saves and a 1.73 ERA on the road. He won the Rolaids National League Relief Man of the Month honors with a 2-0 record, seven saves, and a 1.35 ERA in April and a 1-1 mark, nine saves, and an 0.84 ERA in August. His scoreless streaks included 14 consecutive outings from April 7 through May 14, nine consecutive from July 3 through July 25, and nine from August 25 through September 14.

In eight post-season outings, Hoffman finished 1-1 with three saves and a 2.89 ERA. He performed brilliantly against the Houston Astros in the National League Division Series, posting two saves, yielding no runs in four games, and fanning four batters in three innings. His saves came in Games 1 and 3. He won his lone decision with one save and a 2.08 ERA in the National League Championship Series, fanning seven Atlanta Braves in 4.1 innings. After blowing a save at Turner Stadium in Game 1, Hoffman earned the victory when Ken Caminiti's tenth-inning home run gave the Padres a 3-2 win. He took the loss in Game 3 of the World Series at home against the New York Yankees, allowing an eighth-inning two-run homer to Scott Brosius in a 5-4 setback.

In 1999, Hoffman logged a 2-3 ledger with a 2.14 ERA, 40 saves, and 73 strikeouts in 67.1 innings. He led the major leagues for the second consecutive season in save percentage, converting 40 of 43 save opportunities and a major-league best 31 straight to end the campaign. No other Padre reliever had recorded five consecutive 30-save seasons. Besides making the National League All-Star team for the second consecutive time, Hoffman ranked second behind Ugueth Urbina of the Montreal Expos in saves and limited opponents to a .197 batting average. He won or saved 57 percent of the Padres' 74 victories and garnered his fifth Clyde McCullough Award as the Padres' Pitcher of the Year. In his final 45 appearances, Hoffman finished 2-0 and converted all 31 save opportunities with an 0.96 ERA. He did not blow any of the 24 save opportunities at Qualcomm Stadium.

His blown save on April 28 against the New York Mets at Shea Stadium broke a streak of 181 consecutive Padre victories when leading after eight innings dating back to 1996. Hoffman on May 26 fanned his 500th batter as a Padre, striking out Kelly Stinnett of the Arizona Diamondbacks at Bank One Ballpark. On June 10, he struck out three consecutive Oakland Athletics to preserve a 2-1 home win, becoming the 24th major-leaguer to record 200 career saves. In a 4-2 home victory over the Pittsburgh Pirates eight days later, Hoffman became the first Padre to attain 200 career saves. Only five pitchers had registered more saves with one club. Hoffman recorded eight saves during the club-record 14-consecutive-game winning streak from June 18 through July 2, preserving each of the first five games. He did not allow a run in 11 consecutive stints from June 4 through June 27 or an earned run in 11 straight games from August 5 through September 5. His two victories came on August 29 against the Milwaukee Brewers and on September 8 against the Pittsburgh Pirates.

In 2000, Hoffman logged a 4-7 ledger with a 2.99 ERA and ranked second in the National League with 43 saves. He blew only seven save opportunities, striking out 85 batters in just 72.1 innings. Hoffman made the National League All-Star team for the third straight season and attained several more major milestones. On July 9, he earned his 250th career save, snapping a five-game Texas Rangers winning streak, 4-3, at The Ballpark. His 30th save of the season came on August 7 in a 6-4 triumph over the Philadelphia Phillies at Veterans Stadium, making him just the third major-league reliever to accomplish that feat six consecutive times. On September 15, Hoffman recorded his 40th save of the season, defeating the San Francisco Giants, 5-4, at home. In that game, he joined Dennis Eckersley and Lee Smith as the only closers to post 40 or more saves in three consecutive seasons and Eckersley and John Wettelund as the only relievers to have four 40-save seasons.

In 2001, Hoffman compiled a 3-4 record with a 3.43 ERA and shared second in the National League with 43 saves. He blew only three save opportunities, fanning 63 batters in 60.1 innings and passing several milestones. Hoffman on August 15 became the fourteenth major-league reliever to record 300 career saves, hurling a perfect ninth inning to preserve a 2-1 victory over the visiting New York Mets. He became the second fastest and third youngest to attain 300 career saves. Dennis Eckersley reached 300 saves in 499 appearances, 54 fewer than Hoffman. The following day, Hoffman became the first major-league reliever to record seven straight 30-save seasons, retiring all three New York Mets in the ninth inning to maintain a 6-5 victory. On August 18, he notched his 300th save as a Padre, blanking the Montreal Expos for 1.1 innings to preserve a 4-3 victory. On September 7, Hoffman recorded his twenty-sixth consecutive save, hurling 1.1 innings in a 4-3 road triumph over the Arizona Diamondbacks. The streak ended the next day when he blew a save against Arizona. On September 25, Hoffman became the first major-league reliever to notch four straight 40-save campaigns and to attain five overall in an 8-7 squeaker over the Colorado Rockies at Coors Field, despite surrendering two earned runs in that ninth-inning appearance.

In nine major-league seasons, Hoffman owns a 43-39 record with a 2.79 ERA and 728 strikeouts in 641.2 innings. He holds the Padres' career record for most saves (312) and appearances (543) and shares sixth with 702 strikeouts. Hoffman and his wife, Tracy, reside in Del Mar, California, and have three children, Brody, Quinn, and Wyatt. He was born with one kidney and donates $200 for every save to the National Kidney Foundation.

LAMARR HOYT

LaMarr Hoyt starred as a pitcher for the San Diego Padres in 1985 and 1986 before drug problems sidelined him. The 6-foot 2-inch, 244-pound right-hander was born on January 1, 1955 in Columbia, South Carolina and graduated in 1973 from Keenan High School there. His father, Dewey, pitched in the minor leagues. The New York Yankees selected Hoyt in the fifth round of the June 1973 draft and traded him to the Chicago White Sox in April 1977. Hoyt spent over seven seasons in the minor leagues, briefly appearing with the Chicago White Sox in 1979. He hurled for Chicago from 1980 through 1984, recording more victories than any other major-league pitcher in 1982 and 1983. Besides setting a club record with 14 consecutive victories, he led the American League with 19 triumphs in 1982. His best major-league season came in 1983, when he garnered the American League Cy Young Award and again paced the junior circuit in victories. Hoyt finished with a 24-10 record and a 3.66 ERA, helping Chicago capture the American League West. He accounted for the only White Sox victory in the American League Championship Series against the Baltimore Orioles and was named *The Sporting News'* American League Pitcher of the Year. Hoyt's fortunes reversed in 1984, when he led the junior circuit with 18 losses.

In a seven-player December 1984 transaction, Chicago traded Hoyt to the San Diego Padres. Hoyt logged a 16-8 ledger with a 3.47 ERA in 1985. The control artist walked only 20 batters in 210.1 innings (less than one per game) and did not issue a free pass in his first 30.2 innings. Despite missing four starts with a sore shoulder, he led the Padres in victories. Hoyt struggled in his first eight starts, but survived a bases-loaded jam with no outs in the first inning and hurled a four-hit shutout to defeat the New York Mets, 2-0, on May 20 at Shea Stadium.

The victory began an 11-game winning streak for the big right-hander. In his next 12 starts, Hoyt improved his record to 13-4 with a 2.90 ERA. During the streak, he hurled seven complete games and three road shutouts with a 1.98 ERA. Hoyt blanked the San Francisco Giants, 1-0, at Candlestick Park on June 15 and the Pittsburgh Pirates, 3-0, at Three Rivers Stadium on July 7. He earned the victory as the National League starter in the All-Star Game, allowing two hits and an unearned run in three innings and being named the Most Valuable Player in the 6-1 triumph. On September 10, he defeated the Cincinnati Reds, 3-2, at Riverfront Stadium and won his other two decisions that month. Hoyt fared 2-0 against the New York Mets, Philadelphia Phillies, and Los Angeles Dodgers and 3-0 against the San Francisco Giants.

Hoyt struggled with an 8-11 record and a 5.11 ERA in 1986, fanning 85 batters in 159 innings. He missed about a month at the start of the season in a rehabilitation center for treatment of alcohol dependency. Hoyt rejected the diagnosis that he was an alcoholic and had trouble regaining his pitching form. Upon his May 10 return, he lost to the Chicago Cubs, 6-5, at Wrigley Field. Although winning his other two decisions in May, he lost all three games between June 2 and June 23, four consecutive from July 21 through August 6, and three straight between August 30 and September 22. His best performances came at home before the All-Star break, when he defeated the Chicago Cubs, 4-1, on July 3, the Pittsburgh Pirates, 4-2, on July 8, and the St. Louis Cardinals, 13-6, on July 13.

Commissioner Peter Ueberroth suspended Hoyt for the 1987 season because of persistent drug abuse. After serving a 45-day prison term, Hoyt was invited to the Chicago White Sox training camp in 1988. He was arrested again and returned to prison in February of 1988 after enforcement officials discovered marijuana in his Columbia, South Carolina apartment. In eight major-league seasons, Hoyt compiled a 98-68 mark with a 3.99 ERA and 681 strikeouts in 1,311.1 innings. He resides in Irmo, South Carolina.

BRUCE HURST

Bruce Hurst starred as a pitcher with the San Diego Padres from 1989 through 1993. The 6-foot 3-inch, 219-pound left-hander was born on March 24, 1958 in St. George, Utah and helped Dixie Junior College win the National Junior College basketball tournament. The Boston Red Sox selected him in the first round of the 1976 draft. Hurst spent nearly six seasons in the minor leagues, pitching briefly with Boston in 1980 and 1981.

From 1982 through 1988, Hurst boasted an 88-73 win-loss record as a Red Sox starter and became the second winningest southpaw in club history. In 1986, he helped Boston capture the American League pennant with a 13-8 mark and a 2.99 ERA and averaged nearly a strikeout per inning. Hurst won his only decision in the American League Championship Series against the California Angels and defeated the New York Mets twice in the World Series. In 1987, he triumphed 15 times, made the American League All-Star team, and established a career-best 190 strikeouts. His career-high 18 victories sparked the Red Sox to the 1988 American League East title.

Bruce Hurst

In December 1988, the San Diego Padres signed Hurst as a free agent. In 1989, he attained a 15-11 slate and a 2.69 ERA, a career best and fifth best in the National League. He shared the senior circuit lead in complete games (10), ranked fourth in innings pitched (244), and recorded 179 strikeouts, then second best in Padre history and fifth best in the National League. The Atlanta Braves made only one hit against him on April 10 at home in just his second Padre start as 13 batters struck out. Hurst picked 10 runners off base and won seven of his final 10 decisions. In 1990, he finished 11-9 with a 3.14 ERA, tenth best in the National League. After struggling the first half of the season, Hurst won six of eight decisions following the All-Star break and authored four shutouts. Hurst hurled two-hitters at home on July 7 in a 3-1 win over the St. Louis Cardinals and on July 24 in a 10-0 shutout over the Cincinnati Reds. He shared the National League lead in shutouts (4) and hurled 27 straight scoreless innings.

In 1991, Hurst achieved a 15-8 record with a 3.29 ERA. He won four of his first six starts and five consecutive games from July 16 to August 7. Hurst ranked fifth in the National League with a .652 winning percentage and paced the Padres with six pickoffs. He knocked in a career-high six runs and enjoyed the only multiple-hit game of his career in a 5-4 setback to the Chicago Cubs on August 23 at Wrigley Field. Hurst finished 14-9 with a 3.85 ERA in 1992 and reached 10 consecutive seasons with at least 10 victories. He blanked the New York Mets, 7-0, at Shea Stadium on May 13 and, 3-0, at home on May 18, allowing only a sixth-inning infield single to Chico Walker in the latter. Besides hurling two other shutouts, Hurst allowed one run four times and yielded two runs six times. He struck out 11 San Francisco Giants in an 8-0 home victory on June 25 and won 13 of his last 19 decisions. In October, Hurst underwent arthroscopic surgery on his left shoulder to repair small tears in his labrum and rotator cuff.

The San Diego Padres traded Hurst and Greg Harris to the Colorado Rockies in July 1993. Upon his departure, Hurst ranked third in ERA (3.27), fourth in shutouts (10), and fifth in complete games (29) on the Padre career list. His major-league career ended with the Texas Rangers in 1994. In 15 major-league seasons, Hurst boasted a 145-113 mark and 3.92 ERA with 1,689 strikeouts, 63 pickoffs, and 23 shutouts. He and his wife, Holly, reside in Gilbert, Arizona, and have two sons, Ryan and Kyle, and one daughter, Jordan.

MIKE IVIE

Mike Ivie was the first player selected by the San Diego Padres in the June 1970 free agent draft. The 6-foot 3-inch, 205-pound Ivie, who batted and threw right-handed, was born on August 8, 1952 in Decatur, Georgia and attended high school there. Although an excellent defensive catcher with an outstanding arm, Ivie spent five seasons in the minor leagues, mainly as a first baseman and outfielder. He batted .471 with three RBIs in six games for San Diego as a 19-year-old in 1971, collecting two hits in his first start on September 5 in a 5-2 home loss to the Atlanta Braves and driving in two runs on September 7 in an 8-7 home victory over the Cincinnati Reds. After nearly three more minor-league seasons, Ivie rejoined the Padres in September 1974. He struggled at the plate, but belted one triple and one home run with three RBIs. His first major-league extra-base hit came at home on September 11, when he clouted a two-run homer in the seventh inning to defeat the Houston Astros, 2-0.

In his first full major-league season in 1975, Ivie batted .249 with eight home runs and 46 RBIs. He set the Padre rookie RBI record and tied the club rookie home run mark. Ivie split time between third base and first base, making the Topps and *Baseball Digest* All-Rookie teams. The Padres' manager claimed Ivie "was born to catch," but the latter hated catching and preferred playing first base instead. The Padres even inserted him at third base for 61 games. Besides having 21 multi-hit games and hitting .285 on the road, Ivie batted .359 with 10 RBIs against the Atlanta Braves. He belted a grand slam with five RBIs in a 10-1 rout over the Los Angeles Dodgers at Dodger Stadium on July 1.

Ivie's best major-league season came in 1976, when he played almost exclusively at fist base and batted .291 with 19 doubles, seven home runs, and 70 RBIs. Ivie led the Padres in batting average and RBIs, knocking in three runs in a 4-1 triumph over the Los Angeles Dodgers at Dodger Stadium on October 2 to edge teammate Dave Winfield by one. His 29 multi-hit games included one four-hit and seven three-hit contests. In an 8-7 loss to the San Francisco Giants in the second game of a June 23 doubleheader at Candlestick Park, Ivie made four hits in five plate appearances. He hit safely in 20 of 22 games from August 10 through September 4, collecting four RBIs in a 7-3 home victory over the Pittsburgh Pirates on August 24. Ivie batted over .420 against the St. Louis Cardinals, New York Mets, and Montreal Expos and knocked in 13 runs against the Cincinnati Reds.

Ivie batted .272 with nine home runs and 66 RBIs in 1977, dividing time between first base and third base. He shared the Padre lead in doubles with 29 and finished third with 66 RBIs. Besides collecting three hits in 10 games, Ivie knocked in four runs in a 12-4 slugfest over the Montreal Expos at Olympic Stadium on May 20. His best Padre performance came in a doubleheader against the San Francisco Giants at Candlestick Park on May 30, when he made seven hits, scored three runs, belted five doubles, and knocked in six runs. In a 9-8 second-game triumph, he doubled three times, singled twice, and drove in four runs. Ivie registered nine-game hitting streaks from June 4 through June 14 and from July 21 through July 28. He hit .386 against the St. Louis Cardinals and knocked in 15 runs against the Houston Astros.

In February 1978, the San Diego Padres traded Ivie to the San Francisco Giants for Derrel Thomas.

San Diego disliked Ivie's attitude when he jumped the team for several days after being switched back to third base in 1977. As a Padre, Ivie batted .269 with 356 hits, 64 doubles, 25 home runs, and 188 RBIs in 403 games. Upon his departure from San Diego, he ranked sixth in batting average and RBIs, eighth in doubles, and ninth in hits. Ivie played with the San Francisco Giants through 1981, hitting a career-high .308 with 11 home runs and 55 RBIs as a backup for Willie McCovey in 1978. He matched a major-league record that season by belting two pinch-hit grand slams. In 1979, Ivie batted .286 with career-highs of 27 home runs and 89 RBIs. Ivie spent the remainder of his major-league career with the Houston Astros and Detroit Tigers, retiring following the 1983 season. In 11 major-league seasons, he batted .269 with 81 home runs and 411 RBIs. He and his wife, Pam, reside in Crawfordsville, Georgia and have one son, Michael Steven.

Randy Jones

RANDY JONES

Randy Jones, the first Padre-developed superstar, brought respectability to a struggling franchise from June 1973 through 1980. The 6-foot, 180-pound pitcher, who batted right and threw left-handed, was born on January 12, 1950 in Fullerton, California and grew up in Brea, California. He earned a Bachelor's degree in business in 1972 from Chapman College, where he posted a 12-5 record with a 1.42 ERA in baseball and made the College All-America team as a senior. The San Diego Padres selected him in the fifth round of the June 1972 draft. Jones spent less than one full minor-league season with Tri-City of the Northwestern League in 1972 and Alexandria, Louisiana, of the Texas League in 1972 and 1973. He possessed a good curveball and a slider, which former major-leaguer Claude Osteen taught him.

After joining the San Diego Padres in June 1973, Jones won seven of 13 decisions with a 3.16 ERA and made the Topps Rookie All-Star team. The club's most effective pitcher the second half of the season, Jones set a Padre record for highest winning percentage (.538) by a left-handed pitcher. Jones hurled a 9-0 home shutout over the New York Mets on August 14 and did not allow an earned run in defeating the Los Angeles Dodgers, 4-1, on July 3 and, 3-2, on September 6 at Dodger Stadium. His most effective pitching performances came against the Chicago Cubs, Montreal Expos, New York Mets, and Cincinnati Reds. The hard-luck Jones shared the National League lead with 22 losses and fanned 124 batters in 1974. The Padres were shut out in seven of his losses, scored only once in four of his losses, and scored only twice in six of his losses. He pitched consecutive complete-game home victories over the Montreal Expos, 1-0, on July 12 and the Philadelphia Phillies, 15-1, on July 17.

Jones earned *The Sporting News'* Comeback Player of the Year accolades in 1975 with a 20-12 record, becoming the first Padre 20-game winner and making the AP Major-League All-Star team and the UPI and *The Sporting News'* National League All-Star teams. Besides matching Fred Norman's club record with six shutouts, he led the senior circuit with a career-best 2.24 ERA. Jones finished second to Tom Seaver in the National League Cy Young Award balloting and tenth in the National League Most Valuable Player balloting. He ranked second in the National League in complete games (18) and shutouts (6) and set Padre records for most complete games, wins, innings pitched (285), and winning percentage (.625). Jones allowed only one run in 10 games. Half of his triumphs came against the top four National League clubs, as he defeated the Cincinnati Reds and Philadelphia Phillies three times and the Pittsburgh Pirates and Los Angeles Dodgers twice. He triumphed over every National League club

John Grubb (left) and Randy Jones celebrate after Jones's 10-inning one-hitter against the St. Louis Cardinals.

except the Montreal Expos and Chicago Cubs and struck out eight Los Angeles Dodgers in a 6-4 home win on September 23 to attain his twentieth victory.

Jones fashioned home one-hitters in a 1-0 triumph over the St. Louis Cardinals on May 19 and in a 2-1 win over the Cincinnati Reds on July 3, two-hitters in a 5-1 victory over the Houston Astros on August 6 and in a 2-1 win over the Atlanta Braves on September 10, and a three-hit, 4-0 shutout over the Atlanta Braves on August 1. He was named National League Pitcher of the Week for his May 19 one-hitter and for blanking the Pittsburgh Pirates, 5-0, in a 68-pitch home game on May 24. The first Padre pitcher selected to the All-Star team, Jones earned a save in a scoreless ninth inning to preserve a 6-3 win for the National League in the 1975 Summer Classic. The sinkerball specialist with superb control induced batters to hit ground balls and hurled very short games. His 18 complete games averaged two hours, with the quickest being 1 hour, 37 minutes on August 6 against the Houston Astros. Twelve of his wins came at home, while 17 of his triumphs came at night. The crowd favorite boosted home attendance by several thousand.

Jones's banner 1976 season earned him the National League Cy Young Award over Jerry Koosman. He became only the second pitcher to win the award after placing second the previous season and only the third from a second-division club. Jones finished 1976 with a 22-14 win-loss mark and a 2.74 ERA, recording senior circuit highs and club records for wins, starts (40), complete games (25), innings pitched (315.1), and consecutive complete games (5). His 22 victories represented nearly one-third of the Padre victories. He ranked third in the senior circuit with five shutouts and fifth in ERA. Jones defeated the Houston Astros, Los Angeles Dodgers, Philadelphia Phillies, and San Francisco Giants three times and triumphed over every National League club at least once. He fared 12-5 at home and 12-9 on the road, capturing 16 of 19 decisions before the All-Star break. His 25 complete games averaged just two hours and three minutes, with 11 lasting under two hours. Jones pitched the fastest National League game in 1 hour, 31 minutes in a 3-0 home triumph over the Philadelphia Phillies on July 20 and hurled a 1-hour, 38-minute 2-0 home win over the Montreal Expos on August 27.

From May 17 to June 22, Jones tied Christy Mathewson's National League record of 68 consecutive innings without allowing a walk. His eighth-inning walk on June 22 to Marc Hill of the San Francisco Giants at home on a full count broke the streak. He was the first pitcher since World War II to win 20 games without striking out 100 batters. Half of his losses were by one run, including three games in which the Padres were shut out. Jones also set a major-league record for most chances accepted by a pitcher (112) without making an error and tied the major-league record for highest fielding percentage (1.000) by a pitcher. He established a National League record for inducing the most double plays with 112 and won his start, 7-1, for the National League in the 1976 All-Star Game. His honors included being *The Sporting News'* National League Pitcher of the Year and making the AP, UPI, and *TSN* All-Star teams.

Off-season arm surgery to help repair nerve damage in his left arm limited Jones's effectiveness thereafter. In 1977, he won only six of 18 decisions. His best performances came at home in hurling seven shutout innings in a 5-0 victory over the Chicago Cubs on September 2 and in a 3-2, 10-inning loss to the Los Angeles Dodgers on September 6. In his final five starts, he split two decisions and allowed only five earned runs in 34 innings. The Padres were blanked in four of his 12 losses. In 1978, Jones improved to a 13-14 mark with an excellent 2.88 ERA. Besides toiling 253 innings, he authored 1-0 shutouts at home over the Chicago Cubs on May 10 and over the Los Angeles Dodgers on August 1 and either had no decisions or losses in 11 games in which he allowed two runs or less. Jones boasted a combined 4-1 record against the Cincinnati Reds and Los Angeles Dodgers and compiled a 1.98 ERA in his 19 home starts.

In 1979, Jones logged an 11-12 slate with a 3.68 ERA. He finished 7-4 with a 3.07 ERA in 19 home starts and ranked fourth in the National League with 263 innings pitched. Six times, relievers blew his leads. Jones walked only 2.19 batters per nine innings, seventh best in the senior circuit. He slumped to a 5-13 record in 1980, but hurled three consecutive shutouts. Jones blanked the Chicago Cubs, 4-0, at Wrigley Field on May 6, the Pittsburgh Pirates, 5-0, at home on May 11, and the Chicago Cubs, 3-0, at home on May 16. In December 1980, the Padres traded him to the New York Mets. His final two major-league seasons came with the Mets.

During his major-league career, Jones compiled a 100-123 win-loss record with a 3.42 ERA and struck out 735 batters in 1,933 innings. In eight seasons with the Padres, he tallied 92 wins and 105 losses with 677 strikeouts and a 3.30 ERA. The finesse pitcher still holds Padre career records for most starts (253), innings pitched (1,766), complete games (71), and shutouts (18) and ranks second in victories (92), third in ERA, fifth in appearances (264), and sixth in strikeouts. Teammate Steve Arlin stressed that "Jones always kept his infielders in the game," while announcer Dave Campbell observed: "People reveled in his success. He drew 10,000 to 15,000 additional people to games and received standing ovations even when warming up."

After arranging commissaries on military bases and handling commentary on Padre broadcasts for KFMB-radio, Jones operated a barbecue business at Qualcomm Stadium. The Padres retired his uniform number 35. In August 1999, he was inducted into the San Diego Padres Hall of Fame as a charter member. He lives in Escondido, California and has two children, Staci and Jami.

WALLY JOYNER

Wally Joyner starred at first base for the San Diego Padres from 1996 through 1999. The 6-foot 2-inch, 200-pound Joyner, who batted and threw left-handed, was born on June 16, 1962 in Atlanta, Georgia and graduated from Redan High School in Stone Mountain, Georgia, where he starred in basketball and was named Georgia High School Baseball Player of the Year in 1960. The devout Mormon majored in business administration at Brigham Young University, making second-team All-America in baseball in 1983, and was a teammate of future Padres general manager Kevin Towers.

The California Angels selected Joyner in the third round of the June 1983 draft. Joyner spent three seasons in the minor leagues and played first base for California from 1986 through 1991. In 1986, he finished second in the American League Rookie of the Year balloting, made the American League All-Star team, and batted .455 with a home run in the American League

Wally Joyner

Championship Series against the Boston Red Sox. His best season with the Angels came in 1987, when he attained career highs with 100 runs scored, 34 home runs, and 117 RBIs. Defensively, he led the junior circuit first basemen in putouts three times, chances twice, and assists, double plays, and fielding percentage once. Joyner played with the Kansas City Royals from 1992 through 1995, leading the club in doubles in 1992 and 1993 and in batting average (.311) in 1994. His peak season there came in 1995, when he paced the Royals in batting (.310) and doubles (28), knocked in 83 runs, and led American League first basemen with a .998 fielding percentage.

The Kansas City Royals traded Joyner to the San Diego Padres in December 1995. In 1996, Joyner batted .277 with 29 doubles and paced National League first basemen with a .997 fielding percentage. Despite playing just 121 games, he knocked in 65 runs. He started sensationally, leading the major leagues with a .407 batting average and recording 14 RBIs during April. Joyner hit safely in the first 10 games and in 18 of his first 20 contests. He made his 1,500th major-league hit in the first inning on April 15, singling to right field off Bryan Rekar in an 11-9 loss to the Colorado Rockies at Coors Field. He clouted two home runs and fell one short of his career high with five RBIs in a 5-2 home win over the Philadelphia Phillies on May 22.

Joyner was hitting .321 with five home runs and 33 RBIs on June 2, when a routine double play hurt the Padres' fortunes for the rest of the month. He fractured his left thumb attempting to break up a double play in the fourth inning against the Philadelphia Phillies at Veterans Stadium and spent from June 3 through July 11 on the disabled list. The Padres lost 19 of their first 23 games without Joyner and saw a 5.5-game Western Division lead dissipate into a two-game deficit to the Los Angeles Dodgers. Joyner returned after the All-Star break, but batted just .245 with three homers and 32 RBIs in 65 games.

Defensively, Joyner committed only three errors in 1,151 total chances. The Padres allowed only 17 unearned runs and committed just 34 errors in Joyner's first 56 games but yielded 27 unearned runs with 40 miscues during his absence. After his return in July, the Padres committed only 44 errors.

Joyner helped the Padres win the National League West over the Los Angeles Dodgers, sparking a four-game winning streak in early September. He belted a three-run, sixth-inning homer off Todd Stottlemyre of the St. Louis Cardinals at Busch Stadium to give the Padres a crucial 5-4 victory. He batted .400 with the bases loaded and .305 with 20 doubles and 37 RBIs on the road.

In 1997, Joyner batted a career-high .327 with 149 hits, 29 doubles, 13 home runs, and 83 RBIs, ranking fifth in the National League in batting average, second on the club in hits and fourth in RBIs. Joyner and batting champion Tony Gwynn became the third Padre duo to finish among the top five in batting average in the same season. He recorded 45 multi-hit games, including the lone Padre five-hit contest, and 18 multiple-RBI games.

Joyner batted .324 in April, making two hits in each of the first four games. He batted .392 with nine doubles, four homers, and 26 RBIs in June and fared second best in the major leagues in interleague play with a .442 batting average, trailing only Edgar Martinez of the Seattle Mariners. Joyner homered twice with four RBIs on June 23 in an 11-6 slugfest over the San Francisco Giants at Candlestick Park, connecting off Mark Gardner in the first inning and Jim Poole in the sixth inning. One week later, he posted his second five-hit game in a 15-6 walloping of the Oakland Athletics at the Oakland Coliseum. Joyner enjoyed nine-game hitting streaks to open the season and from August 26 through September 5. His crucial pinch-hit single with two out in the ninth inning at home tied the Cincinnati Reds on August 14, enabling the Padres to win, 5-4, in 10 innings. He batted .455 with five RBIs as a pinch-hitter and .353 with runners in scoring position.

Joyner batted .298 with 12 home runs and 80 RBIs in 131 games for the 1998 National League champions, the second highest batting average and third most RBIs on the Padres. He ranked second in major-league baseball with a .412 batting average with runners in scoring position, trailing only Bobby Abreu of the Philadelphia Phillies. Joyner hit the first major-league home run of the 1998 season, connecting off David Weathers in the sixth inning of the opening game, a 10-2 victory over the Cincinnati Reds at Riverfront Stadium on March 31. He belted his sixth career grand slam and a double off Paul Wagner in a 13-4 trouncing of the Milwaukee Brewers at County Stadium on May 5 and homered and singled twice with five RBIs in a 12-10 setback to the Oakland Athletics at Oakland Coliseum on June 30.

Joyner singled home Ruben Rivera with the winning run in the ninth inning on May 22 in a 9-6 win over the Houston Astros at the Astrodome, drove in Tony Gwynn in the fifth inning to edge the St. Louis Cardinals 3-2 at home on June 1, and plated Quilvio Veras with the winning run on an eighth-inning single in a 2-1 home victory over the Cincinnati Reds on June 10. He collected his 1,000th major-league RBIs with a fourth-inning solo home run off Hideo Nomo in a 7-3 loss to the New York Mets at Shea Stadium on July 28. He batted .321 with eight homers and 49 RBIs on the road and reached base safely in 24 consecutive starts from June 10 through July 15.

In the 1998 post-season, Joyner batted just .200 with one home run and four RBIs in 13 games. A nagging left shoulder strain bothered him throughout the playoffs. His two-run homer with one out in the bottom of the eighth inning gave the host Padres a 6-1 lead in Game 4 of the National League Division Series against the Houston Astros, but he went hitless in his five other at bats. Joyner batted .313 with two RBIs in the National League Championship Series against the Atlanta Braves, singling twice in Game 5 at Qualcomm Stadium and singling in the sixth inning off Tom Glavine to give the Padres a 2-0 lead in decisive Game 6 at Turner Field. San Diego scored three more runs in that inning in the 5-0, series-clinching win. New York Yankee pitchers held him hitless in eight at-bats in the World Series.

Joyner struggled in 1999 with a .248 batting average, five home runs, and 43 RBIs in 110 games, bothered by a bad shoulder. The Padres on December 22 traded Joyner, infielder Quilvio Veras, and outfielder Reggie Sanders to the Atlanta Braves for infielder Bret Boone, outfielder-infielder Ryan Klesko, and pitcher Jason Shiell. As a Padre, Joyner batted .291 with 480 hits, 102 doubles, 38 home runs, and 271 RBIs and ranks twelfth in doubles, RBIs, and walks (229).

Joyner saw limited duty with Atlanta in 2000, hitting .281 with five home runs and 32 RBIs in 119 games. In January 2001, the Anaheim Angels signed him as a free agent. He batted .243 with three home runs and 14 RBIs before retiring in June 2001.

In 16 major-league seasons, Joyner batted .289 with 2,060 hits, 409 doubles, 26 triples, 204 home runs, 1,106 RBIs, 833 walks, and 825 strikeouts in 2,033 major-league games. His .994 fielding percentage ranked ninth of all time among major-league first basemen. Joyner, who hit above .300 four times, rejoined the San Diego Padres as special assistant to the general manager in November 2001. He and his wife, Lesley, a former gymnast, reside in Mapleton, Utah with their four daughters, Jessica, McKenzie, Crosby, and Chase.

FRED KENDALL

Fred Kendall caught for the San Diego Padres from 1969 through 1976 and in 1979 and 1980. The 6-foot, 1-inch 185-pound Kendall, who batted and threw right-handed, was born on January 31, 1949 in Torrance, California. He graduated in 1967 from Torrance High School, where he played baseball and football and was named best senior athlete. The Cincinnati Reds selected Kendall in the fourth round of the June 1967 free agent draft and assigned him to their minor-league system for two years. The San Diego Padres chose Kendall seventh in the October 1968 expansion draft. In 1969, he hit .279 and drove in 61 runs in 136 games for Elmira, New York, of the Eastern League.

Kendall batted .154 in 10 games for the San Diego Padres in 1969. He debuted on September 8 in a 9-2 loss to the Houston Astros at the Astrodome and singled off Scipio Spinks. Kendall singled twice in a 12-3 trouncing by the Atlanta Braves at home on September

Fred Kendall

19 and singled in a 9-4 win over the San Francisco Giants at Candlestick Park on October 1. He batted .307 with Salt Lake City, Utah of the Pacific Coast League in 1970 and went hitless in nine at-bats for San Diego. In 1971, Kendall hit .171 with seven RBIs in 49 Padre games as a reserve catcher. He collected three hits and drove in two runs in a victory over the Montreal Expos and clouted his first major-league home run on July 7 off Bob Gibson in a 4-1 home victory over the St. Louis Cardinals. Kendall's first full major-league season came in 1972, when he batted .216 with six home runs and 18 RBIs and made only three errors in 82 games. He belted three home runs against the Philadelphia Phillies, including two round-trippers in a 6-1 triumph at Veterans Stadium on July 7, and enjoyed two six-game hitting streaks. His .350 batting average with seven hits paced the team against the New York Mets.

New eyeglasses helped Kendall attain his best major-league season and Padre Most Valuable Player honors in 1973 with then career highs in batting average (.282), home runs (10), RBIs (59), and games (145). Kendall hit .304 on the road and shared the club lead with 143 hits. Besides catching more games than any receiver in two years and throwing out one-half of the runners attempting to steal, he produced nine game-winning hits and two four-hit games. Kendall tripled twice in an 8-3 win over the Philadelphia Phillies at Veterans Stadium on August 22. He batted .372 against the New York Mets and .368 against the San Francisco Giants.

In 1974, Kendall batted just .231 with eight home runs and 45 RBIs in 141 games. Besides knocking in eight runs against the San Francisco Giants, he hit .400 against the Philadelphia Phillies with three home runs and seven RBIs. Kendall batted over .300 for the first month, collecting three hits at home in a 9-1 loss to the Houston Astros on April 11 and in a 5-4 win over the Philadelphia Phillies on April 28. His ninth-inning single on May 27 broke up a 6-0 perfect game by Ken Brett of the Pittsburgh Pirates at Three Rivers Stadium. He struggled in 1975, hitting only .199 with 24 RBIs. Kendall drove in three runs in a 5-3 home triumph over the Atlanta Braves on April 25 and batted .308 against the Eastern Division champion Pittsburgh Pirates. He made three hits at home in a 4-3 win over the Pittsburgh Pirates on May 23 and in a 10-8 slugfest loss to the Montreal Expos on August 28.

In 1976, Kendall batted .246 with two home runs and 39 RBIs and led major-league catchers with 146 games. His .994 fielding percentage trailed only Johnny Bench. He caught all of Randy Jones's league-leading 22 victories. Slow afoot, Kendall grounded into a club-record 20 double plays. In December 1976, the Padres traded Kendall, Johnny Grubb, and Hector Torres to the Cleveland Indians for George Hendrick. Kendall, the only remaining Padre from the original 1969 roster, had batted .235 and ranked fourth in games (689), at-bats (2,092), and doubles (70), fifth in RBIs (193) and hits (492), seventh in runs scored (139), and ninth in triples (10) and home runs (29) in franchise history.

After spending 1977 with the Cleveland Indians and 1978 with the Boston Red Sox, Kendall returned to the San Diego Padres as a free agent in February 1979. He batted just .167 with one home run and six RBIs in 46 games in 1979, but hit .500 as a pinch-hitter and homered off John Candelaria of the Pittsburgh Pirates in a 3-1 victory at Three Rivers Stadium on June 2. His two-run double keyed a 5-1 home triumph over the Montreal Expos on July 14. He ended his major-league career in 1980, batting .292 with seven hits and two RBIs.

During 12 major-league seasons, Kendall hit .234 with 130 home runs, 634 RBIs and a .982 fielding average. With the Padres, he batted .233 with 149 runs, 516 hits, 72 doubles, 10 triples, 28 home runs, and 201 RBIs. Kendall has served as a coach for the Colorado Rockies since 2000. He and his wife, Patricia, reside in Torrance, California and have two sons, Michael and Jason, and one daughter, Kathy. Jason has caught for the Pittsburgh Pirates since 1996.

TERRY KENNEDY

Terry Kennedy starred as a catcher for the San Diego Padres from 1981 through 1986. He was born on June 4, 1956 in Euclid, Ohio and is the son of Bob Kennedy, former major-league baseball player, coach, manager, and executive. Kennedy attended Florida State University, batting .348 with 32 career home runs for the Seminoles. He made *The Sporting News'* All-America teams in 1976 and 1977 and was named 1977 College Player of the Year. The St. Louis Cardinals drafted the 6-foot 4-inch, 220-pound catcher, who batted left-handed and threw right-handed, in the first round of the June 1977 draft as the sixth overall pick. Kennedy spent less than three seasons in the minor leagues and joined the St. Louis Cardinals as backup for catcher Ted Simmons in 1980.

In a blockbuster 11-player transaction in December 1980, the Cardinals traded Kennedy to the San Diego Padres. Kennedy made the National League All-Star team in 1981, 1983, and 1985. In 1981, he batted a career-best .301, finished sixth in the National League with 24 doubles, and ranked second on the Padres with 41 RBIs. Kennedy led senior circuit catchers with 12 double plays and placed second with 63 assists. Besides enjoying a 13-game hitting streak from May 22 through June 5, he made four hits in a 10-5 home setback to the Los Angeles Dodgers on September 14 and three hits the next day in an 8-2 victory over the Dodgers.

In 1982, Kennedy became one of the best-hitting major-league catchers, batting .295 with 97 RBIs and a .486 slugging average. He matched the National League record for most doubles by a catcher with 42 and established career highs in runs (75), hits (166), and home runs (21). Kennedy led catchers in most extra-base hits (64) and RBIs, finished second in the senior circuit in doubles, and placed second among catchers in batting average and home runs. He paced the Padres in batting, slugging, doubles, home runs, and RBIs. Kennedy had four hits and four RBIs in a 13-6 home romp over the San Francisco Giants on April

Terry Kennedy

19 and clouted two home runs in a 4-1 home victory over the Chicago Cubs on September 4 and in a 12-6 loss to the Atlanta Braves at Atlanta-Fulton County Stadium.

In 1983, Kennedy made *The Sporting News'* Silver Slugger team as the top National League hitting catcher. His career-high 98 RBIs ranked fifth in the senior circuit and third in Padre history. He batted .284 with 27 doubles, leading National League catchers with 14 game-winning RBIs and nine sacrifice flies and finishing second with 17 home runs. He was named April's National League Player of the Month, hitting a league-leading .390 with 21 RBIs. Kennedy belted seven home runs with 22 RBIs in September. He hit five home runs in six games and set a Padre record by clouting home runs in four consecutive games from September 4 through September 7. In 1984, Kennedy guided the young pitching staff to their first National League pennant. His 147 games paced all major-league catchers. From July 28 through July 31, he helped Padre hurlers garner four consecutive shutouts against the Houston Astros and the Los Angeles Dodgers and set a franchise record with 40.2 consecutive scoreless innings caught. Kennedy batted .222 in the National League Championship Series against the Chicago Cubs and just .211 with one home run and three RBIs in the World Series loss to the Detroit Tigers. In 1985, Kennedy hit .261 with 10 home runs and 74 RBIs. During May, he hit .369 and enjoyed a 12-game hitting streak. Kennedy hit over .400 against the Philadelphia Phillies and Montreal Expos, including a four-hit game in an 8-3 win at Olympic Stadium on May 19. He knocked in a run with a single during the 1985 All-Star Game and set a Padre record by batting .478 as a pinch-hitter in 1986.

In October 1986, the San Diego Padres dealt Kennedy to the Baltimore Orioles. Kennedy spent two seasons with the Orioles and became the second catcher to start All-Star games in both leagues. He caught for the San Francisco Giants from 1989 through 1991, appearing in the 1989 World Series. In 14 major-league seasons, Kennedy batted .264 with 1,313 hits, 244 doubles, 113 home runs, 628 RBIs, and a .986 fielding percentage. Upon leaving the Padres, he ranked second in doubles (158), third in RBI (424), fourth in hits (817) and home runs (76), and fifth in runs (308). He managed Iowa of the Pacific Coast League in 1998 and 1999 and has served as minor-league field coordinator for the Chicago Cubs since 2000. He and his wife, Teresa, reside in Chandler, Arizona and have three children, Suzzana, Sarah, and Bart.

Clay Kirby

CLAY KIRBY

Clay Kirby anchored the San Diego Padres pitching staff in the infant years from 1969 through 1973. The 6-foot 3-inch, 175-pound, right-hander, who was born on June 25, 1948 in Washington, D.C., attended Old Dominion College in Norfolk, Virginia and Benjamin Franklin University in Washington, D.C. The St. Louis Cardinals drafted Kirby in 1966 and assigned him to Sarasota, Florida, of the Florida State League. Although struggling with wildness, Kirby progressed during the next two seasons through the Cardinal farm system.

The San Diego Padres selected Kirby sixth in the October 1968 expansion draft. As a rookie in 1969, Kirby led the major leagues with 20 losses and compiled a 3.79 ERA. The Padres scored only 30 runs in his 20 defeats. Kirby won only seven decisions, but paced San Diego hurlers in innings pitched (215.2) and strikeouts (113). On April 27, he fanned nine Cincinnati Reds in a 5-2 home victory. Kirby lost seven consecutive decisions before winning four of his final six decisions. He defeated the Philadelphia Phillies, 5-2, at home on September 1, the Cincinnati Reds, 2-1, in a three-hit, complete-game effort at Riverfront Stadium on September 10, the Reds, 7-1, at home on September 18, and the San Francisco Giants, 3-2, in the season finale at Candlestick Park on October 2. Kirby's best success came against the Cincinnati Reds with a 3-2 record and 2.25 ERA. Although boasting an excellent ERA, he lost all five decisions to the Atlanta Braves, the New York Mets, and the St. Louis Cardinals.

In 1970, Kirby struggled with a 10-16 win-loss mark and 4.52 ERA. The Padres tallied only 29 runs in his 16 defeats, being blanked three times and held to one run seven times. Kirby started 34 games to share the club lead with Pat Dobson and pitched a home masterpiece on July 21, when he came within three outs of notching a no-hitter against the New York Mets. The Padres were losing, 1-0, on a first-inning walk, two stolen bases, and a groundout. Manager Preston Gomez aroused the ire of the San Diego fans by pinch-hitting for Kirby in the bottom of the eighth inning, denying him an opportunity to complete the no-hitter. No Padre pitcher has yet hurled a no-hitter.

After the All-Star Game, Kirby was one of the most effective National League pitchers. He hurled six complete games, including consecutive home starts on August 3 in a 10-3 victory over the Cincinnati Reds and on August 7 in a 6-1 win over the Atlanta Braves.

Kirby won five of his last eight decisions, and the Padres were blanked in two of his three setbacks. He defeated the Cincinnati Reds three times, fanning 11 for his final 5-4 home victory on September 13.

In 1971, Kirby became San Diego's first 15-game winner and boasted an impressive 2.83 ERA. He ranked fourth in the National League with a team record 231 strikeouts but lost his first three decisions. The Padres failed to score more than two runs in nine of his starts. Kirby set the Padre record for most strikeouts in a nine-inning game with 13 in a 4-2 loss to the New York Mets at Shea Stadium on June 9 and started the season's shortest National League contest, a one-hour, 34-minute July 7 contest, a 4-1 home victory over the St. Louis Cardinals. After the All-Star break, he finished 9-7 with a 2.25 ERA. Kirby authored four memorable games in September, winning two of three decisions. Besides allowing only five earned runs and 19 hits, he fanned 44 batters in 43 innings. He held the Houston Astros hitless for 7.1 innings on September 13 at the Astrodome before John Edwards singled. He eventually lost, 3-2, on an unearned run in the ninth inning.

Five days later, Kirby retired the first 21 San Francisco Giants in a 2-1 victory at Candlestick Park. Willie McCovey led off the eighth inning with a home run for the Giants' only hit. On September 24, Kirby allowed one run and eight hits and struck out 15 batters in 15 innings against the Houston Astros. He was not involved in the decision in the Padres' 2-1, 21-inning loss in the first game of a doubleheader. The senior circuit's longest game of 1971 took 5 hours, 25 minutes. Kirby's 15 strikeouts set the Padre record for most strikeouts in an extra-inning game. On September 29, he hurled a 4-1, seven-hit, 10-inning home victory over the San Francisco Giants that sent the Western Division race into the final day of the season. Kirby retired the last 10 batters consecutively. He defeated the Cincinnati Reds, New York Mets, and San Francisco Giants three times apiece.

In 1972, Kirby won 12 of 26 decisions and paced Padre hurlers in victories, ERA (3.13), and strikeouts (175) in 239 innings. Opponents blanked San Diego in five of his losses and allowed the Padres just one run in three of his setbacks. During a seven-week stretch, Kirby was involved in four heartbreaking extra-inning losses. He pitched 10 innings in a 2-1 home setback to the Chicago Cubs on June 2, 13 innings of an 18-inning home game against the Pittsburgh Pirates on June 7, 11 innings (including 10 scoreless) at home against the Cincinnati Reds on June 30, and 11 innings in a 3-2 home loss to the Philadelphia Phillies on July 19. He won two of his final three decisions and wielded a 2.99 ERA at San Diego Stadium. Kirby finished 3-0 against the Atlanta Braves and allowed only four earned runs in 25 innings against the Chicago Cubs.

Kirby's production declined to an 8-18 mark in 1973, but he still paced San Diego with 129 strikeouts. He whiffed 13 Atlanta Braves in a three-hit, 2-0 home shutout on June 23 and endured the longest losing streak by a Padre pitcher at five games. San Diego traded him to the Cincinnati Reds on November 9, 1973 for outfielder Bobby Tolan and pitcher Dave Tomlin. Kirby posted marks of 12-9 in 1974 and 10-6 in 1975 with the Reds and closed his major-league career with a 1-8 mark and 5.72 ERA for the Montreal Expos in 1976.

From 1969 to 1973, Kirby completed 34 of 170 starts and won 52 of 133 decisions with a 3.30 ERA for San Diego. He hurled seven shutouts and struck out 802 batters in 1,128 innings with a 3.30 ERA. Kirby still ranks fourth in strikeouts, sixth in innings pitched and shutouts, seventh in starts, and eighth in ERA among Padre pitchers. During eight major-league seasons, he compiled a 75-104 record with a 3.83 ERA, eight shutouts, and 1,061 strikeouts in 1,549 innings. He and his wife, Susan, had two children, Teresa and Clayton III. Kirby died on October 11, 1991 in Arlington, Virginia.

RYAN KLESKO

Ryan Klesko has played first base for the San Diego Padres since 2000. The 6-foot 3-inch, 220-pound Klesko, who bats and throws left-handed, was born on June 12, 1971 in Westminster, California and graduated from Westminster High School in 1989. The Atlanta Braves selected him in the fifth round of the June 1989 draft. Klesko spent nearly five seasons in the minor leagues, having brief trials with the Atlanta Braves in 1992 and 1993. He showed considerable promise with Atlanta in 1993, batting .353 with two home runs and five RBIs in 22 games.

Klesko played outfield and first base for the Atlanta Braves from 1994 through 1999, batting .281 with 139 home runs, 450 RBIs, and a .525 slugging percentage in 792 games. Between 1995 and 1999, he clouted at least 20 home runs four times. Forty-three percent of his 297 hits went for extra bases. Klesko batted nearly .400 with the bases loaded, including five doubles, six homers, and 69 RBIs. His best season came in 1996, when he batted .282 with 34 home runs, 90 runs scored, and 93 RBIs. Klesko helped the Atlanta Braves reach the playoffs every season between 1995 and 1999, batting a career-best .310 with a .608 slugging percentage in 1995 and hitting a career-high 29 doubles in 1999. He batted .467 with seven hits against the Colorado Rockies in the 1995 National League Division Series and .313 with three home runs and four RBIs in the World Series triumph over the Cleveland Indians. Klesko also appeared in each National League Division Series and Championship Series between 1996 and 1999 and in the 1996 and 1999 World Series against the New York Yankees.

In a blockbuster December 1999 trade, the San Diego Padres acquired Klesko, second baseman Bret Boone, and pitcher Jason Shiell from the Atlanta Braves for second baseman Quilvio Veras, outfielder Reggie Sanders, and first baseman Wally Joyner. Klesko batted .283 with a .516 slugging percentage in 2000, leading the Padres in runs scored (88) and walks (91). Besides stealing 23 bases, he ranked second to Phil Nevin in doubles (33), home runs (26), and RBIs (92). Klesko hit .256 against left-handed pitchers, much better than he had done the previous two seasons.

Klesko enjoyed several memorable games the first half of his inaugural Padre season. His April 7 home run helped San Diego defeat the Montreal Expos, 10-5, at Olympic Stadium for the third consecutive time. Eleven days later, he clouted a 454-foot two-run homer in the first inning off Andy Benes in a 5-4 setback to the St. Louis Cardinals at Busch Stadium. Klesko on April 21 made two of the seven Padre doubles in a 7-2 victory over the Houston Astros at Enron Field. On June 20, he belted solo home runs off Todd Stottlemyre in the fourth and sixth innings to lift San Diego to a 3-1 win over the Arizona Diamondbacks at Bank One Ballpark. Klesko enjoyed continued success after the All-Star break. On July 23, he slugged the game-tying solo round-tripper in the ninth inning and the game-winning two-run homer in the tenth inning, giving the Padres a 6-4 victory over the Colorado Rockies at Coors Field. On September 11, he recorded one of the six Padre stolen bases in a 7-2 home triumph over the Colorado Rockies.

Klesko's most productive major-league season came in 2001, when he batted .286, led the Padres with a career-high 34 doubles and 88 walks, and finished second on the Padres to Phil Nevin with 30 home runs and a career-high 113 RBIs. The best month of his major-league career came in May, when he hit .354 with 27 runs, 17 home runs, and 40 RBIs in just 27 games. Klesko homered twice on May 4 with three RBIs in an 11-4 rout over the Cincinnati Reds at Riverfront Stadium and on May 11 with four RBIs in a 7-6, 10-inning victory over the visiting Florida Marlins. On May 8, he stole second base twice, as the Padres pilfered eight bases in a 7-1 victory over the visiting Atlanta Braves. On May 17, he hit a home run, a double, and two singles in a 15-3 rout over the New York Mets at Shea Stadium. On May 21, he clouted two three-run homers and a triple, matching a career high with six RBIs in a 7-3 victory over the Houston Astros at Enron Field. Outfielder Greg Vaughn was the only other Padre to homer twice and triple in the same game. The next day, Klesko homered twice for the second consecutive game with three RBIs to key a 6-2 win over the Astros.

Klesko demonstrated a power surge the last two months of the 2001 season. On August 2, he hit his seventh career grand slam in the eighth inning off Jeff Fassero, lifting the host Padres past the Chicago Cubs, 4-3. On August 12, Klesko stole second base in a 7-6 loss to the Pittsburgh Pirates at PNC Park, becoming the first Padre to have two seasons with 20 home runs and 20 stolen bases. On August 28, he knocked in two runs with a homer and a single in a 5-2 triumph over the St. Louis Cardinals at Busch Stadium, reaching 100 RBIs for the first time in his career. The following night, Klesko homered twice, doubled twice, and singled once with five RBIs in a 16-14 loss to the Cardinals. His 472-foot home run off Bud Smith in the second inning was the longest by a visiting player since Busch Stadium opened in 1968. On September 2, his leadoff homer in the thirteenth inning off Byung-Hyun Kim edged the Arizona Diamondbacks, 1-0. On October 6, Klesko homered off Chris Nichting of the visiting Colorado Rockies in the seventh inning in a 10-4 triumph, joining John Mabry as the only players to homer into the Loge Level in right field at Qualcomm Stadium and joining Phil Nevin as the second Padre duo to homer at least 30 times in a season. Ken Caminiti and Steve Finley had accomplished the 30-homer feat in 1996.

During 10 major-league seasons, Klesko has batted .282 with 978 hits, 207 doubles, 195 home runs, 655 RBIs, and 72 stolen bases. He remains single and resides in Covington, Georgia.

JOHN KRUK

John Kruk played outfield and first base with the San Diego Padres from 1986 through June 1989 and ranked among the best hitters in club history. The 5-foot 10-inch, 220-pound Kruk, who batted and threw left-handed, was born on February 9, 1961 in Charleston, West Virginia and attended Allegheny Community College. The San Diego Padres chose him in the June 1981 amateur draft. Kruk played outfield in the minor-leagues and led all Class AAA players in 1985 with a .351 batting average for Las Vegas, Nevada of the Pacific Coast League.

Kruk batted .309 with four home runs and 38 RBIs in his rookie 1986 season with the San Diego Padres. San Diego initially used him mainly as a pinch-hitter. He won the Clyde McCullough Award as the top Padre rookie and was named National League Co-Player of the Week from August 11 to 17, hitting .433 with five RBIs in eight games. He produced four-hit games in a 9-4 home victory over the Atlanta Braves on September 10 and in a 5-0 triumph over the Houston Astros on September 21 at the Astrodome.

In 1987, Kruk finished fourth in the National League in hitting (.313) and sixth in on-base percentage (.406) and led San Diego with 91 RBIs. On April 13, Marvell Wynne, Tony Gwynn, and Kruk set a major-league record by hitting three consecutive home runs at the start of a game off Roger Mason in a 13-6 home loss to the San Francisco Giants. Kruk batted .405 in May, the highest National League batting average that month. He feasted on Atlanta Braves pitching at Atlanta-Fulton County Stadium, getting four hits in a 5-3 triumph on June 6 and producing a career-best seven RBIs with two home runs in a 12-7 setback on August 4. Thirteen of his 20 home runs and 56 of his RBIs came after the All-Star break. Nineteen of his home runs were clouted to the opposite field. During August, he belted seven home runs and set a club record with 30 RBIs.

The injury-prone Kruk batted only .241 in 120 games in 1988, but finished seventh in the National League with 80 walks. He hit .424 in the first eight games, belting a grand slam in the home opener on April 12 to defeat the Los Angeles Dodgers, 5-3. Four days later, his ninth-inning pinch-hit home run defeated the San Francisco Giants, 2-1. An injured right shoulder and jammed thumb caused his batting average to plunge after the All-Star break. Kruk divided time between first base, left field, and right field.

San Diego traded Kruk and infielder Randy Ready to the Philadelphia Phillies in June 1989 for outfielder Chris James. As a Padre, he batted .290 with 60 doubles, 41 home runs, 217 RBIs, and 242 walks in 492 games. Kruk played for the Phillies from 1989 through 1994, batting .316 with 33 doubles in 1993 to spark the Phillies to the National League pennant and starring against the Toronto Blue Jays in the World Series. He retired from baseball following the 1995 season to his farm in Keyser, West Virginia. Kruk, married to Jamie Miller, batted at least .300 seven times and made three All-Star teams. In 10 major-league seasons, he hit .300 with 100 home runs and 592 RBIs.

LERON LEE

Leron Lee played left field for the San Diego Padres from 1971 through 1973. The 6-foot, 192-pound Lee, who batted left-handed and threw right-handed, was born on March 4,1948 in Bakersfield, California and starred in football at Grant Union High School in Sacramento. In one high school game, he carried the ball only three times for touchdowns of 75, 54, and 63 yards. Over two dozen major universities recruited him for football, while the St. Louis Cardinals selected him in the first round of the June 1966 free agent draft. Lee spent nearly four seasons in the minor

Leron Lee

leagues, joining the St. Louis Cardinals briefly in September 1969. He struggled with the Cardinals in 1970 and 1971 before being traded with Fred Norman to the San Diego Padres for Al Santorini.

After joining San Diego in June 1971, Lee batted .273 with four home runs and 21 RBIs in 79 games. He hit .370 his first month with the club and demonstrated good defensive speed. Lee ranked second on the Padres with 20 doubles and set a club record with five hits on September 7 against the Cincinnati Reds, doubling twice, singling three times, and scoring four runs in an 8-7 home victory. He hit over .350 against the Cincinnati Reds and the Los Angeles Dodgers.

In 1972, Lee enjoyed his best major-league season with a .300 batting average, 12 home runs, and 47 RBIs. Despite being sidelined six weeks with a broken finger on his right hand, he became just the second Padre to hit .300 in a season. Lee hit .327 against left-handed pitchers and over .400 against the Philadelphia Phillies and the New York Mets. He made a spectacular catch on June 3 in an 8-3 home loss to the Chicago Cubs and broke up Tom Seaver's no-hitter with a one-out single in the ninth inning in a 2-0 setback in the first game of a July 4 doubleheader at Shea Stadium. After breaking his finger trying to escape a pitch against the Montreal Expos on July 11, he did not return to the lineup until August 23. He drove in four runs in a 10-6 loss to the Houston Astros at the Astrodome on September 14, but a leg injury hindered him thereafter.

In 1973, Lee batted just .237 with three home runs and 30 RBIs. He started the season well but was platooned after the All-Star break. Nevertheless, Lee matched teammate Dave Roberts for having the longest consecutive-game hitting streak with 12 and batted .333 against the St. Louis Cardinals. In March 1974, San Diego sold him to the Cleveland Indians. In three seasons with the Padres, Lee hit .271 with 50 doubles, 19 home runs, and 98 RBIs. Upon his departure, he ranked third among Padres in career batting average, fourth in doubles, fifth in triples (11), eighth in runs (115), ninth in hits (260), and tenth in RBIs.

After playing for the Cleveland Indians in 1974 and 1975, Lee played for the Los Angeles Dodgers in 1975 and 1976. In eight major-league seasons, he batted .250 with 31 home runs and 152 RBIs. He and his wife, Willetta, live in Sacramento, California and have two children, Ron and Kim. He builds and flies gas-powered model airplanes.

CRAIG LEFFERTS

Craig Lefferts pitched for the San Diego Padres from 1984 through July 1987 and 1990 through August 1992. The 6-foot 1-inch, 180-pound left-hander was born on September 29, 1957 in Munich, Germany and graduated from Northeast High School in St. Petersburg, Florida in 1975. Lefferts studied marketing at the University of Arizona, where he pitched in the 1979 and 1980 College World Series. He made the All-College World Series team in 1980, leading the Wildcats to the NCAA title with a tournament-low 0.56 ERA. The Chicago Cubs selected him in the ninth round of the June 1980 free agent draft. After three minor-league seasons, Lefferts pitched for the Chicago Cubs in 1983.

In December 1983, the Chicago Cubs traded Lefferts to the San Diego Padres. Lefferts provided valuable relief with a 3-4 win-loss record, 2.13 ERA, and 10 saves in 1984. He allowed only one earned run in both April and May and made his first save as a Padre on May 17 in a 5-4 home triumph over the Montreal Expos. He recorded his first San Diego victory at home on June 12, defeating the Atlanta Braves, 7-6, in 12 innings. Lefferts helped the Padres' pennant drive by allowing just two earned runs in July and saving four games in August. He surrendered only four home runs in 105.2 innings. In six superb post-season appearances, Lefferts hurled 10 shutout innings, won two decisions, saved a game, fanned eight batters, and allowed only three hits. He won the last two games of the National League Championship Series against the Chicago Cubs at home, benefiting from Steve Garvey's dramatic ninth-inning home run in Game 4 and hurling two frames in Game 5. Lefferts pitched six strong relief innings in the World Series against the Detroit Tigers, permitting only two hits and fanning seven. He earned the save in the Padres' 5-3 home win in Game 2.

In 1985, Lefferts finished 7-6 with a 3.35 ERA and two saves. He had never previously recorded over three victories in a season. Despite a tender left elbow, Lefferts led the San Diego staff with 60 appearances and allowed only one earned run in his first 9.2 innings. His first victory came in a 1-0 triumph over Los Angeles on April 28, when he blanked the Dodgers at Dodger Stadium for 1.1 innings. After struggling during the first half of May, Lefferts won twice and yielded only one earned run in his next nine stints. He blanked the Cincinnati Reds for two innings on June 7 in a 3-2,

11-inning victory at Riverfront Stadium. During 26 appearances between July 10 and September 13, Lefferts recorded three victories and allowed just four earned runs in nearly 34 innings. He defeated the Los Angeles Dodgers twice.

In 1986, Lefferts logged a 9-8 slate with a 3.09 ERA and four saves. He set a durability record for the Padres with a major-league-leading 83 appearances, breaking Rollie Fingers's 1978 mark by five. Lefferts established then career-bests in victories (9), innings (107.2), and strikeouts (72). He boasted a 3-0 record in April and on April 25 clouted his first major-league home run in the twelfth inning to give the Padres a 9-8 home victory over the San Francisco Giants. Lefferts earned the Padres Pitcher of the Month Award in both June and July, winning both decisions with a 1.99 ERA in June and boasting two victories and two saves with a 1.74 ERA in July. In one 12-game stretch, only two of 21 inherited runners scored. He fared 6-1 against Western Division opponents, defeating the San Francisco Giants twice with a 1.74 ERA.

In 1987, Lefferts split four decisions with a 4.38 ERA and two saves. In a blockbuster July 1987 trade, the Padres sent Lefferts, Dave Dravecky, and Kevin Mitchell to the San Francisco Giants for Mark Davis, Mark Grant, and two other players. Lefferts hurled for the Giants through 1989, appearing in the 1987 and 1989 National League Championship Series and the 1989 World Series. In December 1989, Lefferts rejoined the San Diego Padres as a free agent.

Lefferts compiled a 7-5 record in 1990 and shared fourth in the National League with a career-high 23 saves. He converted 23 of 31 save opportunities, including 11 of his first 12. His 2.52 ERA marked his best effort since 1984. In his first 25 stints, Lefferts took five of six decisions with 10 saves and a 1.36 ERA. During that nearly 40-inning span, opposition batters made only 21 hits and whiffed 32 times against him. He won the Padres Pitcher of the Month honors in May with a 1-1 record and six saves and in June with a 3-1 mark and six saves. Lefferts earned Rolaids Reliever of the Month for August, notching eight saves in nine opportunities with a 1.46 ERA. He lost to Los Angeles, 8-7, on October 2, marking his first defeat in 10 decisions against the Dodgers. Lefferts saved six games, including five consecutive in May, against the New York Mets. Only 10 of 45 inherited runners scored.

Lefferts again saved 23 games in 1991, but triumphed only once in seven decisions with a 3.91 ERA. The Padres converted him to a starter in 1992, as he produced a 13-9 record and a 3.69 ERA in 27 games. His 13 wins, 163.1 innings, and 81 strikeouts marked career highs. In August 1992, San Diego traded Lefferts to the Baltimore Orioles. Among Padre career leaders, he still ranks second in appearances (375) and ERA (3.24), fifth in saves (64), and eleventh in wins (42). He led San Diego in appearances from 1984 through 1986 and saves in 1990 and 1991.

Lefferts completed 1992 with the Baltimore Orioles, pitched for the Texas Rangers in 1993, and ended his major-league career with the California Angels in 1994. During 12 major-league seasons, he logged a 58-72 win-loss ledger with a 3.43 ERA and 101 saves. Lefferts struck out 719 batters in 1,145.2 innings and toiled in 696 games, all but 45 in relief. He serves as a pitching coach for the Tennessee Smokies of the Southern League in the Toronto Blue Jays organization and has been elected to the University of Arizona Hall of Fame. He and his wife, Wendy, reside in Poway, California with their two sons, Brock and Brady.

TIM LOLLAR

Tim Lollar pitched for the San Diego Padres from 1981 through 1984. The 6-foot 3-inch, 195-pound left-hander was born on March 17, 1956 in Poplar Bluff, Missouri and graduated from Mineral Area Community College in Flat River, Missouri. He majored in forestry at the University of Arkansas, garnering Southern Conference Most Valuable Player honors and *The Sporting News'* All-America honors as a designated hitter in 1978. The New York Yankees selected him in the fourth round of the June 1978 free agent draft. After dividing his first two minor-league seasons between pitching and first base, Lollar pitched with Columbus, Ohio of the International League in 1980. He joined the New York Yankees that year, boasting a 1-0 record and a 3.38 ERA.

In April 1981, the San Diego Padres acquired Lollar, Ruppert Jones, Joe Lefebvre, and Chris Welsh from the New York Yankees for Jerry Mumphrey and John Pacella. Lollar won only two of 10 decisions with a 6.08 ERA for last-place San Diego in 1981. He began the season in the bullpen, but started 11 of his last 15 games. In his first relief stint, he blanked the Cincinnati Reds on one hit in four innings in a 4-0 home loss on April 14. His initial National League win came three days later, when he shut out the Los Angeles Dodgers for one inning in a 3-2, 10-inning home victory. Lollar recorded his first National League save one week later with one inning of shutout relief in a 6-5 win over the Los Angeles Dodgers at Dodger Stadium. His first major-league hit was a home run off Tom Seaver in an 11-2 trouncing by the Cincinnati Reds at Riverfront Stadium on April 28. He snapped a 10-game losing steak with a 7-2 victory over the San Francisco Giants on October 3 at Candlestick Park.

Lollar became one of the best National League left-handed pitchers in 1982, boasting a 16-9 mark. Besides sharing seventh in victories, he placed eleventh in ERA (3.13) and strikeouts (150) and twelfth in innings (232.2). He matched the club lead in shutouts with two and paced the Padres in victories, ERA, innings, and strikeouts, finishing 8-6 at home and 8-3 on the road. His first major-league shutout and complete game came on April 29, when he blanked the New York Mets, 6-0, at home on a five-hitter. Lollar likewise shut out the Philadelphia Phillies, 6-0, at home with a four-hitter on May 9 and combined with Luis DeLeon to two-hit the Chicago Cubs, 2-0, at home on August 21. He fanned 10 Atlanta Braves at home on April 23 and 10 San Francisco Giants at home on June 27. Lollar won four consecutive games from June 27 through July 11, defeating the San Francisco Giants twice and the Philadelphia Phillies and New York Mets once a piece.

Lollar posted a 10-2 record with a 2.71 ERA at mid-season, but did not make the All-Star team. A .247 batter, he reached base safely in his first seven starts. His 11 RBIs matched Chris Welsh for the most by a Padre pitcher in a season. He clouted three-run homers against Phil Niekro in a 6-3 home win over the Atlanta Braves on April 23, against Charlie Puleo of the New York Mets on April 29, and against Mike Scott in a 6-2 home victory over the New York Mets on July 11.

Lollar, bothered by a tender elbow, slumped to a 7-12 mark with a 4.61 ERA in 1983, but led the staff with 135 strikeouts in 175.2 innings. The Padres scored only 19 runs in his 12 losses and were shut out five times, including 1-0 and 2-0 setbacks. After winning 16-13 on the April 15 opening day slugfest over the San Francisco Giants at Candlestick Park, he did not triumph again until defeating the Cincinnati Reds, 3-1, at home on June 16. After combining with Luis DeLeon to blank the Los Angeles Dodgers, 2-0, on two hits at home on June 21, Lollar took no-hitters into the seventh inning in a 2-0 setback to the San Francisco Giants at Candlestick Park on June 26 and in a 2-1 loss to the Atlanta Braves in the first game of a home doubleheader on July 29. He fanned a career-high 12 San Francisco Giants in a 5-4 loss at Candlestick Park on September 21. Lollar drove in 11 runs for the second consecutive season and homered off Mario Soto in a 10-9 win over the Cincinnati Reds at Riverfront Stadium on August 14.

Lollar logged an 11-13 ledger with a 3.91 ERA in 1984, when San Diego won the National League pennant. Besides pacing the Padres with 131 strikeouts, he shared the club lead with three complete games and two shutouts. He blanked the Philadelphia Phillies, 4-0, at Veterans Stadium on May 27 and the Cincinnati Reds, 6-0, at home on June 8, fanning 12 in the latter. Lollar belted a three-run homer on September 20 to help the Padres defeat the San Francisco Giants, 5-4, for a share of the Western Division title. He surrendered three runs in Game 4 of the National League Championship Series against the Chicago Cubs and fared poorly in Game 3 of the World Series against the Detroit Tigers.

In a seven-player December 1984 transaction, San Diego traded Lollar to the Chicago White Sox. Upon his departure, Lollar ranked third on the Padres in strikeouts (454) and fifth in victories (36). He also recorded 40 losses and four shutouts. He split 1985 between the Chicago White Sox and Boston Red Sox and ended his major-league career with the Boston Red Sox in 1986.

In seven major-league seasons, Lollar fared 47-52 with four shutouts, a 4.27 ERA and 600 strikeouts in 906 innings. He and his wife, Robyn, reside in Golden, Colorado and have one son, Christopher. He met Robyn while she was covering the Padres for a San Diego television station.

GARY LUCAS

Gary Lucas starred as a reliever for the San Diego Padres from 1980 through 1983. The 6-foot 5-inch, 200-pound left-hander was born on November 8, 1954 in Riverside, California. After attending Chapman College in Orange, California, he was chosen by the San Diego Padres in the nineteenth round of the June 1976 free agent draft and spent over three seasons in the minor leagues as a starting pitcher.

In 1980, the San Diego Padres used Lucas as both a starter and a reliever. The sinkerball-slider specialist finished 5-8 with a 3.24 ERA and three saves in 46 games. He began 1980 in the starting rotation and combined with Rollie Fingers on a seven-hit, 3-0 shutout in his first major-league start against the San Francisco Giants at Candlestick Park on April 19. Lucas hurled over eight innings in a 2-1 victory over the New York Mets at Shea Stadium on May 3 and one-hit the Cincinnati Reds for six innings in a 6-1 triumph at Riverfront Stadium on June 7. Three of his losses as a starter were 2-1 and 3-0 to the St. Louis Cardinals on May 14 and July 16 and 2-0 to the Montreal Expos on June 22.

Lucas afforded sensational relief during the last two months of 1980, being called "a left-handed Rollie Fingers" by catcher Gene Tenace. During his final 25 relief appearances, he split two decisions with a 1.46 ERA, three saves, and 29 strikeouts in 36.2 innings. He surrendered just one run in 22 innings from August 13 through September 12.

In 1981, Lucas joined the top National League relievers, leading the senior circuit with 57 appearances and fashioning a 7-7 record and a career-best 2.00 ERA. His 13 saves, all but three before the All-Star break, ranked fifth in the National League. His seven victories and 13 saves contributed to nearly one-half of San Diego's 41 wins. Lucas's longest performance came on April 12, when he hurled 5.1 innings in a 7-6 loss to the San Francisco Giants at Candlestick Park. He also earned consecutive saves against the San Francisco Giants at home on April 21 and April 22 and blanked the Philadelphia Phillies for four innings with four strikeouts to earn a save in the 8-4 win on May 10. After the All-Star break, Lucas allowed only seven runs in 42 innings with a 1.50 ERA and did not surrender a home run in an 83-inning span covering 54 games.

Lucas struggled with a 1-10 mark, a 3.24 ERA, and 16 saves in 1982. Although suffering several heartbreaking losses, he paced National League left-handers with 16 saves and compiled a 1.52 ERA at home. His 10 consecutive losses matched a Padres record for left-handers. Lucas earned saves in his first four opportunities and saved 12 games by the All-Star break. His 10-game losing streak was snapped with three shutout innings in a 3-2 squeaker over the Atlanta Braves at Atlanta-Fulton County Stadium on September 26.

In 1983, Lucas logged a 5-8 slate with a 2.87 ERA and a career-high 17 saves. In December 1983, the San Diego Padres traded Lucas to the Montreal Expos. As a Padre, he won 18 and lost 33 with a 2.90 ERA and 49 saves in 230 games. He ranks sixth in career saves and shares seventh in games on the Padre all-time list, leading San Diego in saves three times and games twice.

Lucas hurled for the Montreal Expos in 1984 and 1985 and ended his major-league career with the California Angels in 1986 and 1987, appearing in the American League Championship Series against the Boston Red Sox. In eight major-league seasons, he finished 29-44 with a 3.01 ERA and 63 saves.

Lucas serves as pitching coach for the Quad City River Bandits of the Midwest League. He and his wife, Taffee, live in Rice Lake, Wisconsin and have two daughters, Mindy and Holly.

CARMELO MARTINEZ

Carmelo Martinez played outfield for the San Diego Padres from 1984 through 1989. The 6-foot 2-inch, 185-pound Martinez, who batted and threw right-handed, was born on July 28, 1960 in Dorado, Puerto Rico. After graduating from Jose S. Alegria High School in Dorado in 1978, he attended Central College of Bayamon, Puerto Rico. In December 1978, the Chicago Cubs signed the first baseman-outfielder as a free agent. Martinez spent nearly five seasons in the minor leagues and batted .258 with six home runs and 16 RBI for the Chicago Cubs in 1983. On August 22, he homered off Frank Pastore of the Cincinnati Reds in his first major-league at-bat. In December 1983, the San Diego Padres acquired Martinez, pitcher Craig Lefferts, and third baseman Fritz Connally from the Cubs for pitcher Scott Sanderson.

In 1984, Martinez batted .250 with 13 home runs and 66 RBIs. He earned the starting left field position on Opening Day and hit .302 through May 2. Martinez batted .323 with four home runs and a team-high 20 RBI in June. He knocked in at least one run in eight consecutive contests and enjoyed the first four-hit game of his major-league career in a 5-3, 15-inning setback to the San Francisco Giants at home on June 17. Martinez hit .308 with seven RBIs in his first 22 September contests, and in a 3-2, 13-inning victory over the New York Mets on September 2 at Shea Stadium, he hit the sixth inside-the-park home run in Padre history. With a strong, accurate throwing arm, he made 15 outfield assists to share second best in the senior circuit with Lonnie Smith. Martinez earned the Clyde McCullough Award as Padre Rookie of the Year. He batted an identical .176 in both the National League Championship Series against the Chicago Cubs and the World Series against the Detroit Tigers.

In 1985, Martinez batted .253 with 130 hits, 21 home runs, and 72 RBIs. In his season debut on April 15 in an 8-3 home triumph over the San Francisco Giants, Martinez belted a grand slam, another round-tripper, and a single in three at-bats and knocked in a career-high five runs. He batted .414 in his first nine games and hit .423 with two doubles, three home runs, seven RBIs, and two game-winners from May 27 through June 2 to earn National League Player of the Week honors. He made three hits in consecutive games against the Montreal Expos and New York Mets on May 30-31, homering three times and driving in two game-winners. Martinez combined two seven-game hitting streaks from August 21 through August 28 and from September 12 through September 19, hitting .435 with two home runs and five RBIs. Martinez hit .320 and drew 20 walks in his final 23 contests. He enjoyed a remarkable .614 on-base percentage in one span of 44 plate appearances, getting 13 hits and 14 walks. Martinez reached safely 44 times in his final 87 plate appearances and produced three consecutive game-winners during the final week. He clouted a home run to defeat the Cincinnati Reds, 5-4, at home on October 2, made three hits including a club-leading twenty-first home run to triumph over the Reds, 9-4, the next day, and edged the Houston Astros, 4-3, with a single on October 4, assuming the team leadership with 13 game-winning RBIs.

His batting average dropped to .238 with just nine home runs and 25 RBIs in 1986. Martinez hit .298 on the road and was relegated to pinch-hitting duties after the All-Star break. He belted two-run homers off Sid Fernandez in a 4-2 victory over the New York Mets on June 3 at Shea Stadium and off Mickey Scott in a 3-2 home win over the Houston Astros. He hit .385 against the eventual World Champion New York Mets.

Although shifting between left field and first base in 1987, Martinez compiled his best batting average (.273) with his second best home run (15) and RBI (70) production. He started 76 games in left field and 50 at first base and enjoyed a career-high 13-game hitting streak in May. Martinez batted .305 in June and knocked in runs in seven straight games. He homered twice off Atlee Hammaker of the San Francisco Giants on June 18 in a 3-1 home victory. Besides homering in three straight games from September 13 through September 15, he enjoyed a 10-game hitting streak that month. He hit .327 with six home runs and 16 RBIs against the division champion San Francisco Giants.

In 1988, Martinez slumped to .236 with 18 home runs and 65 RBIs. He batted under .200 through June, but rebounded to lead the Padres in home runs, finish second in RBIs, and share second in game-winning hits (12). Martinez batted .303 with seven home runs and 18 RBIs in August. He belted a pair of two-run homers in a 9-1 home romp over the Philadelphia Phillies on August 23 and two solo home runs to edge the Los Angeles Dodgers, 5-4, at Dodger Stadium on September 22.

In 1989, Martinez batted just .221 with six home runs and 39 RBIs. He boasted two three-hit contests and knocked in four runs in one game. Martinez clouted a grand slam off Logan Easley in an 8-1 triumph over the Pittsburgh Pirates at Three Rivers Stadium on April 27 and a pinch-hit home run off Miguel Garcia in a 17-4 walloping of the Pittsburgh Pirates on July 18. During six seasons as a Padre, he batted .248 with 577 hits, 111 doubles, 82 home runs, and 337 RBIs. He ranks sixth in slugging percentage (.408) and walks (327), seventh in home runs and on-base percentage (.341), eighth in RBIs, ninth in games (783), and tenth in doubles and strikeouts (403) on the Padre career lists.

In December 1989, the Philadelphia Phillies signed Martinez as a free agent. He split the 1990 season between the Philadelphia Phillies and Pittsburgh Pirates and 1991 between Pittsburgh, the Kansas City Royals, and the Cincinnati Reds. During his nine major-league seasons, he batted .245 with 108 home runs and 424 RBIs. Martinez has managed the Mesa Cubs of the Arizona League since 1999. He and his wife, Gladys, reside in Dorado, Puerto Rico and have one daughter, Natalie.

WILLIE McCOVEY

Willie McCovey played first base for the San Diego Padres from 1974 through August 1976. The 6-foot 4-inch, 225-pound McCovey, who batted and threw left-handed, was born on January 10, 1938 in Mobile, Alabama and became a legendary slugger with the San Francisco Giants. He debuted for San Francisco with two triples and two singles against Robin Roberts of the Philadelphia Phillies on July 30, 1959 and earned National Rookie of the Year honors. In the 1962 World Series against the New York Yankees, McCovey belted a home run in Game 2 and lined out to end the final game. He shared the National League lead in home runs (44) with Hank Aaron in 1963 and led the senior circuit in both home runs and RBIs in 1968 and 1969. McCovey clouted 36 home runs with 105 RBIs in 1968 and 45 home runs with 126 RBIs in 1969. From 1968 through 1970, he won three consecutive slugging titles with percentages of .545, .656, and .612.

In 1969, McCovey earned National League Most Valuable Player honors and set a major-league record with 45 intentional walks. He played on six All-Star teams, belting two home runs in the 1962 Summer Classic. A dead-ball pull hitter, McCovey consistently slashed line drives to right field and set numerous marks with his long clouts. He paced the senior circuit five times in home run percentage, including four consecutive years from 1967 through 1970. McCovey homered three times in three different games and led the National League in walks in 1970. In the 1971 National League Championship Series against the Pittsburgh Pirates, he batted .429 with two home runs and six RBIs.

In October 1973, the San Diego Padres acquired McCovey for pitcher Mike Caldwell. McCovey provided considerable power and leadership for San Diego. Upon joining the Padres, he had already belted 413 career home runs. He batted .253 in 1974 and set club marks for left-handers with 22 home runs and 63 RBIs. McCovey collected three hits in an 8-6 triumph over the Houston Astros at the Astrodome on May 20 and clouted two home runs in a 7-3 home win over the New York Mets on July 21. Besides belting eight round-trippers in August, McCovey knocked in four runs in a 10-7 victory over the San Francisco Giants at Candlestick Park on May 19, against the Houston Astros on May 20, and against the New York Mets on July 21. He batted .385 against the Philadelphia Phillies and belted five home runs against the Atlanta Braves.

McCovey batted .252 in 1975, leading the Padres with 23 home runs and ranking second with 68 RBIs. He hit .367 against the Montreal Expos and .333 against the Pittsburgh Pirates. His home run and RBI marks broke the records he had previously established for a left-hander. McCovey clouted a grand slam in a 6-2 triumph over the New York Mets on May 30 to tie a major-league record with three pinch-hit grand slams and to tie Hank Aaron with 16 career National League grand slams. He doubled three times in a 7-6 home win over the Philadelphia Phillies on August 24 and clouted two home runs in an 8-6 home victory over the San Francisco Giants on September 25. McCovey drove in four runs against the New York Mets on May 30, in a 7-6 home triumph over the San Francisco Giants on June 23 and in an 11-2 home rout over the Cincinnati Reds on September 9. He compiled a .991 fielding percentage and handled 324 consecutive chances at first base without making an error.

McCovey batted only .203 with seven home runs and 36 RBIs in 1976 before being sold to the Oakland A's that August. Although playing less than three years with San Diego, he ranked third with 52 career home runs and sixth in career RBIs with 167 on the Padre all-time list upon his departure. His major-league career ended with the San Francisco Giants from 1977 through 1980. In 2,588 games spanning 22 major-league seasons, McCovey batted .270 with 2,211 hits, 353 doubles, 521 home runs, 1,555 RBIs, and a .515 slugging percentage. He holds the National League record for homers by a first baseman, grand slams (18), and pinch-hit grand slams (3). McCovey, who struck out 1,550 times, twice hit two home runs in the same inning and leads all National League left-handed hitters in round-trippers. He shares eleventh with Ted Williams in career home runs and thirteenth in home run percentage (6.4). The bachelor resides in Woodside, California and was elected to the National Baseball Hall of Fame in 1986.

FRED McGRIFF

Fred McGriff starred as a first baseman for the San Diego Padres from 1991 through July 1993. The 6-foot 3-inch, 215-pound McGriff, who bats and throws left-handed, was born on October 31, 1963 in Tampa, Florida and grew up four blocks from Al Lopez Field. After starring in baseball at Jefferson High School in Tampa, he declined a baseball scholarship from the University of Georgia. The New York Yankees drafted McGriff in the ninth round in June 1981 and traded him to the Toronto Blue Jays in December 1982. McGriff played in the minor leagues through 1986 and with Toronto from 1986 through 1990. Although striking out frequently, he walked often, recorded high on-base percentages, and belted tape-measure home runs. No major-leaguer matched his 106 home runs from 1988 to 1990. In 1988, McGriff led American

League first basemen in fielding (.997) and finished second in home runs (34), slugging percentage (.552) and extra base hits (73). He paced the junior circuit with 36 home runs, knocked in 92 runs, and established a club record with 119 walks in 1989. In 1990, he batted .300 with 35 home runs and a .400 on-base percentage.

In a blockbuster December 1990 trade, the San Diego Padres acquired McGriff and Tony Fernandez from the Toronto Blue Jays for Roberto Alomar and Joe Carter. McGriff in 1991 knocked in a career-pinnacle 106 runs, ranked third in walks (105) and on-base percentage (.393), and ninth in slugging percentage (.494). He belted 31 home runs, sharing fourth in the senior circuit. No Padre had clouted that many round-trippers since Dave Winfield blasted 34 in 1979. McGriff's 106 RBIs ranked fourth in the senior circuit and fourth best in Padre history.

McGriff became the fourth National Leaguer and thirteenth major-leaguer to belt grand slams in consecutive games at home against the Houston Astros,

Fred McGriff

connecting on August 13 against Mark Portugal in a 12-9 loss and the next night against Jim Deshaies in a 4-1 win. During a five-game stretch in August, McGriff belted five home runs with 11 RBIs. He clouted two home runs on May 9 in a 9-6 home setback to the Philadelphia Phillies and enjoyed a career-best 14-game hitting streak from April 24 through May 9. McGriff captured National League Player of the Week honors with a .424 batting average, three home runs, eight RBIs, and a .885 slugging percentage from April 29 through May 5.

In 1992, McGriff batted .286 and led the National League with 35 home runs. Besides becoming the first modern player to win home run titles in both leagues, he became the first Padre to attain the home run crown and post consecutive 30-homer seasons. No major-leaguer since Mike Schmidt had played five straight seasons with at least 30 round-trippers. McGriff ranked third in the National League with 104 RBIs and became the first Padre to knock in at least 100 runs two different seasons. He also ranked second in the senior circuit in walks (96), shared second in intentional walks (23), placed third in slugging percentage (.556), finished fourth in extra-base hits (69) and on-base percentage (.394), and shared fifth in total bases (295). McGriff hit .304 with 21 home runs and 56 RBIs at Jack Murphy Stadium, making *The Sporting News'* National League All-Star and Silver Sluggers teams.

McGriff belted four home runs in his first five games and shared National League Player of the Week honors with Tom Glavine, hitting .348 with nine RBIs. His fourth career grand slam came off John Candelaria in an 8-3 home triumph over the Los Angeles Dodgers on April 10. McGriff enjoyed an eight-game hitting streak from May 23 through May 31 with six multi-hit games. On June 18, he charged the mound and fought San Francisco Giants pitcher Trevor Wilson. McGriff missed some games due to a strained left rib cage from the fight and was suspended by the league for four days. He again captured National League Player of the Week honors from June 29 through July 5, batting .474 with four home runs, seven RBIs, and an incredible 1.105 slugging percentage. His four home runs came in consecutive games, a career first. Fans selected him to start at first base in his first All-Star Game, where he made two hits with one RBI. McGriff hit two home runs off Trevor Wilson of the San Francisco Giants and knocked in five runs in a 6-5 home victory on August 3. Three days later, he combined with Gary Sheffield to blast consecutive home runs in both the first and second innings in a 7-5 home triumph over the Houston Astros. He also belted a 473-foot round-tripper off Doug Drabek in an 11-6 home slugfest over the Pittsburgh Pirates on August 28.

In 1993, McGriff batted .275 with 18 home runs, 46 RBIs, and a .497 slugging percentage. His 18 multi-hit games included one four-hit and three three-hit contests. In July 1993, the San Diego Padres traded him to the Atlanta Braves for three players. Although with San Diego for less than three years, McGriff ranked fourth in Padre history with 84 home runs upon his departure. McGriff finished 1993 with a .291 batting average, a career-high 37 home runs, and 101 RBIs. He played for the Atlanta Braves through 1997, becoming only the ninth major-leaguer to belt at least 30 home runs in seven consecutive seasons. McGriff appeared in the National League Championship Series four times, the World Series twice, and the All-Star game twice as a Brave. In November 1997, the expansion Tampa Bay Devil Rays drafted him. McGriff, in 1999, clouted 32 home runs with 104 RBIs for a last-place club. He became just the second player to clout at least 200 home runs in the American League and National League, batting .277 with 27 home runs and 106 RBIs in 2000. McGriff hit .318 with 19 home runs and 61 RBIs for Tampa Bay before being traded to the Chicago Cubs in July 2001. He provided invaluable support for Cubs slugger Sammy Sosa, batting .282 with 12 home runs and 41 RBIs during the remainder of 2001. McGriff has clouted at least 30 homers eight times and knocked in at least 100 runs six times. In 16 major-league seasons, he has batted .287 with 397 doubles, 448 home runs, and 1,400 RBIs.

McGriff and his wife, Veronica, reside in Tampa, Florida and have one son, Erick, and one daughter, Ericka.

KEVIN McREYNOLDS

Kevin McReynolds starred as an outfielder with the San Diego Padres from 1983 through 1986. The 6-foot 1-inch, 205-pound McReynolds, who batted and threw right-handed, was born on October 16, 1959 in Little Rock, Arkansas and attended the University of Arkansas, where he led the Razorbacks to the 1979 College World Series as a freshman. In 1980, he batted .386 with 17 home runs and 57 RBIs and was selected Southwest Conference Player of the Year. No Razorback has clouted more career home runs.

In June 1981, the San Diego Padres selected McReynolds sixth in the first round of the free agent draft. McReynolds enjoyed a tremendous rookie season with Reno, Nevada of the California League and Amarillo, Texas of the Texas League, batting a combined .368 with 33 home runs and 137 RBIs in 130 games and winning Class A Player of the Year honors. In 1983, McReynolds became the first Padre prospect ever selected Topps/National Association Minor League Player of the Year. He batted .377 with 32 home runs and 116 RBIs for Las Vegas, Nevada, earning the Pacific Coast League Most Valuable Player award.

McReynolds joined the San Diego Padres in June 1983, batting .221 in 39 games. He homered on June 2 in his first major-league game off Ron Reed in a 4-1 home triumph over the Philadelphia Phillies, but was optioned to Las Vegas later that month after hitting under .200. After returning to San Diego on September 19, McReynolds batted .269 in 18 games.

In 1984, McReynolds anchored a young San Diego outfield in center field and helped the Padres win their first National League pennant. He shared the club lead in home runs with 20, batted .275, and knocked in 75 runs. McReynolds enjoyed a sensational April, batting .338 with five home runs,17 RBIs, and a league-best .623 slugging percentage. On April 22, he singled twice, doubled, homered and knocked in three runs in a 15-7 loss to the Los Angeles Dodgers at Dodger Stadium. McReynolds batted .444 with five home runs and 14 RBIs against Los Angeles. He engineered one of the biggest comebacks in Padre history, batting five-for-five on September 5 to help the Padres overcome a 7-0 home deficit after two innings to win a 15-11 slugfest over the Cincinnati Reds. His .991 fielding percentage led all outfielders with 300 or more chances. McReynolds sparked the Padres' dramatic comeback in the National League Championship Series against the Chicago Cubs. After Chicago had won the first two games, he clouted a three-run homer in the sixth inning of Game 3 at home to help San Diego win its first post-season contest. McReynolds batted .300 with four RBIs in the Championship Series, but broke a bone in his left hand while trying to break up a double play in Game 4 and missed the World Series against the Detroit Tigers. Pitcher Ed Whitson lamented, "McReynolds's injury killed us. It took power away from us."

Kevin McReynolds

McReynolds knocked in 75 runs in 1985, but his batting average slumped to .234 and his home runs plunged to 15. He hit safely in 15 consecutive games from May 5 through May 22, clouting four home runs and knocking in 15 runs. He drove in four runs in a 7-2 victory over the Philadelphia Phillies at Veterans Stadium on May 26 and opened June with a 13-game hitting streak. In a June 7 doubleheader sweep over the Cincinnati Reds at Riverfront Stadium, he made three hits in a 9-3 victory in the first game and four in the 3-2, 11-inning triumph in the nightcap. McReynolds doubled, tripled, homered, and drove in four runs in an 8-4 win over the Chicago Cubs at Wrigley Field in the second game of a July 8 doubleheader.

McReynolds emerged as the premier San Diego power hitter in 1986, batting .288 and leading the Padres with 26 home runs, 96 RBIs, and a .504 slugging percentage. Besides recording 31 doubles and six triples, he led the club with 14-game-winning hits. His 50 multi-hit games included two four-hit contests. McReynolds homered twice at home on May 24 in a 5-4 setback to the New York Mets and again on August 20 to edge the Montreal Expos, 3-2, and knocked in five runs on August 19 to spark a 7-1 victory over Montreal. He clouted the only Padre grand slam that year in the third inning on October 4 against Bill Gullickson in a 10-7 loss to the Cincinnati Reds at Riverfront Stadium. In 496 career games with the Padres, McReynolds batted .263 with 84 doubles, 17 triples, 65 home runs and 260 RBIs. He ranks twelfth in triples, thirteenth in RBIs and home runs, and sixteenth in doubles in Padre history.

In December 1986, San Diego traded McReynolds and two other players to the New York Mets for infielder Kevin Mitchell and four young prospects. McReynolds had just completed the fourth year of a six-year contract. His agent rejected the Padres' $4.5 million, five-year contract offer and made demands that the club could not meet. San Diego anticipated that McReynolds would file for free agency and wanted compensation. The trade ultimately disappointed the Padres, who could not fill the power vacuum left by McReynolds's departure. McReynolds played with the New York Mets from 1987 through 1991 and in 1994 and the Kansas City Royals in 1992 and 1993, appearing in the 1988 National League Championship Series. In 12 major-league seasons, he batted .265 with 211 home runs and 807 RBIs in 1,502 games. He and his wife, Jackie, reside in Little Rock, Arkansas.

BUTCH METZGER

Butch Metzger relieved for the San Diego Padres from September 1975 through May 1977. The 6-foot 1-inch, 185-pound right-hander was born on May 23, 1952 in Lafayette, Indiana and starred in baseball at Kennedy High School in Sacramento, California, where he finished 15-5 with a 1.49 ERA and 253 strikeouts in 149 innings. The San Francisco Giants selected him in the second round of the June 1970 draft. He spent nearly five seasons in the minor leagues before winning his only decision with the San Francisco Giants in 1974. In December 1974, the Giants traded Metzger and Tito Fuentes to the San Diego Padres for Derrel Thomas.

Metzger spent 1975 at Hawaii of the Pacific Coast League and struck out six batters in his first two innings after joining the San Diego Padres in September. He appeared in four games and defeated the Los Angeles Dodgers, 6-5, at home on September 22.

Butch Metzger

Metzger enjoyed a spectacular rookie season in 1976, being selected *The Sporting News'* National League Rookie Pitcher of the Year and sharing the Baseball Writers Association of America's National League Rookie of the Year honors with Pat Zachry of the Cincinnati Reds. Metzger logged an 11-4 ledger with 16 saves, a 2.93 ERA, and 89 strikeouts in 123 innings, switching to the bullpen full time. He set a major-league pitching record by appearing in 77 games as a rookie and established Padre marks for appearances, saves, consecutive victories (10), and rookie victories (11). His 16 saves matched the then club career record held by Vincente Romo.

Metzger finished 8-3 with a 2.93 ERA and nine saves against Western Division clubs, with three wins and two saves against the Atlanta Braves and two victories with three saves against the Los Angeles Dodgers. He fared 3-1 with a 2.92 ERA and seven saves against the Eastern Division teams. Opponents did not score off him in nearly two-thirds of his outings. His 77 appearances then ranked seventh in National League history. He pitched 19 innings before yielding his first run against the Chicago Cubs on May 14 and recorded three saves and a win against the Houston Astros between August 5 and August 8. His first loss came in a 7-4 setback to the Montreal Expos at home on August 28.

After Metzger relieved in 17 games in 1977, the San Diego Padres traded him to the St. Louis Cardinals for John D'Aquisto and Pat Scanlon. Metzger relieved for St. Louis in 1978 and completed his major-league career with the New York Mets in 1979. During six major-league seasons, he posted an 18-9 mark and a 3.74 ERA with 23 saves and struck out 175 batters in 293.2 innings. For the Padres, he fashioned a 12-4 mark with a 3.47 ERA and 16 saves. He resides in Sacramento, California and enjoys hunting and fishing.

GRAIG NETTLES

Graig Nettles starred as a third baseman for the San Diego Padres from 1984 through 1986. The 6-foot, 180-pound Nettles, who batted left-handed and threw right-handed, was born on August 20, 1944 in San Diego and attended San Diego State College. His brother, Jim, played for four different major-league teams. Nettles enjoyed a distinguished 22-year major-league career with five different clubs, combining considerable power with sterling defense. The Minnesota Twins selected him in the fourth round of the June 1965 free agent draft.

Nettles's finest seasons came with the New York Yankees from 1973 through 1983. He led the American League with 37 home runs in 1976, won Rawlings Gold Gloves awards in 1977 and 1978, and appeared in five All-Star Games and four World Series. He performed in the 1977 and 1978 World Series championships and earned Most Valuable Player honors in the 1981 American League Championship Series against the Oakland A's.

In March 1984, New York traded Nettles to the San Diego Padres for pitcher Dennis Rasmussen. Nettles platooned at third base with Luis Salazar, facing right-handed hurlers. Although batting only .228 in 1984, he supplied valuable power. Nettles clouted 20 home runs and knocked in 65 runs, sharing the club home run lead with Kevin McReynolds and helping the Padres attain their first post-season appearance. He belted six round-trippers with 17 RBIs in mid-June. From August 11 to August 22, Nettles clouted seven home runs in six games to tie a National League record and became only the eighth major-leaguer to hit round-trippers in six consecutive games. Although batting only .143 in the National League Championship Series

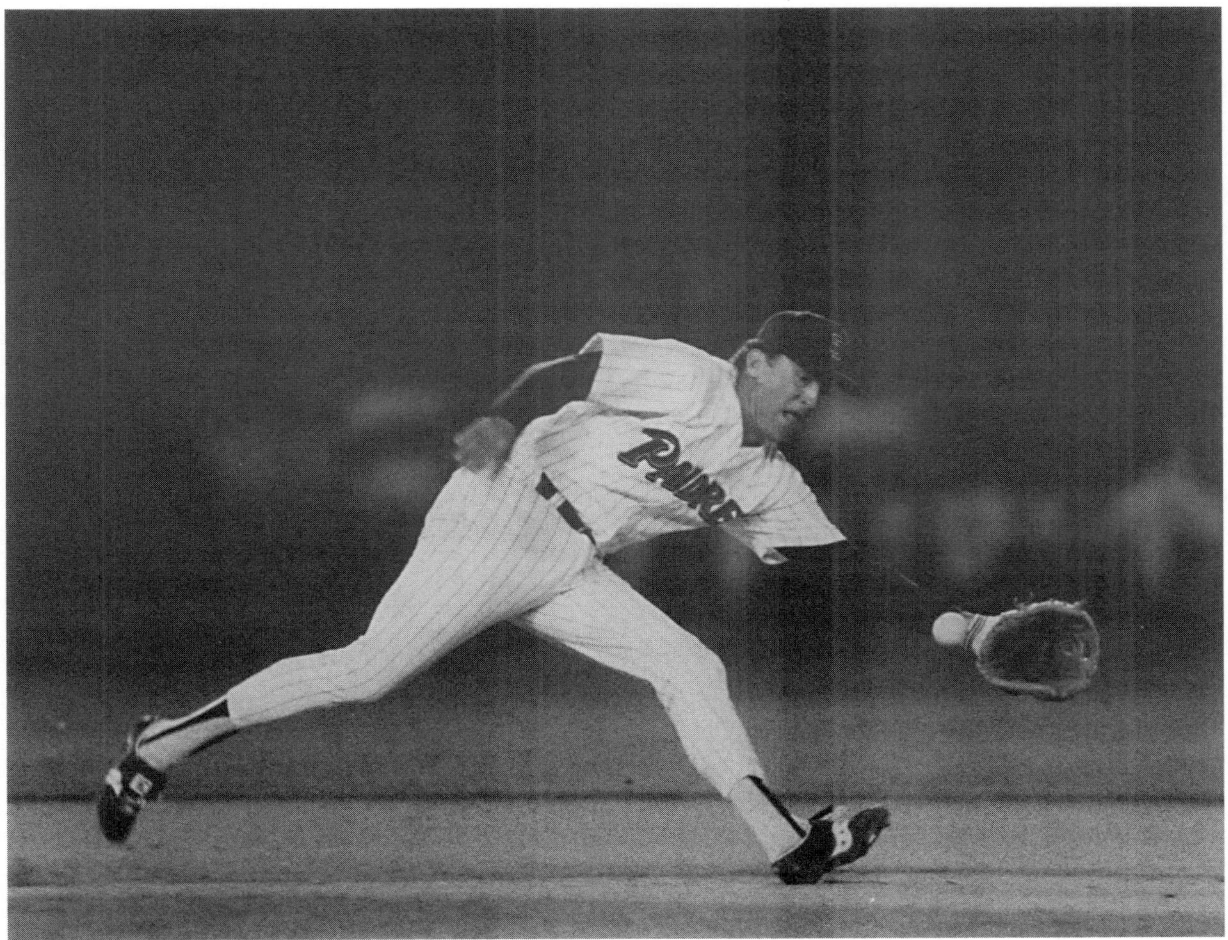

Third baseman Graig Nettles dives for a catch.

against the Chicago Cubs, he hit .250 with two RBIs in the World Series against the Detroit Tigers.

Nettles improved his batting average to .261 in 1985. He clouted 15 home runs with 61 RBIs and 78 walks, appearing in his only All-Star Game as a National Leaguer and sixth altogether. On May 4 at Wrigley Field, Nettles authored the 25th two-homer game of his career in a 12-8 loss to the Chicago Cubs. From May 19 through May 28, he enjoyed an eight-game hitting streak. His four hits on May 19 at Olympic Stadium included the 2,000th of his major-league career, a single in the fifth inning off Steve Rogers in an 8-3 triumph over the Montreal Expos. Nettles clouted three home runs in a six-game stretch in June and batted .337 in July, hitting safely in nine consecutive games. Against the Houston Astros, Nettles homered, doubled, and singled twice in a heartbreaking 2-1 loss on August 4 and attained another four-hit game in a 6-4 home setback on October 6.

Nettles's batting average slumped to .218 in 1986, but he still produced 16 home runs and 55 RBIs. At home, he homered twice in an 8-3 victory over the San Francisco Giants on June 19 and had five RBIs in a 9-3 triumph over the Cincinnati Reds on July 30. Nettles also knocked in four runs once and enjoyed four three-hit contests. After the Padres released him in December 1986, he signed as a free agent with the Atlanta Braves in April 1987. His major-league career ended with the Montreal Expos in 1988.

Nettles batted only .248 lifetime, but supplied impressive power. His 2,235 career major-league hits included 328 doubles and 390 home runs. He knocked in 1,314 runs in 2,700 major-league games. Nettles leads American League third basemen in career home runs with 319 and ranks sixth in Yankee history with

250 round-trippers. The only Yankees to belt more career home runs were Hall of Famers Babe Ruth, Mickey Mantle, Lou Gehrig, Joe DiMaggio, and Yogi Berra. He ranks tenth in Yankee history with 834 RBIs. He rejoined the Padres as a coach for 1995. He and his wife, Ginger, live in Encinitas, California and have one daughter, Barrie, and three sons, Michael, Timothy, and Jeffrey.

PHIL NEVIN

Phil Nevin has played primarily third base for the San Diego Padres since 1999. The 6-foot 2-inch, 231-pound Nevin, who bats and throws right-handed, was born on January 19, 1971 in Fullerton, California. He graduated from El Dorado High School in Placentia, California, playing baseball with Bret Boone. The Los Angeles Dodgers selected Nevin in the third round of the June 1989 free agent draft, but he matriculated instead at California State University, Fullerton. Nevin also played football and won the 1992 Golden Spikes Award as the nation's top amateur baseball player, batting .402 with 22 home runs and 86 RBIs. He was named as the third baseman on *The Sporting News'* All-America team and started at third base for Team USA during the 1992 Summer Olympic Games at Barcelona, Spain.

The Houston Astros made Nevin the first overall pick in the June 1992 free agent draft. Nevin spent over two minor-league seasons with Tucson, Arizona of the Pacific Coast League and struggled in a brief trial with the Houston Astros in 1995. The Houston Astros traded him in August 1995 to the Detroit Tigers for pitcher Mike Henneman. In 1996, Nevin caught for Jacksonville, Florida of the Southern League and batted .292 with eight home runs and 19 RBIs for Detroit after being recalled in August. He slumped with Detroit in 1997 and was traded that November with catcher Matt Walbeck to the Anaheim Angels for pitcher Nick Skuse. After another disappointing season, Nevin in March 1999 was traded with pitcher Keith Volkman to the San Diego Padres for infielder Andy Sheets and outfielder Gus Kennedy.

In 1999, Nevin batted .269 with 24 home runs and a team-best 85 RBIs in 128 games as a third baseman, catcher, and outfielder, attaining Padres' Most Valuable Player honors. He tied outfielder Reggie Sanders for the club lead with a .527 slugging percentage and ranked second to Sanders in home runs and extra base hits (51). After being inserted as clean-up hitter, Nevin batted .320 with 10 doubles, 12 home runs and 40 RBIs between August 1 and September 10. On August 15, he clouted a three-run homer in the first inning and singled twice with four RBIs in a 7-6 home win over the Florida Marlins. The following day against the New York Mets, Nevin broke up Ocatvio Dotel's no-hit bid and erased a 2-0 deficit with a three-run homer in the seventh inning. His two round-trippers and five RBIs triggered a 10-3 home victory over the Montreal Expos on September 10. He also delivered key hits at home in a 4-3 victory over the Los Angeles Dodgers on April 18, in a 4-3 win over the Atlanta Braves on May 7, in a 6-2 triumph over the Texas Rangers on July 11, and in a 7-3 victory over the Chicago Cubs on August 31.

Nevin enjoyed a banner season in 2000, batting .303 with 31 home runs, 107 RBIs, and 34 doubles. He performed well in the clutch, leading the Padres in hits (163), doubles, home runs, and RBIs. At Qualcomm Stadium on April 13, Nevin homered twice in a 5-4 loss to the Arizona Diamondbacks. Three days later knocked in four runs in a 13-3 rout over the Houston Astros. His two two-run homers and five RBIs on May 16 lifted the Padres to a 7-3 win over the Florida Marlins at Pro Player Stadium. Three days later, Nevin contributed a home run and a single with six RBIs in an 11-7 romp over the Atlanta Braves at Turner Field. His three-run homer in the bottom of the eighth inning on May 27 gave the Padres a 4-2 come-from-behind home victory over the Montreal Expos.

Nevin continued to play well after the All-Star break although sidelined for 13 games in September with an abdominal strain. He reached base safely with a hit or walk in 49 consecutive games between July 3 and August 30. The Padres rallied on July 30 from a five-run deficit to defeat the Pittsburgh Pirates, 9-8, at Three Rivers Stadium on Nevin's ninth-inning home run. He and second baseman Bret Boone on August 10 clouted three-run homers in a 15-3 thrashing of the Philadelphia Phillies at Veterans Stadium. Twelve days later, Nevin and right fielder John Mabry hit consecutive second-deck home runs in the third inning at Qualcomm Stadium in a 16-1 romp over the New York Mets. Nevin on August 28 belted a three-run homer in the eighth inning and a three-run double in the ninth inning, tying his career high with six RBIs in an 8-2 triumph over the Chicago Cubs at Wrigley Field. After singling three times the next day against the Cubs,

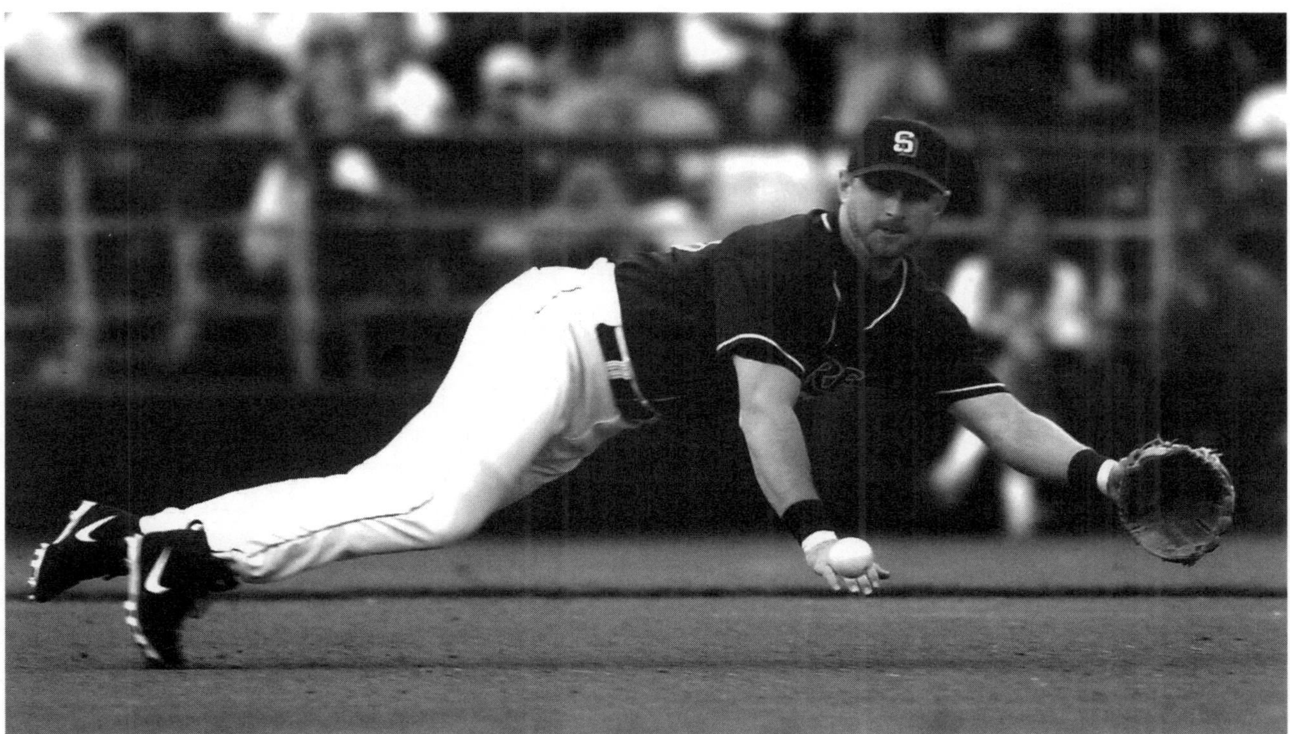

Third baseman Phil Nevin dives to intercept a line drive.

he went hitless in four plate appearances in his next game to end his 49-game streak of reaching base safely.

Nevin enjoyed his best major-league season in 2001, establishing career highs with a .306 batting average, 97 runs scored, 167 hits, 41 home runs, 126 RBIs, 71 walks, 147 strikeouts, and four stolen bases. He led the Padres in hits, home runs, RBIs, and strikeouts, belting a club-record four grand slams, ranking seventh in the National League in home runs and sharing seventh in the senior circuit in RBIs.

Nevin performed well throughout the 2001 campaign. On April 7, he clouted a three-run homer and doubled in a 14-10 slugfest win over the Colorado Rockies at Coors Field. In an outstanding encore performance the next day, Nevin hit a three-run, 453-foot homer and singled twice with five RBIs in an 11-3 rout to give the Padres their first-ever sweep of the Rockies at Coors Field. He homered, doubled, and singled with three RBIs on both April 27 and April 28, sparking 8-1 and 6-1 victories over the visiting Pittsburgh Pirates. On May 1, Nevin clouted a three-run homer, as one of seven consecutive Padres who reached base to start the third inning in a 10-3 victory over the Chicago Cubs at Wrigley Field. On June 14, he belted two home runs, including an eighth-inning grand slam, with five RBIs to lift the Padres to a 6-4 home triumph over the Oakland Athletics. Three days later, Nevin homered and singled three times in an 11-9 win over the visiting Seattle Mariners. He feasted against the visiting Texas Rangers before the All-Star break, homering, doubling, and singling with three RBIs in an 8-3 victory on July 6 and homering and doubling with four RBIs in an 11-2 romp on July 8. He made the National League All-Star team as a reserve.

His power surge continued after the All-Star break. On July 28, Nevin clouted two home runs, including a fourth-inning grand slam, with five RBIs in a 6-2 triumph over the Milwaukee Brewers at Miller Park. His solo home run in the fifth inning on August 4 gave the host Padres a 2-1 win over the Cincinnati Reds, as he joined Fred McGriff as the only Padre to boast consecutive 30-home-run seasons. On August 25, he homered and singled twice with three RBIs in a 16-14 donnybrook loss to the St. Louis Cardinals at Busch Stadium. Ryan Klesko joined him that day as the first Padre duo to knock in 100 runs since Ken Caminiti and Steve Finley in 1996. After homering in three consecutive games from September 7 to September 9. Nevin hit two home runs, including a second-inning grand slam, and doubled with a career-high seven RBIs in a 13-9 slugfest setback to the Colorado Rockies at Coors Field on September 27. On October 6, he tied the club record with three home runs, including a first-inning grand slam, and six RBIs in a 10-4 triumph over the visiting Colorado Rockies. Nevin homered off Scott Elarton in the first and sixth innings and off Chris Nichting in the seventh frame.

On November 15, 2001, San Diego signed him to a four-year $34-million contract extension, the richest in club history. The agreement included a three-year no-trade clause and surpassed the $32 million deal that closer Trevor Hoffman signed in 1999.

In seven major-league seasons through 2001, Nevin has batted .273 with 609 hits, 125 doubles, 122 home runs, and 412 RBIs in 673 games. Since joining the Padres, he has batted .295 with 433 hits, 92 doubles, 96 home runs, and 318 RBIs in 420 games. He and his wife, Kristin, reside in San Diego and have two children, Korel and Tyler.

Bob Owchinko

BOB OWCHINKO

Bob Owchinko pitched for the San Diego Padres from September 1976 through 1979. The 6-foot 2-inch, 185-pound left-hander was born on January 1, 1955 in Detroit, Michigan and starred in baseball at Eastern Michigan University. In 1976, he led Eastern Michigan to second place in the NCAA College World Series and was named All-America. Owchinko finished 14-3 with a 1.95 ERA during the regular season and 4-0 in post-season play. The San Diego Padres selected him in the first round of the June 1976 draft. He pitched just 13 minor-league games for Amarillo of the Texas League before joining the Padres that September. Owchinko lost both starts to the Atlanta Braves and the Los Angeles Dodgers.

Owchinko began 1977 with Hawaii of the Pacific Coast League and finished 9-12 with a 4.45 ERA after rejoining the Padres, winning *The Sporting News'* National League Rookie Pitcher of the Year Award. He ranked second on the staff with nine wins, 28 starts, and 170 innings and third with 101 strikeouts. He blanked the St. Louis Cardinals, 7-0, at Busch Stadium on August 21 and hurled a 1-0 two-hitter against the Los Angeles Dodgers at home on September 5. Steve Garvey bunted down the third base line for a single in the eighth inning to break up a perfect game. Owchinko struck out a season-high eight Cincinnati Reds in a 4-0 home setback on September 20 and authored a 9-2 complete-game home victory over the San Francisco Giants on September 25. He won all four decisions against the St. Louis Cardinals.

In 1978, Owchinko logged a 10-13 ledger with a 3.56 ERA. He shut out the Philadelphia Phillies, 7-0, on seven hits at home on June 17 and pitched very well from early July through mid-August. Owchinko won nine of 15 decisions at home with a 3.10 ERA and surrendered fewer than three runs in eight starts in which he did not get a victory. He blanked the Atlanta Braves for 22 innings and won decisions against Atlanta, the Pittsburgh Pirates, and the St. Louis Cardinals.

In 1979, Owchinko's record slumped to 6-12 with a 3.74 ERA. He started 20 games and relieved in 22 others. The San Diego Padres traded him to the Cleveland Indians for Jerry Mumphrey in February 1980. As a Padre, Owchinko compiled a 25-39 mark, whiffed 265 batters in 526 innings, and hurled three shutouts with a 4.00 ERA. He pitched for the Cleveland Indians in 1980, the Oakland Athletics in 1981 and 1982, the Pittsburgh Pirates in 1983, the Cincinnati Reds in 1984, and the Montreal Expos in 1986. The Oakland Athletics converted him to a reliever. His only winning campaigns were 4-3 at Oakland in 1981 and 1-0 at Montreal in 1986. In 10 major-league seasons, Owchinko won 37 games, lost 60 decisions, struck out 490 batters in 890.2 innings, and logged four shutouts with a 4.28 ERA. He and his wife, Susan, live in Scottsdale, Arizona.

ERIC OWENS

Eric Owens played outfield and infield for the San Diego Padres in 1999 and 2000. The 6-foot, 198-pound Owens, who bats and throws right-handed, was born on February 3, 1971 in Danville, Virginia and graduated from Tunstall High School in Dry Fork, Virginia where he was named All-America in baseball and All-State in football. He played both baseball and football at Ferrum, Virginia, College, batting .430 with 68 stolen bases and 18 triples. His honors include making first team All-America in 1991 and being named Dixie Conference Player of the Year in 1992.

The Cincinnati Reds selected Owens in the fourth round of the June 1992 free agent draft. Owens spent nearly four seasons in the minor leagues with Billings, Montana of the Pioneer League in 1992, Winston-Salem, North Carolina of the Carolina League in 1993, Chattanooga, Tennessee of the Southern League in 1994, and Indianapolis, Indiana of the American Association in 1995, making hits in both at-bats in a brief trial with Cincinnati in 1995. He split the next two campaigns between Cincinnati and Indianapolis, batting .263 for the Reds in 1997. The Florida Marlins acquired him in March 1998 and sold him a week later to the Milwaukee Brewers. After struggling with Milwaukee in 1998, he spent the remainder of the season with Louisville, Kentucky of the American Association.

In December 1998, the San Diego Padres signed Owens as a free agent. His first full major-league season came in 1999 as an outfielder and infielder. He batted .266 and posted career-highs with 22 doubles, nine home runs, 61 RBIs, and 33 stolen bases, including his theft of home in the bottom of the third inning off Brett Tomko of the Cincinnati Reds on May 21. Owens, outfielder Reggie Sanders, shortstop Damian Jackson, and second baseman Quilvio Veras each stole at least 30 bases, becoming the first quartet in Padre history to accomplish that feat. He hit nearly .300 through early August, hitting safely in a career-best 18 consecutive games between June 19 and July 7. Owens recorded 33 multiple-hit games, including four consecutive between July 16 and July 19. He batted .431 in interleague play, second best in major-league baseball.

Owens produced several game-winning hits through early August. His tenth-inning single off Jose Mesa on June 5 plated the winning run in a 3-2 victory over the Seattle Mariners. Three days later, he singled in two runs in the eighth inning to defeat the Oakland A's, 5-3. Owens on June 23 clouted a three-run homer in the fifth inning and sparked a come-from-behind 6-2 victory over the Los Angeles Dodgers at Dodger Stadium. His RBI single in the bottom of the ninth inning on July 10 lifted the Padres to a 5-4 triumph over the Texas Rangers. On July 20, he doubled in the eighth inning to tie the Anaheim Angels at Edison International Field, in a game the Padres won, 2-1, for a three game sweep.

Injuries to Tony Gwynn made Owens a regular outfielder in 2000. Owens enjoyed his best season, attaining career highs with a .293 batting average, 87 runs, 171 hits, and seven triples. He also produced 19 doubles, six home runs, and 51 RBIs and stole 29 bases. Owens led the Padres in hits, triples, and stolen bases and reached base safely in his first 27 games between April 3 and May 5. On April 16, he feasted at home on Houston Astros pitching for four hits in a 13-3 rout. One week later, he hit a double, a triple, and a two-run single in the eighth inning against the Astros to help San Diego sweep its first series at Houston since 1996. On June 10, he made four hits in a 13-2 romp at home over the Houston Astros. The Padres defeated the Anaheim Angels, 6-5, at home on July 16, when pitcher Al Levine made an errant throw on Owens's bunt with the bases loaded. Owens, on August 3, belted a three-run homer and recorded his fifth consecutive multi-hit game in a 6-5 home victory over the Chicago Cubs. On September 11, he recorded two of the six Padre stolen bases in a 7-2 home win over the Colorado Rockies.

In March 2001, San Diego traded Owens and pitchers Matt Clement and Omar Ortiz to the Florida Marlins for outfielder Mark Kotsay and infielder Cesar Crespo. Owens hit .253 with 16 doubles, five home runs, 28 RBIs, and eight stolen bases for Florida in 2001. During his seven major-league seasons, he has batted .262 with 232 runs, 452 hits, 65 doubles, 11 triples, 21 home runs, 157 RBIs, and 89 stolen bases. With the Padres, he batted .282 with 142 runs, 288 hits, 41 doubles, 10 triples, 15 home runs, 112 RBIs, and 62 stolen bases. He and his wife, Cindy, reside in Rocky Mount, Virginia with their two daughters, Makayla and Alyssa.

GAYLORD PERRY

Gaylord Perry starred as a pitcher with the San Diego Padres in 1978 and 1979. The 6-foot 4-inch, 205-pound right-hander was born on September 15, 1938 in Williamston, North Carolina. His older brother, Jim, won 215 games for four major-league clubs between 1959 and 1975. Perry starred in baseball at Williamston High School and attended Campbell College. In June 1958, the San Francisco Giants signed him as a free agent. After just over four minor-league seasons, Perry pitched for the San Francisco Giants from 1962 through 1971, the Cleveland Indians from 1972 through 1975, and the Texas Rangers in 1976 and 1977. With the Giants, he mastered variants of the spitball and authored a 1-0 no-hit masterpiece against the St. Louis Cardinals on September 17, 1968. Perry led the National League in victories (23) and shutouts (5) in 1970 and innings pitched in 1969 (325) and 1970 (329). He paced the American League in victories (24) in 1972 and complete games (29) in 1972 and 1973, earning the American League Cy Young Award in 1972.

In January 1978, the San Diego Padres acquired Perry from the Texas Rangers for Dave Tomlin and cash. Perry performed brilliantly with San Diego in 1978, boasting a 21-6 win-loss record and a 2.72 ERA. His 21 triumphs accounted for 25 percent of the Padre victories. He became the first pitcher to win the Cy Young Award in both major leagues, easily outdistancing Burt Hooton of the Los Angeles Dodgers. *The Sporting News* named him to its National League All-Star team. In 18 home starts, Perry compiled an 11-2 record with a 1.75 ERA. He showed remarkable consistency with a 9-3 ledger and a 2.69 ERA before the All-Star break and a 12-3 slate and a 2.76 ERA the last half. Two weeks after his fortieth birthday, Perry became just the third major-leaguer to strike out 3,000 batters. He fanned Joe Simpson of the Los Angeles Dodgers in the 4-3 season finale at home. At the time, Perry trailed only Walter Johnson and Bob Gibson in career strikeouts. He won nine of his last 10 decisions with a 1.78 ERA, defeating the Houston Astros four times, the Atlanta Braves three times, and every other team at least once. Three of his setbacks were by scores of 1-0, 2-1, and 3-2.

Perry compiled a 12-11 record with a 3.05 ERA in 1979, but left San Diego in September because of personal problems. He led the Padres in victories, ERA, complete games (10), and strikeouts (140), whiffing 10 batters in a 10-5 victory over the New York Mets at Shea Stadium on May 1, in a 6-3 triumph over the Atlanta Braves at home on May 29, and in a 6-3 home win over the Pittsburgh Pirates on June 12. San Diego traded him to the Texas Rangers in February 1980. In two seasons with the Padres, Perry compiled a 33-17 mark, completed 15 of 69 starts, struck out 294 batters in 493.1 innings, and hurled two shutouts.

Perry rounded out his major-league career with the Texas Rangers and the New York Yankees in 1980, the Atlanta Braves in 1981, the Seattle Mariners in 1982 and 1983, and the Kansas City Royals in 1983. His 300th major-league victory came for Seattle against the New York Yankees on May 6, 1982. In 22 major-league seasons, he won 314 games and lost 265 with a 3.10 ERA and fanned 3,534 batters in 5,351.1 innings.

Gaylord Perry sips champagne as he talks with reporters after being named the 1978 National League Cy Young Award winner.

Perry, who recorded 20 or more victories five times, remains one of the few pitchers to win 100 games and strike out at least 1,000 batters in both major leagues. He compiled a 175-135 record in the National League and 139-130 mark in the American League. Perry ranks sixth in innings pitched and losses, seventh in strikeouts and games started (690), fourteenth in wins, fifteenth in shutouts (53), seventeenth in walks (1,379), and thirty-seventh in complete games (303). He made three National League and two American League All-Star teams. He pitched in the 1971 National League Championship Series, but never appeared in a World Series. Perry co-authored a book, *Me and the Spitter* (1974), and was elected to the National Baseball Hall of Fame in 1991. He and his wife, Blanche, live on a Kill Devil Hills, North Carolina ranch and have four children, Amy, Beth, Allison, and Jack.

PHIL PLANTIER

Phil Plantier played outfield for the San Diego Padres from 1993 to 1995 and briefly in 1997. The 5-foot 11-inch, 195-pound Plantier, who batted left-handed and threw right-handed, was born on January 27, 1969 in Manchester, New Hampshire and graduated from Poway, California High School in 1987. The Boston Red Sox selected him in the eleventh round of the June 1987 free agent draft. He played in the minor leagues from 1987 through 1989 and divided the next three campaigns between Pawtucket, Rhode Island of the International League and the Boston Red Sox. In 1991, he batted .331 with 11 home runs and 35 RBIs in 53 games for the Boston Red Sox. In December 1992, Boston traded him to the San Diego Padres.

In his first full major-league season in 1993, Plantier matched the Padre record for home runs by an outfielder with 34 and paced the club with 100 RBIs. He batted just .240 and struck out 124 times. Plantier, the club's Most Valuable Player, became just the fifth Padre to combine 30 home runs with 100 RBIs during the same season. He ranked seventh in home runs and ninth in RBIs. Plantier homered twice in a 10-4 setback to the St. Louis Cardinals at Busch Stadium on May 30, twice in a 10-5 home loss to the Chicago Cubs on June 29, and twice in an 11-9 triumph over the Cincinnati Reds at Riverfront Stadium on July 30. His two-homer games coincidentally came on the next to last day of the month for three consecutive months.

Plantier earned National League Player of the Week honors from August 23 through August 29, batting .409 with five home runs and 18 RBIs. His first career grand slam, off Donovan Osborne, sparked a 7-5 home victory over the St. Louis Cardinals on August 23, while his eleventh-inning home run off Jim Gott defeated the Los Angeles Dodgers, 4-3, at home on September 13. A week later, Plantier knocked in a career-high five runs in an 11-7 slugfest over the Colorado Rockies at Mile High Stadium. He clouted eight home runs between July 26 and August 10 and 19 homers with 55 RBIs in his last 58 games. Plantier batted .429 with five home runs and 14 RBIs against the St. Louis Cardinals and .395 with five home runs and 13 RBIs against the Houston Astros. He ranked third among National League outfielders with 14 assists.

In 1994, Plantier led the Padres with 18 home runs and batted .220 with 21 doubles and 41 RBIs in 96 games. He homered 14 times in his first 170 plate appearances and twice in an 8-0 home romp over the Colorado Rockies on May 6. From April 13 to April 27, Plantier batted safely in 11 of 12 games with five home runs and eight RBIs. On July 15, Tony Gwynn and Plantier hit consecutive home runs in the fourteenth inning off Mike Maddux to edge the New York Mets, 2-1, at Shea Stadium. Plantier doubled three times in three different games and knocked in three runs in four games.

In a blockbuster 12-player December 1994 transaction, the Houston Astros acquired Plantier. Plantier played 22 games for Houston in 1995 before rejoining the Padres in July. He clouted two home runs on August 4 in a 14-12 loss to the Colorado Rockies at Coors Field and hit his second pinch-hit home run as a Padre on September 23 in a 4-2 setback to the Los Angeles Dodgers at Dodger Stadium.

The Detroit Tigers signed Plantier as a free agent in December 1995 and traded him to the Oakland Athletics in March 1996. Plantier split the 1996 season between the Oakland Athletics and their Edmonton, Canada, Pacific Coast League farm team. The San Diego Padres organization re-signed him in January 1997. After starting 1997 at Las Vegas of the Pacific Coast League, Plantier appeared briefly with San Diego and was traded to the St. Louis Cardinals in June. He ended his major-league career with St. Louis in 1997.

In eight major-league seasons, Plantier batted .243 with 91 home runs and 292 RBIs in 610 games. He and his wife, Jennifer, reside in Poway, California and have two sons, Ryan and Tyler.

DENNIS RASMUSSEN

Dennis Rasmussen pitched for the San Diego Padres in September 1983 and from June 1988 through 1991. The 6-foot 7-inch, 233-pound left-hander was born on April 18, 1959 in Los Angeles, California and graduated from Bear Creek High School in Lakewood, Colorado. He attended Creighton University in Omaha, Nebraska, where he played both basketball and baseball. His grandfather, Bill Brubaker, played infield for the Boston Braves and the Pittsburgh Pirates between 1932 and 1943. The California Angels selected Rasmussen in the first round of the June 1981 free agent draft. Rasmussen spent nearly four seasons in the minor leagues, being dealt to the New York Yankees in November 1982 and San Diego Padres in September 1983. His major-league debut came on September 16, 1983 with two scoreless relief innings against the Atlanta Braves at Atlanta-Fulton County Stadium. Rasmussen made his first major-league start on October 1, retiring the first 14 Atlanta Braves and fanning seven in a 4-3, 10-inning home triumph. He did not have any decisions in 1983, logging 13.2 innings with a 1.98 ERA.

Rasmussen began spring training with San Diego in 1984, but was traded to the New York Yankees on March 30. He spent parts of 1984, 1985, and 1987 and all of 1986 with New York, compiling an 18-6 record and 3.88 ERA in 1986. In August 1987, the Yankees traded Rasmussen to the Cincinnati Reds for Bill Gullickson. He finished 4-1 in 1987 with Cincinnati, but struggled in 1988. In June 1988, the San Diego Padres acquired him from the Cincinnati Reds for Candy Sierra.

Rasmussen paid enormous dividends for the Padres in 1988, faring 14-4 with a 2.55 ERA and establishing career bests in innings (204.2), ERA (3.43), and complete games (7). San Diego won 16 of Rasmussen's 20 starts. Rasmussen triumphed in six of seven decisions with a 2.31 ERA at Jack Murphy Stadium. On June 11, he hurled a five-hit, 2-1 victory over the Los Angeles Dodgers at home, fanning a career-high 10 batters. Rasmussen boasted two five-game winning streaks and garnered Padres' Pitcher-of-the-Month honors in June, posting a 4-0 mark with a 2.27 ERA. He won the season finale on October 2 over the Houston Astros, 5-1, at the Astrodome, helping the Padres finish third. Rasmussen led the Padres' staff with seven pickoffs and defeated the Cincinnati Reds and the San Francisco Giants three times each.

Rasmussen split 20 decisions with a 4.26 ERA in 1989 and salvaged a .500 season by winning five of his last six decisions. His lone complete game came on August 21 in an 8-2 victory over the Philadelphia Phillies at Veterans Stadium. Rasmussen posted a 3-6 record in his first 17 starts, but rebounded with a 7-4 ledger in his final 16 starts. He surrendered 18 home runs. He fanned a season-high six batters on April 7 against the Houston Astros and September 5 against the Atlanta Braves.

In 1990, Rasmussen's record slipped to 11-15 with a 4.51 ERA and one shutout. He led the staff with eight pickoffs, but surrendered 28 home runs. The Padres scored only 32 runs in his 15 losses. He fared 7-4 in his first 14 starts and enjoyed a three-game winning streak from May 25 through June 5. Rasmussen hurled a nine-hit, 7-0 shutout of the Houston Astros at the Astrodome on June 26. After losing nine of 10 starts, he posted his second three-game winning streak from September 5 through September 16. Rasmussen won three decisions over the Houston Astros and led the staff with a .290 batting average and eight RBIs. As a pinch-hitter on June 24, he belted a three-run double with the bases loaded in an 11-10 loss to the Atlanta Braves at Atlanta-Fulton County Stadium.

Rasmussen struggled with a 6-13 mark, a 3.74 ERA, and one shutout in injury-riddled 1991. In January 1992, the Baltimore Orioles signed him as a free agent. With the Padres, he had compiled a 41-42 slate with 346 strikeouts, two shutouts, and 11 complete games. Rasmussen appeared briefly with the Chicago Cubs in 1992 and finished his major-league career with the Kansas City Royals between 1992 and 1995. In 12 major-league seasons, he boasted a 91-77 record with a 4.15 ERA, five shutouts, and 835 strikeouts in 1,460.2 innings.

Rasmussen and his wife, Sharon, reside in Tampa, Florida and have four daughters, Ashley, Stephanie, Brynn, and Michelle.

GENE RICHARDS

Gene Richards starred as an outfielder with the San Diego Padres from 1977 through 1983. The 6-foot, 170-pound outfielder, who batted and threw left-handed, was born on September 29, 1953 in

Gene Richards

Monticello, South Carolina and excelled in baseball at South Carolina State College in Orangeburg. He batted .450 with 27 RBIs as a sophomore in 1973 and .414 with 17 RBIs as a junior in 1974. When South Carolina State dropped baseball, the San Diego Padres selected him as the first player in the January 1975 free agent draft. Richards spent only two seasons in the minor leagues before joining San Diego in 1977.

In 1977, Richards blossomed as a rookie left fielder and improved markedly after the All-Star break. Richards batted .290 and set franchise and major-league records for rookies with 56 stolen bases, being caught only 12 times. He matched Bill Almon's Padre mark for most triples with 11. His 38 multi-hit games included one four-hit and 15 three-hit contests. Richards reached base safely in 12 consecutive games from August 7 to August 19, batted .417 against the New York Mets, and stole 10 bases against the Atlanta Braves. In the 15-inning, second-game, 5-2 home loss to the Montreal Expos on July 26, he made six hits in seven at-bats.

Richards finished sixth in the senior circuit in batting with a .3081 mark in 1978, narrowly trailing teammate Dave Winfield's .3083. He began the season as a first baseman, but shifted to the outfield after 26 games. Richards batted .331 after June 9 and performed consistently both at home and on the road. He feasted on Pittsburgh Pirates pitching for a .425 batting average. Richards shared second in the senior circuit with 12 triples, just one behind Garry Templeton, and tied for sixth with 37 stolen bases. Besides enjoying a 12-game hitting streak, he recorded 14 three-hit games and a four-hit effort in a 5-1 home triumph over the San Francisco Giants on September 21.

His batting average dropped to .279 as the regular center fielder in 1979, but he hit .302 the second half of the season and ranked second on the Padres in runs (77), hits (152), triples (9), and stolen bases (24). He reached base with a hit, walk, or as a hit batsman in 24 consecutive games from May 11 through June 1 and enjoyed a 10-game hitting streak. Richards produced 43 multi-hit games, including four-hit games in a 5-3 victory over the New York Mets at Shea Stadium on July 8 and in a 5-2 loss to the Los Angeles Dodgers at Dodger Stadium on September 12. He clouted a triple and a home run off Joe Niekro in a 3-2 setback to the Houston Astros at the Astrodome on May 18 and made 10 putouts in center field against the Los Angeles Dodgers three days later.

Richards enjoyed an outstanding 1980 season as the regular left fielder. He finished second in the National League with 193 hits, fifth in stolen bases with 61, eighth in runs scored with 91, and twelfth in batting at .301 and led major-league outfielders with 21 assists. His hits, stolen bases, and assists set Padre records. Richards led San Diego with eight triples, stole 18 consecutive bases from June 16 through July 19, and joined Ozzie Smith and Jerry Mumphrey as the first trio in senior circuit history to steal at least 50 bases the same season. San Diego led the major leagues in stolen bases. On July 13, Richards stole four bases, including home, in a 4-3 victory over the visiting Los Angeles Dodgers. He pilfered eight bases in that three-game series against the Dodgers from July 12 through July 14 and 14 of 15 bases against the Dodgers that season. Richards recorded a four-hit contest in an 8-7 loss to the Chicago Cubs at Wrigley Field on July 19, another in a 4-3 setback to the Cincinnati Reds at Riverfront Stadium on August 6, and one more in a 5-3 loss to the Montreal Expos at home on September 1 and four consecutive three-hit games from July 11 through July 14. He enjoyed a 13-game hitting streak from June 28 through July 15 and recorded more chances (335) than any other National League left fielder. Richards threw out two runners against the Montreal Expos on June 21 and against the Houston Astros on September 15.

In 1981, Richards batted .288 and exhibited more power in the third position in the lineup, leading the Padres with 42 RBIs. Only teammate Ruppert Jones surpassed his 29 extra-base hits. Richards ranked among the top 10 National League leaders in walks (53) and on-base percentage (.373) and shared the lead with 12 triples. At Atlanta-Fulton County Stadium, he clouted a two-run homer off Gaylord Perry in a 7-6 loss to the Atlanta Braves on May 23 and a three-run homer off Phil Niekro in a 7-5 victory over Atlanta on May 24. Besides batting .440 against the New York Mets, Richards enjoyed a 14-game hitting streak from May 2 through May 16. He produced six three-hit games, but his stolen base production dropped markedly to 20. His 14 outfield assists matched the senior circuit lead with Jack Clark.

Richards hit .286 with 30 stolen bases in 1982. He recorded five hits, including a home run, and three RBIs in a 9-7 setback at home to the New York Mets on July 10 and five hits in a 4-3, 16-inning loss to the Los Angeles Dodgers on September 13. He enjoyed a 13-game hitting streak and recorded four-hit games in a 7-6 victory over the San Francisco Giants at Candlestick Park on June 26 and in a 3-2, 10-inning home triumph over the Cincinnati Reds on September 29. Besides batting .313 against left-handed pitchers, he grounded into only five double plays in 521 official at-bats. After being relegated to part-time duty in 1983, Richards opted for free agency in March 1984 and spent his final major-league campaign with the San Francisco Giants. In 939 games with the Padres, Richards batted .291 with 484 runs, 994 hits, 63 triples, 251 RBIs, and 242 stolen bases. He ranks second in triples and stolen bases, third in runs scored, and fourth in batting average and hits on the all-time Padre list. Richards, who succeeded in stolen base attempts nearly 75 percent of the time, coaches for the San Antonio Missions of the Texas League. He and his wife, Yvette, reside in La Mesa, California, and have one son, Eugene III.

DAVE A. ROBERTS

Dave A. Roberts pitched for the San Diego Padres from July 1969 through 1971. The 6-foot 2-inch, 202-pound Roberts, who batted and threw left-handed, was born on September 11, 1944 in Gallipolis, Ohio, and signed with the Philadelphia Phillies as a free agent in June 1963. He toiled over six seasons in the Phillies', Pittsburgh Pirates', and Kansas City Athletics' minor-league organizations, being named International League Pitcher of the Year in 1968 with Columbus, Ohio.

The San Diego Padres selected Roberts as their 20th choice in the October 1968 expansion draft. Roberts began 1969 with Elmira, New York of the Eastern League and joined San Diego in July, losing all three decisions as a starter with a 4.78 ERA. He made his major-league debut at home on July 6, losing 3-2 to the Houston Astros. Roberts allowed three runs, including one earned, in over six innings. His other losses came to the Atlanta Braves, 3-1, at home on July 10 and to the San Francisco Giants, 4-3, at Candlestick Park on July 16. He relieved in 17 games, fanning 19 batters in nearly 48 innings, and led Padre pitchers with a .267 batting average.

In 1970, Roberts authored a 8-14 record with a 3.81 ERA. Besides twirling two shutouts, he relieved 22 times with one save. Roberts retired 18 consecutive batters in his first relief appearance in a 7-2 victory over the Los Angeles Dodgers at Dodger Stadium on April 10 and performed brilliantly in relief in a 4-0 triumph over the St. Louis Cardinals on June 16, not allowing a runner beyond second base in eight innings. He lost 10 straight decisions from June 22 through September 10. Although Roberts often pitched well, the Padres tallied only 16 runs in those 10 defeats. Roberts defeated the Los Angeles Dodgers three times and established a franchise record by pitching 28.1 scoreless innings from September 10 through September 29, featuring two victories over the Atlanta Braves. He led the Padres with two shutouts, blanking the Los Angeles Dodgers, 4-0, at Dodgers Stadium on September 16 and the Atlanta Braves, 5-0, at Atlanta-Fulton County Stadium on September 24. In the September 16 victory, Roberts set a club record for left-handers by fanning 10 Los Angeles Dodgers. Besides boasting six RBIs during the season, he homered in a 7-6 loss to the Montreal Expos at Jarry Park on May 8 and in a 10-9 win over the Cincinnati Reds at Riverfront Stadium on July 9.

His best season with San Diego came in 1971, when he led the Padres in ERA, innings, and complete games. Roberts fashioned a 14-17 ledger with a 2.10 ERA, setting franchise records for ERA and innings (270) and recording the then second most victories in club history. Besides completing 14 of 34 starts with two shutouts, he fanned 135 batters in 269.2 innings. At home, Roberts blanked the Montreal Expos, 8-0, on June 6 and the Chicago Cubs, 1-0, on July 9. He

Dave A. Roberts

limited the Pittsburgh Pirates to four hits in a 2-1 home triumph on May 12 and lost a three-hitter, 2-1, to the New York Mets at Shea Stadium on August 21.

In three seasons with the Padres, Roberts posted a 22-34 mark with a 2.98 ERA in 102 games. He completed 17 of 60 starts with four shutouts and relieved 42 times with two saves, fanning 256 batters in 500 innings. Upon his departure, Roberts ranked first on the all-time list in ERA, second in innings pitched, victories, and strikeouts, and third in appearances. In December 1971, the San Diego Padres traded him to the Houston Astros. Roberts pitched for Houston from 1972 through 1975, attaining a career-high 17 victories in 1973. He later hurled for the Detroit Tigers, Chicago Cubs, San Francisco Giants, Pittsburgh Pirates, and Seattle Mariners, ending his major-league career with the New York Mets in 1981. In 13 major-league seasons, Roberts compiled a 103-125 record with a 3.78 ERA. He whiffed 957 batters in 2,099 innings with 20 shutouts and 15 saves.

He and his wife, Stella, reside in Fort Ashley, West Virginia and have two children, Christopher and Rick. He enjoys playing the drums, fishing, and golfing.

DAVE W. ROBERTS

Dave W. Roberts played infield and caught for the San Diego Padres between 1972 and 1978. The 6-foot 3-inch, 202-pound Roberts, who batted and threw right-handed, was born on February 17, 1951 in Lebanon, Oregon and attended the University of Oregon. He starred as a third baseman at Oregon and was named on *The Sporting News'* College All-America team in 1972, when he batted .410 with 12 home runs and 47 RBIs and was chosen College Player of the Year. The San Diego Padres selected him as the first player in the June 1972 free agent draft.

Roberts played in his first professional game on June 7, debuting in the twelfth inning against the Pittsburgh Pirates. In 1972, he batted .244 with 17 doubles, five home runs, and 33 RBIs in 100 games and hit .405 against the St. Louis Cardinals. Roberts started on June 10 against St. Louis and remained in the lineup. Besides playing 84 games at third base, he also performed at second base, shortstop, and catcher. Roberts clouted his first major-league home run off George Stone and singled three times in an 8-6 home win over the Atlanta Braves on June 29. He was thrown out three times at the plate the next night against the visiting Cincinnati Reds, but doubled home two runs to tie the game and doubled to start the winning rally in the 13-inning, 4-3 victory. Roberts drove in three runs on July 30 in a 10-7 win over the Houston Astros at the Astrodome, completing the game as a catcher. Defensively, he made difficult plays with seemingly effortless motion at third base.

Roberts's best season with the San Diego came in 1973, when he led the Padres with a .286 batting average and 12 game-winning hits. He attained career highs with 56 runs, 137 hits, 20 doubles, three triples, 21 home runs, 64 RBIs, 11 stolen bases, and a .472 slugging percentage. Roberts hit .307 with 18 home runs and 47 RBIs the second half of the season and enjoyed a 12-game hitting streak from September 2 through September 15. He boasted two four-hit and 11 three-hit games and tripled twice in a 7-4 loss to the Montreal Expos at Jarry Park on June 12. In the season home finale, Roberts clouted an inside-the-park home run in a 3-2 setback to the Los Angeles Dodgers on September 29. He batted .480 against the Chicago Cubs.

Back problems hindered him in 1974. Roberts batted just .167 with five home runs and 18 RBIs in 113 games and never made more than two hits in a

Dave W. Roberts

game. His best performance came in a 5-2 home win over the Philadelphia Phillies on April 27, when he doubled twice and knocked in a season-high three runs.

San Diego used Roberts sparingly thereafter. Roberts spent most of 1975 with Hawaii, but hit .283 with two home runs and 12 RBIs in 33 games for the Padres. After catching for Hawaii in 1976, he was sold to the expansion Toronto Blue Jays that October. In February 1977, Toronto returned him to San Diego for pitcher Jerry Johnson. Roberts batted .220 with one home run and 23 RBIs as a reserve Padre catcher in 1977. He made three hits in an 8-6 victory over the New York Mets at Shea Stadium on July 30, in a 2-1 home loss to the Chicago Cubs on September 4, in a 9-5 triumph over the Houston Astros at the Astrodome on September 7, and in a 6-4 win over the visiting Atlanta Braves on September 14. In the Houston contest, Roberts doubled, homered, and knocked in four runs. He had three RBIs in an 11-8 slugfest over the Astros at the Astrodome in the second game of an April 23 doubleheader and in a 5-4 home loss to the San Francisco Giants on July 13. In his final season with the Padres in 1978, he batted just .216 with one round-tripper and seven RBIs.

In October 1978, the San Diego Padres traded Roberts and Oscar Gamble to the Texas Rangers for three players. Roberts had batted .240 with 67 doubles, 35 home runs, and 157 RBIs as a Padre. He spent 1979 and 1980 with the Texas Rangers and 1981 with the Houston Astros, ending his major-league career with the Philadelphia Phillies in 1982. In 10 major-league seasons, Roberts batted .239 with 49 home runs and 208 RBIs in 709 games. He and his wife, Janie, reside in Portland, Oregon, where he enjoys water skiing and scuba diving.

LEON "BIP" ROBERTS

Leon "Bip" Roberts played infield and outfield in three different stints with the San Diego Padres between 1986 and 1995. The 5-foot 7-inch, 165-pound Roberts, who switch hit and threw right-handed, was born on October 27, 1963 in Berkeley, California and attended Chabot Junior College and the University of Nevada-Las Vegas. The nephew of former NFL player Roy Shivers, he was selected first by the Pittsburgh Pirates in the secondary phase of the June 1982 draft. After spending four seasons in the Pirates' farm system, Roberts was chosen by the San Diego Padres in the Rule V draft and batted .253 in 1986 while splitting second base duties with Tim Flannery. He hit .419 in September and made four hits in a 6-5 loss in the second game of a September 7 doubleheader to the New York Mets at Shea Stadium.

In September 1988, Roberts rejoined the Padres. He hit .301 in 1989, starting 69 games in left field, 46 at third base, 13 at shortstop, and eight at second base. Roberts batted .320 as a leadoff hitter and matched a club record in late June by reaching base nine consecutive times on six hits and three walks. On September 4 at Atlanta-Fulton County Stadium, he made four hits to help edge the Atlanta Braves, 10-9. His .325 batting average marked the sixth best against National League left-handers. In 1990, Roberts earned the Padres' Most Valuable Player honors, ranking sixth in the National League with a .309 batting average, 104 runs, and 36 doubles. He also stole 46 bases with nine home runs and 44 RBIs. Besides leading the senior circuit with a .401 batting average on artificial turf, he ranked second with a .338 road batting average.

Roberts opened the 1991 season as the regular second baseman and divided the rest of the campaign between second base, third base, and the outfield. He batted .281 and clouted two home runs on August 11 in a 13-0 blowout over the visiting Cincinnati Reds. Roberts matched a career-best with four hits on September 21 in a 3-2 home win over the San Francisco Giants. In December 1991, the San Diego Padres traded Roberts to the Cincinnati Reds for pitcher Randy Myers. In 1992, he earned team MVP honors with career highs in batting average (.323) and RBIs (45) and ranked among National League leaders in batting average, on- base percentage, runs, hits, and stolen bases.

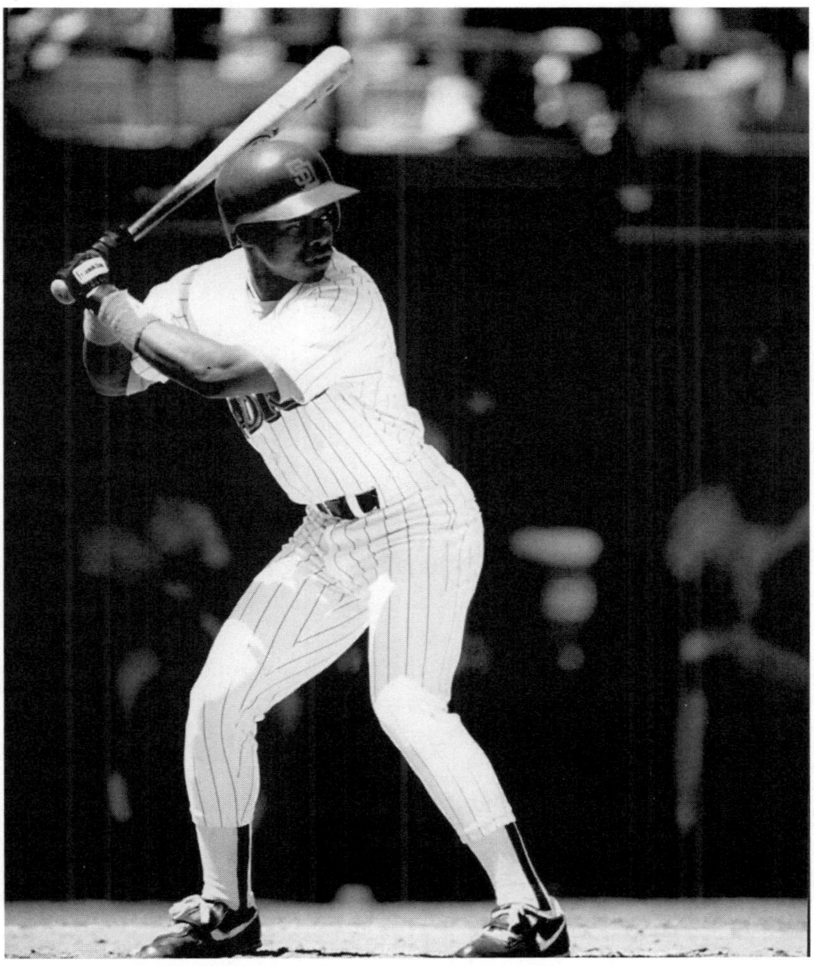

Switch hitter Bip Roberts ready at the plate.

In January 1994, Roberts returned to San Diego as a free agent. That year he stole 21 bases and batted .320, the second highest average of his career. His 23-game hitting streak in May and June marked the longest in the senior circuit and third best in Padre history. No National Leaguer had hit in more consecutive games since 1989. During the hitting streak, Roberts batted .407 with 13 RBIs and recorded 11 multihit games. He made four hits on June 1 in a 6-4 home win over the Pittsburgh Pirates and on June 27 in a 12-7 loss to the Colorado Rockies at Mile High Stadium. Roberts ended 1994 with another 10-game hitting streak and feasted on Chicago Cubs pitchers for a .441 batting average. Injuries sidelined him for part of the 1995 season, as he batted .304 in 73 games. The Padres traded him to the Kansas City Royals for first baseman Wally Joyner in December 1995. On the all-time Padres list, Roberts ranks second in batting average (.298), fourth in stolen bases (148) and on-base percentage (.361), seventh in runs (378), eighth in hits (673), tenth in triples (21), fourteenth in doubles (98), and fifteenth in walks (212).

Roberts remained with the Kansas City Royals until joining the Cleveland Indians in August 1997. He made his only World Series appearance in 1997, batting .273 with four RBIs against the Florida Marlins. Roberts ended his major-league career in 1998 with the Detroit Tigers and Oakland Athletics. During 12 major-league seasons, he batted .293 with 352 RBIs and 264 stolen bases. He and his wife, Janina, reside in Poway, California and have two sons, Lantavio and Markus, and one daughter, Jovan.

LUIS SALAZAR

Luis Salazar played infield for the San Diego Padres three different times between 1980 and 1989. The 5-foot 9-inch, 180-pound Salazar, who batted and threw right-handed, was born on May 19, 1956 in Barcelona, Venezuela and attended Jose Antonio Anzoategui High School there. The Kansas City Royals signed the shortstop as a free agent in November 1973. Salazar played briefly in the minor leagues in 1974 and left organized baseball that July. After signing with the Pittsburgh Pirates in November 1975, he spent nearly five seasons in the minor leagues.

In August 1980, the Pittsburgh Pirates traded Salazar to the San Diego Padres for Kurt Bevacqua and Mark Lee. Salazar joined the Padres in mid-August, batting .337 with 25 RBIs in 44 games as a third baseman-outfielder. He debuted in a doubleheader loss to the Houston Astros on August 17 with four hits in seven plate appearances. His seven three-hit games were in 7-5 and 5-1 victories over the Philadelphia Phillies on August 20 and August 30, an 8-6 triumph over the New York Mets at Shea Stadium on August 26, 12-5 and 12-0 romps over the San Francisco Giants on September 9 and October 3, a 9-4 home win over the Houston Astros on September 23, and a 3-2 home squeaker over the Los Angeles Dodgers on September 26. Salazar drove in four runs and clouted his first major-league home run in the October 3 contest. His season ended with an eight-game hitting streak. He batted over .450 against the Philadelphia Phillies and San Francisco Giants.

In 1981, Salazar batted .303 with three home runs and 38 RBIs. He led the Padres in batting average and hits with 121, which placed eighth in the National League. Salazar enjoyed eight three-hit games and made four hits, including a double and a triple, in a 5-1 home victory over the Atlanta Braves on May 31. Salazar made three hits in a 4-1, opening day triumph over the San Francisco Giants and recorded nine hits in the four-game series. He doubled and tripled in a 13-5 rout over the Montreal Expos at Olympic Stadium on May 6. Salazar boasted an 11-game hitting streak between May 22 and June 4 and made seven consecutive hits between May 30 and June 2. He batted .349 in August, .444 against the Montreal Expos, and over .400 against the Chicago Cubs and Atlanta Braves.

His batting average slipped to .242 in 1982, but he clouted eight home runs and established career bests with 62 RBIs and 32 stolen bases as a regular third baseman. Salazar ranked fourth on the Padres in RBIs and second in stolen bases. He singled, doubled, and homered, and drove in four runs to spark an 8-4 win over the visiting San Francisco Giants on April 20 and collected three hits, including a home run, and four RBIs in a 6-2 home triumph over the Houston Astros on June 11. On July 8, he clouted an inside-the-park home run in a 5-3 victory over the Philadelphia Phillies at Veterans Stadium.

In 1983, Salazar hit .258 with 45 RBIs. His career-high 14 home runs marked the then second highest by a San Diego third baseman. He shared second on the Padres in home runs and ranked third in stolen bases (24), pacing National League third basemen. He batted .302 through late June and clouted nine home runs between July 29 and September 13.

Luis Salazar

Salazar's playing time diminished in 1984, when he batted .241 with three home runs and 17 RBIs in 93 games. Salazar enjoyed one four-hit and one three-RBI game. He tripled in the National League Championship Series against the Chicago Cubs and singled in the World Series against the Detroit Tigers. In a seven-player December 1984 transaction, San Diego traded Salazar to the Chicago White Sox. Salazar played with Chicago in 1985 and spent most of 1986 on the disabled list.

The Padres signed Salazar as a free agent in April 1987. Salazar batted .254 with three home runs and 17 RBIs, boasting one four-hit game and one three-RBI contest. San Diego released him in October 1987. He hit .270 with a career-high 62 RBIs for the Detroit Tigers in 1988 and rejoined the Padres in March 1989. Salazar batted .268 with eight home runs and 22 RBIs before being traded that August to the Chicago Cubs. His major-league career ended with Chicago in 1992. In 13 major-league seasons, he hit .261 with 94 home runs, 455 RBIs, and 117 stolen bases.

On the Padre all-time list, Salazar ranks eighth in career triples (24), ninth in stolen bases (93), tenth in batting average (.267), twelfth in on-base percentage (.298), seventeenth in RBIs (226), and nineteenth in doubles (73). He coached for the Milwaukee Brewers in 2001. Salazar and his wife, Graciela, reside in Guarenas, Venezuela and have one son, Carlos.

BENITO SANTIAGO

Benito Santiago starred as a catcher for the San Diego Padres from September 1986 through 1992. The 6-foot 1-inch, 182-pound Santiago, who bats and throws right-handed, was born on March 25, 1965 in Ponce, Puerto Rico and grew up in low-income Santa Isabel. After his father died of cancer, he was brought up by an uncle and aunt and attended John F. Kennedy High School in Ponce. In September 1982, the San Diego Padres signed him as a free agent.

Santiago spent four seasons in the minor leagues before joining the San Diego Padres in September 1986. He batted .290 with three home runs and six RBIs in 17 games. Santiago doubled to left center field in his first major-league at-bat against Mike Scott in a 3-2 home win over the Houston Astros on September 14 and hit .357 in his first seven contests. His first major-league home run, a solo clout off reliever Mark Davis, gave the Padres a dramatic 5-4, 10-inning home victory over the San Francisco Giants on September 17.

Santiago dramatically improved San Diego's fortunes as a 22-year-old rookie in 1987, catching more games (146) than any other major-league receiver. He unanimously earned National League Rookie of the Year honors, recording a career-high .300 batting average with 21 stolen bases. In the season finale, Santiago made hits in both at-bats in a 5-3 home loss to the Los Angeles Dodgers to become just the second San Diego catcher to bat .300 in a season. He led the Padres in game-winning RBIs (10) and finished second in hits (164), doubles (33), home runs (18), and RBIs (79). His 44 multiple-hit games included 10 three-hit contests. Santiago, who batted .441 against southpaws, belted two home runs with four RBIs to help defeat the Philadelphia Phillies, 9-4, in 11 innings at Veterans Stadium on August 18. Defensively, Santiago tied a club record by throwing out three San Francisco Giants in a 1-0 home loss on April 15. He threw out 43 of 130 runners trying to steal, nailing Vince Coleman of the St. Louis Cardinals three times.

From August 25 through October 2, Santiago batted safely in 34 consecutive games. The streak, the longest in the senior circuit in a decade, established major-league records for a rookie, Latino player, and catcher. No major-league catcher ever had hit in over 30 consecutive games. His streak began on August 25 with one hit against Neal Heaton in a 5-1 home triumph over the Montreal Expos and ended at home on October 3 when Orel Hershiser of the Los Angeles Dodgers blanked him three times and shut out the Padres, 1-0. During the final week, Santiago kept the streak alive three times in his last plate appearance. He bunted for a single in the bottom of the eighth inning at home against Frank Williams in a 4-3 loss to the Cincinnati Reds on October 1 to extend his streak to 33 games. The streak continued twice in the final week against Fernando Valenzuela of the Los Angeles Dodgers, including a second-inning double in a 10-3 loss for the last hit on October 2. During the streak, Santiago batted .346 with 47 hits, 12 doubles, five home runs, and 19 RBIs and raised his batting average from .284 to .299. In August and September, he won the Padres Player of the Month awards. His post-season honors included making *The Sporting News'* Silver Slugger and All-Star teams and earning the Clyde McCullough Award as Padre Rookie of the Year.

Although batting only .248 with 10 home runs and 48 RBIs in 1988, Santiago hit safely in 14 of his first 15 games and made *The Sporting News'* Silver Slugger team. He clouted five round-trippers in late July and early August and homered twice off Zane Smith in a 5-1 victory over the Atlanta Braves at Atlanta-Fulton County Stadium on August 9. In the first game of a September 21 doubleheader, he belted a grand slam off Rick Horton and drove in a career-high five runs to help defeat the Los Angeles Dodgers, 9-3, at Dodger Stadium. Rawlings recognized Santiago as the National League's best defensive catcher with his first Gold Glove Award. Eight runners were picked off base by the Padre catcher, who threw out 45 percent of the 77 runners trying to steal and led major-league catchers with 75 assists. Santiago began throwing out runners while still in a crouch position, nailing 11 of 17 (65 percent) from his knees. He picked off nine runners, including seven at second base and two at first base, and made only 12 errors.

The 1989 season brought Santiago more honors, as fans resoundingly named him starting catcher for the National League All-Stars. Although batting only .236 with 62 RBIs, Santiago earned a second Rawlings Gold Glove Award and made *The Sporting News'* National League All-Star team. He picked off 16 runners from his knees, including nine at first base and seven at second base, and threw out 39 percent of the 51 runners attempting to steal. Santiago enjoyed his first four-hit major-league games in an 8-2 victory over the Philadelphia Phillies at Veterans Stadium on May 19 and in a 17-4 home trouncing of the Pittsburgh Pirates on July 18. He belted 10 home runs in his final 33 contests, including a grand slam off Jeff Parrett of the Philadelphia Phillies on September 3. Right-handers surrendered 14 of his 16 home runs.

Santiago enjoyed his best major-league season in 1990 until June 14, when Jeff Brantley of the San Francisco Giants broke the catcher's left arm and landed him on the disabled list for the first time. At the time, he was batting .317 with nine home runs and 33 RBIs. During a 12-game hitting streak in April, Santiago hit .413 with three homers and 12 RBIs. He clouted a two-run, game-winning home run on April 15 against the San Francisco Giants at Candlestick Park. The round-tripper gave the Padres a 4-3 win and a five-game winning streak. In a 16-11 loss on June 1 to the Atlanta Braves, Santiago made four hits and scored four runs. After returning from his injury in early August, he batted just .215 with two home runs and 20 RBIs. His two home runs came on September 19 and September 20 against the Los Angeles Dodgers at Dodger Stadium. Santiago finished 1990 with a .270 batting average, 11 home runs, and 53 RBIs. Besides earning his third consecutive Rawlings Gold Glove Award, he made *The Sporting News'* Silver Slugger team for the third time and again was voted to start the All-Star Game. He picked off five base runners and threw out 37 percent of the 62 runners trying to steal.

Santiago batted .267 with 17 home runs and a career-high 87 RBIs in 1991 and led National League catchers in assists. The best game of his major-league career came on September 13, when he homered, doubled, and singled three times with five RBIs in a 13-2 victory over the San Francisco Giants at Candlestick Park for his first five-hit major-league game. He also made four hits in two other contests and repeated as a National League All-Star.

Santiago's batting average slumped to .251 in his final San Diego season in 1992. Santiago also clouted 10 home runs with 42 RBIs and tied a Padre record on May 15 by hitting three doubles in a 9-2 victory over the Pittsburgh Pirates at Three Rivers Stadium. He made four hits in a 6-3, 10-inning triumph over the visiting Pittsburgh Pirates on May 26 and homered twice in a 3-0 blanking of the Chicago Cubs at home on August 26. Santiago made only 12 errors and was selected to the National League All-Star team for the final time. In six seasons with San Diego, Santiago batted .264 with 85 home runs and 375 RBIs. On the Padre career list, he ranks fifth in strikeouts (516), sixth in home runs, seventh in hits (757) and RBIs, eighth in games (789), doubles (124), and slugging percentage (.406), ninth in runs (312), eleventh in batting average, twelfth in on-base percentage (.298), thirteenth in triples (15), and fourteenth in stolen bases (62).

Benito Santiago

Santiago caught for the Florida Marlins in 1993 and 1994, the Cincinnati Reds in 1995, the Philadelphia Phillies in 1996, the Toronto Blue Jays in 1997, the Chicago Cubs in 1999, the Cincinnati Reds in 2000, and the San Francisco Giants since 2001. Through 2001, the Pembroke Pines, Florida resident has batted .261 with 184 home runs and 767 RBIs and recorded a .985 fielding percentage in 1,689 games. His exceptional throwing arm enabled him to pick runners off base, throw out runners attempting to steal, and prevent many runners on second base from scoring on singles. Jerry Coleman, who has followed major-league baseball since World War II, remarked, "Santiago has the best throwing arm I've ever seen. He stops runners from stealing." Santiago and his wife, Bianca, had one daughter, Benny Beth, and one son, Benito, Jr., before their separation.

Gary Sheffield

GARY SHEFFIELD

Gary Sheffield starred as a third baseman for the San Diego Padres from 1992 through June 1993. The 5-foot 11-inch, 205-pound Sheffield, who bats and throws right-handed, was born on November 18, 1968 in Tampa, Florida and is the nephew of major-league pitcher Dwight Gooden. He played in the Little League World Series and graduated from Hillsborough High School in Tampa in 1986. The Milwaukee Brewers selected him as the sixth overall pick in the first round of the June 1986 free agent draft. Sheffield spent three seasons in the minor leagues before batting .238 with 12 RBIs in September 1988 with the Milwaukee Brewers. He played shortstop and third base for Milwaukee from 1989 through 1991, batting .294 with 10 home runs and 67 RBIs in 1990.

In March 1992, Milwaukee dealt Sheffield to the San Diego Padres in a five-player transaction. Sheffield batted a career-high .330 in 1992 and set San Diego records for a third baseman with 33 home runs and 100 RBIs, finishing third in the National League Most Valuable Player balloting. His other honors included *The Sporting News'* Comeback Player of the Year and Silver Slugger team, Major-League Player of the Year, and National League All-Star team. Besides being the youngest National League batting champion since Tommy Davis in 1962, he became the first right-hander to win the hitting title since Bill Madlock in 1983. He seriously challenged for the highly-coveted Triple Crown until missing the last six games with a fractured index finger. Sheffield finished third in home runs, two behind teammate Fred McGriff, and fifth in the RBI race. His 33 round-trippers marked the most by a major-league batting champion since Fred Lynn in 1979 and the best in the senior circuit since Billy Williams in 1972.

Before the All-Star break, Sheffield batted .325 with 18 home runs and 62 RBIs. He enjoyed a career-best 18-game hitting streak from May 6 through May 25, batting .411 with seven home runs and 21 RBIs. Sheffield made four hits in a 12-6 home rout of the New York Mets on May 20 and boasted the best Padre offensive performance of the season in a 9-4 victory over the San Francisco Giants at Candlestick Park on June 18, knocking in six runs with his first grand slam off Trevor Wilson and another two-run round-tripper. He made his first All-Star Game appearance as a reserve, making outs both times at Jack Murphy Stadium. Sheffield won the National League Player of the Month Award in August, when he hit .361 with 10 home runs and 26 RBIs. During an 11-game hitting streak in August, Sheffield produced nine multi-hit contests, six home runs, and 17 RBIs. He belted a grand slam off Chris Hammond in a 5-1 triumph over the Cincinnati Reds at Riverfront Stadium on August 14 and homered twice in a 7-5 win over the visiting Houston Astros on August 6 and in a 4-2 home victory over the New York Mets on August 22. In the Houston game, Sheffield and Fred McGriff broke a National League record by hitting consecutive home runs in the first and second innings. He batted .365 with 23 home runs and 58 RBIs at Jack Murphy Stadium and hit .339 with runners in scoring position. His .964 fielding percentage set a record for Padre third baseman.

Sheffield hit .295 with 10 home runs and 36 RBIs in 1993 until traded in June to the Florida Marlins for three young pitchers. His 23 multi-hit games included one four-hit and four three-hit games. He homered twice and knocked in a club-high five runs in a 10-6 home triumph over the St. Louis Cardinals on April 18. Sheffield finished 1993 with a .294 batting average and 20 home runs and became the first player from an expansion team to start in an All-Star Game. He made eight consecutive hits in September 1995 and produced career highs with 42 home runs and 120 RBIs in 1996, making *The Sporting News'* Silver Slugger team. After helping the Florida Marlins win the National League pennant in 1997, Sheffield batted .292 with a double, a home run, and five RBIs in Game 3 of the World Series against the Cleveland Indians. In a blockbuster May 1998 trade, the Los Angeles Dodgers acquired him from the Florida Marlins. His 1999 campaign featured a .301 batting average with 34 home runs and 101 RBIs. He paced the Dodgers with a .325 batting average, 43 home runs, 109 RBIs, and 101 walks in 2000 and hit .311 with 36 home runs and 100 RBIs in 2001. In January 2002, the Los Angeles Dodgers traded the disgruntled Sheffield to the Atlanta Braves for outfielder Brian Jordan and pitchers Odalis Perez and Andy Brown. Through 2001, Sheffield has batted .295 with 315 home runs and 1,016 RBIs. The Los Angeles, California resident has two daughters, Ebony and Carrissa.

BOB SHIRLEY

Bob Shirley pitched for the San Diego Padres from 1977 through 1980. The 5-foot 11-inch, 185-pound Shirley, who batted right-handed and threw left-handed, was born on June 25, 1954 in Cushing, Oklahoma. His high school catcher in Tulsa was Seattle Seahawks wide receiver Steve Largent. Shirley starred in baseball at the University of Oklahoma. The San Diego Padres selected him in the first round of the secondary phase of the January 1976 free agent draft. He spent just one season in the minor leagues, pitching for championship teams at Amarillo of the Texas League and Hawaii of the Pacific Coast League.

Shirley joined the San Diego Padres in 1977, posting a 12-18 record with a 3.70 ERA as a starter. He finished 1977 as one of the top National League rookie pitchers. Shirley led the Padres in wins (12), games started (35), innings pitched (214), and strikeouts (146), setting club records for most home runs (22), walks (100), and balks (6) allowed by a left-hander. In his April 10 major-league debut, he defeated the Cincinnati Reds, 12-4, at Riverfront Stadium. Shirley struck out 11 Reds in 8.2 innings, yielding only four hits and four unearned runs. On April 23, he set a franchise record by retiring 25 consecutive Houston Astros at the Astrodome and hurled 8.2 innings in the 4-2 victory. During his last four outings, Shirley fared 3-0 with a 1.20 ERA. He won four of six decisions against the Cincinnati Reds.

Shirley started 20 games and relieved in 30 contests in 1978, compiling an 8-11 mark with a 3.69 ERA and five saves. He split 10 decisions with a 2.68 ERA at San Diego Stadium and fared 4-1 with a 3.00 ERA in 30 relief appearances. Shirley allowed only one run in 17 innings to the Los Angeles Dodgers and won three of four decisions against the Cincinnati Reds. He did not permit a run in 13.1 innings from July 26 through August 21, recording three saves, and did not surrender a run in his final five appearances.

Shirley slumped to a 8-16 ledger in 1979, but lowered his ERA to 3.38. His ERA ranked fourth best among National League left-handers. He started 25 games and compiled a 4-4 mark with a 1.47 ERA in 24 relief appearances. Shirley hurled the Padres' home opener on April 13, losing, 4-2, to the Cincinnati Reds. He allowed only one unearned run and 13 hits in 22 innings during 10 appearances from May 9 through May 30. On May 30, he relieved in the second inning with no outs and blanked the visiting Atlanta Braves on three hits in the remainder of the game for a 10-2 victory. His first major-league shutout came at home on July 4, when he blanked the Los Angeles Dodgers, 6-0, on a two-hitter. He yielded the St. Louis Cardinals just one run in 10 innings on August 21 at Busch Stadium, eventually winning, 3-2, in 11 innings.

In his final season as a Padre in 1980, Shirley compiled an 11-12 mark with a 3.55 ERA and seven saves. His 11 victories tied Rollie Fingers for the team best. He completed three of 12 starts and relieved in 47 games, mostly as a set-up man for closer Rollie Fingers. In four seasons as a Padre, Shirley boasted a 39-57 mark with a 3.58 ERA in 197 games. He completed 10 of 92 starts with one shutout, relieved 105 times with 12 saves, and fanned 432 batters with 274 walks in 722 innings. On the Padre career list, Shirley ranks tenth in losses, twelfth in walks, thirteenth in innings, fourteenth in wins, games (197), and winning percentage (.406), sixteenth in games started and strikeouts, seventeenth in saves, and nineteenth in complete games.

In a December 1980 11-player blockbuster transaction, the San Diego Padres traded him with Rollie Fingers and Gene Tenace to the St. Louis Cardinals. Shirley spent 1981 with the St. Louis Cardinals, compiling a career-best .600 winning percentage with a 6-4 record. After pitching with the Cincinnati Reds in 1982, he hurled from 1983 through June 1987 with the New York Yankees. In 1985, Shirley split 10 decisions with a career-best 2.64 ERA as a left-handed set-up man. His major-league career ended in 1987 with the Kansas City Royals. In 11 major-league seasons, he recorded 67 wins, 94 losses, and a 3.82 ERA in 434 games. Besides striking out 790 batters in 1,431.2 innings, Shirley completed 16 of 162 starts with two shutouts and saved 18 games. He and his wife, Frances, reside in Tulsa, Oklahoma.

ERIC SHOW

Eric Show, the winningest pitcher in San Diego history, hurled for the Padres from September 1981 through 1990. The 6-foot 1-inch, 180-pound right-hander was born on May 19, 1956 in Riverside, California and majored in physics at the University of California at Riverside. In June 1978, the San Diego Padres selected Show in the 18th round of the free agent draft. Show pitched four seasons in the minor leagues before compiling a 1-3 win-loss record with a 3.13 ERA and 22 strikeouts in 23 innings as a Padre reliever in September 1981. He recorded his first major-league save on September 4 in a 5-4 home triumph over the Pittsburgh Pirates. Show hurled two shutout innings in a 6-3 win over the visiting Atlanta Braves on September 19 for his first major-league victory.

In 1982, Show made 33 relief appearances before joining the starting rotation on July 27. He compiled a 10-6 record and a 2.64 ERA, fourth best in the National League. Show finished 4-3 with a 3.34 ERA as a starter and 6-3 with a 1.62 ERA and three saves as a reliever, making the *Baseball Digest* Rookie All-Star team. In April, he did not surrender any runs and won three consecutive games in his first 18 innings of relief. Show blanked the New York Mets for five innings in a 12-4 home victory on April 27, as the Padres set a then club record with 11 straight victories. He preserved a 9-1 triumph over the Chicago Cubs at Wrigley Field with four shutout innings on June 1 and recorded a 7-6 win over the Cincinnati Reds at Riverfront Stadium with another four shutout innings on June 24. Show hurled his first major-league complete game with a 2-0, seven hit shutout over the Cincinnati Reds at home on August 6 and blanked the visiting Chicago Cubs on a 3-0, five-hitter on September 3.

In 1983, Show paced the young Padre pitching staff with 15 victories, 200.2 innings pitched, and 33 starts and finished second in strikeouts (120) and complete games (4). Only five National League pitchers won more games than Show, who finished 10-3 at home. On April 28, he fashioned a three-hit, 3-1 win over the Chicago Cubs at Wrigley Field and retired the first 16 batters before Larry Bowa reached base. Show blanked the St. Louis Cardinals, 10-0, at home on May 4 with a seven-hit, seven-strikeout effort and the New York Mets, 4-0, on May 27 with a two-hitter. He fanned eight Atlanta Braves in a 3-2 home victory that knocked them out of the Western Division title on September 30.

Show helped the Padres capture their first National League pennant in 1984 with a 15-9 record, 104 strikeouts, and a 3.40 ERA. He matched his career best in victories, led the Padres in starts (32) and innings pitched (206.2), shared the club lead in complete games (3), and finished second in strikeouts. Show defeated the Pittsburgh Pirates, 5-1, on opening day at home, and won five of his first six decisions through May 6 and seven of his last 10 decisions. He blanked the Houston Astros, 2-0, on a two-hitter at the Astrodome on June 19 and hurled a 2-1 complete-game victory over the Montreal Expos at Olympic Stadium on August 26. Show triumphed nine times on the road and batted .246 with three home runs and 10 RBIs. Poor performances, however, plagued him in a National League Championship Series loss in Game 1 against the Chicago Cubs at Wrigley Field and in a World Series loss in Game 4 against the Detroit Tigers at Tiger Stadium.

In 1985, Show won 12 of 23 decisions with a 3.09 ERA and paced the Padre staff in starts (35), innings pitched (233) and strikeouts (141). Opponents, however, clouted a career-high 27 home runs off him. In his season debut, he blanked the San Francisco Giants, 3-0, on a four-hitter with a career-high 11 strikeouts at Candlestick Park on April 10. Show combined with Tim Stoddard on a two-hitter against the San Francisco Giants on June 22 before 53,375 fans. On September 11 at Riverfront Stadium, he surrendered the historic record-breaking 4,192nd hit by Pete Rose of the Cincinnati Reds in the first inning. Show authored three consecutive victories in

September, defeating the Los Angeles Dodgers once and the Atlanta Braves twice and allowing only two earned runs in 25.2 innings. On September 21, he fanned eight Atlanta Braves in a three-hit, 1-0 home shutout. Six days later, Show clouted a three-run homer in a 10-1 triumph over the Atlanta Braves at Atlanta-Fulton County Stadium. He finished 3-0 against the San Francisco Giants with a 1.13 ERA.

Show produced a 9-5 slate with a 2.97 ERA in 1986. On April 26, he fanned a career-high 13 San Francisco Giants in a 10-inning, 3-2 home loss. His 3-1 record and 2.75 ERA earned him Padres Pitcher of the Month honors in May. Show enjoyed a career-high four-game winning streak from June 14 through July 1 and defeated the Cincinnati Reds, 7-1, on August 15 and the Montreal Expos, 3-2, on August 20 before being sidelined with elbow problems for the rest of the season.

Although plunging to a 8-16 mark in 1987, Show paced the Padres in innings pitched (206.1) and recorded a career-high three shutouts. His best performance came at Dodger Stadium on April 26, when he retired 18 consecutive Los Angeles Dodgers in a three-hit, 4-0 shutout. Show earned Padres Pitcher of the Month honors in April, but experienced a career-worst six-game losing streak in May. He defeated the Los Angeles Dodgers, 4-0, on a four-hitter at Dodger Stadium on July 1 and blanked the Houston Astros, 11-0, at home on September 11, yielding only four hits and fanning eight batters. Show finished 2-1 with a 1.95 ERA in September, earning Pitcher of the Month honors again. He fared 7-6 against Western Division clubs, but only 1-10 against Eastern Division teams.

Show enjoyed his best major-league season in 1988 with a 16-11 record, a 3.26 ERA, 13 complete games, and 144 strikeouts. He established personal bests in wins, complete games, innings pitched (234.2), and strikeouts. Show ranked third in complete games among National League pitchers and hurled the most complete games by a Padres pitcher since Randy Jones. He blanked the St. Louis Cardinals, 1-0, on a 10-hitter at home on April 26 and won nine of his last 10 decisions, ending the season with a career-best five-game winning streak. During August and September, he earned Padre Pitcher of the Month honors. He fanned nine San Francisco Giants in a 7-4 victory at Candlestick Park on September 5 and nine Los Angeles Dodgers in an 8-4 home triumph on September 27. San Diego scored over two runs in only one of his 11

Eric Show

losses. Show allowed only 53 walks, matching the sixth best in the senior circuit, and won five games against the Atlanta Braves.

Show finished with an 8-6 record and 4.23 ERA in 1989 before suffering a season-ending back injury in July. He enjoyed a four-game winning streak in April and became the Padre career leader in victories at 93 with a 4-2 home triumph over the Cincinnati Reds on June 14. In his best performance, Show fanned eight Los Angeles Dodgers in a 5-1 home victory on June 19. He won four of his last six decisions prior to back surgery in early August.

Show struggled with a 6-8 mark and 5.76 ERA in 1990 before joining the Oakland Athletics as a free agent in November 1990. With the Padres, he compiled a 100-87 win-loss mark and a 3.59 ERA. He ranks first among San Diego hurlers in victories (100) and walks (593), second in losses, strikeouts (951), innings pitched (1,603.1), and complete games (35), tied for second in shutouts (11), third in appearances (309) and winning percentage (.535), and fifth in ERA. An eccentric personality, Show loved to play the guitar, belonged to the John Birch Society, and often experienced communication problems with managers and teammates. He encountered drug problems and died on March 16, 1994 at a drug rehabilitation center in Dulzura, California.

OZZIE SMITH

Ozzie Smith starred at shortstop for the San Diego Padres from 1978 through 1981. Smith, who batted and threw right-handed, was born on December 26, 1954 in Mobile, Alabama and grew up in the Watts section of Los Angeles, California. One of six children, he played baseball with Eddie Murray at Locke High School. He attended California Polytechnic University in San Louis Obispo on an academic scholarship and played shortstop on their baseball team.

Smith, a 5-foot 10-inch, 155-pound switch hitter, debuted professionally with Walla Walla, Washington of the Northwest League in 1977 after the San Diego Padres selected him in the fourth round of the free agent draft. The shortstop batted .303 while leading the Northwest League in fielding average. Nicknamed "The Wizard of Oz," he spent just 68 games in the minor leagues before becoming the starting San Diego shortstop in 1978. Manager Roger Craig boasted, "Ozzie is the best young infielder I've ever seen . . . very soon he's going to become one of the best shortstops in baseball, if not the best."

As a rookie in 1978, Smith batted .258 and led the San Diego Padres with 40 stolen bases. The acrobatic shortstop finished second to Bob Horner in the National League Rookie of the Year balloting, pacing the senior circuit with 28 sacrifice hits and finishing fourth with 40 stolen bases. Smith registered a nine-game hitting streak from April 25 through May 5, collecting two triples in a 2-1 victory over the St. Louis Cardinals at Busch Stadium on May 5. Besides having 11 three-hit games, he recorded four hits in a 9-2 setback to the Houston Astros at the Astrodome on June 30 and in a 4-3 home triumph over the Los Angeles Dodgers on July 31. Smith stole 12 consecutive bases from May 20 through July 5 and batted .289 against right-handed pitching. His defense impressed baseball followers.

In 1979, Smith ranked just behind Larry Bowa and Tim Foli with a .976 fielding percentage and placed second in assists. "The Octopus" handled 150 more chances than either Bowa or Foli, performing unbelievable feats. In a 19-inning 4-3 home loss to the Pittsburgh Pirates on August 25, 1979, Smith tied a major-league record for most double plays in an extra-inning contest with six. He led the Padres in hitting and RBI during spring training, but suffered a disastrous 0 for 32 start at the plate. Smith never fully recovered from the slump, finishing with a .211 batting average and 27 RBIs. He did not reach the .200 mark until August, batting .242 the second half of the season. His best production came with hitting streaks of seven games from July 7 through July 13 and eight contests from August 17 through August 25. Smith made four hits in a 10-3 triumph over the Atlanta Braves at Atlanta-Fulton County Stadium on July 31 and a trio of three-hit games. He led the Padres with 28 stolen bases and 22 sacrifice hits and finished second with 77 runs scored. National League pitchers found him the fifth-toughest batter to strike out. He stole 11 consecutive bases from July 8 through September 9.

Smith batted .230 in 1980 and led the National League with 23 sacrifice hits. He paced senior circuit shortstops in total chances, putouts, assists, and double plays, earning the first of 13 consecutive Rawlings Gold Gloves awards. His 621 assists broke a record set by Glenn Wright of the Pittsburgh Pirates in 1924. Smith compiled the best fielding percentage (.974) for a shortstop on natural turf and the third best fielding average behind Tim Foli and Dave Concepcion. He handled 16 chances, including 12 assists, on April 12 in a 4-2 home opener over the San Francisco Giants. Offensively, he ranked second on the Padres in at-bats (609) and stolen bases (57), third in games (158), runs (67), and walks (71), and fourth in hits (140). He enjoyed seven three-hit games and compiled an 11-game hitting streak from July 31 through August 9. Smith finished the season with 17 consecutive stolen bases, including three apiece, in losses to the Cincinnati Reds on September 25 and October 1. He, Gene Richards, and Jerry Mumphrey became the first trio from the same team to steal at least 50 bases in a season. Richards stole 61 bases, while Mumphrey pilfered 52.

Smith slumped to a .222 batting average with just 21 RBIs in 1981 but led the Padres with 22 stolen bases and National League shortstops in fielding percentage (.976), total chances, and assists.

Despite Smith's fielding prowess, the Padres needed a better-hitting shortstop. The St. Louis Cardinals, meanwhile, hoped to trade shortstop Garry Templeton, a consistent .300 hitter whose temper had upset manager Whitey Herzog and fans. In February 1982, San Diego dealt Smith to St. Louis for Templeton. The Padres expected to lose Smith to free agency and did not want a repetition of the Dave Winfield case without receiving compensation. With the Padres, overall, Smith batted .231 with 516 hits, 64 doubles, and 147 stolen bases in 583 games. Smith ranks fifth in career stolen bases (147), eleventh in triples (19), fourteenth in runs (266), fifteenth in on-base percentage (.295), seventeenth in hits (516) and slugging percentage (.278), and nineteenth in batting and walks (196) on the Padre all-time list.

Smith gave the Cardinals the defense that they needed on the Busch Stadium Astroturf. He enjoyed an outstanding career with the St. Louis Cardinals, appearing in 13 All-Star Games, four National League Championship Series, and three World Series. *The Sporting News* named him to its National League All-Star team five times. He improved his batting average markedly, batting a career high .303 in 1987.

Sportswriters, announcers, and players described Smith as "poetry in motion," a "combination of baseball and ballet," and "an acrobat on Astroturf." Baseball peers regarded him as the best contemporary defensive shortstop and perhaps the best ever. He led National League shortstops eight times in fielding percentage and assists and compiled a .978 career fielding percentage. In 1991, Smith set a National League record for shortstops with at least 150 games by making only eight errors. His 2,511 games, 8,375 assists, and 1,590 double plays set senior circuit records for shortstops. In 19 major-league seasons, he batted .262 with 793 runs, 2,460 hits, 402 doubles, 69 triples, 793 RBIs, and 580 stolen bases. He was inducted into the National Baseball Hall of Fame in 2002. He has broadcast St. Louis Cardinals games since 1997 and hosted the syndicated television show *This Week in Baseball*. He and his wife, Denise, live in Chesterfield, Missouri and have two sons, Ozzie, Jr. and Dustin.

DAN SPILLNER

Dan Spillner pitched for the San Diego Padres from 1974 through June 1978. The 6-foot 1-inch, 190-pound right-hander was born on November 27, 1951 in Casper, Wyoming and attended Green River Community College in Auburn, Washington. The San Diego Padres selected him in the second round of the June 1970 free agent draft. He pitched just over four seasons in the minor leagues, joining the Padres in mid-May 1974.

Spillner compiled a 9-11 mark with five complete games and a 4.01 ERA in 1974, sharing the team lead in victories and pacing San Diego in shutouts (2). His ERA ranked second best among Padre starters. On June 19, he hurled the fourth one-hitter in Padre history in a 1-0 masterpiece over the Chicago Cubs at Wrigley Field. Rick Monday lined a single off Spillner's leg in the third inning for the lone hit. Spillner outdueled Bob Gibson of the visiting St. Louis Cardinals, 3-1, on August 27 and recorded a career-high 10 strikeouts while blanking the Houston Astros, 2-0, on September 11. He was the only Padre to defeat the Los Angeles Dodgers, besting them, 4-3, on a five-hitter at Dodger Stadium on September 21 and, 3-2, on a six-hitter at home on September 26.

In 1975, Spillner struggled with a 5-13 mark and a 4.26 ERA and led the Padres with 104 strikeouts. He made 25 starts and 12 relief appearances, saving one game. Spillner moved from the starting rotation into the bullpen in the middle portion of the season and returned to the starting rotation for the final third of the campaign. Besides faring well against the Montreal Expos, he fanned eight batters at home in a 5-2 win over the Cincinnati Reds on April 11 and in an 8-3 triumph over the Philadelphia Phillies on August 23. Spillner defeated the Houston Astros, 2-1, on a four-hitter at the Astrodome on April 22 and the Atlanta Braves, 8-1, on a five-hitter at Atlanta-Fulton County Stadium on July 25 and combined with Dave Tomlin to blank the Houston Astros, 1-0, at home on September 12.

Spillner suffered through a disappointing 1976 with only two wins in 13 decisions and a 5.06 ERA, combining 14 starts with 18 relief appearances. He defeated the Montreal Expos, 4-1, at Jarry Park on May 6 and St. Louis Cardinals, 5-4, at Busch Stadium on June 20 in relief. Opponents scored in only six of his 18 relief appearances. He whiffed five batters against the Montreal Expos on May 6 and in a 2-1 victory over the Chicago Cubs at home on July 18.

After starting 1977 with Hawaii of the Pacific Coast League, Spillner compiled a 7-6 record with a 3.73 ERA and six saves for San Diego in 76 relief appearances. He won his first five decisions and did not experience defeat until July 25 against the Philadelphia Phillies. His longest outing came on May 11, when he hurled nearly five scoreless innings to defeat the New York Mets, 6-3, in the first game of a Shea Stadium doubleheader. Spillner fanned five Atlanta Braves in 2.1 innings in a 7-3 loss at Atlanta-Fulton County Stadium on September 11. He fared best against the Chicago Cubs, Houston Astros, and New York Mets.

In 1978, Spillner won his only decision in 17 games with San Diego before being traded to the

Dan Spillner

Cleveland Indians in June. As a Padre, he compiled a 24-41 record with seven saves and a 4.24 ERA in 192 games. Upon his departure, Spillner ranked third in Padre history in appearances (192) and sixth in innings (571), strikeouts (346), and victories. He still ranks fourteenth in walks (255), sixteenth in losses, seventeenth in games, and twentieth in innings pitched in Padre history. He remained with the Cleveland Indians through June 1984, boasting a 16-11 record as a starter in 1980 and a 12-10 mark with 21 saves as a reliever in 1982. The Cleveland Indians traded him to the Chicago White Sox in June 1984. Spillner finished his major-league career with the Chicago White Sox in 1985. In 12 major-league seasons, he compiled a 75-89 record with 50 saves and a 4.21 ERA. He relied mainly on a fastball and was prone to surrendering home runs.

He and his wife, Cathy, reside in Issaquah, Washington, and have one son, Dusty.

GARRY TEMPLETON

Garry Templeton starred as a shortstop for the San Diego Padres from 1982 through May 1991. The 5-foot 11-inch, 170-pound Templeton, who switch hit and threw right-handed, was born on March 24, 1956 in Lockney, Texas. His father, Spiavia, played infield in the Negro Leagues, while his brother, Kenneth, played outfield in the Oakland Athletics organization in the mid-1970s. Templeton signed out of Santa Ana Valley High School for a $40,000 bonus as the St. Louis Cardinals' first draft choice in June 1974. He played less than three minor-league seasons and finished 1976 as starting shortstop for St. Louis, batting .291 in 53 games. Besides hitting .305 for the Cardinals between 1976 and 1981, he led the National League in triples three times, made over 100 hits from each side of the plate in 1979, and reached a personal-high 34 stolen bases in 1978. Although twice pacing senior circuit shortstops in errors, he made exciting defensive plays and displayed excellent range. His temper and sulking irked manager Whitey Herzog. In August 1981, Templeton made obscene gestures to the St. Louis fans who had booed him for lackluster play. Herzog suspended him and sent him to the San Diego Padres for shortstop Ozzie Smith in February 1982.

Templeton helped keep San Diego in the 1982 pennant race until mid-September, batting .247 with six home runs and 64 RBIs. He led National League shortstops in runs (76), RBIs (64), and game-winning RBIs (8) and ranked second on the Padres in triples (8), shared second in stolen bases (27), finished third in extra-base hits (39), and tied for third in hits (139). His eight triples shared fourth best in the senior circuit. Templeton doubled three times in a 6-0 home win over the Philadelphia Phillies on May 9 and enjoyed a 12-game hitting streak from August 14 through August 25.

Templeton hit .263 with three home runs and 40 RBIs in 1983. His batting average was the highest ever for a Padre shortstop and fourth best among shortstops in the National League. He singled, doubled, and homered with four RBIs in the Opening Day, 16-13 slugfest on April 5 over the San Francisco Giants at Candlestick Park. Templeton belted three doubles with three RBIs in a 6-4 home win over the Houston Astros on June 19 and homered off Fernando Valenzuela in a 7-5 triumph over the Los Angeles Dodgers at Dodger Stadium on June 23. He provided three consecutive game-winning RBIs from August 15 through August 17 and batted .300 for the remainder of the season.

Templeton batted .258 with two home runs and 35 RBIs in 1984, appearing in more games (148) than any other National League shortstop. He hit .338 for the first month and authored a nine-game hitting streak. Templeton boasted consecutive three-hit games with two RBIs against the Los Angeles Dodgers in late June and clouted his first grand slam on July 29 off Mike LaCoss in a 9-0 home romp over the Houston Astros. He enjoyed an eight-game hitting streak in September and led the National League with 23 intentional walks. Defensively, he worked closely with new second baseman Alan Wiggins.

During the 1984 National League Championship Series against the Chicago Cubs, Templeton sparked the Padres emotionally and provided some clutch hits. His pre-game enthusiasm enthralled home crowds in the final three games. He doubled home two runs in the fifth inning of Game 3, giving the Padres their first Championship Series lead and sparking their first-ever post-season victory, 7-1. After batting .333 in the Championship Series, he hit .316 with one double in the World Series against the Detroit Tigers.

Templeton enjoyed the best season of any shortstop in San Diego history in 1985, hitting .282 with six home runs and 55 RBIs and earning Padre Most Valuable Player honors. He repeated as the National Leaguer with the most intentional walks (25). His 154 hits marked his best since joining the Padres. Templeton batted .298 with three home runs and 12 RBIs in May, clouting all three round-trippers against the Chicago Cubs in a nine-game span. He batted .356 in June and enjoyed an 11-game hitting streak. Templeton made hits in all three plate appearances and drove in four runs in a 9-1 victory over the Pittsburgh Pirates at Three Rivers Stadium on July 4 and tied a major-league record the next night by being intentionally walked four times in a 5-4, 12-inning loss to Pittsburgh. He made the National League All-Star team for the second time in his career and singled in his only plate appearance. His 44 multiple-hit games included four-hit games in a 3-2 win over the Cincinnati Reds at Riverfront Stadium on September 10 and in an 11-1 home rout over the Atlanta Braves on September 20. He batted over .350 against the Cincinnati Reds and National League champion St. Louis Cardinals.

Nagging back and leg injuries limited Templeton to a .247 batting average in 1986. Templeton collected three hits on April 7 against Fernando Valenzuela in a 2-1, opening day loss to the Los Angeles Dodgers at Dodger Stadium and hit safely in 14 of 15 games in mid-June with two seven-game hitting streaks. He produced consecutive three-hit games with five RBIs in 9-2 and 7-4 victories over the Houston Astros on June 30 and July 1, clouting a three-run homer off Bob Knepper. Templeton batted .346 in September and .371 against the Los Angeles Dodgers.

Garry Templeton

In February 1987, manager Larry Bowa named Templeton as the Padre team captain. Templeton batted only .222 with five home runs and 48 RBIs in 1987. He hit .342 during July with a seven-game hitting streak and two three-hit games. On September 5, Templeton clouted his first home run at Busch Stadium since joining the Padres. The three-run blast lifted the Padres to a 4-1 win over the St. Louis Cardinals. Twelve days later, Templeton clouted the first Padre inside-the-park home run in three years and the first at Jack Murphy Stadium since June 1974. His three-run round-tripper helped the Padres defeat the Atlanta Braves, 7-1. He paced National League shortstops with 253 putouts.

Templeton split shortstop duties with Dickie Thon in 1988, batting .249 with three home runs and 36 RBIs. He enjoyed a 10-game hitting streak in June and hit .275 the second half of the season. He hit .364 against the Cincinnati Reds and .340 with 10 RBIs against the Atlanta Braves.

In 1989, Templeton batted .255 and started 135 games at shortstop. A consistent hitter, he performed at .300 in June and .292 in August. Templeton compiled a seven-game hitting streak in August and connected for a grand slam off Danny Darwin in a 7-3 home triumph over the Houston Astros on September 11. He ranked third among shortstops in putouts.

In 1990, Templeton became the then all-time Padre leader in appearances (1,254) and played 132 games at shortstop. He batted .248 with nine home runs and 59 RBIs and collected his 2,000th major-league hit on August 9 with a ninth-inning single off Tony Castillo in a 7-0 win over the Atlanta Braves at Atlanta-Fulton County Stadium. His 25 doubles moved him into second place on the Padres' all-time list with 194. Templeton also clouted nine home runs for his best output in a decade and hit his third career grand slam on May 18 against Frank Viola in a 6-3 home victory over the New York Mets. His 59 RBIs marked his best power production since 1982. Seven of his home runs and 33 of his RBIs came before the All-Star break. Templeton boasted four-hit home games in a 10-2 rout of the Houston Astros on June 4 and in a 5-2 victory over the Los Angeles Dodgers on September 10, and batted .381 against the Chicago Cubs.

In May 1991, the San Diego Padres traded Templeton to the New York Mets for Tim Teufel. His major-league career ended that year with the Mets. During 16 major-league seasons, he batted .271 with 2,096 hits, 70 home runs, and 728 RBIs. Upon his departure from the Padres, Templeton ranked second in team hits (1,135) and doubles (195), fourth in triples (36) and RBIs (427), and fifth in runs (430). He remains second in games (1,286), hits, doubles, and strikeouts (684), fourth in triples and RBIs, fifth in runs (430), eighth in stolen bases (101), ninth in walks (272), fourteenth in slugging percentage (.339), fifteenth in batting average, and sixteenth in on-base percentage (.293) in Padre history. Templeton managed Cedar Rapids, Iowa of the Midwest League in 1998, Erie, Pennsylvania of the Eastern League in 1999 and 2000, and Salt Lake, Utah of the Pacific Coast League since 2001. He and his wife, Glenda, reside in Poway, California and have two sons, Garry II and Gerome, and a daughter, Genae. He has a daughter, Sharmine, from a previous marriage.

GENE TENACE

Gene Tenace caught and played first base for the San Diego Padres from 1977 through 1980. The 6-foot, 195-pound Tenace, who batted and threw right-handed, was born on October 10, 1946 in Russelton, Pennsylvania and graduated from Valley Local High School in Lucasville, Ohio. The Kansas City Athletics selected him in the 11th round of the June 1965 free agent draft. After spending six seasons in the minor leagues, Tenace joined the Oakland Athletics in 1970. He became the Athletics' regular catcher in August 1972 and moved to first base in 1973. His best season with Oakland came in 1975, when he batted .255 with a career-high 29 home runs and 87 RBIs. Tenace starred in the 1972 World Series against the Cincinnati Reds, becoming the first player to homer in his first two at-bats. The Most Valuable Player set a World Series record for the highest slugging percentage (.913) and tied a fall classic mark with four home runs.

In November 1976, the San Diego Padres signed Tenace via the first reentry draft. Tenace split time between catcher, first base, and third base in 1977, hitting .233 with 15 home runs and 61 RBIs. He set a franchise record with a National League-leading 125 walks, including 10 intentional passes. Tenace hit three doubles and one single with two RBIs in a 9-2 home victory over the San Francisco Giants on September 25 and enjoyed seven three-hit games. He homered twice in a 12-6 romp over the Atlanta Braves at home with five RBIs on April 18, twice with four RBIs in a 10-7 loss to the Pittsburgh Pirates at Three Rivers Stadium on June 10, and twice in an 8-3 triumph over the Montreal Expos at Olympic Stadium on August 9. Besides walking three times in eight different games, he received four free passes at home in a 12-7 loss to the Houston Astros on July 4 and in a 5-2 home setback to the Montreal Expos on July 26. He received free passes 11 times in 16 plate appearances from May 23 through May 26 and in seven straight games from July 2 through July 8.

Tenace caught 79 games and played first base in 80 contests in 1978, batting .224 with 16 home runs and 51 RBIs. He compiled a .393 on-base percentage, reaching base 201 times on hits, walks, or being hit by a pitch. His round-trippers were evenly divided at home and on the road. Tenace homered twice in an 8-5 home loss to the Chicago Cubs on May 9, in a 10-6 setback to the Pittsburgh Pirates at Three Rivers Stadium on July 16, and in a 15-3 home rout over the Cincinnati

Reds on August 10 and knocked in four runs in an 8-3 home win over the St. Louis Cardinals on July 28. Tenace belted three home runs with 12 RBIs against the Cincinnati Reds and three homers with 11 RBIs against the St. Louis Cardinals. He drove in 19 runs in a 20 games between July 28 and August 22.

In 1979, Tenace batted a career-high .263 with 20 home runs and 67 RBIs and led National League catchers with a .998 fielding percentage. He made only one error in 465 chances in 92 games as a catcher and played first base in 70 games. Tenace reached base 40 percent of the time, leading the franchise with 105 walks. Eighteen of his homers and 47 of his RBIs came on the road. Tenace homered and singled three times with three RBIs to edge the New York Mets, 6-5, at Shea Stadium on July 6 and made four hits in a 5-4 triumph over the Cincinnati Reds at home on August 12. He singled, tripled, and homered in a 7-3 victory over the Philadelphia Phillies at Veterans Stadium on July 11. Tenace tripled with three RBIs in a 9-2 win over the Atlanta Braves at Atlanta-Fulton County Stadium on September 8 and closed the season with a game-winning home run in a 5-2 home triumph over the San Francisco Giants on September 30. He clouted six home runs with 21 RBIs against the Atlanta Braves.

His production dropped in 1980, when he batted just .222 with 17 home runs and 50 RBIs and fell below 100 walks. In an 11-player trade December 1980, the San Diego Padres sent Tenace and Rollie Fingers to the St. Louis Cardinals. In four seasons as a Padre, Tenace batted .237 with 384 hits, 69 doubles, 68 home runs, 239 RBIs, and 423 walks in 573 games. He ranks first in on-base percentage (.403), third in walks, fourth in slugging percentage (.422), eleventh in strikeouts (386), twelfth in home runs, fifteenth in triples (13), sixteenth in RBIs, and seventeenth in hitting on the Padres' all-time list.

Tenace was a reserve with the St. Louis Cardinals in 1981 and 1982 and ended his major-league career with the Pittsburgh Pirates in 1983. In 15 major-league seasons, he batted .241 with 1,060 hits, 201 home runs, and 674 RBIs in 1,555 games. Despite his low batting average, he reached base nearly 40 percent of the time and drew over 100 walks in six seasons. After coaching for the Houston Astros in 1986 and 1987 and the Toronto Blue Jays from 1990 through 1997, he coaches for the Trenton, New Jersey Thunder of the Eastern League in the Boston Red Sox farm system. He and his wife, Linda, reside in Redmond, Oregon and have three children, Stacey, Merinda, and Gina.

DERREL THOMAS

Derrel Thomas played infield with the San Diego Padres from 1972 through 1974 and in 1978. The 6-foot, 160-pound Thomas, who switch hit and threw right-handed, was born on January 14, 1951 in Los Angeles, California and starred in football and baseball at Dorsey High School in Los Angeles. The Houston Astros selected him as an infielder as the first pick of the January 1969 free agent draft. Thomas spent three seasons in the minor leagues before joining the Houston Astros in September 1971. Three months later, the San Diego Padres acquired Thomas, Bill Greif, and Mark Schaeffer from Houston for Dave Roberts.

In 1972, Thomas batted just .230 with 115 hits and 36 RBIs as a second baseman and shortstop. His five home runs all came from the left side of the plate. He made three hits in the season-opening 6-5 home victory over the Atlanta Braves on April 15 and in 11 other contests. His first major-league home run came off Gary Gentry in an 8-6 loss to the New York Mets at Shea Stadium on May 7. Thomas drove in three runs in a 6-0 victory over New York two days earlier and the winning run in the seventeenth inning to defeat the Houston Astros, 10-7, in the first game of a July 30 doubleheader at the Astrodome. A fine defensive shortstop, he accepted 10 chances without an error against the St. Louis Cardinals on August 15. Thomas homered off Jim Willoughby in a 1-0 home victory over the San Francisco Giants on September 4. He made the *Baseball Digest* All-Rookie team at shortstop and batted nearly .500 against the Pittsburgh Pirates.

In 1973, the speedy Thomas led the Padres with 15 stolen bases and batted .238 with 22 RBIs. He batted .262 after the All-Star break and made only five errors at second base. Thomas compiled hitting streaks of 10 games from August 10 to August 21 and nine games from September 10 to September 19, batting .355 against the Pittsburgh Pirates.

In 1974, Thomas batted .247 with three home runs and 41 RBIs and paced San Diego with 24 doubles and six triples. Used mostly as a second baseman, he produced six game-winning RBIs. In December 1974, the Padres traded him to the San Francisco Giants for Tito Fuentes and Butch Metzger. At the time of his departure, he ranked third among Padres in career stolen bases (31), fourth in triples (12), fifth in at-bats

Derrel Thomas

(1,427), runs scored (137), and hits (340), seventh in games played (384) and doubles (46), and ninth in RBIs (99). He remains fourteenth in career triples.

After playing with the San Francisco Giants from 1975 through 1977, Thomas returned to the San Diego Padres in a February 1978 trade. He batted only .227 with three home runs and 26 RBIs as a reserve infielder-outfielder in 1978. The Los Angeles Dodgers signed him as a free agent in November 1978. Thomas enjoyed his best seasons with Los Angeles from 1979 through 1983 and performed well in the 1981 and 1983 National League Championship Series. After splitting 1984 between the Montreal Expos and California Angels, he ended his major-league career with the Philadelphia Phillies in 1985. In 15 major-league seasons, he batted .249 with 154 doubles, 54 triples, 43 home runs, 470 RBIs, and 140 stolen bases.

A jack of all trades, Thomas played every position in the major leagues except pitcher. The outspoken speedster was considered among the senior circuit's better defensive players. He and his wife, Eunice, reside in Highland, California and have two children, Derrel Jr. and Dolann.

JERRY TURNER

Jerry Turner played outfield for the San Diego Padres from 1974 through September 1981 and in 1983. The 5-foot 9-inch, 180-pound Turner, who batted and threw left-handed, was born on January 17, 1954 in Texarkana, Arkansas and attended Venice, California High School, where he made All-State in baseball. The San Diego Padres selected him in the tenth round of the June 1972 free agent draft. Turner spent four seasons in the minor leagues, appearing briefly with the San Diego Padres in 1974 and 1975. After joining San Diego in September 1974, he batted .292 with two RBIs in 17 games. He made two hits in a 5-3 loss to the Atlanta Braves at Atlanta-Fulton County Stadium on September 4, in a 4-1 home win over the Houston Astros on September 12, and in a 9-5 triumph over the San Francisco Giants with two RBIs in the October 2 season finale at Candlestick Park. In 1975, he batted .273 in 11 games with the Padres. He appeared seven times as a pinch hitter and made two hits in a 5-0 home loss to the San Francisco Giants on September 26.

Turner emerged among the top rookie major-league outfielders in 1976, batting .267 with five home runs and 37 RBIs in 105 games. He ranked second on the Padres with five triples and eight game-winning hits and third with 12 stolen bases. Turner enjoyed an eight-game hitting streak from April 25 through May 2 and two five-game hitting streaks. He clouted a home run, double, and two singles with four RBIs and four runs in a 9-7 win in the first game of a June 26 doubleheader over the Atlanta Braves. Turner homered and singled three times with three RBIs, sparking a 9-3 home victory over the Houston Astros on August 6, and batted .366 in September. Besides doubling twice in a 5-0 loss to the Pittsburgh Pirates at Three Rivers Stadium on September 2, Turner batted .571 against the Philadelphia Phillies, .500 against the St. Louis Cardinals, and .415 with 11 RBIs against the Atlanta Braves.

Turner produced more power with 10 home runs and 48 RBIs in 1977, but his batting average dropped to .246. He split left field duties with rookie sensation Gene Richards and led the Padres in pinch hitting with 15 RBIs, setting several club single-season and career records. Turner hit safely in six consecutive games from April 14 through April 19 and supplied five doubles, one home run, and six RBIs from September 6 through September 14. His two three-hit games came against the Atlanta Braves in a 7-3 loss at Atlanta-Fulton County Stadium on September 11 and in a 6-4 home triumph on September 14. He doubled twice in a 7-4 win over the Houston Astros at the Astrodome on June 29. He hit .400 against the Pittsburgh Pirates and knocked in 13 runs against the San Francisco Giants and 11 runs against the Atlanta Braves.

In 1978, Turner batted .280 with eight home runs and 37 RBIs. He ranked among the best major-league pinch-hitters with a .408 batting average, 20 hits, five home runs, and 19 RBIs. His five pinch-hit home runs fell just one short of John Frederick's 1932 major-league record. Turner played regularly in the final 34 contests. His seven game-winning hits trailed only teammate Dave Winfield, while his home runs won several games. His first pinch-hit home run came off Randy Moffitt in an 8-4 home loss to the San Francisco Giants in the ninth inning with one runner aboard on April 16. He clouted a two-run pinch-hit homer off Jim Bibby on May 3 to help defeat the Pittsburgh Pirates, 7-5, at Three Rivers Stadium, a dramatic ninth-inning home run off Bruce Sutter on July 22 to triumph over the Chicago Cubs, 4-2, at home, and a three-run pinch-hit homer off Rawley Eastwick on August 22 to edge the Philadelphia Phillies, 6-5, at Veterans Stadium. He also homered on September 6 to help vanquish the Atlanta Braves, 5-3, at Atlanta-Fulton County Stadium, on September 8 to help edge the Cincinnati Reds, 3-2, at Riverfront Stadium, and on September 19 to help defeat the San Francisco Giants, 4-1, at home. He also clouted an eighth-inning pinch-hit home run off Thomas Dixon in a 6-4 win over the Houston Astros at the Astrodome on July 2.

Turner knocked in a career-high 61 runs with nine home runs in 1979, but his batting average declined to .248. He started in left field most of the season and set personal records in nearly every offensive category, including games (138) and plate appearances (448). Turner finished third in the club in RBIs and extra-base hits (34). In a three-game series at Atlanta-Fulton County Stadium from April 20 through April 22, he made eight hits and nine RBIs against the Atlanta Braves. Turner clouted two doubles and a triple to spark a 6-3 home victory over the Atlanta Braves on May 29 and had consecutive three-hit home games on June 17 in an 8-5 loss to the Chicago Cubs and on June 18 to edge the St. Louis Cardinals, 3-2. His ninth-inning home run on July 20 defeated the New York Mets, 2-1, at home. He belted two doubles and two singles in a

Jerry Turner

10-3 win over the Atlanta Braves at Atlanta-Fulton County Stadium on July 31.

Although his playing time diminished in 1980, Turner batted a career-high .288 with three home runs and 18 RBIs. The Padres used him primarily as a pinch hitter, and he hit .277 with one homer and seven RBIs. His eight stolen bases included thefts of home plate on May 8 in a 9-6 home triumph over the Chicago Cubs and on June 20 in a 4-2 win over the visiting Montreal Expos. Turner doubled, homered, and drove in three runs in a 6-6 tie with the Cincinnati Reds at Riverfront Stadium on June 9 and had three-hit games on June 19 in a 4-3 home victory over the Philadelphia Phillies and on July 26 to edge the St. Louis Cardinals, 4-3, at home.

After Turner batted .226 in 33 games in 1981, the San Diego Padres sold him to the Chicago White Sox on September 9. Turner spent 1982 with the Detroit Tigers and rejoined San Diego in February 1983. He hit only .130 for the Padres and split the remainder of the 1983 campaign between Las Vegas, Nevada and Portland, Oregon of the Pacific Coast League. In 10 major-league seasons, he batted .257 with 45 home runs and 238 RBIs. As a Padre, he hit .261

with 37 home runs and 209 RBIs in 613 games and remains fifteenth in games (638) and eighteenth in RBIs (209).

He and his wife, Edith, reside in Santa Monica, California and have one daughter, Erika and one son, Ashton.

FERNANDO VALENZUELA

Fernando Valenzuela pitched for the San Diego Padres from 1995 through June 1997. The 5-foot 11-inch, 200-pound Valenzuela, who bats and throws left-handed, was born on November 1, 1960 in Navajoa, Sonora, Mexico and hurled for numerous Mexican baseball clubs as a teenager. In July 1979, the Los Angeles Dodgers signed Valenzuela, who spent less than two years in the minor leagues. Valenzuela debuted for the Los Angeles Dodgers against the Atlanta Braves in September 1980 with an impressive screwball.

Valenzuela opened 1981 with eight consecutive victories, seven complete games, five shutouts, and a remarkable 0.50 ERA. He rapidly became a folk hero to the large Mexican-American community in the Los Angeles area. In the strike-shortened 1981 season, Valenzuela paced the National League in complete games (11), shutouts (8), innings pitched (192), and strikeouts (180) and became the first player to win both National League Rookie of the Year and Cy Young Award honors. He pitched for the Dodgers through 1990, appearing in six consecutive All-Star Games from 1981 through 1986. Valenzuela led the senior circuit in victories (21) and complete games (20) in 1986 and complete games (12) in 1987. He pitched for the California Angels in 1991, Baltimore Orioles in 1993, and Philadelphia Phillies in 1994.

In April 1995, the San Diego Padres signed Valenzuela as a free agent. His career was rejuvenated with San Diego. Valenzuela split 1995 between the starting rotation and the bullpen, compiling an 8-3 record and a 4.98 ERA. He posted the best winning percentage of his major-league career (.727) and his first winning season since 1986. His eight victories were the second highest on the Padres. Valenzuela finished 1995 with a six-game winning streak, the longest by a Padre since Andy Benes' 10-game streak in 1991.

His first 1995 victory came in a one-inning relief appearance on May 20 in a 9-6 home triumph over the Pittsburgh Pirates, while his first triumph as a starter came on June 6 against the visiting Philadelphia Phillies. Valenzuela tossed six shutout innings, allowing just three hits in the 1-0 win. He compiled six consecutive victories from August 22 to September 27. Three of his triumphs came against the Philadelphia Phillies, while two others were over the Pittsburgh Pirates. He batted .250 with two home runs and eight RBIs, clouting round-trippers against the Pittsburgh Pirates on June 17 and the Chicago Cubs on September 17.

Fernando Valenzuela

Valenzuela enjoyed his best major-league season in a decade in 1996 with a 13-8 record and 3.62 ERA, fanning 95 batters in 171.2 innings. The Padres tallied nearly six runs per game for him. Valenzuela won eight of his last nine decisions, earning his most triumphs since 1990 and recording his lowest ERA since 1989. His .619 winning percentage ranked sixth in the National League.

After two relief appearances, Valenzuela joined the starting rotation on April 9 against the St. Louis Cardinals. He did not win his first decision until a May 1 9-4 home win over the San Francisco Giants. Valenzuela allowed only one earned run in each of three consecutive starts from May 13 through May 24 and recorded the second longest National League winning streak, faring 8-0 with a 2.60 ERA between July 19 and September 8. His streak helped the Padres overtake the Los Angeles Dodgers to win the National League West.

Valenzuela returned to his native Mexico on August 16, as the Padres hosted the New York Mets in Monterrey. The series marked the first major-league games outside the United States or Canada. Valenzuela started the series opener and became the first major-league pitcher to win a regular-season game in Mexico, allowing three runs and six hits in six-plus innings. He cruised through the first six innings without yielding a run and left with a 15-1 lead in the seventh inning. The Padres withstood a furious Met rally to win, 15-10.

Valenzuela, the only Padre hurler with previous post-season experience, made one appearance against the St. Louis Cardinals in the National League Division Series. Although walking two batters, he did not allow a run or hit in two-thirds of an inning in Game 3. Valenzuela struggled in 1997, winning only two of 10 decisions with a 4.75 ERA before being traded in June to the St. Louis Cardinals. His major-league career ended that season with the St. Louis Cardinals. In 17 major-league seasons, he compiled a 173-153 record with a 3.54 ERA. Besides hurling 31 shutouts, he whiffed 2,074 batters in 2,930 innings and completed 113 of 424 starts.

Upon leaving the major leagues, Valenzuela decided to concentrate on winter baseball to allow him to spend more time with his family. He has pitched well since the winter of 1997 for Naranjeros (Orange Growers) of Hermosillo of the Mexican Pacific League, the league's most successful franchise. He and his wife, Linda, reside in Hollywood, California and have four children, Fernando, Jr., Ricardo, Linda, and Maria.

GREG VAUGHN

Greg Vaughn starred as an outfielder for the San Diego Padres from July 1996 through 1998, becoming the first Padre to clout 50 home runs in a season. The 6-foot, 202-pound Vaughn, who bats and throws right-handed, was born on July 3, 1965 in Sacramento, California and graduated from John F. Kennedy High School in 1983. After attending Sacramento City College, he earned a Bachelor's degree in finance in 1986 from the University of Miami in Florida and made the All-America baseball team. His cousin, Mo, starred as a first baseman with the Boston Red Sox, Anaheim Angels, and New York Mets.

The Milwaukee Brewers selected Vaughn in the secondary phase of the June 1986 draft. Vaughn spent nearly four seasons in the minor leagues and played for the Milwaukee Brewers from August 1989 through July 1996. He batted .267 with 30 home runs and 97 RBIs in 1993 and made the American League All-Star team. His best season with Milwaukee came in 1996, when he hit .280 with 31 home runs and 95 RBIs in just 102 games and made the American League All-Star team. In July 1996, the San Diego Padres acquired him for three players. Although clouting 10 home runs with 22 RBIs in 43 games, he struggled with a .206 batting average.

Vaughn's combined 1996 record included a .260 batting average with 41 home runs, 117 RBIs, and a .539 slugging percentage with then career highs in home runs, RBIs, runs (98), slugging percentage, and total bases (278). His home run and RBI production exceeded the 1994 and 1995 seasons combined. Vaughn became the first major-leaguer to knock in over 100 runs in a single season while playing for teams in both leagues. Vaughn's 100th RBI came on August 9, when he homered against Dan Miceli in a 4-1 victory over the Pittsburgh Pirates at Three Rivers Stadium. His 41 home runs marked the most in a season by a player who had worn a Padre uniform part of that campaign.

Although only starting 37 contests in 1996, Vaughn ranked third on the Padres with 10 home runs. Nine of his first 18 hits were home runs. He clouted a two-run, first-inning home run off Andy Benes in an 8-2 loss to the St. Louis Cardinals at Busch Stadium on August 5. Vaughn also homered on August 9 and August 10 in 4-1 and 6-2 wins over the Pittsburgh Pirates at Three Rivers Stadium for his third and fourth hits as a Padre. He belted the first major-league grand slam outside of the United States or Canada off Derek Wallace in a 15-10 slugfest over the New York Mets on August 16 in Monterrey, Mexico. Vaughn clouted a game-winning three-run home run in the bottom of the eighth inning to defeat the Pittsburgh Pirates, 6-5, at home on September 9. His two-out pinch single in the eighth inning against the Los Angeles Dodgers at Dodger Stadium on September 28 paved the way for Tony Gwynn's game-winning two-run single. The Padres clinched a postseason berth with a 4-2 victory. In the National League Division Series, he went hitless in three plate appearances against the St. Louis Cardinals.

Vaughn struggled in 1997 after signing a franchise-record $15 million, three-year contract that February. He batted just .216 with 10 doubles, 18 home

Greg Vaughn

runs, and 57 RBIs and fanned 110 times in 120 games but still ranked third on the Padres in home runs. Thirty-six percent of his 78 hits went for extra bases. Defensively, he fielded .994 with only one error and seven assists in left field. The Padres traded Vaughn to the New York Yankees in July, but the transaction was voided when he failed the team physical.

Vaughn became the first Padre to clout two home runs into the second deck at Qualcomm Stadium, connecting on a 475-foot, seventh-inning blast off Scott Ruffcorn in a 13-3 rout over the Philadelphia Phillies on April 4. He also belted a 415-foot homer that night for his only multi-homer effort of the season. Vaughn became the second major-leaguer to belt home runs as a designated hitter in both leagues. He connected off Dennis Springer of the California Angels in the fourth inning of a June 13 marathon 14-inning, 8-7 nailbiter at Edison International Field. In the sixth inning on July 3, he clouted a two-run pinch-hit game-winning home run off Bobby Ayala in a 10-8 victory over the Seattle Mariners. In a 3-2 home triumph over the Pittsburgh Pirates on July 22, Vaughn delivered a pinch-hit home run off Ricardo Rincon in the eighth inning and contributed a game-winning RBI single off Rich Loiselle in the ninth inning. He led off the ninth inning on August 10 with a 430-foot blast off Kent Bottenfield to edge the Chicago Cubs, 4-3, at Wrigley Field. His fourth game-winner came on August 12 with his two-run double in the seventh inning in a 6-4 triumph over the Montreal Expos at Olympic Stadium.

Vaughn belted a 431-foot sixth-inning homer into the second deck at Qualcomm Stadium off Gabe White in a 5-4 10-inning victory over the Cincinnati Reds on August 14. He also hit a two-run fifth-inning homer that narrowly missed the second deck off Al Leiter in a 7-6 13-inning triumph over the Florida Marlins on September 9. The homer rejuvenated Vaughn, who enjoyed four consecutive two-hit games from September 12 through September 15 and collected 16 RBIs in 11 games from September 9 through September 20. His most productive game came in a 12-2 home rout over the San Francisco Giants on September 20, when he doubled, homered, and knocked in a season-high five RBIs.

Vaughn enjoyed his best season in 1998 with a .272 batting average, 50 home runs, and 119 RBIs, helping the Padres capture the National League West. Besides becoming the first Padre and 28th major-leaguer to clout 50 home runs in a season, he established career highs in games (158), at-bats (573), runs (112), hits (156), doubles (28), home runs, and RBIs. Vaughn led the Padres in runs, hits, home runs, total bases (342), RBIs, and slugging percentage (.597). He also ranked third among National Leaguers in home runs, fourth in extra-base hits (82), fifth in total bases (342) and slugging percentage, ninth in runs, and tenth in RBIs.

Vaughn's 39 multi hit games included 11 three-hit contests, while his 33 multi-RBI games included five four-RBI contests. He set a Padre record by connecting with two home runs in seven contests against the San Francisco Giants on April 14 and June 18 at Candlestick Park, the New York Mets on May 13 and September 1 at home, the Houston Astros on May 22 at the Astrodome, the visiting Colorado Rockies on July 5, and the Cincinnati Reds on July 17 at Riverfront Stadium. Vaughn clouted consecutive home runs with Wally Joyner off Antonio Alfonseca in the ninth inning in a 6-5 loss to the Florida Marlins at Pro Player Stadium on May 1, with Greg Myers off Kevin Millwood in the fourth inning in a 6-4 setback to the Atlanta Braves at Atlanta-Fulton County Stadium on

May 9, with Ken Caminiti off Carl Pavano in the first inning in a 5-4 victory over the Montreal Expos at Olympic Stadium on July 31, and with Mark Sweeney off Javier Vazquez in the fourth inning to key a 12-8 home triumph over the Montreal Expos on August 28. As in 1997, he belted two home runs into the second deck at Qualcomm Stadium. He connected with a 432-foot home run off Bobby Jones of the New York Mets in the fourth inning of a 4-3 loss on May 13 and with a 433-foot home run off Matt Morris of the St. Louis Cardinals in the second inning in a 13-2 loss on July 20.

Vaughn's game-winning sacrifice fly in the tenth inning defeated the Cincinnati Reds, 3-2, in the home opener on April 7. Vaughn enjoyed his best month as a Padre in May, batting .330 with 12 home runs, 32 RBIs, and a .752 slugging percentage. He clouted 10 home runs with 24 RBIs in June, belting his fourth career grand slam off Brett Tomko in the seventh inning of a 5-1 home victory over the Cincinnati Reds on June 9. Vaughn became the first Padre to record 30 home runs before the All-Star break. He made his third trip and first as a National Leaguer to the All-Star Game, singling in two runs. In July, he clouted 11 home runs with 23 RBIs. In his final plate appearance, he belted his 50th home run off Aaron Small in the seventh inning on September 27 to defeat the Arizona Diamondbacks, 3-2, at Bank One Ballpark.

Vaughn batted .333 with one double, one home run, and one RBI against the Houston Astros in the National League Division Series. His solo home run off Randy Johnson of the Houston Astros in the eighth inning of Game 1 gave the Padres a 2-0 lead at the Astrodome. He started Games 1 and 6 of the National League Championship Series at Atlanta-Fulton County Stadium, batting .250 against the Atlanta Braves. He clouted two home runs with three RBIs in Game 1 of the World Series at Yankee Stadium, but made a defensive error against the New York Yankees. Yankee pitchers held him to a .133 batting average for the entire fall classic. *The Sporting News* named him its National League Comeback Player of the Year and as an outfielder on its National League Silver Slugger team. He also won the Padre Most Valuable Player Award and the Chairman's Award for community spirit.

In February 1999, the Padres dealt Vaughn to the Cincinnati Reds. As a Padre, Vaughn batted .245 with 192 runs, 263 hits, 41 doubles, 78 home runs, and 198 RBIs and struck out 262 times in 1,075 plate appearances. He ranks tenth in home runs and twenty-first in strikeouts on the Padre career batting list. His 45 home runs and 118 RBIs helped Cincinnati finish second in the National League Central Division in 1999. In December 1999, the Tampa Bay Devil Rays signed him as a free agent. He batted .254 with 74 RBIs and led the Devil Rays with 28 home runs in 2000. His batting average dropped to .233 in 2001, but he again paced Tampa Bay with 24 home runs and 82 RBIs. During 12 major-league seasons, Vaughn has batted .245 with 271 doubles, 344 home runs, and 1,038 RBIs. He and his wife, Michele, reside in Elk Grove, California and have one son, Cory, and one daughter, Genay.

ED WHITSON

Ed Whitson pitched for the San Diego Padres in two stints between 1983 and 1991. The 6-foot 3-inch, 200-pound right-hander was born on May 19, 1955 in Johnson City, Tennessee and starred in three sports at Unicoi High School in Erwin, Tennessee. The Pittsburgh Pirates selected him in the sixth round of the June 1974 free agent draft. He performed nearly four seasons in the minor leagues before winning his major-league debut against the Montreal Expos in September 1977. In June 1979, the San Francisco Giants acquired Whitson. He remained with the Giants through November 1981 and spent 1982 with the Cleveland Indians. Through 1982, he had compiled a 34-41 record with a 3.54 ERA.

The San Diego Padres acquired Whitson in November 1982. Whitson finished 5-7 with a 4.30 ERA in 1983. He hurled two three-hitters in a 5-1 home victory over the Cincinnati Reds on June 15 and in a 4-1 triumph over the Los Angeles Dodgers at Dodger Stadium on June 20, but he did not triumph again until defeating the Philadelphia Phillies, 7-5, at Veterans Stadium on August 30. He won his last three decisions, including an eight-strikeout, 4-2 win over the San Francisco Giants at Candlestick Park. In 1984, Whitson helped the Padres attain their first National League pennant with a 14-8 record and a 3.24 ERA. Whitson garnered five wins in a row from May 18 through June 15 and eight victories in nine decisions. He recorded the first post-season triumph in Padre history when he defeated the Chicago Cubs, 7-1, in crucial Game 3 at home, but fared poorly in Game 2 of the World Series against the Detroit Tigers.

In December 1984, the New York Yankees signed him as a free agent. Whitson relieved for the Yankees until he was traded to San Diego in July 1986. He struggled in 12 starts with the Padres, winning only one of eight decisions. In 1987, Whitson fashioned a 10-13 record and a 4.73 ERA and established a career high of 135 strikeouts. Besides pacing the Padres in victories, he blanked the New York Mets, 1-0, at home on May 31 and the San Francisco Giants, 5-0, at Candlestick Park on June 12. Whitson two-hit the Houston Astros in a 4-1 home triumph on June 23 and won Padres Pitcher of the Month awards from May through July. He lost all six decisions from August through October, led the National League in surrendering 36 round-trippers, and fanned 10 New York Mets in a 4-3 loss on September 2.

Whitson finished 13-11 with a 3.77 ERA and 118 strikeouts in 1988. Nearly four innings of one-hit relief on June 4 in a 6-5 home win over the Atlanta Braves improved his fortunes. He triumphed in his next five decisions from June 7 through July 21 and pitched brilliantly from August 7 to September 6. Whitson issued only 45 walks and just 17 home runs. His pinnacle came in 1989, when he posted a career-best 16 wins with a 2.66 ERA and 227 innings pitched. He ranked fourth in the National League in ERA and sixth in victories and won nine of his first 11 decisions. Whitson boasted a career-best seven-game winning streak from April 27 to June 5, allowing only 13 earned runs in 63 innings and receiving the Padres Pitcher of the Month Award in May. Whitson garnered the honor again in July with a 4-2 record. He defeated the Pittsburgh Pirates in all four starts and finished 10-3 against the Eastern Division.

In 1990, Whitson attained the Padre Pitcher of the Year Award with a 14-9 mark and a 2.60 ERA. His career-best 2.60 ERA ranked third in the National League. He also set personal highs with three shutouts and 228.2 innings, seventh best in the senior circuit. Whitson yielded only 1.8 walks per nine innings, second best in the major leagues. In eight of his setbacks, the Padres tallied two or fewer runs. Whitson won all five decisions from July 25 to September 2 and earned Padre Pitcher of the Month honors in April with a 2-0 mark and a 1.50 ERA and in August with a 3-0 mark and a 0.86 ERA. He clouted his first career home run in a 3-0 home win over the Chicago Cubs on April 25. His major-league career ended with a 4-6 record in 1991.

In 15 major-league seasons, Whitson compiled a 126-123 mark with a 3.79 ERA and 1,266 strikeouts in 2,240.1 innings. He ranks third in games started (208), wins (77), and innings pitched (1,354.1), fifth in strikeouts (767), losses (72), and winning percentage (.517), seventh in walks (350), complete games (22), and ERA (3.69), tied for eighth in shutouts (6), and tenth in games (227) on the Padre all-time list. He and his wife, Kathleen, reside in Bakersville, North Carolina and have a daughter, Jennifer.

ALAN WIGGINS

Alan Wiggins played infield and outfield for the San Diego Padres from September 1981 through June 1985. The 6-foot 2-inch, 160-pound Wiggins, who switch hit and threw right-handed, was born on February 17, 1958 in Los Angeles, California and attended Pasadena City College. Wiggins signed with the Los Angeles Dodgers organization in January 1979 and stole a then professional baseball record 120 bases for Lodi, California, of the California League in 1980. The San Diego Padres obtained him in the Rule V draft in December 1980.

After playing for Hawaii of the Pacific Coast League in 1981, Wiggins joined the San Diego Padres that September and batted .357 in 15 games. He collected his first major-league hit in a 6-4 victory over the Atlanta Braves at Atlanta-Fulton County Stadium on September 13. Wiggins made his first major-league start as an outfielder in a 5-2 home loss to the Houston Astros on September 16 and stole second base on his first attempt.

Wiggins started 1982 with Hawaii, but replaced the injured Gene Richards in the Padre outfield in May and batted .261 with 35 stolen bases. He finished eleventh in the National League in stolen bases with an 85 percent success rate. Between May 14 and June 10, Wiggins hit safely in 20 of 21 contests, including 13 consecutive. He stole 18 bases and scored 21 runs. He performed very well defensively, making eight assists in only 68 games. After stealing three bases on May 19 in a 5-4 10-inning triumph over the visiting St. Louis Cardinals, Wiggins clouted his first major-league home run the next day off Dave LaPoint in a 6-3 loss to St. Louis. He defeated the Los Angeles Dodgers at home, 7-5, with a ninth-inning hit on June 29 and, 2-1, with a tenth-inning hit on September 22 and tripled with the bases loaded in a 5-1 home victory over the Atlanta Braves on October 3. He underwent treatment from

July 20 through September 19 at the Orange County Drug Rehabilitation Center.

Wiggins batted .276 in 1983 and stole 66 bases, to break Gene Richards's 1980 mark by five. He compiled an 83.5 percent success rate on stolen bases, trailing only Tim Raines of the Montreal Expos. Besides pacing the Padres with 83 runs scored, Wiggins grounded into only three double plays and fanned just 43 times in 503 plate appearances. He played 105 games in the outfield and 45 contests at first base and doubled three times in a 7-3 loss to the Chicago Cubs at Wrigley Field on July 22. Wiggins twice stole 19 consecutive bases and pilfered 19 bases in 16 games from August 22 through September 16. He stole three bases in three different games and pilfered third base 11 times in 13 attempts.

In 1984, Wiggins batted .258 with 34 RBIs and 70 stolen bases to help catapult the Padres to the National League pennant. At first he found it difficult switching to second base, committing 12 errors in his initial 28 games. Wiggins compensated with outstanding range, however, reaching balls that most second basemen could not field and leading second basemen with 391 putouts. His outstanding speed made him one of the best major-league leadoff hitters. Wiggins broke Padre records for stolen bases (70) and runs scored (106), surpassing Dave Winfield's 1977 run output by two. He finished third in the National League in stolen bases and tied Tim Raines for second in runs scored.

Wiggins hit .307 with 14 stolen bases in May and tied a National League record with five stolen bases in a 5-4 home victory on May 17 over the Montreal Expos. He stole home off Jerry Reuss to spark a 9-6 home victory over the Los Angeles Dodgers on April 21 and off Mike LaCoss in a 6-2 triumph over the Houston Astros at the Astrodome on August 24. Wiggins scored 75 percent of the time following stolen bases and boasted two nine-game hitting streaks. He hit .316 with one RBI against the Chicago Cubs in the National League Championship Series and .364 with one double, one RBI, and one stolen base against the Detroit Tigers in the World Series.

In 1985, Wiggins batted just .054 in 10 games and disappeared before an April 25 series with the Los Angeles Dodgers at Dodger Stadium. A drug relapse ended his San Diego career. The Padres traded Wiggins to the Baltimore Orioles for two players in June, but they could not replace his enormous stolen base and run production. San Diego lost its ability to manufacture runs in the late innings without him. During his Padre career, Wiggins batted .260 with 365 hits, 43 doubles, four home runs, and 71 RBIs. His 171 stolen bases rank third in Padre history, trailing only Tony Gwynn and Gene Richards. He also shares nineteenth with 12 triples. Wiggins played with the Orioles from 1985 through 1987 but never solved Baltimore's leadoff problems, and he fell into disfavor with manager Earl Weaver. In seven major-league seasons, he batted .259 with 61 doubles, 118 RBIs, and 242 stolen bases in 631 games.

Wiggins's promising major-league career fizzled amid drug and personality problems. Before his drug relapse, he worked with the San Diego Police Department presenting a program on drug and crime prevention to secondary schools. Wiggins and his wife, Angie, had one daughter, Candace. He died on January 9, 1991 in Los Angeles, California at age 32.

WOODY WILLIAMS

Woody Williams anchored the San Diego pitching staff from 1999 through July 2001, serving as opening day starter twice. The 6-foot 195-pound right-hander was born on August 19, 1966 in Houston, Texas and graduated in 1984 from Cypress–Fairbanks High School, where he starred as a shortstop in baseball and played football and basketball. He earned an associate of arts degree from the University of Houston, making All-Region as a shortstop.

The Toronto Blue Jays selected Williams in the twenty-eighth round of the June 1988 draft. Williams spent five minor-league seasons from 1988 through 1992 with St. Catherines, Ontario of the New York-Pennsylvania League; Knoxville, Tennessee of the Southern League; Dunedin, Florida of the Florida State League; and Syracuse, New York of the International League. He joined Toronto in 1993, posting a 3-1 record and a 4.38 ERA as a reliever. Williams relieved the next two seasons, faring 1-3 and 1-2 in 1994 and 1995, respectively. The Blue Jays converted him to a starter in 1996, when he finished 4-5 with a 4.73 ERA. The workhorse hurler logged 194.2 innings in 1997 and 209.2 innings in 1998, sporting a 9-4 mark and a 4.35 ERA in 1997 and 10-9 mark and a 4.46 ERA in 1998.

In December 1998, Toronto traded Williams, pitcher Carlos Almanzar, and outfielder Peter Tucci to the San Diego Padres for pitcher Joey Hamilton.

Williams, who anchored the Padre staff with Sterling Hitchcock, split 24 decisions with a 4.41 ERA in 1999. He won his final five decisions en route to 12 wins and struck out 137 batters in 208.1 innings, trailing only Hitchcock among Padre hurlers. After struggling until July, Williams fared 8-5 with a 4.30 ERA after the All-Star break. He allowed only six runners (38 percent) to steal against him and walked just 73 batters, but surrendered 33 home runs, fifth worst in the National League. Williams, on August 12 struck out a personal-best 12 batters in a 7-6 win over the Philadelphia Phillies at Veterans Stadium. He paced Padre pitchers with a .178 batting average, four doubles, and six RBIs.

Alan Wiggins

In 2000, Williams won the Clyde McCullough Award as Padre Pitcher of the Year, finishing 10-8 with a 3.75 ERA in 23 starts. He worked six innings of five-hit shutout ball to defeat the New York Mets, 4-0, in the April 5 season opener at Shea Stadium. After experiencing numbness in the finger of his pitching hand in his first six starts, Williams underwent surgery to repair an aneurysm under his right armpit and missed two months from May 4 to July 2. He still led Padre hurlers with a career-best four complete games and struck out 111 batters in 168.0 innings, second best on the club. Williams averaged 7.3 innings per start, trailing only Pedro Martinez of the Boston Red Sox, and limited opponents to a .239 batting average, ninth best in the National League. He did not allow an unearned run until August 21 against the New York Mets.

Williams ranked third among National League pitchers with a .259 batting average. Only teammate Adam Eaton and Mike Hampton of the New York Mets boasted higher batting averages. Williams ranked fifth among senior circuit hurlers in hits (15), shared second in extra base hits (5), and tied for third in RBIs (9), belting four doubles and a home run. His fifth-inning home run off Kirk Reuter of the San Francisco Giants at Pacific Bell Park on July 20 was the first of his career and the first for a Padre pitcher in over two years. He also doubled and singled in that contest and on September 6 singled three times with an RBI against the visiting Milwaukee Brewers.

Williams divided the 2001 season between San Diego and the St. Louis Cardinals, posting a 15-9 record, a 4.05 ERA, and 154 strikeouts in 220 innings. His victories, strikeouts, and innings pitched all marked career bests. He split 16 decisions in 23 starts with a 4.97 ERA for the Padres, fanning 102 batters and allowing 28 home runs in 145.0 innings. San Diego traded him on August 2 to the St.Louis Cardinals for outfielder Ray Lankford. Williams helped lift St. Louis to the playoffs as the wild card team, faring 7-1 with a 2.78 ERA and striking out 52 batters in 75 innings. He completed three starts and hurled one shutout, complementing ace Matt Morris. Williams defeated the Arizona Diamondbacks, 4-1, in Game 2 of the National League Division Series, fanning nine batters in seven innings, doubling off ace Randy Johnson in the third inning, and robbing Tony Womack of a hit in the sixth inning.

In nine major-league seasons, Williams has compiled a 65-63 record with a 4.20 ERA and 841 strikeouts in 1,209.2 innings. Besides completing nine of 165 starts, he has hurled two shutouts and surrendered 179 home runs. As a Padre, he owned a 30-28 record with a 4.35 ERA and struck out 393 batters in 521.1 innings. He and his wife, Kimberli, have two children, Hannah and Caden, and reside in Alvin, Texas.

DAVE WINFIELD

Dave Winfield starred for the San Diego Padres as an outfielder from June 1973 through 1980. The 6-foot 6-inch, 220-pounder, who batted and threw right-handed, was born in St. Paul, Minnesota on October 3, 1951 and did not play baseball until his junior year at St. Paul Central High School. He attended the University of Minnesota, participating in basketball and baseball. During his senior year, Winfield compiled a 13-2 record as a pitcher, batted .385, and slugged nine home runs. He made the College All-America squad and was named Most Valuable Player of the 1973 NCAA College World Series.

Winfield was drafted in all three major professional sports. The Minnesota Vikings selected him as an end, even though he did not play college football. Since Winfield excelled as a basketball forward, the Atlanta Hawks of the National Basketball Association and the Utah Stars of the American Basketball Association chose him. The San Diego Padres selected him in the first round of the June 1973 free agent draft.

Winfield joined San Diego that June directly from the University of Minnesota. As a rookie, he batted .277 with three home runs and 12 RBIs in 56 games. Winfield hit safely in his first six major-league games in June and clouted a home run on June 21 in a 12-2 loss to the visiting Houston Astros. He knocked in four runs in a 9-0 home victory over the New York Mets on August 14 and batted .471 as a pinch hitter, reaching safely in five consecutive appearances.

Blessed with great speed and a powerful throwing arm, Winfield became the most prolific run producer in early franchise history. "Winfield," coach Whitey Wietelmann claimed, "could do everything. He could run, field, throw, hit, hit with power." In 1974, Winfield batted .265, finished second to Willie McCovey with 20 home runs, and led the Padres with 75 RBIs and nine game-winning hits. He collected three hits in eight contests and enjoyed an eight-game hitting streak from August 5 through August 14. He clubbed two home runs in an 8-2 victory over the New York Mets at Shea Stadium on July 10 and knocked in three runs at home in a 7-3 triumph over the New York Mets on July 21 and again in a 6-1 win over the Cincinnati Reds on September 17.

Winfield hit .267 in 1975 and led the Padres with 76 RBIs and 23 stolen bases. He batted .326 against left-handed pitchers and .375 against the Philadelphia Phillies. Winfield finished second on the Padres with 15 home runs and third in hits (136) and doubles (20). He shared the National League lead in home runs and stood among RBI leaders until hurting his hand in July. Winfield collected four hits with five RBIs in an 11-6 home loss to the Los Angeles Dodgers on April 24.

Despite missing the last month of 1976, Winfield paced San Diego in hits (139), doubles (26), home runs (13), stolen bases (26), and runs scored (81) and placed second in RBIs (69). His batting average rose 16 points to .283. He achieved eight three-hit contests, with three consecutive three-hit games in a 4-1 win over the Montreal Expos at Jarry Park on May 6 and in losses to the New York Mets at Shea Stadium on May 7 and May 8. He reached safely in 11 consecutive contests from June 14 through June 24. Winfield doubled twice against the New York Mets on May 8, in a 4-2 setback to the Philadelphia Phillies at Veterans Stadium on May 11, in a 7-3 loss to the Atlanta Braves in the second game of a home doubleheader on June 26, and in a 5-2 victory over Los Angeles Dodgers at Dodger Stadium on July 4. He clouted grand slams in an 8-5 win over the Los Angeles Dodgers at Dodger Stadium on April 13 and in a 4-2 home triumph over the Cincinnati Reds on May 21. He also knocked in four runs in a 5-1 home victory over the St. Louis Cardinals on April 23 and in an 11-9 slugfest over the Pittsburgh Pirates at Three Rivers Stadium on June 5. Winfield stole three bases on September 5 in a 6-1 win over the San Francisco Giants in the second game of a doubleheader at Candlestick Park. He injured his left leg at home plate in that game and missed the remainder of the 1976 season. The fine defensive player with bullet-like throws led National League outfielders with 15 assists.

Winfield's 1977 season saw him pace San Diego in games (157), at-bats (615), runs (104), hits (169), doubles (29), home runs (25), and RBIs (92). Winfield set Padre records for most games, at-bats, and runs

Dave Winfield

scored. He achieved the then longest consecutive-game hitting streak in franchise history with 16 from May 3 through May 21, batting .375 with five doubles, three triples, five home runs, and 19 RBIs. Winfield also reached safely in 13 straight contests from June 14 through June 27. He authored nine three-hit games and singled twice, doubled, and homered with three RBIs in a 9-5 loss to the Atlanta Braves at Atlanta-Fulton County Stadium on June 25. He knocked in four runs in a 12-4 rout over the Cincinnati Reds at Riverfront Stadium on April 10 and in a 5-4 triumph over the Los Angeles Dodgers in the second game of a doubleheader on July 10. He represented the Padres in the All-Star Game, singling in the game-winning run in a 7-5 National League triumph.

Winfield finished fifth in the National League with a .308 batting average in 1978, helping San Diego record its first winning season. He also led the Padres with 181 hits, 30 doubles, 24 home runs, and 97 RBIs. Winfield, named team captain prior to the opening day game against the San Francisco Giants at Candlestick Park, responded with three hits, including a home run, to key a 3-2 victory. He clouted two home runs with six RBIs to spark a 10-8 victory over the Chicago Cubs at Wrigley Field on June 10. At the All-Star Game, Winfield received a thunderous ovation when introduced before a record San Diego Stadium crowd and singled in the eighth inning to help the National League win, 7-3. He made four hits in a 12-3 home victory over the Los Angeles Dodgers on September 22 and authored eight three-hit games, including three consecutive home wins against the Atlanta Braves and the Cincinnati Reds from September 12 through September 14. Altogether, he knocked in 15 runs against the Houston Astros, 13 against the San Francisco Giants, 12 against the Atlanta Braves and New York Mets, and 11 against the Pittsburgh Pirates. He clouted two home runs with six RBIs against the Chicago Cubs at Chicago on June 10 and drove in four runs twice.

Winfield enjoyed his best Padre season in 1979, finishing third in the National League Most Valuable Player voting behind co-winners Willie Stargell and Keith Hernandez. He kept San Diego from last place with a .308 batting average and 34 home runs, leading the National League with 118 RBIs, 333 total bases, and 24 intentional walks. Winfield finished third in home runs, fourth in slugging percentage (.588), eighth in batting, and tenth in runs scored (97) and shared third in game-winning hits (16), fourth in games (159), and seventh in triples (10). He enjoyed six straight two-hit games against the San Francisco Giants and Atlanta Braves from April 17 through April 22. Winfield drove in five runs in a 10-2 home conquest of the Atlanta Braves on May 30 and was selected National League Player of the Week from May 28 through June 3, batting .500 with 12 RBIs. He clouted five home runs against the Atlanta Braves and Pittsburgh Pirates in five games from May 29 through June 1, authored a 10-game hitting streak from June 5 through June 15, and drove in runs in six consecutive games against the Los Angeles Dodgers and New York Mets from July 2 through July 8.

Winfield became the first Padre voted to start an All-Star Game, receiving the second highest total with over three million votes. He made six hits with two home runs and five RBIs in a doubleheader split with the Montreal Expos at Olympic Stadium on July 13. Winfield boasted one five-hit, one four-hit, and 13 three-hit games, as well as one five-RBI game and five four-RBI contests. His best performance came in a 10-

3 victory over the Atlanta Braves at Atlanta-Fulton County Stadium on July 31, when he reached safely in all five at-bats and scored four runs with four RBIs, a double, a home run, and a walk. On September 12, he joined Nate Colbert as the then only Padres to clout 30 home runs in a season. Nine days later, Winfield surpassed Colbert for the most Padre RBIs in a season. He became the first San Diego player to win a Rawlings Gold Glove Award and make *The Sporting News'* All-League team, and received the most votes for both the UPI and AP National League All-Star teams.

Dave Winfield

In 1980, Winfield batted .276 with 25 doubles and 23 stolen bases, paced the Padres with 20 home runs and 87 RBIs, and earned a second Rawlings Gold Glove Award. San Diego lost its most consistent offensive weapon to free agency in December 1980. The Padres negotiated a renewal of Winfield's contract, but he and his agent Al Frohman demanded much more money. When San Diego rejected Winfield's monetary terms, the New York Yankees signed him to a 10-year contract worth up to $25 million. The Padres did not receive any compensation when Winfield departed. Winfield wanted to perform in New York, where he would receive more publicity. On the Padre career list, he still ranks second in runs scored (599), walks (463), home runs (154), RBIs (626), and slugging percentage (.464), third in games (1,117), hits (1,134), doubles (179), and triples (39), fourth in strikeouts (585), fifth in on-base percentage (.357), and sixth in batting average (.284) and stolen bases (133).

Winfield achieved more stardom with the New York Yankees, California Angels, Toronto Blue Jays, Minnesota Twins, and Cleveland Indians from 1981 through 1995. In 22 major-league seasons, he batted .285 with 1,669 runs scored, 3,110 hits, and 223 stolen bases. His 1,093 extra-base hits included 540 doubles, 88 triples, and 465 home runs. He ranks among the top 10 major-leaguers in career at-bats, games, and total bases and among the top 20 in career hits, doubles, home runs, RBIs, and strikeouts. Winfield appeared in every All-Star Game from 1977 to 1988, batting .361, and he also played in the 1981 and 1992 American League Championship Series and World Series. In 1984, he finished second to teammate Don Mattingly for the American League batting title with .340. The next year, Winfield ranked third in the American League with 114 RBIs. In 1993, he became just the seventeenth major-league player to attain 3,000 career hits. As an American Leaguer, Winfield also earned five Rawlings Gold Glove awards.

Winfield donated $20,000 to establish the Winfield Pavilion in right field to provide tickets to selected games for underprivileged youngsters in the San Diego area and set up a college scholarship program in his native Minneapolis-St.Paul area. The Los Angeles, California resident married Tonya Turner on February 18, 1988 and has a daughter, Lauren Shanel, by a previous relationship. He later operated the Winfield Foundation with his brother, Steve. The Foundation has sponsored several charities for underprivileged youth, including free seats for baseball games, All-Star Game children's parties, and yearly scholarships. Winfield was elected to the San Diego Padres Hall of Fame in 2000 and to the National Baseball Hall of Fame in 2001 in his first year of eligibility, becoming the fourth San Diego player so honored and the first to debut as a Padre. He has served on the Padres' board of directors since 2000 and in February 2002 became a vice president and senior adviser for the club. Winfield will concentrate on baseball operations, marketing, player development, community relations, and diversity issues. He also will be involved in the new downtown ballpark.

This Day in Padre History

JANUARY

1 **1977**—Pitcher Danny Frisella dies in a dune buggy accident near Phoenix, Arizona at age 30, becoming the first deceased former Padre.

6 **1984**—The Padres sign free agent pitcher Rich Gossage of the New York Yankees to a multi-year contract worth over $6 million.

7 **1922**—Manager Alvin Dark is born in Comanche, Oklahoma.

7 **1992**—Pitcher Rollie Fingers is elected to the National Baseball Hall of Fame.

8 **1986**—First baseman Willie McCovey is elected to the National Baseball Hall of Fame.

8 **1991**—Pitcher Gaylord Perry is elected to the National Baseball Hall of Fame.

8 **2002**—Shortstop Ozzie Smith becomes the fifth Padre elected to the National Baseball Hall of Fame and the 37th player so honored in his first year of eligibility.

9 **1974**—National League owners veto the sale of the Padres to Marjorie Everett and her associates, ostensibly because of her involvement with a race track scandal.

11 **1974**—Mayor Pete Wilson announces that four separate groups had expressed interest in purchasing the Padres and keeping the team in San Diego.

12 **1950**—Pitcher Randy Jones is born in Fullerton, California.

14 **1984**—Padre Owner Ray Kroc dies at age 81. Joan Kroc becomes owner and chairwoman of the board, while her son-in-law Ballard Smith is named president.

16 **2001**—Dave Winfield, former Padre star outfielder who bypassed the minor leagues, is elected to the National Baseball Hall of Fame in his first year on the ballot.

17 **1931**—Manager Don Zimmer is born in Cincinnati, Ohio.

21 **1960** —Pitcher Andy Hawkins is born in Waco, Texas.

25 **1974**—Ray Kroc, chairman and largest stockholder of the McDonald's restaurant chain, acquires the Padres from C. Arnholdt Smith for $12 million in cash. Signs new San Diego Stadium lease, insuring that the Padres would remain in San Diego at least through 1980 rather than move to Washington, D.C. Kroc initiates special promotions to draw fans to home games and has the players promote the Padres at McDonald's restaurants.

25 **1978**—The Padres acquire pitcher Gaylord Perry from the Texas Rangers for pitcher Dave Tomlin and cash.

27 **1969**—Outfielder Phil Plantier is born in Manchester, New Hampshire.

31 **1974**—The National League owners agree unanimously to the $12 million sale of the Padres from C. Arnholdt Smith to Ray Kroc.

FEBRUARY

2 **1974**—John McNamara, San Francisco Giants third base coach, replaces Don Zimmer as Padre manager.

2 **1999**—The Padres acquire outfielder Reggie Sanders, infielder Damian Jackson, and pitcher

Josh Harris from the Cincinnati Reds for outfielders Greg Vaughn and Mark Sweeney.

5 **1968**—Second baseman Roberto Alomar is born in Ponce, Puerto Rico.

8 **2000**—The Sycuan Band of Mission Indians, which runs a casino in San Diego County, agree to serve as the title sponsor of the Padres' 2000 season. The Sycuan tribe will pay more than $1.5 million, with just under $1 million going to the team and the rest going to radio and television advertising. It is believed to be the first time a major-league franchise has sold such a sponsorship.

9 **1961**—First baseman John Kruk is born in Charleston, West Virginia.

11 **1982**—The Padres trade shortstop Ozzie Smith to the St. Louis Cardinals for shortstop Garry Templeton.

15 **1980**—The Padres acquire outfielder Jerry Mumphrey from the Cleveland Indians for pitcher Bob Owchinko and outfielder Jim Wilhelm. The Padres acquire first baseman Willie Montanez from the Texas Rangers for pitcher Gaylord Perry, third baseman Tucker Ashford, and pitcher Joe Carroll.

15 **2002**—Merrill Lynch buys $169 million in bonds to finance construction of the Padres' new downtown ballpark. A check for $130 million, the proceeds from the sale after closing fees, insurance, and other expenses, is given to San Diego mayor Dick Murphy, ending more than three years of struggle to assemble a financing plan for the new ballpark. Ballpark construction, halted since October 2000 when temporary funding ran out, resumes on February 18.

15 **2002**—Padre outfielder Mike Darr, 25, is killed in Phoenix, Arizona around 2 a.m. when his new sports utility vehicle, a white GMC Yukon, rolls over along Loop 101 near 35th Avenue, five miles from the team's spring training headquarters in Peoria, Arizona. His friend, Duane Johnson, 24, son of UCLA defensive line coach Don Johnson and who was sitting in the passenger seat, is also killed. Padres minor-league pitching prospect Ben Howard, a back seat passenger and the only one wearing a seat belt, survives with minor injuries. Darr, the Padres' minor league player of the year in 1997 and 2000, leaves his wife, Natalie, and two sons, Mike Jr., 7, and Matthew, 2.

17 **1930**—Manager Roger Craig is born in Durham, North Carolina.

17 **1958**—Second baseman Alan Wiggins is born in Los Angeles, California.

17 **1968**—Around 15,000 people tour San Diego Stadium in a two-day open house. The stadium dimensions include the 330-foot foul lines, the 370-foot power alleys, the center-field fence 420 feet away, and the 17-foot high fence surrounding the outfield.

20 **2002**—Pitching coach Dave Smith takes a leave of absence to enter an alcohol rehabilitation program and does not return to the team until May 8.

22 **1978**—The Padres trade infielder Mike Ivie to the San Francisco Giants for outfielder Derrel Thomas.

24 **2001**—Phil Collier, longtime baseball reporter for the *San Diego Union* and former official scorer for the Padres, dies of cancer at age 75 in San Diego. In 1990, he was enshrined in the writers' wing of the National Baseball Hall of Fame.

MARCH

7 **1960**—Outfielder Joe Carter is born in Oklahoma City, Oklahoma.

8 **1964**—Pitcher Lance McCullers is born in Tampa, Florida.

9 **1965**—Catcher Benito Santiago is born in Ponce, Puerto Rico.

9 **2002**—Padre pitcher Bobby Jones and Padre outfielder Ryan Klesko are suspended for seven games and five games, respectively, at the beginning of the 2002 regular season for their participation in two bench-clearing altercations in an exhibition game against the Anaheim Angels at Tempe, Arizona. Klesko charges the mound after being hit by an Aaron Sele, pitch in the first inning, triggering the initial confrontation. Anaheim third baseman Troy Glaus charges the mound after Jones twice comes up and in with fastballs, sparking the second fracas. Anaheim infielder Scott Spiezio and Glaus are suspended six games and

two games, respectively, for their participation. Padre outfielder Ron Gant and Padre first baseman Phil Nevin, along with pitcher Sele are fined.

14 **1965**—Pitcher Kevin Brown is born in McIntyre, Georgia.

14 **1989**—The Padres name Dick Freeman club president.

15 **1919**—Coach Whitey Wietelmann is born in Zanesville, Ohio.

16 **2001**—The Colorado Rockies defeat the Padres, 6-5, in an exhibition game at Culiacan, Mexico.

17 **1944**—Outfielder Cito Gaston is born in San Antonio, Texas.

21 **1978**—The Padres fire manager Alvin Dark 17 days before the National League season, the quickest managerial change in major-league history. Roger Craig, Padre pitching coach, replaces him.

24 **1956**—Shortstop Garry Templeton is born in Cockney, Texas.

24 **1958**—Pitcher Bruce Hurst is born in St. George, Utah.

26 **1987**—Joan Kroc announces plans to sell the Padres to George Argyros, Seattle Mariners owner, for a reported $60 million.

27 **1992**—The Padres acquire third baseman Gary Sheffield and pitcher Geoff Kellogg from the Milwaukee Brewers for pitcher Ricky Bones, shortstop Jose Valentin, and outfielder Matt Mieske.

28 **1969**—The Padres acquire pitcher Tommie Sisk and catcher Chris Cannizzaro from the Pittsburgh Pirates for outfielder Ron Davis and second baseman Bobby Klaus.

30 **1984**—The Padres acquire third baseman Graig Nettles from the New York Yankees for pitchers Dennis Rasmussen and Darin Cloninger.

APRIL

1 **1981**—The Padres trade Jerry Mumphrey and pitcher John Pacella to the New York Yankees for pitchers Tim Lollar and Chris Welsh and outfielders Ruppert Jones and Joe Lefebvre and send pitcher Bob Lacey to the Cleveland Indians for second baseman Juan Bonilla.

1 **1997**—In front of the first opening day sellout crowd since 1985, the Padres explode for 11 runs in the bottom of the sixth inning en route to a 12-5 win over the New York Mets. The inning establishes a modern opening day National League record for runs scored in an inning. Shortstop Chris Gomez, outfielder Rickey Henderson, and second baseman Quilvio Veras clout consecutive home runs to highlight the inning.

1 **1998**—The Padres rally from a 6-1 deficit after two innings to defeat the Cincinnati Reds, 10-9, at Riverfront Stadium.

2 **1990**—Fifteen Southern California businessmen, headed by Tom Werner, sign a letter of intent to purchase the Padres from Joan Kroc.

3 **1984**—The Padres defeat the Pittsburgh Pirates, 5-1, at Jack Murphy Stadium in the then earliest home opener in franchise history.

5 **1968**—The San Francisco Giants play the Cleveland Indians in the first major-league game at San Diego Stadium in an exhibition contest at the end of spring training.

5 **1976**—The Padres acquire outfielder Merv Rettenmund from the Cincinnati Reds for infielder Rudi Meoli.

5 **1979**—Shortstop Ozzie Smith starts the season hitless in his first 34 plate appearances.

5 **1983**—The Padres defeat the San Francisco Giants, 16-13, at Candlestick Park in the highest scoring opening day game in franchise history.

5 **1997**—Pitchers Sterling Hitchcock and Trevor Hoffman combine on a one-hitter in a 4-1 victory over the Philadelphia Phillies at Qualcomm Stadium. First baseman Rico Brogna doubles in the fifth inning for the lone Phillies hit.

5 **1998**—The Padres rally from a 7-3 deficit with five runs in the ninth inning to defeat the St. Louis Cardinals, 8-7, at Busch Stadium.

6 **1969**—Second baseman Bret Boone is born in El Cajon, California.

7 **1970**—First baseman Nate Colbert's three-run homer helps the Padres defeat the Atlanta Braves, 8-3, in the season opener before 25,000 fans at San Diego Stadium.

7 **1978**—Dave Campbell announces his first game for the San Diego Padres. The Padres name outfielder Dave Winfield team captain. Winfield responds with three hits, including a home run, in a 3-2 victory over the San Francisco Giants at Candlestick Park.

7 **1996**—Infielder Craig Shipley makes hits in all five at-bats against the Houston Astros at the Astrodome. Third baseman Ken Caminiti sparks the 8-4 victory with a 13th-inning grand slam home run off Alvin Morman.

7 **1998**—The Padres trail the Cincinnati Reds, 2-0, in the home opener with two outs in the ninth inning when catcher Carlos Hernandez belts a game-tying two-run homer. The Padres win in the tenth inning on outfielder Greg Vaughn's sacrifice fly.

8 **1969**—The Padres win their major-league debut, 2-1, over the Houston Astros before 23,370 fans at San Diego Stadium. Pitcher Dick Selma strikes out 12 batters and yields only five hits. The Padres reach pitchers Don Wilson and Jack Billingham for only four safeties and score their first major-league run in the fifth inning on third baseman Ed Spiezio's home run off Wilson. In that at-bat, Spiezio makes the first hit, first extra-base hit, first home run, and first RBI in Padre history. An inning later, outfielder Ollie Brown doubles home second baseman Roberto Peña with the deciding run.

8 **1997**—Outfielder Steve Finley singles in the first inning off pitcher Steve Cooke for the lone Padres hit in a 2-0 loss to the Pittsburgh Pirates at Qualcomm Stadium.

8 **2001**—Third baseman Phil Nevin clouts a three-run, 453-foot home run in the sixth inning off pitcher Craig Dingman and singles twice with five RBIs in an 11-3 rout to give the Padres their first-ever sweep of the Colorado Rockies at Coors Field.

9 **1946**—First baseman Nate Colbert is born in St. Louis, Missouri.

9 **1974**—Owner Ray Kroc apologizes to the 39,000 San Diego fans over the public address microphone in the eighth inning for the Padres' poor play in a 9-5 season opening day loss to the Houston Astros.

9 **1989**—The Padres turn the earliest triple play in franchise history in the eighth inning during a 5-4 victory over the Houston Astros at the Astrodome.

10 **1969**—The Padres blank the Houston Astros, 2-0, sweeping the first three-game series in franchise history at San Diego Stadium.

10 **1974**—Owner Ray Kroc offers a public apology after being censured by commissioner Bowie Kuhn and Marvin Miller, executive director of the Major-League Baseball Players Association, for denouncing his team's performance over the public address microphone the previous day.

10 **1976**—The Atlanta Braves outbid the Padres for free agent pitcher Andy Messersmith of the Los Angeles Dodgers.

10 **1984**—Pinch hitter Champ Summers's fifth-inning grand slam off pitcher Bob Forsch lifts the Padres to a 7-3 victory over the St. Louis Cardinals at San Diego Stadium.

10 **1989**—Pitcher Bruce Hurst hurls the earliest one-hitter in franchise history in a 5-2 victory over the Atlanta Braves at Jack Murphy Stadium. Outfielder Lonnie Smith homers in the third inning for the lone Braves hit.

10 **1992**—First baseman Fred McGriff's seventh-inning grand slam off pitcher John Candelaria highlights the Padres' 8-3 triumph over the Los Angeles Dodgers at Jack Murphy Stadium.

10 **1998**—Outfielder Steve Finley clouts a two-out grand slam home run in the bottom of the ninth inning to lift the Padres to a 6-4 win over the Arizona Diamondbacks at Qualcomm Stadium.

11 **1971**—First baseman Nate Colbert belts home runs in his first two at-bats in a 9-7 triumph over the Los Angeles Dodgers at Dodger Stadium, giving him three consecutive home runs.

11 **1978**—The Padres turn a triple play in a 3-2 victory over the Atlanta Braves at Atlanta-Fulton County Stadium.

11 **2000**—Outfielder John Roskos becomes the 500th Padre to appear in a major-league game, going hitless in four at-bats in a 3-2, 13-inning victory over the visiting Colorado Rockies.

12 **1969**—The Padres convert their first double play in franchise history in the sixth inning in

a 5-1 loss to the San Francisco Giants at San Diego Stadium. Third baseman Jim Davenport grounds out to shortstop Rafael Robles. The double play goes from Robles to second baseman Roberto Peña to first baseman Bill Davis.

12 **1981**—First baseman Randy Bass clouts the first National League grand slam home run of the season in the third inning in a 7-6, 14-inning loss to the San Francisco Giants at Candlestick Park. The Padres do not hit another grand slam home run that season.

12 **1988**—First baseman John Kruk belts a grand slam home run in the fifth inning off pitcher Brad Havens in a 5-3 triumph over the Los Angeles Dodgers at Jack Murphy Stadium.

13 **1976**—Outfielder Dave Winfield hits the first major-league grand slam home run of the season in the seventh inning in an 8-5 triumph over the Los Angeles Dodgers at Dodger Stadium.

13 **1981**—The Cincinnati Reds defeat the Padres, 7-1, in the first home game played at the rechristened Jack Murphy Stadium. Murphy, a *San Diego Union* sports editor who died in 1980, for years had campaigned vigorously for a modern stadium and major-league franchises in baseball and football.

13 **1987**—Outfielders Marvell Wynne and Tony Gwynn and first baseman John Kruk clout consecutive home runs in the first inning off pitcher Roger Mason in a 13-6 loss to the San Francisco Giants at Jack Murphy Stadium, setting a major-league record for most consecutive home runs to start a game.

13 **1998**—The Padres blank the Arizona Diamondbacks, 1-0, on pitcher Andy Ashby's four-hitter, completing just the second 7-0 homestand in club history.

13 **2001**—Dave Winfield announces that he will enter the National Baseball Hall of Fame as a San Diego Padre, becoming the first to do so. The Padres retire Winfield's uniform number 31 the next day. Outfielder Gary Sheffield of the visiting Los Angeles Dodgers clouts a two-run homer into the second deck in the third inning off Padre pitcher Woody Williams, becoming the first player to hit loge round-trippers for both the Padres and visitors. San Diego, however, comes from behind to win, 5-4, in the 10th inning.

14 **1985**—Steve Garvey sets a major-league record for first basemen by playing in his 193rd consecutive errorless game in a 3-1 loss to the Atlanta Braves at Atlanta-Fulton County Stadium.

14 **1993**—Second baseman Tim Teufel makes five hits in an 11-7 loss to the Pittsburgh Pirates at Jack Murphy Stadium.

15 **1972**—The Padres defeat the Atlanta Braves, 6-5, in the season opener at San Diego Stadium. A strike delays the opening of the season. Jerry Coleman announces his first game for the Padres.

15 **1980**—The Padres steal six bases, including two by first baseman Willie Montanez, in a 9-5 victory over the Los Angeles Dodgers at San Diego Stadium.

15 **1985**—The Padres draw 54,490 fans against the San Francisco Giants to set an opening day club attendance record. The Padres elevate the National League pennant in center field and unveil a new $6.5 million Diamond Vision scoreboard in right field. In the 8-3 Padre victory, outfielder Carmelo Martinez belts a grand slam home run in the fifth inning off pitcher Greg Minton.

15 **1998** —Pitcher Kevin Brown blanks the San Francisco Giants on four hits at Candlestick Park, becoming the second Padre to hurl a 1-0 shutout in three days.

16 **1955**—Manager Bruce Bochy is born in Landes de Boussac, France.

16 **1983**—First baseman Steve Garvey breaks the National League record for most consecutive games played with 1,118 in an 8-5 loss to the Los Angeles Dodgers at Dodger Stadium.

16 **1987**—Outfielder Tony Gwynn makes five hits in a 3-2, 10-inning victory over the Los Angeles Dodgers at Dodger Stadium.

16 **2000**—Outfielder Al Martin sets a franchise record with five runs in a 13-3 triumph over the visiting Houston Astros. The Padres ignite for 18 hits, including four each by Martin and outfielder Eric Owens.

17 **1969**—The Padres trade pitcher Al McBean to the Los Angeles Dodgers for shortstop

Tommy Dean and pitcher Leon Everitt after the former appears in only one game.

17 **2001**—Outfielder Tony Gwynn triples, doubles, and singles for the final three-hit game of his major-league career in a 9-5 home loss to the Colorado Rockies.

18 **1977**—Catcher Gene Tenace's fifth inning grand slam home run off pitcher Bob Johnson lifts the Padres to a 12-6 triumph over the Atlanta Braves at Atlanta-Fulton County Stadium.

18 **1993**—Outfielder Tony Gwynn ties a club record by singling five times in a 10-6 triumph over the St. Louis Cardinals at Jack Murphy Stadium.

19 **1970**—Outfielder Cito Gaston doubles in the seventh inning for the lone Padres hit off pitcher Tom Griffin in a 5-1 loss to the Houston Astros at the Astrodome.

19 **1982**—The Padres set a club record with 24 hits, including 18 singles, and tie a team mark with eight consecutive hits in the fourth inning in a 13-6 triumph over the San Francisco Giants at Candlestick Park.

19 **1997**—The Padres lose a doubleheader, 1-0 and 2-1, to the St. Louis Cardinals in the Padres Paradise Series at Aloha Stadium in Honolulu, Hawaii. The Padres win the series finale, 8-2, the next day.

20 **1923**—Manager Preston Gomez is born in Central Preston, Cuba.

20 **1978**—Rookie shortstop Ozzie Smith makes perhaps the most spectacular defensive play in Padre history, robbing outfielder Jeff Burroughs of a base hit in a 2-0 victory over the Atlanta Braves at San Diego Stadium.

20 **2001**—The Padres become the first major-league team in 56 years to start two players at least 40 years old in the same outfield. Left fielder Rickey Henderson, 42, and right fielder Tony Gwynn, 40, start in the 3-1 loss to the Los Angeles Dodgers at Dodger Stadium. Doc Cramer and Check Hostetler of the 1945 Detroit Tigers were the last two teammates at least 40 years old to start the same game in the outfield. Henderson and Gwynn bat first and second, respectively, each contributing singles.

21 **1963**—Third baseman Ken Caminiti is born in Hanford, California.

21 **2000**—Padre batters hit seven doubles—two each by shortstop Damian Jackson, first baseman Ryan Klesko, and second baseman Bret Boone and one by third baseman Phil Nevin—in a 7-2 win over the Houston Astros at Enron Field.

22 **1970**—Nineteen Padres strike out in a 2-1 loss to the New York Mets at Shea Stadium, tying what was then the major-league record. Pitcher Tom Seaver fans the last 10 Padres in that game.

22 **1977**—Pitcher Bob Shirley sets a club record by retiring 25 consecutive Houston Astros in a 4-2 triumph at the Astrodome.

22 **1984**—The Padres establish a team record with 11 extra-base hits in a 15-7 loss to the Los Angeles Dodgers at Dodger Stadium.

23 **1990**—Outfielder Joe Carter hits a grand slam home run in the first inning off Eric Gunderson in a 13-3 rout of the San Francisco Giants at Jack Murphy Stadium.

23 **1994**—Outfielder Tony Gwynn makes five hits for the seventh time in a 6-2 victory over the Philadelphia Phillies at Jack Murphy Stadium.

23 **2000**—Outfielder Tony Gwynn collects his 2,331st major-league single to move past Cap Anson for tenth place on the all-time list in an 11-10 victory over the Houston Astros at Enron Field. Outfielder Eric Owens doubles, triples, and singles with four RBIs, helping the Padres sweep their first series at Houston since 1996.

24 **1988**—Pitcher Andy Hawkins hurls a one-hit, 3-0 shutout over the Houston Astros at Jack Murphy Stadium. Second baseman Bill Doran singles in the seventh inning for the lone Astros hit.

24 **2001**—Pinch-hitter Rickey Henderson walks off reliever Chris Brock in the sixth inning to tie Babe Ruth's career walk record of 2,062 in a 12-7 loss to the visiting Philadelphia Phillies.

25 **2001**—Outfielder Rickey Henderson walks off reliever Jose Mesa in the ninth inning to break Babe Ruth's career walk record of 2,062 in a 5-3 home loss to the Philadelphia Phillies. Henderson donates the jersey to the National Baseball Hall of Fame in Cooperstown, New

York and the ball to the Babe Ruth Museum in Baltimore, Maryland.

26 **1985**—Outfielder Tony Gwynn singles in the fourth inning off pitcher Orel Hershiser for the lone Padres hit in a 2-0 loss to the Los Angeles Dodgers at Dodger Stadium.

26 **2001**—Pitcher Kevin Jarvis hurls a seven-hit shutout with 10 strikeouts for his initial victory as a Padre and the first shutout by a Padre since 1999 in an 11-0 triumph over the visiting Philadelphia Phillies.

27 **1969**—The Padres win the first extra-inning game in franchise history, a 10-9 victory over the Cincinnati Reds at San Diego Stadium.

27 **1972**—Padre third base coach Don Zimmer replaces Preston Gomez as manager.

27 **1982**—The Padres win a club record eleventh consecutive game, 8-5, over the New York Mets at San Diego Stadium to take first place for a day.

27 **1984**—Third baseman Luis Salazar makes an infield single in the fourth inning off pitcher Rick Honeycutt for the lone Padres hit in a 1-0 loss to the Los Angeles Dodgers at San Diego Stadium.

27 **1989**—Outfielder Carmelo Martinez clouts a grand slam home run in the eighth inning off pitcher Logan Easley in an 8-1 victory over the Pittsburgh Pirates at Three Rivers Stadium.

27 **1997**—Third baseman Ken Caminiti singles in the second inning for the lone Padres hit off pitcher Greg Maddux in a 2-0 loss to the Atlanta Braves at Turner Field.

27 **2000**—The Padres rout the Pittsburgh Pirates, 12-4, at Three Rivers Stadium, tallying six runs in the ninth inning. Pitcher Matt Clement records his seventh consecutive victory dating back to 1999.

28 **1981**—Pitcher Tim Lollar belts a home run for his first major-league hit off pitcher Tom Seaver of the Cincinnati Reds at Riverfront Stadium.

28 **1990**—Outfielder Bip Roberts hits an inside-the-park home run off pitcher Bob Walk in a 4-3 loss to the Pittsburgh Pirates at Jack Murphy Stadium.

28 **1991**—Outfielder Tony Gwynn hits into a triple play in the first inning in a 9-2 loss to the Philadelphia Phillies at Veterans Stadium.

28 **1998**—Outfielder Tony Gwynn posts his eighth career five-hit game, homering with two RBIs in a 7-3 triumph over the Chicago Cubs at Qualcomm Stadium.

29 **1971**—Pitcher Sterling Hitchcock is born in Fayetteville, North Carolina.

30 **1976**—Pitcher Randy Jones becomes the first Padre to win National League Pitcher of the Month honors.

30 **1983**—Catcher Terry Kennedy wins National League Player of the Month honors.

30 **1984**—Outfielder Tony Gwynn wins National League Player of the Month honors.

30 **1986**—Pitcher Mark Thurmond blanks the St. Louis Cardinals, 5-0, on a one-hitter at Jack Murphy Stadium. Outfielder Willie McGee singles in the seventh inning for the lone Cardinals hit.

30 **1989**—Pitcher Mark Davis wins National League Pitcher of the Month honors.

30 **1993**—The Padres play the longest nine-inning home game in franchise history, a 3 hour, 37 minute, 7-6 victory over the New York Mets. Outfielder Tony Gwynn becomes the first Padre to make five hits in a game twice in the same month.

30 **1996**—The Padres set a franchise record by winning 17 games in April.

30 **1998**—The Padres defeat the Florida Marlins, 4-1, at Pro Player Stadium and race out to their quickest start in franchise history, posting a 19-7 mark at the end of April. Closer Trevor Hoffman wins the National League Rolaids Relief Man award for April, posting a 2-0 record with seven saves and a 1.35 ERA. Outfielder Tony Gwynn ends the month batting .362 while third baseman Ken Caminiti clouts seven home runs with 21 RBIs.

MAY

1 **2001**—Catcher Ben Davis clouts his first grand slam home run and third baseman Phil Nevin adds a three-run homer in the third inning to spark a 10-3 victory over the Chicago Cubs at Wrigley Field. Seven consecutive Padres reach base to start the third inning.

2 **1969**—Outfielder Al Ferrara hits the first pinch-hit home run in franchise history with the bases loaded in the fourth inning off pitcher George Culver in an 8-5 triumph over the Cincinnati Reds at Riverfront Stadium.

2 **1980**—Pitcher Rick Wise hurls a 1-0 shutout over the New York Mets at Shea Stadium.

2 **2000**—Shortstop Damian Jackson hits a two-run homer, double, and single in an 8-3 triumph over the visiting Florida Marlins. No Padre ever has hit for the cycle.

2 **2001**—Chicago Cubs outfielder Sammy Sosa hits his 200th career home run at Wrigley Field in the fourth inning off pitcher Kevin Jarvis in an 8-3 win, joining Ernie Banks, Billy Williams, and Ron Santo in that distinct club.

3 **1969**—Outfielder Ollie Brown hits the second grand slam home run in club history, connecting off pitcher Tony Cloninger in the first inning in a 13-5 triumph over the Cincinnati Reds at Riverfront Stadium. The Padres score nine runs that inning.

3 **1986**—The Padre-Pittsburgh Pirates game at Jack Murphy Stadium is delayed seven minutes when a skunk saunters onto the playing field.

4 **1977**—The Padres play the shortest nine-inning home game in franchise history, a 1 hour, 29 minute, 4-1 triumph by pitcher Randy Jones over the Philadelphia Phillies.

4 **2001**—The Padres clout four home runs in an 11-4 rout over the Cincinnati Reds at Riverfront Stadium. First baseman Ryan Klesko and outfielder Bubba Trammell hit two-run homers in the first inning, catcher Wiki Gonzalez contributes a two-run homer in the eighth inning, and Klesko adds a solo homer in the ninth inning. Pitcher Adam Eaton records his third career stolen base, breaking the team record for pitchers.

5 **1978**—The Padres tie a club record with four triples in a 2-1 triumph over the St. Louis Cardinals at Busch Stadium. Shortstop Ozzie Smith connects twice, while outfielders Gene Richards and Oscar Gamble hit one each.

5 **1998**—First baseman Wally Joyner clouts a grand slam home run in the second inning off pitcher Paul Wagner in a 13-4 victory over the Milwaukee Brewers at County Stadium.

5 **2000**—Outfielder Eric Owens reaches base safely in his 27th consecutive game since the start of the season in a 5-3 home loss to the Arizona Diamondbacks.

6 **1971**—Outfielder Ollie Brown singles in the seventh inning for the lone Padres hit off pitcher Larry Dierker in an 8-0 loss to the Houston Astros at San Diego Stadium.

6 **1972**—Pitcher Bill Greif strikes out five consecutive New York Mets in a 6-2 victory at Shea Stadium.

6 **2001**—Manager Bruce Bochy records his 500th victory as Padre pilot, while outfielder Rickey Henderson doubles to reach base safely for the 5,000th time in an 8-2 triumph over the Cincinnati Reds at Cinergy Field.

7 **1928**—Manager Dick Williams is born in St. Louis, Missouri.

8 **1980**—Outfielder Jerry Turner steals home in the eighth inning in a 9-6 triumph over the Chicago Cubs at Wrigley Field, becoming the first Padre to accomplish the feat since 1974.

8 **2001**—The Padres steal eight bases in a 7-1 victory over the visiting Atlanta Braves. Outfielders Mark Kotsay and Rickey Henderson and first baseman Ryan Klesko pilfer two bases each, while outfielder Tony Gwynn and second baseman Damian Jackson steal one apiece.

9 **1960**—Outfielder Tony Gwynn is born in Los Angeles, California.

9 **1971**—Pitcher Clay Kirby throws a franchise-record 161 pitches, including two in the ninth inning, in a 7-2 victory over the Cincinnati Reds at San Diego Stadium.

9 **1974**—Outfielder John Grubb singles in the second inning for the lone Padres hit off pitcher Don Sutton in a 6-0 loss to the Los Angeles Dodgers at San Diego Stadium.

9 **1979**—Outfielder John Briggs doubles in the seventh inning for the lone Padres hit off pitcher Dick Ruthven in a 2-0 loss to the Philadelphia Phillies at San Diego Stadium.

10 **1969**—Shortstop Roberto Peña belts a grand slam home run off pitcher Steve Carlton in the fourth inning in a 5-3 triumph over the St. Louis Cardinals at Busch Stadium.

10 **1991**—The Padres set a club home attendance record for a regular season night game, drawing

54,841 people in a 6-4, 10-inning loss to the Montreal Expos.

12 **1965**—Outfielder Steve Finley is born in Union City, Tennessee.

12 **1993**—Pitcher Andy Benes clouts his fourth career home run in a 3-2 loss to the Cincinnati Reds at Riverfront Stadium.

12 **1998**—Rain forces postponement of the Padres-New York Mets game at Qualcomm Stadium. The home postponement marks San Diego's first since April 20, 1983, breaking a major-league streak of 1,172 home dates (1,184 games).

12 **2001**—Pitcher A.J. Burnett of the Florida Marlins no-hits the Padres, 3-0, at Qualcomm Stadium, striking out seven batters on 128 pitches. His nine bases on balls tie the modern record for most walks in a complete game no-hitter.

14 **1995**—Pinch-hitter Brian Johnson belts an eighth-inning grand slam off pitcher Randy Myers in a 9-7 victory over the Chicago Cubs at Wrigley Field.

16 **2000**—Third baseman Phil Nevin clouts two two-run home runs with five RBIs in a 7-3 win over the Florida Marlins at Pro Player Stadium.

17 **1974**—First baseman Nate Colbert belts his fifth grand slam home run as a Padre, connecting in the first inning off pitcher Ron Bryant in a 7-3 triumph over the San Francisco Giants at Candlestick Park. The grand slam home run ends a team drought dating back to September 7, 1972.

17 **1977**—The Padres trade reliever Butch Metzger to the St. Louis Cardinals for pitcher John D'Acquisto and third baseman Pat Scanlon. The Chicago Cubs score the most runs ever against the Padres in a 23-6 rout at Wrigley Field.

17 **1984**—The Padres set a club record with seven stolen bases, including five by Alan Wiggins, in a 5-4 victory over the Montreal Expos at Jack Murphy Stadium.

17 **1998**—The Padres complete a three-game sweep of the Philadelphia Phillies, 3-1, and end the homestand with six victories in seven games.

17 **2001**—Shortstop Alex Arias, outfielder Rickey Henderson, first baseman Ryan Klesko, and outfielder Bubba Trammell homer off pitcher Steve Trachsel in a seven-run third inning, sparking a 15-3 rout over the New York Mets at Shea Stadium. Trachsel becomes the first Mets pitcher and 19th major-league hurler to allow four home runs in an inning. The Padres collect 17 hits, including a home run, double, and two singles by Klesko. Trammell, a former Met, contributes five RBIs.

18 **1973**—*The San Diego Union* sports editor Jack Murphy writes that owner C. Arnholdt Smith plans to sell the Padres because of financial problems. Smith has secretly juggled millions of dollars to keep his massive financial empire afloat. The Padres lack money to acquire players, develop a strong farm system, or hire enough scouts to make the club competitive.

18 **1990**—Shortstop Garry Templeton clouts a grand slam home run in the second inning off pitcher Frank Viola in a 6-3 victory over the New York Mets at Jack Murphy Stadium.

18 **1992**—Pitcher Bruce Hurst hurls a one-hit, 3-0 victory over the New York Mets at Jack Murphy Stadium. Outfielder Chico Walker makes an infield single in the sixth inning for the lone Mets hit.

19 **1955**—Pitcher Ed Whitson is born in Johnson City, Tennessee.

19 **1956**—Pitcher Eric Show is born in Riverside, California.

19 **1974**—First baseman Willie McCovey hits the second Padre grand slam home run in three days in the fifth inning off pitcher Tom Bradley. The Padres defeat the San Francisco Giants, 10-7, in 12 innings in the second game of a doubleheader at Candlestick Park.

19 **1975**—Pitcher Randy Jones hurls the longest one-hitter in franchise history, a 1- 0, 10-inning masterpiece over the St. Louis Cardinals at San Diego Stadium. The contest takes only two hours, the shortest extra-inning game in franchise history. Outfielder Luis Melendez singles in the seventh inning for the lone Cardinals hit.

19 **2000**—Third baseman Phil Nevin hits a home run and a single with six RBIs in an 11-7 romp over the Atlanta Braves at Turner Field.

19 **2001**—The Padres match a club record for runs scored in a game and collect 20 hits in a 20-7 romp over the Montreal Expos at Olympic Stadium. Outfielder Bubba Trammell registers a career-high six RBIs with a two-run double in the fifth inning, a run-scoring ground out in the sixth inning, and a three-run homer in the seventh inning. Outfielder Mark Kotsay adds four RBIs with a home run, two doubles, and a single. Outfielder Rickey Henderson tallies twice to join Ty Cobb as the only major-league players to score 2,200 career runs.

20 **1977**—The Padres rout the Montreal Expos, 12-4, at Jarry Park, as first baseman Mike Ivie clouts a first-inning grand slam home run off Gerry Hannahs.

20 **1984**—Pitcher Tim Lollar sets a club record by striking out eight consecutive New York Mets in a 4-2, 10-inning loss at Jack Murphy Stadium.

20 **1995**—Bip Roberts hits a ninth-inning grand slam home run off pitcher Dan Miceli in a 9-6 victory over the Pittsburgh Pirates at Jack Murphy Stadium.

21 **1972**—The Padres hit seven doubles in a 7-0 romp over the Cincinnati Reds at San Diego Stadium. First baseman Nate Colbert, third baseman Ed Spiezio, and outfielder Jerry Morales each double twice.

21 **1976**—Outfielder Dave Winfield belts his second grand slam home run of the season off pitcher Gary Nolan in the first inning in a 4-2 victory over the Cincinnati Reds at San Diego Stadium.

21 **1977**—The Padres play their longest road game in history, a 5 hour, 33 minute, 11-8, 21-inning victory over the Montreal Expos at Olympic Stadium.

21 **2001**—First baseman Ryan Klesko clouts two three-run homers and a triple and matches a career high with six RBIs in a 7-3 victory over the Houston Astros at Enron Field. Klesko joins outfielder Greg Vaughn as the only Padres to homer twice and triple in the same game.

22 **1994**—The Padres end a club-record 13-game losing streak, defeating the Houston Astros, 7-6, at the Astrodome.

22 **2001**—First baseman Ryan Klesko hits two home runs for the second consecutive game with three RBIs in a 6-2 win over the Houston Astros at Enron Field. His home runs off pitcher Scott Elarton came leading off the third inning and with one aboard in the fifth inning.

23 **1952**—Pitcher Butch Metzger is born in Lafayette, Indiana.

23 **1970**—The Padres score 17 runs on 21 hits and tie a club record with five home runs in a 17-16, 15-inning marathon victory over the San Francisco Giants at Candlestick Park. First baseman Nate Colbert hits four singles and a home run.

23 **1994**—Pinch hitter Luis Lopez' grand slam home run in the first inning off pitcher Mark Portugal highlights a 4-0 victory over the San Francisco Giants at Jack Murphy Stadium.

23 **2001**—Bruce Bochy manages his 1,000th game with the Padres, recording his 510th career victory, 7-6, over the Houston Astros at Enron Field to give San Diego a share of first place. Outfielder Mark Kotsay clouts a fourth-inning home run and singles three times with two RBIs.

24 **1975**—Pitcher Randy Jones throws only 68 pitches while blanking the Pittsburgh Pirates, 5-0, at San Diego Stadium.

24 **1977**—The Padres set a club record by leaving 17 runners on base in a 4-3 triumph over the Atlanta Braves at San Diego Stadium.

24 **1996**—Catcher Brian Johnson clouts a grand slam home run in the seventh inning off Blas Minor in a 13-1 rout of the New York Mets at Shea Stadium.

24 **2001**—The Padres take over sole possession of first place in the National League West with a 3-1 victory over the visiting Arizona Diamondbacks.

25 **1969**—First baseman Nate Colbert belts the fourth Padre grand slam home run of the month, connecting off Don Nottebart in the third inning in a 10-2 victory over the Chicago Cubs in the first game of doubleheader at San Diego Stadium.

25 **1980**—Third baseman Barry Evans hits the only Padre grand slam home run of the season

in the ninth inning off Pedro Borbon in an 11-5 triumph over the St. Louis Cardinals at Busch Stadium.

26 **1987**—Ballard Smith resigns as Padres president.

26 **2001**—Catcher Ben Davis bloops a bunt safely beyond the pitcher's mound with one out in the eighth inning to break up a bid for a perfect game by pitcher Curt Schilling of the Arizona Diamondbacks. Schilling finishes with a three-hit, 3-1 Arizona victory over the Padres at Qualcomm Stadium.

27 **1968**—The National League owners award the San Diego Padres and Montreal Expos National League franchises during meetings in Chicago, increasing the number of teams to 12. The Padres plan to begin major-league play in 1969, the city of San Diego's 200th anniversary.

28 **1973**—Owner C. Arnholdt Smith sells the Padres for $12 million to a Washington, D.C. group, led by wealthy grocer Joseph Danzansky. Danzansky gives Smith a $100,000 check as a down payment and is granted 45 days to complete financial arrangements, secure a lease for RFK Stadium, and gain support from National League owners. Several obstacles block the proposed sale.

28 **1988**—Jack McKeon replaces Larry Bowa as Padre manager.

28 **1995**—The Padres tie a National League record by tallying nine runs in the tenth inning in a 13-5 victory over the Philadelphia Phillies at Veterans Stadium.

28 **2000**—Outfielder Al Martin singles, doubles, and triples with three RBIs in a 4-3 triumph over the visiting Montreal Expos.

29 **1977**—The Padres fire John McNamara as manager, naming Bob Skinner as interim replacement.

29 **1987**—Owner Joan Kroc cancels plans to sell the Padres to George Argyros.

30 **1975**—Pinch-hitter Willie McCovey ties Hank Aaron's National League mark by belting his 16th career grand slam home run off pitcher Bob Apodaca in the eighth inning to give the Padres a 6-2 win over the New York Mets at Shea Stadium. The grand slam home run marks the first for the Padres since McCovey connected on May 19, 1974.

30 **1977**—The Padres name Alvin Dark manager. First baseman Mike Ivie sets a franchise record with five doubles, including three in the second game, in a doubleheader against the San Francisco Giants at Candlestick Park. The Padres double four times, two by Ivie and one each by third baseman Doug Rader and outfielder Jerry Turner, in the seventh inning of the first game.

30 **1979**—The Padres score seven runs in the fifth inning in a 10-2 romp over the Atlanta Braves at San Diego Stadium.

30 **1985**—Pitcher Andy Hawkins wins his tenth consecutive start, defeating the Montreal Expos, 5-4, at Jack Murphy Stadium.

30 **1994**—Pinch-hitter Craig Shipley sparks the Padres to a 10-2 win over the Pittsburgh Pirates with a seventh-inning grand slam home run off pitcher Dan Miceli.

30 **1997**—The Padres acquire outfielder Ruben Rivera, pitcher Rafael Medina, and $3 million from the New York Yankees for the rights to pitcher Hideki Irabu, infielder Homer Bush, and outfielders Gordon Amerson and Vernon Maxwell.

31 **1976**—Randy Jones wins National League Pitcher of the Month honors for the second consecutive month.

31 **1985**—Andy Hawkins wins National League Pitcher of the Month honors.

31 **1994**—The Padres score a franchise-record 13 runs on nine hits in the second inning during a 15-5 rout of the Pittsburgh Pirates at Jack Murphy Stadium.

31 **1998**—Outfielder Greg Vaughn ends the most productive month of his Padre career with a .330 batting average, 12 home runs, 32 RBIs, and a .752 slugging percentage. Closer Trevor Hoffman records eight saves and a 0.84 ERA in nine outings for the month.

JUNE

1 **1996**—Outfielder Steve Finley sparks an 8-3 victory over the Philadelphia Phillies at Veterans Stadium with a grand slam home run in the sixth inning off pitcher Dave Leiper.

2 **1970**—The Padres hit four triples in a 14-8 triumph over the Pittsburgh Pirates at Three

Rivers Stadium. Catcher Chris Cannizzaro, shortstop Tommy Dean, and second baseman Jose Arcia triple in the seventh inning.

2 **1972**—Second baseman Dave Campbell ruptures an Achilles tendon in his left ankle while running to first base in a 2-1 loss to the Chicago Cubs at San Diego Stadium and misses the rest of the season.

2 **1982**—Pitcher Juan Eichelberger hurls a one-hitter in 3-1 victory against the Chicago Cubs at Wrigley Field. Scot Thompson makes an infield single in the second inning for the lone Cubs hit.

2 **1983**—Outfielder Kevin McReynolds homers in his first major-league game to highlight a 4-1 triumph over the Philadelphia Phillies at San Diego Stadium.

2 **1989**—The Padres trade right fielder-first baseman John Kruk and infielder Randy Ready to the Philadelphia Phillies for outfielder-third baseman Chris James.

2 **1996**—First baseman Wally Joyner breaks his left thumb while sliding into second base in the fourth inning in a 9-8, 12-inning loss to the Philadelphia Phillies at Veterans Stadium. The Padres slump disastrously in Joyner's absence.

3 **1979**—Third baseman Barry Evans doubles in the eighth inning off pitcher Bruce Kison for the sole Padre hit in a 7-0 loss to the Pittsburgh Pirates at Three Rivers Stadium.

3 **1995**—Pitcher Pedro Martinez no-hits the Padres for nine innings before surrendering a tenth-inning leadoff double to outfielder Bip Roberts. The Montreal Expos defeat the Padres, 1-0, in 10 innings.

4 **1932**—Manager John McNamara is born in Sacramento, California.

4 **1956**—Catcher Terry Kennedy is born in Euclid, Ohio.

4 **1972**—The Padres turn a triple play in the ninth inning in a 3-1 setback to the Chicago Cubs at San Diego Stadium.

5 **1973**—The Padres select University of Minnesota star pitcher-outfielder Dave Winfield in the first round of the free agent draft as the fourth overall selection.

5 **1986**—Outfielder Kevin McReynolds hits into a triple play in the third inning in a 4-2 loss to the Atlanta Braves at Jack Murphy Stadium.

6 **1971**—Pitcher Dave Roberts blanks the Montreal Expos, 8-0, in the first game of a doubleheader at San Diego Stadium, while first baseman Nate Colbert clouts a grand slam home run in the fifth inning off pitcher John Strohmayer.

6 **1986**—Padres players criticize owner Joan Kroc and president Ballard Smith after the San Diego management no longer allows players to drink beer in the clubhouse.

6 **1988**—Pitcher Tom Browning hurls a no-hitter until outfielder Tony Gwynn singles in the ninth inning, as the Cincinnati Reds rout the Padres, 12-0.

7 **1972**—Pitcher Clay Kirby tosses 13 consecutive scoreless innings in an 18-inning, 1-0 loss to the Pittsburgh Pirates at San Diego Stadium. Third baseman Dave Roberts jumps directly from the University of Oregon and plays his first major-league game, entering in the twelfth inning.

7 **1985**—Third baseman Kurt Bevacqua clouts a grand slam home run off pitcher Tom Browning in the fifth inning of the first game of a doubleheader in a 9-3 victory over the Cincinnati Reds at Riverfront Stadium.

7 **1998**—The Padres wallop the Texas Rangers, 17-8, at The Ballpark in Arlington, starting an 11-game winning streak, which tied the club record.

7 **2001**—Second baseman Cesar Crespo clouts a solo home run in the seventh inning off pitcher Ryan Vogelson of the San Francisco Giants, while his brother, first baseman Felipe Crespo, homers with the bases empty in the first inning and with one aboard in the sixth inning off Padre pitcher Adam Eaton in a 10-7 San Diego victory at Pacific Bell Stadium.

8 **1973**—The Padres notify the City of San Diego that they intend to play baseball in Washington, D.C. the next season. City attorney John Witt responds that the Padres cannot break their 20 year lease with San Diego Stadium and that the matter would be decided in court, if necessary.

9 **1984**—The Padres take over first place in the Western Division with a 12-2 victory over the

Cincinnati Reds at Jack Murphy Stadium and maintain the lead for the rest of the season.

9 **1985**—Pitcher Andy Hawkins sets a franchise record by winning his eleventh consecutive decision, defeating the Cincinnati Reds, 5-3, at Riverfront Stadium.

9 **1993**—Randy Smith replaces Joe McIlvaine, making the 29-year-old the youngest general manager in major-league history.

9 **1996**—The Padres remain in first place for the 67th consecutive day, their longest run atop the National League West since 1985. C. Arnholdt Smith, the Padres first owner, dies at age 97 at Del Mar, California.

9 **1998**—Outfielder Greg Vaughn clouts a grand slam home run off pitcher Brett Tomko of the Cincinnati Reds in the seventh inning, highlighting a 5-1 Padres victory at Qualcomm Stadium.

9 **2001**—The Padres defeat the Seattle Mariners, 6-3, at Safeco Field, ending the latter's club-record 15-game winning streak and the longest American League winning streak since 1991. The Mariners do not lose another contest on their 12-game homestand.

10 **1971**—Pitcher Clay Kirby strikes out 13 batters in a 4-2 victory over the New York Mets at Shea Stadium.

10 **1972**—The Padres lose their tenth consecutive game, 5-2, to the St. Louis Cardinals at San Diego Stadium, their 21st loss in 25 contests.

10 **1974**—The Padres overcome an 8-0 deficit with nine runs in the last two innings, defeating the Pittsburgh Pirates, 9-8, at San Diego Stadium.

10 **1981**—The Padres defeat the Pittsburgh Pirates, 3-2, at Three Rivers Stadium in the final game before a player's strike cancels the next 52 games.

10 **1987**—Chub Feeney, former National League president, replaces Ballard Smith as Padre president.

10 **1998**—The Padres defeat the Cincinnati Reds, 2-1, at Qualcomm Stadium and hold or share first place in the National League West for the remainder of the season.

10 **2000**—Second baseman Bret Boone hits a home run and three singles with six RBIs and outfielder Eric Owens makes four hits in a 13-2 home rout over the Houston Astros.

11 **1980**—The Padres set a franchise record with 16 singles in a 7-6 loss to the Montreal Expos at Olympic Stadium.

12 **1970**—Pitcher Doc Ellis of the Pittsburgh Pirates hurls the first no-hitter in San Diego Stadium history, blanking the Padres, 2-0, in the first game of a doubleheader.

12 **1971**—Pitcher Clay Kirby retires the first 21 San Francisco Giants batters before Willie McCovey homers in a 2-1 Padres victory. First baseman-outfielder Ryan Klesko is born in Westminster, California.

12 **1973**—The Padres trade pitcher Fred Norman to the Cincinnati Reds for outfielder Gene Locklear, pitcher Mike Johnson, and cash.

12 **1998**—The Padres regain sole possession of first place by defeating the San Francisco Giants, 10-3, before 60,789 fans at Qualcomm Stadium, then the largest crowd ever to see a baseball game in San Diego and the season's largest major-league crowd.

13 **1973**—Outfielder Jerry Morales hits into the first triple play in franchise history in the seventh inning of a 3-2 loss to the Montreal Expos at Jarry Park.

13 **1976**—The Padres set a club attendance record of 43,473 people for a doubleheader in a sweep against the Philadelphia Phillies at San Diego Stadium.

13 **1990**—The National League owners in Cleveland, Ohio unanimously approve the sale of the Padres to 15 partners headed by Tom Werner. Pitcher Trevor Wilson hurls a no-hitter until Mike Pagliarulo singles in the ninth inning, as the San Francisco Giants blank the Padres, 6-0, at Jack Murphy Stadium.

14 **1974**—Second baseman Derrel Thomas belts an inside-the-park home run in the third inning off pitcher Ernie McAnally in a 5-4 win over the Montreal Expos at San Diego Stadium.

14 **1998**—The Padres complete a three-game sweep of the San Francisco Giants, attracting the largest three-game crowd (155,330) in franchise history.

14 **2001**—Third baseman Phil Nevin clouts two home runs, including a grand slam off pitcher

Chad Bradford in the eighth inning, with five RBIs to lift the Padres to a 6-4 triumph over the visiting Oakland Athletics.

15 **1973**—The city of San Diego secures a temporary restraining court order preventing the Padres from completing the sale of the team before a financial agreement is reached with the city.

15 **1974**—The Padres acquire pitchers Brent Strom and Terry Ley for pitcher Steve Arlin.

15 **1977**—The Padres acquire outfielder Dave Kingman from the New York Mets for infielder Bobby Valentine and pitcher Paul Siebert.

15 **1979**—The Padres acquire outfielder Jay Johnstone from the New York Yankees for pitcher Dave Wehrmeister.

16 **1962**—First baseman Wally Joyner is born in Atlanta, Georgia.

16 **1968**—Buzzie Bavasi becomes the club's first president.

16 **1971**—Outfielder Cito Gaston singles in the seventh inning for the lone Padres hit off pitcher Bill Stoneman in a 2-0 loss to the Montreal Expos at Jarry Park.

16 **1985**—Pitcher Mark Thurmond loses both games of a doubleheader, 7-3 and 5-4, in 13 innings, to the San Francisco Giants at Candlestick Park.

16 **2001**—Pitching coach Dave Smith, who had missed the first month of the season to complete an alcohol rehabilitation program, resigns. Bullpen coach Greg Booker replaces him as pitching coach and Darrel Akerfelds, who had been pitching coach for the Class AAA Portland, Oregon Beavers, takes over as bullpen coach.

17 **1969**—Third baseman Van Kelly becomes the first Padre left-handed batter to hit a home run, connecting against pitcher Bill Singer of the Los Angeles Dodgers at Dodger Stadium. The home run comes in the franchise's 65th game.

17 **1970**—Outfielder Ivan Murrell singles in the seventh inning for the Padres lone hit off pitcher Bob Gibson in an 8-0 loss to the St. Louis Cardinals at San Diego Stadium.

17 **1998**—The Padres defeat the Los Angeles Dodgers, 3-2, in 12 innings and extend their Qualcomm Stadium winning streak to nine games, one short of matching their longest home winning streak in franchise history.

18 **1972**—Pitcher Steve Arlin hurls a two-hit, 1-0 victory over the Pittsburgh Pirates at Three Rivers Stadium.

18 **1974**—Outfielder Rich Morales steals home in a 9-4 loss to the Chicago Cubs at Wrigley Field.

18 **1992**—First baseman Fred McGriff charges the mound when pitcher Trevor Wilson of the San Francisco Giants hits him with a delivery in the fourth inning following a grand slam home run by third baseman Gary Sheffield. National League president Bill White suspends McGriff for four games for his role in the bench-clearing incident at Candlestick Park. The Padres triumph over the Giants, 9-4.

19 **1973**—The Padres tie a club record by losing their tenth consecutive home game, 7-3, to the Houston Astros at San Diego Stadium. Outfielder Dave Winfield debuts with a single.

19 **1974**—Pitcher Dan Spillner hurls a one-hit, 1-0 shutout against the Chicago Cubs at Wrigley Field. Outfielder Rick Monday singles in the third inning for the lone Cubs hit.

19 **1998**—The Padres defeat the San Francisco Giants, 9-5, at 3Com Park, tying a club record with 11 consecutive victories.

19 **2001**—The Padres defeat the visiting San Francisco Giants, 4-3, in 15 innings as the two clubs combine for 40 strikeouts. Each team records 20 strikeouts.

20 **1980**—Outfielder Jerry Turner steals home for the second time that season in the fourth inning in a 4-2 triumph over the Montreal Expos at San Diego Stadium.

20 **1994**—Second baseman Bip Roberts hits safely in his 23rd consecutive game, the National League season best, in a 3-2 loss to the Los Angeles Dodgers at San Diego Stadium.

20 **2000**—Pitcher Brian Tollberg, the first Frontier League player to make the major leagues, allows only one unearned run and one hit in his seven-inning debut in a 3-1 win over the Arizona Diamondbacks at Bank One

Ballpark. First baseman Ryan Klesko provides the margin of victory with two solo home runs.

21 **1973**—Outfielder Dave Winfield makes three hits, including his first major-league home run, in a 12-2 loss to the Houston Astros at San Diego Stadium.

21 **1976**—First baseman Willie McCovey hits into a triple play in the third inning in a 6-3 victory over the San Francisco Giants at San Diego Stadium.

21 **1977**—Outfielder Dave Kingman becomes just the third Padre to homer into the second deck in left field in the second inning off pitcher John Candelaria in a 9-2 loss to the Pittsburgh Pirates.

21 **1985**—Second baseman Jerry Royster belts a grand slam home run in the eighth inning off pitcher Greg Minton in a 6-1 triumph over the San Francisco Giants at Jack Murphy Stadium.

21 **1998**—The Padres acquire catcher Jim Leyritz and outfielder Ethan Faggett from the Boston Red Sox for pitchers Carlos Reyes and Dario Veras and catcher Mandy Romero.

22 **1973**—Pitcher Randy Jones makes his major-league debut in a 7-3 loss to the Atlanta Braves at San Diego Stadium.

22 **1976**—Pitcher Randy Jones equals pitcher Christy Mathewson's major-league record of 68 straight innings without walking a batter in a 4-2 triumph over the San Francisco Giants at San Diego Stadium.

22 **1985**—The Padres set a club attendance record for a single day game with 53,375 people in a 2-1 victory over the San Francisco Giants at Jack Murphy Stadium.

23 **1971**—Reliever Bob Miller wins both games of a doubleheader, 3-2 and 4-3, over the Houston Astros at San Diego Stadium.

23 **1972**—Pitcher Steve Arlin hurls a one-hitter in a 4-1 victory over the San Francisco Giants at San Diego Stadium. Outfielder Garry Maddox triples in the second inning for the lone Giants hit.

23 **1973**—Pitcher Clay Kirby blanks the Atlanta Braves, 2-0, with 13 strikeouts at San Diego Stadium.

23 **1985**—Third baseman Kurt Bevacqua clouts his second grand slam home run of the month in the fifth inning off pitcher Atlee Hammaker during a 6-1 triumph over the San Francisco Giants at Jack Murphy Stadium. The Padres hit two grand slam home runs that series.

23 **1996**—Outfielder Steve Finley makes five hits, including a two-run homer, to help the Padres defeat the Philadelphia Phillies, 7-5, at Jack Murphy Stadium.

23 **1997**—Reliever Trevor Hoffman slams the door in an 11-6 triumph over the San Francisco Giants to pass Rollie Fingers as the all-time Padres saves leader with 109.

23 **2000**—Second baseman Bret Boone clouts three home runs with six RBIs and outfielder Ruben Rivera belts a game-winning three-run homer in the 10th inning in a 10-7 triumph over the Cincinnati Reds at Riverfront Stadium. Boone connects off pitchers Scott Sullivan in the fourth inning, Manny Aybar in the sixth frame, and Rob Bell in the eighth inning, becoming the first second baseman in major-league history to have two three-homer games.

24 **1993**—The Padres acquire pitchers Trevor Hoffman, Jose Martinez, and Andres Berumen from the Florida Marlins for third baseman Gary Sheffield and pitcher Rich Rodriguez.

25 **1948**—Pitcher Clay Kirby is born in Washington, D.C.

26 **1997**—Outfielder Tony Gwynn hits an inside-the-park grand slam in the seventh inning off pitcher Mark Guthrie in a 9-7 triumph over the Los Angeles Dodgers at Dodger Stadium.

26 **2000**—Second baseman Bret Boone knocks in five runs with a single, double, and home run in a 9-5 win over the Los Angeles Dodgers at Dodger Stadium.

27 **1985**—The Padres trade second baseman Alan Wiggins to the Baltimore Orioles for pitchers Roy Lee Jackson and Rich Caldwell after Wiggins suffers a drug relapse.

27 **1989**—The Padres defeat the Los Angeles Dodgers, 5-3, in 17 innings at Dodger Stadium.

27 **1995**—Third baseman Ken Caminiti connects for a grand slam home run in the sixth inning off pitcher Greg Hansell in a 14-3 rout over the Los Angeles Dodgers at Dodger Stadium.

27 **1997**—Pitcher Joey Hamilton clouts his second home run of the season and third of his career in a 7-5 victory over the Los Angeles Dodgers at Dodger Stadium.

27 **1998**—The Padres defeat the Anaheim Angels, 5-1, at Qualcomm Stadium for their eighteenth victory of the month, just one shy of the club record. Pitcher Sterling Hitchcock hurls a no-hitter until catcher Phil Nevin homers on the first pitch in the top of the eighth inning.

27 **2001**—The Colorado Rockies edge San Diego, 10-9, preventing the Padres from recording their first-ever six-game road sweep.

28 **1969**—The Padres lose by their largest margin, 19-0, to the Los Angeles Dodgers at San Diego Stadium.

28 **1994**—Outfielder Derek Bell sets a club record with seven hits in a doubleheader split with the Colorado Rockies at Mile High Stadium.

28 **2001**—Outfield Tony Gwynn, on the disabled list since May 11, announces that he will retire at the end of the 2001 season after two decades with the Padres. He is just the 17th major-league player to spend 20 years with only one major-league club.

30 **1972**—Third baseman Dave Roberts is thrown out three times at the plate, but doubles home two runs to tie the game and doubles to start the winning rally in a 13-inning, 4- 3 victory over the Cincinnati Reds at San Diego Stadium.

30 **1978**—Outfielder Dave Winfield becomes the first Padre to win National League Player of the Month honors.

30 **1987**—Outfielder Tony Gwynn earns National League Player of the Month honors for the second time.

JULY

1 **1975**—The Padres trounce the Los Angeles Dodgers, 10-1, at Dodger Stadium, as infielder Mike Ivie clouts a fifth-inning grand slam home run off pitcher Jim Brewer.

2 **1975**—The Padres make eight consecutive hits in the fifth inning in a 6-5 loss to the Los Angeles Dodgers at Dodger Stadium.

2 **1978**—Outfielder Jerry Turner breaks the Padre career record with four pinch-hit home runs, connecting in the eighth inning off pitcher Tom Dixon in a 6-2 victory over the Houston Astros at the Astrodome.

2 **1980**—Outfielder Dave Winfield makes five hits, including a home run, and knocks in four runs in a 10-7 loss to the Los Angeles Dodgers at Dodger Stadium.

3 **1965**—Outfielder Greg Vaughn is born in Sacramento, California.

3 **1975**—Pitcher Randy Jones hurls his second one-hitter of the season in a 2-1 win over the Cincinnati Reds at San Diego Stadium. Catcher Bill Plummer doubles in the eighth inning for the lone Reds hit.

3 **1983**—First baseman Steve Garvey belts his fifth career grand slam home run in the fifth inning off pitcher Mark Davis during a 7-3 triumph over the San Francisco Giants at Candlestick Park.

3 **1994**—Pitcher Andy Benes blanks the New York Mets on one hit in a 7-0 victory at Jack Murphy Stadium. First baseman Rico Brogna doubles in the eighth inning for the lone Mets hit.

3 **1997**—Outfielder Steve Finley belts a grand slam home run in the first inning off pitcher Derek Lowe in a 10-8 victory over the Seattle Mariners at Jack Murphy Stadium.

4 **1972**—Pitcher Tom Seaver hurls a no-hitter until outfielder Leron Lee singles in the ninth inning, as the New York Mets defeat the Padres, 2-0, at Shea Stadium.

4 **1978**—Outfielder Dave Winfield hits his third career grand slam home run in the first inning off pitcher John Montefusco in a 7-5 triumph over the San Francisco Giants at Candlestick Park. The Padres do not clout another grand slam home run until May 25, 1980.

4 **1981**—During the baseball strike, the Reno farm club plays Redwood in a California League game before 37,665 people at Jack Murphy Stadium.

4 **1985**—The Padres defeat the Pittsburgh Pirates, 9-1, at Three Rivers Stadium to widen their Western Division lead to five games.

4 **1987**—The Padres trade pitchers Dave Dravecky and Craig Lefferts, along with third

baseman Kevin Mitchell, to the San Francisco Giants for pitchers Mark Davis, Mark Grant, and Keith Comstock and third baseman Chris Brown.

4 **1998**—The Padres defeat the Colorado Rockies, 9-1, before 61,148 people, the biggest major-league crowd in 1998 and the largest ever to see a regular-season baseball game in San Diego.

5 **1969**—The Padres set a franchise extra-inning record with 21 hits in a 9-8, 12-inning triumph over the Houston Astros at San Diego Stadium.

5 **1994**—Third baseman Eddie Williams lifts the Padres to a 7-2 victory over the Philadelphia Phillies with a fifth-inning grand slam home run off pitcher Bobby Munoz at Jack Murphy Stadium.

5 **1998**—Pitcher Andy Ashby's 75-pitch complete game effort highlights the Padres' 7-2 win over the Colorado Rockies at Qualcomm Stadium. Ashby becomes the first Padre to win 11 games before the All-Star break since Andy Hawkins in 1985. The Padres complete a three-game sweep of the Colorado Rockies and enter the All-Star break with a best-ever 57-31 record, sitting atop the National League West that late for the third time in franchise history. Their 5 1/2-game lead over the second-place San Francisco Giants is the largest they ever have enjoyed at All-Star break.

6 **1969**—Pitcher Dick Kelley hurls the first one-hitter in Padres history in a 1-0 shutout against the Houston Astros at San Diego Stadium. Denis Menke singles in the second inning for the lone Astros hit.

6 **1972**—Pitcher Steve Arlin hurls a one-hitter for the first 10 innings, as the Padres defeat the New York Mets, 1-0, in 14 innings at Shea Stadium.

7 **1980**—Jack McKeon replaces Bob Fontaine as acting general manager.

7 **1993**—Pitchers Andy Benes and Gene Harris combine on a one-hit, 2-0 shutout over the New York Mets at Shea Stadium. Second baseman Jeff Kent makes an infield single in the second inning for the lone Mets hit.

7 **1998**—San Diego sends five players—starting right fielder Tony Gwynn, outfielder Greg Vaughn, and pitchers Andy Ashby, Kevin Brown, and Trevor Hoffman—to the All-Star Game at Coors Field in Denver, Colorado.

8 **1976**—Pitcher Randy Jones improves his win-loss record to 16-3 before the All-Star break, defeating the Chicago Cubs, 6-3, at Wrigley Field.

8 **1982**—Third baseman Luis Salazar belts the first Padre inside-the-park home run since June 1974 in a 5-3 conquest of the Philadelphia Phillies at Veterans Stadium.

8 **1995**—The Houston Astros defeat the Padres, 3-2, in a 17-inning game at the Astrodome.

9 **1944**—Owner John Moores is born in Texas.

9 **1970**—Pitcher Dave Roberts homers for the second time that season in a 10-9 victory over the Cincinnati Reds at Riverfront Stadium.

9 **1986**—The Padres acquire pitcher Ed Whitson from the New York Yankees for reliever Tim Stoddard.

9 **1995**—Third baseman Eddie Williams hits a grand slam home run in the seventh inning off pitcher Doug Brocail in a 9-2 win over the Houston Astros at the Astrodome.

9 **1996**—Third baseman Ken Caminiti becomes the first Padre to clout a home run in an All-Star Game, connecting off pitcher Roger Pavlick of the Texas Rangers in the sixth inning at Veterans Stadium in Philadelphia.

9 **2000**—Reliever Trevor Hoffman earns his 250th career save in a 4-3 victory over the Texas Rangers at The Ballpark in Arlington, breaking a five-game Texas winning streak.

10 **1970**—Outfielder Ivan Murrell, third baseman Ed Spiezio, second baseman Dave Campbell, and outfielder Clarence Gaston hit home runs in the ninth inning in a 9-7 loss to the Los Angeles Dodgers at San Diego Stadium.

10 **1973**—San Diego Superior Court Judge Eli H. Levenson denies the city of San Diego's request for a preliminary injunction to prohibit the Padres from leaving town.

10 **1982**—Outfielder Gene Richards makes five hits, including the second Padre inside-the-park home run in three days, in a 9-7 setback to the New York Mets at Shea Stadium.

10 **2001**—Tony Gwynn and Cal Ripken of the Baltimore Orioles are presented the

Commissioner's Historical Achievement Award by commissioner Bud Selig in a surprise sixth-inning ceremony at the All-Star Game at Safeco Field in Seattle. First baseman Ryan Klesko and third baseman Phil Nevin bat once each as reserves for the National League All-Stars.

11 **1967**—Pitcher Andy Ashby is born in Kansas City, Missouri.

11 **1978**—The Padres host their first All-Star Game, as the National League triumphs, 7-3, before 51,000 spectators. Outfielder Dave Winfield singles in the eighth inning, while pitcher Rollie Fingers hurls two shutout innings in relief. First baseman Steve Garvey earns Most Valuable Player honors for the 49th major-league All-Star game with a triple and two-run single.

11 **1979**—Outfielders Jerry Turner and Dave Winfield and catcher Gene Tenace hit consecutive home runs off pitcher Randy Lerch in the first inning to key a 7-3 victory over the Philadelphia Phillies at Veterans Stadium.

11 **1983**—Third baseman Tim Flannery hits his first San Diego Jack Murphy Stadium home run, a first-inning grand slam off pitcher Ferguson Jenkins, in a 6-5 triumph over the Chicago Cubs.

11 **1990**—Greg Riddoch replaces Jack McKeon as manager to allow the latter to devote all his time to general manager duties.

12 **1979**—The Padres commit their first error in 93 innings dating back to July 3 in a 4-3 loss to the Philadelphia Phillies at Veterans Stadium.

12 **1985**—Pitcher La Marr Hoyt blanks the St. Louis Cardinals, 2-0, at Busch Stadium for his twelfth victory before the All-Star break.

12 **1998**—Third baseman Ken Caminiti becomes the fourth Padre to homer three times in a game and extends his National League career record for home runs from both sides of the plate to nine, as the Padres defeat the Los Angeles Dodgers, 4-1, at Dodger Stadium.

13 **1976**—Manager John McNamara becomes the first Padre to coach in an All-Star Game in a 7-1 National League victory at Veterans Stadium in Philadelphia.

13 **1980**—Outfielder Gene Richards steals four bases, including home in the first inning, in a 4-3 win over the Los Angeles Dodgers at San Diego Stadium. He steals eight bases in the three-game series.

14 **1970**—Outfielder Cito Gaston becomes the first Padre to appear in an All-Star Game, going hitless in two at-bats in a 5-4, 12-inning National League victory at Riverfront Stadium in Cincinnati.

14 **1983**—First baseman Kurt Bevacqua becomes the third Padre in July to belt a grand slam home run, connecting in the seventh inning in an 8-6 loss to the Pittsburgh Pirates at Jack Murphy Stadium.

14 **1991**—Pitchers Greg Harris and Craig Lefferts combine on a one-hit, 2-1 triumph over the New York Mets at Shea Stadium. Mackey Sasser leads off the eighth inning with a ground-rule double for the lone Mets hit.

14 **1992**—Jack Murphy Stadium draws a record crowd of 59,372 fans for the All-Star Game, in which three Padres start. Although first baseman Fred McGriff makes two hits and shortstop Tony Fernandez singles, the American League wins, 13-6. Outfielder Tony Gwynn ties an All-Star Game record with two assists.

14 **2001**—Second baseman Damian Jackson hits a broken-bat grand slam home run to left field off pitcher Wade Miller in the sixth inning, sparking a rally to defeat the Houston Astros, 8-6, at Enron Field. Outfielder Mark Kotsay contributes a two-run homer and a single.

15 **1971**—The Pittsburgh Pirates defeat the Padres, 4-3, in 17 innings at Three Rivers Stadium.

15 **1975**—Pitcher Randy Jones pitches a scoreless ninth inning to save the All-Star Game for the National League at Milwaukee County Stadium.

15 **1994**—Padre pitchers set a then club record by striking out 17 New York Mets in a 2-1 14-inning victory at Shea Stadium.

16 **1977**—Pitcher Bob Owchinko hurls 7.1 consecutive hitless innings in a 1-0 loss to the Los Angeles Dodgers at San Diego Stadium.

16 **1985**—Under manager Dick Williams, the National League defeats the American League,

6-1, in the All-Star Game at the Hubert H. Humphrey Metrodome in Minneapolis. Seven Padres participate, with LaMarr Hoyt winning Most Valuable Player honors.

17 **1945**—Manager Greg Riddoch is born in Greeley, Colorado.

17 **1974**—The Padres defeat the Philadelphia Phillies, 15-1, at San Diego Stadium to tie their largest margin of victory.

17 **1995**—Shortstop Ray Holbert's fifth inning grand slam home run off pitcher C.J. Nitkowski highlights an 8-6 victory over the Cincinnati Reds at Jack Murphy Stadium.

17 **1998**—San Diego crushes a club-record six home runs in a 13-3 win over the Cincinnati Reds at Riverfront Stadium. Outfielder Ruben Rivera belts a grand slam home run in the fourth inning off pitcher Rich Krivda.

18 **1970**—Second baseman Denny Doyle becomes the first major-league player to hit an inside-the-park home run at San Diego Stadium, helping the Philadelphia Phillies win, 7-4.

18 **1972**—Pitcher Steve Arlin hurls the longest hitless game in Padre history in a 5-1 triumph over the Philadelphia Phillies. The no-hitter lasts until second baseman Denny Doyle singles with two strikes and two men out in the ninth inning. Arlin hurls 12 consecutive hitless innings over two successive games.

18 **1989**—The Padres trounce the Pittsburgh Pirates, 17-4, at Jack Murphy Stadium, tying their largest single-game run production. Outfielder Chris James connects for a grand slam home run in the fifth inning off pitcher Bob Walk.

18 **1993**—The Padres trade first baseman Fred McGriff to the Atlanta Braves for outfielders Melvin Nieves and Vince Moore and pitcher Donnie Elliott.

18 **1996**—Padre pitchers blow a 9-2 lead and surrender 11 runs in the seventh inning in a 13-12 loss to the Colorado Rockies at Coors Field.

18 **2000**—Outfielder Ruben Rivera hits an inside-the-park home run, the first for the Padres since June 1997 and the first at home since August 1991, with two strikes and two outs to tie the Anaheim Angels, 2-2, in the bottom of the ninth inning. Anaheim wins the contest, 3-2, in 10 innings.

18 **2001**—Two transformers in the left-field light tower at Qualcomm Stadium blow out in the third inning, postponing the game with the Arizona Diamondbacks. The entire bank of lights stretching from left field to left center field blow out after an explosion which sent out puffs of black smoke.

19 **1973**—An appeals court denies the request of the city attorney's office to prohibit the Padres from moving to Washington, D.C.

19 **1975**—Outfielder John Grubb singles in the seventh inning for the Padres' lone hit off pitcher Steve Stone in a 2-1 victory over the Chicago Cubs at San Diego Stadium.

19 **1980**—Outfielder Gene Richards steals his 18th consecutive base in an 8-7 loss to the Chicago Cubs at Wrigley Field.

19 **1982**—Outfielder Tony Gwynn debuts with two hits in a 7-6 loss to the Philadelphia Phillies at San Diego Stadium.

19 **2001**—San Diego loses the suspended game, 3-0, to the Arizona Diamondbacks. Arizona pitcher Randy Johnson relieves pitcher Curt Schilling in the third inning and sets major-league records for a reliever by striking out seven consecutive batters and 16 batters altogether. He comes within four outs of combining with Schilling on a no-hitter. Catcher Wiki Gonzalez singles for the lone Padre hit in the eighth inning.

20 **1998**—Padre Outfielder Greg Vaughn and St. Louis Cardinals first baseman Mark McGwire become the first players to homer in the second deck in left field at Qualcomm Stadium in the same game in a 13-1 Padre loss. Vaughn accomplishes the feat for the second time in consecutive seasons.

20 **2000**—Pitcher Woody Williams clouts his first major-league home run, doubles, and singles with two RBIs, as San Diego makes just five hits in a 7-3 loss to the visiting San Francisco Giants. His second-inning error marks the first by the Padres in 65.2 innings.

20 **2001**—Larry Lucchino announces that he will resign as Padre president and chief executive officer following the 2001 season. Bob Vizas,

Padre senior vice president and general counsel, will replace him.

21 **1970**—Pitcher Clay Kirby hurls a no-hitter for eight innings against the New York Mets at San Diego Stadium, but outfielder Cito Gaston pinch-hits for him in the bottom of the eighth frame because the Padres trail, 1-0. Two walks, a double steal, and an infield out produce a first-inning run for the Mets, who collect three hits in the ninth inning off pitcher Jack Baldschun and win the contest, 3-0.

21 **1982**—Rookie outfielder Alan Wiggins is arrested on drug charges and checks into a drug rehabilitation center.

21 **1995**—Pinch-hitter Archi Cianfrocco belts the third Padre grand slam home run of the month in the eighth inning off pitcher Steve Bedrosian in a 9-6 victory over the Atlanta Braves at Atlanta-Fulton County Stadium.

22 **1978**—Outfielder Jerry Turner clouts his second pinch-hit home run of the month, connecting off pitcher Bruce Sutter in the ninth inning with two runners aboard to give the Padres a 4-2 victory over the Chicago Cubs at San Diego Stadium.

23 **1969**—Catcher Chris Cannizzaro becomes the first Padre selected for the National League All-Star team.

23 **1971**—The Pittsburgh Pirates blank San Diego, 4-0, at San Diego Stadium, the third consecutive game the Padres fail to score.

23 **2000**—First baseman Ryan Klesko clouts a game-tying solo home run in the ninth inning and a game-winning two-run homer in the 10th inning in a 6-4 triumph over the Colorado Rockies at Coors Field.

24 **2001**—Pitcher Randy Johnson of the Arizona Diamondbacks strikes out 14 Padres in 7.1 innings and surrenders just a single to outfielder Bubba Trammell in an 11-0 rout at Bank One Ballpark.

25 **1972**—First baseman Nate Colbert scores the winning run for the National League in a 4-3 triumph over the American League in the All-Star Game at Atlanta-Fulton County Stadium.

25 **1998**—Pitcher Trevor Hoffman retires the Houston Astros in the ninth inning at Qualcomm Stadium to preserve a 6-5 triumph, tying a major-league record with his 41st consecutive save.

26 **1970**—The Padres trounce the Philadelphia Phillies, 16-2, at Veterans Stadium in their highest scoring game until April 5, 1983.

26 **1977**—Rookie outfielder Gene Richards sets a franchise record and ties a National League mark by making six hits, including five singles and a double, in a 15-inning, 5-2 loss to the Montreal Expos at San Diego Stadium.

26 **1988**—The Houston Astros score a run in the eighth inning of a 5-1 loss at San Diego Stadium to end a consecutive streak of 31.2 scoreless innings by Padre pitchers against them.

27 **1985**—The Padres tie a club mark by turning five double plays in a 12-inning, 2-1 loss to the St. Louis Cardinals at Jack Murphy Stadium.

27 **1993**—Outfielder Tony Gwynn makes five hits and breaks Dave Winfield's club mark of 626 RBIs with a second-inning single in an 8-0 victory over the Chicago Cubs at Wrigley Field. The Padres acquire pitchers Andy Ashby and Bruce Bochtler and catcher Brad Ausmus from the Colorado Rockies for pitchers Greg W. Harris and Bruce Hurst.

27 **1996**—The Padres set a franchise record for runs in a 20-12 rout of the Florida Marlins at Joe Robbie Stadium. The four-hour, 10-minute marathon becomes the longest nine-inning night game in major-league history. First baseman Wally Joyner drives in five runs, while outfielder Steve Finley records four RBIs and tallies four runs. Newly acquired John Flaherty belts a grand slam home run in the eighth inning off pitcher Terry Mathews. Flaherty hits safely in his 27th consecutive game, the second longest hitting streak by a catcher in major-league history.

28 **1960**—Outfielder Carmelo Martinez is born in Dorado, Puerto Rico.

28 **1979**—Pitcher Gaylord Perry fans five batters in a 4-3 win over the San Francisco Giants at San Diego Stadium to move into second place on the all-time list with 3,120 strikeouts.

28 **2001**—Third baseman Phil Nevin clouts two home runs, including a grand slam off pitcher Allen Levreault in the fourth inning, with five RBIs in a 6-2 victory over the Milwaukee Brewers at Miller Park.

29 **1972**—The Padres edge the Cincinnati Reds, 4-3, in a 17-inning game at Riverfront Stadium.

29 **1983**—First baseman Steve Garvey dislocates his left thumb in a collision at home plate in a 6-5 victory over the Atlanta Braves at San Diego Stadium. The injury snaps his National League record at 1,207 consecutive games, the third longest in major-league baseball history at the time.

29 **1984**—Shortstop Garry Templeton's sixth-inning grand slam home run off pitcher Mike LaCoss highlights a 9-0 drubbing of the Houston Astros at San Diego Stadium.

29 **1988**—Outfielder Tony Gwynn clouts his first career inside-the-park home run in a 5-3 triumph over the Cincinnati Reds.

29 **2001**—Outfielder Bubba Trammell homers, doubles, and singles with three RBIs to help the Padres rout the Milwaukee Brewers, 12-5, at Miller Park.

30 **1984**—Pitcher Dave Dravecky hurls a one-hitter in a 12-0 romp over the Los Angeles Dodgers at Jack Murphy Stadium. Shortstop Bill Russell doubles in the seventh inning for the lone Dodgers hit.

30 **2001**—The Padres trade pitcher Sterling Hitchcock to the New York Yankees for pitcher Brett Jodie and outfielder Darren Blakely.

31 **1979**—Outfielder Dave Winfield makes five hits, including a double and home run, in a 10-3 victory over the Atlanta Braves at Atlanta-Fulton County Stadium. Third baseman Kurt Bevacqua and Winfield hit consecutive home runs in the ninth inning off pitcher Adrian Devine.

31 **1983**—The Padres turn a triple play in the fourth inning in a 5-2 win over the Atlanta Braves at Jack Murphy Stadium.

31 **1988**—Outfielder Tony Gwynn wins National League Player of the Month honors for the third time.

31 **1995**—The Padres trade pitchers Andy Benes and Greg Keagle to the Seattle Mariners for pitcher Ron Villone and outfielder Marc Newfield.

31 **1996**—The Padres acquire outfielders Greg Vaughn and Gerald Parent from the Milwaukee Brewers for pitchers Bryce Florie and Ron Villone and outfielder Marc Newfield.

31 **1998**—The Padres edge the Montreal Expos, 5-4, at Olympic Stadium for their third 18-win month of the season and take a commanding 13-game lead in the National League West.

31 **2000**—Pitcher Woody Williams hurls the first complete game of the season for the Padres, allowing just four hits and striking out four in a 4-1 home victory over the Philadelphia Phillies. His performance ends a streak of 126 consecutive starts without a complete game by Padre pitchers. The Padres acquire first baseman-outfielder John Mabry and pitcher Tom Davey from the Seattle Mariners for outfielder Al Martin.

AUGUST

1 **1971**—The Padres turn a triple play in the seventh inning in a 2-0 shutout over the Atlanta Braves at San Diego Stadium.

1 **1972**—First baseman Nate Colbert belts five home runs with 13 RBIs and 22 total bases in a 9-0 and 11-7 doubleheader sweep over the Atlanta Braves at Atlanta-Fulton County Stadium. His RBIs and total bases establish a major-league mark, while his five home runs equal Stan Musial's major-league standard. His three home runs, including a second-inning grand slam off pitcher Pat Jarvis, and eight RBIs in the second game establish Padre records.

1 **1978**—Pitcher Randy Jones outduels Burt Hooton of the Los Angeles Dodgers at San Diego Stadium for his second 1-0 shutout of the season.

1 **1980**—Pitcher Steve Mura blanks the Pittsburgh Pirates, 1-0, at Three Rivers Stadium.

1 **1984**—Padre pitchers surrender a second-inning run in a 4-3 victory over the Los Angeles Dodgers, the first tally given up in 40.2 innings dating back to the seventh inning on July 28.

1 **2000**—Outfielder John Mabry becomes the seventh player to homer in his first at-bat as a

Padre in the 10th inning in a 6-4 triumph over the Colorado Rockies at Coors Field.

2 **1981**—The Padres play their first tie game in franchise history. The contest is halted by rain after three innings with a 3-3 score against the Pittsburgh Pirates at Three Rivers Stadium. The game is rescheduled as part of a doubleheader the next day.

2 **1991**—Second baseman Tim Teufel clouts a grand slam home run in the third inning off pitcher Charlie Leibrandt in a 13-3 romp over the Atlanta Braves at Atlanta-Fulton County Stadium.

2 **1995**—Outfielder Melvin Nieves hits a grand slam home run in the eighth inning off pitcher Terry Mulholland in an 11-3 rout of the San Francisco Giants at Jack Murphy Stadium.

2 **2001**—First baseman Ryan Klesko hits his seventh career grand slam home run in the eighth inning off reliever Jeff Fassero, lifting the host Padres past the Chicago Cubs, 4-3. The Padres trade veteran pitcher Woody Williams to the St. Louis Cardinals for outfielder Ray Lankford.

3 **1983**—Third baseman Tim Flannery singles in the third inning for the lone Padres hit off pitcher Nolan Ryan in a 1-0 loss to the Houston Astros at San Diego Stadium.

3 **1996**—A then club record and National League season-high 55,412 fans witness a 5-2 loss to the Florida Marlins at Jack Murphy Stadium.

4 **1948**—Outfielder John Grub is born in Richmond, Virginia.

4 **1973**—Pitcher Mike Corkins hits his third home run of the season and fifth career home run in a 14-3 loss to the Atlanta Braves at Atlanta-Fulton County Stadium.

4 **1974**—Pitcher Dave Freisleben hurls 13 consecutive scoreless innings in a 1-0, 14-inning triumph over the Cincinnati Reds at San Diego Stadium.

4 **1990**—Outfielder Joe Carter's second grand slam homr run of the season in the eleventh inning off pitcher Rick Mahler lifts the Padres to a 7-3 victory over the Cincinnati Reds at Riverfront Stadium.

4 **1993**—Outfielder Tony Gwynn equals a franchise record by making a career-high six hits in an 11-10, 12-inning triumph over the San Francisco Giants at Jack Murphy Stadium. He joins outfielders Willie Keeler, Ty Cobb, and Stan Musial as the only major leaguers to have at least five hits four times during the same season.

4 **2000**—Pitcher Jay Witasick becomes the 49th player to appear in at least one game for the Padres in an 11-10 win over the visiting Chicago Cubs, setting a season club record. Pitcher Trevor Hoffman records his 254th save as a Padre, tying Rich Aguilera for fourth on the all-time save list with one team.

4 **2001**—Third baseman Phil Nevin clouts a solo home run off pitcher Chris Reitsma in the fifth inning to give host San Diego a 2-1 victory over the Cincinnati Reds, joining Fred McGriff as the only Padres to boast consecutive 30 home-run seasons.

5 **1971**—Outfielder Ollie Brown singles in the fifth inning off pitcher Juan Pizarro for the Padres' lone hit in a 3-0 loss to the Chicago Cubs at Wrigley Field.

5 **1973**—Pitcher Phil Niekro of the Atlanta Braves blanks the Padres, 9-0, on a no-hitter at Atlanta-Fulton County Stadium.

5 **1977**—Outfielder Dave Kingman's sixth-inning grand slam home run off Paul Reuschel highlights an 11-8 victory over the Chicago Cubs at Wrigley Field.

5 **1998**—Pitcher Kevin Brown blanks the Philadelphia Phillies, 4-0, the first of his two shutouts for that month.

6 **1983**—The Padres rout the Cincinnati Reds, 11-4, in the first game of a doubleheader at San Diego Stadium, as outfielder Bobby Brown clouts his first career grand slam home run in the eighth inning off pitcher Tom Hume.

6 **1992**—Third baseman Gary Sheffield and first baseman Fred McGriff become the first Padres to hit consecutive home runs twice in the same game, accomplishing the feat off pitcher Brian Williams in the first and second innings in a 7-5 victory over the Houston Astros at Jack Murphy Stadium.

7 **2000**—Pitcher Trevor Hoffman notches his 30th save for the sixth consecutive season to preserve a 6-4 triumph over the Philadelphia Phillies at Veterans Stadium. Dennis Eckersley

and Lee Smith are the only other relievers to record six straight 30-save seasons.

8 **1936**—Manager Frank Howard is born in Columbus, Ohio.

8 **1972**—Pitcher Bill Greif blanks the Philadelphia Phillies, 3-0, at San Diego Stadium in 1 hour and 30 minutes, the shortest regulation night game in history.

10 **1978**—The Padres defeat the Cincinnati Reds, 15-3, at Jack Murphy Stadium, nearly tying the club record for most runs in a single game.

10 **1981**—Owner Ray Kroc charges no admission when the baseball strike ends after a 52-game interruption since June 11. A Jack Murphy Stadium crowd of 52,608 watches the Atlanta Braves edge the Padres, 3-2.

10 **2000**—Second baseman Bret Boone and third baseman Phil Nevin clout three-run homers in a 15-3 rout over the Philadelphia Phillies at Veterans Stadium. The Padres make 19 hits, including nine for extra bases and three each by second baseman Damian Jackson, catcher Wiki Gonzalez, outfielder Mike Darr, and shortstop Desi Relaford. Relaford and first baseman Joe Vitiello also hit home runs.

11 **1971**—Pitcher Dave Roberts outduels Tom Seaver of the New York Mets, 1-0, in 12 innings before 10,628 fans at San Diego Stadium.

11 **1982**—Catcher Terry Kennedy singles in the fifth inning for the Padres' lone hit off pitcher Nolan Ryan in a 3-0 loss to the Houston Astros at San Diego Stadium.

11 **1987**—Outfielder Tony Gwynn becomes the first Padre to get five hits in a game twice in the same season in a 7-6 victory over the Atlanta Braves at Atlanta-Fulton County Stadium.

11 **1991**—Pitcher Ricky Bones hurls the largest shutout victory in franchise history, 13-0, over the Cincinnati Reds at Jack Murphy Stadium.

11 **1994** —The Padres defeat the Houston Astros, 8-6, at the Astrodome in their last game before a season-ending strike. Outfielder Tony Gwynn wins his fifth National League batting title with a .394 average, the highest major-league mark since outfielder Ted Williams batted .406 in 1941, and leads the National League with 165 hits.

11 **2001**—Tony Gwynn makes his final right field appearance and hits his last home run, a two-run clout off pitcher Joe Beimel in the sixth inning, in a 5-2 victory over the Pittsburgh Pirates at PNC Park.

12 **1984**—The Padres lose to the Atlanta Braves, 5-3, and engage in two brawls at Atlanta-Fulton County Stadium, resulting in a 10-game suspension for manager Dick Williams. The National League also fines seven Padre players and two Padre coaches.

12 **1998**—Pitcher Andy Ashby outduels pitcher Greg Maddux, as the Padres defeat the Atlanta Braves, 5-1, for the second consecutive time at Qualcomm Stadium.

12 **2001**—First baseman Ryan Klesko steals second base in a 7-6 loss to the Pittsburgh Pirates at PNC Park, becoming the first Padre to have two seasons with 20 home runs and 20 stolen bases.

13 **1968**—The San Diego city council agrees to let the Padres use San Diego Stadium for 20 years for major-league baseball and set up a corporation to manage, operate, and promote the $28 million stadium.

13 **1969**—The Padres turn their first triple play in franchise history in the first inning in a 4-2 loss to the Chicago Cubs at San Diego Stadium. Outfielder Billy Williams hit into the triple play involving pitcher Joe Niekro and shortstop Tommy Dean. Second baseman Roberto Peña becomes the first Padre ever thrown out of a game by an umpire. Peña argues with umpire Chris Pelekoudas after being called out attempting to steal second base.

13 **1970**—The Padres defeat the St. Louis Cardinals, 9-7, at Busch Stadium, but trail the Cincinnati Reds by 32 1/2 games and suffer their earliest elimination from the National League pennant race in franchise history.

13 **1996**—Outfielder Tony Gwynn becomes the 71st major leaguer to attain 2,500 hits, singling against reliever Hector Carrasco in a 10-4 loss to the Cincinnati Reds at Riverfront Stadium.

13 **1997**—The Padres trade outfielder Rickey Henderson to the Anaheim Angels for pitchers Ryan Hancock and Stevenson Agosto and third baseman George Arias. Outfielder Mark

Sweeney breaks up pitcher Mike Morgan's bid for a perfect game with a seventh-inning single for the Padres' lone hit in a 2-0 loss to the Cincinnati Reds at Qualcomm Stadium.

14 **1991**—First baseman Fred McGriff becomes the fourth National Leaguer to belt grand slam home run in consecutive games, connecting in the first inning off pitcher Jim Deshaies in a 4-1 victory over the Houston Astros at Jack Murphy Stadium.

14 **1992**—Third baseman Gary Sheffield clouts his second grand slam home run of the season off pitcher Chris Hammond, lifting the Padres to a 5-1 triumph over the Cincinnati Reds at Riverfront Stadium.

15 **1980**—The Padres play their longest game in franchise history, losing, 3-1, to the Houston Astros in a 6-hour, 17-minute, 20-inning contest at San Diego Stadium.

15 **1990**—The Montreal Expos defeat the Padres, 5-3, in 17 innings at Jack Murphy Stadium.

15 **1997**—Outfielder Greg Vaughn becomes the first player to clout two home runs into the second deck in left field at Qualcomm Stadium in the same season in a 5-1 victory over the Chicago Cubs.

15 **2001**—Reliever Trevor Hoffman becomes the 14th major leaguer to record 300 career saves, hurling a perfect ninth inning to preserve a 2-1 win for pitcher Kevin Jarvis over the visiting New York Mets. He becomes the second fastest and third youngest to attain 300 career saves. Reliever Dennis Eckersley reached 300 saves in 499 appearances, 54 fewer than Hoffman.

16 **1973**—The California Supreme Court denies the city of San Diego's petition for a hearing to block the Padres' move to Washington, D.C.

16 **1978**—Pitcher Bob Owchinko picks off catcher John Stearns and first baseman Willie Montanez at second base in the fourth inning in a 2-1 triumph over the New York Mets at Shea Stadium.

16 **1991**—Third baseman Jack Howell clouts an inside-the-park home run in a 3-2 loss to the Atlanta Braves at Jack Murphy Stadium.

16 **1996**—The Padres defeat the New York Mets, 15-10, at Monterrey, Mexico in the first regular-season major-league game played outside the United States or Canada. Pitcher Fernando Valenzuela, a Mexican native, picks up the win. Outfielder Greg Vaughn clouts a grand slam home run in the sixth inning off pitcher Derek Wallace.

16 **1998**—In a 4-0 triumph in the first game of a doubleheader at Qualcomm Stadium, pitcher Kevin Brown hurls a no-hitter until outfielder Jeromy Burnitz singles in the seventh inning for the lone Milwaukee Brewers hit.

16 **2001**—Reliever Trevor Hoffman becomes the first major-league pitcher to record seven 30-save seasons, hurling a perfect ninth inning to preserve a 6-5 home victory over the New York Mets.

18 **1970**—Third baseman Ed Spiezio's grand slam home run in the sixth inning off pitcher Roberto Rodriguez highlights an 11-3 romp over the Chicago Cubs at Wrigley Field.

18 **1972**—The Padres sponsor their first Old-Timers' game before losing to the Pittsburgh Pirates, 4-2, drawing 30,610 people to San Diego Stadium.

18 **1996**—Despite dehydration, third baseman Ken Caminiti headlines an 8-0 victory over the New York Mets with two home runs in Monterrey, Mexico.

18 **2001**—Closer Trevor Hoffman notches his 300th save as a Padre, blanking the visiting Montreal Expos for 1.1 innings to preserve a 4-3 victory.

19 **1969**—Pitcher Al Santorini becomes the first Padre hurler to belt a home run in a 5-4 victory over the Montreal Expos at Jarry Park.

19 **1996**—Ken Caminiti clouts his second grand slam home run in three days, connecting in the first inning off pitcher Pedro Martinez in a 7-3 triumph over the Montreal Expos at Jack Murphy Stadium.

20 **1944**—Third baseman Graig Nettles is born in San Diego, California.

20 **1967**—Pitcher Andy Benes is born in Evansville, Indiana. The dedication ceremonies are held for San Diego Stadium.

20 **1998**—Pitcher Kevin Brown hurls his second shutout of the month, blanking the Atlanta Braves, 2-0, at Turner Field.

21 **1977**—Outfielder Dave Kingman belts his second grand slam home run of the month in the first inning off pitcher Tom Underwood.

Pitcher Bob Owchinko blanks the St. Louis Cardinals, 7-0, at Busch Stadium.

21 **1980**—The Philadelphia Phillies defeat the Padres, 9-8, in 17 innings at Veterans Stadium.

22 **1977**—Catcher Gene Tenace hits a home run for the Padres' lone run in a 1-0 victory over the Pittsburgh Pirates at Three Rivers Stadium. Pitcher Bob Shirley blanks the Pirates.

22 **1978**—Outfielder Jerry Turner sets a franchise record by belting his fifth pinch-hit home run of the season in the sixth inning with two runners on base against pitcher Rawley Eastwick in a 5-3 loss to the Philadelphia Phillies at Veterans Stadium. Outfielder Johnny Frederick of the Brooklyn Dodgers holds the major-league record with six pinch-hit home runs in 1932.

22 **1995**—Outfielder Tony Gwynn belts a grand slam home run in the fifth inning off pitcher Tommy Greene to spark a 5-3 victory over the Philadelphia Phillies at Veterans Stadium.

22 **2000**—Third baseman Phil Nevin and outfielder John Mabry belt consecutive second deck home runs in the third inning at Qualcomm Stadium in a 16-1 rout over the New York Mets. Mabry becomes the first player to clout a homer in the second deck in right field, built in the 1997 stadium expansion. Second baseman Damian Jackson records a career-high five RBIs and makes three hits, including his first grand slam home run in the second inning. His homer, the 141st major-league grand slam of the season, ties the major-league record. The Padres match the club record for the largest margin of victory and attain their highest run total since June 7, 1998.

23 **1979**—Commissioner Bowie Kuhn fines owner-chairman-president Ray Kroc an unprecedented $100,000 for tampering when Kroc announces publicly that he would seek both second baseman Joe Morgan of the Cincinnati Reds and third baseman Graig Nettles of the New York Yankees if they become free agents. Kroc resigns as president and assigns daily club operations to his son-in-law Ballard Smith.

23 **1982**—Outfielder Dave Edwards hits into a triple play in the first inning in a 5-3 triumph over the Pittsburgh Pirates at Three Rivers Stadium.

23 **1993**—Outfielder Phil Plantier clouts a grand slam home run in the first inning off pitcher Donovan Osborne in a 7-5 victory over the St. Louis Cardinals at Jack Murphy Stadium.

24 **1981**—Outfielder Jerry Turner extends his club record with his ninth pinch-hit home run, connecting in the fifth inning off Mike Krukow in a 9-8 loss to the Chicago Cubs at Wrigley Field.

24 **1993**—The Padres belt five home runs in trouncing the St. Louis Cardinals, 17-4, at Busch Stadium, tying club records for most home runs and second largest run production.

25 **1946**—Pitcher Rollie Fingers is born in Steubenville, Ohio.

25 **1979**—The Pittsburgh Pirates edge the Padres, 4-3, in a 19-inning, 6-hour, 12-minute contest, the second longest in San Diego history.

25 **1987**—Catcher Benito Santiago begins his 34-game consecutive hitting streak in a 5-1 victory over the Montreal Expos at Jack Murphy Stadium.

25 **1991**—Outfielder Darrin Jackson belts the fourth Padre grand slam home run of the month in the sixth inning off pitcher Bob Scanlan in a 12-9 triumph over the Chicago Cubs at Wrigley Field.

26 **1980**—Outfielder Jerry Mumphrey makes five hits in an 8-6, 18-inning victory over the New York Mets at Shea Stadium.

26 **1995**—Outfielder Melvin Nieves clouts his second grand slam home run of the month off pitcher Doug Henry in the ninth inning in a 7-6 loss to the New York Mets at Shea Stadium.

28 **1996**—Third baseman Ken Caminiti sets a National League record by homering from both sides of the plate for seventh time in his major-league career in a 3-2, 12-inning win over the New York Mets at Shea Stadium.

28 **1998**—The Padres defeat the Montreal Expos, 12-9, at Qualcomm Stadium, stretching their lead in the National League West to a club-record 16 games.

29 **1967**—The final step toward a major-league baseball franchise is taken when San Diego Stadium is formally dedicated with an

exhibition football game between the San Diego Chargers and Detroit Lions.

28 **2000**—Third baseman Phil Nevin belts a three-run homer in the eighth inning and a three-run double in the ninth inning, tying a career-high with six RBIs in an 8-2 triumph over the Chicago Cubs at Wrigley Field.

29 **1968**—The Padres name Preston Gomez, a Los Angeles Dodgers coach, as their first manager.

29 **1974**—Catcher Fred Kendall singles in the eighth inning for the Padres' lone hit off pitcher John Curtis in a 3-1 loss to the St. Louis Cardinals at San Diego Stadium.

29 **1977**—Lou Brock of the St. Louis Cardinals steals second base in the seventh inning for his second stolen base of the night and the 893rd of his career in a 4-3 Padre victory at Jack Murphy Stadium, breaking Ty Cobb's major-league record for most career stolen bases.

29 **1986**—Owner Joan Kroc suspends relief pitcher Goose Gossage indefinitely without pay for making comments critical of management.

29 **1988**—Outfielder Tony Gwynn doubles in the fourth inning for the Padres' only hit off pitcher David Cone in a 6-0 loss to the New York Mets at Shea Stadium.

29 **1997**—The California Angels defeat the Padres, 3-1, before 60,230 fans at Jack Murphy Stadium, the year's largest major-league crowd.

29 **2001**—The Padres lose a 16-14 slugfest to the St. Louis Cardinals, combining for the most runs in a game in Busch Stadium history. First baseman Ryan Klesko homers twice, doubles twice, and singles once with five RBIs, while third baseman Phil Nevin homers and singles twice with three RBIs to join Klesko in the 100 RBI club.

29 **2000**—Third baseman Phil Nevin reaches base safely with a hit or walk for the 49th consecutive game beginning July 3rd in a 7-6, 13-inning loss to the Chicago Cubs at Wrigley Field. He singles three times with two RBIs, but goes hitless in four plate appearances in his next game.

30 **1967**—The dedication ceremonies are held for San Diego Stadium.

30 **1971**—Pitcher Clay Kirby ties the club record for most season strikeouts with 185 in a 4-3 victory over the Cincinnati Reds at Riverfront Stadium.

31 **1973**—The city of San Diego demands $12 million from the Padres for breaking the lease agreement for using San Diego Stadium. The city bases the amount on income expected by the city from the Padres over the next 15 years plus money the city would lose in taxes with the move of the team.

31 **1992**—Third baseman Gary Sheffield wins National League Player of the Month honors. The Padres trade relief pitcher Craig Lefferts to the Baltimore Orioles.

31 **1993**—Outfielder Tony Gwynn wins National League Player of the Month honors for the fourth time.

SEPTEMBER

1 **1970**—The Padres trade pitcher Ron Herbel to the New York Mets for infielder Rod Gaspar. Herbel, who appears in 64 games before being swapped, leads the National League with 76 appearances altogether and becomes the first Padre to pace the senior circuit in any category.

1 **1997**—Outfielder Steve Finley clouts his second grand slam home run of the season in the ninth inning off pitcher Bobby Ayala in a 9-6 loss to the Seattle Mariners at The Kingdome.

1 **2001**—Outfielder Ray Lankford clouts a grand slam home run off pitcher Byung-Hyun Kim to spark a six-run rally in the eighth inning in a come-from-behind 7-5 victory over the visiting Arizona Diamondbacks.

2 **1972**—Pitcher Milt Pappas of the Chicago Cubs hurls an 8-0 no-hitter against the Padres at Wrigley Field.

2 **1984**—Outfielder Carmelo Martinez hits an inside-the-park home run in a 3-2, 12-inning loss to the New York Mets at Shea Stadium.

2 **2001**—First baseman Ryan Klesko hits a game-winning home run in the 13th inning off pitcher Byung-Hyun Kim to give the Padres a 1-0 home victory over the Arizona Diamondbacks. Arizona pitcher Randy Johnson holds Padre batters hitless until the sixth inning and strikes out 14 batters in 7.1 innings.

3 **1936**—Manager Steve Boros is born in Flint, Michigan.

3 **1979**—Pitcher Gaylord Perry blanks the San Francisco Giants, 3-0, at San Diego Stadium, and is the oldest Padre to appear in a major-league game at 40 years, 11 months, 18 days. Infielder Tim Flannery singles and knocks in a run in his major-league debut.

3 **1989**—Catcher Benito Santiago's seventh-inning grand slam home run off pitcher Jeff Parrett lifts the Padres to a 9-5 victory over the Philadelphia Phillies at Jack Murphy Stadium.

3 **2001**—Pitcher Bud Smith of the visiting St. Louis Cardinals becomes the sixteenth rookie in modern major-league history to hurl a no-hitter and the second pitcher to no-hit San Diego in 2001 in a 4-0 masterpiece over the Padres. He becomes the first rookie to throw a no-hitter since pitcher Jose Jimenez of the Cardinals no-hit the Arizona Diamondbacks in June 1999. Smith walks four, including outfielder Rickey Henderson twice, and strikes out seven.

4 **1970**—Pitcher Mike Corkins belts a grand slam home run off pitcher Jim Merritt in the fourth inning, as the Padres trounce the Cincinnati Reds, 15-2, at Riverfront Stadium.

4 **1971**—Pitcher Jay Franklin becomes the youngest Padre to appear in a major-league game at age 18 years, 6 months, 19 days in an 11-7 loss to the Atlanta Braves at San Diego Stadium. His battery mate is 19-year-old catcher Mike Ivie. Franklin makes two more appearances for the Padres that season, but never hurls in the major leagues again. Ivie develops a mental block against catching after just six games and spends the next two seasons in the minor leagues learning to play first base.

4 **1981**—Outfielder Alan Wiggins makes his major-league debut as a pinch runner in a 5-4 triumph over the Pittsburgh Pirates at Jack Murphy Stadium.

4 **1989**—First baseman Jack Clark clouts the second Padre grand slam homer in two days, connecting in the seventh inning off pitcher Mark Eichorn in a 10-9 triumph over the Atlanta Braves at Atlanta-Fulton County Stadium.

4 **2000**—Tom Davey becomes the 28th different pitcher used by the Padres, hurling the eighth inning for the victory in a 4-3 home triumph over the Milwaukee Brewers. The Padres break the National League record for most pitchers used in a season, formerly shared by the 1967 New York Mets and 1995 Florida Marlins.

5 **1979**—Catcher Bill Fahey makes five hits in a 4-3, 10-inning loss to the Houston Astros at the Astrodome.

5 **1984**—Outfielder Kevin McReynolds sets a franchise record with five singles in a 15-11 triumph over the Cincinnati Reds at Jack Murphy Stadium.

5 **1991**—First baseman Jack Clark hits into a triple play in the second inning in a 3-1 victory over the St. Louis Cardinals at Jack Murphy Stadium.

5 **1997**—Pitcher Andy Ashby loses his bid for the first no-hitter in Padres history when outfielder Kenny Lofton of the Atlanta Braves leads off the ninth inning with a single to right field on a 3-2 pitch.

5 **2001**—San Diego sends the minimum 27 batters to the plate in being shut out a league-leading 14th time in a 2-0 loss to the visiting St. Louis Cardinals. Pitcher Woody Williams of the Cardinals returns to San Diego to hurl a two-hitter, fanning six and not allowing a Padre to reach base until shortstop D'Angelo Jimenez singles in the seventh inning.

6 **1945**—President and chief executive officer Larry Lucchino is born in Pittsburgh, Pennsylvania.

6 **1983**—The Padres triumph for the sixth consecutive time at Dodger Stadium with an 8-3 win over the Los Angeles Dodgers.

6 **1984**—Pitcher Eric Show homers for the third time that season in a 10-3 loss to the Cincinnati Reds at Jack Murphy Stadium.

7 **1969**—The Padres defeat the Los Angeles Dodgers, 4-2, to complete their first four-game series sweep at San Diego Stadium in franchise history.

7 **1970**—First baseman Ramon Webster clouts the second Padre grand slam home run in four

days in the ninth inning off pitcher Ken Forsch in a 10-5 loss to the Houston Astros in the first game of a doubleheader at San Diego Stadium.

7 **1971**—Outfielder Leron Lee becomes the first Padre to make five hits in a major-league game, doubling twice with four runs scored in an 8-7 triumph over the Cincinnati Reds at San Diego Stadium.

7 **1972**—First baseman Nate Colbert surpasses 100 RBIs with his second grand slam home runs of the season in the sixth inning off pitcher Jack Billingham in a 5-1 victory over the Cincinnati Reds at San Diego Stadium.

7 **1974**—Pinch-hitter Enzo Hernandez singles twice in the same inning in an 8-4 win over the Houston Astros at the Astrodome.

7 **1992**—Outfielder Jerald Clark clouts a fourth-inning grand slam home run off pitcher Bud Black in a 5-4 triumph over the San Francisco Giants at Candlestick Park.

7 **2001**—Closer Trevor Hoffman records his 26th consecutive save, hurling 1.1 innings to preserve a 4-3 road triumph over the Arizona Diamondbacks. The streak ends the next day when he blows a save against Arizona.

7 **2000**—Third baseman Gabe Alvarez becomes the 54th different player used by the Padres, tying the National League record shared by the 1967 New York Mets and 1996 Philadelphia Phillies, in a 13-0 loss to the San Francisco Giants at Pacific Bell Stadium.

8 **1992**—The Padres set a franchise record with eight doubles in a 6-5, 16-inning loss to the San Francisco Giants at Candlestick Park. Outfielder Tony Gwynn makes five hits, doubling twice.

9 **1970**—Pitcher Joey Hamilton is born in Statesboro, Georgia.

9 **1993**—Second baseman Luis Lopez singles in the eighth inning off pitcher Mark Wohlers for his first major-league hit and the Padres' lone safety in a 1-0, 10-inning loss to the Atlanta Braves at Jack Murphy Stadium.

10 **1972**—Pitcher Mike Corkins hurls his second consecutive 1-0 shutout, blanking the Atlanta Braves at San Diego Stadium.

10 **1992**—Outfielder Jerald Clark steals home in the seventh inning in a 3-1 victory over the Los Angeles Dodgers at Dodger Stadium.

10 **1998**—Pitcher Kevin Brown becomes the Padres' single-season strikeout king with 232, fanning Trenidad Hubbard in the fourth inning in a 4-3 loss to the Los Angeles Dodgers. He finishes the season with 257 strikeouts, ranking second in the National League.

11 **1973**—The Padres draw only 1,413 fans in a 4-2 loss to the Houston Astros at San Diego Stadium.

11 **1985**—Pitcher Eric Show surrenders first baseman Pete Rose's historic record-breaking 4,192nd hit in a 3-2 setback to the Cincinnati Reds at Riverfront Stadium.

11 **1988**—Outfielder Marvell Wynne's second-inning grand slam homer off pitcher Charlie Puleo highlights an 8-2 win over the Atlanta Braves at Jack Murphy Stadium.

11 **1990**—Shortstop Garry Templeton hits a sixth-inning grand slam home run off pitcher Danny Darwin to give the Padres a 7-3 victory over the Houston Astros at Jack Murphy Stadium.

11 **1991**—Pitchers Kent Mercker, Mark Wohlers, and Alejandro Peña of the Atlanta Braves blank the Padres, 1-0, on a no-hitter at Atlanta-Fulton County Stadium.

11 **1996**—Third baseman Ken Caminiti breaks his own major-league records by homering from both sides of the plate for the fourth time that season in an 8-7 triumph over the Pittsburgh Pirates at Jack Murphy Stadium.

11 **2001**—The terrorist attacks upon the World Trade Center in New York City and the Pentagon in Washington, D.C. caused postponement of the Padres' home game with the Los Angeles Dodgers and five subsequent home games.

11 **2000**—The Padres steal six bases in a 7-2 home victory over the Colorado Rockies. Outfielders Eric Owens and Mike Darr steal two bases apiece, the latter pilfering home in the seventh inning. Second baseman Damian Jackson and first baseman Ryan Klesko also record stolen bases.

12 **1956**—Pitcher Mark Thurmond is born in Houston, Texas.

12 **1998**—The Padres rally from a 7-0, fifth-inning deficit to defeat the Los Angeles

Dodgers, 8-7, before 60,823 people at Qualcomm Stadium, clinching their second National League West title in three years.

13 **1971**—Pitcher Clay Kirby hurls a no-hitter until catcher John Edwards singles in the eighth inning in a 3-2 loss to the Houston Astros at the Astrodome.

13 **1982**—Outfielder Joe Lefebvre ties a franchise record for most hits in a single game with six and becomes the first National Leaguer in five years to get six hits in the same contest in a 4-3, 16-inning loss to the Los Angeles Dodgers at Dodger Stadium. Outfielder Gene Richards makes five hits in the same game for the second time that season.

13 **1991**—Catcher Benito Santiago makes five hits in a 13-2 victory over the San Francisco Giants at Candlestick Park.

14 **1924**—Announcer and former manager Jerry Coleman is born in San Jose, California.

15 **1938**—Pitcher Gaylord Perry is born in Williamston, North Carolina.

15 **1972**—Pitcher Fred Norman establishes club records for shutouts in a season with six and strikeouts in a nine-inning game with 15 in a 1-0 victory over the Cincinnati Reds at Riverfront Stadium. The 28 strikeouts by both clubs in that game set a then National League record.

15 **2000**—Pitcher Trevor Hoffman becomes the third major-league closer to have three consecutive 40-save seasons in a 5-4 home victory over the San Francisco Giants. Dennis Eckersley and Lee Smith are the only other closers to post three straight 40-save seasons. Hoffman joins Eckersley and John Wettelund as the only relievers to have four 40-save seasons.

16 **1986**—The Padres set a club record by using eight pinch-hitters in a 4-1 loss to the San Francisco Giants at Jack Murphy Stadium.

16 **1996**—Pitcher Fernando Valenzuela wins his eighth consecutive decision, 5-4, over the St. Louis Cardinals at Busch Stadium, ending the latter's eight-game winning streak.

17 **1975**—The Padres trade pitcher Gary Ross to the California Angels for infielders Bobby Valentine and Rudi Meoli.

17 **1987**—Shortstop Garry Templeton hits the Padres' first inside-the-park home run in over three years in a 7-1 win over the Atlanta Braves at Jack Murphy Stadium.

17 **1993**—Outfielder Jarvis Brown's sixth-inning bunt single is the Padres' sole hit off Pete Harnisch in a 3-0 loss to the Houston Astros at the Astrodome.

17 **1995**—Third baseman Ken Caminiti belts home runs from both sides of the plate for the second consecutive game in an 11-3 victory over the Chicago Cubs. Pitcher Fernando Valenzuela clouts his second home run of the season.

17 **2001**—The Padres play their first game since the terrorist attacks, defeating the Los Angeles Dodgers, 6-4, at Dodger Stadium. Jason Middlebrook allows just two hits in six innings for his first major-league victory in his major-league debut.

18 **1971**—Pitcher Clay Kirby hurls a no-hitter until first baseman Willie McCovey homers in the eighth inning for the lone San Francisco Giants hit in a 2-1 triumph at Candlestick Park.

18 **1974**—The Padres surpass one million fans in attendance for the first time in a 6-5 victory over the Cincinnati Reds at San Diego Stadium.

19 **1973**—National League owners delay a vote for 30 days on the proposed Padre move to Washington, D.C.

19 **1990**—Catcher Benito Santiago clouts a grand slam home run in the sixth inning off pitcher Darrin Holmes in a 9-4 win over the Los Angeles Dodgers at Dodger Stadium.

19 **1995**—Third baseman Ken Caminiti homers from both sides of the plate for the third time in four games and becomes the first major-league player to accomplish that three times in a season in a 15-4 rout over the Colorado Rockies at Jack Murphy Stadium.

19 **2001**—The Padres defeat the Los Angeles Dodgers, 4-3, in 10 innings, recording their first three-game sweep at Dodger Stadium since 1983. Outfielder Bubba Trammell hits a solo home run in the ninth inning and singles twice with three RBIs. Pinch hitter Tony Gwynn singles in the tenth inning for his final

hit at Dodger Stadium, the park of his boyhood.

20 **1984**—Pitcher Tim Lollar belts a three-run homer to help the Padres edge the San Francisco Giants, 5-4, at Jack Murphy Stadium for a share of the National League Western Division title. The Padres clinch their first Western Division crown three hours later when the Los Angeles Dodgers defeat the Houston Astros.

20 **1986**—Outfielder Tony Gwynn ties a franchise record by stealing five bases in a 10-6 loss to the Houston Astros at the Astrodome.

20 **2000**—Outfielder John Mabry, third baseman Dave Magadan, and catcher Ben Davis clout home runs to help the Padres defeat the Colorado Rockies, 15-11, at Coors Field. Magadan and outfielder Mike Darr record four RBIs apiece, while Mabry, Darr, and shortstop Desi Relaford each contribute three hits. Pitcher Buddy Carlyle relieves in the eighth inning to become the 55th different player used by the Padres, breaking the National League record formerly held by the 1967 New York Mets and 1996 Philadelphia Phillies.

21 **1986**—Pitcher Jimmy Jones blanks the Houston Astros, 5-0, on a one-hitter in his major-league debut at the Astrodome. Pitcher Bob Knepper triples in the third inning for the lone Astros hit.

21 **1988**—Catcher Benito Santiago clouts a grand slam home run off pitcher Rick Horton in the second inning of the first game of a doubleheader, as the Padres defeat the Los Angeles Dodgers, 9-3, at Dodger Stadium.

21 **1990**—The Padres fire general manager Jack McKeon.

22 **1969**—Willie Mays of the San Francisco Giants joins Babe Ruth as the then only major leaguers to clout 600 career home runs, connecting with a two-run pinch-hit homer off Mike Corkins in the seventh inning for a 4-2 Giants victory at San Diego Stadium.

22 **1978**—The Padres record 20 hits to set a franchise record for a nine-inning game in a 12-3 romp over the Los Angeles Dodgers at Dodger Stadium.

22 **1979**—The Padres steal six bases, including three by third baseman Paul Dade, in a 10-8 triumph over the Los Angeles Dodgers at San Diego Stadium.

22 **1986**—The Padres use a franchise record 22 players in a 9-8 loss to the Atlanta Braves at Atlanta-Fulton County Stadium.

22 **1996**—Third baseman Ken Caminiti ties first baseman Nate Colbert's team record for most home runs in a season with 38 in a 4-2 triumph over the Los Angeles Dodgers at Jack Murphy Stadium. The Padres reach the two-million attendance mark for the third time in franchise history. The four-game home series with Los Angeles from September 19-22 draws a club-record 197,225 fans, including the first three non-opening day advance sellouts in club history.

22 **2001**—Pinch hitter Tony Gwynn singles in two runs in the seventh inning and pinch hitter Mike Darr clouts a solo game-winning home run in the 10th inning to defeat the visiting San Francisco Giants, 4-3.

23 **1975**—Pitcher Randy Jones becomes the first 20-game winner in Padre history, defeating the Los Angeles Dodgers, 6-4, at San Diego Stadium.

23 **1980**—The Padres appoint Jack McKeon general manager and vice-president of baseball operations.

23 **1992**—Jim Riggleman replaces Greg Riddoch as Padre manager.

24 **1969**—The Padres defeat the San Francisco Giants, 3-2, at San Diego Stadium, ending their first major-league home season with 512,970 paid attendance.

24 **1970**—Pitcher Dave Roberts becomes the first Padre to hurl two consecutive shutouts, blanking the Atlanta Braves, 5-0, at Atlanta-Fulton County Stadium.

24 **1971**—The Padres play their longest home game in franchise history, losing the first game of a doubleheader, 2-1, in 21 innings to the Houston Astros. The doubleheader ends at 2:29 a.m. Pitcher Clay Kirby sets a club record by striking out 15 Astros in the first 15 innings.

24 **1972**—Pitcher Clay Kirby becomes the club's first 15-game winner, triumphing over the Atlanta Braves, 4-1, at Atlanta-Fulton County Stadium.

24 **1977**—Pitcher Randy Jones sets a club record with his 22nd victory in a 6-4 triumph over the Atlanta Braves at Atlanta-Fulton County Stadium.

24 **1980**—Jack Murphy, sports editor and columnist for *The San Diego Union*, dies of cancer at age 57 in San Diego. After his death, San Diego Stadium is renamed Jack Murphy Stadium.

24 **1987**—First baseman John Kruk clouts an inside-the-park home run to left field in a 5-4 loss to the Cincinnati Reds at Riverfront Stadium.

24 **1988**—During Fan Appreciation Night, president Chub Feeney makes a one-finger obscene gesture from his private box high above the field to two fans parading around Jack Murphy Stadium with a sign imploring owner Joan Kroc to "Scrub Chub."

24 **2001**—Second baseman Cesar Crespo homers twice, doubles, and singles, while outfielder Rickey Henderson records four hits and outfielder Ray Lankford and catcher Ben Davis make three hits each in a 15-11 setback to the Colorado Rockies at Coors Field.

25 **1974**—Outfielder John Scott singles off pitcher Mike Caldwell in an 8-6 victory over the San Francisco Giants for his only major-league hit in 24 at bats.

25 **1988**—Chub Feeney resigns as Padres' president.

25 **1991**—Pitcher Andy Benes wins his tenth consecutive decision in an 8-2 triumph over the Los Angeles Dodgers at Jack Murphy Stadium.

25 **2001**—Pitcher Trevor Hoffman becomes the first major-league reliever to notch four consecutive 40-save seasons and five overall in an 8-7 squeaker over the Colorado Rockies at Coors Field. He surrenders two hits and two earned runs in his ninth-inning appearance.

26 **1974**—Although losing his final start, pitcher Randy Jones ends the season leading the National League with a 2.24 ERA.

26 **1978**—Pitcher Gaylord Perry wins his 21st game in a 4-1 triumph over the San Francisco Giants at Candlestick Park.

26 **1980**—Ozzie Smith sets a single-season major-league record for most assists by a shortstop with 602 in a 3-2 triumph over the Los Angeles Dodgers at San Diego Stadium.

26 **1995**—Randy Smith resigns as Padres' general manager.

27 **1985**—Pitcher Eric Show hits his fourth career home run in a 10-1 romp over the Atlanta Braves at Atlanta-Fulton County Stadium.

27 **1996**—Third baseman Ken Caminiti extends a franchise record with his 40th home run in a 5-3, 10-inning victory over the Los Angeles Dodgers at Dodger Stadium to stave off elimination.

27 **1998**—The Padres defeat the Arizona Diamondbacks, 3-2, at Bank One Ballpark for their club-record 98th regular-season victory. In the season finale, outfielder Greg Vaughn becomes the first Padre and the 28th major leaguer to hit 50 home runs in a season. He connects off pitcher Aaron Small in his final season at-bat, giving him 119 RBIs for the season. Reliever Trevor Hoffman works a perfect ninth inning to record his 53rd save, matching Randy Myers's 1993 National League record for the second-highest season total in major-league history.

27 **2001**—Third baseman Phil Nevin homers twice, including a grand slam off pitcher Kane Davis in the second inning, and doubles with seven RBIs in a 13-9 loss to the Colorado Rockies at Coors Field. Shortstop D'Angelo Jimenez also doubles and singles twice with one RBI.

28 **1979**—Pitcher Eric Rasmussen hurls a one-hitter against the San Francisco Giants in a 2-0 victory at Candlestick Park. Third baseman Darrell Evans singles in the second inning for the lone Giants hit.

28 **1997**—Outfielder Tony Gwynn wins his eighth National League batting title with a .372 average, tying Honus Wagner's National League record. His 220 hits and 49 doubles establish Padres records. The Padres set club records with 795 runs scored, 1,519 hits, 761 RBIs, 2,282 total bases, and 604 bases on balls.

29 **1953**—Outfielder Gene Richards is born in Monticello, South Carolina.

29 **1957**—Infielder Tim Flannery is born in Tulsa, Oklahoma. Pitcher Craig Lefferts is born in Munich, Germany.

29 **1971**—Pitcher Clay Kirby extends his club season record for most strikeouts with his 231st in a 4-1 triumph over the San Francisco Giants at San Diego Stadium.

29 **1973**—The Los Angeles Dodgers edge the Padres, 3-2, before 14,846 people at San Diego Stadium in what many expected would be the last Padres game in San Diego. In the fourth inning, infielder Dave Roberts becomes the first Padre to hit an inside-the-park home run.

29 **1976**—Infielder Doug Rader in the first inning hits the last grand slam home run of the National League season in a 6-1 triumph over the Cincinnati Reds at San Diego Stadium.

29 **1977**—Reliever Rollie Fingers ties a National League record with his 37th save in a 3-1 victory over the Los Angeles Dodgers at San Diego Stadium.

29 **1992**—Third baseman Gary Sheffield misses the rest of the season with a broken right index finger, but wins the National League batting title with a .330 average and finishes third with a career-high 33 home runs.

29 **1996**—Outfielder Chris Gwynn breaks a scoreless tie with a two-run pinch-hit double in the eleventh inning to give the Padres a 2-0 victory and three-game sweep over the Los Angeles Dodgers at Dodger Stadium for their second National League West crown in club history. The Padres compile their second best record in franchise history with a 91-71 mark and set a club record by winning 46 of 81 road games. Outfielder Tony Gwynn wins his seventh National League batting title with a .353 batting average, tying him with Hall of Famers Rogers Hornsby, Stan Musial, and Rod Carew for third on the all-time list.

29 **1998**—Pitcher Kevin Brown fans a Division Series-record 16 Houston Astros and strikes out every Houston batter at least once in a 2-1 victory at the Astrodome, outdueling Randy Johnson.

30 **1970**—Pat Dobson becomes the first Padre hurler to win 14 games in a season with a 2-1 victory over the Los Angeles Dodgers at San Diego Stadium.

30 **1971**—Pitcher Dave Roberts loses, 5-1, to the San Francisco Giants at San Diego Stadium, but finishes second in the National League in ERA with 2.10.

30 **1978**—Gaylord Perry wins National League Pitcher of the Month honors.

30 **1979**—The Padres fire manager Roger Craig. Veteran Whitey Wietelmann retires as bullpen coach. Outfielder Dave Winfield wins the National League RBI title with 118.

30 **1980**—The Padres lead the major leagues in stolen bases with 239, as outfielder Gene Richards, shortstop Ozzie Smith, and outfielder Jerry Mumphrey become the first three teammates to steal 50 bases the same season. Padre runners swipe second base 221 times, third base 15 times, and home three times.

30 **1984**—The Padres lose, 4-3, to the Atlanta Braves at Atlanta-Fulton County Stadium, but finish the season with a franchise best 92-70 mark. Outfielder Tony Gwynn wins his first National League batting title with a .351 average and leads the National League with 213 hits.

30 **2000**—Infielder Xavier Nady becomes the 56th different player used by the Padres, tying the major-league record set by the 1915 Philadelphia Athletics. He singles as a pinch-hitter in the seventh inning in a 10-2 home loss to the Los Angeles Dodgers.

OCTOBER

1 **1970**—Outfielder Cito Gaston ends the campaign with a .318 batting average, making him the first Padre to bat over .300 in a season. The team ends the season with a club-record 172 home runs.

1 **1973**—Outfielder John Grubb ends an outstanding rookie season, setting a Padre record for highest batting average by a lefthander (.311) and fielding brilliantly in center field.

1 **1978**—The Padres defeat the Los Angeles Dodgers, 4-3, at San Diego Stadium, earning their first winning record with an 84-78 mark. Pitcher Gaylord Perry strikes out outfielder Joe Simpson for his 3,000th career strikeout.

Outfielders Dave Winfield and Gene Richards compile .308 batting averages, giving the Padres two starters above .300 for the first time in franchise history. Padre relievers lead the National League with 60 saves. Padre pitchers allow fewer home runs than any team since 1968.

1 **1979**—The Padres name broadcaster Jerry Coleman as manager.

1 **1981**—Pitcher Fred Kuhaulua bests pitcher Fernando Valenzuela of the Los Angeles Dodgers, 1-0, at Dodger Stadium.

1 **1989**—Outfielder Tony Gwynn who made six hits in his final eight at-bats, edges first baseman Will Clark for his fourth National League batting title with a .336 average and leads the National League with 203 hits. Relief pitcher Mark Davis paces the National League with his then club record 44 saves.

1 **1995**—Outfielder Tony Gwynn wins his sixth National League batting title with a .368 average, ties for the National League lead with 197 hits and 33 doubles, and leads the National League with a .404 on-base percentage.

1 **1996**—The St. Louis Cardinals defeat the Padres, 3-1, in the first game of the National League Division Series on third baseman Gary Gaetti's three-run homer off pitcher Joey Hamilton in the first inning at Busch Stadium.

1 **1998**—The Houston Astros triumph over the Padres, 5-4, in the second game of the National League Division Series at the Astrodome. Third baseman Bill Spiers strokes his third hit of the night in the bottom of the ninth inning, scoring shortstop Ricky Gutierrez and knotting the series at one game apiece.

2 **1969**—The Padres defeat the San Francisco Giants, 3-2, at Candlestick Park, but finish their first season with a 52-110 record, 41 games behind the Western Division champion Atlanta Braves.

2 **1974**—The Padres set a franchise single-season record by using 43 different players. The record lasts 17 seasons.

2 **1977**—Outfielder Merv Rettenmund finishes the season with a club-record 21 pinch hits. Outfielder Gene Richards sets a rookie major-league record with 56 stolen bases, being caught just 12 times. Reliever Rollie Fingers leads the National League with 78 appearances, while pitchers Dan Spillner and Dave Tomlin follow close behind with 76 to rank as the top three in the major leagues in that category.

2 **1984**—The Chicago Cubs clobber the Padres, 13-0, at Wrigley Field in San Diego's first National League Championship Series appearance. The Cubs set National League Championship Series records for runs, home runs, and total bases.

2 **1987**—Catcher Benito Santiago hits safely in his 34th consecutive game, a 10-3 loss to the Los Angeles Dodgers at San Diego Stadium, to extend a major-league record for catchers and rookies.

2 **1988**—Outfielder Tony Gwynn wins his third National League batting title with a .313 average.

2 **1990**—The Padres select Joe McIlvaine as general manager.

3 **1951**—Outfielder Dave Winfield is born in St. Paul, Minnesota.

3 **1976**—The Padres finish the season with a statistical oddity, having played 82 road games and only 80 home games.

3 **1980**—Second baseman Dave Cash hits into a triple play in the fourth inning in a 12-0 romp over the San Francisco Giants at Candlestick Park.

3 **1984**—The Chicago Cubs defeat the Padres, 4-2, in Game 2 of the National League Championship Series at Wrigley Field. Thousands of fans greet the Padres at Jack Murphy Stadium upon their arrival home.

3 **1990**—Pitcher Eric Show sets a club career record for victories with 100 in the season finale, defeating the Los Angeles Dodgers, 7-3, at Dodger Stadium.

3 **1993**—Padre pitchers tie a then club record by striking out 15 batters in a 4-1 loss to the Chicago Cubs at Jack Murphy Stadium.

3 **1996**—The St. Louis Cardinals defeat the Padres, 5-4, in Game 2 of the National League Division Series at Busch Stadium. Pitcher Andy Benes retires the first 12 Padres before third baseman Ken Caminiti clouts a home run in the fifth inning.

3 **1998**—The Padres defeat the Houston Astros, 2-1, in Game 3 of the National League Division Series at Qualcomm Stadium. Catcher Jim Leyritz breaks a 1-1 tie with a 402-foot home run into the left field stands in the seventh inning.

3 **2001**—Outfielder Rickey Henderson walks off pitcher Eric Gagne with none out in the third inning and scores on first baseman Ryan Klesko's double down the right-field line, matching Ty Cobb's major-league runs record of 2,245 in a 12-5 setback to the visiting Los Angeles Dodgers. He receives a standing ovation from the crowd and is greeted by his teammates in front of the Padre dugout. Pitcher Bobby Jones surrenders a three-run homer to Garry Sheffield in the first inning, setting a new team record with 37 home runs allowed in a single season.

4 **1972**—First baseman Nate Colbert ends the season with a then-club record 38 home runs and 111 RBIs. The strike helps the Padres avoid a 100 loss season.

4 **1980**—The Padres replace Jerry Coleman as manager.

4 **1984**—The Padres defeat the Chicago Cubs, 7-1, in Game 3 of the National League Championship Series at Jack Murphy Stadium, sparked by shortstop Garry Templeton's two-run double and outfielder Kevin McReynolds' three-run homer.

4 **1986**—Outfielder Kevin McReynolds clouts the only Padre grand slam home run of the season in the third inning off pitcher Bill Gullickson in a 10-7 loss to the Cincinnati Reds at Riverfront Stadium.

4 **1987**—Outfielder Tony Gwynn wins his second National League batting title with the highest average (.370) since outfielder Stan Musial of the St. Louis Cardinals in 1948. He also paces the National League with a franchise record 219 hits and sets club record with 119 runs scored and 13 triples.

4 **1988**—The Padres name Dick Freeman as interim president.

4 **1992**—First baseman Fred McGriff edges outfielder Barry Bonds for the National League home run crown with 35, becoming the first player to lead both leagues in round-trippers.

4 **1998**—Pitcher Sterling Hitchcock strikes out 11 Houston Astros in six innings, giving the Padres a 6-1 victory over pitcher Randy Johnson in the National League Division Series at Qualcomm Stadium. Catcher Jim Leyritz clouts his third home run in three games in the second inning to help the Padres wrap up the series, three games to one.

4 **2000**—The Padres decline to exercise their $6 million option on outfielder Tony Gwynn for 2001. Gwynn holds most Padre career batting records.

4 **2001**—Outfielder Rickey Henderson hits a solo home run with one out in the third inning off pitcher Luke Prokopec to become major-league baseball's career run leader, passing Ty Cobb with run number 2,246 and celebrating with a feet-first slide at the plate. His record-setting home run, off the top of the left-field fence, helps the Padres defeat the visiting Los Angeles Dodgers, 6-3.

5 **1902**—Owner Ray Kroc is born in Chicago, Illinois.

5 **1973**—National League owners postpone the sale of the Padres after learning that owner C. Arnholdt Smith had found a partner who would help keep the club in San Diego.

5 **1986**—Outfielder Tony Gwynn leads the National League with 211 hits.

5 **1996**—The St. Louis Cardinals defeat the Padres, 7-5, to sweep the three-game National League Division Series on outfielder Brian Jordan's two-run homer in the ninth inning at Jack Murphy Stadium. Third baseman Ken Caminiti hits two home runs in a losing cause.

5 **2001**—The Padres set a club record by being shut out for the thirteenth time at home and sixteenth time overall, in a 4-0 loss to the Colorado Rockies. Pitcher Kevin Jarvis surrenders his 37th home run of the season, a solo round tripper by outfielder Larry Walker in the sixth inning, to tie the club record for most home runs allowed in a single season. Pitcher Bobby Jones had set the mark two days earlier.

6 **1980**—The Padres appoint Milwaukee Brewers coach Frank Howard as manager.

6 **1984**—First baseman Steve Garvey belts a dramatic two-run homer in the ninth inning

for his fourth hit to give the Padres a 7-5 victory over the Chicago Cubs in Game 4 of the National League Championship Series.

6 **2001**—Third baseman Phil Nevin ties a Padre record with three home runs, including a grand slam off pitcher Scott Elarton in the first inning, with six RBIs in a 10-4 triumph over the visiting Colorado Rockies. He becomes the first Padre to homer three times in a San Diego home game. His solo home runs come off Elarton in the sixth inning and pitcher Chris Nichting in the seventh inning. First baseman Ryan Klesko hits a solo home run off Nichting in the seventh inning, joining John Mabry as the only players to homer into the loge level in right field at Qualcomm Stadium and joining Nevin as the second pair of Padres to homer at least 30 times in the same season. Ken Caminiti and Steve Finley accomplished the 30-homer feat in 1996. Catcher Wiki Gonzalez also clouts a solo homer run off Elarton in the sixth inning. Tony Gwynn doubles in a run in the sixth inning as a pinch-hitter for pitcher Brian Tollberg for his 3,141st and final hit of his illustrious major-league career.

7 **1984**—The Padres overcome an early three-run deficit to defeat the Chicago Cubs, 6-3, in decisive Game 5 of the National League Championship Series and become the first National League team to win the Championship Series after trailing by two games. First baseman Steve Garvey wins the National League Championship Series Most Valuable Player Award.

7 **1998**—The Padres edge the Atlanta Braves, 3-2 in 10 innings in Game 1 of the National League Championship Series at Turner Field. Third baseman Ken Caminiti clouts an opposite-field home run in the top of the tenth inning for the victory.

7 **2001**—Outfielder Rickey Henderson leads off the home half of the first inning with a bloop double down the right-field line off pitcher John Thomson, becoming the 25th major leaguer and first player in October to reach 3,000 hits in a 14-5 loss to the Colorado Rockies. His teammates rush to congratulate him at second base. He is presented with a plaque and given the ball by shortstop Juan Uribe. Henderson scores on a single by third baseman Phil Nevin to extend his already established career runs record with 2,248. He joins outfielder Tony Gwynn as the only players to reach 3,000 hits with the Padres. Gwynn appears in his final game after 20 seasons with the Padres, grounding out as a pinch-hitter for pitcher Jeremy Fikac in the ninth inning. The Padres honor Gwynn before and after the game, attended by a sellout crowd of 60,013 at Qualcomm Stadium.

8 **1998**—Pitcher Kevin Brown blanks the Atlanta Braves, 3-0, in Game 2 of the National League Championship Series at Turner Field, fanning 11 batters and allowing only three hits.

9 **1984**—The Detroit Tigers edge the Padres, 3-2, in Game 1 of the World Series at Jack Murphy Stadium on outfielder Larry Herndon's two-run homer.

10 **1984**—The Padres come from behind to defeat the Detroit Tigers, 5-3, in Game 2 of the World Series at Jack Murphy Stadium, keyed by designated hitter Kurt Bevacqua's three-run homer and pitcher Andy Hawkins' brilliant relief.

10 **1998**—The Padres triumph over the Atlanta Braves, 4-1, in Game 3 of the National Championship Series at Qualcomm Stadium, scoring twice in the fifth inning on outfielder Steve Finley's double and third baseman Ken Caminiti's single.

11 **1998**—The Atlanta Braves rally for six runs in the seventh inning to defeat the Padres, 8-3, in Game 4 of the National League Championship Series at Qualcomm Stadium. First baseman Andres Galarraga clouts a grand slam home run off relief pitcher Dan Miceli.

12 **1984**—The Detroit Tigers defeat the Padres, 5-2, in Game 3 of the World Series at Tiger Stadium, as San Diego pitchers tied a World Series record by walking 11 batters.

12 **1998**—The Atlanta Braves rally for five runs in the eighth inning and hold on to defeat the Padres, 7-6, in Game 5 of the National League Championship Series at Qualcomm Stadium. Outfielder Michael Tucker clouts a three-run homer off Padre relief pitcher Kevin Brown.

13 **1967**—Pitcher Trevor Hoffman is born in Bellflower, California.

13 **1981**—The Padres fire manager Frank Howard.

13 **1984**—The Detroit Tigers prevail over the Padres, 4-2, in Game 4 of the World Series, sparked by shortstop Alan Trammell's two home runs.

14 **1968**—The Padres select 30 players in the expansion draft, making outfielder Ollie Brown, pitcher Dave Guisti, pitcher Dick Selma, second baseman Jose Arcia, and pitcher Al Santorini their first five choices. Pitcher Clay Kirby, catcher Fred Kendall, outfielder Julio Morales, first baseman Nate Colbert, and shortstop Zoilo Versalles are chosen in the next rounds.

14 **1984**—The Detroit Tigers clinch the World Series with an 8-4 victory over the Padres in Game 5, as outfielder Kirk Gibson cracks two home runs.

14 **1996**—Third baseman Ken Caminiti makes *The Sporting News'* Major-League All-Star and Silver Slugger teams for the first time. He and outfielder Steve Finley earn their second Gold Glove awards. Relief pitcher Trevor Hoffman earns *The Sporting News'* and Rolaids' National League Fireman of the Year honors.

14 **1998**—The Padres blank the Atlanta Braves, 5-0, at Turner Field to clinch the National League Championship Series in six games. Pitcher Sterling Hitchcock hurls a two-hit shutout for the first five innings and earns Series Most Valuable Player honors, thwarting Atlanta's attempt to stage the greatest single-series comeback in baseball history.

15 **1973**—*The Washington Post* reports that Marjorie Everett, the largest stockholder in the Hollywood Park race track, will co-own the Padres and keep the team in San Diego.

16 **1959**—Outfielder Kevin McReynolds is born in Little Rock, Arkansas.

17 **1998**—The New York Yankees defeat the Padres, 9-6, in Game 1 of the World Series at Yankee Stadium. First baseman Tino Martinez clouts a grand slam home run off pitcher Mark Langston to spark a seven-run, seventh-inning Yankee rally. Outfielder Greg Vaughn clouts two home runs with three RBIs in a losing cause.

18 **1949**—Outfielder George Hendrick is born in Los Angeles, California.

18 **1973**—The Internal Revenue Service indicts owner C. Arnholdt Smith on income tax evasion charges, while the Securities and Exchange Commission sues Smith and other top executives of the Westgate Corporation for trying to defraud stockholders of Westgate and the United States National Bank of San Diego. The comptroller of the currency declares Smith's bank insolvent.

18 **1998**—The New York Yankees triumph over the Padres, 9-3, in Game 2 of the World Series at Yankee Stadium. Every Yankee starting batter manages at least one hit.

19 **1960**—Pitcher Mark Davis is born in Livermore, California.

20 **1975**—The Padres acquire outfielder Willie Davis from the St. Louis Cardinals for outfielder Dick Sharon.

20 **1998**—The New York Yankees rally to defeat the Padres, 5-4, in Game 3 of the World Series at Qualcomm Stadium. Third baseman Scott Brosius launches two home runs, including a three-run homer to center field in the eighth inning.

21 **1994**—Bruce Bochy replaces Jim Riggleman as manager.

21 **1998**—The New York Yankees blank the Padres, 3-0, in decisive Game 4 of the World Series at Qualcomm Stadium. Pitcher Andy Pettit e allows only five hits in 7.1 innings to key the World Series sweep. Outfielder Tony Gwynn bats .500 with a home run and three RBIs in a losing cause.

24 **1988**—The Padres acquire first baseman Jack Clark and pitcher Pat Clements from the New York Yankees for pitchers Lance McCullers and Jimmy Jones and outfielder Stan Jefferson.

25 **1973**—The Padres acquire first baseman Willie McCovey and outfielder Bernie Williams from the San Francisco Giants for pitcher Mike Caldwell. The Padres acquire outfielder Matty Alou from the St. Louis Cardinals.

25 **1978**—The Padres acquire first baseman Mike Hargrove, infielder Kurt Bevacqua, and catcher

Bill Fahey from the Texas Rangers for outfielder Oscar Gamble, infielder Dave Roberts, and $300,000.

26 **1987**—Outfielder Tony Gwynn makes *The Sporting News'* National League All-Star team for the third time, while catcher Benito Santiago makes it for the first time. *The Sporting News* names the latter National League Rookie of the Year.

26 **1992**—The Padres trade shortstop Tony Fernandez to the New York Mets for pitcher Wally Whitehurst, outfielder D. J. Dozier, and catcher Raul Casanova.

26 **1998**—*The Sporting News* names Kevin Brown National League Pitcher of the Year, outfielder Greg Vaughn National League Comeback Player of the Year, and Bruce Bochy National League Manager of the Year. The *Sporting News* and Rolaids both select pitcher Trevor Hoffman National League Fireman of the Year. Vaughn makes *The Sporting News* National League Silver Slugger and All-Star teams, while Brown also makes the latter team.

27 **1963**—Infielder-outfielder Bip Roberts is born in Berkeley, California.

27 **1997**—Outfielder Tony Gwynn makes *The Sporting News'* National League All-Star and Silver Slugger teams for the sixth time, while third baseman Ken Caminiti wins a third consecutive Rawlings Gold Glove Award.

28 **1986**—Larry Bowa replaces Steve Boros as manager.

28 **1991**—Outfielder Tony Gwynn earns his fifth Rawlings Gold Glove Award, while catcher Benito Santiago makes his fourth *The Sporting News'* National League Silver Slugger team.

29 **1973**—Negotiations between the city of San Diego and the Everett group for the sale of the Padres temporarily collapse when the latter asks for too many financial concessions from the city.

29 **1990**—Outfielder Tony Gwynn wins his fourth Rawlings Gold Glove Award, while catcher Benito Santiago receives his third Rawlings Gold Glove Award and makes his third *The Sporting News'* National League Silver Slugger team.

30 **1986**—The Padres trade catcher Terry Kennedy and pitcher Mark Williamson to the Baltimore Orioles for pitcher Storm Davis.

31 **1963**—First baseman Fred McGriff is born in Tampa, Florida.

31 **1978**—Pitcher Gaylord Perry becomes the second Padre to win the National League Cy Young Award, making him the first hurler to earn this honor in both leagues and the oldest recipient. He paced National League hurlers with 21 victories, suffered only six losses, and boasted a 2.72 ERA.

31 **1994**—Outfielder Tony Gwynn makes *The Sporting News'* National League All-Star and Silver Slugger teams for the fifth time.

NOVEMBER

2 **1992**—*The Sporting News* names third baseman Gary Sheffield Major-League Player of the Year. Sheffield leads the National League with a .330 batting average, finishing third with 33 home runs and producing 100 RBIs. He and first baseman Fred McGriff make *The Sporting News'* National League Silver Slugger team.

3 **1998**—San Diego voters approve a proposition to move the Padres from Qualcomm Stadium to a new downtown ballpark near San Diego Bay and the City's convention center. The Padres pledge to stay in San Diego until at least 2024 while the City agrees to pay $275 million of the cost, including $225 million from a hotel tax and $50 million from the City's redevelopment agency.

6 **1989**—*The Sporting News* and Rolaids name left-handed reliever Mark Davis the National League Pitcher of the Year and Fireman of the Year. Outfielder Tony Gwynn makes *The Sporting News'* National League All-Star team for the fourth time, while catcher Benito Santiago makes it for the second time. *The Sporting News* names Andy Benes National League Rookie Pitcher of the Year.

7 **1988**—Catcher Benito Santiago makes *The Sporting News'* National League Silver Slugger team for the second time.

8 **1974**—The Padres trade outfielder Cito Gaston to the Atlanta Braves for pitcher Danny Frisella.

8 **1996**—Bruce Bochy becomes the first Padre to win the Baseball Writers Association of America's and *The Sporting News'* National League Manager of the Year honors, guiding his club to the National League West crown with a 91-71 record.

9 **1973**—The Padres trade pitcher Clay Kirby to the Cincinnati Reds for outfielder Bobby Tolan and pitcher Dave Tomlin.

10 **1955**—First baseman Jack Clark is born in New Brighton, Pennsylvania.

11 **1961**—Senior vice president and general manager Kevin Towers is born in Medford, Oregon.

12 **2001**—Major League Baseball guarantees the last $48 million the Padres need to complete financing for their new downtown ballpark.

13 **1996**—Third baseman Ken Caminiti becomes the first Padre to win the National League Most Valuable Player Award and only the fourth player to receive a unanimous vote. He set club records with 40 home runs, 130 RBIs, and a .621 slugging percentage.

14 **1989**—Mark Davis becomes the third Padre to win the National League Cy Young Award and just the fourth reliever to earn both the National League Cy Young and Rolaids Relief awards. He set a Padre mark with 44 saves, either winning or saving 48 of San Diego's 89 triumphs.

15 **2001**—Third baseman Phil Nevin agrees to a four-year, $34 million contract extension, the most lucrative in club history. The agreement includes a three-year, no-trade clause and surpasses the $32 million deal that closer Trevor Hoffman signed in 1999. The Padres name Wally Joyner, former Padre first baseman, special assistant to the general manager.

16 **1976**—Randy Jones wins the National League Cy Young Award for his 22-14 record, leading the National League in victories, innings pitched (315.1), and complete games (25), setting club records in each category. Butch Metzger shares National League Rookie of the Year honors from the Baseball Writers Association of America and earns National League Rookie Pitcher of the Year honors from *The Sporting News.*

16 **1987**—Outfielder Tony Gwynn makes *The Sporting News'* National League Silver Slugger team for the third time, while catcher Benito Santiago makes it for the first time.

17 **1977**—Rollie Fingers wins The *Sporting News'* and Rolaids National League Fireman of the Year awards, while Bob Owchinko earns *The Sporting News'* National League Rookie Pitcher of the Year honors.

17 **1995**—The Padres name scouting director Kevin Towers as general manager.

17 **1998**—The Houston Astros sign third baseman Ken Caminiti as a free agent.

18 **1968**—Third baseman Gary Sheffield is born in Tampa, Florida.

18 **1974**—The Padres trade first baseman Nate Colbert to the Detroit Tigers for shortstop Ed Brinkman, pitcher Bob Stampe, and outfielder Dick Sharon.

18 **1981**—The Padres sign Dick Williams to a three-year pact as manager.

18 **1982**—The Padres acquire pitcher Ed Whitson from the Cleveland Indians for pitcher Juan Eichelberger and first baseman Broderick Perkins.

19 **1945**—Outfielder Bobby Tolan is born in Los Angeles, California.

19 **1979**—The Padres sign pitcher Rick Wise of the Cleveland Indians as a free agent for nearly $2 million.

19 **1997**—The Padres acquire pitchers Dan Miceli and Donne Wall and third baseman Ryan Balfe from the Detroit Tigers for pitcher Tim Worrell and outfielder Trey Beamon.

20 **1986**—Owner Joan Kroc puts the Padres up for sale.

20 **1989**—Outfielder Tony Gwynn makes *The Sporting News'* National League Silver Slugger team for the fourth time.

20 **1995**—Third baseman Ken Caminiti and outfielder Steve Finley earn their first Rawlings Gold Glove awards. Outfielder Tony Gwynn makes *The Sporting News'* National League Silver Slugger team for the sixth time.

20 **2001**—The San Diego City Council votes, 8-1, to approve a $166 million bond issue to fund construction of the Padres' downtown ballpark, enabling the resumption of construction after a delay of nearly 14 months. The new stadium is expected to be ready for the 2004 season.

23 **1930**—Manager Jack McKeon is born in South Amboy, New Jersey.

23 **1973**—Owner C. Arnholdt Smith sells the Padres to Marjorie Everett and other investors for a reported $10 million subject to National League approval. The owners could buy or sell out of the lease if they want to sell or move the team from San Diego.

26 **1979**—The Padres sign pitcher John Curtis of the San Francisco Giants as a free agent for $1.75 million.

27 **1979**—The Padres acquire second baseman Dave Cash from the Montreal Expos for infielder Bill Almon and first baseman Dan Briggs.

29 **1977**—The Padres sign outfielder Oscar Gamble of the Chicago White Sox as a free agent.

DECEMBER

1 **1973**—Topps Chewing Gum produces 1974 cards of 13 Padre players with the Washington inscription.

3 **1968**—The Padres make their first trade in franchise history, sending pitcher Dave Giusti to the St. Louis Cardinals for third baseman Ed Spiezio, outfielder Ron Davis, catcher Danny Breeden, and pitcher Phil Knuckles.

3 **1971**—The Padres trade pitcher Dave Roberts to the Houston Astros for second baseman Derrel Thomas and pitchers Bill Greif and Mark Schaeffer.

5 **1973**—National League owners again postpone their vote over the future of the Padres.

5 **1990**—The Padres trade outfielder Joe Carter and second baseman Roberto Alomar to the Toronto Blue Jays for first baseman Fred McGriff and shortstop Tony Fernandez.

6 **1945**—Manager Larry Bowa is born in Sacramento, California.

6 **1973**—The National League owners approve the move of the Padres to Washington, D.C. and award the franchise to Joseph Danzansky, who is given until December 21 to pay the city of San Diego $5 million in damages for breaking the 15-year lease on San Diego Stadium.

6 **1985**—The Padres acquire pitchers LaMarr Hoyt, Todd Simmons, and Kevin Kristan from the Chicago White Sox for shortstop Ozzie Guillen, pitchers Tim Lollar and Bill Long, and third baseman Luis Salazar.

6 **1989**—The Padres acquire outfielder Joe Carter from the Cleveland Indians for catcher Sandy Alomar, outfielder Chris James, and third baseman Carlos Baerga.

6 **1996**—The Padres acquire pitcher Sterling Hitchcock from the Seattle Mariners for pitcher Scott Sanders.

7 **1979**—The Padres purchase third baseman Aurelio Rodriguez from the Detroit Tigers for $200,000.

7 **1983**—The Padres acquire pitcher Craig Lefferts, outfielder Carmelo Martinez, and third baseman Fritz Connally from the Chicago Cubs for pitcher Scott Sanderson in three-way trade also involving the Montreal Expos.

7 **1987**—Outfielder Tony Gwynn earns his second Rawlings Gold Glove Award.

7 **2000**—The Padres sign outfielder Tony Gwynn to an incentive-laden $2 million one-year contract. The 2001 season marks Gwynn's 20th in a Padres uniform. Gwynn becomes the 17th major leaguer to play at least 20 seasons and spend his entire career with one team.

8 **1976**—The Padres acquire outfielder George Hendrick from the Cleveland Indians for outfielder Johnny Grubb, catcher Fred Kendall, and shortstop Hector Torres.

8 **1980**—The Padres trade pitcher Rollie Fingers, catchers Gene Tenace and Bob Geren, and pitcher Bob Shirley to the St. Louis Cardinals for catchers Terry Kennedy and Steve Swisher, shortstop Mike Phillips, and pitchers John Littlefield, John Urrea, Kim Seaman, and Al Olmsted.

8 **1988**—Pitcher Bruce Hurst of the Boston Red Sox signs a $5.25 million, three year contract with the Padres as a free agent.

8 **1991**—The Padres acquire pitcher Randy Myers from the Cincinnati Reds for infielder Bip Roberts and outfielder Craig Pueschner.

8 **1998**—The Arizona Diamondbacks sign outfielder Steve Finley as a free agent.

9 **1980**—The Padres draft outfielder Alan Wiggins out of the Los Angeles Dodgers minor league organization.

11 **1975**—The Padres acquire third baseman Doug Rader from the Houston Astros for pitchers Joe McIntosh and Larry Hardy.

11 **1986**—The Padres trade outfielder Kevin McReynolds, pitcher Gene Walter, and infielder Adam Ging to the New York Mets for outfielders Shawn Abner and Stan Jefferson, third baseman Kevin Mitchell, and pitchers Kevin Armstrong and Kevin Brown.

11 **1989**—Outfielder Tony Gwynn earns his third Rawlings Gold Glove Award, while catcher Benito Santiago earns his second Rawlings Gold Glove Award.

11 **2000**—The Padres trade pitcher Donne Wall to the New York Mets for outfielder Bubba Trammell.

11 **2001**—The Padres trade catcher Ben Davis, pitcher Wascar Serrano, and shortstop Alex Arias to the Seattle Mariners for pitcher Brett Tomko, catcher Tom Lampkin, and shortstop Ramon Vazquez.

12 **1973**—The city of San Diego files an antitrust civil suit asking for $72 million in damages from the National League and other defendants.

12 **1988**—Catcher Benito Santiago earns his first Rawlings Gold Glove Award.

12 **1998**—The Los Angeles Dodgers sign free agent pitcher Kevin Brown.

13 **1998**—The Padres trade pitcher Joey Hamilton to the Toronto Blue Jays for pitchers Woody Williams and Carlos Almanzar and outfielder Peter Tucci.

14 **1976**—Relief pitcher Rollie Fingers of the Oakland Athletics signs a $1.6 million, six-year contract with the Padres as a free agent.

15 **1980**—The Padres lose free agent outfielder Dave Winfield to the New York Yankees and trade pitcher Randy Jones to the New York Mets for pitcher John Pacella and outfielder Jose Moreno.

15 **1994**—The National League owners approve the sale of the Padres to John Moores, a Texas computer software manufacturer, for $80 million.

15 **1997**—The Padres acquire pitcher Kevin Brown from the Florida Marlins for pitchers Rafael Medina and Steve Hoff and first baseman Derrek Lee.

18 **1973**—A federal judge declines to issue a preliminary restraining order to block the Padres from moving to Washington, D.C.

18 **1995**—The Padres sign free agent pitcher Bob Tewksbury of the Texas Rangers.

19 **1973**—Superior Court Judge Eli Levenson again denies city attorney John Witt's demand for a writ of attachment on the assets of the San Diego Padres.

21 **1973**—The National League voids its approval of the sale of the San Diego Padres to the Washington, D.C. group, headed by Joseph Danzansky. Danzansky's group fails to deliver the money to protect the National League from damage suits by the city of San Diego and to meet the deadline to purchase the Padres.

21 **1982**—First baseman Steve Garvey of the Los Angeles Dodgers signs a $6.6 million, five-year contract with the Padres as a free agent.

21 **1994**—Arrangements are completed for the sale of the Padres to a partnership led by John Moores and Larry Lucchino. Moores becomes chairman of the board, while Lucchino becomes president and chief executive officer.

21 **1995**—The Padres acquire first baseman Wally Joyner and pitcher Aaron Dorlarque from the Kansas City Royals for infielder Bip Roberts and pitcher Bryan Wolff.

22 **1948**—First baseman Steve Garvey is born in Tampa, Florida.

22 **1999**—The Padres acquire first baseman Ryan Klesko, second baseman Brett Boone, and pitcher Jason Shiell from the Atlanta Braves for second baseman Quilvio Veras, left fielder Reggie Sanders, and first baseman Wally Joyner.

24 **1967**—Groundbreaking ceremonies are held for the natural turf facility at San Diego Stadium.

26 **1954**—Shortstop Ozzie Smith is born in Mobile, Alabama.

28 **1972**—General Manager Eddie Leishman dies of complications from pneumonia.

28 **1973**—Owner C. Arnhholdt Smith sells the Padres to Marjorie Everett and her associates for $12 million.

28 **1994**—The Padres acquire infielders Ken Caminiti, Andujar Cedeno, and Roberto Petagine, outfielder Steve Finley, pitcher Brian Williams, a player to be named later (Sean Fesh) from the Houston Astros for outfielders Derek Bell and Phil Plantier, infielders Ricky Gutierrez and Craig Shipley, and pitchers Doug Brocail and Pedro A. Martinez in the biggest trade in team history and the largest transaction in major-league baseball since 1957.

29 **1995**—The Padres sign free agent outfielder Rickey Henderson of the Oakland Athletics.

31 **1974**—The New York Yankees outbid owner Ray Kroc for pitcher Catfish Hunter as a free agent from the Oakland Athletics.

Trades

The following contains a chronological listing of Padres trades, sales, and free agent signings since the inception of the franchise.

1968

October 21—The Padres purchased first baseman Bill Davis from the Cleveland Indians. The deal was completed when the Indians acquired shortstop Zoilo Versalles from the Padres on December 2.

December 3—The Padres traded pitcher Dave Giusti to the St. Louis Cardinals for third baseman Ed Spiezio, outfielder Ron Davis, catcher Dan Breeden, and pitcher Phil Knuckles. Knuckles was assigned to Elmira, New York.

1969

March 21—The Padres signed pitcher Johnny Podres, a free agent.

March 28—The Padres traded outfielder Ron Davis and infielder Bobby Klaus to the Pittsburgh Pirates for pitcher Tommie Sisk and catcher Chris Cannizzaro.

April 11—The Padres signed catcher Everett (Chris) Krug as a coach, placed him on the active player roster on April 14, and assigned him to Elmira, New York on May 23.

April 17—The Padres traded pitcher Al McBean to the Los Angeles Dodgers for infielder Tommy Dean and pitcher Leon Everitt.

April 23—The Padres released catcher Jesse Gonder.

April 25—The Padres traded pitcher Dick Selma to the Chicago Cubs for pitchers Joe Niekro and Gary Ross and infielder Francisco Libran.

May 22—The Padres traded shortstop Jerry DaVanon and first baseman Bill Davis to the St. Louis Cardinals for shortstop John Sipin and catcher John (Sonny) Ruberto.

June 12—The Padres traded outfielder Tony Gonzalez to the Atlanta Braves for catcher Walt Hriniak, infielder Van Kelly, and outfielder Andy Finlay. Finlay was assigned to Lodi, California.

June 27—The Padres placed pitcher Johnny Podres on the voluntary retired list and made him a minor league pitching instructor.

June 30—The Padres sold catcher Danny Breeden to the Cincinnati Reds.

October 22—The Padres purchased pitcher Danny Coombs from the Houston Astros.

December 4—The Padres traded pitcher Joe Niekro to the Detroit Tigers for pitcher Pat Dobson and infielder Dave Campbell.

December 5—The Padres traded pitcher Frank Reberger to the San Francisco Giants for pitcher Ron Herbel, catcher Bob Barton, and third baseman Bob Etheridge.

1970

March 24—The Padres traded infielder Roberto Peña to the Oakland Athletics for first baseman Ramon Webster.

March 30—The Padres traded pitcher Tommie Sisk to the Chicago White Sox for pitcher Gerry Nyman.

April 2—The Padres traded pitcher Billy McCool to the St. Louis Cardinals for shortstop Steve Huntz.

April 5—The Padres released pitcher Jack Baldschun.

May 25—The Padres purchased pitcher Roberto Rodriguez from the Oakland Athletics.

June 23—The Padres sold pitcher Roberto Rodriguez to the Chicago Cubs.

July 15—The Padres purchased pitcher Earl Wilson from the Detroit Tigers.

August 25—The Padres purchased pitcher Paul Doyle from the California Angels.

September 1—The Padres sold pitcher Ron Herbel to the New York Mets. The deal was completed when the Padres acquired outfielder Rod Gaspar on October 20.

October 19—The Padres sold first baseman Ramon Webster to the Oakland Athletics.

December 1—The Padres traded pitchers Pat Dobson and Tom Dukes to the Baltimore Orioles for pitchers Tom Phoebus, Al Severinsen, and Fred Beene and shortstop Enzo Hernandez.

December 4—The Padres traded infielder Steve Huntz to the San Francisco Giants for second baseman Don Mason and pitcher Bill Frost. Frost was assigned to Hawaii.

1971

January 13—The Padres released pitcher Earl Wilson.

April 26—The Padres purchased first baseman Ramon Webster from the Oakland Athletics. Webster returned to the Athletics on May 14.

May 11—The Padres signed pitcher Robert L. Miller, released by the Chicago Cubs.

May 13—The Padres traded outfielder Al Ferrara to the Cincinnati Reds for outfielder Angel Bravo.

May 19—The Padres traded catcher Chris Cannizzaro to the Chicago Cubs for infielder Garry Jestadt and cash.

May 22—The Padres purchased pitcher Camilo Pascual conditionally from the Cleveland Indians, but returned him to the Cleveland Indians on May 26.

June 11—The Padres traded pitcher Al Santorini to the St. Louis Cardinals for outfielder Leron Lee and pitcher Fred Norman.

August 10—The Padres traded pitcher Robert L. Miller to the Pittsburgh Pirates for outfielder John Jeter and pitcher Eduardo Acosta.

December 3—The Padres traded pitcher David A. Roberts to the Houston Astros for infielder Derrel Thomas and pitchers Bill Greif and Mark Schaeffer, the latter assigned to Hawaii.

1972

April 20—The Padres signed pitcher Ron Taylor, formerly of the Montreal Expos.

April 20—The Padres traded pitcher Tom Phoebus to the Chicago Cubs for a player to be named later and cash.

May 17—The Padres traded outfielder Ollie Brown to the Oakland Athletics for catcher-outfielder Curt Blefary, pitcher Mike Kilkenny, and a player to be named later. The Padres acquired outfielder Greg Schubert to complete the deal on September 11 and assigned him to Hawaii.

June 11—The Padres traded pitcher Mike Kilkenny to the Cleveland Indians for infielder Fred Stanley.

June 11—The Padres traded catcher Bob Barton to the Cincinnati Reds for catcher Pat Corrales.

June 20—The Padres traded infielder Rafael Robles to the St. Louis Cardinals for first baseman Mike Fiore and pitcher Bob Chlupsa, the latter transferred to Hawaii.

July 3—The Padres returned first baseman Mike Fiore to the St. Louis Cardinals.

July 9—The Padres traded third baseman Ed Spiezio to the Chicago White Sox. The Padres acquired pitcher Don Eddy on July 16 to complete the deal. Eddy was assigned to Hawaii.

October 28—The Padres traded outfielder John Jeter to the Chicago White Sox for pitcher Vicente Romo.

November 30—The Padres traded pitcher Al Severinsen to the New York Mets for outfielder Dave Marshall.

December 1—The Padres sold outfielder Larry Stahl to the Cincinnati Reds.

December 27—The Padres released outfielder-catcher Curt Blefary.

1973

April 2—The Padres signed pitcher Robert L. Miller, formerly with the Pittsburgh Pirates.

May 26—The Padres purchased infielder Rich Morales from the Chicago White Sox.

June 7—The Padres traded second baseman Dave Campbell to the St. Louis Cardinals for infielder Dwain Anderson.

June 12—The Padres traded pitcher Fred Norman to the Cincinnati Reds for outfielder Gene Locklear, pitcher Mike Johnson, and cash. Johnson was assigned to Alexandria, Louisiana.

June 22—The Padres sold pitcher Robert L. Miller to the Detroit Tigers.

October 25—The Padres purchased outfielder Matty Alou from the St. Louis Cardinals.

October 25—The Padres traded pitcher Mike Caldwell to the San Francisco Giants for first baseman Willie McCovey and outfielder Bernie Williams.

November 7—The Padres traded outfielder Jerry Morales to the Chicago Cubs for second baseman Glenn Beckert and infielder Bob Fenwick, the latter transferred to Hawaii.

November 9—The Padres traded pitcher Clay Kirby to the Cincinnati Reds for outfielder Bobby Tolan and pitcher Dave Tomlin.

December 20—The Padres traded pitcher Steve Simpson to the New York Mets for pitcher Jim McAndrew.

1974

March 28—The Padres sold outfielder Leron Lee to the Cleveland Indians.

April 1—The Padres sold outfielder Ivan Murrell to the Atlanta Braves.

April 2—The Padres signed catcher Bob Barton, a free agent.

May 31—The Padres purchased second baseman Horace Clarke from the New York Yankees.

May 31—The Padres purchased pitcher Lowell Palmer from the New York Yankees.

June 1—The Padres released pitcher Jim McAndrew.

June 15—The Padres traded pitcher Steve Arlin to the Cleveland Indians for two players to be named later. The Padres acquired pitchers Terry Ley and Brent Strom on June 21 to complete the deal and assigned them to Hawaii.

July 11—The Padres released outfielder Matty Alou.

October 3—The Padres released catcher Bob Barton and infielders Rich Morales and Horace Clarke.

November 8—The Padres traded outfielder Cito Gaston to the Atlanta Braves for pitcher Danny Frisella.

November 18—In a three-club deal, the Padres traded first baseman Nate Colbert to the Detroit Tigers for shortstop Ed Brinkman, pitcher Bob Strampe, and outfielder Dick Sharon. The Padres then traded Brinkman and a player to be named later for pitchers Alan Foster, Rich Folkers, and Sonny Siebert. The deal was completed December 12, when the Padres traded catcher Danny Breeden to the Cardinals.

December 6—The Padres traded infielder-outfielder Derrel Thomas to the San Francisco Giants for second baseman Tito Fuentes and pitcher Butch Metzger.

1975

March 28—The Padres released pitcher Vicente Romo.

April 3—The Padres signed catcher Randy Hundley, a free agent.

April 28—The Padres released second baseman Glenn Beckert.

April 28—The Padres purchased catcher Gerry Moses from the New York Mets.

May 16—The Padres traded pitcher Sonny Siebert to the Oakland Athletics for infielder Ted Kubiak.

June 24—The Padres purchased outfielder Don Hahn from the St. Louis Cardinals.

July 18—The Padres sold catcher Gerry Moses to the Chicago White Sox.

September 17—The Padres traded pitcher Gary Ross to the California Angels for infielder-outfielder Bobby Valentine and a player to be named later. The Padres acquired infielder Rudy Meoli to the Padres to complete the deal on November 4.

October 20—The Padres traded outfielder Dick Sharon to the St.Louis Cardinals for outfielder Willie Davis.

December 11—The Padres traded pitchers Joe McIntosh and Larry Hardy to the Houston Astros for third baseman Doug Rader.

1976

April 5—The Padres traded shortstop Rudy Meoli and cash to the Cincinnati Reds for outfielder Merv Rettenmund.

April 8—The Padres traded pitcher Danny Frisella to the St. Louis Cardinals for pitcher Ken Reynolds.

April 13—The Padres sold catcher Randy Hundley to the Chicago Cubs.

May 19—The Padres traded pitcher Bill Greif to the St. Louis Cardinals for outfielder Luis Melendez.

July 10—The Padres traded outfielder Gene Locklear to the New York Yankees for a player to be named later. The Padres acquired pitcher Rick Sawyer to complete the deal on July 31.

August 3—The Padres purchased pitcher Tom Griffin from the Houston Astros.

August 30—The Padres sold first baseman Willie McCovey to the Oakland Athletics.

October 22—The Padres sold infielder Dave Hilton, outfielder John Scott, and infielder-catcher David W. Roberts to the Toronto Blue Jays.

December 8—The Padres traded outfielder Johnny Grubb, catcher Fred Kendall, and shortstop Hector Torres to the Cleveland Indians for outfielder George Hendrick.

December 14—The Padres signed pitcher Rollie Fingers, a free agent formerly with the Oakland Athletics.

December 14—The Padres signed catcher-first baseman Gene Tenace, a free agent formerly with the Oakland Athletics.

1977

January 20—The Padres released outfielder Willie Davis.

February 16—The Padres traded pitcher Jerry Johnson to the Toronto Blue Jays for catcher-third baseman Dave Roberts.

February 23—The Detroit Tigers signed infielder Tito Fuentes, a free agent formerly with the Padres.

March 21—The Padres sold pitcher Ken Reynolds to the Toronto Blue Jays.

March 23—The Padres sold pitcher Rich Folkers to the Milwaukee Brewers.

March 29—The Padres released pitcher Alan Foster.

April 5—The Padres signed second baseman Gary Sutherland, a free agent.

May 17—The Padres traded pitcher Butch Metzger to the St. Louis Cardinals for pitcher John D'Acquisto and infielder Pat Scanlon, the latter transferred to Hawaii.

June 8—The Padres sold third baseman Doug Rader to the Toronto Blue Jays.

June 15—The Padres traded third baseman-outfielder Bobby Valentine and pitcher Paul Siebert to the New York Mets for first baseman-outfielder Dave Kingman.

September 6—The Padres sold outfielder-first baseman Dave Kingman to the California Angels.

September 29—The Padres sold pitcher Rick Sawyer to the Montreal Expos.

November 29—The Padres signed outfielder Oscar Gamble, a free agent formerly with the Chicago White Sox.

1978

January 25—The Padres traded pitcher Dave Tomlin and an estimated $125,000 cash to the Texas Rangers for pitcher Gaylord Perry.

February 28—The Padres traded infielder Mike Ivie to the San Francisco Giants for infielder-outfielder Derrel Thomas.

March 14—The Padres released shortstop Enzo Hernandez.

March 28—The Padres released pitcher Brent Strom.

May 26—The Cardinals traded pitcher Eric Rasmussen to the Padres for outfielder George Hendrick.

June 5—The Padres purchased infielder Fernando Gonzalez from the Pittsburgh Pirates.

June 14—The Padres traded pitcher Dan Spillner to the Cleveland Indians for pitcher Dennis Kinney.

June 22—The Padres traded pitcher Dave Freisleben to the Cleveland Indians for pitcher Bill Laxton.

September 12—The Padres traded pitcher Mark Wiley to the Toronto Blue Jays for outfielder Andy Dyes.

October 25—The Padres traded outfielder Oscar Gamble, catcher Dave Roberts, and an estimated $300,000 cash to the Texas Rangers for first baseman Mike Hargrove, third baseman Kurt Bevacqua, and catcher Bill Fahey.

November 14—The Los Angeles Dodgers signed infielder-outfielder Derrel Thomas, a free agent formerly with the Padres.

1979

February 22—The Padres signed catcher Fred Kendall, a free agent formerly with the Boston Red Sox.

March 30—The Padres acquired outfielder Dan Briggs from the Cleveland Indians for a player to be named later. The Padres traded second baseman Mike Champion to complete the deal on April 3.

June 14—The Padres traded first baseman Mike Hargrove to the Cleveland Indians for outfielder-third baseman Paul Dade.

June 15—The Padres traded pitcher Dave Wehrmeister to the New York Yankees for outfielder Jay Johnstone.

July 5—The Padres signed first baseman-outfielder Bobby Tolan, a free agent.

October 3—The Padres released pitcher Mickey Lolich.

October 25—The Padres released outfielder Bobby Tolan.

November 20—The Padres signed pitcher Rick Wise, a free agent formerly with the Cleveland Indians.

November 26—The Padres signed pitcher John Curtis, a free agent formerly with the San Francisco Giants.

November 27—The Padres traded infielder Bill Almon and first baseman-outfielder Dan Briggs to the Montreal Expos for second baseman Dave Cash.

December 4—The Los Angeles Dodgers signed outfielder Jay Johnstone, a free agent formerly with the Padres.

December 4—The Padres obtained outfielder Von Joshua from the Los Angeles Dodgers on waivers.

December 7—The Padres acquired third baseman Aurelio Rodriguez from the Detroit Tigers for a player to be named later.

1980

January 29—The Padres sold second baseman Sam Perlozzo to the Yakult, Japan Swallows.

February 15—The Padres traded pitcher Gaylord Perry, third baseman Tucker Ashford, and pitcher Joe Carroll to the Texas Rangers for first baseman Willie Montanez.

February 15—The Padres traded pitcher Bob Owchinko and outfielder Jim Wilhelm to the Cleveland Indians for outfielder Jerry Mumphrey.

February 15—The Padres released second baseman Fernando Gonzalez.

August 4—The Padres sold third baseman Aurelio Rodriguez to the New York Yankees.

August 5—The Padres traded third baseman Kurt Bevacqua and a player to be named later to the Pittsburgh Pirates for outfielder Rick Lancellotti, and third baseman-outfielder Luis Salazar. The Padres traded pitcher Mark Lee to complete the deal on August 12. The Padres assigned Lancellotti to Amarillo and Salazar to Hawaii.

August 11—The Padres traded pitcher John D'Acquisto to the Montreal Expos for a player to be named and cash . The Padres purchased outfielder Randy Bass to complete the deal September 5.

August 11—The Padres released outfielder Von Joshua and catcher Fred Kendall.

August 31—The Padres traded first baseman Willie Montanez to the Montreal Expos for infielder Tony Phillips and cash.

December 8—The Padres traded pitchers Rollie Fingers and Bob Shirley, catcher-first baseman Gene Tenace, and a player to be named to the St. Louis Cardinals for catchers Terry Kennedy and Steve Swisher, infielder Mike Phillips, and pitchers John Littlefield, John Urrea, Kim Seaman, and Alan Olmsted. The Padres traded catcher Bob Geren to complete the deal on December 10.

December 8—The Padres released third baseman-outfielder Paul Dade.

December 8—The Padres traded infielder Chuck Baker to the Minnesota Twins for outfielder Dave Edwards.

December 9—The Padres drafted infielder Mario Ramirez from the New York Mets and outfielder Alan Wiggins from the Los Angeles Dodgers in the Rule V draft.

December 12—The Padres traded pitcher Dennis Kinney to the Detroit Tigers for outfielder Dave Stegman, who was assigned to Hawaii.

December 15—The New York Yankees signed outfielder Dave Winfield, a free agent formerly with the Padres.

December 15—The Padres traded pitcher Randy Jones to the New York Mets for pitcher John Pacella and infielder Jose Moreno, assigned to Hawaii.

1981

March 24—The Padres sold catcher Bill Fahey to the Detroit Tigers.

March 27—The Padres traded pitcher Eric Mustad and infielders Kevin Bell and Tony Phillips to the Oakland Athletics for pitcher Bob Lacey.

March 27—The Padres released pitcher Eric Rasmussen.

April 1—The Padres traded pitcher Bob Lacey to the Cleveland Indians for second baseman Juan Bonilla.

April 1—The Padres traded outfielder Jerry Mumphrey and pitcher John Pacella to the New York Yankees for outfielders Ruppert Jones and Joe Lefebvre and pitchers Tim Lollar and Chris Welsh.

April 4—The Padres released second baseman Dave Cash.

April 5—The Padres traded outfielder Bobby Mitchell to the Pittsburgh Pirates for pitcher Dave Dravecky.

May 10—The Padres sold infielder Mike Phillips to the Montreal Expos.

September 9—The Padres sold outfielder Jerry Turner to the Chicago White Sox.

December 8—The Padres drafted infielder Clifton Wherry from the Houston Astros organization.

December 10—The Padres traded pitcher Steve Mura and a player to be named to the St. Louis Cardinals for outfielder Sixto Lezcano and a player to be named.

1982

January 27—The Padres sold catcher Craig Stimac to the Cleveland Indians.

February 11—The Padres traded shortstop Ozzie Smith to the St. Louis Cardinals for shortstop Garry Templeton.

February 19—The Padres traded pitcher Al Olmsted to the St. Louis Cardinals for pitcher Luis DeLeon, completing the December 10, 1981 deal.

February 22—The Padres sold third baseman Barry Evans to the New York Yankees.

February 25—The Padres released pitcher John Littlefield.

March 6—The Padres signed pitcher John Montefusco, a free agent formerly with the Atlanta Braves.

March 26—The Padres released pitcher John Urrea.

March 29—The Houston Astros reclaimed infielder Clifton Wherry from the Padres, who had selected him in the 1981 major-league draft.

April 4—The Padres sold pitcher Mike Armstrong to the Kansas City Royals.

April 16—The Padres released pitcher Rick Wise.

May 17—The Padres sold first baseman-outfielder Randy Bass to the Texas Rangers.

May 22—The Padres traded pitcher Kim Seaman to the Montreal Expos for infielder Jerry Manuel.

June 8—The Padres traded pitcher Dan Boone to the Houston Astros for infielder Joe Pittman.

June 8—The Padres traded infielder Jerry Manuel to the Montreal Expos for a player to be named. The Padres acquired pitcher Mike Griffin to complete the deal on August 30.

August 31—The Padres sold pitcher John Curtis to the California Angels.

October 7—The Padres purchased pitcher Elias Sosa from the Detroit Tigers.

October 7—The Padres sold outfielder Rick Lancellotti to the Montreal Expos.

October 15—The Padres traded pitcher Tom Tellman to the Milwaukee Brewers for pitchers Weldon Swift and Tim Cook.

November 3—The Padres released outfielder Dave Edwards.

November 18—The Padres traded pitcher Juan Eichelberger and first baseman-outfielder Broderick Perkins to the Cleveland Indians for pitcher Ed Whitson.

December 15—The Padres acquired pitcher Ray Searage from the Cleveland Indians for a player to be named.

December 21—The Padres signed first baseman Steve Garvey, a free agent formerly with the Los Angeles Dodgers.

1983

February 23—The Padres signed catcher Bruce Bochy, a free agent, and assigned him to Las Vegas, Nevada.

February 28—The Padres signed outfielder Jerry Turner, a free agent, and assigned him to Las Vegas, Nevada.

March 27—The Padres released pitcher Tom Griffin.

March 28—The Padres returned pitcher Ray Searage, conditionally purchased on December 15, 1982, to the Cleveland Indians.

April 19—The Padres signed outfielder Bobby Brown, a free agent, and assigned him to Las Vegas, Nevada.

May 4—The Padres sold pitcher Chris Welsh to the Montreal Expos.

May 22—The Padres traded outfielder Joe Lefebvre to the Philadelphia Phillies for pitcher Sid Monge.

July 26—The Padres released outfielder Jerry Turner.

August 26—The Padres traded pitcher John Montefusco to the New York Yankees for two players to be named. The Padres acquired pitcher Dennis Rasmussen and infielder Edwin Rodriguez to complete the deal on September 12.

August 31—The Padres traded outfielder Sixto Lezcano and a player to be named to the Philadelphia Phillies for four players to be named. The Padres acquired pitchers Marty Decker, Ed Wojna, Darren Burroughs, and Lance McCullers on September 20. The Phillies acquired pitcher Steve Fireovid on October 11.

December 5—The Padres traded infielder Joe Pittman and a player to be named to the San Francisco Giants for outfielder-first baseman Champ Summers. The Giants acquired outfielder Tommy Francis to complete the deal on December 7.

December 7—In a three-team deal, the Padres traded pitcher Gary Lucas to the Montreal Expos for pitcher Scott Sanderson. The Padres then traded Sanderson to the Chicago Cubs for pitcher Craig Lefferts, first baseman Carmelo Martinez, and third baseman Fritz Connally.

1984

January 6—The Padres signed pitcher Rich Gossage, a free agent formerly with the New York Yankees.

March 26—The Padres released second baseman Juan Bonilla.

March 28—The San Francisco Giants signed outfielder Gene Richards, a free agent formerly with the Padres.

March 30—The Padres traded pitcher Dennis Rasmussen and a player to be named to the New York Yankees for third baseman Craig Nettles. The Padres traded pitcher Darin Cloninger on April 26.

April 18—The Detroit Tigers signed outfielder Ruppert Jones, a free agent formerly with the Padres.

June 10—The Padres sold pitcher Sid Monge to the Detroit Tigers.

July 20—The Padres traded infielder Al Newman to the Montreal Expos for pitcher Greg Harris.

November 1—The Padres released outfielder Ed Miller.

December 6—The Padres traded pitchers Tim Lollar and Bill Long, third baseman Luis Salazar, and shortstop Ozzie Guillen to the Chicago White Sox for pitchers LaMarr Hoyt, Kevin Kristan, and Todd Simmons. The Padres assigned Simmons to Reno, Nevada and Kristan to Beaumont, Texas.

December 7—The Padres traded pitcher Floyd Chiffer to the Minnesota Twins for catcher Ray Smith. The Padres assigned Smith to Las Vegas, Nevada.

December 27—The New York Yankees signed pitcher Ed Whitson, a free agent formerly with the Padres.

1985

January 3—The Padres signed infielder-outfielder Jerry Royster, a free agent formerly with the Atlanta Braves.

January 8—The Padres signed pitcher Tim Stoddard, a free agent formerly with the Chicago Cubs.

February 7—The Padres traded third baseman Fritz Connally to the Baltimore Orioles for second baseman Vic Rodriguez. The Padres assigned Rodriguez to Las Vegas, Nevada.

February 13—The Padres sold pitcher Greg Harris to the Texas Rangers.

March 28—The Padres signed outfielder Al Bumbry, a free agent formerly with the Baltimore Orioles.

March 30—The Padres released outfielder Ron Roenicke.

March 31—The Padres traded outfielder-first baseman Rick Lancellotti to the New York Mets for outfielder Rusty Tillman. The Padres assigned Tillman to Las Vegas, Nevada.

April 6—The Padres reclaimed pitcher Mitch Williams from the Texas Rangers, who had selected him in the 1984 major-league draft. The Padres then traded Williams to the Texas Rangers for third baseman Randy Asadoor.

June 28—The Padres traded second baseman Alan Wiggins to the Baltimore Orioles for pitcher Roy Lee Jackson and a player to be named. The Padres assigned Jackson to Las Vegas, Nevada and acquired pitcher Rich Caldwell on September 16.

July 27—The Padres organization signed outfielder Miguel Dilone, a free agent.

1986

January 28—The Padres signed first baseman-outfielder Dane Iorg, a free agent formerly with the Kansas City Royals.

March 23—The Padres released pitcher Roy Lee Jackson.

March 25—The Padres released shortstop Mario Ramirez.

April 3—The Padres traded pitcher Bob Patterson to the Pittsburgh Pirates for outfielder Marvell Wynne.

April 18—The Padres traded outfielder Kerry Tillman to the Oakland Athletics for pitcher Bob Stoddard and outfielder Kevin Russ. The Padres assigned Stoddard to Las Vegas, Nevada and Russ to Charleston, South Carolina.

June 12—The Padres traded a player to be named to the Milwaukee Brewers for infielder Randy Ready. The Brewers acquired infielder Tim Pyznarski on October 29.

July 9—The Padres traded pitcher Mark Thurmond to the Detroit Tigers for pitcher Dave LaPoint.

July 9—The Padres traded pitcher Tim Stoddard to the New York Yankees for pitcher Ed Whitson.

October 9—The Padres released outfielder Dane Iorg.

October 30—The Padres traded catcher Terry Kennedy and pitcher Mark Williamson to the Baltimore Orioles for pitcher Storm Davis.

November 1—The Padres released pitcher Bob Stoddard.

December 10—The Padres drafted infielder Leon (Bip) Roberts from the Pittsburgh Pirates organization in the Rule V draft.

December 11—The Padres traded outfielder Kevin McReynolds, pitcher Gene Walter, and infielder Adam Ging to the New York Mets for outfielders Shawn Abner and Stanley Jefferson, third baseman Kevin Mitchell, and pitchers Kevin Armstrong and Kevin Brown.

December 18—The Padres released third baseman Graig Nettles and pitcher Dave LaPoint.

1987

January 13—The Padres organization signed pitcher Tom Gorman, a free agent.

January 21—The Chicago White Sox signed infielder Jerry Royster, a free agent formerly with the Padres.

April 1—The Atlanta Braves signed third baseman Graig Nettles, a free agent formerly with the Padres.

April 2—The Padres signed infielder Luis Salazar, a free agent, and assigned him to Las Vegas, Nevada.

April 25—The Padres traded pitcher Tim Meagher and infielder Mark Wasinger to the San Francisco Giants for pitcher Colin Ward and infielder Steve Miller. The Padres assigned Ward and Miller to Las Vegas, Nevada.

June 4—The Padres traded pitcher Tom Gorman to the Minnesota Twins for pitcher Dave Blakley and assigned Blakley to Reno, Nevada.

June 17—The Padres released pitcher LaMarr Hoyt.

July 1—The Chicago White Sox signed pitcher LaMarr Hoyt, a free agent formerly with the Padres.

July 5—The Padres traded pitchers Dave Dravecky and Craig Lefferts and infielder Kevin Mitchell to the San Francisco Giants for third baseman Chris Brown and pitchers Keith Comstock, Mark Davis, and Mark Grant.

August 30—The Padres traded pitcher Storm Davis to the Oakland Athletics for two players to be named. The Padres acquired pitcher Dave Leiper on August 31 and first baseman Rob Nelson on September 8.

October 5—The Padres traded pitcher Ed Wojna to the Chicago White Sox for a player to be named.

1988

February 11—The Padres acquired pitcher Joel McKeon from the Chicago White Sox, completing the October 5, 1987 deal. The Padres assigned McKeon to Las Vegas, Nevada.

February 12—The Padres traded pitchers Goose Gossage and Ray Hayward to the Chicago Cubs for infielders Keith Moreland and Mike Brumley.

February 18—The Padres signed shortstop Dickie Thon, a free agent formerly with the Houston Astros.

June 8—The Padres traded pitcher Candy Sierra to the Cincinnati Reds for pitcher Dennis Rasmussen.

October 24—The Padres traded pitchers Jimmy Jones and Lance McCullers and outfielder Stan Jefferson to the New York Yankees for outfielder Jack Clark and pitcher Pat Clements.

October 28—The Padres traded infielders Chris Brown and Keith Moreland to the Detroit Tigers for pitcher Walt Terrell.

December 8—The Padres signed pitcher Bruce Hurst, a free agent formerly with the Boston Red Sox.

December 13—The Padres traded pitcher Ed Vosberg to the Houston Astros for catcher Dan Walters.

1989

January 27—The Padres sold infielder Dickie Thon to the Philadelphia Phillies.

February 15—The Padres traded pitchers Todd Simmons and James Austin to the Milwaukee Brewers for pitcher Dan Murphy.

March 23—The Padres traded shortstop Mike Brumley to the Detroit Tigers for infielder Luis Salazar.

June 2—The Padres traded infielder Randy Ready and outfielder John Kruk to the Philadelphia Phillies for outfielder Chris James.

June 29—The Padres traded pitcher Greg Booker to the Minnesota Twins for pitcher Fred Toliver.

July 22—The Padres traded pitcher Walt Terrell and a player to be named to the New York Yankees for third baseman Mike Pagliarulo and pitcher Don Schulze. The Yankees acquired pitcher Fred Toliver on September 27.

August 30—The Padres traded outfielder Marvell Wynne and infielder Luis Salazar to the Chicago Cubs for pitcher Calvin Schiraldi, outfielder Darrin Jackson, and a player to be named. The Padres acquired first baseman Phil Stephenson on September 5.

November 16—The Padres released pitcher Don Schulze.

December 1—The Philadelphia Phillies signed outfielder-first baseman Carmelo Martinez, a free agent formerly with the Padres.

December 6—The Padres traded catcher Sandy Alomar, outfielder Chris James, and third baseman Carlos Baerga to the Cleveland Indians for outfielder Joe Carter.

December 6—The Padres signed outfielder Fred Lynn, a free agent formerly with the Detroit Tigers.

December 6—The Padres signed pitcher Craig Lefferts, a free agent formerly with the San Francisco Giants.

December 11—The Kansas City Royals signed pitcher Mark Davis, a free agent formerly with the Padres.

December 19—The Padres released pitcher Dave Leiper.

1990

February 27—The Padres traded pitcher Omar Olivares to the St.Louis Cardinals for outfielder Alex Cole and pitcher Steve Peters.

July 11—The Padres traded outfielder Alex Cole to the Cleveland Indians for catcher Tom Lampkin.

July 12—The Padres traded pitcher Mark Grant to the Atlanta Braves for pitcher Derek Lilliquist.

August 24—The Padres signed pitcher Atlee Hammaker, a free agent formerly with the San Francisco Giants.

November 9—The Padres traded pitcher Brian Harrison to the Montreal Expos for pitcher John Costello.

December 2—The Padres sold third baseman Eddie Williams to the Daiei Hawks of the Japanese Baseball League.

December 3—The Padres traded a player to be named to the New York Yankees for outfielder Oscar Azocar.

December 5—The Padres traded outfielder Joe Carter and second baseman Roberto Alomar to the Toronto Blue Jays for first baseman Fred McGriff and shortstop Tony Fernandez.

December 10—The Oakland Athletics signed pitcher Eric Show, a free agent formerly with the Padres.

December 12—The Padres traded catcher Mark Parent to the Texas Rangers for third baseman Scott Coolbaugh.

December 15—The Boston Red Sox signed first baseman Jack Clark, a free agent formerly with the Padres.

December 15—The Padres traded first baseman-outfielder Steve Hendricks and pitcher Brad Hoyer to the Boston Red Sox for pitcher Wes Gardner.

December 21—The Padres signed pitcher Larry Andersen, a free agent formerly with the Boston Red Sox.

1991

January 8—The Padres signed second baseman Marty Barrett, a free agent.

January 15—The Padres signed catchers Dann Bilardello and Brian Dorsett, both free agents.

January 25—The Minnesota Twins signed third baseman Mike Pagliarulo, a free agent formerly with the Padres.

February 7—The Padres traded outfielder Mike Humphreys to the New York Yankees to complete the December 3, 1990 trade.

February 8—The Padres claimed outfielder Jim Vatcher on waivers from the Atlanta Braves.

February 8—The Padres signed third baseman Jim Presley, a free agent.

February 14—The Padres released pitcher Matthew Maysey.

March 19—The Padres released pitcher Candy Sierra.

March 25—The Padres released pitcher Mike Dunne.

March 26—The Padres claimed pitcher Jose Melendez on waivers from the Seattle Mariners.

March 30—The Padres released pitcher Calvin Schiraldi.

March 31—The Padres traded second baseman Joey Cora, outfielder Warren Newson, and infielder Kevin Garner to the Chicago White Sox for pitchers Adam Peterson and Steve Rosenberg.

April 5—The Padres signed outfielder Mike Aldrete.

May 10—The Padres released outfielder Mike Aldrete.

May 20—The Padres released pitcher Eric Nolte.

May 31—The Padres traded shortstop Garry Templeton to the New York Mets for infielder Tim Teufel

May 31—The Padres released pitcher Wes Gardner.

June 8—The Padres released third baseman Jim Presley.

June 14—The Padres released second baseman Marty Barrett.

July 30—The Padres traded outfielder Shawn Abner to the California Angels for third baseman Jack Howell.

November 19—The Padres released pitcher John Costello.

November 21—The Cleveland Indians acquired pitcher Derek Lilliquist on waivers from the Padres.

December 8—The Padres traded infielder-outfielder Bip Roberts and a player to be named to the Cincinnati Reds for pitcher Randy Myers. The Reds acquired outfielder Craig Pueschner to complete the deal on December 9.

December 11—The Padres traded pitcher Steve Rosenberg to the New York Mets for second baseman Jeff Gardner.

1992

January 8—The Padres signed infielder Tim Teufel, a free agent.

February 17—The Padres traded pitcher Jim Lewis and outfielder Steve Martin to the Baltimore Orioles for third baseman Craig Worthington and pitcher Tom Martin. Martin was assigned to Waterloo, Iowa.

February 21—The Padres signed shortstop Kurt Stillwell, a free agent.

March 26—The Padres traded pitcher Ricky Bones, infielder Jose Valentin, and outfielder Matt Mieske to the Milwaukee Brewers for third baseman Gary Sheffield and pitcher Geoff Kellogg.

March 26—The Padres reacquired outfielder Darrell Sherman from the Baltimore Orioles, who had selected him in the 1991 Rule 5 major-league draft.

March 30—The Padres traded third baseman Craig Bullock to the New York Mets for pitcher Terry Bross and assigned Bross to Las Vegas, Nevada.

March 30—The Padres released third baseman Craig Worthington.

April 14—The Padres signed outfielder Garry Pettis, a free agent.

April 14—The Padres traded outfielder Thomas Howard to the Cleveland Indians for shortstop Jason Hardtke and a player to be named later. The Padres acquired catcher Christopher Maffet to complete the deal on July 10 and assigned him to Spokane.

April 28—The Padres organization signed pitcher Jim Deshaies, a free agent.

May 11—The Padres traded outfielder Will Taylor to the Seattle Mariners for pitcher Gene Harris.

July 6—The Padres traded infielder Scott Coolbaugh to the Cincinnati Reds for infielder Lenny Wentz and assigned Wentz to Charleston, South Carolina.

July 9—The Baltimore Orioles claimed pitcher Pat Clements on waivers from the Padres.

August 31—The Padres traded pitcher Craig Lefferts to the Baltimore Orioles for pitcher Erik Schullstrom and a player to be named. The Padres acquired infielder Ricky Gutierrez to complete the deal on September 4 and assigned him to Las Vegas, Nevada.

October 7—The Padres granted outfielder-first baseman Oscar Azocar and outfielder-first baseman Kevin Ward free agency.

October 8—The Padres released outfielder-first baseman Phil Stephenson.

October 26—The Padres traded shortstop Tony Fernandez to the New York Mets for pitcher Wally Whitehurst, outfielder D. J. Dozier, and a player to be named. The Padres acquired catcher Raul Casanova to complete the deal on December 7.

October 27—The Padres released catcher Dann Bilardello.

November 20—The Padres signed free agent outfielder Jarvis Brown.

December 2—The Padres organization signed catcher Bob Geren, a free agent.

December 8—The Minnesota Twins signed pitcher Jim Deshaies, a free agent formerly with the Padres.

December 9—The Chicago Cubs signed pitcher Randy Myers, a free agent formerly with the Padres.

December 9—The Padres traded pitcher Jose Melendez to the Boston Red Sox for outfielder Phil Plantier.

December 10—The Padres traded infielder Paul Faries to the San Francisco Giants for pitcher Jim Pena.

December 16—The Florida Marlins signed catcher Benito Santiago, a free agent formerly with the Padres.

December 16—The Padres traded pitcher Terry Bross to the Texas Rangers for pitcher Pat Gomez.

December 17—The Padres traded pitcher Mike Maddux to the New York Mets for pitchers Roger Mason and Mike Freitas.

1993

February 11 -The Padres signed catcher Mike Scioscia, a free agent formerly with the Los Angeles Dodgers.

March 25—The Padres sold catcher Tom Lampkin to the Milwaukee Brewers.

March 30—The Padres traded outfielder Darrin Jackson to the Toronto Blue Jays for outfielders Derek Bell and Stoney Briggs.

April 2—The Padres claimed outfielder Phil Clark on waivers from the Detroit Tigers.

May 20—The Padres organization released pitcher Juan Agosto.

May 27—The Padres granted pitcher Dave Eiland free agency.

June 1—The Padres traded pitcher Jeremy Hernandez to the Cleveland Indians for outfielder Tracy Sanders and pitcher Fernando Hernandez.

June 23—The Padres traded pitcher Tim Scott to the Montreal Expos for infielder-outfielder Archi Cianfrocco.

June 24—The Padres traded third baseman Gary Sheffield and pitcher Rich Rodriguez to the Florida Marlins for pitchers Trevor Hoffman, Jose Martinez, and Andres Beruman. The Padres assigned Martinez to Las Vegas, Nevada and Beruman to Wichita, Kansas.

July 3—The Padres traded pitcher Roger Mason to the Philadelphia Phillies for pitcher Tim Mauser.

July 10—The Padres signed pitcher Mark Davis, a free agent.

July 18—The Padres traded first baseman Fred McGriff to the Atlanta Braves for outfielder Melvin Nieves, pitcher Donnie Elliott, and outfielder Vince Moore.

July 22—The Padres organization signed pitcher Rudy Seanez, a free agent.

July 26—The Padres traded pitchers Bruce Hurst and Greg W. Harris to the Colorado Rockies for catcher Brad Ausmus, pitcher Doug Bochtler, and a player to be named. The Padres acquired pitcher Andy Ashby to complete the deal on July 27.

July 26—The Padres released infielder Kurt Stillwell.

October 15—The Padres released catcher Mike Scioscia.

November 18—The Atlanta Braves claimed outfielder Jarvis Brown on waivers from the Padres.

November 18—The Padres released pitcher Rudy Seanez.

November 18—The Colorado Rockies claimed outfielder Darrell Sherman on waivers from the Padres.

December 10—The Padres traded pitcher Frank Seminara, outfielder Tracy Sanders, and a player to be named to the New York Mets for outfielder Randy Curtis and a player to be named. The Padres acquired pitcher Marc Kroon and the Mets acquired shortstop Pablo Martinez to complete the deal on December 13.

1994

January 7—The Padres organization signed infielder Keith Lockhart, a free agent formerly with the St. Louis Cardinals organization.

January 10—The Padres signed second baseman Bip Roberts, a free agent formerly with the Cincinnati Reds.

January 20—The Padres released second baseman Jeff Gardner.

January 28—The Padres organization signed infielder Harold Reynolds, a free agent formerly with the Baltimore Orioles.

February 27—The San Francisco Giants signed pitcher Pat Gomez, a free agent formerly with the Padres.

March 29—The Padres traded second baseman Harold Reynolds to the California Angels for pitcher Hilly Hathaway.

March 29—The Padres released first baseman Guillermo Velasquez.

May 11—The Padres traded pitcher Gene Harris to the Detroit Tigers for third baseman Scott Livingstone.

May 12—The Padres claimed pitcher Jeff Tabaka on waivers from the Pittsburgh Pirates.

May 24—The Padres released pitcher Mark Davis.

November 23—The Baltimore Orioles organization signed pitcher Frank Seminara, a free agent formerly with the Padres.

November 28—The Padres released pitcher Wally Whitehurst and infielder Archi Cianfrocco.

December 1—The Padres re-signed third baseman Archi Cianfrocco.

December 28—The Padres traded outfielders Phil Plantier and Derek Bell, pitchers Pedro A. Martinez and Doug Brocail, and infielders Craig Shipley and Ricky Gutierrez to the Houston Astros for third baseman Ken Caminiti, outfielder Steve Finley, infielders Andujar Cedeno and Roberto Petagine, pitcher Brian Williams, and a player to be named later (Sean Fesh). The Padres acquired pitcher Sean Fesh to complete the deal on May 1, 1995.

1995

April 5—The Padres signed pitcher Fernando Valenzuela, a free agent formerly with the Philadelphia Phillies.

April 19—The Padres signed second baseman Jody Reed, a free agent formerly with the Milwaukee Brewers.

April 30—The Padres returned pitcher Nate Cromwell, whom they had selected in Rule 5 Draft, to the Houston Astros organization.

July 19—The Padres traded pitcher Jeff Tabaka and Rich Loiselle to the Houston Astros for outfielder Phil Plantier.

July 31—The Padres traded pitcher Andy Benes to the Seattle Mariners for pitcher Ron Villone, outfielder Marc Newfield, and a player to be named. The Mariners acquired pitcher Greg Keagle to complete the deal on September 17.

October 10—The Padres traded infielder Ray Holbert to the Houston Astros for pitcher Pedro A. Martinez.

December 7—The Detroit Tigers signed outfielder Phil Plantier, a free agent formerly with the Padres.

December 15—The Padres traded pitcher Pedro A. Martinez to the New York Mets for outfielder Jeff Barry.

December 18—The Padres signed pitcher Bob Tewksbury, a free agent formerly with the Texas Rangers.

December 21—The Padres traded infielder Bip Roberts and pitcher Bryan Wolff to the Kansas City Royals for first baseman Wally Joyner and pitcher Aaron Dorlarque.

December 21—The Montreal Expos claimed outfielder Ray McDavid on waivers from the Padres.

December 21—The Padres released pitchers Willie Blair and Brian Williams and third baseman Eddie Williams.

December 21—The Padres signed shortstop Andujar Cedeno.

December 29—The Padres signed outfielder Rickey Henderson, a free agent formerly with the Oakland Athletics.

1996

January 5—The Padres signed shortstop Craig Shipley.

January 13—The Padres organization signed outfielder Chris Gwynn.

June 18—The Padres traded catcher Brad Ausmus, shortstop Andujar Cedeno, and pitcher Russ Spear to the Detroit Tigers for catcher John Flaherty and shortstop Chris Gomez.

July 31—The Padres traded pitchers Bryce Florie and Ron Villone and outfielder Marc Newfield to the Milwaukee Brewers for outfielder Greg Vaughn and a player to be named. The Padres acquired outfielder Gerald Parent to complete the deal on September 16.

August 1—The Padres organization signed pitcher Al Osuna.

November 21—The Padres traded pitcher Dustin Hermanson to the Florida Marlins for infielder Quilvio Veras.

December 2—The Padres signed catcher Carlos Hernandez.

December 6—The Padres traded pitcher Scott Sanders to the Seattle Mariners for pitcher Sterling Hitchcock.

December 17—The Padres traded catcher Brian Johnson and pitcher Willie Blair to the Detroit Tigers for pitchers Joey Eischen and Cam Smith.

December 23—The Padres organization signed catcher Don Slaught.

1997

January 3—The Padres released first baseman Jason Thompson.

January 9—The Padres traded catcher Leroy McKinnis to the Baltimore Orioles for outfielder Mark Smith.

January 17—The Padres organization signed outfielder Phil Plantier.

January 22—The Padres sold catcher Sean Mulligan to the Cleveland Indians.

March 15—The Padres traded pitcher Joey Eischen to the Cincinnati Reds for a player to be named. The Padres acquired infielder Ray Brown to complete the deal on March 19.

March 15—The Padres traded infielder Luis Lopez to the Houston Astros for pitcher Sean Runyan. Runyan was assigned to Mobile, Alabama

March 22—The Padres traded second baseman Jody Reed to the Detroit Tigers for outfielder Mike Darr and pitcher Matt Skrmetta.

March 29—The Padres traded outfielder Mark Smith and pitcher Hal Garrett to the Pittsburgh Pirates for outfielder Trey Beamon and catcher Angelo Encarnacion.

April 22—The Padres traded the rights to pitcher Hideki Irabu, second baseman Homer Bush, outfielder Gordon Amerson, and a player to be named to the New York Yankees for outfielder Ruben Rivera, pitcher Rafael Medina, and $3 million. The Yankees signed Irabu on May 29 and acquired outfielder Vernon Maxwell to complete the deal on June 9.

May 16—The Padres released pitcher Tim Scott.

June 10—The Padres traded pitcher Andres Berumen to the Seattle Mariners for pitcher Paul Menhart.

June 13—The Padres traded pitcher Fernando Valenzuela, third baseman Scott Livingstone, and outfielder Phil Plantier to the St. Louis Cardinals for pitcher Danny Jackson, Rich Batchelor, and outfielder Mark Sweeney.

August 9—The Padres announced the retirement of pitcher Danny Jackson.

August 13—The Padres traded outfielder Ricky Henderson to the Anaheim Angels for pitchers Ryan Hancock and Stevenson Agosto and a player to be named. The Padres acquired third baseman George Arias to complete the deal on August 19.

October 13—The Padres claimed infielder Ed Giovanola on waivers from the Atlanta Braves.

November 18—The Padres traded catcher John Flaherty to the Tampa Bay Devil Rays for pitcher Brian Boehringer and shortstop Andy Sheets.

November 19—The Padres traded outfielder Trey Beamon and pitcher Tim Worrell to the Detroit Tigers for pitchers Dan Miceli and Donne Wall and third baseman Ryan Balfe.

November 20—The Padres traded pitcher Chris Clark to the Florida Marlins for pitcher Ed Vosberg.

November 25—The Padres signed catcher Greg Myers.

November 25—The Padres released pitcher Rich Batchelor.

November 26—The Padres traded pitcher Doug Botchler and infielder Jorge Velandia to the Oakland Athletics for pitcher Don Wengert and infielder David Newhan.

December 15—The Padres traded pitchers Rafael Medina and Steve Hoff and first baseman Derrek Lee to the Florida Marlins for pitcher Kevin Brown.

1998

January 7—The Padres organization signed pitcher Mark Langston.

January 13—The Padres organization signed first baseman Eddie Williams.

January 14—The Padres traded pitcher Sean Bergman to the Houston Astros for outfielder James Mouton.

April 8—The Padres traded pitcher Marc Kroon to the Cincinnati Reds for pitcher Buddy Carlyle.

April 23—The Padres organization signed pitcher Roberto Ramirez.

May 5—The Padres traded pitcher Don Wengert to the Chicago Cubs for pitcher Ben VanRyn.

May 6—The Padres traded a player to be named to the Detroit Tigers for pitcher Scott Sanders. The Tigers acquired outfielder Rod Lindsey to complete the deal on June 1.

June 9—The Padres traded pitcher Pete Smith to the Baltimore Orioles for pitcher Eric Estes.

June 20—The Padres traded pitchers Carlos Reyes and Dario Veras and catcher Mandy Romero to the Boston Red Sox for catcher Jim Leyritz and outfielder Ethan Faggett.

July 23—The Padres traded pitcher Widd Workman to the Los Angeles Dodgers for pitcher Jim Bruske.

August 6—The Padres traded catcher Brian Loyd and a player to be named to the Toronto Blue Jays for pitcher Randy Myers.

August 31—The Padres traded a player to be named to the Colorado Rockies for outfielder John Vander Wal. The Rockies acquired outfielder Kevin Burford to complete the deal on October 29.

November 14—The Houston Astros signed third baseman Ken Caminiti, a free agent formerly with the Padres.

November 17—The Padres released infielder Archi Cianfrocco and pitcher Scott Sanders.

December 7—The Arizona Diamondbacks signed outfielder Steve Finley, a free agent formerly with the Padres.

December 12—The Padres traded pitcher Joey Hamilton to the Toronto Blue Jays for pitchers Woody Williams and Carlos Almanzar and outfielder Peter Tucci.

December 12—The Los Angeles Dodgers signed pitcher Kevin Brown, a free agent formerly with the Padres.

1999

February 2—The Padres traded outfielder Greg Vaughn and first baseman-outfielder Mark Sweeney to the Cincinnati Reds for outfielder Reggie Sanders, shortstop Damian Jackson, and pitcher Josh Harris.

February 4—The Padres organization signed pitcher Carlos Reyes.

March 29—The Padres traded infielder Andy Sheets and outfielder Gus Kennedy to the Anaheim Angels for catcher Phil Nevin and pitcher Keith Volkman.

April 1—The Padres released pitcher Mark Langston.

June 5—The Padres organization released pitcher Ed Vosberg.

June 5—The Padres organization signed second baseman Carlos Baerga.

July 8—The Padres traded shortstop Juan Melo to the Toronto Blue Jays for pitcher Isabel Giron.

July 26—The Padres traded catcher Greg Myers to the Atlanta Braves for pitcher Doug Dent.

July 31—The Padres traded catcher-first baseman Jim Leyritz to the New York Yankees for pitcher Geraldo Padua.

August 16—The Padres sold second baseman Carlos Baerga to the Cleveland Indians.

August 20—The Padres signed pitcher Matt Whisenant.

October 6—The Cincinnati Reds claimed pitcher Heath Murray on waivers from the Padres.

October 6—The Philadelphia Phillies claimed pitcher Carlos Reyes on waivers from the Padres.

October 25—The Padres organization signed pitcher Matt Whiteside.

November 4—The Padres organization signed pitcher Vicente Palacios.

November 10—The Padres traded pitcher Andy Ashby to the Philadelphia Phillies for pitchers Carlton Loewer, Steve Montgomery, and Adam Eaton.

November 15—The Padres traded pitcher Dan Miceli to the Florida Marlins for pitcher Brian Meadows.

November 22—The Padres organization signed first baseman Joe Vitiello, pitcher Stan Spencer, and catchers George Williams and John Roskos.

December 13—The Padres selected outfielder Kory DeHaan from the Pittsburgh Pirates in the Rule V Draft.

December 22—The Padres traded outfielder Brandon Pernell to the Chicago Cubs for pitcher Dan Serafini.

December 22—The Padres traded second baseman Quilvio Veras, first baseman Wally Joyner, and outfielder Reggie Sanders to the Atlanta Braves for first baseman Ryan Klesko, second baseman Bret Boone, and pitcher Jason Shiell.

2000

February 3—The Padres organization signed third baseman Ed Sprague as a free agent.

February 23—The Padres traded outfielder John Vander Wal and pitchers Jim Sak and Geraldo Padua to the Pittsburgh Pirates for outfielder Al Martin.

March 24—The Padres traded outfielder Gary Matthews, Jr. to the Chicago Cubs for pitcher Rodney Myers.

June 30—The Padres traded third baseman Ed Sprague to the Boston Red Sox for pitcher Dennis Tankersley and infielder Cesar Saba.

July 12—The Padres claimed pitcher Todd Erdos of the New York Yankees on waivers.

July 17—The Padres traded outfielder Dusty Allen to the Detroit Tigers for third baseman Gabe Alvarez.

July 31—The Padres traded pitcher Brian Meadows to the Kansas City Royals for pitcher Jay Witasick.

July 31—The Padres traded catcher Carlos Hernandez and infielder Nathan Tebbs to the St. Louis Cardinals for pitcher Heathcliffe Slocumb and outfielder Ben Jackson.

July 31—The Padres traded outfielder Al Martin to the Seattle Mariners for outfielder John Mabry and pitcher Tom Davey.

August 4—The Padres acquired shortstop Desi Relaford from the Philadelphia Phillies for second baseman David Newhan.

August 31—The Padres signed third baseman Ed Sprague, a free agent formerly with the Boston Red Sox.

October 5—The New York Mets claimed pitcher Jason Middlebrook, formerly with the Padres, on waivers.

October 6—The Padres acquired pitcher Sean Lawrence from Schaumburg, Illinois of the Northern League.

October 12—The New York Mets claimed shortstop Desi Relaford, formerly with the Padres, on waivers.

October 17—The Padres claimed outfielder Mike Colangelo, formerly with the Arizona Diamondbacks, on waivers.

October 31—The Padres declined to exercise their option on second baseman Bret Boone.

November 3—The Padres sold pitcher Buddy Carlyle to the Hanshin Tigers of the Japanese Central League.

November 22—The Padres claimed pitcher Jason Middlebrook, formerly with the New York Mets, on waivers.

December 1—The Padres traded pitcher Brandon Kolb and a player to be named or cash to the Milwaukee Brewers for shortstop Santiago Perez.

December 11—The Padres traded pitcher Donne Wall to the New York Mets for outfielder Bubba Trammell.

December 13—The Padres signed third baseman Alex Arias, formerly with the Philadelphia Phillies, as a free agent.

December 13—The Padres selected shortstop Donaldo Mendez from the Houston Astros in the Rule V draft.

December 14—The New York Yankees organization signed pitcher Brian Boehringer, formerly with the Padres, as a free agent.

December 14—The Los Angeles Dodgers organization signed pitcher Matt Whisenant, formerly with the Padres, as a free agent.

December 17—The Padres organization signed outfielder/first baseman Kevin Witt, and second baseman Adam Riggs.

December 20—The Padres traded pitcher Will Cunnane to the Milwaukee Brewers for outfielder Chad Green to complete an earlier trade.

December 22—The Seattle Mariners signed second baseman Bret Boone, formerly with the Padres, as a free agent.

2001

January 5—The St. Louis Cardinals organization signed outfielder John Mabry, formerly with the Padres, as a free agent.

January 5—The Padres signed pitcher Kevin Jarvis, formerly with the Colorado Rockies, as a free agent.

January 12—The Padres released pitcher Heathcliff Slocumb.

January 26—The Padres sold first baseman Joe Vitiello to the Orix Blue Wave of the Japanese Pacific League.

January 29—The Padres organization signed catcher Rick Wilkins, formerly with the St. Louis Cardinals, as a free agent.

February 14—The Padres organization signed pitcher Rudy Seanez, formerly with the Atlanta Braves, as a free agent.

February 15—The Padres signed pitcher Bobby J. Jones, formerly with the New York Mets, as a free agent.

March 14—The Padres released outfielder Ruben Rivera.

March 19—The Padres organization signed outfielder Rickey Henderson, formerly with the Seattle Mariners, as a free agent.

March 21—The Cincinnati Reds signed outfielder Ruben Rivera, formerly with the Padres, as a free agent.

March 25—The Padres traded pitcher Carlos Almanzar to the New York Yankees for pitcher David Lee.

March 28—The Padres traded pitchers Matt Clement and Omar Ortiz and outfielder Eric Owens to the Florida Marlins for outfielder Mark Kotsay and infielder Cesar Crespo.

March 28—The Padres released infielder Ed Sprague.

April 11—The Padres claimed pitcher Jimmy Osting, formerly with the Colorado Rockies, on waivers.

May 11—The Padres claimed pitcher Jose Nunez, formerly with the Los Angeles Dodgers, on waivers.

June 22—The Padres released shortstop Chris Gomez.

June 23—The Padres acquired shortstop D'Angelo Jimenez from the New York Yankees for pitcher Jay Witasick.

June 27—The Florida Marlins signed shortstop Chris Gomez, formerly with the Padres, as a free agent.

July 10—The Padres traded minor league pitcher Shawn Camp and outfielder Shawn Garrett to the Pittsburgh Pirates for outfielder Emil Brown.

July 23—The Padres signed pitcher Chuck McElroy, formerly with the Baltimore Orioles, as a free agent.

July 30—The Padres traded pitcher Sterling Hitchcock to the New York Yankees for pitcher Brett Jodie and outfielder Darren Blakely.

August 2—The Padres acquired outfielder Ray Lankford from the St. Louis Cardinals for pitcher Woody Williams.

August 31—The Atlanta Braves claimed pitcher Rudy Seanez from the Padres on waivers for a player to be named later.

September 6—The Padres acquired pitcher Winston Abreu off waivers from the Atlanta Braves to complete the earlier trade.

October 11—The Padres released catcher Rick Wilkins.

November—The Padres released outfielder Rickey Henderson and pitcher Chuck McElroy. Infielder Dave Magadan retired as a player and became the club's roving batting instructor.

November 19—The Padres acquired infielder Tag Bozied from Joliet, Illinois of the Northern League.

November 20—The Padres claimed pitcher Rob Ramsay off waivers from the Seattle Mariners.

December 6—The Padres organization acquired outfielder Scott Morgan and pitchers Jason Kershner, Jason Boyd, and Brandon Villafuerte as free agents.

December 11—The Padres traded catcher Ben Davis, pitcher Wascar Serrano, and shortstop Alex Arias to the Seattle Mariners for pitcher Brett Tomko, catcher Tom Lampkin, shortstop Ramon Vazquez, and $1 million.

December 13—The Padres selected pitcher Ryan Baerlocher from the Kansas City Royals in the Rule V draft.

December 14—The Padres acquired infielder Bernabel Castro from the New York Yankees for outfielder Kevin Reese.

December 27—The Padres signed pitcher Alan Embree, formerly with the Chicago White Sox, as a free agent.

2002

January 2—The Padres organization signed catcher Mike Walbeck, formerly with the Anaheim Angels, as a free agent.

January 3— The New York Yankees claimed pitcher Brett Jodie, formerly with the Padres, off waivers.

January 18—The Padres organization signed outfielder Ron Gant, formerly with the Atlanta Braves, as a free agent.

January 23—The Padres organization signed pitcher Steve Reed, formerly with the Atlanta Braves, as a free agent.

January 30—The Padres organization signed infielder Deivi Cruz, formerly with the Detroit Tigers, as a free agent.

February 6—The Houston Astros organization signed pitcher Chuck McElroy, formerly with the Padres, as a free agent.

February 11—The Padres organization signed catcher Adam Amezcua.

February 13—The Boston Red Sox organization signed outfielder Rickey Henderson, formerly with the Padres, as a free agent.

February 22—The Padres organization signed outfielder Trenidad Hubbard, formerly with the Kansas City Royals, as a free agent.

March 16—The Padres organization signed outfielder Mark Sweeney, formerly with the New York Mets, as a free agent.

March 20—The Padres traded pitcher Winston Abreau to the Chicago Cubs for outfielder Keto Anderson.

March 23—The Padres traded infielder Damian Jackson and catcher Matt Walbeck to the Detroit Tigers for catcher Javier Cardona and outfielder Rich Gomez.

March 25—The Padres returned pitcher Brian Baerlocher, a selection in the Rule V draft, to the Kansas City Royals organization for $25,000 after he failed to make the Padres' major-league squad.

Padres All-Time Roster 1969-2001

Through the end of the 2001 season, 552 players have appeared in at least one game for the San Diego Padres.

Players

A (22)

Abner, Shawn (1987-91)
Acota, Ed (1971-72)
Aldrete, Mike (1991)
Allen, Dusty (2000)
Almanzar, Carlos (1999-2000)
Almon, Bill (1974-79)
Alomar, Roberto (1988-90)
Alomar, Jr., Sandy (1988-89)
Alou, Matty (1974)
Alvarez, Gabe (2000)
Andersen, Larry (1991-92)
Anderson, Dwain (1973)
Arcia, Jose (1969-70)
Arias, Alex (2001)
Arias, George (1997-99)
Arlin, Steve (1969-74)
Armstrong, Mike (1980-81)
Asadoor, Randy (1986)
Ashby, Andy (1993-99)
Ashford, Tucker (1976-78)
Ausmus, Brad (1993-96)
Azocar, Oscar (1991-92)

B (42)

Baerga, Carlos (1999)
Baker, Chuck (1978, 1980)
Baldschun, Jack (1969-70)
Barrett, Marty (1991)
Barton, Bob (1970-72, 1974)
Bass, Randy (1980-82)
Batchelor, Rich (1997)
Beamon, Trey (1997)
Bean, Billy (1993-95)
Beckert, Glenn (1974-75)
Bell, Derek (1993-94)
Benes, Andy (1989-95)
Bergman, Sean (1996-97)
Bernal, Victor (1977)
Berumen, Andres (1995-96)
Beswick, Jim (1978)
Bevacqua, Kurt (1979-80, 1982-85)
Bilardello, Dann (1991-92)
Blair, Dennis (1980)
Blair, Willie (1995-96)
Blefary, Curt (1972)
Bochtler, Doug (1995-97)
Bochy, Bruce (1983-87)
Boehringer, Brian (1998-2000)
Bones, Ricky (1991)
Bonilla, Juan (1981-83)
Booker, Greg (1983-89)
Boone, Bret (2000)
Boone, Dan (1981-82)
Bravo, Angel (1971)
Briggs, Dan (1979)
Brocail, Doug (1992-94)
Brown, Bobby (1983-85)
Brown, Chris (1987-88)
Brown, Emil (2001)
Brown, Jarvis (1993)
Brown, Kevin (1998)
Brown, Ollie (1969-72)
Bruske, Jim (1997)
Bumbry, Al (1985)
Burrows, Terry (1997)
Byers, Randell (1987-88)

C (32)

Caldwell, Mike (1971-73)
Caminiti, Ken (1995-98)
Campbell, Dave (1970-73)
Campbell, Mike (1994)
Cannizzaro, Chris (1969-71,1974)
Carlyle, Buddy (1999-2000)
Carter, Joe (1990)
Cash, Dave (1980)
Castillo, Tony (1978)
Cedeno, Andujar (1995-96)
Champion, Mike (1976-78)
Chiffer, Floyd (1982-84)
Cianfrocco, Archi (1993-98)
Clark, Jack (1989-90)
Clark, Jerald (1988-92)
Clark, Phil (1993-95)
Clarke, Horace (1974)
Clement, Matt (1998-2000)
Clements, Pat (1989-92)
Colangelo, Mike (2001)
Colbert, Nate (1969-74)
Comstock, Keith (1987-88)
Coolbaugh, Scott (1991)
Coombs, Danny (1970-71)
Cora, Joey (1987, 1989-90)
Corkins, Mike (1969-1974)
Corrales, Pat (1972-73)
Costello, John (1991)
Couchee, Mike (1983)
Crespo, Cesar (2001-)
Cunnane, Will (1997-2000)
Curtis, John (1980-82)

D (29)

D'Acquisto, John (1977-80)
Dade, Paul (1979-80)
Darr, Mike (1999-2001)
Dascenzo, Doug (1996)
DaVanon, Jerry (1969)
Davey, Tom (2000-)
Davis, Ben (1998-2001)
Davis, Bill (1969)
Davis, Bob (1973, 1975-78)
Davis, Jerry (1983, 1985)
Davis, John (1990)
Davis, Mark (1987-89, 1993-94)
Davis, Storm (1987)
Davis, Willie (1976)
Dean, Tommy (1969-71)

Decker, Marty (1983)
Deer, Rob (1996)
DeHaan, Kory (2000)
DeLeon, Luis (1982-85)
Deshaies, Jim (1992)
Dilone, Miguel (1985)
Dishman, Glenn (1995-96)
Dobson, Pat (1970)
Dorsett, Brian (1991)
Doyle, Paul (1970)
Dravecky, Dave (1982-87)
Dukes, Tom (1969-70)
Dunne, Mike (1990)
Dupree, Mike (1976)

E (10)

Eaton, Adam (2000-)
Edwards, Dave (1981-82)
Eichelberger, Juan (1978-82)
Eiland, David (1992-93)
Elliott, Donnie (1994-95)
Elliott, Randy (1972, 1974)
Erdos, Todd (1997, 2000)
Ettles, Mark (1993)
Evans, Barry (1978-81)
Everitt, Leon (1969)

F (18)

Fahey, Bill (1979-80)
Faries, Paul (1990-92)
Fernandez, Tony (1991-92)
Ferrara, Al (1969-71)
Fikac, Jeremy (2001-)
Fingers, Rollie (1977-80)
Finley, Steve (1995-98)
Fiore, Mike (1972)
Fireovid, Steve (1981, 1983)
Flaherty, John (1996-97)
Flannery, Tim (1979-89)
Florie, Bryce (1994-96)
Folkers, Rich (1975-76)
Foster, Alan (1975-76)
Franklin, Jay (1971)
Freisleben, Dave (1974-78)
Frisella, Danny (1975)
Fuentes, Tito (1975-76)

G (31)

Gamble, Oscar (1978)
Garcia, Carlos (1999)
Garcia, Ralph (1972, 1974)
Gardner, Jeff (1992-93)
Gardner, Wes (1991)
Garvey, Steve (1983-87)
Gaspar, Rod (1971, 1974)
Gaston, Clarence (1969-74)
Geren, Bob (1993)
Gerhardt, Rusty (1974)
Giovanola, Ed (1998-99)
Goddard, Joe (1972)
Gomez, Chris (1996-2001)
Gomez, Pat (1993)
Gonzalez, Fernando (1978-79)
Gonzalez, Tony (1969)
Gonzalez, Wiki (1999-)
Gorman, Tom (1987)
Gossage, Rich (1984-87)
Grant, Mark (1987-90)
Green, Gary (1986, 1989)
Greer, Brian (1977, 1979)
Greif, Bill (1972-76)
Griffin, Mike (1982)
Griffin, Tom (1976-77)
Grubb, John (1972-76)
Gutierrez, Ricky (1993-94)
Guzman, Domingo (1999-2000)
Gwosdz, Doug (1981-84)
Gwynn, Chris (1996)
Gwynn, Tony (1982-2001)

H (32)

Hahn, Don (1975)
Hamilton, Joey (1994-98)
Hammaker, Atlee (1990-91)
Hardy, Larry (1974-75)
Hargrove, Mike (1979)
Harris, Gene (1992-94)
Harris, Greg A. (1984)
Harris, Greg W. (1988-93)
Hawkins, Andy (1982-88)
Hayward, Ray (1986-87)
Henderson, Rickey (1996-97, 2001)
Hendrick, George (1977-78)
Herbel, Ron (1970)
Hermanson, Dustin (1995-96)
Hernandez, Carlos (1997-2000)
Hernandez, Enzo (1971-77)
Hernandez, Jeremy (1991-93)
Herndon, Junior (2001)
Higgins, Kevin (1993)
Hilton, Dave (1972-75)
Hinshaw, George (1982-83)
Hitchcock, Sterling (1997-2001)
Hoffman, Trevor (1993-)
Holbert, Ray (1994-95)
Howard, Thomas (1990-92)
Howell, Jack (1991)
Hoyt, LaMarr (1985-86)
Hriniak, Walt (1969)
Hundley, Randy (1975)
Huntz, Steve (1970, 1975)
Hurst, Bruce (1989-93)
Hyers, Tim (1994-95)

I (2)

Iorg, Dane (1986)
Ivie, Mike (1971, 1974-77)

J (22)

Jackson, Damian (1999-2001)
Jackson, Danny (1997)
Jackson, Darrin (1989-92)
Jackson, Roy Lee (1985)
James, Chris (1989)
Jarvis, Kevin (2001-)
Jefferson, Stan (1987-88)
Jestadt, Garry (1971-72)
Jeter, John (1971-72)
Jimenez, D'Angelo (2001-)
Jodie, Brett (2001-)
Johnson, Brian (1994-96)
Johnson, Jerry (1975-76)
Johnson, Mike (1974)
Johnstone, Jay (1979)
Jones, Bobby (2001-)
Jones, Chris (1997)
Jones, Jimmy (1986-88)
Jones, Randy (1973-80)
Jones, Ruppert (1981-83)
Joshua, Von (1980)
Joyner, Wally (1996-99)

K (17)

Kelley, Dick (1969-71)
Kelly, Van (1969-70)
Kendall, Fred (1969-76, 1979-80)
Kennedy, Terry (1981-86)
Kilkenny, Mike (1972)
Kingman, Dave (1977)
Kinney, Dennis (1978-80)
Kirby, Clay (1969-73)
Klesko, Ryan (2000-)
Kolb, Brandon (2000)
Kotsay, Mark (2001-)
Kroon, Marc (1995, 1997-98)
Krueger, Bill (1994-95)

Krug, Chris (1969)
Kruk, John (1986-89)
Kubiak, Ted (1975-76)
Kuhaulua, Fred (1981)

L (34)

Lampkin, Tom (1990-92)
Lancellotti, Rick (1982)
Langston, Mark (1998)
Lankford, Ray (2001-)
Lansford, Joe (1982-83)
LaPoint, Dave (1986)
LaRocca, Greg (2000)
Lawrence, Brian (2001-)
Laxton, Bill (1971, 1974)
Lee, David (2001)
Lee, Derrek (1997)
Lee, Leron (1971-73)
Lee, Mark (1978-79)
Lefebvre, Joe (1981-83)
Lefferts, Craig (1984-87, 1990-92)
Leiper, Dave (1987-89)
Lewis, Jim (1991)
Leyritz, Jim (1998-99)
Lezcano, Sixto (1982-83)
Libran, Francisco (1969)
Lilliquist, Derek (1990-91)
Littlefield, John (1981)
Livingstone, Scott (1994-97)
Lockhart, Keith (1994)
Locklear, Gene (1973-76)
Loewer, Carlton (2000-01)
Lolich, Mickey (1978-79)
Lollar, Tim (1981-84)
Long, Joey (1997)
Lopez, Luis (1993-94, 1996)
Lopez, Rodrigo (2000)
Lucas, Gary (1980-83)
Lynn, Fred (1990)

M (56)

Mabry, John (2000)
Mack, Shane (1987-88)
Maddux, Mike (1991-92)
Magadan, Dave (1999-2001)
Manuel, Jerry (1982)
Marshall, Dave (1973)
Martin, Al (2000)
Martinez, Carmelo (1984-89)
Martinez, Jose (1994)
Martinez, Pedro (1993-94)
Mason, Don (1971-73)
Mason, Roger (1993)
Matthews, Jr., Gary (1999)
Maurer, Dave (2000-01)
Mauser, Tim (1993-95)
McAndrew, Jim (1974)
McBean, Alvin (1969)
McCool, Billy (1969)
McCovey, Willie (1974-76)
McCullers, Lance (1985-88)
McDavid, Ray (1994-95)
McElroy, Chuck (2001)
McGriff, Fred (1991-93)
McIntosh, Joe (1974-75)
McReynolds, Kevin (1983-86)
Meadows, Brian (2000)
Melendez, Jose (1991-92)
Melendez, Luis (1976-77)
Mendez, Donaldo (2001)
Menhart, Paul (1997)
Metzger, Butch (1975-77)
Miceli, Dan (1998-99)
Middlebrook, Jason (2001-)
Miller, Bob (1971, 1973)
Miller, Ed (1984)
Mitchell, Kevin (1987)
Monge, Sid (1983-84)
Montanez, Willie (1980)
Montefusco, John (1982-83)
Montgomery, Steve L. (2000-01)
Morales, Jerry (1969-73)
Morales, Rich (1973-74)
Moreland, Keith (1988)
Moreno, Jose (1981)
Moses, Jerry (1975)
Mota, Jose (1991)
Mouton, James (1998)
Mulligan, Sean (1996)
Mumphrey, Jerry (1980)
Mura, Steve (1978-81)
Murphy, Dan (1989)
Murray, Heath (1997, 1999)
Murrell, Ivan (1969-73)
Myers, Greg (1998-99)
Myers, Randy (1992, 1998-00)
Myers, Rodney (2000-)

N (13)

Nady, Xavier (2000)
Nelson, Rob (1987-90)
Nevin, Phil (1999-)
Newfield, Marc (1995-96)
Newhan, David (1999-2000)
Nettles, Graig (1984-86)
Nicholson, Kevin (2000)
Niekro, Joe (1969)
Nieves, Melvin (1993-95)
Nolte, Eric (1987-89, 1991)
Norman, Fred (1971-73)
Nunez, Jose (2001-)
Nyman, Gerry (1970)

O (5)

Oquist, Mike (1996)
Osting, Jimmy (2001)
Osuna, Al (1996)
Owchinko, Bob (1976-79)
Owens, Eric (1999-2000)

P (20)

Pagliarulo, Mike (1989-90)
Palacios, Vicente (2000)
Palmer, Lowell (1974)
Parent, Mark (1986-90)
Patterson, Bob (1985)
Pena, Roberto (1969)
Perez, Santiago (2001)
Perkins, Broderick (1978-82)
Perlozzo, Sammy (1979)
Perry, Gaylord (1978-79)
Petagine, Roberto (1995)
Peterson, Adam (1991)
Pettis, Gary (1992)
Phillips, Mike (1981)
Phoebus, Tom (1971-72)
Pittman, Joe (1982)
Plantier, Phil (1993-95, 1997)
Podres, Johnny (1969)
Presley, Jim (1991)
Pyznarski, Tim (1986)

Q (0)

None

R (35)

Rader, Doug (1976-77)
Ramirez, Mario (1981-85)
Ramirez, Roberto (1998)
Rasmussen, Dennis (1983, 1988-91)
Rasmussen, Eric (1978-80)
Ready, Randy (1986-89)
Reberger, Frank (1969)
Reed, Jody (1995-96)
Relaford, Desi (2000)
Rettenmund, Merv (1976-77)

Reyes, Carlos (1998, 1999, 2000)
Reynolds, Don (1978-79)
Reynolds, Ken (1976)
Reynolds, Ronn (1990)
Richards, Gene (1977-83)
Riggs, Adam (2001)
Rivera, Roberto (1999)
Rivera, Ruben (1997-2000)
Roberts, David A. (1969-71)
Roberts, David W. (1972-75, 1977-78)
Roberts, Leon (1986, 1988-91, 1994-95)
Robinson, Dave (1970-71)
Robles, Rafael (1969-70, 1972)
Rodriguez, Aurelio (1980)
Rodriguez, Edwin (1983, 1985)
Rodriguez, Rich (1990-93)
Rodriguez, Roberto (1970)
Roenicke, Ron (1984)
Romero, Mandy (1997-98)
Romo, Vicente (1973-74)
Rosenberg, Steve (1991)
Roskos, John (2000)
Ross, Gary (1969-74)
Royster, Jerry (1985-86)
Ruberto, Sonny (1969)

S (61)

Sager, A. J. (1994)
Salazar, Luis (1980-84, 1987, 1989)
Sanders, Reggie (1999)
Sanders, Scott (1993-96, 1998)
Santiago, Benito (1986-92)
Santorini, Al (1969-71)
Sawyer, Rick (1976-77)
Scanlon, Pat (1977)
Schaeffer, Mark (1972)
Schiraldi, Calvin (1989-90)
Schulze, Don (1989)
Scott, John (1974-75)
Scott, Tim (1991-93, 1997)
Seanez, Rudy (1993, 2001)
Selma, Dick (1969)
Seminara, Frank (1992-93)
Serafini, Dan (2000)
Serrano, Wascar (2001)
Severinsen, Al (1971-72)
Sharon, Dick (1975)
Sheets, Andy (1998)
Sheffield, Gary (1992-93)
Sherman, Darrell (1993)
Shipley, Craig (1991-94, 1996-97)
Shirley, Bob (1977-80)
Show, Eric (1981-90)
Shumpert, Terry (1997)
Siebert, Paul (1977)
Siebert, Sonny (1975)
Sierra, Candy (1988)
Simpson, Steve (1972)
Sipin, John (1969)
Sisk, Tommie (1969)
Slaught, Don (1997)
Slocum, Ron (1969-71)
Slocumb, Heathcliff (2000)
Smith, Ozzie (1978-81)
Smith, Pete (1997-98)
Snook, Frank (1973)
Sosa, Elias (1983)
Spencer, Stan (1998-2000)
Spiezio, Ed (1969-72)
Spillner, Dan (1974-78)
Sprague, Ed, Jr. (2000)
Stablein, George (1980)
Stahl, Larry (1969-72)
Stanley, Fred (1972)
Staton, Dave (1993-94)
Steels, James (1987)
Stephenson, Phil (1989-92)
Steverson, Todd (1996)
Stilwell, Kurt (1992-93)
Stimac, Craig (1980-81)
Stoddard, Bob (1986)
Stoddard, Tim (1985-86)
Strom, Brent (1975-77)
Summers, Champ (1984)
Sutherland, Gary (1977)
Sweeney, Mark (1997-98)
Sweet, Rick (1978)
Swisher, Steve (1981-82)

T (23)

Tabaka, Jeff (1994-95)
Tatum, Jim (1996)
Taylor, Kerry (1993-94)
Taylor, Ron (1972)
Tellman, Tom (1979-80)
Tenace, Gene (1977-80)
Templeton, Garry (1982-91)
Terrell, Walt (1989)
Teufel, Tim (1991-93)
Tewksbury, Bob (1996)
Thomas, Derrel (1972-74, 1978)
Thompson, Jason (1996)
Thon, Dickie (1988)
Thurmond, Mark (1983-86)
Tingley, Ron (1982)
Tolan, Bobby (1974-75, 1979)
Toliver, Fred (1989)
Tollberg, Brian (2000-)
Tomlin, Dave (1974-77)
Torres, Hector (1975-76)
Trammell, Bubba (2001-)
Troedsen, Rich (1973-74)
Turner, Jerry (1974-81, 1983)

U (1)

Urrea, John (1981)

V (14)

Valdez, Rafael (1990)
Valentine, Bobby (1975-77)
Valenzuela, Fernando (1995-97)
Vander Wal, John (1998-99)
Van Ryn, Ben (1998)
Vatcher, Jim (1991-92)
Vaughn, Greg (1996-98)
Velandia, Jorge (1997)
Velasquez, Guillermo (1992-93)
Veras, Dario (1996-98)
Veras, Quilvio (1997-99)
Villone, Ron (1995-96)
Vitiello, Joe (2000)
Vosberg, Ed (1986, 1998-99)

W (34)

Walker,Kevin (2000-)
Walker, Pete (1996)
Wall, Donne (1998-2000)
Walter, Gene (1985-86)
Walters, Dan (1992-93)
Ward, Kevin (1991-92)
Wasinger, Mark (1986)
Webster, Ramon (1970-71)
Wehrmeister, Dave (1976-78)
Welsh, Chris (1981-83)
Wengert, Don (1998)
Whisenant, Matt (1999-2000)
Whitehurst, Wally (1993-94)
Whiteside, Matt (1999-2000)
Whitson, Ed (1983-84, 1986-91)
Wiggins, Alan (1981-85)
Wiley, Mark (1978)
Wilhelm, Jim (1978-79)
Wilkins, Rick (2001)
Williams, Bernie (1974)
Williams, Brian (1995)
Williams, Eddie (1990, 1994-95, 1998)
Williams, George (2000)

Williams, Jim (1969-70)
Williams, Woody (1999-2001)
Willis, Ron (1970)
Wilson, Earl (1970)
Winfield, Dave (1973-80)
Wise, Rick (1980-82)
Witasick, Jay (2000-01)
Witt, Kevin (2001)
Wojna, Ed (1985-87)
Worrell, Tim (1993-97)
Wynne, Marvell (1986-89)

X (0)

None

Y (0)

None

Z (0)

None

Managers (15)

Bochy, Bruce (1995-)
Boros, Steve (1986)
Bowa, Larry (1987-88)
Coleman, Jerry (1980)
Craig, Roger (1978-79)
Dark, Alvin (1977)
Gomez, Preston (1969-72)
Howard, Frank (1981)
McKeon, Jack (1988-90)
McNamara, John (1974-77)
Riddoch, Greg (1990-92)
Riggleman, Jim (1992-94)
Skinner, Bob (1977)
Williams, Dick (1982-85)
Zimmer, Don (1972-73)

Coaches (60)

Akerfelds, Darrel (2001)
Alomar, Sandy (1986-90)
Amalfitano, Joe (1976-77)
Anderson, Sparky (1969)
Bialas, Dave (1993-94)
Bloomfield, Jack (1974)
Bochy, Bruce (1993-94)
Booker, Greg (1997-)
Brinkman, Eddie (1981)
Cisco, Galen (1985-87)
Craig, Roger (1969-72, 1976-78)
Davenport, Jim (1974-75)
Dobson, Pat (1988-90)
Dunlop, Harry (1983-87)
Espy, Duane (2000-)
Estrada, Chuck (1978-81)
Flannery, Tim (1996-)
Garcia, Dave (1970-73)
Heist, Al (1980)
Herman, Billy (1978-79)
Jones, Deacon (1984-87)
Kimm, Bruce (1991-92)
Krol, Jack (1981-86)
Little, Grady (1996)
Lopes, Davey (1995-99)
Maloof, Jack (1990)
McCullough, Clyde (1980-82)
Moon, Wally (1969)
Morgan, Tom (1975)
Nettles, Graig (1995)
Oglivie, Ben (2000)
Otis, Amos (1988-90)
Phillips, Dick (1980)
Picciolo, Rob (1990-)
Podres, John (1973)
Posedel, Bill (1974)
Rader, Doug (1978-79)
Radison, Dan (1993-94)
Rettenmund, Merv (1991-99)
Riddoch, Greg (1987-90)
Rigney, Bill (1975)
Roarke, Mike (1991-93)
Roof, Phil (1978)
Sherry, Norm (1982-84)
Siebert, Sonny (1994-95)
Sisler, Dick (1975-76)
Skinner, Bob (1970-73, 1977)
Smith, Dave (1999-2001)
Snyder, Jim (1991-92)
Sommers, Denny (1988-90)
Stevens, Ed (1981)
Stewart, Dave (1998)
Tolan, Bobby (1980-83)
Trammell, Alan (2000-)
Virgil, Ozzie (1982-85)
Waller, Tye (1995)
Warthen, Dan (1996-97)
Wietelmann, Whitey (1969-79)
Williams, Don (1977-80)
Zimmer, Don (1972-73)

Statistics

The San Diego Padres media guides provided the information for the various statistical charts in the remainder of this section, except for the sections on All-Time Padre Batting Statistics and All-Time Padre Pitching Statistics. The authors are grateful to the Padres for granting permission to use this material.

ANNUAL STANDINGS AND ATTENDANCE

Year	Home W-L	Away W-L	Total W-L	Pct.	Pos.	GB	Home Attendance
1969	28-53	24-57	52-110	.321	6	41	613,327
1970	31-50	32-49	63-99	.389	6	39	633,439
1971	33-48	28-52	61-100	.379	6	28.5	549,085
1972	26-54	32-41	58-95	.379	6	36.5	644,272
1973	31-50	29-52	60-102	.370	6	39	611,826
1974	36-45	24-57	60-102	.370	6	42	1,075,399
1975	38-43	33-48	71-91	.438	4	37	1,281,747
1976	42-38	31-51	73-89	.451	5	29	1,458,478
1977	35-46	34-47	69-93	.426	5	29	1,376,269
1978	50-31	34-47	84-78	.519	4	11	1,670,107
1979	39-42	29-51	68-93	.422	5	22	1,456,967
1980	45-36	28-53	73-89	.451	6	19.5	1,139,026
1981	20-35	21-34	41-69	.373	6	26	519,161
1982	43-38	38-43	81-81	.500	4	8	1,607,516
1983	47-34	34-47	81-81	.500	4	10	1,539,819
1984	48-33	44-37	92-70	.568	1	(12)	1,983,904
1985	44-37	39-42	83-79	.512	T3	12	2,210,352
1986	43-38	31-50	74-88	.457	4	22	1,805,776
1987	37-44	28-53	65-97	.401	6	25	1,454,061
1988	47-34	36-44	83-78	.516	3	11	1,506,896
1989	46-35	43-38	89-73	.549	2	3	2,009,032
1990	37-44	38-43	75-87	.463	T4	16	1,856,395
1991	42-39	42-39	84-78	.519	3	10	1,804,289
1992	45-36	37-44	82-80	.506	3	16	1,722,102
1993	34-47	27-54	61-101	.377	7	43	1,375,432
1994	26-31	21-39	47-70	.402	4	12.5	953,857
1995	40-32	30-42	70-74	.486	3	8	1,041,805
1996	45-36	46-35	91-71	.562	1	(1)	2,187,886
1997	39-42	37-44	76-86	.469	4	14	2,089,333
1998	54-27	44-37	98-64	.604	1	(9.5)	2,555,901
1999	46-35	28-53	74-88	.457	4	26	2,523,538
2000	41-40	35-46	76-86	.469	5	21	2,423,149
2001	35-46	44-37	79-83	.488	4	13	2,378,116

ALL-TIME WIN-LOSS BREAKDOWN

	Home All-Time	Road All-Time	All-Time
Season	1,293-1,319	1,101-1,506	2,394-2,825
Day Games	351-351	377-530	732-881
Night Games	938-968	724-876	1662-1,944
vs. RHP	970-952	784-1081	1,754-2,033

	Home All-Time	Road All-Time	All-Time
vs. LHP	364-407	352-471	716-878
One-Run Games	511-464	316-511	827-975
Extra Innings	134-129	107-139	241-268
Shutouts	179-190	129-202	308-392
Doubleheaders	24-19	17-43	41-62
March	0-0	1-0	1-0
April	184-193	132-197	316-390
May	223-237	197-255	420-492
June	238-216	181-259	419-475
July	213-225	181-252	394-477
August	214-200	212-289	426-489
September	207-228	175-239	382-467
October	17-16	19-19	36-35
First Half	687-698	545-742	1,232-1,440
Second Half	627-638	556-764	1,183-1,402

ANNUAL RECORDS AGAINST OPPONENTS

Team	1969	1970	1971	1972	1973	1974	1975	1976	1977
Atlanta	5-13	9-9	7-11	11-6	6-12	1-17	11-7	8-10	7-11
Chicago	1-11	3-9	3-9	3-9	5-7	6-6	7-5	6-6	5-7
Cincinnati	7-11	10-8	8-10	10-8	5-13	6-12	7-11	5-13	7-11
Houston	8-10	4-14	8-10	2-12	8-10	7-11	9-9	8-10	10-8
Los Angeles	6-12	7-11	5-13	5-13	9-9	2-16	7-11	12-6	6-12
Montreal	8-4	6-6	5-6	6-6	5-7	6-6	5-7	8-4	7-5
New York	1-11	6-6	5-7	5-7	4-8	6-6	4-8	5-7	6-6
Philadelphia	4-8	3-9	8-4	6-6	3-9	7-5	5-7	4-8	3-9
Pittsburgh	2-10	6-6	3-9	2-10	4-8	3-9	4-8	5-7	2-10
St. Louis	4-8	4-8	4-8	4-8	4-8	5-7	4-8	4-8	8-4
San Francisco	6-12	5-13	5-13	4-10	7-11	11-7	8-10	8-10	8-10

Team	1978	1979	1980	1981	1982	1983	1984	1985	1986
Atlanta	10-8	12-6	6-12	6-9	7-11	9-9	11-7	11-7	6-12
Chicago	5-7	3-9	8-4	3-3	8-4	7-5	6-6	4-8	6-6
Cincinnati	9-9	7-10	3-15	2-10	12-6	9-9	11-7	9-9	9-9
Houston	10-8	4-14	7-11	3-11	9-9	7-11	12-6	6-12	8-10
Los Angeles	9-9	9-9	9-9	5-6	9-9	12-6	8-10	10-8	12-6
Montreal	6-6	5-7	2-10	2-4	5-7	4-8	5-7	7-5	8-4
New York	7-5	8-4	11-1	5-2	6-6	6-6	6-6	5-7	2-10
Philadelphia	4-8	3-9	4-8	2-4	5-7	7-5	5-7	7-5	6-6
Pittsburgh	7-5	5-7	6-6	4-6	6-6	3-9	8-4	8-4	4-8
St. Louis	9-3	4-8	7-5	3-7	4-8	6-6	7-5	4-8	5-7
San Francisco	8-10	8-10	10-8	6-7	10-8	11-7	13-5	12-6	8-10

Team	1987	1988	1989	1990	1991	1992	1993	1994	1995
Atlanta	12-6	10-8	11-7	10-8	7-11	5-13	4-9	1-6	2-5
Chicago	3-9	4-8	4-8	4-8	8-4	7-5	4-8	3-6	7-5
Cincinnati	6-12	8-10	9-9	9-9	10-8	7-11	4-9	2-8	6-3
Colorado							7-6	5-5	4-9
Florida							5-7	1-5	2-3
Houston	13-5	12-6	10-8	14-4	12-6	11-7	5-8	5-5	4-7
Los Angeles	7-11	11-7	12-6	9-9	8-10	9-9	4-9	4-6	6-7
Montreal	3-9	8-4	7-5	5-7	6-6	4-8	2-10	0-12	5-7
New York	4-8	5-7	7-5	7-5	5-7	8-4	7-5	6-6	7-6
Philadelphia	4-8	7-4	10-2	5-7	3-9	9-3	6-6	8-4	6-6
Pittsburgh	4-8	4-8	9-3	2-10	5-7	7-5	3-9	3-3	8-4
St. Louis	4-8	6-6	2-10	3-9	9-3	4-8	7-5	4-2	7-5
San Francisco	5-13	8-10	8-10	7-11	11-7	11-7	3-10	5-2	6-7

Team	1996	1997	1998	1999	2000	2001
Anaheim		2-2	2-1	3-0	1-2	1-2
Arizona			9-3	2-11	4-9	7-12
Atlanta	4-9	3-8	4-5	4-5	1-8	3-3
Chicago	6-6	5-6	4-5	3-6	5-3	4-2
Cincinnati	3-9	6-5	11-1	3-6	5-4	4-2
Colorado	5-8	8-4	7-5	9-4	6-7	10-9
Florida	9-3	6-5	5-4	6-3	7-2	4-3
Houston	6-6	5-6	4-5	1-8	7-2	6-3
Los Angeles	8-5	7-5	7-5	9-3	5-8	10-9
Milwaukee			6-3	5-3	7-2	5-1
Montreal	8-4	3-8	4-4	3-5	6-3	3-3
New York	10-3	6-5	5-4	2-7	6-3	5-1
Oakland		1-3	1-2	2-1	0-3	1-2
Philadelphia	8-4	4-7	8-1	3-6	5-2	2-5
Pittsburgh	9-4	6-5	4-5	6-3	2-7	4-2
Seattle		3-1	2-2	4-2	3-3	2-4
St. Louis	4-8	5-6	6-3	2-7	0-9	1-5
San Francisco	11-2	4-8	8-4	5-7	5-7	5-14
Texas		2-2	1-2	2-1	1-2	2-1

PADRES AWARD WINNERS

National League Most Valuable Player
1996—Ken Caminiti, 3B (BBWAA)

National League Cy Young Award
1976—Randy Jones (BBWAA)
1978—Gaylord Perry (BBWAA)
1989—Mark Davis (BBWAA)

Rawlings Gold Glove Award
1979—Dave Winfield, OF
1980—Dave Winfield, OF, Ozzie Smith, SS
1981—Ozzie Smith, SS
1986—Tony Gwynn, OF
1987—Tony Gwynn, OF
1988—Benito Santiago, C
1989—Tony Gwynn, OF, Benito Santiago, C
1990—Tony Gwynn, OF, Benito Santiago, C
1991—Tony Gwynn, OF
1995—Ken Caminiti, 3B, Steve Finley, CF
1996—Ken Caminiti, 3B, Steve Finley, CF
1997—Ken Caminiti, 3B

The Sporting News All-League Team
1975—Randy Jones, LHP
1976—Randy Jones, LHP
1978—Gaylord Perry, RHP
1979—Dave Winfield, OF
1984—Tony Gwynn, OF, Mark Thurmond, LHP
1986—Tony Gwynn, OF
1987—Tony Gwynn, OF, Benito Santiago, C
1989—Tony Gwynn, OF, Benito Santiago, C
1994—Tony Gwynn, OF
1995—Ken Caminiti, 3B
1996—Ken Caminiti, 3B

Player of the Year
1992—Gary Sheffield, 3B (*The Sporting News*)
1996—Ken Caminiti, 3B (ESPN)

National League Pitcher of the Year
1976—Randy Jones, LHP (*The Sporting News*)
1989—Mark Davis, LHP (*The Sporting News*)

National League Manager of the Year
1996—Bruce Bochy (BBWAA, *The Sporting News*)
1998—Bruce Bochy (*The Sporting News*)

National League Fireman of the Year
1977—Rollie Fingers (*The Sporting News*, Rolaids)
1978—Rollie Fingers (*The Sporting News*, Rolaids)
1980—Rollie Fingers (Rolaids, share of *The Sporting News*)
1989—Mark Davis (*The Sporting News*, Rolaids)
1996—Trevor Hoffman (*The Sporting News*)
1998—Trevor Hoffman (*The Sporting News*, Rolaids)

National League Rookie of the Year
1987—Benito Santiago (*The Sporting News*)

National League Rookie Pitcher of the Year
1976—Butch Metzger (*The Sporting News*, share of BBWAA)
1977—Bob Owchinko (*The Sporting News*)
1989—Andy Benes (*The Sporting News*)

Silver Slugger Team

1983—Terry Kennedy, C
1984—Tony Gwynn, OF, Garry Templeton, SS
1986—Tony Gwynn, OF
1987—Tony Gwynn, OF, Benito Santiago, C
1988—Benito Santiago, C
1989—Tony Gwynn, OF
1990—Benito Santiago, C
1991—Benito Santiago, C
1992—Fred McGriff, 1B, Gary Sheffield, 3B
1994—Tony Gwynn, OF
1995—Tony Gwynn, OF
1996—Ken Caminiti, 3B
1997—Tony Gwynn, OF
1998—Greg Vaughn, OF

National League Championship Series Most Valuable Player

1984—Steve Garvey
1998—Sterling Hitchcock

National League Pitcher of the Month

April 1976—Randy Jones
May 1976—Randy Jones
September 1978—Gaylord Perry
May 1985—Andy Hawkins
April 1989—Mark Davis

National League Player of the Month

June 1978—Dave Winfield
April 1983—Terry Kennedy
April 1984—Tony Gwynn
June 1987—Tony Gwynn
July 1988—Tony Gwynn
August 1992—Gary Sheffield
August 1993—Tony Gwynn
August 1996—Ken Caminiti
September 1996—Ken Caminiti
May 1997—Tony Gwynn

Roberto Clemente Man Of The Year

1999—Tony Gwynn

PADRES CLUB AWARDS

San Diego Padres Most Valuable Player

The San Diego Padres Most Valuable Player Award is selected annually by the San Diego Chapter of the Baseball Writers' Association of America (BBWAA)

1969—Nate Colbert
1970—Cito Gaston
1971—Clay Kirby
1972—Nate Colbert
1973—Fred Kendall
1974—Bobby Tolan
1975—Randy Jones
1976—Randy Jones
1977—George Hendrick
1978—Dave Winfield
1979—Dave Winfield
1980—Gene Richards
1981—Juan Bonilla
1982—Terry Kennedy
1983—Alan Wiggins
1984—Tony Gwynn
1985—Garry Templeton
1986—Tony Gwynn
1987—Tony Gwynn
1988—Tony Gwynn
1989—Mark Davis
1990—Bip Roberts
1991—Fred McGriff
1992—Gary Sheffield
1993—Phil Plantier
1994—Tony Gwynn
1995—Tony Gwynn
1996—Ken Caminiti
1997—Tony Gwynn
1998—Greg Vaughn
1999—Phil Nevin
2000—Phil Nevin
2001—Phil Nevin

Clyde McCullough Award

The Clyde McCullough Award for Padres Pitcher of the Year, selected annually by the San Diego Chapter of the Baseball Writers' Association of America, is named in honor of the former San Diego bullpen coach who died September 18, 1982. McCullough, whose career as a player, coach, instructor, and scout spanned nearly five decades, was an inspirational and popular figure. The award originally honored the Padres' top rookie, but has recognized the club's best pitcher since 1990.

1982—Luis DeLeon
1983—Mark Thurmond
1984—Carmelo Martinez
1985—Lance McCullers
1986—John Kruk
1987— Benito Santiago
1988—Roberto Alomar
1989—Greg Harris
1990—Ed Whitson
1991—Andy Benes
1992—Bruce Hurst
1993—Andy Benes
1994—Trevor Hoffman
1995—Andy Ashby
1996—Trevor Hoffman
1997—Trevor Hoffman
1998—Trevor Hoffman
Kevin Brown
1999—Trevor Hoffman
2000—Woody Williams
2001—Trevor Hoffman

The Chairman's Award

The Padres' Community Relations Department founded The Chairman's Award in 1995 to honor the Padres player who best exemplifies the community spirit of Club Chairman John Moores and his family.

1995—Tony Gwynn
1996—Brian Johnson
1997—Steve Finley
1998—Greg Vaughn
1999—Trevor Hoffman
2000—Woody Williams
2001—Ryan Klesko

Favorite New Padre Award

The Favorite New Padre Award, also established in 1995, is selected by the Madres, a group of volunteers who have been helping the Padres front office and serving San Diego youth baseball since 1972.

1995—Steve Finley
1996—John Flaherty
1997—Mark Sweeney
1998—Kevin Brown
1999—Eric Owens
2000—Ryan Klesko
2001—Bubba Trammell

Community Hero Award

1998—Rob Picciolo

OPENING DAY LINEUPS (1969-2001)

April 8, 1969
Houston 1
San Diego 2
Attendance—23,370
R. Robles SS
B. Pena 2B
T. Gonzalez CF
O. Brown RF
B. Davis 1B
L. Stahl LF
E. Spiezio 3B
C. Cannizzaro C
D. Selma P

April 7, 1970
Atlanta 3
San Diego 8
Attendance—28,215
T. Dean SS
V. Kelly 3B
O. Brown RF
N. Colbert 1B
C. Gaston CF
J. Morales LF
D. Campbell 2B
C. Cannizzaro C
P. Dobson P

April 6, 1971
San Francisco 4
San Diego 0
Attendance—34,554
D. Campbell 2B
L. Stahl LF
C. Gaston CF
N. Colbert 1B
O. Brown RF
E. Spiezio 3B
C. Cannizzaro C
T. Dean SS
T. Phoebus P

April 15, 1972
Atlanta 5
San Diego 6
Attendance—16,555
E. Hernandez SS
D. Thomas 2B
L. Lee LF
N. Colbert 1B
L. Stahl RF
J. Morales CF
B. Barton C
D. Campbell 3B
C. Kirby P

April 6, 1973
Los Angeles 4
San Diego 2
Attendance—32,019
E. Hernandez SS
J. Grubb CF
L. Lee LF
N. Colbert 1B
C. Gaston RF
D. Hilton 3B
D. Roberts 2B
B. Davis C
C. Kirby P

April 5, 1974
San Diego 0
Los Angeles 8
Attendance—31,556
B. Tolan RF
G. Beckert 2B
J. Grubb CF
W. McCovey 1B
N. Colbert LF
F. Kendall C
D. Hilton 3B
E. Hernandez SS
B. Greif P

April 10, 1975
San Francisco 2
San Diego 0 (10)
Attendance—17,670
B. Tolanlf
T. Fuentes 2B
D. Winfield RF
W. McCovey 1B
J. Grubb CF
G. Beckert 3B
R. Hundley C
E. Hernandez SS
R. Jones P

April 9, 1976
Atlanta 2
San Diego 8
Attendance—44,728
J. Grubb LF
T. Fuentes 2B
W. Davis CF
D. Winfield RF
M. Ivie1b
D. Rader 3B
H. Torres SS
B. Davis C
R. Jones P

April 6, 1977
San Diego 3
Cincinnati 5
Attendance—51,869
G. Richards LF
M. Champion 2B
D. Winfield RF
G. Hendrick CF
G. Tenace C
M. Ivie 1B
D. Rader 3B
B. Almon SS
R. Jones P

April 7, 1978
San Diego 3
San Francisco 2
Attendance—36,131
G. Richards 1B
D. Thomas 2B
O. Gamble LF
D. Winfield RF
G. Hendrick CF
G. Tenace C
B. Almon 3B
O. Smith SS
G. Perry P

April 5, 1979
San Diego 4
Los Angeles 3
Attendance—46,536
G. Richards CF
O. Smith SS
M. Hargrove 1B
D. Winfield RF
J. Turner LF
B. Evans 3B
G. Tenace C
F. Gonzalez 2B
G. Perry P

April 10, 1980
San Francisco 4
San Diego 6
Attendance—29,535
O. Smith SS
D. Cash 2B
G. Richards LF
D. Winfield RF
J. Mumphrey CF
G. Tenace 1B
B. Fahey C
A. Rodriguez 3B
R. Jones P

April 9, 1981
San Diego 4
San Francisco 1 (10)
Attendance—54,520
G. Richards LF
O. Smith SS
R. Jones CF
L. Salazar 3B
R. Bass 1B
D. Edwards RF
T. Kennedy C
J. Bonilla 2B
J. Curtis P

April 6, 1982
Atlanta 1
San Diego 0
Attendance—30,188
G., Richards LF
J. Bonilla 2B
G. Templeton SS
R. Jones CF
S. Lezcano RF
T. Kennedy C
L. Salazar 3B
B. Perkins 1B
J. Eichelberger P

April 5, 1983
San Diego 16
San Francisco 13
Attendance—49,519
G. Richards LF
J. Bonilla 2B
S. Garvey 1B
T. Kennedy C
S. Lezcano RF
R. Jones CF
G. Templeton SS
L. Salazar 3B
T. Lollar P

April 3, 1984
Pittsburgh 1
San Diego 5
Attendance—44,553
A. Wiggins 2B
T. Gwynn RF
G. Nettles 3B
S. Garvey 1B
T. Kennedy C
C. Martinez LF
K. McReynolds CF
G. Templeton SS
E. Show P

April 9, 1985
San Diego 3
San Francisco 5
Attendance—52,714
J. Davis LF
M. Ramirez 2B
T. Gwynn RF
S. Garvey 1B
K. McReynolds CF
T. Kennedy C
J. Royster 3B
G. Templeton SS
L. Hoyt P

April 7, 1986
San Diego 1
Los Angeles 2
Attendance—49,444
B. Roberts 2B
T. Gwynn RF
K. McReynolds CF
S. Garvey 1B
C. Martinez LF
G. Templeton SS
T. Kennedy C
J. Royster 3B
E. Show P

April 6, 1987
San Diego 3
San Francisco 4 (12)
Attendance—52,020
M. Wynne CF
G. Templeton SS
T. Gwynn RF
C. Martinez LF
K. Mitchell 3B
S. Garvey 1B
B. Santiago C
J. Cora 2B
E. Show P

April 5, 1988
San Diego 3
Houston 6
Attendance—39,906
S. Jefferson CF
T. Gwynn RF
K. Moreland LF
J. Kruk 1B
R. Ready 2B
B. Santiago C
C. Brown 3B
G. Templeton SS
E. Whitson P

April 3, 1989
San Francisco 4
San Diego 3
Attendance—52,763
R. Alomar 2B
T. Flannery 3B
T. Gwynn CF
J. Clark 1B
C. Martinez LF
J. Kruk RF
B. Santiago C
G. Templeton SS
E. Show P

April 9, 1990
San Diego 2
Los Angeles 4
Attendance—48,686
B. Roberts 3B
R. Alomar 2B
T. Gwynn RF
J. Clark 1B
J. Carter CF
F. Lynn LF
B. Santiago C
G. Templeton SS
B. Hurst P

April 9, 1991
San Francisco 4
San Diego 7
Attendance—48,089
B. Roberts 2B
T. Fernandez SS
T. Gwynn RF
F. McGriff 1B
B. Santiago C
J. Clark LF
J. Presley 3B
S. Abner CF
E. Whitson P

April 6, 1992
San Diego 4
Cincinnati 3
Attendance—55,356
T. Fernandez SS
T. Gwynn RF
G. Sheffield 3B
F. McGriff 1B
B. Santiago C
J. Clark LF
D. Jackson CF
K. Stilwell 2B
B. Hurst P

April 6, 1993
San Diego 4
Pittsburgh 9
Attendance—44,103

April 4, 1994
Atlanta 4
San Diego 1
Attendance—42,251

April 26, 1995
Houston 10
San Diego 2
Attendance—38,124

April 6, 1993 contd.
T. Gwynn RF
J. Gardner 2B
G. Sheffield 3B
F. McGriff 1B
P. Plantier LF
D. Bell CF
D. Walters C
C. Shipley SS
A. Benes P

April 4, 1994 contd.
B. Roberts 2B
R. Gutierrez SS
T. Gwynn RF
P. Plantier LF
D. Bell CF
A. Cianfrocco 3B
D. Staton 1B
B. Ausmus C
A. Benes P

April 26, 1995 contd.
B. Roberts LF
S. Finley CF
T. Gwynn RF
E. Williams1b
K. Caminiti 3B
A. Cedeno SS
J. Reed 2B
B. Ausmus C
A. Benes P

April 1, 1996
San Diego 4
Chicago 5 (10)
Attendance—38,734
R. Henderson LF
S. Finley CF
T. Gwynn RF
K. Caminiti 3B
W. Joyner 1B
B. Ausmus C
A. Cedeno SS
J. Reed 2B
A. Ashby P

April 1, 1997
New York 5
San Diego 12
Attendance—43,005
Q. Veras 2B
T. Gwynn RF
S. Finley CF
K. Caminiti 3B
G. Vaughn LF
W. Joyner 1B
J. Flaherty C
C. Gomez SS
J. Hamilton P

March 31, 1998
San Diego 10
Cincinnati 2
Attendance—54,578
Q. Veras 2B
S. Finley CF
T. Gwynn RF
K. Caminiti 3B
G. Vaughn LF
W. Joyner 1B
C. Hernandez C
C. Gomez SS
K. Brown P

April 4, 1999
Monterrey, Mexico
Colorado 8
San Diego 2
Attendance—60,021
Q. Veras 2B
R. Sanders LF
T. Gwynn RF
W. Joyner 1B
G. Myers C
G. Arias 3B
R. Rivera CF
C. Gomez SS
A. Ashby P

April 10, 2000
Arizona 8
San Diego 4

Attendance —40,930
A. Martin LF
D. Jackson SS
T. Gwynn RF
P. Nevin 3B
R. Klesko 1B
B. Boone 2B
E. Owens CF
W. Gonzalez C
W. Williams P

April 2, 2001
San Diego 2
San Francisco 3

Attendance—27,104
D. Jackson 2B
M. Kotsay LF
R. Klesko 1B
P. Nevin 3B
T. Gwynn RF
M. Darr CF
W. Gonzalez C
C. Gomez SS
W. Williams P

ANNUAL BATTING TOTALS

Year	Avg.	R	H	2B	3B	HR	RBI	SB
1969	.225	468	1203	180	42	99	431	45
1970	.246	681	1353	208	36	172	629	60
1971	.233	486	1250	184	31	96	447	70
1972	.227	488	1181	168	38	102	452	78
1973	.244	548	1330	198	26	112	516	88
1974	.229	541	1239	196	27	99	506	85
1975	.244	552	1324	215	22	78	505	85
1976	.247	570	1327	216	37	64	528	92
1977	.249	692	1397	245	49	120	652	133
1978	.252	591	1349	208	42	75	542	152
1979	.242	603	1316	193	53	93	559	100
1980	.255	591	1410	195	43	67	546	239
1981	.256	382	963	170	35	32	350	83
1982	.257	675	1435	217	52	81	611	165
1983	.250	563	1384	207	34	93	592	179
1984	.259	586	1425	207	42	109	629	152
1985	.255	650	1405	241	28	109	611	60
1986	.261	656	1442	239	25	136	629	96
1987	.260	668	1419	209	48	113	621	198
1988	.247	594	1325	205	35	94	566	123
1989	.251	642	1360	215	32	120	598	136
1990	.257	673	1429	243	35	123	628	138
1991	.244	636	1321	204	36	121	591	101
1992	.255	617	1396	255	30	135	576	69
1993	.252	679	1386	239	28	153	633	92
1994	.275	479	1117	200	19	92	445	79
1995	.272	668	1345	231	20	116	618	124
1996	.265	771	1499	285	24	147	718	109
1997	.271	795	1519	275	16	152	761	140
1998	.253	749	1390	292	30	167	715	79
1999	.252	710	1360	256	22	153	671	174
2000	.254	752	1413	279	37	157	714	131
2001	.252	789	1379	273	26	161	753	129

ANNUAL PITCHING TOTALS

Year	W	L	ERA	CG	SV	SHO	H	R	ER	HR	BB	SO
1969	52	110	4.24	16	25	9	1454	746	670	113	592	764
1970	63	99	4.36	24	32	9	1483	788	697	149	611	886
1971	61	100	3.22	47	17	10	1351	610	515	93	559	923
1972	58	95	3.78	39	19	17	1350	665	589	121	618	960
1973	60	102	4.16	34	23	10	1461	770	661	157	548	845
1974	60	102	4.58	25	19	7	1536	830	736	124	715	855
1975	71	91	3.48	40	20	12	1494	683	566	99	521	713
1976	73	89	3.65	47	18	11	1368	662	581	87	543	652
1877	69	93	4.43	6	44	5	1556	834	722	160	673	827
1978	84	78	3.28	21	55	10	1385	598	522	74	483	744
1979	58	93	3.69	29	25	7	1438	681	596	108	513	779
1980	73	89	3.65	19	39	9	1474	654	595	97	536	728
1981	41	69	3.72	9	23	6	1013	455	414	64	414	492
1982	81	81	3.52	20	41	11	1348	658	578	139	502	765
1983	81	81	3.62	23	44	5	1389	653	590	144	528	850
1984	92	70	3.48	13	44	17	1327	634	565	122	563	812

Year	W	L	ERA	CG	SV	SHO	H	R	ER	HR	BB	SO
1985	83	79	3.40	26	44	19	1399	622	549	127	443	727
1986	74	88	3.99	13	32	7	1406	723	640	150	607	934
1987	65	97	4.27	14	33	10	1402	763	680	175	602	897
1988	83	78	3.28	30	39	9	1332	583	528	112	439	885
1989	89	73	3.38	21	52	11	1359	626	547	133	481	933
1990	75	87	3.68	21	35	12	1437	673	597	147	507	928
1991	84	78	3.57	14	47	11	1385	646	577	139	457	921
1992	82	80	3.56	9	46	11	1444	636	578	111	439	971
1993	61	101	4.23	8	32	6	1470	772	675	148	558	957
1994	47	70	4.08	8	27	6	1008	531	474	99	393	862
1995	70	74	4.13	6	35	10	1242	672	590	142	512	1047
1996	91	71	3.72	5	47	11	1395	682	616	147	506	1194
1997	76	86	4.99	5	43	0	1581	891	804	172	596	1059
1998	98	64	3.63	14	59	11	1384	635	587	139	501	1217
1999	74	88	4.47	5	43	6	1454	781	705	193	529	1078
2000	76	86	4.52	5	46	0	1443	815	733	191	649	1071
2001	79	83	4.52	5	46	6	1519	812	724	219	476	1088

ANNUAL BATTING LEADERS

	Batting Average		Hits		Doubles	
1969	O. Brown	.264	O. Brown	150	A. Ferrara	22
1970	C. Gaston	.318	C. Gaston	186	O. Brown	34
1971	O. Brown	.273	N. Colbert	149	N. Colbert	25
1972	C. Gaston	.269	N. Colbert	141	N. Colbert	27
1973	D. Roberts	.286	N. Colbert F. Kendall	143	N. Colbert	25
1974	J. Grubb	.286	D. Winfield	132	D. Thomas	24
1975	T. Fuentes	.280	T. Fuentes	158	J. Grubb	36
1976	M. Ivie	.291	D. Winfield	139	D. Winfield	26
1977	G. Hendrick	.311	D. Winfield	169	M. Ivie D. Winfield	29
1978	D. Winfield	.308	D. Winfield	181	D. Winfield	30
1979	D. Winfield	.308	D. Winfield	184	D. Winfield	29
1980	G. Richards	.301	G. Richards	193	G. Richards	26
1981	L. Salazar	.303	L. Salazar	121	R. Jones	34
1982	T. Kennedy	.295	T. Kennedy	166	T. Kennedy	42
1983	T. Kennedy	.284	T. Kennedy	156	T. Kennedy	27
1984	T. Gwynn	.351	T. Gwynn	213	C. Martinez	28
1985	T. Gwynn	.317	T. Gwynn	197	S. Garvey	34
1986	T. Gwynn	.329	T. Gwynn	211	T. Gwynn	33
1987	T. Gwynn	.370	T. Gwynn	218	T. Gwynn	36
1988	T. Gwynn	.313	T. Gwynn	163	R. Alomar	24
1989	T. Gwynn	.336	T. Gwynn	203	R. Alomar T. Gwynn	27
1990	T. Gwynn B. Roberts	.309	T. Gwynn	177	B. Roberts	36
1991	T. Gwynn	.317	T. Gwynn	168	T. Fernandez T. Gwynn	27
1992	G. Sheffield	.330	G. Sheffield	184	G. Sheffield	34
1993	T. Gwynn	.358	T. Gwynn	175	T. Gwynn	41
1994	T. Gwynn	.394	T. Gwynn	165	T. Gwynn	35
1995	T. Gwynn	.368	T. Gwynn	197	K. Caminiti T. Gwynn	33
1996	T. Gwynn	.353	S. Finley	195	S. Finley	45
1997	T. Gwynn	.372	T. Gwynn	220	T. Gwynn	49

Year	Batting Average		Hits		Doubles	
1998	T. Gwynn	.321	G. Vaughn	156	S. Finley	40
1999	T. Gwynn	.339	T. Gwynn	139	T. Gwynn	27
					P. Nevin	27
2000	P. Nevin	.303	E. Owens	171	P. Nevin	34
2001	P. Nevin	.306	P. Nevin	167	R. Klesko	34

Year	Triples		Home Runs		Runs Batted In	
1969	N. Colbert	9	N. Colbert	24	N. Colbert	66
1970	C. Gaston	9	N. Colbert	38	C. Gaston	93
1971	C. Gaston	9	N. Colbert	27	N. Colbert	84
1972	L. Lee	7	N. Colbert	38	N. Colbert	111
	J. Morales					
1973	C. Gaston	4	N. Colbert	22	N. Colbert	80
1974	D. Thomas	6	W. McCovey	22	D. Winfield	75
1975	B. Tolan	4	W. McCovey	23	D. Winfield	76
1976	W. Davis	10	D. Winfield	13	M. Ivie	70
1977	B. Almon	11	D. Winfield	25	D. Winfield	92
	G. Richards					
1978	G. Richards	12	D. Winfield	24	D. Winfield	97
1979	D. Winfield	10	D. Winfield	34	D. Winfield	118
1980	G. Richards	8	D. Winfield	20	D. Winfield	87
1981	G. Richards	12	J. Lefebvre	8	G. Richards	42
1982	G. Richards	8	T. Kennedy	21	T. Kennedy	97
	G. Templeton					
1983	J. Bonilla	4	T. Kennedy	17	T. Kennedy	98
1984	T. Gwynn	10	K. McReynolds	20	S. Garvey	86
			G. Nettles			
1985	S. Garvey	6	C. Martinez	21	S. Garvey	81
1986	T. Gwynn	7	K. McReynolds	26	K. McReynolds	96
1987	T. Gwynn	13	J. Kruk	20	J. Kruk	91
1988	G. Templeton	7	C. Martinez	18	T. Gwynn	70
1989	B. Roberts	8	J. Clark	26	J. Clark	94
1990	T. Gwynn	10	J. Clark	25	J. Carter	115
1991	T. Gwynn	11	F. McGriff	31	F. McGriff	106
1992	J. Clark	6	F. McGriff	35	F. McGriff	104
1993	J. Gardner	7	P. Plantier	34	P. Plantier	100
1994	B. Roberts	5	P. Plantier	18	T. Gwynn	64
1995	S. Finley	8	K. Caminiti	26	K. Caminiti	94
1996	S. Finley	9	K. Caminiti	40	K. Caminiti	130
1997	S. Finley	5	S. Finley	28	T. Gwynn	119
1998	S. Finley	6	G. Vaughn	50	G. Vaughn	119
1999	E. Owens	3	R. Sanders	26	P. Nevin	85
2000	E. Owens	7	P. Nevin	31	P. Nevin	107
2001	R. Klesko	6	P. Nevin	41	P. Nevin	126
	D. Jackson	6				

Year	Runs		Stolen Bases	
1969	O. Brown	76	J. Arcia	14
1970	C. Gaston	92	D. Campbell	18
1971	N. Colbert	81	E. Hernandez	21
1972	N. Colbert	87	E. Hernandez	24
1973	N. Colbert	73	E. Hernandez	15
			D. Thomas	
1974	D. Winfield	57	E. Hernandez	37
1975	D. Winfield	74	D. Winfield	23
1976	D. Winfield	81	D. Winfield	26
1977	D. Winfield	104	G. Richards	56
1978	G. Richards	90	O. Smith	40

	Runs		Stolen Bases	
1979	D. Winfield	97	O. Smith	28
1980	G. Richards	91	G. Richards	61
1981	R. Jones	53	O. Smith	22
	O. Smith			
1982	G. Templeton	76	A. Wiggins	33
1983	A. Wiggins	83	A. Wiggins	66
1984	A. Wiggins	106	A. Wiggins	70
1985	T. Gwynn	90	G. Templeton	16
1986	T. Gwynn	107	T. Gwynn	37
1987	T. Gwynn	119	T. Gwynn	56
1988	R. Alomar	84	T. Gwynn	26
1989	R. Alomar	82	R. Alomar	42
	T. Gwynn			
1990	B. Roberts	104	B. Roberts	46
1991	F. McGriff	84	B. Roberts	26
1992	G. Sheffield	87	T. Fernandez	20
1993	R. Gutierrez	76	D. Bell	26
1994	T. Gwynn	79	D. Bell	24
1995	S. Finley	104	S. Finley	36
1996	S. Finley	126	R. Henderson	37
1997	S. Finley	101	Q. Veras	33
1998	G. Vaughn	112	Q. Veras	24
1999	Q. Veras	95	R. Sanders	36
2000	R. Klesko	88	E. Owens	29
2001	R. Klesko	105	R. Henderson	25

ANNUAL PITCHING LEADERS

	Wins		ERA		Strikeouts	
1969	J. Niekro	8	J. Niekro	3.70	C. Kirby	113
	A. Santorini					
1970	P. Dobson	12	D. Coombs	3.30	P. Dobson	185
1971	C. Kirby	15	D. Roberts	2.10	C. Kirby	231
1972	C. Kirby	12	C. Kirby	3.13	C. Kirby	175
1973	S. Arlin	11	B. Greif	3.21	C. Kirby	129
1974	D. Freisleben	9	D. Freisleben	3.65	B. Greif	137
	B. Greif					
	L. Hardy					
	D. Spillner					
1975	R. Jones	20	R. Jones	2.24	D. Spillner	104
1976	R. Jones	22	R. Jones	2.74	B. Storm	103
1977	B. Shirley	12	B. Shirley	3.70	B. Shirley	146
1978	G. Perry	21	G. Perry	2.72	G. Perry	154
1979	G. Perry	12	G. Perry	3.05	G. Perry	140
1980	B. Shirley	11	J. Curtis	3.51	S. Mura	107
	R. Fingers					
1981	J. Eichelberger	8	J. Eichelberger	3.51	J. Eichelberger	81
1982	T. Lollar	16	T. Lollar	3.13	T. Lollar	150
1983	E. Show	15	D. Dravecky	3.58	T. Lollar	135
1984	E. Show	15	M. Thurmond	2.97	T. Lollar	131
1985	A. Hawkins	18	D. Dravecky	2.93	E. Show	141
1986	A. Hawkins	10	D. Dravecky	3.07	A. Hawkins	117
	L. McCullers					
1987	E. Whitson	10	E. Show	3.84	E. Whitson	135
1988	E. Show	16	E. Show	3.26	E. Show	144
1989	E. Whitson	16	E. Whitson	2.66	B. Hurst	179

	Wins		ERA		Strikeouts	
1990	E. Whitson	14	E. Whitson	2.60	B. Hurst	162
1991	A. Benes	15	A. Benes	3.03	A. Benes	167
	B. Hurst					
1992	B. Hurst	14	A. Benes	3.35	A. Benes	169
1993	A. Benes	15	A. Benes	3.35	A. Benes	179
1994	J. Hamilton	9	J. Hamilton	2.98	A. Benes	189
1995	A. Ashby	12	A. Ashby	2.94	A. Ashby	150
1996	J. Hamilton	15	F. Valenzuela	3.62	J. Hamilton	184
1997	J. Hamilton	12	A. Ashby	4.13	A. Ashby	144
1998	K. Brown	18	K.Brown	2.38	K. Brown	257
1999	A. Ashby	14	A. Ashby	3.80	S. Hitchcock	194
2000	M. Clement	13	M. Williams	3.75	M.Clement	170
2001	K. Jarvis	12	K. Jarvis	4.79	K. Jarvis	133

	Innings Pitched		Complete Games		Shutouts	
1969	C. Kirby	215.2	J. Niekro	8	J. Niekro	3
1970	P. Dobson	215.0	P. Dobson	8	D. Roberts	2
1971	D. Roberts	269.2	D. Roberts	14	S. Arlin	4
1972	S. Arlin	250.0	S. Arlin	12	F. Norman	6
1973	B. Greif	199.1	B. Greif	9	S. Arlin	3
					B. Greif	
1974	B. Greif	226.0	B. Greif	7	D. Spillner	2
1975	R. Jones	285.0	R. Jones	18	R. Jones	6
1976	R. Jones	315.1	R. Jones	25	R. Jones	5
1977	B. Shirley	214.0	B. Owchinko	3	B. Owchinko	2
1978	G. Perry	260.2	R. Jones	7	R. Jones	2
					G. Perry	
					E. Rasmussen	
1979	R. Jones	263.0	G. Perry	10	E. Rasmussen	3
1980	J. Curtis	187.0	J. Curtis	6	R. Jones	3
1981	J. Eichelberger	141.1	C. Welsh	4	C. Welsh	2
1982	T. Lollar	232.2	J. Eichelberger	8	T. Lollar	2
					E. Show	
1983	E. Show	200.2	D. Dravecky	9	E. Show	2
1984	E. Show	206.2	D. Dravecky	3	D. Dravecky	2
			T. Lollar		T. Lollar	
			E. Show			
1985	E. Show	233.0	L. Hoyt	8	L. Hoyt	3
1986	A. Hawkins	209.1	D. Dravecky	3	Four Tied at	1
			A. Hawkins			
1987	E. Show	206.1	E. Show	5	E. Show	3
1988	E. Show	234.2	E. Show	13	A. Hawkins	2
1989	B. Hurst	244.2	B. Hurst	10	B. Hurst	2
1990	E. Whitson	228.2	B. Hurst	9	B. Hurst	2
1991	A. Benes	223.0	A. Benes	4	Gr. Harris	2
			Hurst			
1992	A. Benes	231.1	B. Hurst	6	B. Hurst	4
1993	A. Benes	230.2	A. Benes	4	A. Benes	2
			Gr. Harris			
1994	A. Benes	172.1	A. Ashby	4	A. Benes	2
1995	J. Hamilton	204.1	A. Ashby	2	A. Ashby	2
			J. Hamilton		J. Hamilton	
1996	J. Hamilton	211.2	J. Hamilton	3	J. Hamilton	1
1997	A. Ashby	200.2	A. Ashby	2	None	
1998	K. Brown	257.0	K. Brown	7	K. Brown	3
1999	W. Williams	208.1	A. Ashby	4	A. Ashby	3
2000	M. Clement	205.0	W. Williams	4	None	
2001	B. Jones	195.0	A. Eaton	2	K. Jarvis	1

	Saves		Appearances	
1969	B. McCool	7	J. Baldschun	61
1970	T. Dukes	10	R. Herbel	64
1971	A. Severinsen	8	A. Severinsen	59
1972	M. Corkins	6	G. Ross	58
1973	M. Caldwell	10	L. Hardy	76
1974	V. Romo	9	D. Tomlin	67
1975	D. Frisella	9		
	B. Greif		B. Metzger	77
1976	B. Metzger	16	R. Fingers	78
1977	R. Fingers	35	R. Fingers	67
1978	R. Fingers	37	R. Fingers	54
1979	R. Fingers	13	R. Fingers	66
1980	R. Fingers	23	G. Lucas	57
1981	G. Lucas	13	G. Lucas	65
1982	G. Lucas	13	L. DeLeon	63
1983	G. Lucas	17	R. Gossage	62
1984	R. Gossage	25	C. Lefferts	
			C. Lefferts	60
1985	R. Gossage	26	C. Lefferts	83
1986	R. Gossage	21	L. McCullers	78
1987	L. McCullers	16	M. Davis	62
1988	M. Davis	28	M. Davis	70
1989	M. Davis	44	Gr. Harris	73
1990	C. Lefferts	23	M. Maddux	64
1991	C. Lefferts	23	R. Rodriguez	
			R. Myers	66
1992	R. Myers	38	Ge. Harris	59
1993	Ge. Harris	23	P. Martinez	48
1994	T. Hoffman	20	T. Hoffman	55
1995	T. Hoffman	31	T. Hoffman	70
1996	T. Hoffman	42	T. Hoffman	70
1997	T. Hoffman	37	D. Miceli	67
1998	T. Hoffman	53	D. Miceli	66
1999	T. Hoffman	40	T. Hoffman	70
2000	T. Hoffman	43	K. Walker	70
			T. Hoffman	62
2001	T. Hoffman	43	J. Nunez	62

PADRES CAREER BATTING LEADERS

Batting Average (500 G)		Hits		Games	
T. Gwynn	.338	T. Gwynn	3,141	T. Gwynn	2,440
B. Roberts	.298	G. Templeton	1,135	G. Templeton	1,286
K. Caminiti	.295	D. Winfield	1,134	D. Winfield	1,117
G. Richards	.291	G. Richards	994	T. Flannery	972
J. Grubb	.286	T. Kennedy	817	G. Richards	939
D. Winfield	.284	N. Colbert	780	N. Colbert	866
S. Finley	.276	B. Santiago	758	T. Kennedy	835
S. Garvey	.275	B. Roberts	673	B. Santiago	789
T. Kennedy	.274	C. Gaston	672	C. Martinez	783
L. Salazar	.267	S. Finley	662	C. Gaston	766
B. Santiago	.264	T. Flannery	631	F. Kendall	754
J. Turner	.259	S. Garvey	631	E. Hernandez	710
C. Gaston	.257	L. Salazar	598	L. Salazar	704
T. Flannery	.255	K. Caminiti	592	B. Roberts	667
N. Colbert	.253	C. Martinez	577	J. Turner	638
G. Templeton	.252	E. Hernandez	522	S. Garvey	605

Batting Average (500 G)

C. Martinez	.248
D. Roberts	.240
G. Tenace	.237
D. Thomas	.236

Hits

F. Kendall	516
O. Smith	516
J. Grubb	513
R. Alomar	497

Games

S. Finley	602
O. Smith	583
G. Tenace	573
K. Caminiti	557

Doubles

T. Gwynn	534
G. Templeton	195
D. Winfield	179
T. Kennedy	158
S. Finley	134
N. Colbert	130
K. Caminiti	127
B. Santiago	124
G. Richards	123
C. Martinez	111
S. Garvey	107
W. Joyner	102
J. Grubb	101
B. Roberts	98
C. Gaston	93
P. Nevin	92
K. McReynolds	84
R. Alomar	78
C. Gomez	78
T. Flannery	77

Triples

T. Gwynn	85
G. Richards	63
D. Winfield	39
G. Templeton	36
C. Gaston	29
S. Finley	28
T. Flannery	25
L. Salazar	24
N. Colbert	22
B. Roberts	21
O. Smith	19
K. McReynolds	17
B. Santiago	15
D. Jackson	14
D. Thomas	14
I. Murrell	13
E. Hernandez	13
B. Almon	13
G. Tenace	13
A. Wiggins	12
R. Alomar	12

Home Runs

N. Colbert	163
D. Winfield	154
T. Gwynn	134
K. Caminiti	121
P. Nevin	96
B. Santiago	85
F. McGriff	84
C. Martinez	82
S. Finley	82
G. Vaughn	78
C. Gaston	77
T. Kennedy	76
G. Tenace	68
K. McReynolds	65
S. Garvey	61
P. Plantier	57
R. Klesko	56
O. Brown	52
W. McCovey	52
G. Nettles	51
J. Clark	51

Runs Batted In

T. Gwynn	1,138
D. Winfield	626
N. Colbert	481
G. Templeton	427
T. Kennedy	424
K. Caminiti	396
B. Santiago	375
C. Martinez	337
P. Nevin	318
C. Gaston	316
S. Garvey	316
S. Finley	298
W. Joyner	271
K. McReynolds	260
F. McGriff	256
G. Richards	251
G. Tenace	239
L. Salazar	226
J. Turner	209
T. Flannery	209

Runs

T. Gwynn	1,383
D. Winfield	599
G. Richards	484
N. Colbert	442
G. Templeton	430
S. Finley	423
B. Roberts	378
K. Caminiti	362
B. Santiago	312
T. Kennedy	308
S. Garvey	291
C. Martinez	286
C. Gaston	269
O. Smith	266
T. Flannery	255
Q. Veras	248
R. Alomar	246
R. Henderson	243
E. Hernandez	241
A. Wiggins	236
P. Nevin	236

At Bats

T. Gwynn	9,288
G. Templeton	4,512
D. Winfield	3,997
G. Richards	3,414
N. Colbert	3,080
T. Kennedy	2,987
B. Santiago	2,872
C. Gaston	2,615
T. Flannery	2,473
S. Finley	2,396
C. Martinez	2,325
E. Hernandez	2,324
S. Garvey	2,292
B. Roberts	2,258
L. Salazar	2,237
O. Smith	2,236
F. Kendall	2,218
K. Caminiti	2,010
J. Grubb	1,791
K. McReynolds	1,789

Walks

T. Gwynn	790
D. Winfield	463
G. Tenace	423
N. Colbert	350
G. Richards	338
C. Martinez	327
K. Caminiti	298

Strikeouts

N. Colbert	773
G. Templeton	684
C. Gaston	595
D. Winfield	585
B. Santiago	516
T. Kennedy	508
T. Gwynn	434

Stolen Bases

T. Gwynn	319
G. Richards	242
A. Wiggins	171
B. Roberts	148
O. Smith	147
D. Winfield	133
E. Hernandez	129

Walks

T. Flannery	277
R. Henderson	277
G. Templeton	272
F. McGriff	243
J. Clark	236
W. Joyner	229
Q. Veras	221
J. Kruk	215
B. Roberts	212
J. Grubb	208
S. Finley	203
T. Kennedy	200
O. Smith	196

Strikeouts

K. Caminiti	419
G. Richards	408
C. Martinez	403
G. Tenace	386
L. Salazar	369
P. Nevin	350
S. Finley	344
R. Rivera	341
D. Jackson	341
C. Gomez	333
B. Roberts	305
F. McGriff	298
T. Flannery	293

Stolen Bases

G. Templeton	101
L. Salazar	93
R. Henderson	91
R. Alomar	90
Q. Veras	87
S. Finley	85
D. Jackson	85
E. Owens	62
B. Santiago	62
J. Mumphrey	52
D. Bell	50
B. Brown	49
N. Colbert	48

On Base Percentage (500 G)

G. Tenace	.403
T. Gwynn	.388
K. Caminiti	.386
J. Grubb	.363
B. Roberts	.361
D. Winfield	.357
G. Richards	.357
C. Martinez	.341
T. Flannery	.335
S. Finley	.333
N. Colbert	.331
J. Turner	.321
T. Kennedy	.319
S. Garvey	.309
C. Gaston	.298
B. Santiago	.298
L. Salazar	.298
O. Smith	.295
G. Templeton	.293
F. Kendall	.287

Slugging Percentage (500 G)

K. Caminiti	.540
N. Colbert	.469
D. Winfield	.464
T. Gwynn	.459
S. Finley	.458
G. Tenace	.422
S. Garvey	.409
C. Martinez	.408
T. Kennedy	.407
B. Santiago	.406
C. Gaston	.403
J. Grubb	.397
J. Turner	.390
G. Richards	.387
B. Roberts	.387
L. Salazar	.375
D. Roberts	.354
G. Templeton	.339
T. Flannery	.317
F. Kendall	.312

PADRES CAREER PITCHING LEADERS

Wins

E. Show	100
R. Jones	92
E. Whitson	77
A. Ashby	70
A. Benes	69
A. Hawkins	60
J. Hamilton	55
B. Hurst	55
D. Dravecky	53
C. Kirby	52
C. Lefferts	42
D. Rasmussen	41
Gr. Harris	41
T. Hoffman	41
B. Shirley	39
T. Lollar	36
R. Fingers	34
S. Hitchcock	34
G. Perry	33

Losses

R. Jones	105
E. Show	87
C. Kirby	81
A. Benes	75
E. Whitson	72
S. Arlin	62
A. Ashby	62
B. Greif	61
A. Hawkins	58
B. Shirley	57
D. Freisleben	53
D. Dravecky	50
J. Hamilton	44
T. Lollar	42
D. Rasmussen	42
D. Spillner	41
R. Fingers	40
C. Lefferts	40
B. Owchinko	39

Winning Percentage (75 dec.)

B. Hurst	.591
J. Hamilton	.556
E. Show	.535
A. Ashby	.530
T. Hoffman	.526
E. Whitson	.517
D. Dravecky	.515
Gr. Harris	.513
C. Lefferts	.512
A. Hawkins	.508
D. Rasmussen	.494
A. Benes	.479
R. Jones	.467
T. Lollar	.462
B. Shirley	.406
C. Kirby	.391
D. Freisleben	.369
S. Arlin	.340
B. Greif	.322

Wins

S. Arlin	32

Losses

Gr. Harris	39
S. Hitchcock	39

Games

T. Hoffman	543
C. Lefferts	375
E. Show	309
R. Fingers	265
R. Jones	264
D. Tomlin	239
M. Davis	230
G. Lucas	230
L. McCullers	229
E. Whitson	227
G. Ross	219
D. Dravecky	199
A. Hawkins	199
G. Gossage	197
B. Shirley	197
Gr. Harris	194
D. Spillner	192
R. Rodriguez	191
A. Benes	187
A. Ashby	185
L. DeLeon	185

Games Started

R. Jones	253
E. Show	230
E. Whitson	208
A. Benes	186
A. Ashby	185
A. Hawkins	172
C. Kirby	170
J. Hamilton	142
B. Hurst	131
D. Dravecky	119
S. Arlin	113
D. Rasmussen	110
D. Freisleben	109
T. Lollar	106
S. Hitchcock	102
B. Greif	94
B. Shirley	92
M. Thurmond	85
B. Owchinko	83
W. Williams	79

Complete Games

R. Jones	71
E. Show	35
C. Kirby	34
S. Arlin	31
B. Hurst	29
D. Dravecky	23
E. Whitson	22
A. Hawkins	19
A. Ashby	18
B. Greif	18
D. Freisleben	17
D. Roberts	17
F. Norman	16
A. Benes	15
G. Perry	15
B. Strom	14
J. Eichelberger	12
D. Rasmussen	11
B. Shirley	10
Seven Tied At	9

Innings Pitched

R. Jones	1,766.0
E. Show	1,603.1
E. Whitson	1,354.1
A. Benes	1,235.0
A. Ashby	1,210.0
C. Kirby	1,128.0
A. Hawkins	1,102.2
J. Hamilton	934.2
B. Hurst	911.2
D. Dravecky	900.1
S. Arlin	745.0
D. Freisleben	730.0
B. Shirley	722.0
T. Lollar	680.2
D. Rasmussen	680.0
Gr. Harris	673.1
C. Lefferts	659.0
B. Greif	645.0
S. Hitchcock	627.2
T. Hoffman	606.0

Shutouts

R. Jones	18
S. Arlin	11
E. Show	11
B. Hurst	10
A. Benes	8
A. Hawkins	7
C. Kirby	7
A. Ashby	6
D. Dravecky	6
D. Freisleben	6
F. Norman	6
E. Whitson	6
B. Greif	5
E. Rasmussen	5
J. Hamilton	4
T. Lollar	4
D. Roberts	4
15 Tied At	3

Saves

T. Hoffman	312
R. Fingers	108
G. Gossage	83
M. Davis	78
C. Lefferts	64
G. Lucas	49
R. Myers	38
L. McCullers	36
L. DeLeon	31
Ge. Harris	23
B. Metzger	16
V. Romo	16
L. Andersen	15
Gr. Harris	15
J. D'Acquisto	13
B. Greif	13
M. Caldwell	12
B. Shirley	12
T. Dukes	11
Four Tied At	10

Walks

E. Show	593
C. Kirby	505
R. Jones	414
A. Hawkins	412
A. Benes	402
S. Arlin	351
E. Whitson	350
D. Freisleben	346
J. Hamilton	343
T. Lollar	328

Strikeouts

A. Benes	1,036
E. Show	951
A. Ashby	827
C. Kirby	802
E. Whitson	767
T. Hoffman	702
R. Jones	677
J. Hamilton	639
B. Hurst	616
S. Hitchcock	534

Strikeouts Per 9 Innings (750 inn.)

A. Benes	7.55
C. Kirby	6.40
A. Ashby	6.15
J. Hamilton	6.15
B. Hurst	6.08
E. Show	5.34
E. Whitson	5.10
D. Dravecky	4.56
A. Hawkins	3.99
R. Jones	3.45

Walks

A. Ashby	324
B. Shirley	274
D. Dravecky	270
D. Spillner	255
B. Greif	253
M. Corkins	248
B. Hurst	242
D. Rasmussen	227
J. D'Acquisto	225
J. Eichelberger	214

Strikeouts

A. Hawkins	489
Gr. Harris	462
D. Dravecky	456
T. Lollar	454
S. Arlin	443
B. Shirley	432
S. Sanders	417
C. Lefferts	404
B. Greif	396
D. Freisleben	376

Earned Run Average (750 inn.)

D. Dravecky	3.12
B. Hurst	3.27
R. Jones	3.30
A. Benes	3.57
E. Show	3.59
A. Ashby	3.60
E. Whitson	3.69
C. Kirby	3.73
J. Hamilton	3.83
A. Hawkins	3.84

Opponents Average (750 inn.)

A. Benes	.242
D. Dravecky	.243
C. Kirby	.243
B. Hurst	.244
E. Show	.245
R. Jones	.256
E. Whitson	.256
A. Ashby	.257
A. Hawkins	.261

PADRES SINGLE-SEASON BATTING LEADERS

Games

D. Winfield	1980	162
S. Garvey	1985	162
J. Carter	1990	162
S. Garvey	1984	161
S. Finley	1996	161
J. Mumphrey	1980	160
T. Gwynn	1986	160
O. Smith	1978	159
D. Winfield	1979	159
S. Finley	1998	159
D. Winfield	1978	158
G. Richards	1980	158
O. Smith	1980	158
A. Wiggins	1984	158
T. Gwynn	1984	158
K. McReynolds	1986	158
T. Gwynn	1989	158
R. Alomar	1989	158
G. Vaughn	1998	158
D. Winfield	1977	157
T. Gwynn	1987	157

At-Bats

S. Finley	1996	655
S. Garvey	1985	654
G. Richards	1980	642
T. Gwynn	1986	642
J. Carter	1990	634
R. Alomar	1989	623
T. Gwynn	1985	622
T. Fernandez	1992	622
S. Finley	1998	619
S. Garvey	1984	617
D. Winfield	1977	615
B. Almon	1977	613
O. Smith	1980	609
T. Gwynn	1984	606
T. Gwynn	1989	604
D. Winfield	1979	597
A. Wiggins	1984	596
T. Gwynn	1997	592
O. Smith	1978	590
T. Gwynn	1987	589

Runs

S. Finley	1996	126
T. Gwynn	1987	119
G. Vaughn	1998	112
R. Henderson	1996	110
K. Caminiti	1996	109
T. Gwynn	1986	107
A. Wiggins	1984	106
R. Klesko	2001	105
D. Winfield	1997	104
B. Roberts	1990	104
S. Finley	1995	104
S. Finley	1997	101
D. Winfield	1979	97
T. Gwynn	1997	97
P. Nevin	2001	97
Q. Veras	1999	95
C. Gaston	1970	92
K. Caminiti	1997	92
S. Finley	1998	92
R. Sanders	1999	92

Hits

T. Gwynn	1997	220
T. Gwynn	1987	218
T. Gwynn	1984	213
T. Gwynn	1986	211
T. Gwynn	1989	203
T. Gwynn	1985	197
T. Gwynn	1995	197

Doubles

T. Gwynn	1997	49
S. Finley	1996	45
T. Kennedy	1982	42
T. Gwynn	1993	41
S. Finley	1998	40
K. Caminiti	1996	37
J. Grubb	1975	36

Triples

T. Gwynn	1987	13
G. Richards	1978	12
G. Richards	1981	12
B. Almon	1977	11
G. Richards	1977	11
T. Gwynn	1991	11
W. Davis	1976	10

Hits

S. Finley	1996	195
G. Richards	1980	193
C. Gaston	1970	186
D. Winfield	1979	184
S. Garvey	1985	184
R. Alomar	1989	184
G. Sheffield	1992	184
D. Winfield	1978	181
K. Caminiti	1996	178
T. Gwynn	1990	177
S. Garvey	1984	175
T. Gwynn	1993	175
B. Roberts	1990	172

Doubles

T. Gwynn	1987	36
B. Roberts	1990	36
T. Gwynn	1994	35
T. Gwynn	1998	35
O. Brown	1970	34
R. Jones	1981	34
S. Garvey	1985	34
G. Sheffield	1992	34
P. Nevin	2000	34
R. Klesko	2001	34
T. Gwynn	1986	33
B. Santiago	1987	33
T. Gwynn	1995	33
K. Caminiti	1995	33
R. Klesko	2000	33

Triples

D. Winfield	1979	10
T. Gwynn	1984	10
T. Gwynn	1990	10
N. Colbert	1969	9
C. Gaston	1970	9
C. Gaston	1971	9
G. Richards	1979	9
S. Finley	1996	9
G. Richards	1980	8
G. Richards	1982	8
G. Templeton	1982	8
B. Roberts	1989	8
S. Finley	1995	8

Home Runs

G. Vaughn	1998	50
P. Nevin	2001	41
K. Caminiti	1996	40
N. Colbert	1970	38
N. Colbert	1972	38
F. McGriff	1992	35
D. Winfield	1979	34
P. Plantier	1993	34
G. Sheffield	1992	33
F. McGriff	1991	31
P. Nevin	2000	31
S. Finley	1996	30
R. Klesko	2001	30
C. Gaston	1970	29
K. Caminiti	1998	29
S. Finley	1997	28
N. Colbert	1971	27
K. McReynolds	1986	26
J. Clark	1989	26
K. Caminiti	1995	26
K. Caminiti	1997	26
R. Sanders	1999	26
R. Klesko	2000	26

Runs Batted In

K. Caminiti	1996	130
P. Nevin	2001	126
T. Gwynn	1997	119
G. Vaughn	1998	119
D. Winfield	1979	118
J. Carter	1990	115
R. Klesko	2001	113
N. Colbert	1972	111
P. Nevin	2000	107
F. McGriff	1991	106
F. McGriff	1992	104
G. Sheffield	1982	100
P. Plantier	1993	100
T. Kennedy	1983	98
D. Winfield	1978	97
T. Kennedy	1982	97
K. McReynolds	1986	96
S. Finley	1996	95
Ja. Clark	1989	94
K. Caminiti	1995	94

Batting Average
(3.1 plate appearances per game)

T. Gwynn	1994	.394
T. Gwynn	1997	.372
T. Gwynn	1987	.370
T. Gwynn	1995	.368
T. Gwynn	1993	.358
T. Gwynn	1984	.351
T. Gwynn	1989	.336
G. Sheffield	1992	.330
T. Gwynn	1986	.329
W. Joyner	1997	.327
K. Caminiti	1996	.326
T. Gwynn	1998	.321
B. Roberts	1994	.320
C. Gaston	1970	.318
T. Gwynn	1985	.317
T. Gwynn	1991	.317
T. Gwynn	1992	.317
J. Kruk	1987	.313
T. Gwynn	1988	.313
G. Hendrick	1977	.311
D. Bell	1994	.311

Walks

Ja. Clark	1989	132
G. Tenace	1977	125
R. Henderson	1996	125
G. Tenace	1979	105
F. McGriff	1991	105
Ja. Clark	1990	104
G. Tenace	1978	101
W. McCovey	1976	96
F. McGriff	1992	96
G. Tenace	1980	92
R. Klesko	2000	91
R. Klesko	2001	88
C. Martinez	1985	87
D. Winfield	1979	85
Q. Veras	1998	84
T. Gwynn	1987	82

Strikeouts

N. Colbert	1970	150
P. Nevin	2001	147
N. Colbert	1973	146
Ja. Clark	1989	145
R. Rivera	1999	143
C. Gaston	1970	142
R. Rivera	2000	137
F. McGriff	1991	135
D. Jackson	2001	128
N. Colbert	1972	127
P. Plantier	1993	124
N. Colbert	1969	123
D. Bell	1993	122
C. Gaston	1971	121
G. Vaughn	1998	121
P. Nevin	2000	121

Stolen Bases

A. Wiggins	1984	70
A. Wiggins	1983	66
G. Richards	1980	61
O. Smith	1980	57
G. Richards	1977	56
T. Gwynn	1987	56
J. Mumphrey	1980	52
B. Roberts	1990	46
R. Alomar	1989	42
O. Smith	1978	40
T. Gwynn	1989	40
E. Hernandez	1974	37
G. Richards	1978	37
T. Gwynn	1986	37
R. Henderson	1996	37
S. Finley	1995	36

Walks

R. Henderson	2001	81
J. Kruk	1988	79
K. Caminiti	1997	80
D. Winfield	1980	79
G. Vaughn	1998	79

Strikeouts

N. Colbert	1971	119
G. Tenace	1977	119
K. Caminiti	1997	118
C. Gaston	1969	117

Stolen Bases

R. Sanders	1999	36
S. Jefferson	1987	34
D. Jackson	1999	34
A. Wiggins	1982	33
T. Gwynn	1984	33
Q. Veras	1997	33
E. Owens	1999	33

On Base Percentage
(3.1 plate appearances per game)

T. Gwynn	1994	.454
T. Gwynn	1987	.447
G. Tenace	1977	.415
T. Gwynn	1984	.410
Ja. Clark	1989	.410
R. Henderson	1996	.410
T. Gwynn	1997	.409
K. Caminiti	1996	.408
J. Kruk	1987	.406
T. Gwynn	1995	.404
G. Tenace	1979	.403
T. Gwynn	1993	.398
F. McGriff	1991	.396
D. Winfield	1979	.395
F. McGriff	1992	.394
R. Klesko	2000	.393
G. Tenace	1978	.392
W. Joyner	1997	.390
T. Gwynn	1989	.389
K. Caminiti	1997	.389

Slugging Percentage
(3.1 plate appearances per game)

K. Caminiti	1996	.621
G. Vaughn	1998	.597
P. Nevin	2001	.588
G. Sheffield	1992	.580
T. Gwynn	1994	.568
D. Winfield	1979	.558
F. McGriff	1992	.556
T. Gwynn	1997	.547
C. Gaston	1970	.543
P. Nevin	2000	.543
R. Klesko	2001	.539
S. Finley	1996	.531
R. Klesko	2000	.516
K. Caminiti	1995	.513
T. Gwynn	1987	.511
N. Colbert	1970	.509
P. Plantier	1993	.509
K. Caminiti	1998	.509
N. Colbert	1972	.508
K. Caminiti	1997	.508

PADRES SINGLE-SEASON PITCHING LEADERS

Wins

R. Jones	1976	22
G. Perry	1978	21
R. Jones	1975	20
A. Hawkins	1985	18
K. Brown	1998	18
A. Ashby	1998	17
T. Lollar	1982	16
L. Hoyt	1985	16
E. Show	1988	16
E. Whitson	1989	16
C. Kirby	1971	15
E. Show	1983	15
E. Show	1984	15
B. Hurst	1989	15
B. Hurst	1991	15
A. Benes	1991	15
A. Benes	1993	15
J. Hamilton	1996	15
Ten Tied At		14

Losses

R. Jones	1974	22
S. Arlin	1972	21
C. Kirby	1969	20
S. Arlin	1971	19
B. Greif	1974	19
B. Jones	2001	19
C. Kirby	1973	18
B. Shirley	1977	18
J. Niekro	1969	17
D. Roberts	1971	17
B. Greif	1973	17
M. Clement	2000	17
C. Kirby	1970	16
B. Greif	1972	16
B. Strom	1976	16
B. Shirley	1979	16
E. Show	1987	16
P. Dobson	1970	15
J. McIntosh	1975	15
D. Rasmussen	1990	15
A. Benes	1993	15

Winning Percentage (15 dec.)

G. Perry	1978	.778
D. Rasmussen	1988	.778
B. Metzger	1976	.733
K. Brown	1998	.720
A. Hawkins	1985	.692
L. Hoyt	1985	.667
A. Ashby	1998	.654
B. Hurst	1991	.652
T. Lollar	1982	.640
E. Whitson	1984	.636
M. Thurmond	1984	.636
J. Hamilton	1997	.632
R. Jones	1975	.625
E. Show	1982	.625
E. Show	1984	.625
G. Gossage	1984	.625
J. Hamilton	1996	.625
F. Valenzuela	1996	.619
R. Jones	1976	.611
E. Whitson	1990	.609
B. Hurst	1992	.609

Games

C. Lefferts	1986	83
R. Fingers	1977	78
L. McCullers	1987	78
B. Metzger	1976	77
L. Hardy	1974	76
D. Tomlin	1977	76
D. Spillner	1977	76
Gr. Harris	1990	73
L. McCullers	1986	70
M. Davis	1989	70
T. Hoffman	1996	70
T. Hoffman	1997	70
T. Hoffman	2000	70
K. Walker	2000	70
F. Reberger	1969	67
D. Tomlin	1975	67
R. Fingers	1978	67
D. Miceli	1998	67
R. Fingers	1980	66
R. Myers	1992	66
T. Hoffman	1998	66
D. Miceli	1999	66

Games Started

R. Jones	1976	40
R. Jones	1979	39
S. Arlin	1972	37
G. Perry	1978	37
C. Kirby	1971	36
R. Jones	1975	36
R. Jones	1978	36
C. Kirby	1969	35
B. Greif	1974	35
B. Shirley	1977	35
E. Show	1985	35
A. Hawkins	1986	35
K. Brown	1998	35
Thirteen tied at		34

Complete Games

R. Jones	1976	25
R. Jones	1975	18
D. Roberts	1971	14
C. Kirby	1971	13
E. Show	1988	13
S. Arlin	1972	12
S. Arlin	1971	10
F. Norman	1972	10
G. Perry	1979	10
B. Hurst	1989	10
C. Kirby	1972	9
B. Greif	1973	9
D. Dravecky	1983	9
B. Hurst	1990	9
J. Niekro	1969	8
P. Dobson	1970	8
B. Strom	1976	8
J. Eichelberger	1982	8
L. Hoyt	1985	8
Five tied At		7

Innings Pitched

R. Jones	1976	315.1
R. Jones	1975	285.0
D. Roberts	1971	269.2
C. Kirby	1971	267.1
R. Jones	1979	263.0
G. Perry	1978	260.2
K. Brown	1998	257.0
R. Jones	1978	253.0
P. Dobson	1971	251.0
S. Arlin	1972	250.0
B. Hurst	1989	244.2
C. Kirby	1972	238.2
E. Show	1988	234.2
E. Show	1985	233.0
G. Perry	1979	232.2
T. Lollar	1982	232.2
A. Benes	1992	231.1
A. Benes	1993	230.2
A. Hawkins	1985	228.2
E. Whitson	1990	228.2

Shutouts

F. Norman	1972	6
R. Jones	1975	6
R. Jones	1976	5
S. Arlin	1971	4
B. Hurst	1990	4
B. Hurst	1992	4
J. Niekro	1969	3
S. Arlin	1972	3
S. Arlin	1973	3
B. Greif	1973	3
D. Freisleben	1976	3
E. Rasmussen	1979	3
R. Jones	1980	3
L. Hoyt	1985	3
E. Show	1987	3
E. Whitson	1990	3
K. Brown	1998	3
A. Ashby	1999	3

Saves

T. Hoffman	1998	53
M. Davis	1989	44
T. Hoffman	2000	43
T. Hoffman	2001	43
T. Hoffman	1996	42
T. Hoffman	1999	40
R. Myers	1992	38
R. Fingers	1978	37
T. Hoffman	1997	37
R. Fingers	1977	35
T. Hoffman	1995	31
M. Davis	1988	28
R. Gossage	1985	26
R. Gossage	1984	25
R. Fingers	1980	23
C. Lefferts	1990	23
C. Lefferts	1991	23
Ge. Harris	1993	23
R. Gossage	1986	21
T. Hoffman	1994	20

Walks

M. Clement	2000	125
S. Arlin	1972	122
C. Kirby	1970	120
C. Kirby	1972	116
D. Freisleben	1974	112
J. Hamilton	1998	106
T. Lollar	1984	105
S. Arlin	1971	103
C. Kirby	1971	103
C. Kirby	1969	100
B. Shirley	1977	100
B. Greif	1974	95
F. Norman	1972	88

Strikeouts

K. Brown	1998	257
C. Kirby	1971	231
S. Hitchcock	1999	194
A. Benes	1994	189
P. Dobson	1970	185
J. Hamilton	1996	184
B. Hurst	1989	179
A. Benes	1993	179
C. Kirby	1972	175
M. Clement	2000	170
A. Benes	1992	169
F. Norman	1972	167
A. Benes	1991	167

Strikeouts Per 9 Innings

A. Benes	1994	9.87
K. Brown	1998	9.00
S. Hitchcock	1999	8.49
A. Eaton	2001	8.41
S. Hitchcock	1998	8.06
J. Hamilton	1996	7.82
C. Kirby	1971	7.78
M. Clement	2000	7.46
F. Norman	1972	7.10
A. Ashby	1995	7.01
A. Benes	1993	6.98
T. Lollar	1983	6.92
A. Benes	1991	6.74

Walks

T. Griffin	1977	88
E. Show	1984	88
T. Lollar	1982	87
E. Show	1985	87
J. D'Acquisto	1979	86
S. Mura	1980	86
A. Benes	1993	86
M. Clement	1999	86

Earned Run Average

D. Roberts	1971	2.10
R. Jones	1975	2.24
K. Brown	1998	2.38
E. Whitson	1990	2.60
E. Whitson	1989	2.66
B. Hurst	1989	2.69
G. Perry	1978	2.73
R. Jones	1976	2.74
C. Kirby	1971	2.83
R. Jones	1978	2.88
D. Dravecky	1985	2.93
A. Ashby	1995	2.94
M. Thurmond	1984	2.97
A. Benes	1991	3.03
G. Perry	1979	3.06
J. Hamilton	1995	3.08
E. Show	1985	3.09
C. Kirby	1972	3.13
T. Lollar	1982	3.13
B. Hurst	1985	3.15

Strikeouts

B. Hurst	1990	162
S. Arlin	1972	159
S. Hitchcock	1998	158
S. Sanders	1996	157
S. Arlin	1971	156
C. Kirby	1970	154
G. Perry	1978	154

Opponents Average

C. Kirby	1971	.216
T. Lollar	1982	.224
C. Kirby	1972	.226
B. Hurst	1990	.228
E. Show	1988	.231
R. Jones	1975	.232
A. Benes	1991	.232
A. Benes	1993	.232
A. Ashby	1994	.233
R. Jones	1976	.234
E. Show	1984	.234
T. Lollar	1984	.234
K. Brown	1998	.235
E. Whitson	1989	.235
S. Arlin	1972	.237
B. Hurst	1989	.237
A. Benes	1994	.237
B. Strom	1976	.239
W. Williams	2000	.239
D. Freisleben	1974	.241
B. Hurst	1991	.241
A. Eaton	2001	.241

Strikeouts Per 9 Innings

M. Clement	1999	6.72
P. Dobson	1970	6.63
A. Ashby	1994	6.63
C. Kirby	1972	6.60
B. Lawrence	2001	6.59
B. Hurst	1989	6.58
A. Benes	1992	6.57

ALL-TIME PADRE BATTING STATISTICS

Player, Years, Position	G	AB	R	H	2B	3B	HR	RBI	SB	BB	SO	AVE
Abner, Shawn 87-91 OF	254	531	56	110	23	2	8	46	4	27	100	.207
Acosta, Ed 71-72 P	54	29	1	1	0	0	0	0	0	1	15	.034
Aldrete, Mike 91 OF	12	15	2	0	0	0	0	1	0	3	4	.000
Allen, Dusty 00 OF	9	12	0	0	0	0	0	0	0	2	5	.000
Almanzar, Carlos 99-00 P	90	4	0	0	0	0	0	0	0	0	3	.000
Almon, Bill 74-79 IF	429	1321	144	337	44	13	4	81	47	95	255	.255
Alomar, Roberto 88-90 2B	448	1754	246	497	78	12	22	157	90	148	231	.283
Alomar, Sandy, Jr. 88-89 C	8	20	1	4	1	0	1	6	0	3	4	.200
Alou, Matty 74 OF	48	81	8	16	3	0	0	3	0	5	6	.198
Alvarez, Gabe 00 3B	11	13	1	2	1	0	0	0	0	1	1	.154
Andersen, Larry 91-92 P	72	3	1	0	0	0	0	0	0	1	2	.000
Anderson, Dwain 73 SS	53	107	11	13	0	0	0	3	2	14	29	.121
Arcia, Jose 69-70 2B	234	531	63	116	20	6	0	27	17	26	83	.218
Arias, Alex 01 3B	70	137	19	31	9	0	2	12	1	17	22	.226
Arias, George 97-99 3B	86	222	26	52	10	1	8	26	0	9	71	.234
Arlin, Steve 69-74 P	130	230	13	32	3	2	0	12	0	15	74	.139
Armstrong, Mike 80-81 P	21	3	0	0	0	0	0	0	0	0	3	.000
Asadoor, Randy 86 3B	15	55	9	20	5	0	0	7	1	3	13	.364
Ashby, Andy 93-99 P	207	373	18	52	12	0	0	14	1	11	149	.139
Ashford, Tucker 76-78 3B	160	409	36	95	30	0	6	50	5	36	66	.232
Ausmus, Brad 93-96 C	303	964	123	246	40	6	18	83	24	80	174	.235
Azocar, Oscar 91-92 OF	137	225	20	46	8	0	0	17	3	10	21	.204
Baerga, Carlos 99 IF	33	80	6	20	1	0	2	5	1	6	14	.250
Baker, Chuck 78, 80 2B-SS	53	80	8	15	2	0	0	3	0	2	19	.188
Baldschun, Jack 69-70 P	73	4	0	1	0	0	0	0	0	1	3	.250
Barrett, Marty 91 2B	12	16	1	3	1	0	1	3	0	0	3	.188
Barton, Bob 70-72, 74 C	271	814	47	190	26	2	9	62	3	65	122	.233
Bass, Randy 80-82 1B	101	255	19	57	4	2	8	36	0	29	35	.224
Batchelor, Rich 97 P	13	0	0	0	0	0	0	0	0	0	0	.000
Beamon, Trey 97 OF	43	65	5	18	3	0	0	7	1	2	17	.277
Bean, Billy 93-95 OF	176	319	27	76	14	1	5	46	2	14	58	.238
Beckert, Glenn 74-75 2B	73	188	13	50	2	0	0	7	0	12	8	.266
Bell, Derek 93-94 OF	258	976	127	277	39	1	35	126	50	52	250	.284
Benes, Andy 89-95 P	187	374	20	47	8	0	4	24	0	16	168	.126
Bergman, Sean 96-97 P	87	43	3	6	1	0	1	5	0	0	16	.140
Bernal, Victor 77 P	15	1	0	0	0	0	0	0	0	0	1	.000
Berumen, Andres 95-96 P	40	1	0	0	0	0	0	0	0	0	1	.000
Beswick, Jim 78 OF	17	20	2	1	0	0	0	0	0	1	7	.050
Bevacqua, Kurt 79-80, 82-85 IF	444	865	83	212	43	5	8	128	5	118	117	.245
Bilardello, Dann 91-92 C	32	59	6	11	3	1	0	6	0	7	12	.186
Blair, Dennis 80 P	5	5	0	1	0	0	0	0	0	0	2	.200
Blair, Willie 95-96 P	100	27	2	0	0	0	0	1	0	1	18	.000
Blefary, Curt 72 OF	74	102	10	20	3	0	3	9	0	19	18	.196
Bochtler, Doug 95-97 P	151	2	0	0	0	0	0	0	0	0	0	.000
Bochy, Bruce 83-87 C	209	448	52	104	20	2	20	64	1	34	104	.232
Boehringer, Brian 98-00 P	40	20	0	2	1	0	0	2	0	2	9	.100
Bones, Ricky 91 P	11	13	1	1	0	0	0	1	0	2	5	.077
Bonilla, Juan 81-83 2B	296	1107	106	290	36	8	5	78	7	86	78	.262
Booker, Greg 83-89 P	153	23	2	4	2	0	0	1	0	0	9	.174
Boone, Bret 00 2B	127	463	61	116	18	2	19	74	8	50	97	.251
Boone, Dan 81-82 P	47	9	0	3	1	0	0	0	0	0	0	.333
Bravo, Angel 71 OF	52	58	6	9	2	0	0	6	0	8	12	.155
Briggs, Dan 79 1B	104	227	34	47	4	3	8	30	2	18	45	.207
Brocail, Doug 92-94 P	47	40	6	7	0	0	0	0	2	0	9	.175
Brown, Bobby 83-85 OF	221	480	76	116	15	5	8	57	49	39	91	.242
Brown, Chris 87-88 3B	124	402	31	94	9	0	8	42	3	30	79	.234
Brown, Emil 01 OF	13	14	3	1	0	0	0	0	2	1	3	.071
Brown, Jarvis 93 OF	47	133	21	31	9	2	0	8	3	15	26	.233
Brown, Kevin 98 P	36	82	4	17	3	0	0	10	0	4	29	.207
Brown, Ollie 69-72 OF	458	1656	194	450	70	4	52	208	18	135	258	.272
Bruske, Jim 97 P	29	6	0	1	1	0	0	0	0	0	1	.167
Bumbry, Al 85 OF	68	95	6	19	3	0	1	10	2	7	9	.200
Burrows, Terry 97 P	13	0	0	0	0	0	0	0	0	0	0	.000
Byers, Randell 87-88 OF	21	26	1	7	2	0	0	1	1	1	10	.269
Caldwell, Mike 71-73 P	104	86	3	13	1	0	0	8	0	1	32	.151
Caminiti, Ken 95-98 3B	557	2010	362	592	127	2	121	396	40	298	419	.295
Campbell, Dave 70-73 2B	328	1144	117	256	50	4	19	80	28	95	217	.224
Campbell, Mike 94 P	3	3	0	1	0	0	0	2	0	0	1	.333
Cannizzaro, Chris 69-71, 74 C	292	882	54	210	29	6	10	87	2	101	140	.238
Carlyle, Buddy 99-00 P	11	9	1	2	0	0	0	1	0	2	3	.222
Carter, Joe 90 OF	162	634	78	147	27	1	24	115	22	48	93	.232
Cash, Dave 80 2B	130	397	25	90	14	2	1	23	6	35	21	.227
Castillo, Tony 78 C	5	8	0	1	0	0	0	1	0	0	2	.225
Cedeno, Andujar 95-96 SS	169	544	52	118	18	3	9	49	8	37	124	.217
Champion, Mike 76-78 2B	193	598	42	137	16	8	2	49	3	33	101	.229
Chiffer, Floyd 82-84 P	81	12	0	0	0	0	0	0	0	0	4	.000
Cianfrocco, Archi 93-98 1B	402	1027	108	248	53	5	27	154	13	69	289	.241

Player, Years, Position	G	AB	R	H	2B	3B	HR	RBI	SB	BB	SO	AVE
Clark, Jack 89-90 1B	257	789	135	199	31	2	51	156	10	236	236	.252
Clark, Jerald 88-92 OF	340	1022	88	242	45	7	28	126	5	61	224	.237
Clark, Phil 93-95 OF	238	486	59	128	26	0	16	60	3	21	66	.263
Clarke, Horace 74 2B	42	90	5	17	1	0	0	4	0	8	6	.189
Clement, Matt 98-00 P	69	114	10	8	0	1	0	3	0	8	63	.070
Clements, Pat 89-92 P	71	8	0	0	0	0	0	0	0	0	5	.000
Colangelo, Mike 01 OF	50	91	10	22	3	3	2	8	0	8	30	.242
Colbert, Nate 69-74 1B	866	3080	442	780	130	22	163	481	48	350	773	.253
Comstock, Keith 87-88 P	48	2	0	0	0	0	0	0	0	0	1	.000
Coolbaugh, Scott 91 3B	60	180	12	39	8	1	2	15	0	19	45	.217
Coombs, Danny 70-71 P	54	66	5	8	3	0	0	2	0	4	37	.121
Cora, Joey 87, 89-90 2B	140	360	40	90	11	2	0	16	24	35	35	.250
Corkins, Mike 69-74 P	164	119	16	24	2	0	5	12	0	10	54	.202
Corrales, Pat 72-73 C	72	191	13	38	2	1	0	9	0	17	36	.199
Costello, John 91 P	27	1	0	0	0	0	0	0	0	0	1	.000
Couchee, Mike 83 P	8	2	0	1	0	0	0	0	0	0	0	.500
Crespo, Cesar 01 2B, OF	55	153	27	32	6	0	4	12	6	25	50	.209
Cunnane, Will 97-00 P	109	24	4	6	1	1	0	4	0	2	8	.250
Curtis, John 80-82 P	85	112	4	24	1	1	0	9	0	2	52	.214
D'Acquisto, John 77-80 P	152	66	2	8	3	0	0	7	0	6	38	.121
Dade, Paul 79-80 3B	144	336	55	88	19	2	1	22	17	26	58	.262
Darr, Mike 99-01 OF	188	542	63	148	28	5	5	67	17	67	135	.273
Dascenzo, Doug 96 OF	21	9	3	1	0	0	0	0	0	1	2	.111
Davanon, Jerry 69 SS, 2B	24	59	4	8	1	0	0	3	0	3	12	.136
Davey, Tom 00- P	50	0	0	0	0	0	0	0	0	1	0	.000
Davis, Ben 98-01 C	258	845	97	201	40	1	19	101	7	105	217	.238
Davis, Bill 69 1B	31	57	1	10	1	0	0	1	0	8	18	.175
Davis, Bob 73, 75-78 C	166	356	26	73	6	3	1	24	0	22	78	.205
Davis, Jerry 83, 85 OF	49	73	13	22	5	1	0	3	1	8	11	.301
Davis, John 90 P	6	1	0	0	0	0	0	0	0	0	0	.000
Davis, Mark 87-89, 93-94 P	276	57	6	10	1	1	1	3	1	1	15	.175
Davis, Storm 87 P	21	16	1	1	0	0	0	0	0	0	10	.063
Davis, Willie 76 OF	141	493	61	132	18	10	5	46	14	19	34	.268
Dean, Tommy 69-71 SS	203	501	34	91	14	3	4	23	3	42	96	.203
Decker, Marty 83 P	4	0	0	0	0	0	0	0	0	0	0	.000
Deer, Rob 96 OF	25	50	9	9	3	0	4	9	0	14	30	.180
DeHaan, Kory 00 OF	90	103	19	21	7	0	2	13	4	5	39	.204
DeLeon, Luis 82-85 P	185	34	4	4	1	0	0	0	0	2	19	.118
Deshaies, Jim 92 P	15	29	3	6	0	0	0	0	0	1	9	.207
Dilone, Miguel 85 OF	27	46	8	10	0	1	0	1	10	4	8	.217
Dishman, Glenn 95-96 P	22	30	4	6	0	0	0	4	0	0	13	.200
Dobson, Pat 70 P	40	71	5	10	1	0	0	4	0	5	17	.141
Dorsett, Brian 91 1B	11	12	0	1	0	0	0	1	0	0	3	.083
Doyle, Paul 70 P	9	1	0	0	0	0	0	0	0	0	0	.000
Dravecky, Dave 82-87 P	210	262	15	31	5	1	1	14	1	13	75	.118
Dukes, Tom 69-70 P	66	8	0	0	0	0	0	0	0	0	6	.000
Dunne, Mike 90 P	10	6	0	0	0	0	0	0	0	0	2	.000
Dupree, Mike 76 P	11	1	1	1	0	0	0	0	0	0	0	1.000
Eaton, Adam 00- P	45	76	9	15	3	0	0	6	3	10	22	.197
Edwards, Dave 81-82 OF	129	167	20	34	6	1	3	15	3	12	38	.204
Eichelberger, Juan 78-82 P	77	133	3	14	2	1	0	4	1	4	63	.105
Eiland, Dave 92-93 P	17	21	2	2	0	0	1	2	0	0	8	.095
Elliott, Donnie 94-95 P	31	1	0	0	0	0	0	0	0	0	1	.000
Elliott, Randy 72, 74 OF	27	82	10	17	4	1	1	8	0	9	20	.207
Erdos, Todd 97, 00 P	33	3	0	0	0	0	0	0	0	0	1	.000
Ettles, Mark 93 P	14	2	0	0	0	0	0	0	0	0	0	.000
Evans, Barry 78-81 3B	207	470	38	118	14	3	2	39	3	35	36	.251
Everitt, Leon 69 P	6	3	0	0	0	0	0	0	0	1	0	.000
Fahey, Bill 79-80 C	166	450	32	122	12	1	4	41	3	42	33	.271
Faries, Paul 90-92 2B	81	178	20	35	5	1	0	10	3	19	30	.197
Fernandez, Tony 91-92 SS	300	1180	165	323	59	9	8	75	43	111	136	.274
Ferrara, Al 69-71 OF	293	755	83	200	38	5	27	109	0	94	142	.265
Fikac, Jeremy 01- P	23	0	0	0	0	0	0	0	0	0	0	.000
Fingers, Rollie 77-80 P	265	62	1	9	3	0	0	6	0	0	19	.145
Finley, Steve 95-98 OF	602	2396	423	662	134	28	82	298	85	203	344	.276
Fiore, Mike 92 OF	7	6	0	0	0	0	0	0	0	1	3	.000
Fireovid, Steve 81, 83 P	8	7	0	1	0	0	0	0	0	0	4	.143
Flaherty, John 96-97 C	201	703	60	200	33	1	18	87	6	42	98	.284
Flannery, Tim 79-89 IF	972	2473	255	631	77	25	9	209	22	277	293	.255
Florie, Bryce 94-96 P	95	5	0	0	0	0	0	0	0	0	3	.000
Folkers, Rich 75-76 P	78	40	2	6	1	0	0	4	0	4	15	.150
Foster, Alan 75-76 P	47	29	2	2	0	0	0	2	0	3	9	.069
Franklin, Jay 71 P	3	1	0	0	0	0	0	0	0	0	0	.000
Freisleben, Dave 74-78 P	48	192	13	27	3	2	0	8	0	19	43	.141
Frisella, Danny 75 P	65	5	1	1	0	0	0	0	0	0	2	.200
Fuentes, Tito 75-76 2B	281	1085	105	295	39	0	6	79	13	42	89	.272
Gamble, Oscar 78 OF	126	375	46	103	15	3	7	47	1	51	45	.275
Garcia, Carlos 99 3B-1B	6	11	1	2	0	0	0	0	0	1	3	.182

Player, Years, Position	G	AB	R	H	2B	3B	HR	RBI	SB	BB	SO	AVE
Garcia, Ralph 72, 74 P	11	0	0	0	0	0	0	0	0	0	0	.000
Gardner, Jeff 92-93 2B	145	423	53	108	21	7	1	24	2	46	77	.255
Gardner, Wes 91 P	14	2	0	0	0	0	0	0	0	0	2	.000
Garvey, Steve 83-87 1B	605	2,292	291	631	107	8	61	316	6	112	252	.275
Gaspar, Rod 71, 74 OF	49	31	5	5	0	0	0	3	0	7	6	.161
Gaston, Cito 69-74 OF	766	2615	269	672	93	29	77	316	9	147	595	.257
Geren, Bob 93 C	58	145	8	31	6	0	3	6	0	13	28	.214
Gerhardt, Rusty 74 P	23	6	0	1	0	0	0	0	0	0	3	.167
Giovanola, Ed 98-99 IF	148	197	29	43	3	4	1	12	3	31	30	.218
Goddard, Joe 72 C	12	35	0	7	2	0	0	2	0	5	9	.200
Gomez, Chris 96-01 SS	533	1699	179	430	78	7	13	147	10	186	333	.253
Gonzalez, Fernando 78-79 2B	215	643	49	150	23	5	11	63	4	36	66	.233
Gonzalez, Tony 69 OF	53	182	17	41	4	0	2	8	1	19	24	.225
Gonzalez, Wiki 99- C	189	527	48	131	23	2	16	69	3	42	67	.249
Gorman, Tom 87 P	6	0	0	0	0	0	0	0	0	0	0	.000
Gossage, Rich 84-87 P	197	41	1	4	0	0	0	0	0	3	18	.098
Grant, Mark 87-90 P	143	82	9	6	0	0	0	1	0	9	33	.073
Green, Gary 86, 89 SS	28	60	6	14	4	0	0	2	0	2	12	.233
Greer, Brian 77, 79 OF	5	4	0	0	0	0	0	0	0	0	2	.000
Greif, Bill 72-76 P	180	159	6	11	0	0	0	1	0	15	69	.069
Griffin, Mike 82 P	7	1	0	0	0	0	0	0	0	0	1	.000
Griffin, Tom 76-77 P	51	71	4	8	3	0	2	4	0	0	30	.113
Grubb, John 73-77 OF	513	1781	235	513	101	11	25	145	16	208	212	.288
Gutierrez, Ricky 93-94 SS	273	713	103	176	21	7	6	54	6	82	151	.247
Guzman, Domingo 99-00 P	8	0	0	0	0	0	0	0	0	0	0	.000
Gwosdz, Doug 81-84 C	69	104	9	15	3	0	1	8	0	14	37	.144
Gwynn, Chris 96 OF	81	90	8	16	4	0	1	10	0	10	28	.178
Gwynn, Tony 1982-01 OF	2440	9288	1383	3141	543	85	135	1138	319	790	434	.338
Hahn, Don 75 OF	34	26	7	6	1	2	0	3	1	10	2	.231
Hamilton, Joey 94-98 P	147	298	16	35	4	1	4	20	0	8	151	.117
Hammaker, Atlee 90-91 P	35	20	2	2	0	0	0	0	0	1	7	.100
Hardy, Larry 74-75 P	79	10	1	0	0	0	0	0	0	1	7	.000
Hargrove, Mike 79 1B	52	125	15	24	5	0	0	8	0	25	15	.192
Harris, Gene 92-94 P	87	5	0	1	0	0	0	0	0	0	1	.200
Harris, Greg A. 84 P	19	8	3	3	1	0	0	0	0	0	1	.375
Harris, Greg W. 88-93 P	172	105	5	9	1	1	0	3	0	8	48	.086
Hawkins, Andy 82-88 P	184	310	12	38	1	0	0	9	0	10	92	.123
Hayward, Ray 86-87 P	8	5	0	0	0	0	0	0	0	0	0	.000
Henderson, Rickey 96-97, 01 OF	359	1132	243	277	45	5	23	98	91	277	236	.245
Hendrick, George 77-78 OF	188	652	84	195	29	2	26	89	12	73	90	.299
Herbel, Ron 70 P	64	13	0	0	0	0	0	0	0	1	8	.000
Hermanson, Dustin 95-96 P	34	0	0	0	0	0	0	0	0	0	0	.000
Hernandez, Carlos 97-00 C	237	715	65	192	33	1	14	91	3	35	107	.269
Hernandez, Enzo 71-77 SS	710	2324	241	522	66	13	2	113	129	189	150	.225
Hernandez, Jeremy 91-93 P	56	5	0	0	0	0	0	0	0	0	2	.000
Herndon, Junior 01 P	12	12	0	0	0	0	0	0	0	0	11	.000
Higgins, Kevin 93 C	71	181	17	40	4	1	0	13	0	16	17	.221
Hilton, Dave 72-75 3B	161	506	40	108	19	3	6	33	6	35	69	.213
Hinshaw, George 82-83 OF	13	31	2	11	1	0	0	5	1	8	15	.355
Hitchcock, Sterling 97-01 P	118	191	14	18	0	0	0	5	0	7	103	.094
Hoffman, Trevor 93- P	571	33	1	3	2	0	0	5	0	0	10	.091
Holbert, Ray 94-95 SS	68	78	12	14	2	1	2	5	4	8	24	.179
Howard, Thomas 90-92 OF	131	328	35	83	14	3	4	22	10	24	68	.253
Howell, Jack 91 3B	58	160	24	33	3	1	6	16	0	18	33	.206
Hoyt, LaMarr 85-86 P	66	110	7	10	1	0	0	3	0	2	39	.091
Hrniak, Walt 69 C	31	66	4	15	0	0	0	1	0	8	11	.227
Hundley, Randy 75 C	74	180	7	37	5	1	2	14	0	19	29	.206
Huntz, Steve 70, 75 OF, 3B	128	405	57	85	12	0	11	41	0	73	77	.210
Hurst, Bruce 89-93 P	139	274	11	31	5	0	0	8	0	20	141	.113
Hyers, Tim 94-95 1B	58	123	13	30	3	0	0	7	3	9	16	.244
Iorg, Dane 86 1B, P	90	106	10	24	2	1	2	11	0	2	21	.226
Ivie, Mike 71, 74-77 1B	403	1322	154	356	64	9	25	188	13	92	170	.269
Jackson, Damian 99-01 SS 2B, OF	393	1298	191	313	68	14	19	114	85	159	341	.241
Jackson, Danny 97 P	13	13	0	1	0	0	0	0	0	1	4	.076
Jackson, Darrin 89-92 OF, P	360	1146	143	287	41	6	44	140	22	65	213	.250
Jackson, Roy Lee 85 P	22	5	0	0	0	0	0	0	0	0	3	.000
James, Chris 89 OF	76	303	41	80	13	2	11	46	2	22	45	.264
Jarvis, Kevin 01- P	34	61	8	11	3	0	1	10	0	5	20	.180
Jefferson, Stan 87-88 OF	165	533	75	113	9	9	9	33	39	48	114	.212
Jestadt, Garry 71-72 2B, 3B	167	445	32	118	18	1	6	35	1	24	45	.265
Jeter, John 71-72 OF	128	401	33	96	8	3	8	24	13	20	92	.239
Jimenez, D'Angelo 01- SS	86	308	45	85	19	0	3	33	2	39	68	.276
Jodie, Brett 01 P	7	4	0	0	0	0	0	0	0	0	2	.000
Johnson, Brian 94-96 C	186	543	45	141	26	2	14	80	0	20	96	.260
Johnson, Jerry 75-76 P	45	15	1	1	1	0	0	0	0	0	6	.067
Johnson, Mike 74 P	18	0	0	0	0	0	0	0	0	0	0	.000
Johnstone, Jay 79 OF	75	201	10	59	8	2	0	32	1	18	21	.294
Jones, Bobby 01- P	33	57	5	8	2	0	0	1	0	3	18	.140
Jones, Chris 97 OF	92	152	24	37	9	0	7	25	7	16	45	.243

Player, Years, Position	G	AB	R	H	2B	3B	HR	RBI	SB	BB	SO	AVE
Jones, Jimmy 86-88 P	67	110	10	18	0	0	2	7	0	6	34	.164
Jones, Randy 73-80 P	277	556	36	73	8	0	0	20	1	19	216	.131
Jones, Ruppert 81-83 OF	354	1156	164	297	66	6	28	149	36	140	214	.257
Joshua, Von 80 OF	53	63	8	15	2	1	2	7	0	5	15	.238
Joyner, Wally 96-99 1B	497	1650	210	480	102	6	38	271	9	229	220	.291
Kelley, Dick 69-71 P	75	50	0	6	1	0	0	2	0	0	25	.120
Kelly, Van 69-70 3B	111	298	25	66	10	1	4	24	0	27	45	.221
Kendall, Fred 69-75, 79-80 C	754	2218	149	516	72	10	28	201	5	173	211	.233
Kennedy, Terry 81-86 C	835	2987	308	817	158	7	76	424	3	200	508	.274
Kilkenny, Mike 72 P	5	0	0	0	0	0	0	0	0	0	0	.000
Kingman, Dave 77 OF	56	168	16	40	9	0	11	39	2	12	48	.238
Kinney, Dennis 78-80 P	70	14	0	1	0	0	0	0	0	1	8	.071
Kirby, Clay 69-73 P	181	354	14	33	3	0	0	7	0	23	161	.093
Klesko, Ryan 00- 1B	291	1032	193	294	67	8	56	205	46	179	170	.285
Kolb, Brandon 00 P	11	1	1	0	0	0	0	0	0	0	0	.000
Kotsay, Mark 01-OF	119	406	67	118	29	1	10	58	13	48	58	.291
Kroon, Marc 95, 97-98 P	16	0	0	0	0	0	0	0	0	0	0	.000
Krueger, Bill 94-95 P	14	12	1	6	1	0	0	0	0	0	3	.500
Krug, Chris 69 C	8	17	0	1	0	0	0	0	0	1	6	.059
Kruk, John 86-89 OF, 1B	411	1179	166	331	47	5	36	179	25	215	233	.281
Kubiak, Ted 75-76 3B	183	408	29	94	10	2	0	40	3	49	46	.230
Kuhaulua, Fred 81 P	5	9	0	1	0	0	0	1	0	0	5	.111
Lampkin, Tom 90-92 C	73	138	11	29	3	2	1	7	2	13	19	.210
Lancelotti, Rick 82 1B	17	39	2	7	2	0	0	4	0	2	8	.179
Langston, Mark 98 P	23	24	0	2	1	0	0	2	0	2	9	.083
Lankford, Ray 01- OF	40	125	20	36	10	1	4	19	6	18	40	.288
Lansford, Joe 82-83 1B	25	30	7	6	0	0	1	5	0	6	7	.200
LaPoint, Dave 86 P	24	8	0	0	0	0	0	0	0	0	1	.000
LaRocca, Greg 00 3B	13	27	1	6	2	0	0	2	0	1	4	.222
Lawrence, Brian 01- P	27	26	0	3	2	0	0	3	0	0	7	.115
Laxton, Bill 71, 74 P	48	5	0	1	0	0	0	0	0	1	3	.200
Lee, David 01 P	41	1	0	0	0	0	0	0	0	0	1	.000
Lee, Derrek 97 1B	22	54	9	14	3	0	1	4	0	9	24	.259
Lee, Leron 71-73 OF	298	959	115	260	50	11	19	98	10	80	164	.271
Lee, Mark 78-79 P	102	11	0	2	0	0	0	0	0	0	5	.182
Lefebvre, Joe 81-83 OF	206	505	57	125	22	4	12	53	6	55	86	.248
Lefferts, Craig 84-87, 90-92 P	376	94	3	13	1	0	1	2	0	0	41	.138
Leiper, Dave 87-89 P	69	1	0	0	0	0	0	0	0	0	1	.000
Lewis, Jim 91 P	12	2	0	0	0	0	0	0	0	0	1	.000
Leyritz, Jim 98-99 C, 1B	112	277	34	70	15	0	12	40	0	36	77	.253
Lezcano, Sixto 82-83 OF	235	787	114	210	37	8	24	133	2	125	135	.267
Libran, Francisco 69 SS	10	10	1	1	1	0	0	1	0	1	2	.100
Lilliquist, Derek 90-91 P	22	22	3	3	0	0	0	1	0	1	4	.136
Littlefield, John 81 P	42	1	0	0	0	0	0	0	0	0	0	.000
Livingstone, Scott 94-97 3B	281	574	58	170	32	2	9	65	4	32	67	.296
Lockhart, Keith 94 2B, 3B	27	43	4	9	0	0	2	6	1	4	10	.209
Locklear, Gene 73-76 OF	249	532	67	148	23	4	9	63	13	51	75	.278
Loewer, Carlton 01 P	2	0	0	0	0	0	0	0	0	0	0	.000
Lolich, Mickey 78-79 P	47	9	0	0	0	0	0	0	0	1	6	.000
Lollar, Tim 81-84 P	122	229	27	53	3	3	8	38	0	18	64	.231
Long, Joey 97 P	10	0	0	0	0	0	0	0	0	0	0	.000
Lopez, Luis 93-94, 96 2B, SS	157	417	40	95	20	1	4	32	3	24	82	.228
Lopez, Rodrigo 00 P	6	9	1	1	0	0	0	0	0	0	4	.111
Lucas, Gary 80-83 P	230	71	2	7	0	0	0	5	0	2	26	.099
Lundquist, David 01- P	17	0	0	0	0	0	0	0	0	0	0	.000
Lynn, Fred 90 OF	90	196	18	47	3	1	6	23	2	22	44	.240
Mabry, John 00 OF	48	123	17	28	8	0	7	25	0	5	38	.228
Mack, Shane 87-88 OF	161	357	41	86	14	3	4	37	9	32	68	.241
Maddux, Mike 91-92 P	114	22	1	2	0	0	0	0	0	3	8	.091
Magadan, Dave 99-01 3B, 1B	302	508	445	136	26	1	5	63	1	89	79	.268
Manuel, Jerry 82 IF	2	5	0	1	0	1	0	1	0	1	0	.200
Marshall, Dave 73 OF	39	49	4	14	5	0	0	4	0	8	9	.286
Martin, Al 00 OF	93	346	62	106	13	6	11	27	6	28	54	.306
Martinez, Carmelo 84-89 OF	783	2325	286	577	111	0	82	337	8	327	403	.248
Martinez, Jose 94 P	4	2	0	0	0	0	0	0	0	0	1	.000
Martinez, Pedro A. 93-94 P	80	9	0	0	0	0	0	1	0	0	4	.000
Mason, Don 71-73 2B	130	363	44	75	12	1	2	11	6	28	38	.207
Matthews, Gary, Jr. 99 OF	23	36	4	8	0	0	0	7	2	9	9	.222
Maurer, Dave 00-01 P	17	1	0	0	0	0	0	0	0	0	1	.000
Mauser, Tim 93-95 P	76	11	1	1	0	0	0	0	0	2	7	.091
McAndrew, Jim 74 P	15	7	0	1	0	0	0	0	0	1	1	.143
McBean, Alvin 69 P	1	2	0	1	0	0	0	0	0	0	1	.500
McCool, Billy 69 P	54	1	0	0	0	0	0	0	0	0	0	.000
McCovey, Willie 74-76 1B	321	959	116	232	45	1	52	167	2	174	195	.242
McCullers, Lance 85-88 P	235	48	5	5	2	0	0	4	1	5	23	.104
McDavid, Ray 94-95 OF	20	45	4	10	1	0	0	2	2	3	14	.222
McElroy, Chuck 01 P	31	3	0	0	0	0	0	0	0	0	1	.000
McGriff, Fred 91-93 1B	388	1361	215	382	60	6	84	256	16	243	298	.281

Player, Years, Position	G	AB	R	H	2B	3B	HR	RBI	SB	BB	SO	AVE
McIntosh, Joe 74-75 P	48	58	6	9	2	0	0	5	0	4	12	.155
McReynolds, Kevin 83-86 OF	496	1789	233	470	84	17	65	260	17	155	262	.263
Meadows, Brian 00 P	22	40	2	6	0	0	0	2	0	0	17	.150
Melendez, Jose 91-92 P	87	25	1	2	1	0	0	0	0	1	18	.080
Melendez, Luis 76-77 OF	98	146	16	32	5	0	0	5	1	4	16	.219
Mendez, Donaldo 01 SS	46	118	11	18	2	1	1	5	1	5	37	.153
Menhart, Paul 97 P	9	12	0	0	0	0	0	0	0	0	4	.000
Metzger, Butch 75-77 P	98	11	1	0	0	0	0	0	0	2	5	.000
Miceli, Dan 98-99 P	134	2	0	1	0	0	0	0	0	0	1	.500
Middlebrook, Jason 01- P	4	7	0	1	0	0	0	1	0	0	6	.143
Miller, Bob 71, 73 P	56	12	0	0	0	0	0	0	0	4	0	.000
Miller, Ed 84 OF	13	14	4	4	0	1	1	2	0	0	4	.286
Mitchell, Kevin 87 3B	62	196	19	48	7	1	7	26	0	20	38	.245
Monge, Sid 83-84 P	60	11	0	1	0	0	0	0	0	0	3	.091
Montanez, Willie 80 1B	128	481	39	132	12	4	6	63	3	36	52	.274
Montefusco, John 82-83 P	63	77	3	6	1	0	0	3	0	6	41	.078
Montgomery, Steve 00 P	7	0	0	0	0	0	0	0	0	0	0	.000
Morales, Jerry 69-73 OF	296	851	97	211	40	10	15	63	11	72	129	.248
Morales, Rich 73-74 2B, SS	144	305	17	52	9	1	1	21	1	35	42	.170
Moreland, Keith 88 1B, OF	143	511	40	131	23	0	5	64	2	40	51	.256
Moreno, Jose 81 2B	34	48	5	11	2	0	0	6	4	1	8	.229
Moses, Gerry 75 C	13	19	1	3	2	0	0	1	0	2	3	.158
Mota, Jose 91 2B	17	36	4	8	0	0	0	2	0	2	7	.222
Mouton, James 98 OF	55	63	8	12	2	1	0	7	4	7	11	.190
Mulligan, Sean 96 C	2	1	0	0	0	0	0	0	0	0	0	.000
Mumphrey, Jerry 80 OF	160	564	61	168	24	3	4	59	52	49	90	.298
Mura, Steve 78-81 P	106	106	6	13	3	0	0	12	0	5	33	.123
Murphy, Dan 89 P	7	0	0	0	0	0	0	0	0	0	0	.000
Murray, Heath 97, 99 P	39	19	1	2	0	0	0	0	0	1	10	.105
Murrell, Ivan 69-73 OF	437	1066	108	257	38	13	31	106	5	37	273	.241
Myers, Greg 98-99 C	119	299	28	79	14	0	7	35	0	30	50	.264
Myers, Randy 92, 98 P	87	7	0	1	0	0	0	0	0	0	5	.143
Myers, Rodney L. 00-01 P	40	2	0	0	0	0	0	0	0	0	0	.000
Nady, Xavier 00 PH	1	1	1	1	0	0	0	0	0	0	0	1.000
Nelson, Rob 87-90 1B	64	119	10	21	0	1	4	11	1	23	50	.178
Nettles, Graig 84-86 3B	387	1189	158	282	43	2	51	181	0	171	176	.237
Nevin, Phil 99 C, 3B	420	1467	236	433	92	1	96	318	7	181	350	.295
Newfield, Marc 95-96 OF	105	246	33	65	16	1	6	33	1	18	52	.264
Newhan, David 99-00 2B	44	63	12	9	2	0	3	7	2	7	18	.143
Nicholson, Kevin 00 SS	37	97	7	21	6	1	1	8	1	4	31	.216
Niekro, Joe 69 P	38	51	1	6	1	0	0	2	0	6	17	.118
Nieves, Melvin 93-95 OF	127	300	38	62	7	1	17	45	2	25	119	.207
Nolte, Eric 87-89, 91 P	23	32	2	3	0	0	0	0	0	1	18	.094
Norman, Fred 71-73 P	80	127	7	20	2	0	0	3	0	12	31	.161
Nunez, Jose 01- P	56	3	0	0	0	0	0	0	0	0	2	.000
Nyman, Gerry 70 P	3	0	0	0	0	0	0	0	0	0	0	.000
Oquist, Mike 96 P	8	0	0	0	0	0	0	0	0	0	0	.000
Osting, Jimmy 01 P	3	0	0	0	0	0	0	0	0	0	0	.000
Osuna, Al 96 P	10	1	0	0	0	0	0	0	0	0	0	.000
Owens, Eric 99-00 IF, OF	294	1023	142	288	41	10	15	112	62	83	113	.282
Owchinko, Bob 76-79 P	110	146	6	19	2	0	0	5	0	9	58	.130
Pagliarulo, Mike 89-90 3B	178	546	41	130	30	2	10	52	3	57	105	.238
Palacios, Vicente 00 P	7	0	0	0	0	0	0	0	0	0	0	.000
Palmer, Lowell 74 P	23	23	2	2	0	1	0	0	0	0	15	.097
Parent, Mark 86-90 C	178	487	35	96	18	9	16	54	2	31	98	.197
Patterson, Bob 85 P	3	0	0	0	0	0	0	0	0	0	0	.000
Pena, Roberto 69 SS	139	472	44	118	16	3	4	30	0	21	63	.250
Perez, Santiago 01 SS, OF	43	81	13	16	1	0	0	4	5	15	29	.198
Perkins, Broderick 78-82 1B	379	1005	99	277	51	8	8	129	8	64	87	.276
Perlozzo, Sammy 79 2B	2	2	0	0	0	0	0	0	0	1	0	.000
Perry, Gaylord 78-79 P	59	158	7	14	4	0	1	5	0	4	50	.089
Petagine, Roberto 95 1B	89	124	15	29	8	0	3	17	0	26	41	.234
Peterson, Adam 91 P	13	13	0	0	0	0	0	0	0	2	9	.000
Pettis, Gary 92 OF	30	30	0	6	1	0	0	0	1	2	11	.200
Phillips, Mike 81 2B	14	29	1	6	0	1	0	0	1	0	3	.207
Phoebus, Tom 71-72 P	30	38	2	6	2	0	0	0	0	3	19	.158
Pittman, Joe 82 2B	55	118	16	30	2	0	0	7	8	9	13	.254
Plantier, Phil 93-95, 97 OF	296	959	132	225	45	1	57	160	8	116	247	.235
Podres, Johnny 69 P	17	16	0	1	0	0	0	1	0	0	3	.063
Presley, Jim 91 3B	20	59	3	8	0	0	1	5	0	4	16	.136
Pyznarski, Tim 86 1B	15	42	3	10	1	0	0	0	2	4	11	.238
Rader, Doug 76-77 3B	191	641	64	167	30	7	14	82	3	88	142	.261
Ramirez, Mario 81-85 SS	166	262	31	50	8	3	4	28	0	40	57	.191
Ramirez, Roberto 98 P	21	0	0	0	0	0	0	0	0	0	0	.000
Rasmussen, Dennis 83, 88-91 P	115	222	18	44	7	0	0	13	0	12	69	.198
Rasmussen, Eric 78-80 P	113	103	1	11	2	0	0	1	0	3	25	.107
Ready, Randy 86-89 3B, 2B	267	751	116	213	44	9	19	98	13	117	89	.284
Reberger, Frank 69 P	67	5	0	1	0	0	0	0	0	0	3	.200

Player, Years, Position	G	AB	R	H	2B	3B	HR	RBI	SB	BB	SO	AVE
Reed, Jody 95-96 2B	277	940	103	235	38	1	6	89	8	108	91	.250
Relaford, Desi 00 SS	45	157	26	32	2	0	2	16	8	27	26	.204
Rettenmund, Merv 76-77 OF	191	266	39	68	13	1	6	28	5	62	51	.256
Reyes, Carlos 98-00 P	77	1	0	0	0	0	0	0	0	0	0	.000
Reynolds, Ken 76 P	19	5	0	0	0	0	0	0	0	0	0	.000
Reynolds, Ronn 90 C	8	15	1	1	1	0	0	1	0	1	6	.067
Richards, Gene 77-83 OF	939	3414	484	994	123	63	26	251	242	338	408	.291
Riggs, Adam 01 2B	12	36	2	7	1	0	0	1	1	2	8	.194
Rivera, Roberto 99 P	12	0	0	0	0	0	0	0	0	0	0	.000
Rivera, Ruben 97-00 OF	394	1026	160	209	42	9	46	135	33	129	341	.204
Roberts, David A. 69-71 P	104	160	8	32	3	0	2	9	0	1	44	.200
Roberts, David W. 72-75, 77-78 3B, C	509	1611	149	386	67	6	35	157	25	103	292	.240
Roberts, Leon 86, 88-91, 94-95 2B, 3B, OF	667	2258	378	673	98	21	20	169	148	212	305	.298
Robinson, Dave 70-71 OF	22	44	5	12	2	0	2	6	2	6	7	.273
Robles, Rafael 69-70, 72 SS	47	133	7	25	1	0	0	3	4	6	17	.188
Rodriguez, Aurelio 80 3B	89	175	7	35	7	2	2	13	1	6	26	.200
Rodriguez, Edwin 83, 85 2B	8	13	1	2	1	0	0	0	0	1	3	.154
Rodriguez, Rich 90-93 P	191	14	1	0	0	0	0	0	0	2	3	.000
Rodriguez, Roberto 70 P	10	3	0	0	0	0	0	0	0	0	0	.000
Roenicke, Ron 84 OF	12	20	4	6	1	0	1	2	0	2	5	.300
Romero, Mandy 97-98 C	27	57	8	10	0	0	2	4	1	3	21	.175
Romo, Vicente 73-74 P	103	22	2	2	0	0	0	1	0	1	3	.091
Rosenberg, Steve 91 P	10	1	0	0	0	0	0	0	0	0	1	.000
Roskos, John 00 OF	14	27	0	1	1	0	0	1	0	3	7	.037
Ross, Gary 69-74 P	229	50	1	6	0	0	0	3	0	1	18	.120
Royster, Jerry 85-86 IF	208	506	62	136	25	2	10	57	9	64	76	.269
Ruberto, Sonny 69 C	19	21	3	3	0	0	0	0	0	1	7	.143
Sager, A. J. 94 P	22	10	0	1	0	1	0	2	0	0	5	.100
Salazar, Luis 80-84, 87, 89 IF, OF, P	704	2237	232	598	73	24	40	226	113	93	69	.267
Sanders, Reggie 99 OF	133	478	92	136	24	7	26	72	36	65	108	.285
Sanders, Scott 93-96, 98 P	118	111	4	20	4	0	0	7	1	5	36	.180
Santiago, Benito 86-92 C	789	2872	312	758	124	15	85	375	62	139	516	.264
Santorini, Al 69-71 P	71	86	2	9	0	0	1	3	0	3	46	.105
Sawyer, Rick 76-77 P	69	44	4	8	0	0	0	4	0	7	10	.182
Scanlon, Pat 77 2B	47	79	9	15	3	0	1	11	0	12	20	.190
Schaeffer, Mark 72 P	41	3	0	0	0	0	0	0	0	0	1	.000
Schiraldi, Calvin 89-90 P	47	28	3	5	2	0	2	4	0	2	8	.179
Schulze, Don 89 P	7	4	1	0	0	0	0	0	0	0	3	.000
Scott, John 74-75 OF	39	24	9	1	0	0	0	0	3	4	2	.042
Scott, Tim 91-93, 97 P	109	4	0	0	0	0	0	0	0	0	4	.000
Seanez, Rudy 93, 01 P	29	0	0	0	0	0	0	0	0	0	0	.000
Selma, Dick 69 P	4	7	0	2	0	0	0	1	0	0	2	.286
Seminara, Frank 92-93 P	37	44	4	6	0	0	0	0	0	1	10	.136
Serrano, Wascar 01 P	20	9	0	1	0	0	0	0	0	0	4	.111
Sevirensen, Al 71-72 P	76	2	0	0	0	0	0	0	0	0	2	.000
Sharon, Dick 75 OF	91	160	14	31	7	0	4	20	0	26	35	.193
Sheets, Andy 98 IF	88	194	31	47	5	3	7	29	7	21	62	.242
Sheffield, Gary 92-93 3B	214	815	121	260	46	5	43	136	10	66	70	.319
Sherman, Darrell 93 OF	37	63	8	14	1	0	0	2	2	6	8	.222
Shipley, Craig 91-94, 96-97 IF	371	897	105	252	46	4	15	91	27	32	129	.281
Shirley, Bob 77-80 P	197	199	14	20	3	0	0	5	0	12	82	.101
Show, Eric 81-90 P	310	510	33	81	10	0	4	28	0	4	179	.159
Shumpert, Terry 97 IF	13	33	4	9	3	0	1	6	0	3	4	.273
Siebert, Paul 77 P	4	0	0	0	0	0	0	0	0	0	0	.000
Siebert, Sonny 75 P	7	8	1	3	1	0	0	1	0	2	2	.375
Sierra, Candy 88 P	15	3	0	0	0	0	0	0	0	0	3	.000
Simpson, Steve 72 P	9	0	0	0	0	0	0	0	0	0	0	.000
Sipin, John 69 2B	68	229	22	51	12	2	2	9	2	8	44	.223
Sisk, Tommie 69 P	63	25	2	3	1	0	0	0	0	3	12	.120
Slaught, Don 97 C	20	20	2	0	0	0	0	0	0	5	4	.000
Slocum, Ron 69-71 3B	80	113	15	17	3	2	2	16	0	8	32	.150
Slocumb, Heathcliff 00 P	22	1	0	0	0	0	0	0	0	0	1	.000
Smith, Ozzie 78-81 SS	583	2236	266	516	64	19	1	129	147	196	166	.231
Smith, Pete 97-98 P	39	44	3	6	1	1	0	4	0	3	22	.136
Snook, Frank 73 P	18	2	0	0	0	0	0	0	0	0	2	.000
Sosa, Elias 83 P	41	7	0	1	0	0	0	1	0	0	2	.143
Spencer, Stan 98-00 P	23	31	0	5	1	0	0	1	0	0	13	.161
Spiezio, Ed 69-72 3B	348	1008	92	248	39	2	32	125	12	84	162	.246
Spillner, Dan 74-78 P	193	130	8	10	1	0	0	1	0	18	73	.077
Sprague, Ed, Jr. 00 1B, 3B	73	157	19	41	12	0	10	27	0	13	40	.261
Stablein, George 80 P	4	3	0	0	0	0	0	0	0	0	2	.000
Stahl, Larry 69-72 OF	368	833	73	189	30	9	18	69	10	76	171	.227
Stanley, Fred 72 2B	39	85	15	17	2	0	0	2	1	12	19	.200
Steels, James 87 OF	62	68	9	13	1	1	0	6	3	11	14	.191
Stephenson, Phil 89-92 1B	177	277	35	57	11	2	6	29	2	45	59	.206
Steverson, Todd 96 OF	1	1	0	0	0	0	0	0	0	0	1	.000

Player, Years, Position	G	AB	R	H	2B	3B	HR	RBI	SB	BB	SO	AVE
Stillwell, Kurt 92-93 2B	171	500	44	112	19	3	3	35	8	27	80	.224
Stimac, Craig 80-81 C	20	59	5	12	2	0	0	7	0	1	9	.203
Stoddard, Bob 86 P	18	1	0	0	0	0	0	0	0	0	0	.000
Stoddard, Tim 85-86 P	74	9	1	1	0	0	1	1	0	0	2	.111
Strom, Brent 75-77 P	64	96	7	8	1	1	0	1	0	7	25	.083
Summers, Champ 84 1B	49	54	5	10	3	0	1	12	0	4	15	.185
Sutherland, Gary 77 2B	80	103	5	25	3	0	1	11	0	7	15	.243
Sweeney, Mark 97-98 OF	193	295	28	78	12	3	4	34	3	37	55	.264
Sweet, Rick 78 C	88	226	15	50	8	0	1	11	1	27	22	.221
Swisher, Steve 81-82 C	42	86	4	14	1	0	2	3	0	7	35	.163
Tabaka, Jeff 94-95 P	44	1	1	1	1	0	0	0	0	1	0	1.000
Tatum, Jim 96 C	5	3	0	0	0	0	0	0	0	0	1	.000
Taylor, Kerry 93-94 P	37	14	0	0	0	0	0	0	0	0	9	.000
Taylor, Ron 72 P	4	0	0	0	0	0	0	0	0	0	0	.000
Tellman, Tom 79-80 P	7	8	0	1	0	0	0	1	0	0	5	.125
Templeton, Garry 82-91 SS	1286	4512	430	1135	195	36	43	427	101	272	684	.252
Tenace, Gene 77-80 C	573	1617	233	384	69	13	68	239	17	423	386	.237
Terrell, Walt 89 P	19	40	2	4	2	0	0	2	0	3	22	.100
Teufel, Tim 91-93 2B	294	753	88	175	37	2	24	98	12	107	153	.232
Tewksbury, Bob 96 P	36	65	1	2	1	0	0	2	0	3	27	.031
Thomas, Derrel 72-74, 78 IF, OF	512	1779	173	420	56	14	11	125	42	161	220	.236
Thompson, Jason 76 1B	13	49	4	11	4	0	2	6	0	1	14	.224
Thon, Dickie 88 SS	95	258	36	68	12	2	1	18	19	33	49	.264
Thurmond, Mark 83-86 P	107	153	4	22	3	0	0	12	0	6	29	.144
Tingley, Ron 82 C	8	20	0	2	0	0	0	0	0	0	7	.100
Tolan, Bobby 74-75, 79 OF	264	884	105	228	35	6	13	85	18	48	88	.258
Toliver, Fred 89 P	9	0	0	0	0	0	0	0	0	0	0	.000
Tollberg, Brian 00- P	38	72	5	11	0	0	0	2	0	2	28	.153
Tomlin, Dave 74-77 P	239	24	5	3	0	0	0	0	0	4	5	.125
Torres, Hector 75-76 SS, 3B	186	567	39	133	18	0	9	41	4	38	63	.235
Trammell, Bubba 01- OF	142	490	66	128	20	3	25	92	2	49	70	.261
Troedsen, Rich 73-74 P	65	41	1	7	0	0	0	1	0	1	19	.171
Turner, Jerry 74-81, 83 OF	638	1521	199	394	70	9	37	209	44	138	206	.259
Urrea, John 81 P	38	4	0	1	0	0	0	0	0	0	1	.250
Valdez, Rafael 90 P	3	1	0	0	0	0	0	0	0	0	0	.000
Valentine, Bobby 75-77 OF	66	131	10	32	7	0	2	15	1	17	12	.244
Valenzuela, Fernando 95-97 P	79	112	7	20	3	0	2	11	0	0	24	.179
Vander Wal, John 98-99 OF	152	271	29	73	21	0	6	41	2	43	64	.269
Vatcher, Jim 91-92 OF	30	36	4	8	1	0	0	4	1	7	12	.222
Vaughn, Greg 96-98 OF	321	1075	192	263	41	5	78	198	22	159	262	.245
Velandia, Jorge 97 SS	14	29	0	3	2	0	0	0	0	1	7	.103
Velasquez, Guillermo 92-93 1B	94	166	8	37	2	0	4	25	0	14	42	.223
Veras, Dario 96-97 P	46	0	0	0	0	0	0	0	0	0	0	.000
Veras, Quilvio 97-99 2B	415	1531	248	414	72	5	15	131	87	221	250	.270
Villone, Ron 95-96 P	40	1	0	0	0	0	0	0	0	0	0	.000
Vitiello, Joe 00 1B	39	52	7	13	3	0	2	8	0	10	9	.250
Vosberg, Ed 86, 99 P	20	2	0	0	0	0	0	0	0	0	1	.000
Walker, Kevin 00- P	86	4	0	1	1	0	0	0	0	0	1	.000
Walker, Pete 96 P	1	0	0	0	0	0	0	0	0	0	0	.000
Wall, Donne 1998-00 P	145	9	0	2	0	0	0	0	0	0	5	.222
Walter, Gene 85-86 P	72	11	0	2	1	0	0	0	0	2	4	.182
Walters, Dan 92-93 C	84	273	20	64	14	1	5	32	1	17	41	.234
Ward, Kevin 91-92 OF	125	254	25	55	12	2	5	20	3	23	65	.217
Wasinger, Mark 86 3B	3	8	0	0	0	0	0	1	0	0	2	.000
Webster, Ramon 70-71 1B	105	124	12	31	3	0	2	11	1	13	13	.250
Wehrmeister, Dave 76-78 P	41	18	2	2	1	0	0	0	0	0	7	.111
Welsh, Chris 81-83 P	57	87	8	17	4	0	0	12	0	5	29	.195
Whisenant, Matt 99-00 P	43	0	0	0	0	0	0	0	0	0	0	.000
Whitehurst, Wally 93-94 P	34	43	1	4	0	0	0	0	0	3	19	.093
Whiteside, Matt 99-00 P	38	0	0	0	0	0	0	0	0	0	0	.000
Whitson, Ed 83-84, 86-91 P	236	417	18	56	9	0	1	20	0	13	112	.134
Wiggins, Alan 81-85 OF, 2B	399	1404	236	365	43	12	4	71	171	156	123	.260
Wiley, Mark 78 P	4	2	0	0	0	0	0	0	0	0	1	.000
Wilhelm, Jim 78-79 OF	49	122	10	32	6	3	0	12	2	2	14	.262
Wilkins, Rick 01 C	12	22	3	4	1	0	1	8	0	2	8	.182
Williams, Bernie 74 OF	14	15	1	2	0	0	0	0	0	0	6	.133
Williams, Brian 95 P	44	14	1	1	1	0	0	0	0	0	4	.071
Williams, Eddie 90, 94-95, 98 3B, 1B	177	536	73	151	25	2	26	96	0	45	85	.282
Williams, George 00 C	11	16	2	3	0	0	1	2	0	0	4	.188
Williams, Jim 69-70 OF	24	39	8	11	1	0	0	2	1	4	14	.282
Williams, Woody 99-01 P	83	187	21	37	11	0	1	19	0	8	64	.198
Willis, Ron 70 P	42	5	0	0	0	0	0	0	0	0	2	.000
Wilson, Earl 70 P	15	17	2	1	0	0	1	2	0	2	12	.059
Winfield, Dave 73-80 OF	1117	3997	599	1134	179	39	154	626	133	463	585	.284
Wise, Rick 80-82 P	47	83	2	9	3	0	0	5	0	3	32	.108
Witasick, Jay 00-01 P	42	27	0	3	0	0	0	3	0	1	11	.111
Witt, Kevin 01 1B	14	27	5	5	0	0	2	5	0	2	7	.185
Wojna, Ed 85-87 P	27	31	1	4	0	0	0	0	0	0	20	.129

Player, Years, Position	G	AB	R	H	2B	3B	HR	RBI	SB	BB	SO	AVE
Worrell, Tim 93-97 P	143	69	6	8	1	0	0	4	0	4	34	.116
Wynne, Marvell 86-89 OF	468	1103	107	285	41	9	26	138	29	84	185	.258

ALL-TIME PADRE PITCHING STATISTICS

Player	W	L	Pct	ERA	G	GS	CG	SH	SV	IP	H	R	ER	BB	SO
Acosta	3	9	.250	3.87	54	8	3	1	0	135	148	67	58	37	69
Almanzar	4	5	.444	5.46	90	0	0	0	0	107	121	67	65	40	86
Andersen	4	5	.444	2.74	72	0	0	0	15	82	55	27	25	21	75
Arlin	32	62	.340	4.19	130	113	31	11	1	745	733	397	347	351	443
Armstrong	0	2	.000	5.88	21	0	0	0	0	26.1	30	19	17	24	23
Ashby	70	62	.530	3.60	185	185	18	6	0	1210	1185	553	484	324	827
Baldschun	8	2	.800	5.60	73	0	0	0	1	90.1	104	60	56	33	79
Batchelor	3	1	.750	5.97	23	0	0	0	0	28.2	40	23	19	14	18
Benes	69	75	.479	3.57	187	186	15	8	0	1235	1128	539	490	402	1036
Bergman	8	12	.400	5.17	85	23	0	0	0	212.1	245	135	122	71	159
Bernal	1	1	.500	5.32	15	0	0	0	0	20.1	23	13	12	9	6
Berumen	2	3	.400	5.66	40	0	0	0	0	47.2	40	31	30	38	46
Blair, D	0	1	.000	6.43	5	1	0	0	0	14	18	10	10	3	11
Blair, W	9	11	.450	4.46	100	12	0	0	1	202	192	112	100	74	150
Bochtler	9	14	.391	3.78	151	0	0	0	6	171.1	134	78	72	108	159
Boehringer	11	10	.524	3.62	152	15	0	0	0	186.1	190	91	75	90	140
Bones	4	6	.400	4.83	11	11	0	0	0	54	57	33	29	18	31
Booker	5	7	.417	3.80	153	4	0	0	1	253.1	260	129	107	116	115
Boone	2	0	1.000	3.40	47	0	0	0	3	79.1	84	33	20	21	51
Brocail	4	13	.235	4.86	39	27	0	0	0	159.1	181	98	86	52	96
Brown	18	7	.720	2.38	36	35	7	3	0	257	225	77	68	49	257
Bruske	4	1	.800	3.63	28	0	0	0	0	44.2	37	22	18	25	32
Burrows	0	2	.000	10.45	13	0	0	0	0	10.1	12	13	12	8	8
Caldwell	13	25	.342	3.81	103	33	7	3	12	319.1	333	169	135	105	193
Campbell	1	1	.500	12.96	3	2	0	0	0	8.1	13	12	12	5	10
Carlyle	1	3	.250	7.08	11	7	0	0	0	40.2	42	35	32	20	31
Chiffer	5	5	.500	4.02	81	1	0	0	5	130	132	67	58	60	83
Clement	25	29	.463	4.82	69	67	0	0	0	399.1	399	245	214	218	318
Clements	7	2	.777	3.60	71	1	0	0	0	90	97	43	36	43	43
Comstock	2	1	.667	4.87	48	0	0	0	1	71	66	36	35	34	68
Coombs	11	20	.355	3.99	54	34	5	1	0	246	266	135	109	101	142
Corkins	19	28	.396	4.39	157	44	5	1	9	459.1	458	257	224	248	335
Costello	1	0	1.000	3.09	27	0	0	0	0	35.0	37	15	12	17	24
Couchee	0	1	.000	5.14	8	0	0	0	0	14	12	8	8	6	5
Cunnane	9	5	.643	5.33	108	11	0	0	0	163.2	187	111	97	83	136
Curtis	20	20	.500	3.99	84	53	7	1	0	370	375	187	164	143	156
D'Acquisto	16	21	.432	4.18	152	26	1	1	13	337.2	316	177	157	225	190
Davey	4	5	.444	3.60	50	0	0	0	0	50.2	53	23	20	19	43
Davis, J	0	1	.000	5.79	6	0	0	0	0	9.1	9	7	6	4	5
Davis, M	14	20	.412	2.75	23	0	0	0	78	308	251	104	94	137	298
Davis, S	2	7	.222	6.18	21	10	0	0	0	62.2	70	48	43	36	37
Decker	0	0	.000	2.08	4	0	0	0	0	8.2	5	2	2	3	9
DeLeon	17	16	.515	3.06	185	0	0	0	31	294.1	249	111	100	65	225
Deshaies	4	7	.364	3.28	15	15	0	0	0	96	92	40	35	33	46
Dishman	4	8	.333	5.08	22	16	0	0	0	99.1	107	62	56	35	44
Dobson	14	15	.483	3.76	40	34	8	1	1	251	257	126	105	78	185
Doyle	0	2	.000	6.43	9	0	0	0	2	7	9	5	5	6	2
Dravecky	53	50	.515	3.12	199	119	23	6	10	900.1	812	354	312	270	456
Dukes	2	6	.250	4.88	66	0	0	0	11	90.1	88	57	49	35	71
Dunne	0	3	.000	5.65	10	6	0	0	0	28.2	28	21	18	17	15
Dupree	0	0	.000	9.19	11	0	0	0	0	15.2	18	17	16	7	5
Eaton	15	9	.625	4.22	39	39	2	0	0	251.2	242	124	118	101	199
Eichelberger	20	25	.444	3.87	77	64	12	1	0	432	399	213	186	214	209
Eiland	0	5	.000	5.38	17	16	0	0	0	75.1	91	54	45	22	24
Elliott	0	1	.000	3.09	31	1	0	0	0	35	33	12	12	22	27
Erdos	2	0	1.000	6.23	33	0	0	0	1	43.1	49	33	30	21	29
Ettles	1	0	1.000	6.50	14	0	0	0	0	18	23	16	13	4	9
Everitt	0	1	.000	7.88	5	0	0	0	0	15.2	18	14	14	12	11
Fikac	2	0	1.000	1.37	23	0	0	0	0	26.1	15	6	4	5	19
Fingers	34	40	.459	3.13	265	0	0	0	108	426.1	399	162	148	134	319
Fireovid	0	1	.000	2.59	8	4	0	0	0	31.1	34	10	9	9	12
Florie	4	4	.500	3.25	95	0	0	0	1	127.1	102	55	46	68	127
Folkers	8	14	.364	4.50	78	18	4	0	0	201.2	222	109	101	64	113
Foster	6	7	.462	2.92	43	15	3	0	0	131.1	116	50	43	56	42
Franklin	0	1	.000	6.00	3	1	0	0	0	5.2	5	5	4	4	4
Freisleben	31	53	.369	3.80	148	109	17	6	1	730	744	383	308	346	376
Frisella	1	6	.143	3.12	65	0	0	0	9	97.2	86	36	34	51	67

Player	W	L	Pct	ERA	G	GS	CG	SH	SV	IP	H	R	ER	BB	SO
Garcia	0	0	.000	4.70	11	0	0	0	0	15.1	19	9	8	10	12
Gardner	0	1	.000	7.08	14	0	0	0	1	20.1	27	16	16	12	9
Gerhardt	2	1	.667	7.07	23	1	0	0	1	35.2	44	28	28	17	22
Giavanola	0	0	.000	0.00	1	0	0	0	0	1.1	1	0	0	2	0
Gomez	1	2	.333	5.12	27	1	0	0	0	31.2	35	19	18	19	26
Gorman	0	0	.000	4.09	6	0	0	0	0	11	11	5	5	8	5
Gossage	25	20	.555	2.99	197	0	0	0	83	298	255	109	99	92	243
Grant	17	18	.486	3.98	126	28	2	1	2	355.1	353	168	157	139	217
Greif	29	61	.322	4.42	177	94	18	5	13	645	669	364	317	253	396
Griffin, M	0	1	.000	3.48	7	0	0	0	0	10.1	9	4	4	3	4
Griffin, T	10	12	.455	3.98	49	31	2	0	0	221.1	200	115	98	130	115
Guzman	0	1	.000	19.50	8	0	0	0	0	6.0	14	13	13	4	4
Hamilton	55	44	.556	3.83	146	142	7	4	0	934.2	912	442	398	343	639
Hammaker	0	5	.000	4.87	10	2	0	0	0	24	24	18	13	9	17
Hardy	9	4	.692	4.89	79	1	0	0	2	104.1	137	64	57	46	60
Harris, Gen	7	7	.500	3.89	72	0	0	0	23	71.2	78	38	31	45	48
Harris, Gr A	2	1	.667	2.70	19	1	0	0	1	36.2	28	14	11	18	30
Harris, Gr W	41	39	.513	2.95	194	71	9	2	15	673.1	591	250	221	205	462
Hawkins	60	58	.508	3.84	199	172	19	7	0	1102.2	1089	531	471	412	489
Hayward	0	2	.000	11.81	7	3	0	0	0	16	28	23	21	7	8
Herbel	7	5	.583	4.95	64	1	0	0	9	111	114	69	61	39	53
Hermanson	4	1	.800	7.35	34	0	0	0	0	45.1	53	41	37	26	30
Hernandez	1	6	.143	3.69	56	0	0	0	3	85.1	88	36	35	23	60
Herndon	2	6	.250	6.33	12	9	0	0	0	42.2	55	34	30	25	14
Hitchcock	34	39	.466	4.40	118	102	4	1	1	627.2	634	331	307	208	534
Hoffman	41	37	.526	2.72	543	0	0	0	312	616	450	208	186	17	702
Hoyt	24	19	.558	4.19	66	56	9	3	0	369.1	380	185	172	88	168
Hurst	55	38	.591	3.27	131	131	29	10	0	911.2	835	361	331	242	616
Iorg	0	0	.000	12.00	2	0	0	0	0	3.0	5	4	4	1	2
Jackson, Darrin	0	0	.000	0.00	1	0	0	0	0	2.0	3	2	2	2	0
Jackson, Donny	1	7	.125	7.53	13	9	0	0	0	49	72	47	41	20	19
Jackson, R	2	3	.400	2.70	22	2	0	0	2	40	32	13	12	13	28
Jarvis	12	11	.522	4.79	32	32	1	1	0	193.1	190	107	103	49	133
Jodie	0	1	.000	4.63	7	2	0	0	0	23.1	19	12	12	12	13
Johnson, J	4	4	.500	5.23	45	5	0	0	0	93	99	64	54	57	45
Johnson, M	0	2	.000	4.64	18	0	0	0	0	21.1	29	13	11	15	15
Jones, B	8	19	.296	5.12	33	33	1	0	0	195.0	250	137	111	38	113
Jones, J	20	21	.488	4.07	62	54	6	2	0	340.2	356	189	154	101	148
Jones, R	92	105	.467	3.30	264	253	71	18	2	1766	1720	759	648	414	677
Kelley	6	11	.353	3.54	75	24	1	1	2	196	165	88	77	84	138
Kilkenny	0	0	.000	8.31	5	0	0	0	0	4.1	7	4	4	3	5
Kinney	4	7	.364	4.29	70	0	0	0	1	107.2	102	58	51	49	53
Kirby	52	81	.391	3.73	177	170	34	7	0	1128	1026	534	468	505	802
Kolb	0	1	.000	4.50	11	0	0	0	0	14	16	8	7	11	12
Kroon	0	2	.000	5.15	16	0	0	0	0	15.1	15	11	11	8	16
Krueger	3	2	.600	5.18	14	7	1	0	0	48.2	55	30	28	11	36
Kuhaulua	1	0	1.000	2.48	5	4	0	0	0	29.1	28	10	8	9	16
LaPoint	1	4	.200	4.26	24	4	0	0	0	61.1	67	37	29	24	41
Lawrence	5	5	.500	3.45	27	15	1	0	0	114.2	107	53	44	34	84
Laxton	0	3	.000	5.10	48	1	0	0	0	72.1	69	47	41	64	63
Lee, D	1	0	1.000	3.70	41	0	0	0	0	48.2	52	20	20	27	42
Lee, M.	7	5	.583	3.72	102	1	0	0	7	150	162	68	62	61	56
Lefferts	42	40	.512	3.24	375	27	0	0	64	659	639	270	237	184	404
Leiper	4	1	.800	3.38	69	0	0	0	1	98.2	101	46	37	30	50
Lewis	0	0	.000	4.15	12	0	0	0	0	13	14	7	6	11	10
Llilliquist	3	5	.375	5.18	22	9	1	1	0	74.2	86	43	43	27	36
Littlefield	2	3	.400	3.66	42	0	0	0	2	64	53	28	26	28	21
Loewer	0	2	.000	24.92	2	2	0	0	0	4.1	13	12	12	3	1
Lolich	2	3	.400	3.43	47	7	0	0	1	84	89	39	32	33	33
Lollar	36	42	.462	4.07	119	106	8	4	1	325	617	325	308	328	454
Long	0	0	.000	8.18	10	0	0	0	0	11	17	11	10	8	8
Lopez	0	3	.000	8.76	6	6	0	0	0	24.2	40	24	24	13	17
Lucas	18	33	.353	2.90	230	18	0	0	49	428.1	390	165	138	142	262
Lundquist	0	1	.000	5.95	17	0	0	0	0	19.2	20	13	13	7	19
Maddux, M	9	4	.692	2.42	114	2	0	0	10	178.1	149	55	48	51	117
Martinez, J	0	2	.000	6.75	4	1	0	0	0	12	18	9	9	5	7
Martinez, P	6	3	.667	2.73	80	1	0	0	3	105.1	75	42	32	62	84
Maurer	10	1	.000	5.49	17	0	0	0	0	19.2	23	14	12	9	17
Mauser	2	6	.250	3.90	68	0	0	0	2	92.1	90	46	40	45	73
McAndrew	1	4	.200	5.62	15	5	1	0	0	41.2	48	30	26	13	16
McBean	0	1	.000	5.14	1	1	0	0	0	7	10	4	4	2	1
McCool	3	5	.375	4.27	54	0	0	0	7	58.2	59	32	28	42	35
McCullers	21	28	.429	2.96	229	7	0	0	36	392	311	150	129	188	326
McElroy	1	1	.500	5.16	31	0	0	0	0	29.2	38	24	17	18	25
McIntosh	8	19	.296	3.68	47	33	4	1	0	220.1	231	107	90	77	93
Meadows	7	8	.467	5.34	22	22	0	0	0	124.2	150	80	74	50	53

Player	W	L	Pct	ERA	G	GS	CG	SH	SV	IP	H	R	ER	BB	SO
Melendez	14	12	.538	3.10	87	12	0	0	3	183	159	67	63	44	142
Menhart	2	3	.400	4.70	9	8	0	0	0	44	42	23	23	13	22
Metzger	12	4	.750	3.47	98	1	0	0	16	150.2	152	64	58	68	101
Miceli	14	10	.583	3.82	133	0	0	0	4	141.1	131	67	60	63	129
Middlebrook	2	1	.667	5.12	4	3	0	0	0	19.1	18	11	11	10	10
Miller	7	3	.700	2.29	56	0	0	0	7	94.1	82	30	24	38	51
Monge	9	4	.692	3.44	60	0	0	0	7	83.2	82	34	32	48	39
Montefusco	19	15	.559	3.77	63	42	2	0	4	279.2	271	131	117	73	135
Montgomery	0	2	.000	7.94	7	0	0	0	0	5.2	6	6	5	4	3
Mura	17	26	.395	3.94	103	52	5	1	4	388	377	186	170	178	203
Murphy	0	0	.000	5.68	7	0	0	0	0	6.1	6	6	4	4	1
Murray	1	6	.143	6.16	39	11	0	0	0	83.1	110	58	57	47	41
Myers, Randy	4	9	.308	4.60	87	0	0	0	38	94	99	48	48	41	75
Myers, Rodney	1	2	.333	5.29	40	0	0	0	1	49.1	55	32	29	20	32
Niekro	8	17	.320	3.70	37	31	8	3	0	202	213	91	83	45	55
Nolte	5	8	.385	5.68	23	19	1	0	0	101.1	112	69	64	55	68
Norman	13	30	.302	3.55	74	57	16	6	2	414.1	381	171	163	173	293
Nunez	4	1	.800	3.31	56	0	0	0	0	51.2	48	20	19	20	49
Nyman	0	2	.000	16.20	2	2	0	0	0	5.1	8	9	9	2	2
Oquist	0	0	.000	2.35	8	0	0	0	0	7.2	6	2	2	4	4
Osting	0	0	.000	.000	3	0	0	0	0	2	1	0	0	2	3
Osuna	0	0	.000	2.25	10	0	0	0	0	4	5	1	1	2	4
Owchinko	25	39	.391	4.00	110	83	9	3	0	526	544	261	234	203	265
Palacios	0	1	.000	6.75	7	0	0	0	0	10.2	12	10	8	5	8
Palmer	2	5	.286	5.67	22	8	1	0	0	73	68	48	46	59	52
Patterson	0	0	.000	24.75	3	0	0	0	0	4	13	11	11	3	1
Perry	33	17	.660	2.88	69	69	15	2	0	493.1	466	186	158	133	294
Peterson	3	4	.429	4.45	13	11	0	0	0	54.2	50	33	27	28	37
Phoebus	3	12	.200	4.55	30	22	2	0	0	140.1	147	72	71	70	88
Podres	5	6	.455	4.29	17	9	1	0	0	64.2	66	34	31	28	17
Ramirez	1	0	1.000	6.14	21	0	0	0	0	14.2	12	13	10	12	17
Rasmussen, D	41	42	.494	3.80	113	110	11	2	0	680	703	338	287	227	346
Rasmussen, E	22	30	.423	3.85	112	58	8	5	4	414.1	426	191	177	118	163
Reberger	1	2	.333	3.58	67	0	0	0	6	87.2	83	38	35	41	65
Reyes	5	7	.417	4.02	99	0	0	0	3	123	114	61	55	38	94
Reynolds	0	3	.000	6.40	19	2	0	0	1	32.1	38	27	23	29	18
Rivera	1	2	.333	3.86	12	0	0	0	0	7	6	4	3	3	3
Roberts	22	34	.393	2.99	102	60	17	4	2	500	485	189	166	123	256
Rodriguez, Rich	12	8	.600	2.86	191	2	0	0	3	248.2	229	91	79	98	148
Rodriguez, Roberto	0	0	.000	6.75	10	0	0	0	3	16.1	26	16	12	5	8
Romo	7	8	.467	4.08	103	2	0	0	16	158.2	163	90	72	83	77
Rosenberg	1	1	.500	6.94	10	0	0	0	0	11.2	11	9	9	5	6
Ross	14	25	.359	4.12	219	9	0	0	7	382.1	406	201	175	191	210
Sager	1	4	.200	5.98	22	3	0	0	0	46.2	62	34	31	16	26
Sanders	24	22	.522	4.08	118	60	1	0	1	428	386	219	194	155	417
Santorini	9	24	.273	4.45	71	45	2	1	1	298.2	328	170	148	127	173
Sawyer	12	9	.571	4.44	69	20	4	2	0	192.2	220	101	95	93	78
Schaeffer	2	0	1.000	4.61	41	0	0	0	1	41	52	21	21	28	25
Schiraldi	6	9	.400	4.09	47	12	0	0	1	125.1	117	65	57	73	91
Schulze	2	1	.667	5.55	7	4	0	0	0	24.1	38	20	15	6	15
Scott	7	2	.777	4.66	64	0	0	0	0	94.2	104	56	49	41	75
Seanez	0	2	.000	3.95	29	0	0	0	1	27.1	23	14	12	17	25
Selma	2	2	.500	4.09	4	3	1	0	0	22	19	10	10	9	20
Seminara	12	7	.632	3.93	37	25	0	0	0	146.2	151	76	64	67	83
Serafini	0	0	.000	18.00	3	0	0	0	0	3	9	6	6	2	3
Serrano	3	3	.500	6.56	20	5	0	0	0	46.2	60	37	34	21	39
Sevirensen	2	6	.250	3.25	76	0	0	0	9	91.1	90	38	33	37	40
Shirley	39	57	.406	3.58	197	92	10	1	2	722	718	329	287	274	432
Show	100	87	.535	3.59	309	230	35	1	17	1603.1	1464	703	639	593	951
Siebert P	0	0	.000	2.50	4	0	0	0	0	3.2	3	4	1	4	1
Siebert S	3	2	.600	4.33	6	6	0	0	0	26.2	37	15	13	10	10
Sierra	0	1	.000	5.70	15	0	0	0	0	23.2	36	15	15	11	20
Simpson	0	2	.000	4.76	9	0	0	0	2	11.1	10	6	6	8	9
Sisk	2	13	.133	4.78	53	13	1	0	6	143	160	81	76	48	59
Slocumb	0	1	.000	3.79	22	0	0	0	0	19	19	11	8	13	12
Smith	10	8	.555	4.80	48	23	0	0	1	161.1	165	89	86	70	104
Snook	0	2	.000	3.62	18	0	0	0	1	27.1	19	15	11	18	13
Sosa	1	4	.200	4.35	41	1	0	0	1	72.1	72	41	35	30	45
Spencer	3	9	.250	5.54	23	21	0	0	0	118.2	129	82	73	34	107
Spillner	24	41	.369	4.25	192	64	8	2	7	570	629	317	269	255	346
Stablein	0	1	.000	3.00	4	2	0	0	0	11.2	16	4	4	3	4
Stoddard, Bob	1	0	1.000	2.31	18	0	0	0	1	23.1	20	7	6	11	17
Stoddard, T	2	9	.182	4.27	74	0	0	0	1	105.1	96	55	50	71	89
Strom	20	26	.435	3.47	62	52	14	3	0	347.2	314	167	134	118	167
Tabaka	3	1	.750	4.36	44	0	0	0	1	43.1	38	26	21	24	36

Player	W	L	Pct	ERA	G	GS	CG	SH	SV	IP	H	R	ER	BB	SO
Taylor, Kerry	0	5	.000	6.56	37	8	0	0	0	72.2	81	57	53	50	48
Taylor, Ron	0	0	.000	12.80	4	0	0	0	0	5	9	7	7	0	0
Tellman	3	0	1.000	2.88	7	3	2	0	1	25	30	10	9	8	10
Terrell	5	13	.278	4.01	19	13	1	1	0	123.1	134	65	55	26	63
Tewksbury	10	10	.500	4.31	36	33	1	0	0	206.2	224	116	99	44	126
Thurmond	31	29	.517	3.67	106	85	6	3	2	503	528	238	205	159	195
Toliver	0	0	.000	7.07	9	0	0	0	0	14	17	14	11	9	14
Tollberg	14	9	.609	3.94	38	38	1	0	0	235.1	259	116	103	60	147
Tomlin	10	7	.588	3.28	239	1	0	0	5	315.2	306	129	115	113	175
Troedsen	8	10	.444	4.74	65	19	2	0	3	171	191	95	90	67	92
Urrea	2	2	.500	2.39	38	0	0	0	2	49	43	14	13	28	9
Valdez	0	1	.000	11.12	3	0	0	0	0	5.2	11	7	7	2	3
Valenzuela	23	19	.548	4.22	75	59	1	0	0	328.1	362	173	154	133	203
Veras	5	2	.714	3.86	46	0	0	0	0	53.2	52	28	23	22	44
Villone	3	2	.600	3.68	40	0	0	0	1	44	41	18	18	18	56
Vosberg	0	1	.000	7.77	20	3	0	0	0	22	33	22	19	12	14
Walker, K	7	1	.875	4.00	86	0	0	0	0	78.2	54	39	35	46	73
Walker, P	0	0	.000	0.00	1	0	0	0	0	.2	0	0	0	3	1
Wall	17	10	.630	2.92	145	1	0	0	2	194.1	144	71	63	76	138
Walter	2	4	.333	3.53	72	0	0	0	4	120	101	53	47	57	102
Wehrmeister	2	7	.222	6.35	41	10	0	0	0	96.1	116	75	68	60	44
Welsh	14	16	.467	4.28	57	40	7	3	0	277.1	281	148	132	106	104
Whisenant	2	3	.400	3.75	43	0	0	0	0	36	26	18	15	27	22
Whitehurst	8	14	.364	4.24	34	32	0	0	0	169.2	193	84	80	56	100
Whiteside	3	3	.500	6.37	38	0	0	0	0	48	51	38	34	22	36
Whitson	77	72	.517	3.69	227	208	22	6	1	1354.1	1314	596	555	350	767
Wiley	1	0	1.000	5.63	4	1	0	0	0	8	11	6	5	1	1
Williams, B	3	10	.231	6.00	44	6	0	0	0	72	79	54	48	38	75
Williams, W	30	28	.517	4.35	79	78	4	0	0	521.1	535	268	252	164	350
Willis	2	2	.500	4.02	42	0	0	0	4	56	53	33	25	28	20
Wilson	1	6	.143	4.85	15	9	0	0	0	65	82	36	35	19	29
Wise	10	16	.385	3.75	46	45	1	0	0	254.1	291	115	106	56	86
Witasick	8	4	.667	4.17	42	11	0	0	0	99.1	100	56	46	50	107
Wojna	4	9	.308	4.80	27	17	1	0	0	99.1	120	66	53	50	41
Worrell	16	23	.410	4.30	143	40	0	0	4	356	354	189	170	143	259

ALL-TIME PADRE MANAGERIAL STATISTICS

Manager	Years	W	L	Pct.
Preston Gomez	1969-72	180	316	.363
Don Zimmer	1972-73	114	190	.375
John McNamara	1974-1977	224	310	.419
Bob Skinner	1977	1	0	1.000
Alvin Dark	1977	48	65	.425
Roger Craig	1978-79	152	171	.471
Jerry Coleman	1980	73	89	.451
Frank Howard	1981	41	69	.373
Dick Williams	1982-85	337	311	.520
Steve Boros	1986	74	88	.457
Larry Bowa	1987-88	81	127	.389
Jack McKeon	1988-90	193	164	.541
Greg Riddoch	1990-92	200	194	.508
Jim Riggleman	1992-94	112	179	.385
Bruce Bochy	1995-	564	552	.505

LOW-HIT GAMES

Padre No-Hitters (None)

The San Diego Padres have never thrown a no-hitter.

Opponents No-Hitters (6)

Pitcher	Date	Opponent	Score
Dock Ellis	June 12, 1970	Pittsburgh Pirates	0-2
Milt Pappas	Sept. 2, 1972	at Chicago Cubs	0-8
Phil Niekro	August 5, 1973	at Atlanta Braves	0-9
Kent Mercker Mark Wohlers Alejandro Pena	Sept. 11, 1991	at Atlanta Braves	0-1
A. J. Burnett	May 12, 2001	Florida Marlins	0-3
Bud Smith	Sept. 3, 2001	St. Louis Cardinals	0-4

Close Calls

Nine Padres pitchers have carried no-hitters into the eighth inning:

Pitcher	Date	Result
Clay Kirby	July 21, 1970	Manager Preston Gomez lifted Kirby after eight no-hit innings against the New York Mets. Jack Baldschun allowed a Bud Harrelson single to open the ninth inning.
Clay Kirby	Sept. 13, 1971	John Edwards of the Houston Astros doubled with one out in the eighth inning.
Clay Kirby	Sept. 18, 1971	Willie McCovey of the San Francisco Giants homered with no outs in the eighth inning.
Steve Arlin	July 18, 1972	Denny Doyle of the Philadelphia Phillies singled with two outs in the ninth inning.
Randy Jones	July 3, 1975	Bill Plummer of the Cincinnati Reds doubled in the eighth inning, the lone hit off Jones.
Greg Harris	July 14, 1991	Mackey Sasser of the New York Mets led off the eighth inning with a ground-rule double.
Andy Benes	July 3, 1994	Rico Brogna of the New York Mets hit a leadoff double in the eighth inning for the lone hit.
Andy Ashby	Sept. 5, 1997	Kenny Lofton of the Atlanta Braves hit a leadoff single in the ninth inning.
Sterling Hitchcock	June 27, 1998	Phil Nevin of the Anaheim Angels homered on the first pitch in the eighth inning.

One-Hitters by San Diego Padres (19)

Pitcher	Date	Opponent	Score	Hit/Inning
D. Kelley	7/6/69	Houston	1-0	D. Menke, single, 2nd
C. Kirby	9/18/71	San Francisco	2-1	W. McCovey, homer, 8th
S. Arlin	6/23/72	San Francisco	4-1	G. Maddox, triple, 2nd
D. Spillner	6/19/74	Chicago	1-0	R. Monday, single, 3rd
R. Jones	5/19/75	St. Louis	1-0 (10)	L. Melendez, single, 7th
R. Jones	7/3/75	Cincinnati	2-1	B. Plummer, double, 8th
E. Rasmussen	9/28/79	San Francisco	2-0	D. Evans, single, 2nd
J. Eichelberger	6/2/82	Chicago	3-1	S. Thompson, infield single, 2nd
D. Dravecky	7/30/84	Los Angeles	12-0	B. Russell, double, 7th

Pitcher	Date	Opponent	Score	Hit/Inning
M. Thurmond	4/30/86	St. Louis	5-0	W. McGee, single, 7th
J. Jones	9/21/86	Houston	5-0	B. Knepper, triple, 3rd
A. Hawkins	4/24/88	Houston	3-0	B. Doran, single, 7th
B. Hurst	4/10/89	Atlanta	5-2	L. Smith, homer, 3rd
Gr. Harris	7/14/91	New York	2-1	M. Sasser, double, 8th
C. Lefferts				
B. Hurst	5/18/92	New York	3-0	C. Walker, infield single, 6th
A. Benes	7/7/93	New York	2-0	J. Kent, infield single, 2nd
Ge. Harris				
A. Benes	7/3/94	New York	7-0	R. Brogna, double, 8th
S. Hitchcock	5/5/97	Philadelphia	4-1	R. Brogna, double, 5th
T. Hoffman				
K. Brown	8/16/98	Milwaukee	4-0 (G1)	J. Burnitz, single, 7th

One-Hitters by Opponents (26)

Pitcher	Date	Opponent	Score	Hit/Inning
T. Griffin	4/19/70	Houston	1-5	C. Gaston, double, 7th
B. Gibson	6/17/70	St. Louis	0-8	I. Murrell, single, 7th
L. Dierker	5/6/71	Houston	0-8	O. Brown, single, 7th
B. Stoneman	6/16/71	Montreal	0-2	C. Gaston, single, 7th
J. Pizarro	8/5/71	Chicago	0-3	O. Brown, single, 5th
T. Seaver	7/4/72	New York	0-2	L. Lee, single, 9th
D. Sutton	5/9/74	Los Angeles	0-6	J. Grubb, single, 2nd
J. Curtis	8/29/74	St. Louis	1-3	F. Kendall, single, 8th
S. Stone	7/19/75	Chicago	2-1	J. Grubb, single, 7th
T. Dettore				
D. Ruthven	7/9/79	Philadelphia	0-2	D. Briggs, double, 7th
B. Kison	6/3/79	Pittsburgh	0-7	B. Evans, double, 8th
N. Ryan	8/11/82	Houston	0-3	T. Kennedy, single, 5th
N. Ryan	8/3/83	Houston	0-1	T. Flannery, single, 3rd
R. Honeycutt	4/27/84	Los Angeles	0-1 (6.2)	L. Salazar, infield single, 4th
O. Hershiser	4/26/85	Los Angeles	0-2	T. Gwynn, single, 4th
T. Browning	6/6/88	Cincinnati	0-12	T. Gwynn, single, 9th
D. Cone	8/29/88	New York	0-6	T. Gwynn, double, 4th
T. Wilson	6/13/90	San Francisco	0-6	M. Pagliarulo, single, 9th
K. Mercker	9/9/93	Atlanta	0-1 (l0)	L. Lopez, single, 8th
M. Wohlers				
G. McMichael				
P. Harnisch	9/17/93	Houston	0-3	J. Brown, bunt single, 6th
P. Martinez	6/3/95	Montreal	0-1 (10)	B. Roberts, double, 10th
M. Rojas				
S. Cooke	4/8/97	Pittsburgh	0-2	S. Finley, single, 1st
R. Loiselle				
J. Ericks				
G. Maddux	4/27/97	Atlanta	0-2 (5)	K. Caminiti, single, 2nd
M. Morgan	8/13/97	Cincinnati	0-2	M. Sweeney, single, 7th
S. Belinda				
J. Shaw				
C. Schilling	7/18-19/01	Arizona	0-3	W. Gonzalez, single, 8th
R. Johnson				
R. Johnson	7/24/01	Arizona	0-11	B. Trammell, single, 1st
T. Brohawn				
E. Sabel				

HOME RUN HISTORY

Padre Pitchers with Home Runs (48)

Pitcher	Date	Opponent
Al Santorini	August 19, 1969	at Montreal Expos
Dave Roberts	May 8, 1970 (Game 2)	at Montreal Expos
Dave Roberts (2)	July 9, 1970	at Cincinnati Reds
Mike Corkins	Sept. 4, 1970	at Cincinnati Reds
Earl Wilson	Sept. 9, 1970 (Game 2)	Atlanta Braves
Mike Corkins	June 28, 1972 (Game 1)	Atlanta Braves
Mike Corkins	May 23, 1973	at Los Angeles Dodgers
Mike Corkins	May 28, 1973	Montreal Expos
Mike Corkins (5)	August 4, 1973 (Game 2)	at Atlanta Braves
Tom Griffin	May 12, 1977	at New York Mets
Tom Griffin (2)	June 27, 1977	at Houston Astros
Gaylord Perry	May 10, 1979	Philadelphia Phillies
Tim Lollar	April 28, 1981	at Cincinnati Reds
Tim Lollar	April 18, 1982	at Atlanta Braves
Tim Lollar	April 29, 1982	New York Mets
Tim Lollar	July 11, 1982	at New York Mets
Tim Lollar	August 14, 1983	at Cincinnati Reds
Tim Lollar	April 11, 1984	St. Louis Cardinals
Tim Lollar	May 14, 1984	Montreal Expos
Eric Show	June 24, 1984	at Cincinnati Reds
Eric Show	July 22, 1984 (Game 2)	at Pittsburgh Pirates
Eric Show	Sept. 6, 1984	Cincinnati Reds
Tim Lollar (8)	Sept. 20, 1984	San Francisco Giants
Eric Show (4)	Sept. 27, 1985	at Atlanta Braves
Dave Dravecky	April 16, 1986	Los Angeles Dodgers
Craig Lefferts	April 24, 1986	San Francisco Giants
Tim Stoddard	June 18, 1986	San Francisco Giants
Jimmy Jones	July 30, 1987	at Cincinnati Reds
Mark Davis	June 13, 1988	San Francisco Giants
Jimmy Jones (2)	August 22, 1988	Philadelphia Phillies
Andy Benes	Sept. 3, 1989	Philadelphia Phillies
Calvin Schiraldi	Sept. 23, 1989	Philadelphia Phillies
Ed Whitson	April 25, 1990	Chicago Cubs
Calvin Schiraldi (2)	July 25, 1990 (Game 2)	Cincinnati Reds
Andy Benes	April 27, 1991	at Philadelphia Phillies
Dave Eiland	April 10, 1992	Los Angeles Dodgers
Andy Benes	August 13, 1992	at Atlanta Braves
Andy Benes (4)	May 12, 1993	at Cincinnati Reds
Fernando Valenzuela	June 17, 1995	at Pittsburgh Pirates
Fernando Valenzuela (2)	Sept. 17, 1995	Chicago Cubs
Sean Bergman	June 12, 1996	Cincinnati Reds
Joey Hamilton	August 18, 1996	New York Mets*
Joey Hamilton	May 22, 1997	Los Angeles Dodgers
Joey Hamilton	June 27, 1997	at Los Angeles Dodgers
Joey Hamilton (4)	July 12, 1998	at Los Angeles Dodgers
Woody Williams	July 20, 2000	at San Francisco Giants
Kevin Jarvis	May 23, 2001	at Houston Astros

*in Monterrey, Mexico

Padres Pitchers Home Run Leaders

Pitcher	Number
Tim Lollar	8
Mike Corkins	5
Andy Benes	4
Joey Hamilton	4
Eric Show	4
Tom Griffin	2
Jimmy Jones	2
Dave Roberts	2
Calvin Schiraldi	2
Fernando Valenzuela	2

Loge Launches

Twenty-nine home runs have been hit into the second deck (Loge Level) in left field and three home runs into the second deck (Loge Level) in right field at Qualcomm Stadium. These included a record setting seven in 1998. Mark McGwire (July 20) and Sammy Sosa (September 16) reached the Loge Level in 1998 on their way to shattering Roger Maris' single-season home run record. Greg Vaughn accomplished the feat twice in 1997 and 1998, the second coming in the same game that McGwire reached the second deck. Phil Nevin and John Mabry on August 22, 2000 combined for the first consecutive Loge Level home runs in Qualcomm Stadium history when they connected in the third inning off Pat Mahomes of the New York Mets. Mabry's clout became the first to reach the Loge Level in right field since the seats were installed during the 1997 stadium expansion. Ryan Klesko on October 6, 2001 hit a solo home run in the seventh inning into the Loge Level in right field off Chris Nichting of the Colorado Rockies, joining Phil Nevin as the second pair of Padres to homer at least 30 times in the same season. Gary Sheffield of the Los Angeles Dodgers on April 13, 2001 clouted a two run homer into the Loge Level in left field in the third inning off Woody Williams, becoming the first player to hit Loge Level home runs for both the Padres and visitors. The complete list of the 12 Padres and 13 opponents is:

Padres (16)	Opponents (16)
Dave Kingman	Dick Allen
Nate Colbert	Chris James
Ivan Murrell	Kevin Mitchell
Kevin McReynolds	Cory Snyder
Gary Sheffield	Jeff Bagwell
Dave Staton	Andres Galarraga
Greg Vaughn (4)	Mike Piazza (2)
Ken Caminiti	Cecil Fielder
Carlos Hernandez	Mark McGwire (2)
Reggie Sanders	Sammy Sosa
Phil Nevin	Alex Rodriguez
John Mabry (RF)	Gary Sheffield (2)
Ryan Klesko (RF)	John Olerud (RF)

Inside-the-Park Home Runs by Padres (14)

Player	Date	Opponent
Dave Roberts	Sept. 29, 1973	Los Angeles Dodgers
Derrel Thomas	June 14, 1974	Montreal Expos
Luis Salazar	July 8, 1982	at Philadelphia Phillies
Gene Richards	July 10, 1982	at New York Mets
Gene Richards (2)	Sept. 26, 1982	at Atlanta Braves
Carmelo Martinez	Sept. 2, 1984	at New York Mets
Garry Templeton	Sept. 17, 1987	Atlanta Braves
John Kruk	Sept. 24, 1987	at Cincinnati Reds
Tony Gwynn	July 29, 1988	Cincinnati Reds
Bip Roberts	April 28, 1990	Pittsburgh Pirates
Jack Howell	August 16, 1991	Atlanta Braves
Tony Gwynn (2)*	June 26, 1997	at Los Angeles Dodgers
Bret Boone	May 11, 2000	at Cincinnati Reds
Ruben Rivera	July 18, 2000	Anaheim Angels

Inside-the-Park Home Runs Against Padres (23)

Player	Date	Team
Denny Doyle	July 18, 1970	Philadelphia Phillies
Cesar Geronimo	July 2, 1972	Cincinnati Reds
Joe Morgan	May 18, 1973	at Cincinnati Reds
Pete Rose	June 29, 1973	at Cincinnati Reds
Paul Casanova	August 5, 1973	at Atlanta Braves
Tito Fuentes	Sept. 23, 1973	at San Francisco Giants
Mike Schmidt	April 27, 1974	Philadelphia Phillies
Heity Cruz	June 18, 1976	at St. Louis Cardinals
Lou Brock	June 18, 1976	at St. Louis Cardinals
Bob Boone	July 10, 1976	at Philadelphia Phillies
Ellis Valentine	May 21, 1977	at Montreal Expos
Pete Rose	Sept. 7, 1978	Cincinnati Reds
Jerry White	June 12, 1980	at Montreal Expos
Larry Bowa	Aug. 21, 1980	at Philadelphia Phillies
Tim Raines	May 7, 1981	at Montreal Expos
Larry Walker	May 5, 1992	at Montreal Expos
Ken Caminiti	May 22, 1993	Houston Astros
Mitch Webster	June 21, 1994	Los Angeles Dodgers
Reggie Sanders	April 29, 1995	Cincinnati Reds
Ron Gant	April 20, 1997	St. Louis Cardinals*
Kenny Lofton	May 27, 1997	Atlanta Braves
Barry Bonds	Sept. 21, 1997	San Francisco Giants
Mike Lansing	Sept. 6, 1998	at Colorado Rockies

*During the Padres Paradise Series in Honolulu, Hawaii.

First Inning Leadoff Home Runs by Padres (44)

Player	Date	Opponent	Pitcher
Tommy Dean	April 27, 1969	Cincinnati	George Culver
Dave Campbell	Sept. 15, 1970	at Los Angeles	Don Sutton
Jerry Morales	Aug. 12, 1973	Montreal	Steve Renko
Jerry Morales (2)	Aug. 28, 1973	at New York	Jon Matlack
Bobby Tolan	May 27, 1974	at Pittsburgh	Bruce Kison
Bobby Tolan (2)	July 13, 1974	Montreal	Steve Rogers
John Grubb	June 21, 1976	San Francisco	John Montefusco
John Grubb (2)	Aug. 2, 1976	at Atlanta	Frank LaCorte
Merv Rettenmund	June 11, 1977	at Pittsburgh	John Candelaria
Gene Richards	Sept. 12, 1977	at Los Angeles	Don Sutton
Gene Richards	May 7, 1978	at St. Louis	Bob Forsch
Gene Richards (3)	April 6, 1983	at San Francisco	Bill Laskey
Alan Wiggins	July 8, 1984	Pittsburgh	John Candelaria
Jerry Royster	Aug. 18, 1985	Atlanta	Craig McMurtry
Marvell Wynne	July 6, 1986	Chicago	Scott Sanderson
Marvell Wynne (2)	Apr. 13, 1987	San Francisco	Roger Mason
Stan Jefferson	July 11, 1987	at Pittsburgh	Brian Fisher
Shane Mack	July 26, 1987	Pittsburgh	Bob Kipper
Stan Jefferson (2)	Aug. 11, 1987	Atlanta	Rick Mahler
John Kruk	July 24, 1988	at Chicago	Rick Sutcliffe
Roberto Alomar	Sept. 17, 1989	at San Francisco	Rick Reuschel
Bip Roberts	Aug. 25, 1990	at Montreal	Chris Nabholz
Roberto Alomar (2)	Sept. 1,1990	at Philadelphia	Tommy Greene
Bip Roberts	Aug. 11, 1991	Cincinnati	Kip Gross
Darrin Jackson	Aug. 25, 1991	at Chicago	Danny Jackson
Darrin Jackson (2)	Sept. 12, 1991	at Atlanta	Charlie Leibrandt

Player	Date	Opponent	Pitcher
Tony Fernandez	Sept. 15, 1992	Los Angeles	Orel Hershiser
Jeff Gardner	July 20, 1993	New York	Dave Telgheder
Bip Roberts (3)	Aug. 31, 1995	Montreal	Pedro Martinez
Steve Finley	April 24, 1996	Chicago	Kevin Foster
Rickey Henderson	June 4, 1996	St. Louis	Mike Morgan
Rickey Henderson	Aug. 24, 1996	Philadelphia	Matt Beech
Rickey Henderson	Sept. 1,1996	at Montreal	Jeff Fassero
Quilvio Veras	April 6, 1997	Philadelphia	Curt Schilling
Rickey Henderson	July 2, 1997	Seattle	Jeff Fassero
Quilvio Veras	June 17, 1998	Los Angeles	Ismael Valdes
Quilvio Veras	July 21, 1998	St. Louis	Kent Mercker
Quilvio Veras	Aug. 22, 1998	at Milwaukee	Rafael Roque
Steve Finley (2)	Sept. 9, 1998	San Francisco	Shawn Estes
Quilvio Veras	Sept. 7, 1999	at Pittsburgh	Jason Schmidt
Quilvio Veras	Sept. 18, 1999	San Francisco	Mark Gardner
Quilvio Veras (7)	Sept. 30, 1999	at Arizona	Randy Johnson
Rickey Henderson (5)	May 16, 2001	at New York	Glendon Rusch
Damian Jackson	Aug. 8, 2001	at Philadelphia	Dave Coggin

Pinch Hit Home Runs by Padres (124)

Player	Date	Inning	On	Opponent	Pitcher
Al Ferrara	May 2, 1969	4	3	at Cincinnati	George Culver
Al Ferrara (2)	May 16, 1969	7	0	St. Louis	Ray Washburn
Ivan Murrell	April 16, 1970	10	0	at Atlanta	Phil Niekro
Ramon Webster	July 3, 1970 (2)	5	0	at Atlanta	Phil Niekro
Ed Spiezio	July 18, 1970	9	0	Philadelphia	Dick Selma
Ivan Murrell (2)	July 15, 1971	13	0	at Pittsburgh	Mudcat Grant
Garry Jestadt	May 14, 1972	8	1	at Montreal	Mike Torrez
Larry Stahl	May 31, 1972	9	1	at Atlanta	Ron Reed
Jerry Morales	June 7, 1972 (1)	9	0	Pittsburgh	Bob Johnson
Clarence Gaston	June 14, 1972	6	3	at Chicago	Ferguson Jenkins
Curt Blefary	June 21, 1972	8	0	at St. Louis	Moe Drabowsky
Jerry Morales	April 7, 1973	9	0	Los Angeles	Jim Brewer
Jerry Morales (3)	June 5, 1973	7	1	at St. Louis	Alan Foster
Dave Winfield	August 3, 1973	5	0	at Atlanta	Ron Schueler
Clarence Gaston	June 4, 1974	8	0	Chicago	Dave LaRoche
Clarence Gaston (3)	June 16, 1974	8	1	at Montreal	Chuck Taylor
Gene Locklear	August 21, 1974	8	0	at Montreal	Chuck Taylor
Willie McCovey	May 30, 1975	8	3	at New York	Bob Apodaca
Willie McCovey	June 12, 1975	8	0	Montreal	Chuck Taylor
Merv Rettenmund	May 18, 1976	9	1	at San Francisco	Gary Lavelle
Willie McCovey (3)	August 8, 1976	8	2	Houston	J. R. Richard
Merv Rettenmund	Sept. 6, 1976	9	0	Los Angeles	Don Sutton
Merv Rettenmund (3)	April 14, 1977	7	0	San Francisco	Jim Barr
Gary Sutherland	April 25, 1977	9	0	Los Angeles	Rick Rhoden
Jerry Turner	June 17, 1977	4	2	St. Louis	John Denny
Jerry Turner	April 16, 1978	9	1	San Francisco	Randy Moffitt
Jerry Turner	May 3, 1978	6	1	at Pittsburgh	Jim Bibby
Jerry Turner	July 2, 1978	8	0	at Houston	Tom Dixon
Jerry Turner	July 22, 1978	9	2	Chicago	Bruce Sutter
Jerry Turner	August 22, 1978	6	2	at Philadelphia	Rawley Eastwick
Gene Tenace	July 13, 1979 (2)	9	0	at Montreal	Dave Palmer
Dave Winfield (2)	April 22, 1980	9	0	at Pittsburgh	Kent Tekulve
Jerry Turner	May 29, 1980	8	1	Cincinnati	Frank Pastore
Von Joshua	June 26, 1980	8	0	San Francisco	Ed Whitson
Jerry Mumphrey	July 3, 1980	7	1	at Los Angeles	Burt Hooten
Gene Tenace (2)	Aug. 17, 1980 (2)	7	0	Houston	Joe Niekro

Player	Date	Inning	On	Opponent	Pitcher
Jerry Turner	April 23, 1981	8	0	at Los Angeles	Rick Sutcliffe
Joe Lefebvre	April 30, 1981	8	0	at Cincinnati	Mike LaCoss
Joe Lefebvre	August 19, 1981	8	0	at St. Louis	Bruce Sutter
Jerry Turner (9)	August 24, 1981	5	2	at Chicago	Mike Krukow
Dave Edwards	June 29, 1982	9	0	at Los Angeles	Jerry Reuss
Terry Kennedy	June 30, 1982 (2)	5	2	at Los Angeles	Dave Stewart
Garry Templeton	July 4, 1982	7	1	San Francisco	Atlee Hammaker
Joe Lefebvre (3)	August 3, 1982	9	0	at Houston	Frank LaCorte
Kurt Bevacqua	July 14, 1983	7	3	Pittsburgh	Rod Scurry
Joe Lansford	Sept. 21, 1983	8	1	at San Francisco	Mark Davis
Champ Summers	April 10, 1984	5	3	St. Louis	Bob Forsch
Kurt Bevacqua (2)	June 14, 1984	7	1	San Francisco	Mark Davis
Graig Nettles	July 14, 1984	9	1	at St. Louis	Bruce Sutter
Kevin McReynolds	August 8, 1984	9	0	at Cincinnati	Mario Soto
Mario Ramirez	June 28, 1985	5	1	Cincinnati	Joe Price
Al Bumbry	August 4, 1985	9	0	at Houston	Mike Scott
Marvell Wynne	April 13, 1986	7	0	Cincinnati	Tom Browning
Bruce Bochy	April 14, 1986	11	0	Los Angeles	Ed Vande Berg
Graig Nettles (2)	May 16, 1986	9	0	Montreal	Jeff Reardon
Terry Kennedy (2)	June 21, 1986	8	1	at Los Angeles	Tom Niedenfuer
Bruce Bochy (2)	July 4, 1986	9	0	Chicago	Ray Fontenot
Carmelo Martinez	August 5, 1986	9	0	Atlanta	Ed Olwine
Dane Org	Sept. 7, 1986 (1)	6	0	at New York	Dwight Gooden
Carmelo Martinez	Sept. 14, 1986	9	1	Houston	Mike Scott
John Kruk	July 10, 1987	9	0	at Pittsburgh	Don Robinson
John Kruk (2)	April 16, 1998	9	0	San Francisco	Don Robinson
Marvell Wynne (2)	May 19, 1988	9	0	New York	Terry Leach
Dickie Thon	Sept. 18 1988	9	0	at Atlanta	Paul Assenmacher
Mark Parent	Sept. 28, 1988	16	1	Los Angeles	Rick Horton
Luis Salazar	April 13, 1989	8	0	Atlanta	Derek Lilliquist
Carmelo Martinez (3)	July 18, 1989	8	2	Pittsburgh	Miguel Garcia
Luis Salazar	August 12, 1989	7	1	Atlanta	Tom Glavine
Luis Salazar (3)	August 16, 1989	8	0	at New York	Ron Darling
Mark Parent (2)	Sept. 14, 1989	9	0	Atlanta	Sergio Valdez
Darrin Jackson	April 27, 1990	7	0	Pittsburgh	Bob Patterson
Fred Lynn	June 18, 1990	8	0	at San Francisco	Jeff Brantley
Mike Pagliarulo	Sept. 19, 1990	7	1	at Los Angeles	Don Aase
Marty Barrett	April 11, 1991	9	2	San Francisco	Dave Righetti
Garry Templeton	May 28, 1991	7	2	Atlanta	Kent Mercker
Darrin Jackson (2)	June 14, 1991	7	1	Chicago	Chuck McElroy
Thomas Howard	August 11, 1991	7	0	Cincinnati	Gino Minutelli
Kevin Ward	April 15, 1992	8	1	at San Francisco	Bryan Hickerson
Guillermo Velasquez	Sept. 23,1992	7	1	Houston	Pete Harnisch
Tim Teufel	June 10, 1993	8	1	Los Angeles	Todd Worrell
Phil Clark	July 26, 1993	9	0	at Chicago	Randy Myers
Guillermo Velasquez (2)	July 28, 1993	8	1	at Chicago	Bob Scanlan
Dave Staton	Sept. 15, 1993	3	0	Los Angeles	Kevin Gross
Craig Shipley	May 30, 1994	7	3	Pittsburgh	Dan Miceli
Brian Johnson	July 25, 1994	9	0	Colorado	Bruce Ruffin
Brian Johnson (2)	May 14, 1995	8	3	at Chicago	Randy Myers
Phil Clark (2)	May 21, 1995	6	0	Pittsburgh	Danny Neagle
Scott Livingstone	May 27, 1995	5	0	at Philadelphia	Mike Williams
Roberto Petagine	June 19, 1995	7	2	Chicago	Kevin Foster
Melvin Nieves	July 5, 1995	10	1	at Florida	Randy Veres
Archi Cianfrocco	July 21, 1995	8	3	at Atlanta	Steve Bedrosian
Eddie Williams	August 23, 1995	9	1	at Philadelphia	Mike Mimbs
Archi Cianfrocco	Sept. 1, 1995	5	2	Philadelphia	Russ Springer
Archi Cianfrocco (3)	Sept. 9, 1995	7	2	at St. Louis	Jeff Parrett
Phil Plantier	Sept. 23, 1995	8	0	at Los Angeles	Ismael Valdes

Player	Date	Inning	On	Opponent	Pitcher
Marc Newfield	June 20, 1996	8	1	Chicago	Jaimie Navarro
Rob Deer	July 6, 1996	7	1	San Francisco	Rich Delucia
Scott Livingstone (2)	July 12, 1996	9	2	at Colorado	Curtis Leskanic
Steve Finley	Sept. 9, 1996	9	0	Pittsburgh	Rich Loiselle
Rickey Henderson	April 1, 1997	6	0	New York	Pete Harnisch
Carlos Hernandez	May 19, 1997	9	0	at Cincinnati	Stan Belinda
Greg Vaughn	July 3, 1997	6	1	Seattle	Bobby Ayala
Greg Vaughn (2)	July 22, 1997	8	0	Pittsburgh	Ricardo Rincon
Mike Sweeney	July 28, 1997	9	0	Philadelphia	Ricky Bottalico
Mike Sweeney	August 16, 1997	8	1	Chicago	Kevin Foster
Craig Shipley (2)	August 23, 1997	7	0	New York	Dave Mlicki
Mark Sweeney (3)	April 23, 1998	9	0	at Chicago	Amaury Telemaco
George Arias	August 31, 1998	6	0	Montreal	Anthony Telford
Jim Leyritz	April 7, 1999	9	0	Colorado	Bobby Jones
Geg Myers	May 11,1999	5	0	Florida	Ryan Dempster
Jim Leyritz (2)	May 29, 1999	5	0	at Milwaukee	Rafael Roque
Phil Nevin	July 2, 1999	9	1	at Colorado	Dave Wainhouse
Carlos Baerga	July 2, 1999	9	1	at Colorado	Dave Wainhouse
Phil Nevin (2)	July 23, 1999	9	0	at Houston	Billy Wagner
Wiki Gonzalez	Sept. 9, 1999	8	1	Montreal	Ted Lilly
Ryan Klesko	April 26, 2000	9	1	at Pittsburgh	Mike Williams
Carlos Hernandez (2)	May 20, 2000	7	1	at Atlanta	John Burkett
Al Martin	May 21, 2000	9	1	at Atlanta	Greg McMichael
Ed Sprague	June 18, 2000	5	2	Cincinnati	Dennys Reyes
Ryan Klesko (2)	June 21, 2000	9	1	at Arizona	Byung-Hyun Kim
Dave Magadan	July 14, 2000	9	0	Seattle	Kazuhiro Sasaki
Kory DeHaan	August 31, 2000	6	1	at Chicago	Kyle Farnsworth
Cesar Crespo	August 29, 2001	9	1	at St. Louis	Dave Veres
Mike Darr	Sept. 22, 2001	10	0	San Francisco	Brian Boehringer

Padres All-Time Pinch Hit Home Run Leaders

Player	Home Runs
Jerry Turner	9
Archi Cianfrocco	3
Clarence Gaston	3
Joe Lefebvre	3
Carmelo Martinez	3
Willie McCovey	3
Merv Rettenmund	3
Luis Salazar	3
Mark Sweeney	3

Grand Slam Home Runs by Padres (100)

Player	Date	Inning	Opponent	Pitcher
*Al Ferrara	May 2, 1969	4	at Cincinnati	George Culver
Ollie Brown	May 3, 1969	1	at Cincinnati	Tony Cloninger
Roberto Pena	May 10, 1969	4	at St. Louis	Steve Carlton
Nate Colbert	May 25, 1969	3	Chicago	Don Nottebart
Ed Spiezio	August 18, 1970	6	at Chicago	Roberto Rodriguez
+Mike Corkins	Sept. 4, 1970	4	at Cincinnati	Jim Merritt
Ramon Webster	Sept. 7, 1970 (1)	9	Houston	Ken Forsch
Nate Colbert	June 6, 1971	5	Montreal	John Strohmayer
Bob Barton	June 18, 1971	9	at San Francisco	Jerry Johnson
*Clarence Gaston	June 14, 1972	6	at Chicago	Ferguson Jenkins
Nate Colbert	August 1, 1972	2	at Atlanta	Pat Jarvis
Nate Colbert	Sept. 7, 1972	6	Cincinnati	Jack Billingham

Player	Date	Inning	Opponent	Pitcher
Nate Colbert	May 17, 1974	1	at San Francisco	Ron Bryant
Willie McCovey	May 19, 1974	5	at San Francisco	Tom Bradley
Willie McCovey	May 30, 1975	8	at New York	Bob Apodaca
Mike Ivie	July 1, 1975	5	at Los Angeles	Jim Brewer
Dave Winfield	April 13, 1976	7	at Los Angeles	Stan Wall
Dave Winfield	May 21, 1976	1	Cincinnati	Gary Nolan
Doug Rader	Sept. 29 1976	1	Cincinnati	Fred Norman
Gene Tenace	April 18, 1977	5	at Atlanta	Bob Johnson
Mike Ivie	May 20, 1977	1	at Montreal	Gerry Hannahs
Dave Kingman	August 5, 1977	6	at Chicago	Paul Reuschel
Dave Kingman	August 21, 1977	1	at St. Louis	Tom Underwood
Dave Winfield	July 4, 1978	1	at San Francisco	John Montefusco
Barry Evans	May 25, 1980	9	at St. Louis	Pedro Borbon
Randy Bass	April 12, 1981	3	at San Francisco	Tom Griffin
Steve Garvey	July 3, 1983	5	at San Francisco	Mark Davis
Tim Flannery	July 11, 1983	1	Chicago	Ferguson Jenkins
*Kurt Bevacqua	July 14, 1983	7	Pittsburgh	Rod Scurry
Bobby Brown	August 6, 1983	8	Cincinnati	Tom Hume
*Champ Summers	April 10, 1984	5	St. Louis	Bob Forsch
Garry Templeton	July 29, 1984	6	Houston	Mike LaCoss
Carmelo Martinez	April 15, 1985	7	San Francisco	Greg Minton
Kurt Bevacqua	June 7, 1985 (1)	5	at Cincinnati	Tom Browning
Jerry Royster	June 21, 1985	8	San Francisco	Greg Minton
Kurt Bevacqua	June 23, 1985	5	San Francisco	Atlee Hammaker
Kevin McReynolds	October 4, 1986	3	at Cincinnati	Bill Gullickson
John Kruk	April 12, 1988	5	Los Angeles	Brad Havens
Marvell Wynne	Sept. 11, 1988	2	Atlanta	Charlie Puleo
Benito Santiago	Sept. 21, 1988 (1)	2	at Los Angeles	Rick Horton
Carmelo Martinez	April 27, 1989	8	at Pittsburgh	Logan Easley
Chris James	July 18, 1989	5	Pittsburgh	Bob Walk
Benito Santiago	Sept. 3, 1989	7	Philadelphia	Jeff Parrett
Jack Clark	Sept. 4, 1989	7	at Atlanta	Mark Eichorn
Garry Templeton	Sept. 11, 1989	6	Houston	Danny Darwin
Joe Carter	April 23, 1990	1	San Francisco	Eric Gunderson
Garry Templeton	May 18, 1990	2	New York	Frank Viola
Joe Carter	August 4, 1990	11	at Cincinnati	Rick Mahler
Benito Santiago	Sept. 19, 1990	6	at Los Angeles	Darrin Holmes
Tim Teufel	August 2, 1991	3	at Atlanta	Charlie Leibrandt
Fred McGriff	August 13, 1991	3	Houston	Mark Portugal
Fred McGriff	August 14, 1991	1	Houston	Jim Deschaies
Darrin Jackson	August 25, 1991	6	at Chicago	Bob Scanlan
Fred McGriff	April 10, 1992	7	Los Angeles	John Candelaria
Gary Sheffield	June 19, 1992	4	at San Francisco	Trevor Wilson
Gary Sheffield	August 14, 1992	2	at Cincinnati	Chris Hammond
Jerald Clark	Sept. 7, 1992	4	at San Francisco	Bud Black
Billy Bean	August 11, 1993	3	Houston	Darryl Kile
Phil Plantier	August 23, 1993	1	St. Louis	Donovan Osborne
+Luis Lopez	May 23, 1994	1	San Francisco	Mark Portugal
*Craig Shipley	May 30, 1994	7	Pittsburgh	Dan Miceli
Brian Johnson	July 1, 1994	7	New York	Roger Mason
Eddie Williams	July 5, 1994	5	Philadelphia	Bobby Munoz
*Brian Johnson	May 14, 1995	8	at Chicago	Randy Myers
Bip Roberts	May 20, 1995	9	Pittsburgh	Dan Miceli
Ken Caminiti	June 27, 1995	6	at Los Angeles	Greg Hansell
Eddie Williams	July 9, 1995	7	at Houston	Doug Brocail
Ray Holbert	July 17, 1995	5	Cincinnati	C. J. Nitkowski
*Archi Cianfrocco	July 21, 1995	8	at Atlanta	Steve Bedrosian
Melvin Nieves	August 2, 1995	8	San Francisco	Terry Mulholland
Tony Gwynn	August 22, 1995	5	at Philadelphia	Tommy Greene

Player	Date	Inning	Opponent	Pitcher
Melvin Nieves	August 26, 1995	9	at New York	Doug Henry
Ken Caminiti	April 6, 1996	13	at Houston	Alvin Morman
Brian Johnson	May 24, 1996	7	at New York	Blas Minor
Steve Finley	June 1, 1996	6	at Philadelphia	Dave Leiper
John Flaherty	July 27, 1996	8	at Florida	Terry Mathews
!Greg Vaughn	August 16, 1996	6	New York	Derek Wallace
Ken Caminiti	August 19, 1996	1	Montreal	Pedro Martinez
@Tony Gwynn	June 26, 1997	7	at Los Angeles	Mark Guthrie
Steve Finley	July 3, 1997	1	Seattle	Derek Lowe
Steve Finley	Sept. 1, 1997	9	at Seattle	Bobby Ayala
%Steve Finley	April 10, 1998	9	Arizona	Felix Rodriguez
Wally Joyner	May 5, 1998	2	at Milwaukee	Paul Wagner
Greg Vaughn	June 9, 1998	7	Cincinnati	Brett Tomko
Ruben Rivera	July 17, 1998	4	at Cincinnati	Rick Krivda
Tony Gwynn	August 4, 1999	5	at St. Louis	Kent Mercker
Phil Nevin	May 19, 2000	7	at Atlanta	Kevin McGlinchey
Bret Boone	June 10, 2000	1	Houston	Scott Elarton
Ruben Rivera	July 30, 2000	7	at Pittsburgh	Josias Manzanillo
Damian Jackson	August 22, 2000	2	New York	Pat Mahomes
Ben Davis	May 1, 2001	3	at Chicago	Jason Bere
Phil Nevin	June 14, 2001	8	Oakland	Chad Bradford
Bubba Trammell	July 4, 2001	7	Colorado	Juan Acevedo
Damian Jackson	July 14, 2001	6	at Houston	Wade Miller
Phil Nevin	July 28, 2001	4	at Milwaukee	Allen Levrault
Ryan Klesko	August 2, 2001	8	Chicago	Jeff Fassero
Bubba Trammell	August 25, 2001	9	at Florida	Ricky Bones
Ray Lankford	September 1, 2001	8	Arizona	Byung-Hyun Kim
Phil Nevin	September 27, 2001	2	at Colorado	Kane Davis
Phil Nevin	October 6, 2001	1	Colorado	Scott Elarton

*Pinch hitter +First major league home run !In Monterrey, Mexico
@Inside-the-park %Game-Ending

Padres All-Time Grand Slam Home Run Leaders

Player	Home Runs	Player	Home Runs
Nate Colbert	5	Mike Ivie	2
Phil Nevin	5	Damian Jackson	2
Steve Finley	4	Dave Kingman	2
Kurt Bevacqua	3	Carmelo Martinez	2
Tony Gwynn	3	Willie McCovey	2
Brian Johnson	3	Melvin Nieves	2
Fred McGriff	3	Ruben Rivera	2
Benito Santiago	3	Gary Sheffield	2
Garry Templeton	3	Bubba Trammell	2
Dave Winfield	3	Greg Vaughn	2
Ken Caminiti	2	Eddie Williams	2
Joe Carter	2		

PADRES SINGLE-SEASON RECORDS

CLUB GENERAL

Wins and Losses

Best Overall Record—98-64, 1998
Best Home Record —54-27, 1998
Best Road Record —46-35, 1996
Most Home Wins —54, 1998
Fewest Home Wins —26, 1972
Most Road Wins —46, 1996
Fewest Road Wins—23, 1969
Most Home Losses —54, 1972
Fewest Home Losses—27, 1998
Most Road Losses —59, 1969
Fewest Road Losses—37, 1984
Wins Against One Club —14, vs. Houston, 1990
Home Wins Against One Club— 8, 12 times
Road Wins Against One Club — 7, seven times
Losses Against One Club —17, vs. Atlanta, 1974
Home Losses Against One Club — 9, vs. Los Angeles, 1971, vs. Atlanta, 1974
Away Losses Against One Club — 9, at Atlanta, 1980
Most Wins in a Month —19, in June 1984, July 1984, September 1989
Most Losses in a Month —22, in June 1969, August 1969, May 1974

Shutouts

Most Played—34, 1972, 1976
Most Won—19, 1985
Most Lost—23, 1969, 1976
Most Won, Home— 9, 1978, 1982, 1984
Most Won, Away—13, 1985
Most Lost, Home —13, 2001
Most Lost, Away—15, 1969
Most Wins by Shutout Against One Club—5, vs. Houston, 1984
Most Losses by Shutout Against One Club—5, four times

Season Series

Swept by Padres at San Diego—15 times
Swept by Opposition at San Diego—13 times
Swept by Padres on road—3 times, at Philadelphia, 3-0, 1998; at Houston, 3-0, 2000; at Cincinnati, 3-0, 2001
Swept by Opposition on Road—13 times

One-Run Games

Most Played—64, 1980
Most Won—34, 1978, 1984
Fewest Won—12, 1994
Most Lost—37, 1970
Fewest Lost—13, 1974
Most Won, Home—24, 1979
Fewest Won, Home—5, 1969
Most Won, Road—15, 1978, 1984
Fewest Won, Road—4, 1995
Most Lost, Home—20, 1972
Fewest Lost, Home—3, 1974
Most Lost, Road—23, 1970
Fewest Lost, Road—9, 1977

Extra-Inning Games
Most—24, 1996, 2000
Most Won—13, 1996
Most Lost—14, 1972

Doubleheaders
Most Won—5, 1977
Most Lost—8, 1969
Best Record—5-1-2, 1977

1-0 Games
Most Won—7, 1985
Most Lost—5, 1976, 1996

Vs. Righthanders
Most won—71, 1998
Most Lost—93, 1969

Vs. Left handers
Most Won—32, 1990
Most Lost—36, 1979

Players Used
Season, Most—56, 2000 (ties major league record)
Season, Fewest—31, 1984

Pitchers Used
Season, Most—29, 2000 (National League record)

Longest Padres Winning Streaks

Streak	Dates
14 games	June 18-July 2, 1999
11 games	April 14-27, 1982
11 games	June 7-19, 1998
10 games	July 25-August 4, 1978
8 games	July 26-August 3, 1980
8 games	April 5-13, 1998

CLUB BATTING

Batting Average	Highest—.275, 1994	Lowest—.225, 1969
At-Bats	Most—5,655, 1996	
Runs Scored	Most—795, 1997	Fewest—468, 1969
Hits	Most—1,519, 1997	Fewest—1,181, 1972
Singles	Most—1,105, 1980	
Doubles	Most—292, 1998	Fewest—168, 1972
Triples	Most—53, 1979	Fewest—16, 1997
Home Runs	Most—172, 1970	Fewest—64, 1976
At Home	Most—87, 1992, 1993	Fewest—30, 1976
Away	Most—104, 1970	Fewest—34, 1976
Grand Slams	Most—10, 2001	Fewest—0, 1973, 1979, 1982, 1987
Extra-Base Hits	Most—489, 1998	
Total Bases	Most—2,282, 1997	
Slugging Pct.	Highest—.409, 1998	Lowest—.329, 1969
Pinch Hits	Most—74, 1986	Fewest—35, 1985, 1988

Pinch-Hit Average	Highest—.274, 1994	
Pinch-Hit HR	Most—10, 1995	Fewest—1, 1971, 1979, 1987
Stolen Bases	Most—239, 1980	Fewest—45, 1969
Caught Stealing	Most—91, 1987	
Home Runs vs. One NL Team	Most—25, vs. Atlanta, 1970	Fewest—1, vs. Montreal, 1987
Home Runs vs. Padres	Most—28, by Atlanta, 1973	Fewest—2, by St. Louis, 1969; by Montreal, 1971
Strikeouts	Most—1,273, 2001	Fewest—716, 1976
Bases on Balls	Most—678, 2001	Fewest—401, 1973
Left on Base	Most—1,239, 1980	Fewest—998, 1995
Hit by Pitch	Most—59, 1993	Fewest—9, 1989
Sacrifice Hits	Most—133, 1975	
Sacrifice Flies	Most—58, 1997	
Double Plays	Most—146, 1996	Fewest—81, 1978

CLUB PITCHING

Earned Run Average	Lowest—3.22, 1971	Highest—4.99, 1997
Complete Games	Most—47, 1976	Fewest—5, 1996, 1997, 1999, 2000, 2001
Strikeouts	Most—1,217, 1998	Fewest—652, 1976
Base on Balls	Most—715, 1974	Fewest—443, 1985
Hits	Most—1,581, 1997	Fewest—1,242, 1995
Runs Allowed	Most—891, 1997	Fewest—583, 1988
Saves	Most—59, 1998	Fewest—17, 1971
Wild Pitches	Most—73, 1999	Fewest—23, 1979
Balks	Most—25, 1977	Fewest—3, 1973
Hit Batsmen	Most—68, 2000	Fewest—12, 1978, 1980
Home Runs, Allowed	Most—219, 2001	Fewest—74, 1978

CLUB FIELDING

Fielding Pct.	Highest—.983, 1998	Lowest—.971, 1975, 1977
Errors	Most—189, 1977	Fewest—104, 1998
Double Plays	Most—171, 1978	Fewest—126, 1974
Putouts	Most—4,467, 1996	Fewest—4,211, 1972
Assists	Most—2,012, 1980	Fewest—1,607, 2001
Chances	Most—6,411, 1980	Fewest—5,832, 1972
Passed Balls	Most—22, 1987	Fewest—2, 1992

INDIVIDUAL BATTING

Batting Average	.394	Tony Gwynn, 1994
Slugging Percentage	.621	Ken Caminiti, 1996
Games Played	162	Dave Winfield, 1980; Steve Garvey, 1985; Joe Carter, 1990
Runs Scored	126	Steve Finley, 1996
Hits	220	Tony Gwynn, 1997
Total Bases	348	Steve Finley, 1996
Singles	177	Tony Gwynn, 1984
Doubles	49	Tony Gwynn, 1997
Triples	13	Tony Gwynn, 1987
Home Runs	50	Greg Vaughn, 1998
Games, HR Both Sides	4	Ken Caminiti, 1996
Runs Batted In	130	Ken Caminiti, 1996

Grand Slams	4	Phil Nevin, 2001
Game-Winning RBI	15	Terry Kennedy, 1982; Steve Garvey, 1984
Pinch Hit Average	.478	Terry Kennedy, 1986
Most Pinch Hits	21	Merv Rettenmund, 1977
Stolen Bases	70	Alan Wiggins, 1970
Strikeouts, Most	150	Nate Colbert, 1970
Strikeouts, Fewest (502ab)	16	Tony Gwynn, 1992
Base on Balls	132	Jack Clark, 1989
Intentional Walks	26	Tony Gwynn, 1987; Fred McGriff, 1991
Sacrifice Hits	28	Ozzie Smith, 1978
Hit By Pitch	13	Gene Tenace, 1977
Most Double Plays	25	Steve Garvey, 1984, 1985
Fewest Double Plays	2	Alan Wiggins, 1984

INDIVIDUAL PITCHING

Most Appearances	83	Craig Lefferts, 1986
Most Games, Rookie	77	Butch Metzger, 1976
Complete Games	25	Randy Jones, 1976
Starts	40	Randy Jones, 1976
Games Finished	69	Rollie Fingers, 1977
Shutouts	6	Fred Norman, 1972 Randy Jones, 1975
Most Victories	22	Randy Jones, 1976
Most Victories, Rookie	12	Bob Shirley, 1977
Most Victories, Relief	11	Rollie Fingers, 1980
Win-Loss Pct., Starter	.778	Gaylord Perry, 1978 Dennis Rasmussen, 1988
Losses	22	Randy Jones, 1974
Innings Pitched	315.1	Randy Jones, 1976
Runs Allowed	137	Bobby Jones, 2001
Earned Runs Allowed	117	Bill Greif, 1974; Matt Clement, 2000
Hits	274	Randy Jones, 1976
Base on Balls	125	Matt Clement, 2000
Strikeouts	257	Kevin Brown, 1998
Lowest ERA, Starter	2.10	Dave Roberts, 1971
Home Runs Allowed	37	Bobby Jones, 2001; Kevin Jarvis, 2001
Saves, Lefthander	44	Mark Davis, 1989
Saves, Righthander	53	Trevor Hoffman, 1998 (ties National League record)
Hit Batsmen	16	Matt Clement, 2000
Wild Pitches	23	Matt Clement, 2000
Balks	6	Tom Griffin, 1977 Bob Shirley, 1977

INDIVIDUAL FIELDING PERCENTAGE

First Baseman	1.000	Steve Garvey, 1984
Second Baseman	.994	Jody Reed, 1995
Third Baseman	.961	Gary Sheffield, 1992
Shortstop	.983	Tony Fernandez, 1992
Outfielder	1.000	Eric Owens, 2000
Catcher	.998	Gene Tenace, 1979
Pitcher	1.000	14 times

PADRES SINGLE-GAME RECORDS

CLUB GENERAL

Players Used	Padres—22, at Atlanta, September 22, 1996 Both Teams—50, at Los Angeles, Sept. 13, 1982 (16 innings) Extra Inning Game—26, vs. Florida, Sept. 9, 1997 (13 innings)
Longest Game Time, Nine Innings	Home—3:51 vs. San Francisco, May 6, 1995 Road—4:10 at Florida July 27, 1996
Shortest Game Time, Nine Innings	Home—1:29 vs. Philadelphia, May 4, 1997
Longest Game Time, Extra Innings	Home—6:17 vs. Houston, August 15, 1980 (20 innings) Road—5:53 at Montreal, May 21, 1977 (21 innings)
Shortest Game Time, Extra Innings	Home—2:00 vs. St. Louis, May 19, 1975 (10 innings)
Longest Game, Innings	Home—21, vs. Houston, September 24, 1971 (1st game) Road—21, at Montreal, May 21, 1977
Largest Margin of Victory	15, at Houston (17-2), April 7, 1996; vs. New York (16-1), August 22, 2000
Largest Margin of Defeat	19, at Chicago (19-0), May 13, 1969; vs. Los Angeles (19-0), June 28, 1969
Largest Shutout Victory	13-0, vs. Cincinnati, August 11, 1991
Largest Shutout Loss	19-0, at Chicago, May 13, 1969; vs. Los Angeles, June 28, 1969

CLUB BATTING

Runs Scored, Padres	20, at Florida, July 27, 1996; at Montreal, May 19, 2001
Runs Scored, Opponents	23, at Chicago, May 17, 1977
Runs Scored, Padres Extra Inning Game	17 vs. San Francisco, May 23, 1970 (15 innings)
Runs Batted In, Padres	20, at Florida, July 27, 1996
Runs Batted In, Opponents	22, at Chicago, May 17, 1977
Hits, Padres	24 vs. San Francisco, April 19, 1982
Hits, Opponents	24, at Chicago, May 17, 1977
Hits, Padres, Extra Innings	21, vs. Houston, July 5, 1969; at San Francisco, May 23, 1970
Singles, Padres	18 vs. San Francisco, April 19, 1982; vs. Houston, April 27, 1995
Doubles, Padres	8 vs. San Francisco, Sept. 8, 1992; vs. Colorado, April 16, 1996
Doubles, Opponents	8 vs. Houston, August 6, 1970
Triples, Padres	4, at Pittsburgh, June 2, 1970; at St. Louis, May 5, 1978
Triples, Opponents	4 vs. Montreal, July 8, 1994; at Chicago, May 15, 1997
Home Runs, Padres	6, at Cincinnati, July 17, 1998
Home Runs, Opponents	7, twice
Home Runs, Padres, Extra Inning Game	5, vs. San Francisco, May 23, 1970 (15 innings)
Extra-Base Hits, Padres	11, at Los Angeles, April 22 1984; at New York, May 17, 2001
Extra-Base Hits, Opponents	11, twice
Total Bases, Padres	39, vs. San Francisco, May 23, 1970
Most Left on Base, Padres	17, vs. Atlanta, May 24, 1977
Most Left on Base, Opponents	15, four times
Most Left on Base, Padres Extra Innings	26, vs. Pittsburgh, August 25, 1979 (19 innings)
Most Left on Base, Opponents 23, Extra Innings	at Montreal, May 21, 1977 (21 innings)
Fewest Left on Base, Padres	0, 10 times

Fewest Left on Base, Opponents	0, vs. Houston, August 6 1975
Fewest Left on Base, Padres Extra Innings	1, vs. St. Louis, July 20, 1975 (11 innings)
Pinch Hitters Used	8 vs. San Francisco, September 16, 1986
Times Striking Out	19, at New York, April 22, 1970
Times Striking Out, Extra Inning Game	20, vs. San Francisco, June 19, 2001 (15 innings)
Walks Received	12, three times
Intentional Walks Received	4, three times
Stolen Bases	9, vs. Colorado, June 28, 1999
Sacrifice Flies	4, vs. Colorado, July 3, 2001

CLUB PITCHING

Runs Allowed, 9-Inning Game	23, at Chicago, May 17, 1977
Hits Allowed, 9-Inning Game	24, at Chicago, May 17, 1977
Doubles Allowed, 9-Inning Game	8, vs. Houston, August 6, 1970
Triples Allowed, 9-Inning Game	4, vs. Montreal, July 8, 1994; at Chicago, May 15, 1997
Home Runs Allowed, 9-Inning Game	7, twice
Extra-Base Hits Allowed, 9-Inning Game	20, vs. Sam Francisco, June 19, 2001 (15 innings)
Strikeouts, 9-Inning Game	17, vs. Montreal, August 29, 1998
Strikeouts, Extra-Inning Game	17, twice
Walks Issued, 9-Inning Game	13, four times
Walks Issued, Extra-Inning Game	12, at Chicago, June 17, 1974 (13 innings)
Hit Batsmen, 9-Inning Game	4, at Montreal, May 14, 1997
Pitchers Used, 9-Inning Game	7, 13 times
Pitchers Used, Extra-Inning Game	9, vs. Florida, September 9, 1997 (13 innings)

CLUB FIELDING

Double Plays, 9-Inning Game	5, three times
Double Plays by Opponents, 9-Inning Game	5, three times
Double Plays, Both Teams, 9-Inning Game	7, vs. St. Louis, July 27, 1985
Triple Plays by Padres	1, seven times
Triple Plays by Opponents	1, eight times
Errors by Padres, 9-Inning Game	6, five times
Errors by Opponents, 9-Inning Game	6, vs. Houston, June 25, 1978
Errors, Both Teams, 9-Inning Game	11, at Chicago, April 29, 1989 (San Diego—6)

INDIVIDUAL BATTING

Hits	5, 22 times (including 3 in extra innings)
Hits, Extra Innings	6 (Gene Richards vs. Montreal, 15 innings, July 26, 1977; Joe Lefebvre at Los Angeles, 16 innings, September 13, 1982; Tony Gwynn vs. San Francisco, 12 innings, August 4, 1993)
Runs Scored	5, Albert Martin vs. Houston, April 16, 2000
At-Bats	7, Mark Hotsay and Ryan Klesko, at Montreal, May 19, 2001
At-Bats, Extra Innings	8, five times
Hit for Cycle	Never Accomplished
Singles	5, Kevin McReynolds vs. Cincinnati, September 4, 1984; Tony Gwynn vs. St. Louis, April 18, 1993
Doubles	3, 23 times
Triples	2, 12 times
Home Runs	3, six times, Nate Colbert at Atlanta, August 1, 1972, Game 1; Steve Finley at Cincinnati, May 19, 1997; Steve Finley at San Francisco, June 23, 1997; Ken Caminiti at Los Angeles, July 12, 1998; Bret Boone at Cincinnati, June 23, 2000; Phil Nevin vs. Colorado, October 6, 2001
Consecutive Home Runs Twice by Same Two Players	Gary Sheffield and Fred McGriff, vs. Houston, August 6, 1992, First and Second Innings

Runs Batted In	8, Nate Colbert at Atlanta, August 1, 1972 (Game 2); Ken Caminiti vs. Colorado, September 19, 1995
Stolen Bases	5, Alan Wiggins vs. Montreal, May 17, 1984; Tony Gwynn at Houston, September 20, 1986; Damian Jackson vs. Colorado, June 28, 1999
Walks	4, 15 times

INDIVIDUAL PITCHING

Strikeouts, 9-Inning Game	15, Fred Norman at Cincinnati, September 15, 1972; Sterling Hitchcock vs. Montreal, August 29, 1998
Strikeouts, Extra-Inning Game	15, Clay Kirby vs. Houston (Game 1), September 24, 1971 (15 innings)
Walks	10, Clay Kirby at San Francisco, July 15, 1969
Runs Allowed	11, Junior Herndon at St. Louis, August 30, 2001
Home Runs Allowed	5, Woody Williams at Houston, July 13, 2001
Innings Pitched, Starter	15, Clay Kirby vs. Houston, September 24, 1971, Complete Game
Innings Pitched, Reliever	8, Jimmy Jones vs. Los Angeles, June 29, 1987

INDIVIDUAL FIELDING

Double Plays

First Baseman	5, Bill Davis vs. St. Louis, May 16, 1969
Second Baseman	5, Roberto Pena vs. St. Louis, May 16, 1969
Third Baseman	3, Ed Spiezio vs. Los Angeles, July 3, 1971
Shortstop	4, twice (Tommy Dean vs. St. Louis, May 16, 1969; Garry Templeton vs. San Francisco, April 16, 1985)

Putouts

First Baseman, 9-Inning Game	19, three times (last time Gene Tenace vs. Philadelphia, May 4, 1977)
First Baseman, Extra-Inning Game	23, Nate Colbert vs. Pittsburgh, June 7, 1972 (18 innings)
Second Baseman, 9-Inning Game	9, Tim Flannery at Atlanta, September 29, 1985
Third Baseman, 9-Inning Game	4, six times (last time Gene Tenace vs. St. Louis, June 17, 1977)
Shortstop, 9-Inning Game	6, eight times (last time Craig Shipley at San Francisco, September 25, 1993)
Outfielder, 9-Inning Game	10, Phil Clark vs. New York, May 1, 1993
Outfielder, Extra-Inning Game	10, Gene Richards vs. Los Angeles, May 22, 1979 (10 innings)
Catcher, 9-Inning Game	16, twice (last time Fred Kendall at Cincinnati, September 15, 1972)
Pitcher, 9-Inning Game	5, Jimmy Jones vs. Houston, April 22, 1988

Assists

First Baseman, 9-Inning Game	6, Keith Moreland at Cincinnati, September 19, 1988
Second Baseman, 9-Inning Game	10, twice (last time Fernando Gonzalez vs. Chicago, June 17, 1979)
Second Baseman, Extra-Inning Game	11, Derrel Thomas vs. Pittsburgh, June 7, 1972 (18 innings)
Third Baseman, 9-Inning Game	8, five times (last time Randy Ready at San Francisco, June 21, 1988)
Shortstop, 9-Inning Game	13, Bill Almon vs. Philadelphia, May 4, 1977
Outfielder, 9-Inning Game	3, twice (last time Tony Gwynn vs. New York, August 27, 1986)
Catcher, 9-Inning Game	7, Benito Santiago at Montreal, May 15, 1989
Pitcher, 9-Inning Game	7, Rich Troedsen vs. Montreal, August 12,1973

PADRES INNING RECORDS

BIGGEST INNING

The Padres scored 11 runs on seven hits in the sixth inning of their April 1, 1997 season opener against the New York Mets at Qualcomm Stadium. After trailing 4-0 through the fifth inning, the Padres eventually won the contest, 12-5. The 11 runs established a modern National League record for most runs plated in a single inning on Opening Day. The incredible inning played out as follows:

Chris Gomez homered off Pete Harnisch to left center. Rickey Henderson pinch hit for pitcher Joey Hamilton and homered to left. Quilvio Veras homered to right. After Yorkis Perez relieved Harnisch, Tony Gwynn singled to left. Steve Finley struck out swinging. Gwynn stole second. Ken Caminiti singled to shallow right center, scoring Gwynn. Toby Borland relieved Perez. Greg Vaughn walked.

Wally Joyner grounded out to first, moving Caminiti to third and Vaughn to second. John Flaherty walked. Gomez walked, scoring Caminiti. Barry Manuel relieved Borland. Henderson was hit by a pitch, scoring Vaughn. Veras walked, scoring Flaherty. Gwynn singled to left, scoring Gomez and Henderson. Gwynn advanced to second on the throw. Finley doubled to deep right center, scoring Veras and Gwynn. Caminiti struck out swinging.

CLUB BATTING

Plate Appearances	17, vs. Pittsburgh, May 31, 1994 (2nd inning)
Runs Scored	13, vs. St. Louis, August 24, 1993 (1st inning); vs. Pittsburgh, May 31, 1994 (2nd inning)
Hits	9, three times
Home Runs	4, vs. Los Angeles, July 10, 1970 (9th inning); at New York, May 17, 2001 (3rd inning)
Stolen Bases	5, at Pittsburgh, September 11, 1995 (9th inning)

INDIVIDUAL BATTING

RBIs	5, Bret Boone, at Los Angeles, June 26, 2000 (2nd inning)

INDIVIDUAL PITCHING

Home Runs Allowed	3, seven times

PADRES DOUBLEHEADER RECORDS

CLUB GENERAL

Players, Padres, Both Games	41, at San Francisco, May 30, 1977
Players, Opponents, Both Games	33, at San Francisco, May 30, 1977
Players, Both Teams, Both Games	74, at San Francisco, May 30, 1977
Longest, Innings	30 innings, vs. Houston, September 24, 1971 (1st game, 21 innings)
Longest, Time	7:39, vs. Houston, September 24, 1971 (1st game 5:25; 2nd game, 2:14)

CLUB BATTING

Times Striking Out, Padres	15, vs. New York, May 29 1971 (1st game 8; 2nd game 7); vs. Arizona, August 31, 2001 (1st game 11; 2nd game 4)
Times Striking Out, Padres, Extra-Inning Game	23, at Houston (1st game 18; 2nd game 5)
Times Striking Out, Opponents	26, vs. New York, May 29, 1971 (1st game 10, 2nd game 16)
Times Striking Out, Both Teams	43, at Houston, July 8, 1995 (1st game 31; 2nd game 12)
Pitchers Used by Padres	13, at San Francisco, May 30, 1977
Pitchers Used by Padres, Extra Innings	15, at San Francisco, June 18, 1985 (1st game 5; 2nd game 10, 13 innings)

INDIVIDUAL BATTING

Hits	7, three times
Doubles	5, Mike Ivie, at San Francisco, May 30, 1977
Home Runs	5, Nate Colbert at Atlanta, August 1, 1972
Runs Batted In	13, Nate Colbert at Atlanta, August 1, 1972
Extra Base Hits	5, twice
Total Bases	22, Nate Colbert at Atlanta, August 1, 1972

INDIVIDUAL PITCHING

Won Both Games	Bob Miller vs. Houston, June 23, 1971
Lost Both Games	Mark Thurmond at San Francisco, June 16, 1985
Saved Both Games	Never accomplished

LONGEST DOUBLEHEADER

The Padres made major league history against the Phillies on July 2, 1993 in Philadelphia with a twi-night doubleheader that lasted until 4:40 a.m. the following morning. The start of the first game, scheduled for 4:35 p.m., was delayed one hour and 10 minutes by rain. During the game, there were two more delays that totaled 4 hours and 44 minutes before play was resumed just before midnight. After 5 hours and 54 minutes of rain delays and a game time of 2 hours, 34 minutes, game one, a 5-2 Padres victory, concluded at 1:03 a.m. Game 2 started at 1:28 a.m. and went 10 innings before the Phillies won, 6-5. The game-winning run crossed the plate at 4:40 a.m. It is the latest a major league game has ever ended. The previous mark was 3:55 a.m., when the New York Mets and Atlanta Braves played into the wee hours on July 4-5, 1985.

LONGEST GAMES IN PADRES HISTORY

Innings	Date	Opponent	Score (SD 1st)	Time
21	Sept. 24, 1971	Houston	1-2	5:25
21	May 21, 1977	at Montreal	11-8	5:33
20	August 15, 1980	Houston	1-3	6:17
19	August 25, 1979	Pittsburgh	3-4	6:12
18	June 7, 1972	Pittsburgh	0-1	4:27
18	August 26, 1980	at New York	8-6	5:01
17	July 15, 1971	at Pittsburgh	3-4	4:12
17	July 29, 1972	at Cincinnati	4-3	4:11
17	August 21, 1980	at Philadelphia	8-9	5:13
17	June 27, 1989	at Los Angeles	5-3	5:21
17	August 15, 1990	Montreal	3-5	5:15
17	July 8, 1995	at Houston	2-3	4:29
16	Sept. 13, 1982	at Los Angeles	3-4	5:20
16	August 10, 1988	at Atlanta	5-4	4:24
16	April 24, 1992	Cincinnati	6-7	5:01
16	Sept. 8, 1992	at San Francisco	5-6	5:04
16	June 22, 1996	Chicago	6-9	5:14
16	April 25, 1998	Pittsburgh	4-3	4:31

PADRES CONSECUTIVE RECORDS

CLUB GENERAL

Games Won, Overall	14, June 18-July 2, 1999
Games Won, Home	10, 1978, 1980, 1999
Games Won, Road	7, 1985
Games Won vs. One Club, Home	15 vs. St. Louis, 1992-1995
Games Lost, Overall	13, 1994
Games Lost, Home	12, 1972
Games Lost, Road	11, 1969
Games Lost vs. One Club, Home	12, Los Angeles, 1970-1972
Games Lost vs. One Club, Road	14, at Montreal, 1993-1995

CLUB BATTING

Hits, One Game, Padres	8, twice
Hits, One Game, Opponents	9, at Philadelphia, June 13, 1980 (1st inning)
Batters Hitting Home Runs, Padres	4 vs. Los Angeles, July 10, 1970 (9th inning: Ivan Murrell, Ed Spiezio, Dave Campbell, Cito Gaston)
Batters Reaching Base Safely, Padres	10, vs. Pittsburgh, May 31, 1994 (2nd inning)
Batters Reaching Base Safely, Opponents	9, at Philadelphia, June 13, 1980 (1st inning)

Games Hitting a Home Run, Padres	14, July 14-29, 1998 (23 home runs)

CLUB PITCHING

Shutouts Won	4, 1984
Shutouts Against One Club	2, 11 times
Scoreless Innings Pitched, Padres	40.2, July 28 (7th inning) August 1 (1st inning) 1984
Scoreless Innings Pitched, Opponents	37.2, July 21-24, 1971
Scoreless Innings Pitched Against One Club	31.2, vs. Houston, April 22 (4th inning), July 26 (8th inning) 1988
Hitless Innings at Start of Game	8.2, vs. Philadelphia, July 18, 1972 (Steve Arlin)

CLUB FIELDING

Games Turning Double Plays, Padres	11, August 29-September 10, 1997
Games Without Errors	9, July 3-12, 1979
Innings Without Errors	92.0, July 2-12 (1st game), 1979
Games Making Errors	12, August 12-15, 2000

INDIVIDUAL GENERAL

Games Played	305, Steve Garvey, 1984-1986
Stolen Bases Without Being Caught	27, Jerry Mumphrey, 1980

INDIVIDUAL BATTING

Games With One or More Hits	34, Benito Santiago, August 25-October 2, 1987
Hits Without Making an Out	8, Dave Winfield, 1979; Tony Gwynn, 1994
Times Reaching Base Safely	9, Bip Roberts, 1989; Tony Gwynn, 1989, 1994; Quilvio Veras, 1997
Games, Hitting Home Runs	6, Graig Nettles, 1984
At Bats, Hitting a Home Run, Same Batter	3, Nate Colbert, 1971; Steve Finley, 1996
Pinch Hits	5, Terry Kennedy, 1986; Tim Flannery, 1988; Billy Bean, 1994

INDIVIDUAL PITCHING

Winning Decisions, Starter	11, Andy Hawkins, 1985; LaMarr Hoyt, 1985; Kevin Brown, 1998
Winning Decisions, Reliever	10, Butch Metzger, 1976
Losing Decisions	11, Gary Ross, 1969; Steve Arlin, 1972
Complete Games	5, Randy Jones, 1976, twice
Winning Decisions Against One Club	9, Bruce Hurst vs. New York, 1989-1992
Hitless Innings, Start of Game	8.2, Steve Arlin vs. Philadelphia, July 18, 1972
Hitless Innings	12, Steve Arlin, 1972
Shutouts	3, Randy Jones, 1980
Scoreless Innings, Starter	30.0, Randy Jones, 1980
Scoreless Innings, Reliever	27.2, Mark Davis, 1988
Strikeouts	8, Tim Lollar vs. New York, May 20, 1984
Batters Retired	25, Bob Shirley vs. Houston, April 22, 1977

INDIVIDUAL FIELDING

Errorless Games, First Baseman	193, Steve Garvey, June 26, 1983 (2nd game) April 14, 1985

STEALS OF HOME BY A PADRE

Player	Opponent	Inning	Date
Rich Morales	at Chicago	6	June 18, 1974
Jerry Turner	at Chicago	8	May 8, 1980
Jerry Turner	Montreal	4	June 20, 1980
Gene Richards	Los Angeles	1	July 13, 1980
Alan Wiggins	at Houston	1	April 21, 1984

Player	Opponent	Inning	Date
Alan Wiggins	at Houston	3	August 4, 1984
Jerald Clark	at Los Angeles	7	September 10, 1992
Greg Vaughn	Los Angeles	3	September 10, 1998
Eric Owens*	Cincinnati	3	May 21, 1999
Gary Matthews, Jr.	Seattle	4	June 4, 1999
Damian Jackson	Colorado	6	June 28, 1999
Ruben Rivera	at Montreal	8	August 6, 1999
Ryan Klesko	Los Angeles	1	July 5, 2000
Mike Darr	Colorado	1	September 11, 2000

Bibliography

Anderson, Bruce, "A Most Unlikely Slugger," *Sports Illustrated* 68 (May 23, 1988), p. 77.

Armstrong, L., "St. Louis' Wizard Named Oz is the Slickest Fielding Shortstop in Baseball," *People Weekly* 19 (June 20, 1983), pp. 119-120.

"The Arnholdt Smith Affair," *Newsweek* 82 (August 20, 1973), p. 57.

Axthelm, Pete with Vern E. Smith, "The Amazing Randy," *Newsweek* 87 (June 21, 1976), p. 57.

Baker, Kevin, "The Great San Diego Fire Sale," *Harper's* 288 (April 1994), pp. 72-73.

Ballew, Bill, "Steve Arlin: Ohio State Star May Have Been Best Ever in College Ranks," *Sports Collectors Digest* 21 (September 23, 1994), pp. 140-141.

Bamberger, Michael, "Grit vs. Glamour," *Sports Illustrated* 89 (October 19, 1998), pp. 32-37.

Barman, Russell William, "From Smith and Bavasi to Kroc: A History of the San Diego Padres 1968-1974," master's thesis, History, University of San Diego, March 2, 1987.

Bavasi, Buzzie, with John Strege, *Off the Record.* Chicago, IL: Contemporary Books, 1987.

Berger, Phil, "The Yankees' $20 Million Gamble," *New York Times Magazine* (March 29, 1981), pp. 26-40.

Bloom, Barry, "Alomar, As in All-Star," *Sport* 82 (March 1991), pp. 46-48, 50-51.

Bloom, Barry, "Mission Accomplished," *Sport* 88 (September 1997), pp. 46-49.

Bloom, Barry, "One on One . . . Tony Gwynn," *Sport* 85 (September 1994), pp. 26-27.

Bloom, Barry, "San Diego Padres + Steve Garvey = ?," *Sport* 74 (April 1983), p. 60.

Bloom, Barry, "Tony Gwynn," *Sport* 85 (September 1994), pp. 26-27.

Broome, Tol, "Gutierrez Cards May Draw Collectors' Interest," *Sports Collectors Digest* 20 (October 15, 1993), p. 130.

Broome, Tol, "Highlights of the San Diego Sports Museum," *Sports Collectors Digest* 20 (October 8, 1993), p. 228.

"The Burger That Conquered the Country," *Time* 102 (September 17, 1973), pp. 84-92.

California, State of, Superior Court of the State of California for the County of San Diego, No. 343508. June 15, 1973.

Callahan, Tom, "A Not-So-Classic Fall Classic," *Time* 124 (October 22, 1984), pp. 82-83.

Callahan, Tom, "Wait Until This Year," *Time* 124 (October 8, 1984), pp. 72-74.

Cannella, Stephen, and Jeff Pearlman, "A Run for the Money," *Sports Illustrated* 91 (July 21, 1999), pp. 68-70.

Castle, George, "The Goose Again," *Sport* 80 (March 1989), pp. 38-40.

Chung, Mark, "Eric Show: A Thinking Man's Pitcher," *Sports Collectors Digest* 18 (July 5, 1991), p. 258.

Cobbs, Chris, "How Garry Templeton Emerged as Leader of the Padres," *Baseball Digest* 44 (July 1985), pp. 37-39.

"Crime in the Suites," *Forbes* 116 (August 15, 1975), pp. 17-20.

Curtis, John, "How We Did It," *San Diego Magazine* 34 (September 1982), pp. 132-135.

D'Agostino, John, "Trader Jack McKeon's Wish List," *San Diego Magazine* 39 (April 1987), pp. 128-131, 269-271, 277.

Davis, Craig, "Ozzie Smith: Baseball's Most Graceful Fielder of Them All," *Baseball Digest* 42 (July 1983), pp. 80-82.

Delsohn, Steve, "Beers with . . . Jack McKeon," *Sport* 80 (July 1989), pp. 19ff.

Diaz, Jaime, "A First Breeze Cools the Desert Air," *Sports Illustrated* 64 (March 10, 1986), pp. 18-21.

Dravecky, Dave, with Tim Stafford, *Dravecky.* Grand Rapids, MI: Zondervan Publishing House, 1990.

Fall, Steve, "San Diego Baseball Update," March 1991-January 1993.

Farber, Michael, "Battle Royal," *Sports Illustrated* 89 (October 12,1998), pp. 48-51.

Fimrite, Ron, "A Son of San Diego Pounds the Padres," *Sports Illustrated* 61 (October 22, 1984), pp. 34-35.

Fimrite, Ron, "Baseball Games Back to the Big Time," *Sports Illustrated* 55 (July 13, 1981), pp. 22-24ff.

Fimrite, Ron, "Bound for Glory," *Sports Illustrated* 55 (August 24, 1981), pp. 92-96ff.

Fimrite, Ron, "Cable Cars, the Fog—and Willie," *Sports Illustrated* 48 (April 17, 1978), pp. 36-38ff.

Fimrite, Ron, "Good Hit, Better Man," *Sports Illustrated* 51 (July 9, 1979), pp. 32-34.

Fimrite, Ron,"Has Typewriter, Will Pitch," *Sports Illustrated* 52 (May 12, 1980), pp. 46ff.

Fimrite, Ron, "He is Not Just a Wild and Crazy Guy," *Sports Illustrated* 59 (August 8, 1983), pp. 38-41ff.

Fimrite, Ron, "Padre with a Passion," *Sports Illustrated* 66 (May 4, 1987), pp. 52-54ff.

Fimrite, Ron, "Playing Ketchup Out West," *Sport* Illustrated 42 (May 12,1975), pp. 26-27.

Fimrite, Ron, "Richest Kid on the Block," *Sports Illustrated* 54 (January 5, 1981), pp. 22-26.

Fimrite, Ron, "San Diego Finds a Sugar Padre," *Sports Illustrated* 40 (February 11, 1974), pp. 56-58.

Fimrite, Ron, "Small Stick, Tall Stats," *Sports Illustrated* 64 (April 14, 1986), pp. 50-52.

Fimrite, Ron, "Take Me Out to the Brawl Game," *Sports Illustrated* 61 (August 24,1984), pp. 22-27.

Fimrite, Ron, "Uncommon Success for a Common Man," *Sports Illustrated* 45 (July 12, 1976), pp. 20-22.

Forman, Ross, "Dick Williams Talks Candidly About Baseball," *Sports Collectors Digest* 19 (December 18, 1992), p. 200.

Forman, Ross, "Ex-Cy Young Winner Jones is Barbecuing with Gas," *Sports Collectors Digest* 24 (December 19, 1997), pp. 138-139.

Forman, Ross, "Fred Kahaulua's Career Produced One Win . . . and a Topps Card," *Sports Collectors Digest* 24 (September 12, 1997), p. 120.

Forman, Ross, "Nate Colbert: Former Padre Now a Pastor in California," *Sports Collectors Digest* 21 (June 17, 1994), pp. 152-153.

Freeman, Don, "San Diego is Crowing About the Red Rooster," *Sport* 63 (September 1976), pp. 57-63.

Freeman, Don, "San Diego Love Story: Two Big Macs with Lots of Trimmings," *Sport* 58 (September 1974), pp. 79-88.

Furlong, William, "Ray Kroc: Burger Master," *Saturday Evening Post* 253 (March 1981), p. 64.

Garvey, Steve, with Skip Rozin, *Garvey.* New York: Times Books, 1986.

Gergen, Joe, "San Diego Padres Survived a Most Humble Beginning," *Baseball Digest* 44 (February 1985), pp. 55-58.

Geschke, Jim, "Padres 20th Anniversary: The Building of Tradition 1969-1988," *Padres Magazine* 2 (September 1988), pp. 26-28, 31, 55, 61.

Greenwood, Chuck, "Coleman's MLB Career Interrupted by Wars," *Sports Collectors Digest* 25 (April 17, 1998), p. 50.

Greenwood, Chuck, "From Backup Catcher to Manager of Year: Bochy Has Basketball to Thank for Baseball Success," *Sports Collectors Digest* 23 (December 6, 1996), p. 180.

Greenwood, Chuck, "McKeon Has a Story for Every Situation," *Sports Collectors Digest* 21 (December 23, 1994), pp. 150-151.

Grover, P., "So You Want to Own a Baseball Team," *Business Week* 80 (July 22, 1991), p. 80.

Gutierrez, Paul, "Catching Up with Randy Jones," *Sports Illustrated* 89 (August 3, 1998), pp. 70-71.

Gwynn, Tony, with Jim Geschke, *Tony!* Chicago, IL: Contemporary Books, 1986.

Heins, J., "Stepping into the Vacuum," *Forbes* 133 (April 30, 1984), p. 134.

Herron, Gary, "Former Infielder Flannery Has an Interesting Life On and Off the Diamond . . .He has Cut His Own CD," *Sports Collectors Digest* 22 (August 18, 1995), pp. 158-159.

Herron, Gary, "The Kennedys Are Part of a Famous American Family in Baseball, Too," *Sports Collectors Digest* 22 (July 21, 1995), pp. 154-155.

Hinz, Bob, *San Diego Padres.* Minneapolis, MN: Creative Education, 1982.

Hoffer, Richard, "Every Game is a Home Game," *Sports Illustrated* 72 (April 16, 1990), pp. 78-80.

Hoffer, Richard, "Fear of Failure," *Sports Illustrated* 83 (September 18, 1995), pp. 67-70.

"How C. Arnholdt Smith's Empire Came Apart," *Business Week* (October 27, 1973), pp. 85-86ff.

Howard, Johnette, "Better Late Than Never," *Sports Illustrated* 88 (June 22, 1998), pp. 72-73.

Howerton, Darryl, "Image is Nothing," *Sport* 89 (October 1998), pp. 70-71.

Hultman, Tom, "Destined to be a Dodger," *Sports Collectors Digest* 24 (June 20, 1997), pp. 170-171.

Hultman, Tom, "Gwynn Speaks Softly, Carries Big Stick," *Sports Collectors Digest* 19 (March 20, 1992), p. 101.

Hultman, Tom, "Smith Still the Wizard of Oz," *Sports Collectors Digest* 24 (July 11, 1997), pp. 130-131.

Jacobs, Barry, "The Wizardry of Ozzie Smith," *Saturday Evening Post* 255 (May/June 1983), pp. 64-65ff.

Johnson, Paul M., "Encore," *Sport* 88 (July 1997), pp. 67-69.

Johnson, William Oscar, "Al Gave It His All," *Sports Illustrated* 54 (January 5, 1981), pp. 26-35.

Jordan, Pat, "The Last Inning," *Los Angeles* 40 (June 1995), pp. 88-96ff.

Kaplan, Jim, "The Padres' Persnickety Papa," *Sports Illustrated* 56 (June 28, 1982), pp. 22-24ff.

Kaplan, Jim, "Taking a Run at Monumental Success," *Sports Illustrated* 54 (April 20, 1981), pp. 42-44ff.

Keidan, Bruce and William Ladson, "Compadres," *Sport* 84 (March 1993), pp. 58-61.

Kennedy, Ray, "San Diego Wins the Palm as Sports Town, U. S. A.," *Sports Illustrated* 49 (December 25, 1978-January 1, 1979), pp. 48-50, 55-56, 58.

Kernan, Kevin, "Tony Gwynn," *Sport* 82 (July 1991), pp. 34-38.

Keteyian, Armen, "Inside Stuff," *Sport* 90 (April 1999), pp. 30-31.

King, Peter, "Padres Hit Parade," *Sports Illustrated* 76 (June 15, 1992), pp. 36-37.

Klein, Moss, "The Old Champ Went Down Swinging," *Sports Illustrated* 63 (September 30, 1985), pp. 38-39.

Knobler, Danny, "Psst. . . Heard About Tony Gwynn?," *Sport* 80 (August 1989), pp. 22-24, 26, 28.

Kowet, Don, The Rich Who Own Sports. New York: Random House, 1977.

Korn, Peter, "The Clean and Mean Machine," Inside Sports 6 (July 1984), pp. 24-31.

Kravitz, Bob, "*Sport* Interview," *Sport* 75 (October 1984), pp. 23-26ff.

Kroc, Ray, and Robert Anderson, Grinding It Out: The Making of McDonald's. Chicago, IL: Contemporary Books, 1985.

Kurkjian, Tim, "A Blessing for the Padres," *Sports Illustrated* 76 (April 27, 1992), p. 54.

Kurkjian, Tim, "Beginning Again," *Sports Illustrated* 74 (March 11, 1991), pp. 44-47.

Kurkjian, Tim, "Penny Pinchin' Padres," *Sports Illustrated* 78 (March 29, 1993), pp. 28-32.

Kurkjian, Tim, "San Diego Hits a Sour Note," *Sports Illustrated* 73 (May 6, 1990), pp. 38-40ff.

Landsverck, Rocky, "3,000 Hit, Onward and Upward," *Sports Collectors Digest* 25 (June 10, 1998), pp. 106-107.

Leavy, Walter, "Is Tony Gwynn the Greatest Hitter in Baseball History?," *Ebony* 52 (August 1997), pp. 132ff.

Leerhsen, Charles, "A Surprise Series: Tigers vs. the Padres," *Newsweek* 104 (October 15, 1984), pp. 94-95.

Leerhsen, Charles, "The Tigers Take It All," *Newsweek* 104 (October 22,1984), p. 59.

Leggett, William, "Celestial Decision in Houston; San Diego Padres' Possible Move to Washington, D. C.," *Sports Illustrated* 39 (December 17, 1973), pp. 77ff.

Leggett, William, "These Men for Sale," *Sports Illustrated* 29 (September 9, 1968), p. 29.

Lidz, Franz, "All's Right with His World," *Sports Illustrated* 61 (August 6, 1984), pp. 76ff.

Lidz, Franz, "Benito Finito at 34 Games," *Sports Illustrated* 67 (October 12,1987), pp. 26-27.

Lidz, Franz, "Tale of a Trade," *Sports Illustrated* 70 (June 26, 1989), p. 44.

Lincoln, Melissa Ludtke, "Rollie's Rolling Again," *Sports Illustrated* 49 (September 11,1978), pp. 81-82.

Louis, A. M., "The Hall of Fame for U. S. Business Leadership," *Fortune* 107 (April 4, 1983), pp. 144-149.

Lucas, Ed, and Paul Post, "'Popeye' Had Strength to Battle Through Two Beanings," *Sports Collectors Digest* 26 (May 7, 1999), pp. 112-113.

Ludtke, Melissa, "Nobody Knows the Doubles I've Creamed," *Sports Illustrated* 47 (July 11, 1977), pp. 44-47.

Lupica, Mike, "The Unnatural," *Esquire* 124 (August 1995), pp. 40ff.

Maisel, Ivan, "San Diego: A Case of Padrecide," *Sports Illustrated* 63 (August 5, 1985), pp. 16-17.

Marazzi, Rich, "Don Zimmer: A Half Century as a Major Leaguer," *Sports Collectors Digest* 25 (February 6, 1998), pp. 142-144.

Marazzi, Rich, "Don Zimmer Remembers a Generation of Legendary Players," *Sports Collectors Digest* 25 (February 20, 1998), pp. 70-71.

Marazzi, Rich, "Manager of the Year Award in 1989 Was a Highlight for Zimmer," *Sports Collectors Digest* 25 (February 13, 1998), pp. 80-81.

Marazzi, Rich, "Steve Boros Recalls Long Baseball Career," *Sports Collectors Digest* 21 (July 8, 1994), pp. 140-141.

Marquis, Alice, "Smith Who Knew Nixon: 'Mr. San Diego' is in Trouble," *Nation* 217 (September 24, 1973), pp. 268-271.

Martin, J., "Can Baseball Make it in Mexico?," *Fortune* 134 (September 30, 1996), pp. 32ff.

Mayer, Allen J. and A. Bentley, "Richest Men in America," *Newsweek* 88 (August 2, 1976), pp. 56-59.

McDevitt, Sean, "Crime Dog Speaks Softly, Carries a Big Stick," *Sports Collectors Digest* 18 (August 23, 1991), p. 40.

McDevitt, Sean, "Tony Gwynn: On a Crash Course with Cooperstown," *Sports Collectors Digest* 18 (July 12, 1991), pp. 100-101.

McKeon, Jack and Tom Friend, *Jack of All Trades.* Chicago, IL: Contemporary Books, 1988.

Miller, Cary S., "Gwynn Our Way?," *Sports Collectors Digest* 16 (November 3, 1989), pp. 170-171.

Mitchell, Greg, "The Great Shortstop Swap," *Sport* 73 (August 1982), pp. 62-63ff.

"Mr. San Diego in Dutch," *Time* 101 (June 11, 1973), pp. 77-78.

Moriah, David, "Steady Personality Keeps Fernandez in Game," *Sports Collectors Digest* 26 (January 15, 1999), p. 106.

Murphy, Katie, "Team Player," *Texas Monthly* 24 (May 1996), p. 28.

Nack, William, "A Team in Trouble," *Sports Illustrated* 53 (August 11,1980), pp. 50-53.

Neff, Craig, "Picking Up Where They Left Off," *Sports Illustrated* 62 (May 13, 1985), pp. 32-34ff.

New York Times, 1969-2000.

Newman, Bruce, "He Has Georgia on His Mind," *Sports Illustrated* 53 (July 28, 1980), pp. 36-38.

Newman, Bruce, "Home Suite Home," *Sports Illustrated* 76 (June 8, 1992), pp. 36-39.

Newman, Bruce, "Man with the Golden Gun," *Sports Illustrated* 74 (February 11, 1991), pp. 60-62.

Newman, Bruce, "Way Above Average," *Sports Illustrated* 71 (September 25, 1989), pp. 24-26ff.

Nightengale, Barry, "The *Sport* Q & A: Jack Clark," *Sport* 82 (April 1991), pp. 82-84.

Norris, Frank, "San Diego Baseball: The Early Years," *Journal of San Diego History* 30 (Winter 1984), pp. 1-13.

"Now Pitching, Randy Jones," *New York Times Biographical Service* 8 (March 1977), pp. 400-401.

Olberman, Keith, "Hitting the Wall," *Sports Illustrated* 89 (July 27, 1998), p. 71.

"Padres Cut Payroll, Trade Fred McGriff to the Atlanta Braves," *Jet* 84 (August 9, 1993), p. 46.

"Padres 25th Anniversary," *The San Diego Union Tribune*, June 25, 1993.

Pate, Steve, "He's Stranger than His Rangers," *Sport* 74 (September 1983), pp. 73-75ff.

Peterson, Harold, "The Padres Are No Longer Patsies," *Sports Illustrated* 36 (May 29, 1972), pp. 73-74.

Phillips, B. J., "Baseball's $20 Million Man," *Time* 116 (December 29, 1980), p. 43.

"Playing One on One," *Essence* 22 (March 1992), p. 126.

Porter, David L., Interviews with Steve Arlin, San Diego, CA, July 26, 1989; Dave Campbell, San Diego, CA, July 24,1989; Jerry Coleman, San Diego, CA, July 23,1989; Rollie Fingers, Dyersville, Iowa, September 1, 1996; Tim Flannery, San Diego, CA, July 21,1989; Dick Freeman, San Diego, CA, July 25, 1989; Steve Garvey, San Diego, CA, July 27, 1989; Tony Gwynn, San Diego, CA, July 21, 1989; Jay Johnstone, Dyersville, Iowa, September 2, 1995; Frank Kern, San Diego,CA, July 25, 1989; Gary Lucas, San Diego, CA, July 25, 1989; Jack McKeon, San Diego, CA, July 21, 1989; Luis Salazar, San Diego, CA, July 28,1989; Elten Schiller, San Diego, CA, July 24, 1989; Eric Show, San Diego, CA, July 23, 1989; Garry Templeton, San Diego, CA, July 28, 1989; Ed Whitson, San Diego, CA, July 22, 1989; Whitey Wietelmann, San Diego, CA, July 21, 1989.

Porter, David L., "San Diego Padres: The Saga of Big Mac and Trader Jack," in Peter C. Bjarkman, ed., *Encyclopedia of Major League Baseball Team Histories: National League.* Westport, CT: Meckler Publishing, 1991.

"Ray Kroc," *Current Biography* (1973), pp. 230-232.

Reid, Ron, "He Stoops to Low Tricks," *Sports Illustrated* 44 (May 17, 1976), pp. 56, 59.

Reidenbaugh, Lowell, *Take Me Out to the Ballpark.* St. Louis, MO: The Sporting News, 1983.

Reilly, Rick, "America's Sweetheart," *Sports Illustrated* 71 (November 27, 1989), pp. 92-96ff.

Reilly, Rick, "Andy's in Lone Star State," *Sports Illustrated* 62 (June 10, 1985), pp. 62-64ff.

Reilly, Rick, "Can't Take Nothin' Off," *Sports Illustrated* 77 (September 14, 1992), pp. 54-56.

Reilly, Rick, "This is the House that Jack Built," *Sports Illustrated* 75 (July 22, 1991), pp. 60-66ff.

Robbins, Tim, "Ray Kroc Did It All for You," *Esquire* 100 (December 1983), pp. 340-342ff.

Rothaus, James R., *San Diego Padres.* Minneapolis, MN: Creative Education, 1987.

San Diego, City of, Lease between the City of San Diego and the San Diego Padres. August 14, 1968.

San Diego Padres, *San Diego Padres Media Guide*, 1975-2000.

San Diego Padres, *San Diego Padres Press-Radio-TV Guide,* 1969-1974.

San Diego Padres, *San Diego Padres Yearbook,* 1969, 1979-1985.

The San Diego Union Tribune, 1968-2000.

Seixas, S., "When a Young Pitcher Strikes It Rich," *Money* 12 (June 1983), pp. 108-112ff.

Shaw, David, "Dave Winfield: The Prince of the Padres," *Sport* 70 (January 1980), pp. 78-80ff.

"Short Cut to Texas," *Newsweek* 78 (October 4, 1971), p. 49.

Smith, George L., "Man Named Smith and the President," *Progressive* 38 (February 1974), pp. 27-30.

Smith, Ozzie, with Rob Rains, *Ozzie.* Chicago, IL: Contemporary Books, 1988.

Smith, R., "Crime and Punishment," *New York Biographical Service* 10 (August 1979), p. 1073.

The Sporting News Official Baseball Guide, 1969-2000.

The Sporting News Official Baseball Register, 1969-2000.

Stein, Harry, "Ozzie Smith," *Sport* 68 (March 1979), pp. 60-61.

Strasberg, Andy, and Mark Guglielmo, *Nineteen Summers: Padres* 1969-1988 VHS.

Swank, Bill, *Echoes from Lane Field: A History of the San Diego Padres 1936-1957.* Paducah, KY: Turner Publishing Company, 1999.

Swanson, Mike, et al., *A Dedicated Season: 1984 San Diego Padres Post Season Media Guide.*

"Tony Gwynn," *Current Biography* 57 (October 1996), pp. 23-27.

USA Today, 1988-2000.

Verducci, Tom, "Bat Man," *Sports Illustrated* 87 (July 28, 1997), pp. 40-44.

Verducci, Tom, "The Best Years of their Lives," *Sports Illustrated* 85 (July 29, 1996), pp. 90-92.

Verducci, Tom, "Crowd Pleasers,"*Sports Illustrated* 89 (November 2, 1998), pp. 46-52ff.

Verducci, Tom, "Game Show," *Sports Illustrated* 85 (October 14, 1996), pp. 22-27.

Verducci, Tom, "Scary Man," *Sports Illustrated* 85 (September 9, 1996), pp. 48-50, 55.

Verducci, Tom, "Single Minded," *Sports Illustrated* 91 (August 9, 1999), pp. 44-50.

Verducci, Tom, "Suffering an Identity Crisis," *Sports Illustrated* 80 (April 4, 1994), p. 111.

Verducci, Tom, "Topsy Turvy," *Sports Illustrated* 89 (July 6, 1998), pp. 48-52.

Verducci, Tom, "Tourist Trap," *Sports Illustrated* 89 (October 26, 1998), pp. 40-45.

Walker, S., "A Trip to the San Diego Bullpen Turns 'Pussycat' Padre Pitcher into a Tiger," *People Weekly* 24 (July 8, 1985), pp. 48-49.

Washington Post, 1972-1974.

Weinberg, Rick, "Super Joe," *Sport* 83 (June 1992), pp. 22-23, 26, 28-29.

"Westgate Scandal," *Time* 102 (October 29, 1973), pp. 115-116.

Whiteside, Kelly, "The Survival Game," *Sports Illustrated* 80 (February 14, 1994), pp. 136-138ff.

Who's Who in Baseball, 1969-2000.

Will, George F., "It's April, so 'Work Ball,'" *Newsweek* 111 (April 11, 1988), p. 92.

Will, George F., "Tony Gwynn, Union Man," *Newsweek* 124 (August 22, 1994), p. 70.

Winfield, Dave, with Tom Parker, *Winfield: A Player' Life.* New York: W. W. Norton and Company, 1988.

Williams, Dick and Bill Plaschke, *No More Mr. Nice Guy.* San Diego, CA: Harcourt Brace Jovanovich, 1990.

Wolff, Craig, "$24 Million Man Tells Why," *Sport* 72 (March 1981), pp. 15-16ff.

Wulf, Steve, "All My Padres," *Sports Illustrated* 70 (April 5,1989), pp. 42-50.

Wulf, Steve, "Baseball as Usual," *Sports Illustrated* 68 (January 18, 1988), p. 12

Wulf, Steve, "The Beast Team in Baseball," *Sports Illustrated* 60 (April 16, 1984), pp. 18-23.

Wulf, Steve, "Big Wheels Make Big Deals in Big D," *Sports Illustrated* 53 (December 22-29, 1980), pp. 18-19.

Wulf, Steve, "Detroit Jumped All Over Them," *Sports Illustrated* 61 (October 22, 1984), pp. 26-44.

Wulf, Steve, "How the Mighty Have Fallen," *Sports Illustrated* 63 (August 26, 1985), pp. 30-35.

Wulf, Steve, "It Was Too Good to be True," *Sports Illustrated* 58 (April 25, 1983), pp. 20-25.

Wulf, Steve, "Plenty More After Nomo," *Time* 149 (March 24, 1997), p. 84.

Wulf, Steve, "You've Got to Hand it to the Padres," *Sports Illustrated* 61 (October 15, 1984), pp. 28-34.

Wulff, Alexander, "They Were Playing His Song," *Sports Illustrated* 56 (May 31, 1982), pp. 52-54.